The Sociology of
Religious Movements

The Sociology of

Religious Movements

William Sims Bainbridge

ROUTLEDGE
New York   London

Published in 1997 by

Routledge
29 West 35th Street
New York, NY 10001

Published in Great Britain by

Routledge
11 New Fetter Lane
London EC4P 4EE

Library of Congress Cataloging-in-Publication Data is available upon request.

Contents

Contents

THE DYNAMICS OF TRANSFORMATION

CONCLUSION

Introduction

1

The Religious Impulse

A religious movement is a relatively organized attempt by a number of people to cause or prevent change in a religious organization or in religious aspects of life. Religious movements have some similarities with political, cultural, and social movements, in that they are collective human attempts to create or to block change. But their religious character is a decisive part of their definition, and we cannot understand them unless we recognize their connection to human feelings about the divine. Such movements are special expressions of the impulse that motivates religion of all kinds, so before we can examine them we need an overview of the general meaning of the sacred. That will be the task of this chapter. Before we can analyze our topic scientifically, we need a vivid illustration that presents the central issues in a clear and powerful manner. Therefore we will begin with a true story that illustrates some of the chief features of religion and of the human needs that faith serves. The incident took place on and near Manhattan island many years ago, and the story is chiefly based on information taken from issues of the *New York Times* published immediately afterward (cf. Nash 1976).

A Church Catastrophe

The band played a lively tune as the women and children of St. Mark's German Evangelical Lutheran Church boarded the steamer *General Slocum* on Wednesday morning, June 15, 1904, unaware that their annual excursion was destined for disaster. Reverend George C. F. Haas greeted his parishioners at Manhattan's East Third Street pier, in the company of his wife Anna, his daughter Gertrude, and his sister Emma. Mary Abendschein, chairwoman of the church social committee that organized the trip, had complete confidence in Captain William Van Schaick and his crew of twenty-three men. The three-deck *General Slocum* was two hundred and fifty feet long, built of white oak and yellow pine, propelled by two huge paddle wheels mounted on its sides. Hass and Abendschein did not keep an exact count, and many stray children ran on without tickets, but about fifteen hundred souls were aboard the ship as it chugged away from the pier and headed up the East River.

With no sign of trouble, the *Slocum* passed through the narrows aptly called Hell Gate, and the mood was so happy that mothers let their children run freely around the ship and made no effort to keep their groups together. A few noticed smoke emanating from the kitchen but assumed it was simply the chowder cooking. Then there was a muffled explosion, and a sheet of flame engulfed the bow of the ship, apparently promoted by the fresh white paint on the old pine superstructure and perhaps by painting supplies that had not been cleaned up. The fire spread with amazing swiftness, and in absolute panic everyone rushed toward the stern. The boat was less than a hundred yards distant from the city, so the captain could easily have turned toward it to let his passengers escape, or nearly as quickly he could had beached the *Slocum* on nearby Randall's Island. But instead he steered it on a long course around into a rocky cove on North Brother Island where there was no place to beach the ship, condemning hundreds of souls to a horrible death.

Passengers fought over the life preservers only to find that they were rotten and useless. Mrs. Lembesk became separated from three of her five children, and desperately threw Ernestine and Albert overboard when their clothing caught fire. Ida Hayden, stepdaughter of the superintendent of St. Mark's Parish School, watched in awe and horror as Reverend Haas struggled to save a group of children by standing in the very midst of the flames to hold a cabin door shut against the conflagration. Haas later described the hellish scene to the *New York Times*. "Women and children were shrieking and crying in their terror at the frightful doom facing them. Some of the poor mothers had three or four little children with them, and their attempts to save the little ones were heart rending beyond description. Everything seemed hopeless.

"When the fire first shot up through the hurricane deck and drove the crowd back, the panic was simply terrible. Those in the rear were swept along by the crowd in front, the women and children trying in vain to hold on to the railings and stanchions. Those first to fall, I believe, were crushed. My wife and daughter and myself were among those swept along in the rush. There seemed to be a general inclination to jump, and the women and children were swept over the rails like so many flies. In the terrific rush many were trampled upon. Little children were crushed, while mothers and their babes would give wild, heart-breaking screams and then jump into the water.

"Soon we saw that boats from the shore were making for us, and then we had a ray of hope. It looked up to then as if no one would be saved, and with my wife and daughter I went overboard. I do not know whether we jumped or whether we were pushed over. When I rose from the water I saw scores and scores of people fighting to keep afloat, and then one by one they would sink the last time. It was awful, and I was powerless to do anything. By a great effort I managed to keep above water, but my strength was about gone when a boat picked me up."

River men on other boats came as quickly as they could to help. The tug-boat *Wade* rushed alongside the blazing *Slocum* as it was fully engulfed in flames, saving more than a hundred and catching fire itself in its courageous effort. One of its crew, Edward Carroll dove into the water and seized three drowning children, but they were too much for him, so he let one sink to save the other two. Policeman Thomas Cooney saved eleven people until exhaustion made him drown with the woman who would have been his twelfth rescue. Hospital matron Nellie O'Donnell had never learned to swim, but when she saw the children drowning she dove in anyway and somehow managed to save ten. In a heap of bodies on the *Slocum's* paddle box, the boatmen found little Lizzie Krieger crying piteously for her mother. They took her to Alexander Avenue Station, where for the rest of the day she sat in a back room in sight of rows of bodies, crying "Mamma is all burned up!"

Eight-year-old Freda Gardner had slipped aboard the *Slocum* without her mother's permission, and she had no one to turn to when the fire and panic broke out. A man she had never seen before, who was praying at the top of his lungs, strapped a life preserver on her, but then a woman tore it off for her own use. Freda stood at the rail uncertain what to do, as the smoke rose around her. Another man threw her into the water, then jumped in himself, but the swirling mass of wreckage and thrashing humanity was too much for him, and he disappeared beneath the water before he could swim to her. She grabbed a floating plank. The hand of a drowning person seized her foot and nearly pulled her under before it lost its grip. A man tried to climb onto the plank, but a woman seized him around the neck and they both fell back into the deep water. Freda tried to pray for her life, but she felt so guilty for going on the excursion against her mother's wishes that the words would not come. A man in a rowboat rescued her, and she was still wet when she returned home. She and her mother knelt by the sofa and prayed together for a long time.

That first day, six hundred bodies were pulled from the water, and many of them were laid out in double rows at the Twenty-sixth Street pier near the New York City Morgue. Ten thousand people milled around searching for relatives, assisted by the staff of Bellevue hospital and Commissioner James Tully of the Department of Charities. Police swarmed over the pier to restrain grief-stricken individuals from leaping into the water and to pick up the many who fainted. Clerks from the coroner's office stood ready to fill out death certificates instantly, and a line of undertakers' wagons extended from the pier to First Avenue.

Reverend John A. W. Hass, the brother of George and himself the pastor of St. Paul's Lutheran Church uptown, found George and their sister Emma alive in Lincoln Hospital. When the doctors revived George, he asked desperately, "Where are they? Where is my family? Are they dead or alive?" His parishioner, Mrs. Lembesk, ran shrieking through the hospital corridors, her head and neck wrapped in bandages, wild at the loss of all her five children. Their friend, Reverend Julius J. Schultz, who had escaped the fire nearly unscathed, found the body of Mrs. Haas at the morgue, but twelve-year-old Gertrude remained missing. Exhausted and grief-stricken, George let his brother take him home.

Most husbands and fathers had been at work when their wives and children went on the *Slocum* excursion, and as the dreadful news swept New York scenes of unendurable shock spread across the city. When John Woll learned that all five of his children were lost, he wrung his hands, weeping, and begged anyone to kill him and end his misery. When Edmund Butler read his wife's name among a list of the dead, he instantly attempted suicide. Another man tried to stab himself with a butcher's knife, but two friends were able to restrain him. When Edward Skepter recognized the body of his beloved daughter Elsie in a plain white box on the pier, he threw his watch, ring and wallet into the coffin, screaming, "Take all, take all! I do not want to live now that my baby is dead!"

A man came to the Alexander Avenue Station, and looked over the bodies of women and children laid out on the floor. Then his glance turned to the chair where Lizzie Krieger was sitting in her ruined red dress, sobbing about her lost mother and watching the corpses being dragged in. He swept her up in his arms, exclaiming, "My dear Lizzie, my dear Lizzie! How glad I am to find you!" After telling the coroner where he lived, he carried Lizzie off in search of his four other lost children.

Little Germany, the section of the city covered by St. Mark's, extended from First Street to Seventh. The thousand families that formed the large congregation were linked together by marriage and ties of friendship as well as by the common experience of immigrating to America not too many years before. More than a thousand individuals had been killed, thus averaging one per family, including half the church choir and many Sunday-school teachers, elders, and other officers. One large, extended family lost twenty-nine members. Only one person regularly involved in church activities, the sexton John Holthusen, did not lose a single member of his immediate family.

The day after the disaster, Reverend Holter from New Jersey sat at a table in St. Mark's churchyard, taking contributions, and hundreds of people pressed dimes, quarters, and even hundred-dollar bills into his hands. The mayor appointed a committee of wealthy men, including Morris K. Jesup the benefactor of the New York City Mission Society, to collect donations on a larger scale, and within minutes they had delivered ten thousand dollars to Reverend Haas for immediate needs. The fifty nurses and social workers of the Mission Society went through the tenements, offering prayer and practical assistance to the bereaved. J. P. Sloane, president of the Cedar Grove Cemetery, offered free graves for the unidentified dead, but the Lutherans decided to bury them in their own yard, in a common grave. The Lutheran Pastor's Assembly met to organize help for the neediest survivors. The twenty-five Lutheran pastors of Hudson Country, New Jersey, volunteered to help their 169 New York brethren conduct the vast number of funerals that would be required. The Roman Catholic archbishop expressed the sympathy of his flock, "May the Giver of all strength comfort you and yours in this the dreadful hour of your sorrow." Help and prayers were offered by Episcopal, Methodist, Presbyterian, and Jewish clergy, who stood together at St. Mark's and sang in German, "Who knows how near my end may be?"

The funerals began on Friday, a hundred every day. At eight o'clock on Saturday, a procession of thirteen hearses brought twenty-seven unidentified bodies to St. Mark's. Despite his burns and knowing that his daughter had still not been found, Reverend George Haas sat beside his wife's casket in the St. Mark's parsonage, as Reverend Doctor Alexander A. Richter preached a stoic sermon. "We should all be good Christians, recognizing in this tragedy, no matter how appalling, the inscrutable hand of Providence. Everything that has happened to us has happened with God's will. We as Christians should bear with composure whatever the good Lord sees fit to inflict upon us. In times like this we should show the world that our faith stands conquering and supreme on the ruins of our shattered homes. All we need to know is that God did not prohibit this accident. Whether it was due to the negligence of the ship owners or anybody on board cannot be said at the present time, but God has his hand in it, and we must recognize that."

A Theory of Religion

The story of the *Slocum* catastrophe reminds us how precious yet precarious human life really is. Everyone dies eventually, and although we hide death away in hospitals and anesthetize the physical pain, all death is horrible. Each of us knows that he or she will die, and during our lifetimes most of us lose loved ones. As we rejoice to see our darling children play, in the backs of our minds we know that some day they, too, will die, hopefully long after we have gone so that we will not have to endure their deaths. As George Haas sat beside his wife's coffin, knowing that at any moment the salvage crew might rip his daughter's missing body from the wreck of the *Slocum*, his bandaged burns still raw, the familiar words of the Lutheran funeral service helped him, at least to some degree. Clearly, one of the functions of religion is to soothe grief.

But religion is not just a passive drug that dulls pain. It is an active force that seeks to overcome death. By now, nearly a century after the catastrophe, George Haas himself is long dead, and according to his faith he has now rejoined his wife and daughter in Heaven. Many religions set down rules for belief or behavior that must be followed if a person is to escape death, thus (as they believe) giving the person the strength to achieve immortality. Other religions demand less of their adherents, yet still provide some means for overcoming human mortality. Indeed, there is a tremendous variety of religious responses to death, but every major religious tradition responds in some way to this greatest of human challenges (Chidester 1990).

Death is not the only problem that people face, however, and religion addresses many of the others. At the height of the *Slocum* disaster, there were countless acts of altruism and of selfishness. The man who strapped the life preserver on little Freda Gardner was praying as he did so, but the women who ripped it off again was not. In its formal commandments and the examples of its saints, religion tells us how to behave. However, we all know superficially religious people who do wicked things, and some atheists seem to be very nice folk. In recent years, many researchers have addressed the question of how much power religion has to make people conform to societal norms (Bainbridge and Stark 1996), but clearly one of the chief goals of religion is enforcement of morality.

Religion offers guidance on how to achieve a prosperous life, secure in the respect of the community and the love of one's family members. When St. Mark's parishioners immigrated to the United States, few of them could speak English and few brought much in the way of material resources with them. Other ethnic groups had a rougher time, but these Germans did face a measure of prejudice and discrimination from the earlier English immigrants who were in control of American business and community life. The simple fact that their church brought together a thousand families facing similar difficulties gave them a community of their own that could offer help and guidance to newcomers. Through religious support for the institution of marriage, and through innumerable church-based activities, it strengthened families. And the Lutheran denomination reinforced traditional German norms of hard work, sobriety, and frugality that stood them in good stead as they struggled to get a footing in the new land. But even when the church could not help a particular individual succeed in worldly terms, it offered comfort.

Everyone who has given the matter a moment's thought understands that one function of religion is to compensate people for the terrible deficiencies of life in this world of pain and disappointment. A few years ago, Rodney Stark and I attempted to sketch a general theory of religion based on this familiar insight (Stark and Bainbridge 1985, 1987). Our work was not particularly original, because it drew upon the earlier efforts of scores of social scientists who had studied religion and upon theoretical developments in sociology more generally, notably the work of my chief mentor, George Homans (1967, 1974, 1984). Our aim was to create a formal theory, almost like a deductive branch of mathematics—and that is far too abstract a goal for this volume. But it is worth sketching the outlines of the theory of religion because we will find that it explains much about the forces that give rise to religious movements.

Human beings seek goals, from something as immediate as lunch to long-term objectives such as a college degree. Put in crude psychological language, humans seek pleasure and avoid pain. Following Homans, we preferred words that were a little broader and more economic in flavor: rewards and costs. We feel pleasure and pain directly, but many rewards and costs are indirect steps on the way to these emotions. Money does not taste anywhere near as good as lunch does, but we all know that money can buy us lunch. People can be mistaken, of course, in believing that something they are seeking will actually be rewarding. The money we work for may turn out to be counterfeit, and the lunch we buy might be rancid. Thus, Stark and I stated a key axiom of our theory in slightly tentative terms: "Humans seek what they perceive to be rewards and avoid what they perceive to be costs."

The manner in which human beings perceive things is extremely complex, but a key element is our ability to develop theories about the world and to plan courses of action based on them. That is, we have minds. With our minds, we remember the consequences of past actions, evaluate different kinds of rewards or costs, and plan future actions. Some rewards are far more valuable than others. Costs are negative rewards, with values less than zero, and they vary as well. Both rewards and costs vary greatly in how general they are. Death is a very general cost, because in dying we may lose everything. Thus triumph over death would be a very general reward, because it enables us to obtain so many less general rewards. Money is a fairly general reward, because we can spend it to buy many different things—except perhaps love and respect—but even very large sums of money are not so valuable as eternal life would be.

In seeking a particular reward, our clever minds develop explanations that tell us the circumstances under which we can find it. These explanations are instructions, plans, recipes, lists of things to do to get the reward, but they also are theories about the reward that tell us something about its nature and origins. For example, an explanation about how to catch fish not only tells us to tie a hook to a string, stick a worm on it, and drop it in the water. It also tells us that fish are living things that dwell in the water, that swim around looking for something to eat, and are not smart enough to learn from other fish the secret of our hook-filled worm. But humans are smart. We readily trade rewards with each other, and we tell each other how to obtain various rewards. Indeed, humans tend to get many of their effective explanations from each other, especially when the desired reward is very difficult to obtain by our own individual efforts.

That is, we rely upon each other for much of the information we have about the world and the way to live a successful life. Although we constantly check what other people tell us against our own experience, we accept a good deal on faith. This is especially true for explanations about how to get rewards that are highly general, valuable, and difficult to obtain. If somebody tells us it is easy to catch fish simply by reaching down into the water and grabbing them, it will not take us many minutes to prove this person wrong. But many explanations are much harder to test. Suppose somebody says we should buy some dynamite, explode it on top of the water, and use a big net to scoop up all the fish. We will soon find it is difficult to get dynamite, and that a casual attempt on a summer's afternoon without extensive preparation is not possible. These difficulties do not invalidate the idea that dynamite would be a good method of fishing, if only we could get some. When a desired reward is relatively unavailable, explanations that promise to provide it are often costly and difficult for the individual to evaluate correctly, so we often rely upon faith in the people who offer the explanation. This faith is typically based on our memory of the valuable rewards we have gotten from these people in the past.

In the absence of a desired reward, explanations often will be accepted which posit the attainment of the reward in the distant future or in some other nonverifiable context. Consider poor George Hass, sitting through his wife's funeral. When he was dragged from the water, he looked around for his daughter Gertrude, but he did not see her. Burned and exhausted, he did not have the strength to rush back into the water and look for her, himself. At that point, hundreds of people were mounting a massive rescue effort, and he was forced to rely upon them to save her if it was at all possible. A rumor said that a small boy had found her alive on the island, and for some hours Haas thought that at any moment she might run to his hospital bed and embrace him.

But by the time of the funeral for her mother, all earthly hope was lost. The salvage team had begun firing canon into the water to dislodge bodies from the wreck, and they were preparing to employ dynamite, but the city's efficient rescue operation had found and identified every survivor. The only way Haas could ever hear his daughter's sweet laughter again was in the afterlife. Short of killing himself on the spot, he could not enter the realm where his religious belief told him she might be found, except by waiting for his own life to run its course. He wept only once during his wife's funeral, at the moment when the presiding minister spoke his daughter's name. Thus, even though he was a clergyman with a lifetime of religious instruction, his faith may not have been complete. He would have far better preferred his daughter to turn up alive, unconscious but recovering in a hospital, than to seek her in Heaven. But he had no other choice than to cling to the religious explanation he possessed, and pray to see her in the great beyond.

Explanations that cannot readily be evaluated often turn out to be correct. Get a good education, work hard, and you will become prosperous. At least this is what the colleges of the world tell their students. And for many students, after years of effort, the promise is fulfilled. Based on the skills and wisdom they acquired during sixteen to twenty years of formal education, they acquire good jobs, purchase houses, build families, and ultimately find that their faith in higher education was well placed. So there is nothing disparaging about saying that people take some explanations on faith. But for purposes of sociological analysis it is worth having a special term to refer to explanations that require faith. Because these explanations psychologically compensate people for the lack of immediately rewards, we like to call them compensators.

Compensators are postulations of reward according to explanations that are not readily susceptible to unambiguous evaluation. To say that a particular explanation is a compensator is merely to note that it is taken on faith. Like rewards themselves, compensators vary in terms of how specific or general they are, and in how valuable people consider them to be. The very most general and valuable compensators can be supported only by religious assumptions, because only religion has access to the supernatural world where the ordinary laws of physical nature can be suspended. A religion is a system of general compensators based on supernatural assumptions.

Table 1.1 lists eleven key definitions related to rewards, explanations, compensators, and religion. We cannot do full justice to the entire complex theory here, and those who want to explore it more fully will need to consult our technical volume (Stark and Bainbridge 1987). Indeed, much of this book will merrily ignore the details of our theory as it describes and explains various features of religious movements. But a few words will indicate why this theory is a fruitful basis for understanding the nature and variations in religious movements.

One key issue concerns specific compensators. Everybody faces death, so all people are potential customers for the general compensators that form the defining core of religion. But people vary greatly in their need for more specific compensators. Some people are rich and influential, so they can directly enjoy the palpable rewards of wealth and power. Others are poor and lack any influence, so they are open to religious compensators that substitute for wealth and power. For example, they may join a religious sect that tells them they will be rewarded in Heaven (perhaps for their piety or the good judgment to join the particular sect) whereas the rich will be humbled and possibly even damned.

Thus we can see a need for two kinds of religion. Both kinds are built on the basis of general compensators of potential interest to all human beings. But one kind also includes a number of specific compensators attractive to the poor and powerless, whereas the other rejects them. This is a remarkably simple idea, yet we will find that it explains much about the dynamics of religious sects. It tells us a lot about the style of sects, compared with churches having prosperous congregations, and about who will join them. Combined with a few other simple ideas, it helps us understand the dynamics of sect formation and the evolution of intense sects as their members' needs change over the years. Indeed, a chief feature of the theory is its dynamism, the fact that it explains religion in terms of individual actions and social processes that change with time. Before we can fully grapple with change, however, we must consider some of the dimensions of variation along which change can occur.

Dimensions of Religious Variation

Sociologists of religion have devoted considerable energy to charting two kinds of religious variation: the dimensions of individual religious commitment and the dimensions along which religious organizations differ. Groups are composed of individuals, and religious individuals tend to belong to groups, so a research technique designed to study individuals often can also be applied to groups, and vice versa. We will start from an approach designed to measure the religiousness of individuals, but very quickly we will find ourselves also comparing groups.

We often say that one person is more religious than another, or that a particular person has become more or less religious over the years, speaking as if there were a single dimension of religiousness along which all people could be arranged unambiguously. But quick reflection tells us that this is far too simple a model. Imagine Tom, Dick, and Harry. Tom attends religious services frequently and always participates in the rituals flawlessly, but when asked he admits he doesn't believe the doctrines of his denomination and he habitually cheats his neighbors in business. Dick, on the other hand, says that his faith is extremely powerful and his religious beliefs matter to him very much, but he doesn't treat his neighbors any better than Tom does and he never participates in religious observances. Harry, in contrast, says he doesn't know what he believes and never attends religious services, but he

Table 1.1: Definitions from a Theory of Religion

---

1. *Rewards* are anything, including valuable information, that humans will incur costs to obtain.
2. *Costs* are whatever humans attempt to avoid.
3. Reward A is more *valuable* than B if a person will usually exchange B for A.
4. Rewards are *general* to the extent that they include other (less general) rewards.
5. *Explanations* are statements about how and why rewards may be obtained and costs are incurred.
6. *Evaluation* is the determination of the value of any reward, including explanations.
7. *Compensators* are postulations of reward according to explanations that are not readily susceptible to unambiguous evaluation.
8. Compensators which substitute for single, specific rewards are *specific compensators*.
9. Compensators which substitute for a cluster of many rewards and for rewards of great scope and value are *general compensators*.
10. A *religion* is a system of general compensators based on supernatural assumptions.
11. *Supernatural* forces are those that exist beyond or outside nature and can suspend, alter, or ignore physical forces.

---

gives liberally to charities without demanding any credit for his generosity and always deals fairly with the people in his community. Who is most religious among these men?

Now consider Joan and Jane. Both are very decent people, and both attend church regularly. Joan's denomination emphasizes prayer and intense religious experiences, while Jane's stresses elaborate formal rituals and social-service programs for the poor. Can we say which of these two women is more religious than the other, or which of their denominations is closer to God? Probably not. True, we can imagine a sixth person, June, who goes to church all the time, prays and has intense spiritual experiences, believes her denomination's doctrines without the shadow of a doubt, is constantly active in social service volunteer activity, and practices the Golden Rule in her dealings with her neighbors. Presumably, she is more religious than any of the other five, but her type is also very rare, and we will need a more subtle approach if we are to understand the religious variations that exist among most people.

In the 1950s and 1960s, sociologists of religion who wanted to measure religiousness in questionnaire surveys realized that religiousness probably has several dimensions (McGuire 1992:102). The most influential approach is probably the one devised by Charles Y. Glock and developed by him in collaboration with Rodney Stark. It postulates five dimensions of religious commitment: belief, practice, knowledge, experience, and consequences (Stark and Glock 1968:14). Here we will emphasize the ways that these five help us understand variations across the spectrum of religious organizations, but they have special relevance for religious movements. This is true because a religious movement generally seeks to move people along one or more of these five dimensions, usually a combination of belief and practice.

Belief refers to the acceptance of the truth of religious doctrines. In a study of northern California church members, Glock and Stark found that questionnaire items about individual belief were an effective tool for charting the differences among Christian denominations. For instance, 68 percent of Catholics but only 26 percent of Protestants were convinced it was completely true that "a child is born into the world already guilty of sin." Among the Protestants, Lutherans were more likely to agree with this statement than were members of other denominations (Stark and Glock 1968:40). This item illustrates the fact that separate religious traditions may vary in their acceptance of particular articles of belief. But it is also possible to find clusters of items that correlate with each other and measure an entire dimension of variation.

The Glock and Stark "orthodoxy index" is a good example. It was created by combining responses to four questionnaire items: "I know God exists and I have no doubts about it." "Jesus is the Divine Son of God and I have no doubts about it." "Miracles actually happened just as the Bible says they did." "It is completely true that the Devil actually exists." A respondent who agreed with all four of these statements would get four points on the orthodoxy index, whereas somebody who disagreed with all four would get zero points. In their survey data, Stark and Glock (1968:60) found a tremendous variation across denominations in the percentage who scored high on orthodoxy. Among Roman Catholics, 62 percent had a top score of four, compared with 33 percent of the Protestants. But an even greater variation occurred among the Protestants, from just 4 percent fully orthodox among the Presbyterians to 88 percent among Southern Baptists. And within a single denomination, individuals sometimes varied considerably. Of Episcopalians, 24 percent had zero points on the orthodoxy scale, 18 percent had one point, 21 percent had two, 23 percent had three, and 14 percent had the high score of four points.

Religious *practices* are actions individuals perform that directly concern their religion. Stark and Glock identified two kinds of religious practice, ritual and devotion. *Rituals* are the formal public rites of religious observance, which may be elaborate, precisely scripted ceremonies lasting an hour or more, or may be single actions. Conventional Christian examples are church attendance and participation in communion. *Devotion* refers to more private actions, such as private prayer and Bible reading.

In principle, beliefs and practices reinforce each other, and rituals are often symbolic expressions of beliefs. The Process Church of the Final Judgement, which is the subject of Chapter 9, made extensive use of water and fire in its rituals. For the weekly Sabbath Assembly, a circular altar would be placed in the center of the room, with stands on either side holding two bowls, one of which contained water, and the other, fire either from a short fat candle or a sterno can. At one point in the ceremony, the presiding Sacrifist would point one hand with the first two fingers outstretched at one bowl, and then do the same with the other hand toward the other bowl, saying "May the life-giving water of the Lord Christ and the purifying fire of the Lord Satan bring the presence of Love and Unity into this assembly." With the last words, the Sacrifist would bring his or her hands together in a prayerful pose. This ritualistic sentence, with the movements of the two arms, reminded the group of its core element of belief. In Process theology, Christ and Satan were now joining in "Unity" for an apocalyptic "end and a new beginning" of all existence. As the group knew full well, the water symbolized Christ, and the fire, Satan. By pointing at each when mentioning its name, then bringing his or her two separated hands together, the Sacrifist acted out the coming together of Christ and Satan, which also meant the unification of all members of the group.

Knowledge is different from belief in the Glock and Stark scheme, because some people seem to have great conviction in the truth of their religion without really knowing much about it, whereas other people are very well informed doubters. To evaluate their Christian respondents' religious knowledge, Glock and Stark included a little test in their questionnaire. One part listed six statements and the respondent was supposed to say which were direct quotes from the Bible. One was: "Blessed are the strong: for they shall be the sword of God." Of course, as 59 percent of the Catholics and 72 percent of the Protestants realized, this is not a Biblical quotation. Another test question asked, "Which one of Christ's Disciples denied Him three times?" Respondents were supposed to pick one of the following: James, Paul, Judas, Mark, Peter, Jacob. One does not have to believe in the divinity of Jesus to know that the right answer is Peter, and many Jewish or Buddhist students of religious studies presumably learn this striking example of human frailty from the *New Testament*. At the time Glock and Stark did their survey, private Bible reading was not a widespread custom among Catholics, and the fact that Protestants outscored them on this test of biblical knowledge says little about the level of Catholic devotion. Thus the knowledge of key facts about a religion is not the same thing as belief or practice.

The intensity and kind of religious *experiences* vary across denominations, but every major tradition is rooted in experiences that people feel are direct contact with the divine, transcendent or sacred. In the northern California survey of church members, 45 percent of the Protestants and 43 percent of the Catholics reported having had "a feeling that you were somehow in the presence of God." Many religious practices stimulate spiritual experiences, and

15

some seem fundamentally designed to produce them, such as fasting, meditation, extended prayer, and the various physical techniques of Yoga. In some Asian faiths, religious experiences often involve detachment, a sense of peace, and direct awareness of the paradoxical or unreal nature of existence. In the Judeo-Christian-Islamic tradition, religious experiences more commonly involve a sense of communication with supernatural beings, most specially the deity. Such experiences may vary in terms of the degree to which the person feels a complete and intimate communication with God, and what specific message if any God has for him or her (Stark 1965a, 1965b). Beliefs help a person interpret his or her experiences, and experiences reinforce beliefs.

The possible *consequences* of religious commitment are many. Perhaps the religious faith of Reverend George C. F. Haas comforted him after his wife was killed and his daughter lost on the *Slocum*. Another consequence might be altruistic and benevolent behavior, as when Haas stood in the flames to protect children, or when the praying man strapped the life jacket on little Freda Gardner. Religion may enforce morality more generally, and religiously committed people may be less likely to commit some kinds of crime than irreligious people (Bainbridge and Stark 1996). And some of the consequences may directly concern religion itself, as when religious people donate money to their church or make a special effort to share their faith with people who are not members. Because Stark and I have examined some of the consequences of religion in a recent volume, we will not consider them all here. However, Chapters 12 and 13 of this book directly concern the consequences of religion for social welfare and political freedom, and we will see the consequential dimension of religion in the background of all other chapters.

A National Survey

A quick overview of American religion can come from the most widely used sociological questionnaire study, the General Social Survey (Davis and Smith 1991). First administered in 1972, the GSS is a continuing, nearly annual national survey of about 1,500 non-institutionalized adults. Prior to this book, more than 3,000 scientific publications or dissertations had used the GSS, and now we will add one more item to that immense library. The questionnaire is administered face-to-face by a trained interviewer in the home of the respondent, taking about ninety minutes. A core set of items is asked every time, and other items are asked occasionally or only in one year. Fortunately for us, some very good religion questions have been asked many times, so we have really large numbers of respondents to work with. Here in this chapter, and later in the book, we will use data from the first eighteen surveys; because two years were skipped in the sequence, they cover 1972–1991.

A pivotal question is, "What is your religious preference? Is it Protestant, Catholic, Jewish, some other religion, or no religion?" Note that this item refers to *preference*, not formal membership in a denomination, nor to baptism, confirmation, or some other very explicit connection. Thus, some respondents will answer in terms of their feelings or the denomination of their parents, rather than being currently involved in the denomination. Fully 26,997 respondents answered this question. Of these, 64 percent were Protestant, 25 percent Catholic, and 2 percent Jewish. The "Other" category, which contained about 2 percent, includes an unknown number of people whom we might have called Protestant, but who did not give this label to themselves, plus the Eastern Orthodox churches. And this is where all the members of groups outside the Judeo-Christian tradition are categorized: Islam, Buddhism, Hinduism, and so forth. The "None" category includes atheists (who are convinced God does not exist), agnostics (who doubt we can know with certainty about God's existence), and people largely indifferent to religion. But some people with a strong personal faith may say their religion is "none" because they have no connection to any particular denomination.

Table 1.2 shows how respondents in these five categories responded to a variety of other religion questions. The figures are the percentages giving the indicated response, with the number of respondents on which the particular percentage is based given in parentheses. The first item in the table asks respondents to judge the strength of their religious affiliation. If the respondent had just said he or she was a Roman Catholic, the interviewer would ask, "Would you call yourself a strong Roman Catholic or not a very strong Roman Catholic?" If the respondent had named a different denomination, then the question would have referred to it. If somebody claimed a religious affiliation of "None," then the interviewer would skip this question. Interestingly, almost identical percentages of Protestants, Catholics and Jews said they were strong members of their denominations, about 40 percent. For decades, Americans have recognized these three major traditions as coequal ways of being religious (Herberg 1955), and the GSS respondents in these three categories apparently consider themselves equally religious.

The GSS does not explicitly ask if the respondent belongs to a particular congregation, but one question comes close to this. The interviewer says, "Now we would like to know something about the groups or organizations to which individuals belong" and lists sixteen different kinds, including labor unions, youth groups, and hobby or garden clubs. By far the most popular kind of membership was "church-affiliated (or synagogue-related) groups," selected by nearly twice as many respondents as "sports groups" which was in second place. Table 1.2 shows that Protestants are most likely to belong to a religion-related group, with Jews close behind in second place.

Introduction

Table 1.2: Religious Commitment—Percent

	Protestant	Catholic	Jewish	Other	None
Respondent is a strong member of his or her denomination.	43 (14,634)	40 (5,930)	41 (475)	51 (372)	- -
Respondent belongs to a church-affiliated group.	43 (11,008)	29 (4,327)	37 (361)	26 (289)	3 (1,255)
Respondent attends religious services weekly.	30 (17,087)	40 (6,839)	9 (593)	25 (455)	1 (1,891)
Respondent believes there is a life after death.	77 (11,302)	70 (4,552)	26 (362)	64 (328)	41 (1,313)
Respondent believes the Bible is the actual word of God and is to be taken literally.	43 (4,407)	23 (1,774)	4 (119)	17 (149)	11 (504)
Respondent says somebody who is against all churches should be allowed to speak.	62 (11,941)	71 (4,751)	81 (419)	79 (323)	89 (1,273)
Respondent approves of Supreme Court's ban on prayer in public schools.	34 (8,051)	39 (3,205)	81 (270)	56 (201)	68 (891)

Unfortunately, we do not know which respondents answered in terms of whether they belonged to a congregation, or only whether they belonged to some group in addition to their congregation, such as a church committee, Bible-study class, or the like. In a portion of the interviews administered in 1987, the GSS asked, "You said you were a member of a church affiliated group. Is that group or organization the church (synagogue) itself, or some other group related to the church?" Only 307 people answered this question, and about 54 percent of them said "the church itself." Another 29 percent said "other group," and 17 percent said "both." Thus, the item about involvement in church-related groups is somewhat ambiguous, but it is worth considering because involvement in such groups is a major way of being religious.

One of the most effective and commonly used variables in the sociology of religion is frequency of participation in religious services. This not only taps the ritual aspect of religious commitment but presumably measures how closely the person is embedded in the social network around the congregation. The GSS asks, "How often do you attend religious services?" The respondent was asked to choose one of nine answers, from "never" to "several times a week." This item shows substantial differences among Protestants, Catholics, and Jews, and quite reasonably few people whose religion is "none" participate weekly in religious services.

As the Slocum disaster demonstrated, a key feature of religious belief is the way it deals with death. The GSS asks, "Do you believe there is a life after death?" The respondent could select one of three responses: yes, no, undecided. More than two-thirds of Christians, compared with about a quarter of Jews, believe in an afterlife, reminding us that religious traditions differ in the way they deal with the greatest challenges of life. But mutual respect and sympathy are possible in a society that possesses religious freedom. Recall that moment in the Slocum story when clergy of many faiths, including Catholics and Jews, rallied around the bereaved Lutheran Protestants to offer comfort and prayers.

People differ in how they conceptualize the afterlife, and in 1983 through 1987, the GSS sought to determine which conceptions were most common. If a respondent had said they believed in an afterlife or were undecided about it, the interviewer would say, "Of course, no one knows exactly what life after death would be like, but here are some ideas people have had." The interviewer then handed the respondent a card that had ten different descriptions of the afterlife on it and asked, "How likely do you feel each possibility is?" Following are the ten, listed in order from the one judged most likely to least likely:

1. Union with God
2. Reunion with loved ones
3. A life of peace and tranquillity
4. A place of loving intellectual communion
5. A spiritual life, involving our mind but not our body
6. A paradise of pleasure and delights
7. A life like the one here on earth only better
8. A life without many things which make our present life enjoyable
9. A life of intense action
10. A pale, shadowy form of life, hardly life at all

The chief source of religious beliefs in Western civilization is the Bible, although of course denominations differ in terms of which translations they prefer, only Christians include the New Testament, and a few groups add other sacred writings. (For example, the Church of Jesus Christ of Latter-Day Saints considers the *Book of Mormon* to be "Another Testament of Jesus Christ.") Starting in the mid-1980s, the GSS included an item asking, "Which of the following three statements comes closest to describing your feelings about the Bible?" Of the 6,962 who answered, 35 percent said, "The Bible is the actual word of God and is to be taken literally, word for word." Fully 49 percent said, "The Bible is the inspired word of God but not everything in it should be taken literally, word for word." And only one in seven, about 15 percent, described the Bible in nonreligious terms: "The Bible is an ancient book of fables, legends, history, and moral precepts recorded by men." Table 1.2 shows that Protestants are twice as likely as Catholics to say the Bible is the "actual word of God," and Jews are especially unlikely to express this opinion.

Although the majority believe the Bible contains religious truth, the majority are also prepared to allow people to disagree with them. One series of GSS questions measures attitudes toward people with minority opinions: "There are always some people whose ideas are considered bad or dangerous by other people, for instance, somebody who is against all churches and religion. If such a person wanted to make a speech in your community against churches and religion, should he be allowed to speak, or not?" Notice that this person is not simply an atheist who wants to express his view that God does not exist. It is entirely possible for an atheist to respect churches—for their art and music, for the good deeds they do, and even for the comfort they provide their members, despite the fact the atheist does not accept the beliefs on which the comfort is based. No, this troublesome person is not merely an atheist but a vocal opponent of churches and religion. Yet, a majority of respondents in each religious tradition favor letting him speak. There are noticeable difference across the groups, however, with fewer Protestants prepared to allow the speech than Catholics, who are slightly less accepting than Jews and those with no religion.

Many people are willing to let an opponent of the churches speak but want official support for religion nonetheless. The GSS asks, "The United States Supreme Court has ruled that no state or local government may require the reading of the Lord's Prayer or Bible verses in public schools. What are your views on this—do you approve or disapprove of the court ruling?" Altogether, 13,406 respondents answered this question, and just 37 percent approved of the Supreme Court decision. Fully 60 percent of them disapproved, and 3 percent had no opinion. Table 1.2 shows that approval of the court ban is lowest among Christians. Other groups might well predict that if prayers are mandated in school, they will reflect the Christian majority in the nation. In addition, denominations may differ in terms of their concern about government interference in private matters, including spiritual ones.

The GSS once included a related item: "What are your views on the reading of the Lord's Prayer or Bible verses in public schools? Do you think it should be required in all public schools, not allowed in any public schools, or that it should be up to each state or local community to decide?" Of the 723 respondents who answered, 31 percent said it should be required, and 58 percent said it should be left up to the state or local community, which

20

seems to imply they would be happy for prayer to be required by local governments whatever a few individual students and their families might feel. Perhaps respondents did not understand the local option this way, but if they did fully 89 percent feel it is all right to require prayer in schools so long as the decision results from local democratic processes. This forcefully raises the issue of the rights of religious minorities.

Churches, Sects, and Cults

If a respondent said he or she was a Protestant, the GSS interviewer would then ask, "What specific denomination is that, if any?" In the first decade of the GSS, the interviewer did not probe deeply to learn the precise name of the denomination, but was content with a general label, such as Baptist or Lutheran. More recently, interviewers have tried to distinguish the American Baptist Association (northern Baptists) from the Southern Baptist Convention, Missouri Synod Lutherans from Wisconsin Synod Lutherans, and so on. But often respondents don't know what kind of Baptists or Lutherans they are. In addition, many denominations are so small we cannot do reliable statistical analysis with data about them unless we combine numbers into general groupings such as Holiness or Pentecostal. Table 1.3 tells us how many respondents were in each of twenty-four categories of Protestants. Perhaps only two of these, Episcopal and Jehovah's Witness, are really single denominations.

Some of the categories require explanation. There are probably three kinds of nondenominational Protestant. Some are members of mainstream community churches that do not owe allegiance to any particular national denomination; these include local fusion churches with ties to two or more denominations. Others respondents are members of tiny sects, some consisting of a single congregation, that have not yet created a denominational identity, if they ever will. Still others are unchurched Protestants who have a sentimental attachment to their tradition but no current involvement in a church. The Christian Church is another name of the Disciples of Christ, a mainline denomination, but many other people may have said their denomination was Christian, including Born-Again Christian members of various sects and some unchurched people like those who wound up in the nondenominational category. Table 1.3 lists separately every denominational category with at least twenty-five members, and the rest are combined under the Other Protestant label, along with a few who simply said they were Protestants.

In later chapters, we will see that several of these groups came into being by splitting off from large denominations on the list. For example, Chapter 3 will examine the Holiness movement, in which several schismatic groups erupted from the Methodists, and a few of these combined to form the Nazarenes. Other groups emerged from disorganized mass movements, what sociologists often call *collective behavior*, without the clear denominational ruptures we call schisms. Chapter 4 looks at the widespread Adventist movement that includes Jehovah's Witnesses. Of course, once the Adventist movement became relatively well-organized, schisms were possible, and the Branch Davidians who died in the 1993 holocaust in Waco, Texas, were the result of a whole series of schisms. At least four of the groups in Table 1.3 represent major new departures, adding fresh beliefs to the existing Protestant traditions shared by most of the other groups: Latter-Day Saints (Mor-

Table 1.3: Major Denominational Groupings

Denomination	Respondents	Percent
Baptist	5,539	20.5
Methodist	3,000	11.1
Lutheran	2,021	7.5
Presbyterian	1,240	4.6
Episcopal	684	2.5
Pentecostal	475	1.8
Christian Church	439	1.6
United Church of Christ	376	1.4
Latter-Day Saints (Mormon)	375	1.4
Church of Christ	351	1.3
Holiness	213	0.8
Church of God	180	0.7
Assemblies of God	174	0.6
Jehovah's Witnesses	157	0.6
Nazarene	139	0.5
Reform	128	0.5
Adventist	117	0.4
Christian Scientist	90	0.3
Unitarian-Universalist	65	0.2
Brethren	55	0.2
Quakers (Friends)	33	0.1
Menonites	25	0.1
Nondenominational Protestant	992	3.7
Other Protestant	309	1.1
Total Protestant	17,177	63.6
Catholic	6,852	25.4
Jewish	595	2.2
Other	456	1.7
None	1,917	7.1
Total	26,997	100.0

mons), Adventists, Jehovah's Witnesses, and Christian Scientists. What should we call groups of these different kinds?

Many religious movements are commonly called *sects*. In recent decades, sociologists have tended to mean either or both of two things by this term. First, sects could be defined as schismatic religious groups, ones that came into existence through the rupture of an existing denomination. Often, the term is reserved for the smaller pieces that broke off, letting the major piece retain its identity as a denomination. Second, the term sect can be applied to groups that possess a very intense form of the religious tradition to which they belong. The stereotypical member is practically a fanatic, observing the faith's traditional practices with excessive zeal and promoting an unreasonably rigid version of the belief system with great energy and often little politeness.

There are two problems here. First, the word *sect* carries unnecessary negative connotations. A *denomination* is a moderate, respectable religious organization. whereas a *sect* is a troublesome one. As we shall see in greater detail in the next chapter, sociologists traditionally referred to the state-supported, established religious organization in a society as a *church* or ecclesia, in distinction with sects, but in modern pluralistic societies there is no single dominant church, and we often call the several moderate groups denominations. When referring to the brand of religion dominant in Iran, however, journalists often call it the Shiite "sect" of Islam. But they do not refer to the Episcopal "sect" of Christianity. Properly, they should speak of the Shiite "denomination" or "church" because it is a well-established, even ancient variety of Islam that is the official faith of a major nation. It used to be said that a gentleman does not offend unintentionally. Perhaps sociologists of religion should not use potentially offensive four-letter words like sect, except advisedly when forced to refer to the offense that many people express concerning groups that receive the label from the mass media or other powerful elements of society.

The second problem is that defining *sect* as an intense, schismatic group leaves one in an awkward position for speaking of groups that are schismatic but not intense, or intense but not schismatic. An alternative term has been proposed for moderate groups that arose through schism, *church movement*, and the example usually given is Reform Judaism (Steinberg 1965; Stark and Bainbridge 1985:123–124). There are several ways an intense religious group can arise, but scholars generally restrict the term *sect* to groups within a religious tradition that also contains moderate groups. The Episcopalians are a Protestant denomination, for example, whereas Pentecostal groups are Protestant sects. Logically, the chief way a group can belong to an established religious tradition is through its historical roots, so it must have been born out of an existing denomination, often a more moderate one. We will consider the dynamics of schism in Chapter 2 and Chapter 3, and here we merely note that the standard definition of "sect" is not perfect. But it alerts us to the fact that many groups represent an intense form of a standard religious tradition and were born in schism.

But many groups offer religion that is distinctively new. Their detailed histories vary considerably, although the popular image of their origins is often not far from the mark. An individual of unusual talent and strange visions establishes a tiny group out of his or her friends and family, then succeeds in recruiting many individuals to it and forming them into a solid organization based on novel beliefs and practices. The mass media occasionally call these groups sects, but often they came into being without a schism and they do not belong to familiar religious traditions. Consequently, many sociologists have used the word "cult" for culturally innovative new groups. Others feel that the mass media have brought the word "cult" into disrepute, applying it only when they want to disparage a group. Therefore, many scholars now employ the phrase "new religious movement," often abbreviated *NRM*. This also is an unfortunate term. Sects, too, are new. Rodney Stark has suggested to me that NRM should mean *novel* religious movement.

These are unfortunate responses to an unfortunate situation, because the word *cult* had much to recommend it. "Cult is culture writ small" and has been defined as "a culturally innovative cohesive group oriented to supernatural concerns" (Bainbridge 1978:14). The word need not carry any negative connotations. In Roman Catholicism, for example, devotions dedicated to Mary can be called the cult of the Virgin, carrying neutral or even positive connotations (O'Dea 1966:39). The word is connected to the favorable concept "cultivate" which means devoting oneself to something to make it grow. Ultimately, we like the word "cult" because it is a short version of *culture*, and surely religious cults are subcultures.

In our favorably received theoretical treatise, Stark and I offered formal definitions (Stark and Bainbridge 1987:328). A *church* (or denomination) is a conventional religious organization. A *sect* movement is a deviant religious organization with traditional beliefs and practices. A *cult* movement is a deviant religious organization with novel beliefs and practices. The second and third of these refer to deviance, which some readers might mistake as a synonym for bad, so we should also define it. *Deviance* is departure from the norms of a culture in such a way as to incur the imposition of extraordinary costs from those who maintain the culture. Finally, we just suggested that sects arise through schism, so we need a definition of that as well. A *schism* is the division of the social structure of an organization into two or more independent parts.

But in this book we will take a newer approach, one that naturally extends the terminological trends of contemporary social science of religion. With care we may use a variety of words to refer informally to different religious organizations, when we want to move a discussion forward swiftly.

But when we want to be scientifically precise, we will use none of these terms at all. Rather, we will recognize that each religious organization is unique and cannot be placed perfectly in any category. Instead of thinking in terms of restrictive categories, we will concentrate on understanding the social and cultural processes that create and sustain the differences we observe between religious groups. That is, we will view religion not as a set of distinct organizations arranged in conceptual boxes, but as dynamic systems of beliefs, practices, socioeconomic structures and human beings.

Conclusion: A System Perspective

When the *General Slocum* burned, a religious system responded to the loss of a thousand human souls and the grief of those who loved them. Indeed, we can conceptualize this massive response as coming from a vast interconnected system of systems. The organizational system of the Lutheran Church responded as dozens of clergy converged upon St. Mark's Church. The Lutheran cultural system provided a funeral ritual, the German words of prayers, and the dignified hymn music for which Lutheranism is justly famous. The system of American Judeo-Christian denominationalism for once responded cooperatively rather than competitively, as many other denominations offered material aid and comfort to the Lutherans. The surrounding secular system, consisting of businesses and the city government, rich and poor citizens alike, offered material aid. Thus, St. Mark's existed as part of an immense network of organizations, individual people, and cultural traditions, rendered especially visible by their common response to the great tragedy.

Throughout this book, we will continually see that each particular religious phenomenon is inextricably tied to others and to phenomena of the secular world. At times, we will offer theoretical models that help us understand the dynamics of these systems. But we will also constantly offer vivid pictures of how human beings experience and create their religion. Each of the fourteen chapters starts with a little story that illustrates principles to be discussed later in the chapter. Usually these are historical, because the chief source of data about religious movements has always been the histories (including primary sources such as documents) of particular movements.

This chapter has introduced the topic of religion, and the final chapter will sum things up and contemplate the great questions of the future. The twelve chapters between them are structured in three blocks of four. The first chapter in each block provides an overview and some theoretical models. Each of the three chapters that follow it in the block documents a particular religious movement, usually a single organization but sometimes a set of related or comparable organizations.

Chapter 2 introduces the chief sociological findings concerning sectarian religious movements, especially the way that sects serve the needs of deprived members of society and exist in tension with the dominant secular institutions and religious denominations. Chapter 3 examines the largest system of religious movements in American history, Methodism and the swarm of sects that erupted from it. Chapter 4 considers the highly significant system of Adventist movements that arose from the Millerite "Great Disappointment" of 1844, including the Seventh-day Adventists and Jehovah's Witnesses. The concluding section of the sectarian block, Chapter 5, examines the extreme in schismatic groups, the communes of the nineteenth century that sought to break away entirely from American society.

In Chapter 6, we consider how individuals might be recruited to a tiny religious movement, perhaps of the radical kind often disparagingly called "cults," as a preparation for understanding the dynamics of religious innovation. Chapter 7 looks at the simplest form of religious innovation, the importation of movements from the alien religious traditions of Asia. Chapter 8 focuses on the inventiveness of a small but worldwide movement that arose from the American counterculture of the 1960s, called The Family or The Children of God. Further insights about how tiny religious groups innovate in beliefs and practices come in Chapter 9, from an examination of The Process Church of the Final Judgement, a group that began as an uninhibited psychotherapy service but evolved into a flamboyant communal religion that worshipped four gods.

The grand interaction between religion and the world, in which each transforms the other, is the topic of Chapter 10. In Chapter 11 we see how a religious charity or social-service movement operates, through the example of the New York City Mission Society in the 1890s. Chapter 12 considers the involvement of religion in the worldwide Democratization Movement that is especially visible in Eastern Europe and the former Soviet Union. A specific example of how phenomena on the margins of religion can potentially affect it is the New Age Movement, covered by Chapter 13, which prepares the way for the concluding chapter which looks at the long-term potential for religious change.

Most of the knowledge on which this book rests was developed over a long period of time by a large number of sociologists of religion and religious scholars. But this volume also reports a good deal of original research by the author, employing historical, ethnographic, and statistical methods. Instances of primary historical research appear throughout, notably including some work on the nineteenth-century communes, employing manuscripts of the U.S. Census, and documentation of the New York City Mission Society based on a variety of records. Extensive participant observation provided the data for the chapter on The Process, and other ethnographic work (in descending order of extensiveness) was done on the Family, the Unification Church, the New Age Movement, Transcendental Meditation, and the International Society for Krishna Consciousness. We have already begun to see statistical analysis in this chapter, and more will come in Chapter 2, always limited to simple numbers and percentages, so the tables will not require any formal statistical training to understand. This diversity of data sources, and the many theoretical models quoted or proposed in this book, testify to the present maturity of the sociology of religion.

In sociology, anthropology, and even psychology, religion was a prime topic for the pioneers of social science. But despite occasional upsurges like the extensive survey research of the 1960s, the sociology of religion has languished in a peripheral status since those pioneers departed. Today, however, this discipline is primed for a renaissance through which it takes its rightful place at the center of social science. No sphere of human activity is so thoroughly social as religion, in part because it is not severely constrained by the physical laws that so powerfully shape technology, economy, and even family life. Nowhere are so many fundamental theories about human interaction so ready for empirical examination as in religious movements. The research methods and analytical perspectives of the sociology of religion have reached a level of maturity conducive to rapid progress. After decades of little respect from social scientists in other specialties, and even less support from grant-giving agencies, the sociology of religion is rapidly gaining stature within the intellectual community, because of a renewed recognition of the importance of its theme. All around the world, religious movements are energizing social change and shaping the transformation of entire societies.

The Dynamics of Schism

2

Tension with the Sociocultural Environment

We should be prepared to go beyond typological language to escape the confinement of categories like "sect," but this chapter of necessity is deeply rooted in traditional theories of sects. For many decades, sociologists have noted that the groups commonly called sects possess three related characteristics. First, their religious beliefs and practices stand in the same cultural tradition as the mainstream denominations of their society, but they are unusually intense, even exaggerated. Second, the members of sects appear to come disproportionately from the poor and uneducated classes of society. Third, sects come into being through the social fragmentation of denominational schism. In fact, many groups people might call sects lack one or more of these characteristics, and in the previous chapter we already argued that rigid categories can impede sociological theory and research. But these three characteristics are often found together in a religious movement, and theories can link them together. Therefore we will structure this chapter around the traditional perspective on sects, from which a more dynamic analysis can be built. And we begin with Liston Pope's (1942) classic study of the way that churches often reinforce social stratification in a community.

The Gastonia Strike

Gaston County, North Carolina, twenty miles west of Charlotte on the other side of the Catawba River, was an obscure backwoods area until catapulted into worldwide notoriety by the great Communist uprising of 1929. Popular histories of the Civil War fail to mention anything that happened in Gaston, and the first event of real significance was the arrival of the Southern Railway in 1872. Three years later a second railroad met it at right angles, and the previously rural spot where they crossed became the town of Gastonia. The surrounding territory was devoted to agriculture, but many of the farms were small and their land poor, so the chief resource was the availability of cheap labor. This gave the county the opportunity to compete with the New England textile industry, because labor in Massachusetts had become relatively costly and the evolving technology did not require as much skill on the part of mill workers as it had previously.

All across the South, community leaders decided that industrialization could achieve a level of prosperity that a purely agricultural economy could not. There were no rich people in Gaston County in the 1880s, but merchants and modest property owners were able to pool small investments to build the area's first textile mills. These were community projects, built and managed by local people. The clergy vigorously promoted the new industry, praising the mill builders as saviors of the community and giving them leading roles in their churches. For religious leaders, the textile industry provided an alternative to the dreaded liquor distilleries that had started popping up across the landscape, and the ministers predicted that the mills would provide stable congregations while ensuring the economic survival of the entire community. The churches could return this favor to the mills by ensuring that the work force would be well-disciplined and docile, although critics could later charge that preachers had become the "moral police for the mill owners." As the mills grew, so did the churches. In 1880, the county contained just five mills and forty-one churches, but by 1930 there were 102 mills and 121 churches (Pope 1942:21–35, 3, 43).

In 1900, John F. Love and George A. Gray, together with other capitalists of the Gastonia Cotton Manufacturing Company, built the Loray Mill on the west side of town. The name "Loray" came from the names of the two local entrepreneurs (LOve-gRAY), but much of the money came from distant northern financiers. Around the mill they constructed a company town of two hundred and fifty tiny houses, later increased to more than six hundred. By providing homes for the workers the mill gained a considerable amount of power over them, but the fact is that most of them were in no position to provide lodging for themselves. They were impoverished farmers, or the children of farmers, who had lost their poor land in the foothills or the mountains and came to the mill job dispirited and destitute. Many members of these families worked in the mill, including children.

The mill jobs were the last chance for many of the workers, and without them they would fall into absolute poverty and starvation. Thus they were willing to work painfully long hours at low wages. In 1925–1926, Loray workers labored fifty-five hours per week. Men's wages ran from $2.54 to

$4.36 per day, and women's from $1.81 to $3.27 (Pope 1942:226–227). The mill-town houses cost between $700 and $2,000 to build, and while their tenants were struggling to buy them from the company they were required to pay a weekly rent averaging twenty-five cents per room (Pope 1942:63). Labor in the Loray mill was hot, exhausting, demanding work, tending and constantly replacing the spindles on machines that spun yarn used in making cotton cord automobile tires.

In 1906, the mill donated land near its front gate for construction of Loray Baptist Church, which steadily added members and meeting rooms, until in the 1920s about 1,200 people were formally listed on the membership rolls. In 1925, forceful Julius W. Whitley became pastor. A native of Stanly County just the other side of Charlotte, he had studied law in his home state, then went north to the influential Rochester Divinity School, where he took a degree in theology, and then earned a Ph.D. at the University of Chicago. Despite a certain lack of interest on the part of his mill-worker parishioners, he sought to teach some of them Latin, Greek, and Hebrew. Considered "a stern disciplinarian" (Ellis and Hasty 1995:18) he set demanding standards for membership.

At the end of the 1920s, the county contained about equal numbers of conventional Baptist and Methodist churches, thirty-five and twenty-nine respectively. Two other denominations were prominent, the Presbyterians with twenty-four congregations, and the Lutherans with thirteen (Pope 1942:97). The mills tended to favor the Methodist churches, often directly subsidizing the pastor's salary and contributing to the cost of church buildings. Three Episcopal churches completed the roster of fully "respectable" Protestant congregations, and there were also three Roman Catholic churches. The spectrum of religious organizations was completed by fourteen congregations that a sociologist might call "sects" but local community leaders tended to disparage as "Holy Rollers." These included five Wesleyan Methodist churches, a Pentecostal Holiness church, and one belonging to the Church of the Nazarene, all identified with the controversial Holiness Movement. The following chapter will examine the relationship of the Holiness Movement to the Methodist tradition from which it chiefly sprang. There were also two congregations of the Church of God, which may also have been Holiness groups, and one congregation each of isolated sects: the Van Dyke Auditorium, the Church of God Undenominational, the Gastonia Gospel Tabernacle, the Dallas House of God Tabernacle, and the Tomlinson Church of God (Pope 1942:103, 128).

By this time, distinct social classes had emerged in Gaston County, with most of the mills becoming the property of a dozen rich families, and the denominations tended to represent different socioeconomic strata. This can be seen in the educational level of clergy, for example. Liston Pope (1942:108) collected data on fourteen Presbyterian ministers plus nine Lutherans, and every single one of them had earned a college degree. Of the twenty Methodist clergy, seventeen held college degrees, compared with nineteen out of the thirty-four Baptist ministers. But not a single one of the eleven clergy in the Church of God possessed a degree. Pope (1942:109) commented, "The newer sects in the county are led by ministers almost wholly uneducated. Several of them find it necessary to have some more literate person read the Scriptures in their services." But they were effective with the mill populations, whereas the highly educated Presbyterian and Lutheran clergy found it difficult to communicate with the workers or to understand the conditions of their lives.

Compared with those of the upper-class churches, the religious services of the sects were informal and unstructured, but they had a powerful rhythm all their own. As people moved about and chatted with their neighbors, the choir would begin to sing a hymn, in the style of a mountain ballad, stanza after stanza, building the crowd's excitement. People would begin clapping their hands to the pulse of the song, and voices would shout "Hallelujah" when the spirit moved them, which it did increasingly often. A few folk would start prancing around in jerks and jumps. After the hymn's climax, a prayer might follow, with everyone pouring his or her heart out to the Lord in whatever words they were moved to utter. More hymns would lead to an informal Scripture lesson then an emotional sermon that a seminary graduate would find ungrammatical, but which called forth spontaneous Amens from the congregation, on topics a conventional church might find disruptive, such as sanctification and the Second Coming. Individual members would testify to the power of Holiness, and sinners would kneel to receive the group's prayers. This intense and noisy throng might not reach complete exhaustion until after three hours of religious ecstasy, and many would be ready for another session of divine power long before the week had come back around (Pope 1942:130–133).

Liston Pope (1942:134–135) noted a number of theories explaining the strength of these tiny sects among the poorest members of the community. Perhaps "an otherworldly emphasis in the newer sects affords compensation for poverty and transcendence of poor estate." The emotionality of the Holy Roller services provided relief from the monotony of life in a mill village. In the individual expressions of religious feeling permitted by sect services, a worker could find release from the oppression of a life devoid of choices. The fact that the sects were largely lay movements provided roles and statuses for people who were nothing more than the servants of brute machines at work. Lacking any of the symbols of status in the secular community, such as fine clothing and jewelry, they rejected those trifles in favor of the divinely conferred status of being sanctified or reborn in the Holy Spirit. "They transmute poverty into a symptom of Grace. Having no money, they redeem their economic status by rigid tithing of the small income they do possess, and thus far surpass members of churches of any other type or denomination in per capita contributions, despite the fact that they stand at the bottom of the economic scale" (Pope 1942:137).

A later Gastonia clergyman and student of Liston Pope, Donald W. Shriver (1976:18), developed a theory of church attendance during his three-year ministry in a more restrained Presbyterian church just a mile from the Loray Mill. He observed four motivations that drew people to his church: First, "because they have been hurt and need comforting." To provide this comfort, the pastor needs to offer "peace, forgiveness, and love." Second, "because they are tired and lonely." Here the church can help with "many informal social gatherings." Third, "because they are often reminded in their work that they are relatively low on the social totem pole, and they want to enjoy a different status somewhere." To give them the opportunity to feel they have status in the church, it must minimize competition between members and develop a social life that is separate from "the world of everyday work." Fourth, "because almost anyone can participate in the control of the church." One requirement to achieve this is to have a pastor who is close to the congregation and does not flaunt a better education than his flock possesses. The first of these four reasons, and to some extent the second, may be motivations for attending churches of any kind, but the third and fourth take on special significance with churches like those clustered around Gastonia's mills, that serve the lower social classes.

None of the churches opposed the prevailing socioeconomic system, and the sects preached otherworldly compensators rather than political revolution. There were no labor unions, and the political system was so completely in the hands of the wealthier people that it was irrelevant to the problems of the mill workers. By 1929, the Loray Mill had become the property of a company based in far-away Rhode Island, with neither understanding nor concern for the welfare of Gastonia. The local managers had been instructed to make the mill more profitable without much concern how they did so. To them the logical course was to reduce wages, reduce the number of workers, and require the remaining workers to handle more machines. Many of the veteran employees collapsed under the strain, and the mill hired newcomers who were neither members of the community nor churchgoers. The result was an increasing level of social disorganization that weakened the restraints that earlier had prevented social disaster.

At this point, a contingent of Communist agitators, led by Fred Beal, came to Gastonia, hoping to make the obscure mill town the beginning of a labor struggle that would sweep the South. The Communists operated under the banner of the National Textile Workers' Union, which was a Marxist organization unrelated to the moderate unions of the American Federation of Labor. When they followed Beal's call to go out on strike, April 1, 1929, few workers were clear what a Marxist was, and most did not even know that Beal and his crew were members of the international Communist movement (Pope 1942:261). For their part, the Communists made a pretense of representing the workers interests against those of the mill, but they really wanted to exploit the incident to radicalize workers across the South (Beal 1937).

Immediately the mill owners launched countermeasures. Chief among their allies were the pastors of respectable churches, led by Reverend Whitley of Loray Baptist Church. He said he sympathized with the strikers, but they should respectfully send a committee to the mill superintendent and trust him to respond justly. On Sunday he preached against Communism, scornfully reading aloud from a Communist pamphlet that advocated racial equality and atheism. The overwhelming majority of town clergy quietly let their antistrike sentiments be known, and they refrained from criticizing police brutality or mob violence against the strikers (Pope 1942:281–283). However, two Baptist preachers who lacked churches and had been working in the mill instantly supported the strike, as did an evangelist, a traveling Holiness preacher, and a handful of local Holiness and Church of God clergy. H. J. Crabtree, of the Church of God, prayed publicly for the workers' success.

Pope (1942:274) observed, "Salaried ministers of 'respectable' churches, with assured status in the prevailing culture, universally opposed the strike; a few ministers of the newer sects and a few lay preachers and ministers without churches supported the strike." Beal (1937:156) recalled that a few "lay-preachers who made something of a spiritual revival of the strike" joined his movement. The rank-and-file strikers seemed more open to a religious than a Marxist understanding of events. After a few choruses of "Solidarity Forever!" or other labor songs, "the singer would drift into spirituals or hymns and many a 'praise-the-Lord' would resound through the quiet night. Although most of the local ministers held against them, the strikers had faith that a Superior Court would reverse their verdict on the great Judgment Day" (Beal 1937:159). The Communists were dedicated atheists, and their disdain of religion eventually eroded the loyalty of the strikers and prevented them from building an effective partnership with the Holiness clergy who were sympathetic toward the strike.

At first, there were as many as two thousand strikers, but by the end of April the number had dwindled to perhaps two hundred. On April 18, a band of somewhere between fifty and two hundred masked men destroyed the equipment and supplies the strikers had collected. The defection of half-hearted supporters left a hard core of committed strikers who constructed a tent city when they were evicted from company houses, staged parades after the city had banned them, and willingly risked arrest and beatings by company-hired thugs and sympathizers.

On June 7, the Communists planned to revive the strike. At dusk, a crowd assembled. A young divinity student named Paul Shepherd told them "that a great test awaited them that night" (Beal 1937:164). After confused actions and counteractions in the deepening darkness, shooting broke out at the tent colony, and Police Chief O. F. Aderholt was killed. Beal barely escaped lynching by a town mob, and along with more than seventy strikers he was arrested.

Aderholt was not the only victim of the strike. After Beal, the best-known of the Communists was Ella May Wiggins, a tobacco-chewing mother of five children who wrote revolutionary songs. On September 14, she was shot dead when a mob blocked her truck from entering Gastonia for a rally (Yellen 1936:313; Beal 1937:159, 193). Five employees of the Loray mill were charged in the murder of Wiggins, but despite several eyewitnesses who identified the man who fired the fatal shot, they were acquitted. Beal and sixteen others faced trial for Aderholt's murder, even though no one saw who shot him.

The case against Beal and his codefendants was proceeding rather blandly, when the prosecution took an idea from the then popular movie, "The Trail of Mary Dugan," and brought in a dummy made up to look like the departed police chief, complete with simulated wounds. This phantom, or the wails of Aderholt's widow and children who were strategically stationed near the jury box, apparently drove one of the jurors insane, leading to a mistrial. In a second trial, the prosecution employed the tactic of asking defense witnesses about their religious beliefs, then painted them as untrustworthy when many admitted they were not believers. The judge found nothing wrong with this, commenting, "If I believed that life ends with death and that there is no punishment after death, I would be less apt to tell the truth" (Pope 1942:298).

This time Beal and six others were convicted and given sentences ranging from five to twenty years. Remarkably, the defendants were allowed out on bail pending appeal, whereupon some vanished and others including Beal immediately fled to the Soviet Union. After several years experiencing what Communism was really like, he returned utterly disillusioned to the United States, published his autobiography from hiding, was captured and served four years in prison before regaining his freedom. In 1943, while living peacefully in New York, he wrote the Gastonia newspaper that American's wartime alliance with the Soviet Union was ironic. "So now it turns out that the Fred E. Beal of 1929, who followed Stalin, almost to the point of landing in the hot seat, now is the enemy of all that Stalin holds dear, while my antagonists of 1929 are now groveling at his feet. Justice, where art thou!" (Earle et al. 1976:58).

Life and socioeconomic stratification in Gastonia returned quickly to normal, without benefit of labor unions. The mill's management noted that few strikers had been members of Loray Baptist Church, so they went to Reverend Whitley and to other trusted clergy of workers' churches, asking them to take on the responsibility of screening prospective employees. This they gladly did for a decade, and no one could get a job without being a church member in good standing (Ellis and Hasty 1995:20). Conditions for mill workers improved slightly, until the Depression devastated the economy and led to bankruptcy of the mill. It continued in operation at a reduced level until purchased by the Firestone Tire and Rubber company, and real prosperity did not come until the Second World War.

After all these decades, it is far too late to offer Gastonia a more progressive solution to its labor-management problems. Politically moderate labor unions did not successfully penetrate the county for many years, and the law of economics saying that production will move in search of low wage rates has not been repealed. The whole church-supported socioeconomic system of Gastonia was designed to lure textile production from New England to the South, and in recent years a very different highly effective system has lured it to Asia. As Beal painfully discovered for himself, Communism was not the answer. Perhaps there was no better solution for the poor mill workers of Gastonia than the social rewards and emotional compensators of religion, in a sociocultural system that provided one kind of church for the rich and comfortable citizens, and quite another kind for the desperate and downtrodden folk.

Church-Sect Theory

Perhaps the cornerstone of the sociology of religion is church-sect theory, a set of ideas that we will begin to explore here and will examine closely over the next three chapters. As the name suggests, the root of this theory is a distinction between religious movements called sects and a kind of religious institution called a church. Here the common word "church" refers to a very specific variety of religious institution called an *established church*, and "established" here is a technical term referring to a special relationship with the government or other rulers of the society. This word has a prominent place in the First Amendment to the United States Constitution, the first two phrases of the Bill of Rights: "Congress shall make no law respecting an establishment of religion, or prohibiting the free exercise thereof." Establishment of a religious denomination would mean that the government recognized it as the official religion of the nation, giving it a unique legal status with potentially many economic and political benefits.

Earlier we have noted the negative connotations and confusions associated with the term sect (and even more so with cult), but there is a different set of problems with "church." Unlike "sect" and "cult," "church" has a positive connotation. The problem is that "church" means too many different things. It can refer to a house of worship, a local congregation, a denomination, or even organized religion in the abstract. Church-sect theory is first and foremost about a particular kind of church, the denomination that is officially established by a society as the best religion, or even the only legitimate religion. We have called this an *established church*, but we might prefer a single word. And indeed, a perfectly good English word of Greek origins is often employed for this concept: ecclesia. Some English dictionaries do not have it, but they are bound to have "ecclesiastical" (church-related). So let us use "ecclesia" as the technical term for the established state church of a society.

The classical definition of this concept is imbedded in Ernst Troeltsch's massive historical study, *The Social Teaching of the Christian Churches* (1911:331). Actually, this English title leaves off the last two words of the original German, "... *and Groups*," so the treatise really covers a wide range of religious movements, beyond simply the established churches. Troeltsch says an ecclesia is "overwhelming conservative," "to a certain extent accepts the secular order, and dominates the masses." It intends to be "universal," encompassing the entire population. It "utilizes the State and the ruling classes" and "becomes an integral part of the existing social order."

In contrast, sects "are comparatively small groups; they aspire after personal inward perfection, and they aim at a direct personal fellowship between the members of each group." Sects vary in their attitudes toward the state and the society, although many try to avoid them whereas others wish "to replace these social institutions by their own society." Sects "are connected with the lower social classes, or at least with those elements in Society which are opposed to the State and to Society; they work upwards from below, and not downwards from above."

Table 2.1 shows how Thomas O'Dea (1966:68) attempted to summarize the concepts of church and sect as formulated by Troeltsch and later writers. An ecclesia claims to be the proper church for all persons born into a particular territory or ethnic group, and anybody born in the particular place or group is under pressure to belong. An elaborate system of priests and other religious professionals is organized into a formal structure that delivers divine grace or assists the believer in attaining it by adherence to the society's official religious dogma. Perhaps the key point for much modern church-sect theory is that the ecclesia has accommodated itself to the prevailing secular powers, intertwining with the secular institutions and supporting their values.

A sect, in contrast, has withdrawn from the secular world and even defies the chief institutions of the society. Stated most strongly, the sect is at war with the ecclesia, and any stranger who comes upon their battlefield by accident can tell the two armies apart because the ecclesia has the secular institutions on its side, whereas the outnumbered sect opposes both of them. In O'Dea's formulation, the sect is exclusive in membership, not considering everybody born in a particular country or ethnic group to be a member. Instead, a person has to join voluntarily, typically through a conversion experience in which the individual is regenerated. The austerity and asceticism of sects is connected to the fact that members tend to be poor in terms of worldly wealth, although not poor in spirit, whereas the members of the ecclesia include the richest members of the society.

Although this church-sect typology provided a conceptual orientation for much good sociology of religion, there are severe difficulties with it. For one thing, modern advanced industrial nations are filled with competing religious movements of many kinds, but lack an ecclesia. Certainly, there is no single religious organization that proudly represents the United States. The "National Cathedral" in Washington, D.C., may be Episcopalian. But the Episcopal is an Americanized version of the Church of England (or Anglican) denomination, which lost whatever vestiges of official establishment it possessed when the armies of England lost the Revolutionary War. In 1776, there were already more Congregational congregations, or Presbyterian ones, or Baptist ones than there were Episcopal churches in the thirteen colonies (Stark and Finke 1988). In Canada, three denominations compete for the honor of being the national ecclesia (Roman Catholics, Anglicans, United Church), and that is two too many to have a fully established state church (Oliver 1930; Clark 1948; Westhues 1976, 1978). All across Western Europe, the state-favored denominations are gradually losing their special privileges. Yet an opposition between relatively conventional denominations and radical sects continues to exist. So, church-sect theory needs to be modified so that it can apply even when a society lacks an ecclesia.

Furthermore, once scholars began describing religious movements as sects they ran into difficulties. Many of the supposed features of the ideal sect were frequently missing. For example, many groups which everybody wanted to call sects did not emphasize conversion. A familiar example is the Amish or "Pennsylvania Dutch" who try to keep outsiders out and who base membership exclusively on birth (Hostetler 1968; Keim 1975). Scholars began to realize that church-sect theory had been developed to describe relations between established religious institutions and dissenting religious movements in Europe during a particular historical period. Thus, it consisted of a tangle of concepts that might better be pulled apart. Many social scientists attempted to expand church-sect typology or criticized its inadequacies (B. Wilson 1961, 1970; Eister 1967; Goode 1967; Gustafson 1967; Dittes 1971; Welch 1977; Knudsen et al. 1978).

In a series of influential papers, Benton Johnson (1957, 1963, 1971) argued that the church-sect distinction should be pared down to its essentials, so it would really constitute a clear dimension of variation that could be employed to analyze a variety of religious groups. He wrote, "A church is a religious

Table 2.1: Thomas O'Dea's Ideal Types of Church (Ecclesia) and Sect

---

Ecclesia:
1. Membership in fact upon the basis of birth
2. Administration of the formalized means of grace and their sociological and theological concomitants — hierarchy and dogma
3. Inclusiveness of social structure, often coinciding with geographical or ethnic boundaries
4. Orientation toward the conversion of all
5. The tendency to adjust to and compromise with the existing society and its values and institutions

Sect:
1. Separatism from the general society, and withdrawal from or defiance of the world and its institutions and values
2. Exclusiveness both in attitude and in social structure
3. Emphasis upon a conversion experience prior to membership
4. Voluntary joining
5. A spirit of regeneration
6. An attitude of ethical austerity, often of an ascetic nature

---

group that accepts the social environment in which it exists. A sect is a religious group that rejects the social environment in which it exists" (Johnson 1963:542). Subsequently, Stark and Bainbridge (1979) picked up Johnson's passing use of the word "tension" to describe a sect's relationship with society, and proposed that the categorical "church-sect typology" be abandoned in favor of a dimension of variation, *tension* with the sociocultural environment. Religious groups could be placed at various points along this spectrum, rather than merely put in one of two categories, in terms of how thoroughly they accepted or rejected secular culture and societal institutions. Thus in a pluralistic society lacking an ecclesia, the church-sect distinction becomes a dimension running from low-tension denominations at one end, to high-tension sects at the other. A religious group might be found at any point along this dimension, and over time it may move a significant distance, either increasing or decreasing its relative tension with the surrounding sociocultural environment.

Johnson's simplification of church-sect typology did not immediately achieve widespread acceptance, however. Historical sociologist T. Scott Miyakawa, found it difficult to apply the concept of tension to the early nineteenth-century religious movements he was studying, notably the Methodists and Baptists. Although he saw some merit in Johnson's idea, he wrote "It would be difficult, however, to evaluate the variables to determine the degree of the popular denominational acceptance of their secular environment, since they continued to be suspicious of the arts and some intellectual interests, even while they encouraged their members in their calling

41

and participation in civic life" (Miyakawa 1964:83–84). All sociological concepts present problems of measurement, and in a moment we shall see that it is possible to distinguish various aspects of tension, even though it is frequently appropriate to treat it as a single, well-defined dimension, perhaps taking an average of a number of different measures.

In the most detailed classic examination of the differences between low-tension and high-tension religious groups, Liston Pope (1942:122–124) listed fully twenty-one different "facets" of religious life that might distinguish relatively established denominations from high-tension sects. Table 2.2 shows that these facets range from having no property to celebration of religion in the home. Several of these could be reduced to tension, including renunciation of the prevailing society and culture, lack of cooperation with established religion, and feelings of persecution. But it might be most profitable to identify each of these twenty-one variables as a different way that religious groups can differ, correlating more or less strongly with the abstract concept of tension. Especially important are the distinctively religious variables, such as an emphasis on evangelism, on the afterlife, on strict Biblical standards of behavior, and on emotive, spontaneous forms of worship. In many respects, sects are more orthodox in their religion than are low tension denominations, and it should be possible to measure this orthodoxy in questionnaire surveys.

Religious Orthodoxy

The chief virtue of questionnaire survey research is its ability to map the variations in beliefs, attitudes, and behavior across groups in a population. The classic study of northern California church members, carried out in the 1960s by Charles Glock and Rodney Stark, provides excellent data to compare sects with mainline denominations (Glock and Stark 1965, 1966; Stark and Glock 1968; Bainbridge and Stark, 1980b). Among the 2,326 Protestant respondents, 235 belonged to five good-sized sects: Church of God, Church of Christ, Nazarenes, Assemblies of God, and Seventh-day Adventists. Another 1,032 belonged to "liberal" or "low-tension" denominations: Episcopalians, Methodists, the United Church of Christ, and the Disciples of Christ. In the "medium-tension" category are 844 Presbyterians, American Lutherans, and American Baptists. Table 2.3 shows how they answered representative questions about religious beliefs, behavior, and social relations.

Among the liberal Protestants, only 14 percent said it was completely true that the Devil actually exists, compared with 89 percent among sect members, about as great a difference as there could possibly be. Similarly, sectarians were far more likely to say that biblical miracles "actually happened just as the Bible says they did" and to be "definitely" sure that "Jesus will actu-

Table 2.2: Liston Pope's 21 Facets of Religious Variation

Facet of a Religious Group	Low-Tension Denomination	High-Tension Sect
1. Members' property	Property-owners	Propertyless
2. Economic status	Wealth	Poverty
3. Relation to surrounding culture	At the center	At the periphery
4. Prevailing society & culture	Affirmation	Renunciation or indifference
5. Style of religion	Social institution	Personal experience
6. Attitude to established religion	Cooperation	No cooperation, ridicule
7. Attitude to (other) sects	Disdain or pity	Suspicion
8. Membership requirements	Social acceptability	Moral worthiness
9. Ministry	Professional, full-time	Unprofessional, part-time
10. Psychology	Success, dominance	Persecution
11. Basis of membership	Social prerequisites	Voluntary, confessional
12. Age group emphasis	Adults and children	Principal concern with adults
13. Socialization emphasis	Religious education	Evangelism, conversion
14. Primary interest in the future	This world (earth)	The next world (heaven)
15. Source of formal norms	General cultural standards	Strict biblical standards
16. Members in the administration	A small percentage	High degree of participation
17. Behavior in worship services	Restraint, passive listening	Fervor, positive action
18. Number of religious services	At stated regular intervals	Large number of special ones
19. Structure of religious service	Fixed order of worship	Spontaneous spirit leadings
20. Kind of hymns	Stately and classical	Contemporary folk music
21. Location of religious life	Church organizations	The home

ally return to the earth some day." The liberal Protestants in this study were all church members, and all would have considered themselves to be religious people, but only a minority of them fully accepted any of these beliefs. Yet, the beliefs are clearly part of the Christian tradition, so the fact that the sectarians accept them does not place the members of these high-tension groups outside the majority religious tradition of their society. Rather, they hold an especially intense version of the standard religious beliefs.

The next three items in Table 2.3 concern some of the highly varied religious actions that a Christian may perform frequently. The first focuses on home and family: "How often, if at all, are table prayers or grace said before or after meals in your home?" The next may involve the family but could be a solitary behavior: "How often do you read the Bible at home?" And the third concerns church-related activities other than the traditional Sunday-morning services: "In an average week, how many evenings do you spend in church, including church meetings such as study groups which may not actually meet in the church building?" In each case, few of the members of low-tension denominations perform the religious action frequently, but more than half of the high-tension members do.

Table 2.3 concludes with three measures of the degree of social separation between the religious group and the surrounding society, and the corre-

Table 2.3: Sectarian Tension of Protestants—Percent

	Low Tension (1,032)	Medium Tension (844)	High Tension (235)
BELIEFS:			
The Devil actually exists	14	38	89
Biblical miracles happened	39	61	91
Jesus will return to earth	22	48	89
BEHAVIOR:			
Grace said at all home meals	16	25	71
Reads Bible at home regularly	12	24	56
Two or more evenings in church per week	6	10	57
SOCIAL RELATIONS:			
Disapproves of religiously mixed marriages	31	39	78
Associates most with congregation	29	37	71
Most friends are in congregation	22	25	67

sponding closeness of members to each other. One item concerned "mixed religious marriages." It was included in a list of things, from "dancing" to "racial mixing," that asked the respondent to say whether his or her pastor would approve of each thing, and whether the respondent approved or disapproved. Here we focus just on the respondent's disapproval of religiously mixed marriages. The final two items directly measure the respondent's social relations with members of his or her religious congregation, compared with nonmembers: "Generally speaking, would you say most of the people you associate with in activities aside from church affairs are or are not members of your congregation (or parish)?" "Of your five closest friends, how many are members of your congregation (or parish)?" Again, the difference between low-tension and high-tension respondents is great, always more than twice as great a percentage of sect members showing a high level of religious separation.

Religious beliefs, behavior, and social relations probably reinforce each other. It is only common sense that groups with the highest levels of religious belief will also tend to perform religious rituals and participate more frequently in religious meetings. Religious beliefs, we have suggested, are essentially explanations about the nature of existence and how to achieve a good life in this world and the next. These explanations stipulate or imply religious actions to achieve the great rewards promised by the religion. It might be interesting to examine the conditions under which religious beliefs and practices diverge from each other, but it is safe to assume that most of the time they tend rather to reinforce each other and to harmonize.

The three items about social relations add an interesting dimension, however. Why should people who share strong religious beliefs and behavior tend to associate disproportionately with each other? Certainly one possibility is simply that sects draw their membership from more narrow segments of the population, such as just the Swedes in the neighborhood or just the poor farmers who live in Lost Valley. But the sects in the Glock and Stark survey are neither ethnic or rural, so an explanation along these lines would have to be rather complicated. Instead it might be more profitable to explain the concentration of sectarian social relations within the congregation in terms of the religion itself.

Religion is a social phenomenon, and religious faith can be strengthened by social support. Most people belong to low- or medium-tension denominations, and their relatively undemanding form of religion sets the standard for what kind of religion is expected, tolerated, and even supported across the entire society. A lone individual who departs from this low-tension standard will constantly experience unpleasant encounters with other people, in which his or her style of religion elicits disapproval, scorn, and even mild punishment. Thus, the costs are high for professing intense religion. There are two ways for the individual to lower these costs. First, the person could reduce the intensity of his or her religion. Second, the person could reduce interactions with the majority of people having low-tension religion. This second response would turn the person into a hermit, unless he or she found like-minded coreligionists with whom to interact.

High-tension religion demands frequent participation in religious activities that have the effect of strengthening social bonds among participants. Furthermore, high-tension religion offers specific compensators for low social status, which means that the sect considers itself superior to other people by virtue of its intense religion, a belief that is easier to sustain if intimate relations with outsiders are avoided. Given all these features of high-tension religion, nonmembers themselves are apt to find relations with members uncomfortable and thus to discourage them. The result of all these intertwined processes is that high-tension religious groups tend to be socially encapsulated, with members chiefly socializing with each other to the extent possible given the structure of their neighborhoods and families.

Before we leave this topic, we need to confirm that the northern California survey, done many years ago in one part of the country, reflects more general religious trends. To do so, we return to the General Social Survey and examine the same items we did in the previous chapter. Table 2.4 (which can be compared with Table 1.2) shows responses from five large Protestant denominational groups (Episcopal, Presbyterian, Lutheran, Methodist, and Baptist) plus a "sects" category that includes the five large sectarian groups studied by Glock and Stark plus the diffuse categories of little groups often called Holiness and Pentecostal. In comparing the Baptists with the sects, we should keep in mind that "Baptist" in the General Social Survey means not only members of the relatively moderate northern Baptists, but also the rather more intense Southern Baptists plus many small sects that have "Baptist" in their names.

Even compared with the rather fervent Baptists, members of the sects reveal intense involvement in their religion. A majority of them consider themselves strong members of their denomination, belong to a church-affiliated group, and attend religious services at least as often as every week. In contrast, these things are true only of minorities of the other Protestant groups. Although a majority in all groups believe in an afterlife, this view is nearly unanimous among sect members. Only among sect members and Baptists do a majority believe that the Bible is the actual word of God. Just a third of Lutherans believe this, compared with two-thirds of sect members. The proportion is closer to a sixth among Episcopalians. The last two items in Table 2.4 measure acceptance of a secular definition of society. A majority of every group except the sects is willing to let someone speak against the churches. Approval of the Supreme Court's ban on prayer in the public schools is lowest among sect members. The GSS items are not arranged in neat groups, as

Table 2.4: Religious Commitment of Protestants - Percent

	Epis-copal	Presby-terian	Meth-odist	Luth-eran	Baptist	Sects
Respondent is a strong member of his or her denomination	32 (594)	32 (1,070)	33 (2,514)	41 (1,707)	45 (4,765)	58 (1,447)
Respondent belongs to a church affiliated group	35 (420)	41 (800)	41 (1,878)	41 (1,287)	41 (3,573)	52 (1,094)
Respondent attends religious services weekly	18 (683)	23 (1,230)	22 (2,983)	24 (2,014)	30 (5,515)	53 (1,642)
Respondent believes there is a life after death	68 (449)	74 (825)	75 (1,909)	76 (1,301)	78 (3,649)	87 (1,125)
Respondent believes the Bible is the actual word of God and is to be taken literally	19 (151)	25 (334)	34 (693)	33 (447)	59 (1,461)	67 (459)
Respondent says somebody who is against all churches should be allowed to speak	84 (475)	73 (886)	62 (2,128)	70 (1,359)	54 (3,856)	48 (1,128)
Respondent approves Supreme Court's ban on prayer in public schools.	53 (329)	41 (551)	33 (1,355)	42 (992)	26 (2,576)	23 (791)

was the case for the survey of northern California church members, but they confirm that the religious intensity of sects is a national phenomenon.

Social Class of Sectarians

Among the best-established principles of the sociology of religion is the proposition that people who join radical religious movements tend to come from deprived groups, such as the poor and downtrodden (Pope 1942; Clark 1937; Cohn 1961; Demerath 1965). The General Social Survey provides ample evidence that this is true, summarized here in Table 2.5.

The first line of Table 2.5 reports the percentage in each group of Protestants who are of African descent. Naturally, just like other citizens African Americans belong to all social classes and income levels. Given the long-standing deprivations suffered by African Americans as a group, however, sociolo-

Table 2.5: Social Class of Protestant Denominations—Percent

	Episcopal (611)	Presbyterian (1,082)	Lutheran (1,737)	Methodist (2,570)	Baptist (4,847)	Sects (1,368)
Percent black	6	2	1	11	31	17.5
Lower class or working class	26	36	50	46	61	65
College Graduate	34.5	29	16	17	8	6
High-prestige occupation	43	38	26	28	16	15
Low-prestige occupation	12	13.5	22	21	33	34.5
High income	35	30	20	20	12	10
Low income	18	20	24	25	34	38

gists always like to check whether class differences across groups might merely reflect differences in racial composition. The table reveals substantial differences across denominations in the percentage of members who are Black, from only 1 percent among Lutherans to 31 percent among Baptists. Historically, of course, Lutherans were Protestants of German or Scandinavian descent, and for whatever reason the blending of American ethnic groups has not yet brought many African Americans into the church that Martin Luther built. The largest Baptist denomination by far is the Southern Baptists, and it has proved to be a comfortable home for large numbers of African Americans. The sects, which are the focus of our interest in this chapter, contain a substantial proportion of African Americans, but a proportion that is not very different than for the nation as a whole. In any case, I repeated the analyses that follow for just the white respondents, and while individual numbers changed slightly, the patterns did not.

One item in the GSS asked respondents, "If you were asked to use one of four names for your social class, which would you say you belong in: the lower class, the working class, the middle class or the upper class?" Only about 5 percent of the population admits belonging to the lower class, so to identify substantial numbers of people in the less-affluent classes of society, we need to combine the lower class with the working class. This puts about a quarter (26 percent) of Episcopalians in the lower classes, compared with nearly two-thirds (65 percent) of sect members.

Education is among the standard aspects of social status, and, for contrast with self-reported social class, Table 2.5 examines the high end of the spectrum rather than the low one. More than a third of Episcopalians have graduated from college, compared with just 6 percent of sect members. Another way of comparing the figures is to say that an Episcopalian is more than five times as likely as a sect member to have completed college.

Another key element of social status is the prestige of the work an individual does, and the National Opinion Research Center developed measures of the prestige of the occupations of respondents to the GSS (Davis and Smith 1991:817–835). Back in the early 1960s, an NORC project asked a number of respondents to rate the social standing of occupations (from the 1960 U.S. Census occupational categories) on a nine-step scale. Over the years, prominent sociologists worked with NORC to update and expand the ratings. The data set we are analyzing assigned a two-digit prestige number to the occupation of every employed respondent to the GSS, ranging from a low of twelve points to a high of eighty-two points. In 1970 data, for example, low-prestige occupations included hucksters and peddlers (eighteen points), teamsters (twelve points), and farm laborers (eighteen points). Near the top end of the scale were judges (seventy-six points), bank officers (seventy-two points), and physicians (eighty-two points). Sociologists rated sixty-six points, compared with sixty-nine for clergy and fifty-six for nonordained religious workers. There are bound to be uncertainties and errors in any coding system like this, and the original data were simply the name of the job the respondent said he or she did. Sometimes, that is, a person who has a low-prestige job will get credit for having a high-prestige one, and vice versa.

Simplifying the analysis somewhat for our present, limited purposes, I recoded these prestige scores into low (twelve to twenty-nine points), medium (thirty to forty-nine) and high (fifty to eighty-two). Among the low-tension Episcopalians, 43 percent have high-prestige occupations, compared with only 15 percent among sect members. And just 12 percent of Episcopalians have low-prestige jobs, compared with fully 35 percent of sect members. Clearly, occupational prestige and sectarian tension are negatively correlated. High prestige goes with low tension, and low prestige goes with high tension. This fully accords with the theory that high-tension religion compensates believers for the lack of prestige in the surrounding secular society.

Honor, of course, is not the chief benefit of a job; money is. One question in the GSS simply asked people how much money they earned, but this changed over the years of the survey and varied from one region of the country to another. Another item asked, "Compared with American families in general, would you say your family income is far below average, below average, average, above average, or far above average?" By asking people to compare their incomes with those they imagine other people have, we are measuring the subjective side of relative deprivation. This is a good approach because it is a person's feeling of deprivation that provides the motivation for high-tension religious involvement. In Table 2.5, persons with high income are above average or far above average, whereas low income is below average or far below average. Well over three times as high a proportion of Episcopalians say they have high incomes as do sect members. And as we would expect, sect members are more likely than Episcopalians to say their incomes are below average.

Relative Deprivation

It used to be traditional in sociology to begin theoretical analysis of a social movement with a discussion of the severe frustrations that might drive someone to join it. The assumption was that joining a social movement was an unreasonable thing to do, and only unusual motivations could overcome a person's natural reluctance. In its more sober versions, this theoretical approach is not very far from the compensator theory of religion, and we shall examine it again in Chapter 6. As Hans Toch (1965:5) put the idea, "A social movement represents an effort by a large number of people to solve collectively a problem that they feel they have in common." Two generations ago, Hadley Cantril and Muzafer Sherif (1941) argued that the religious movement of Father Divine offered poor, oppressed African Americans a sense of self-worth and compensators for their economic and political deprivations.

Sociologists distinguish between absolute deprivation and relative deprivation, and they have given the latter a far greater role to play in their theories (Davies 1962; Gurr 1970; Bainbridge 1992). A person suffering absolute deprivation lacks something he objectively needs. For instance, someone dying of a disease lacks good health. A person suffering relative deprivation lacks something that a person in a different status possesses. For example, the poor do not have the wealth and power of the elite in their society. Relative deprivation always exists in terms of a standard of comparison, but different standards may be used. People may compare themselves with the other people with whom they associate closely. Or they may compare themselves with the rich and powerful they only see from a distance. Or the standard is the level of reward that the people themselves used to have in the past. Or it can be an imagined happy state the people could achieve in the future.

Thus, to say that followers of sectarian movements tend to be relatively deprived is not the same thing as to assert that they are poor. It is entirely possible for a member of a religious group to have more than the average wealth and power in the general population, and still be deprived relative to other members of the same denomination. That is, if most members of a particular church are rich, a member who has only moderate wealth is relatively deprived. And this may be enough to attract the person to a schismatic movement.

In the 1820s, the Quakers (Society of Friends) were one of the most prosperous groups in Pennsylvania. Originally their denomination had encouraged emotional displays in group meetings, "quaking," and had peculiarities of dress and speech that earlier in American history had caused them to be the victims of harsh religious persecution. But in Philadelphia and other parts of the state many had become wealthy and influential in the affairs of the wider community. Not surprisingly, the leading cliques among the Quakers were rapidly reducing their church's tension with the sociocultural environment so that they would fit into the upper echelons of secular society. But members who were not quite so prosperous were a natural constituency that wanted to preserve the relatively high tension that had marked Quakerism. The result was a schism that split Pennsylvania Quakers roughly in half, producing a low-tension church called Orthodox Quakers and a higher-tension sect called Hicksites after their leader, Elias Hicks.

Robert W. Doherty (1967) has carefully analyzed old financial and land-ownership records, discovering that Orthodox Quakers tended to be wealthier than Hicksites. But, interestingly, both varieties of Quaker were much more prosperous than non-Quakers. If Doherty had merely compared Hicksites with the average for the general population, he would have been baffled by the finding of a sect movement composed of people who were not apparently deprived. But because he also compared them with Orthodox Quakers, we know that what counted was their relative deprivation within the Quaker community.

Conceivably, anyone could come to feel deprived if offered convincing evidence that life could be much better than it is. And everyone is deprived in an absolute sense, because we are all going to die, we all fall ill, and life is filled with petty annoyances and tragic losses. The foregoing analysis of relative deprivation offers a partial explanation of why high-tension sects contain some members from the upper social classes, and low-tension denominations contain some poor people, but it is worth reviewing four plausible explanations so we can fully appreciate what the quantitative data have to tell us.

First, every set of data contains some error. In particular, with questionnaire data like the General Social Survey, it is unreasonable to expect every respondent to give accurate answers. Social class and income are notoriously anxiety-provoking questions, and even people who generally tell the truth may feel great pressure to claim a higher income than they actually receive, simply to appear respectable in the eyes of the interviewer. This is the opposite bias we might expect to find on their income tax forms, but with good justification the Internal Revenue Service does not provide us our respondents' tax returns for comparison. Another source of error is simple lack of knowledge, and this is aggravated when questions ask for subjective judgments that are outside a person's daily experience. The fact is that people do not unambiguously belong to a particular social class, and respondents are unlikely to share the particular definitions of the classes that the researcher prefers. In high-quality data collection efforts like the General Social Survey, crude errors of recording data are rare, but sometimes the interviewer may check the wrong box on the interview schedule even if the respondent gave the right answer.

Second, personal needs and motivations are not the only factors that determine which religious denomination a person will belong to. Many people stay in a denomination that does not fit their needs especially well simply because they were born into it. In many cases, church affiliation is a family affair, and different branches of a close-knit family may actually belong to different classes even while attending the same church. This may be a case of remaining in the church of their ancestors, or it may be a matter of joining the church that best fits the needs of the average family member or of the most influential members. Typically a church draws its congregation from a particular neighborhood, and if families can contain several social classes, neighborhoods can, as well. In the extreme case of an isolated small town with one church, everybody who wants religion has to belong to it regardless of what its level of tension might be. All of these are examples of ways that an individual's church affiliation may be determined not by their own religious needs, but by the individual's social network.

Third, we should remember that a person gains not only compensators but also rewards from membership in a church. Relatively affluent people may take pride in being the major financial contributors to a church in which most members are poorer than they. Often, the dominant leadership positions in a church are taken by members who also enjoy relatively high status in the surrounding secular society. There are rewards for members who are poorer than the average of the congregation, as well. A social connection to more affluent people can provide a subjective sense of status, but it also may be the means of obtaining jobs in the business of the affluent members, or upscale marriage partners. The very poorest members may explicitly receive charity.

Fourth, as we suggested above, people may be motivated by deprivations other than those associated with social class. High-tension religious groups are much more likely than low-tension denominations to provide effective healing ministries for people with chronic medical complaints. Even in this age of antibiotics, some parents must cope with the unendurable fact that their children have died, a dreadful experience that often contains guilt as well as grief. For all the hope that attended the rise of psychoanalysis in the middle of the twentieth century, the century ends without reliable ways of curing chronic anxiety, neurosis, and moderate depression, so the emotionally powerful brands of religion still have a contribution to make in dealing with mild mental problems. No one should ignore that fact that many clergy in low-tension denominations still know how to minister. A good Episcopal service can communicate forcefully the impression that human existence is meaningful, that beyond this vale of tears lies a land of holy grandeur, and that there is good reason to hope that one's daily cares will ultimately dissolve into heavenly bliss. The religious services of low-tension denominations often seem well-designed to create a mood of peace and tranquillity, framed by a mild sense of community. But desperate people may respond better to intense displays of emotion than to an hour of tranquillity.

Of all the kinds of relative deprivation, social class is most conducive to the development of somewhat specialized religious movements. This is true because differences of power and money create and stem from social cleavages in society. The poor tend to live in poor neighborhoods, so it is easy for a local church to minister to their distinctive needs. Although many other kinds of relative deprivation may correlate with social class, they have their own social patterns that are less conducive to the emergence of specialized religious movements. Ill health, for example, is found in every stratum of society, although it especially afflicts the elderly. It would be unreasonable to expect people in their sixties to convert en masse from the well-people's denomination to the sick-people's denomination, at the very least because they could not bring their entire families and neighborhoods with them. The fact that many people in the lower social classes lack the means to obtain the best medical care for their problems only increases the importance of their churches.

Thus, high-tension religious movements come into being and sustain themselves on the frustrations of people who are economically deprived. Secondarily, they may then serve the special needs of people with chronic health problems or other less socially structured miseries. A moderately high-tension movement, based in relative economic deprivation but not so far out on the sectarian limb that it cannot appeal to economically comfortable people, may be especially well positioned to recruit almost anybody. It is sufficiently intense in its displays of faith to provide efficacious specific compensators for the poor, and beyond them to the chronically ill and others with special suffering. But this same faith can raise the value of the general compensators as well. People in every social class need general rewards that are unavailable in this life, so they may be attracted to a strong religious movement that provides credible general compensators, almost regardless of its social origins. And we must not forget that every religion is primarily in the business of providing general compensators based on supernatural assumptions. Specific compensators that address relative deprivation are the distinctive feature of high-tension religious movements, but at heart all of them are based on the quest for general compensators, just as is true for the low-tension denominations.

Converts and Defectors

We have described sects as relatively high-tension religious movements within the conventional tradition, and we have argued that such groups disproportionately attract persons suffering from relative deprivation. But we have not actually presented any data about people who were attracted from one religious affiliation to another. That is, our theory would seem to apply best to converts and defectors. People who are in a religious denomination that is at the wrong tension level for persons of their particular social class will tend to leave. People will tend to join religious groups that are at the typical level of tension for their particular social class. Thus, we need data on the flow of membership from low-tension denominations to sects, and from sects to low-tension denominations.

Table 2.6 compares a number of groups of converts with people who have stayed in their original denomination, again using the General Social Survey. Luckily, the GSS not only asks people their current religious affiliation, but also what it was at age sixteen. Thus it is a straightforward, if complex and tedious, matter of variable-recoding to divide people in terms of their religious change rather than just their current status. For example, ninety-eight people who were Roman Catholic at age sixteen had converted to a Protestant sect by the time they were surveyed by the GSS. In contrast, more than 5,700 had stayed Catholic. Here we are not interested in the Catholics who became low-tension Protestants or abandoned religion altogether, nor are we interested in the Protestants who became Catholics. Rather, the aim is to look at social-class differences between sect-related converts and the logical comparison groups.

The table employs five social-class measures, three of which were already introduced for Table 2.5 (family income, social class, occupational prestige). "Did not complete high school," is simply a different educational range in the same item from which we took college graduation for Table 2.5. And for sake of variety we have added a fresh item: "We are interested in how people are getting along financially these days. So far as you and your family are concerned, would you say that you are pretty well satisfied with your present financial situation, more or less satisfied, or not satisfied at all?" Of course a middle-class person who is obsessed with the goal of being rich can express dissatisfaction, whereas the mythical contentedly poor person could be satisfied, so this is not a pure social-class question. But it does bear on the person's motivation for change and thus perhaps their openness to specific compensators. Here we focus on the people who are not at all satisfied, and thus might be susceptible to conversion.

Comparing the first two columns of Table 2.6, we see that former Catholics who have joined a Protestant sect are more likely than lifelong

Table 2.6: Socioeconomic Status of Converts to Sects—Percent

	Raised Roman Catholic		Raised Mainline Protestant		Current Sect Members		Raised in a Sect but Converted to Mainline Protestant
	Still Catholic	Joined Sect	Still Mainline	Joined Sect	Raised in a Sect	Converted to Sect	
Below-average family income	26 (5,706)	38 (97)	23 (5,639)	38 (253)	36 (799)	41 (826)	26 (103)
Not satisfied with family finances	25 (5,727)	34 (98)	20 (5,656)	30 (256)	29 (807)	34 (837)	18 (103)
Did not complete high school	27 (5,739)	45 (97)	22 (5,664)	43 (255)	41 (810)	47 (834)	26 (103)
Lower class or working clas	50 (5,362)	64 (94)	43 (5,271)	59 (240)	66 (752)	65 (792)	48 (100)
Low-prestige occupation	23 (5,376)	36 (83)	19 (5,305)	35 (231)	34 (721)	37 (748)	21 (99)

Catholics to have below-average incomes, be dissatisfied with family finances, to have failed to complete high school, to consider themselves working or lower class, and to have low-prestige incomes. The third and fourth columns make the same comparison for Protestants. We see a larger number of people who converted, and this makes sense because these converts were able to stay within the same religious tradition, but Catholics who joined sects had to accept a greater change in many aspects of doctrine, religious behavior, and style of church. Again, Protestants who converted to sects are substantially more apt to report low socioeconomic status, than are Protestants who did not convert. Thus, the first four columns of the table provide ample confirmation of the theory that sects attract the relatively deprived.

In the previous section we noted that some people may belong to a particular church less because of their own needs than because family and friends were members. Imagine that Pete, who is a low-tension Presbyterian, has become best friends with Seth, who belongs to a sect. Then Seth introduces Pete to his equally sectarian sister, Sally, and within a few months Pete marries Sally. The end result may be that Pete leaves the local Presbyterian church and joins the sect. If this is the predominant route by which people join sects, then converts would tend to be of higher social class than are people born into the sects. They may still be lower social class than the people in the churches they left, because people tend to make friendships and to marry roughly along social-class lines, but on average they should not be quite as deprived as the people they join.

Our theory of sectarian tension disagrees, saying that relative deprivation is such a powerful motivation for joining a sect that it will overwhelm any contrary effects of joining via randomly created friendships and marriages. Undoubtedly, scenarios like Pete's story in the previous paragraph happen frequently, and Chapter 6 will examine the importance of social relationships in recruitment to religious movements. But we are here predicting that the social class of recruits to a sect will be as low as that of lifelong members. Given that abandoning one religious affiliation for another involves costs, we would even predict that the social class of recruits will be lower than that of lifelong sect members, because people need a stronger motivation to move than they do to stay where they are.

A decade ago, Stark and I (1985:160) analyzed data from the study of northern California church members, examining the social class of sect members. At that point, we wanted to focus explicitly on people who had individually chosen to switch affiliations, so we excluded people who joined the sect after marrying a member. This left us with 110 adult converts to sects and 110 members whom we called "socialized" because they had grown up in the sect. Among converts, just 39 percent had attended college, compared with 57 percent of the socialized. In contrast, 26 percent of converts but only 8 percent of socialized members had not completed high school. So in terms of education, at least, people who joined a sect were clearly more likely to be deprived than people who grew up in it. The study was done in the 1960s, when incomes were far lower in nominal dollars than today, so we should not be terribly shocked to learn that something like a quarter of sect members had annual incomes below $4,000. But it is interesting that the percentage is higher among converts than among socialized, 32 percent versus eighteen. Among converts, 46 percent judged themselves to be working class, compared with 37 percent of socialized respondents. Thus, when marital converts are excluded from the analysis, recruits are substantially more deprived than are lifelong members of high-tension religious movements.

In analyzing our more recent data from the General Social Survey, I have not removed marital converts, so we are giving the deprivation theory of sects a tougher test. But as the fifth and sixth columns of Table 2.4 show, on four out of five measures converts to a sect are more likely to be relatively deprived than are persons raised in it. The differences are certainly not huge, but with the very large number of respondents in the GSS, we can be especially confident in them. Converts are more likely to report a below-average income, to be dissatisfied with family finances, to have failed to complete high school, and to have a low-prestige occupation. There is only a one percentage point difference on claiming membership in the lower class or working class. Actually, the deprivation theory of conversion to sects does not absolutely need converts to be lower class than lifelong sect members. It merely requires that they be more deprived than are people who do not join sects. But here we have shown the great power of the theory, because the data show that deprivation is so powerful a driver of conversion that converts are even more deprived than are members raised in a sect.

The final process to consider is transfer from a sect into a mainline denomination. If relative deprivation draws recruits into a sect, members who are not relatively deprived may be likely to defect from it. Within any sect, some members get good educations, become prosperous, and may be attracted by the social status and other features of a low-tension denomination. They may no longer find the sect's emphasis on specific compensators particularly satisfying, and they may even dislike it. Thus they are open to recruitment by a mainline denomination. Just over a hundred GSS respondents had been raised in a sect but switched to a mainline Protestant denomination, and we see data on their social class in the last column of Table 2.4. Clearly on average they are far less deprived than are current sect members. On four of five measures they are slightly more deprived that people raised in mainline Protestant denominations, but the differences are small. Even with the very large number of respondents in the GSS we are not prepared to do a more detailed analysis of how they compare with socialized members of the particular mainline denominations, some of which are at moderate rather than low tension with the surrounding sociocultural environment. Of course, our theory does not predict that converts to low-tension denominations will be less deprived that people born into them. The theory of relative deprivation explains much about why people join sects and about the characteristics that sects have. Escape from deprivation allows a person to switch from a sect to a low-tension denomination, but lack of deprivation does not have the driving force that deprivation does.

Conclusion: The Shape of Tension

Societies vary in how clearly their stratification systems are divided into classes and castes, but all large societies possess substantial socioeconomic inequality. Gastonia, North Carolina, was divided into mill owners and mill workers, with farmers, shopkeepers, and professionals standing to some extent on the sidelines of class conflict. Few contemporary American communities are as clearly divided along class lines, but the connection of religious denomination to class found in Gastonia also shows up in the General Social Survey. The majority of clergymen in Gastonia in 1929 gave at least tacit support to the mill owners, and only a few Holiness preachers joined the strike by the mill workers. There are two ways to look at this, and we shall not try to decide between them here. First, one could criticize most of the clergy for being the servants of wealth and power, rather than siding with the exploited workers. Or, second, one could argue that the prosperity of the entire community—workers and owners alike—depended upon low wages that would allow the local mills to compete with those in New England, so the clergy were right to try to hold the community together behind the leadership of the owners. In either case, Liston Pope's study illustrates clearly that society contains different socioeconomic strata, and that each seeks a distinctive style of religion.

Traditional church-sect theory postulates a system of religious institutions and movements, in which an ecclesia (or established church) has formed an alliance with the powerful members of society, and small dissenting sects break away in social opposition and religious fervor. These sectarian movements tend to attract poor and uneducated converts, in contrast to the ecclesia which comprises the rich and educated. Throughout the first half of the twentieth century, sociologists tended to construct complex descriptions of an ecclesia and of sects that listed a number of attributes of each. But many examples did not fit these typologies at all well. Following the ideas of sociologist Benton Johnson, expressed early in the second half of the century, it is useful to arrange religious groups along a dimension of their degree of tension with the surrounding sociocultural environment.

By definition, an ecclesia is at very low tension with the standard institutions of the society, and in theocratic societies like the ancient Byzantine Empire or contemporary Iran, the state and the ecclesia are merged. In modern America and Western Europe, a number of low-tension denominations take the place of the ecclesia, because these secularized societies are not dominated by religious monopolies. These denominations are not at zero tension, because they do disagree with some secular norms and assert a more supernatural view of reality than that promulgated by secular institutions. In all societies, short of instant execution of all religious heretics, there will always be supernaturally oriented movements that stand in significant opposition to secular standards and thus are relatively high tension. These are commonly called sects or sectarian movements, although they differ greatly among themselves and may share only the single characteristic of religious high tension.

All forms of religion offer general compensators, which are promises to be taken on faith that extremely general and valuable rewards will be forthcoming if a person adheres to the sacred norms. In addition, high-tension religious movements within the standard tradition of the society tend to offer specific compensators that substitute for wealth, power, and status. In so doing they attract a membership who disproportionately suffer relative deprivation with respect to other citizens of the society. At the end of the chapter we saw survey data from the General Social Survey which illustrated this exactly. Some of the people raised in low-tension denominations who suffered relative deprivation, were converted to high-tension sects. Indeed, on average converts to sects were more deprived than were members raised in the sect. Some sect members defected from these high-tension religious movements to join low-tension denominations, and these people tended not to be as deprived as fellow sect members who did not defect. This flow of people between low-tension and high-tension religious groups links these organizations into a larger system that encompasses them and in which each type plays a distinctive role. To understand the dynamics of this system more fully, we need to become familiar with some particular sectarian systems: the Holiness Movement, the Adventist Movement, and the cluster of communal movements that flourished in the first century of the United States.

3

The Holiness Movement

The grandest single drama of American religious history is the rise of the Methodist Movement, its gradual loss of fervor, and the eruption from it of dozens of small sects that together constitute the Holiness Movement. This dynamic story illustrates classical church-sect theory, which says that high-tension religious movements often will reduce their tension and form an accommodation with the surrounding society. When they do this, the religious needs of relatively deprived members will no longer be met, and the stage will be set for a new act of the drama, in which new high-tension sects explode out of the old movement. In the context of Methodism and Holiness, the psychological theme is the search for sanctification (or holiness), which may be a common quest among poor people of strong religious faith, but which also can seize the attention of the rich and well-educated. Thus, some key leaders of these "poor people's movements" have themselves not been poor and uneducated at all, notably John Wesley and Phoebe Palmer. Securely achieving sanctification within this life is exceedingly difficult, and thus religious movements frequently back away from it years after they committed themselves to its attainment. But in a sense holiness is the goal of all religion, and the quest for sanctification continually reignites itself.

The Holiness of Phoebe Palmer

Phoebe Worrall, better known by her married name of Phoebe Palmer, was born in New York City in 1807 to wealthy Henry and Dorothea Worrall, an exceedingly devout Methodist couple (White 1986:2). Early every morning, they would ring one bell to get everybody up, and a second bell to call the family to an hour of Bible reading, hymn singing, and prayer. Every meal began with a blessing and ended with a thanksgiving. Phoebe was the fourth of sixteen children, and the entire Worrall tribe trooped regularly to the Duane Street Methodist Episcopal Church. This upbringing gave Phoebe the most solid possible religious commitment, but it also created a slightly embarrassing problem. If Phoebe was already so completely pious, how could she have the transformation experience of salvation?

In 1826, Phoebe met Walter Clarke Palmer, an equally devout Methodist physician who was just then establishing what would become an exceedingly successful medical practice, and the following year they were married. The harmonious linkage of these two ideal, prosperous Christian families was further cemented when her sister, Hannah, married his brother, Miles. Phoebe gave birth to her first child, Alexander, on her first wedding anniversary, but he was a sickly child and she fretted over him. Years later, she wrote, "The duty of consecrating our children to God in the holy ordinance of baptism was clear to my mind; but the responsibility I should thereby bring upon myself, caused me from week to week to delay this act of consecration with our first-born; little adornments, requiring, as I feared, a useless expenditure of *time* and expense, were indulged in, and I waited to feel a perfect clearness relative to the fact that I *really* gave him up, *body*, as well as soul, to God.

"With thousands of mothers, I had spent hours of precious time in embroidering his garments; hours, which, as they winged their report to eternity, had left traces of painful uncertainty upon my mind, that I *might* be wrong. 'If I give up this child in baptism, I virtually take upon myself the acknowledgment that he is the *Lord's*, and if the *Lord's*, should I adorn him thus?' It was thus I reasoned, and (while lingering from week to week) God suddenly took our firstborn to himself" (Palmer 1845:254–255).

Soon after Alexander's death, Samuel was born, and he died even more quickly than had Alexander. Death was a constant companion of children prior to the medical advances of the twentieth century, and of Phoebe's own ten brothers and five sisters only eight lived to adulthood. In poetry, she sought to assuage her grief with piety:

> O! there our Alexander lives,
> > Where beauty's bud ne'er dies!
> Though snatched from love's maternal arms,
> He's safe from all impending harms,
> > And calls us to the skies. (Palmer 1988:77)

On her third wedding anniversary, Phoebe placed in her diary a hint of her feelings about Samuel and of the means by which she managed them: "The treasure was lent but seven short weeks, and was then recalled; giving us two angel children in heaven, and leaving us childless on earth. I will not attempt to describe the pressure of this last crushing trial. Surely I needed it, or it would not have been given. God takes our treasure to heaven, that our hearts may be there also. The Lord has declared himself a jealous God, He will have no other Gods before Him. After my loved ones were snatched away, I saw that I had concentrated my time and attentions far too exclusively, to the neglect of the religious activities demanded. Though painfully learned, yet I trust the lesson has been fully apprehended. From henceforth, Jesus must and shall have the uppermost seat in my heart" (quoted in Wheatley 1881:26).

Phoebe and Walter were active members of the Allen Street Methodist Episcopal Church, where Reverend Samuel Merwin launched a series of preaching meetings that grew into a local revival. Walter drove himself to exhaustion, attending all the meetings and assisting the newcomers by praying with them and urging them to come to Jesus. Although the revival made Phoebe feel closer to God, it accentuated her concern that she had never experienced the intense emotional experience her religious tradition associated with dedication to God.

In 1833, Phoebe gave birth to a healthy daughter named Sarah, and a second but less healthy girl, Eliza, was born in 1835. Illness struck mother and daughter, bringing both to the door of death, but they recovered. This new torment ratcheted up Phoebe's religiousness another notch, and she began writing sacred poetry regularly. The Palmer family moved to a house on the Lower East Side of Manhattan, which they shared with Phoebe's elder sister Sarah, who had married an architect named Thomas Lankford. In the new home, everybody was healthy, prosperous, and optimistic. Then tragedy struck again.

Phoebe wrote, "Just before the great trial came upon me, I had attended a camp-meeting, where the Lord was most graciously present, and my own soul shared in the general refreshing from on high. Soon after my return home, I observed that my lovely little daughter, Eliza, about eleven months old, though not really ill, appeared to be drooping in health. I don't know why it was, but a feeling came over me that she might not be with me long. My motherly fondness might have drawn the picture too strongly, but I thought her an angel-like child, both in disposition and beauty of form. She was robed in virgin white, and her every look seemed so angelic, that I clasped her yet more closely to my breast, and with inexpressible love, exclaimed, 'O you little angel!' I sat clasping her in my arms, till she fell into a soft beautiful slumber" (quoted in Wheatley 1881:30–31).

Just then a gentleman came to visit, and Phoebe laid Eliza in her soft cradle, all festooned with white gauze, and told the nursemaid to watch the child. While Phoebe was in another room, talking with the visitor, the nurse noticed that her alcohol lamp needing filling. Too lazy to blow out the flame before adding more of the incendiary liquid, she simply set about to pour it in. It spilled, caught fire, and burned her hands. Without thinking, the nurse-maid hurled the blazing lamp away from her, and it landed in the cradle, engulfing Eliza and all the flammable bedding with fire. Eliza's screams alerted her mother (White 1986:7–8).

"I flew to the spot, and what a scene met my gaze! The gauze curtains that surrounded the cradle of the sleeping infant, through the carelessness of the nurse, had caught fire. I grasped my darling from the flames. She darted one inexpressible look of amazement and pity, on her agonized mother, and then closed her eyes forever on the scenes of earth. After a few hours the sweet spirit of my darling passed away, leaving me, from the suddenness of the shock, in an inexpressible bewilderment of grief. Turning away from human comforters, I coveted to be alone with God.

"After the angel spirit winged its way to paradise, I retired alone, not willing that any one should behold my sorrow. While pacing the room, crying to God, amid the tumult of grief, my mind was arrested by a gentle whisper, saying, 'Your Heavenly Father loves you. He would not permit such a great trial, without intending that some great good, proportionate in magnitude and weight should result. He means to teach you some great lesson that might not otherwise be learned. He doth not willingly grieve or afflict the children of men. If not *willingly*, then he has some specific design, in this, the greatest of all the trials you have been called to endure.'

"In the agony of my soul I had exclaimed, 'O, what shall I do!' And the answer now came,—'Be still, and know that I am God.' I took up the precious WORD, and cried, 'O, teach me the lesson of this trial,' and the first lines to catch my eye on opening the Bible, were these, 'O, the depth of the riches, both of the wisdom and knowledge of God! How unsearchable are his judgements and his ways past finding out!'

"It is the Holy Spirit alone that can take of the things of God, and reveal them to the waiting soul. The tumult of feeling was hushed, and with the words came a divine conviction, that it was a loving Father's hand, that had inflicted the stroke. 'What thou knowest not now, thou shalt know hereafter,' was assuringly whispered. Wholly subdued under the wing of the Holy Comforter.

"From that moment the very distressing keenness of the trial passed away, and my loved little one, who during her brief stay on earth, had seemed so akin to heaven's inhabitants, appeared scarcely separated from me. The vale separating the two worlds was so slight, that things unseen became a living reality. Never before have I felt such a deadness to the world, and my affections so fixed on things above. God takes our treasures to heaven, that our hearts may be there also. My darling is in heaven doing an angel service. And now I have resolved, that the service, or in other words, the time I would have devoted to her, shall be spent in work for Jesus. And if diligent and self-sacrificing in carrying out my resolve, the death of this child may result in the spiritual life of many" (quoted in Wheatley 1881:31–32). Eventually, Phoebe bore a total of six children, and the other three survived to adulthood. But the loss of half her children, with the tremendous investment of love and effort they represented, drove her still deeper into religion, and give her the mission to save souls.

Phoebe believed she could not save others unless she, herself, had already been saved. Her doubts about her own spiritual status were conditioned by the traditional Methodist belief, originating from founder John Wesley himself, that there were two different works of grace, "justification" and "sanctification." Phoebe's understanding of these two concepts is very important, because she transformed Methodist theology in a manner that encouraged the later development of breakaway Holiness movements, at the same time that she was merely trying to apply Wesley's doctrines to her own emotional situation.

Put simply, justification is the moment early in a person's religious quest when he or she decides to be a Christian, and sanctification comes later after the person has achieved considerable progress toward fulfilling the requirements of living a fully Christian life. Phoebe's biographer, Charles Edward White, describes the two concepts more formally from a theological point of view: "Justification occurs when a sinner is forgiven, regenerated, and made right with God. Entire sanctification happens when the carnal nature within a Christian is finally destroyed, and the believer is then enabled to love God with the whole heart, soul, mind, and strength. Entire sanctification makes Christians perfect in their love for God, but in no other way. Their hearts are so filled with their love of God that there is no room for a contrary affection. Hence they are sinless in that while in this state they do not willingly violate the known law of God. Although believers' hearts are filled with love and freed from sin, sanctified people still suffer the effects of sin on their minds and bodies. They are not free from errors in judgment or mistakes in action. Thus, they continually need the blood of Christ to cleanse them from these accidental 'fallings short of the glory of God' " (White 1986:121).

At about the age of thirteen, Phoebe "acknowledged herself, before the world, as a seeker of salvation" (Palmer 1845:76), thus achieving justification. John Wesley had originally felt sanctification might come soon afterward, but he eventually came to feel that it might be delayed until the very end of life, after a slow process of increasing piety. But like many others, Phoebe was impatient, and the sorrows of her three lost children goaded her to gain entire sanctification immediately. Yet these driving feelings did not lead to the overwhelming emotive transformation expected in the tradition of American revivalists (Raser 1987:265). As Phoebe later wrote about herself, "Not unfrequently she felt like weeping because she could not weep, imagining if she could plunge herself into those overwhelming sorrows, and despairing views of relationship to God, spoken of by some, she could then come and throw herself upon his mercy with greater probability of success" (Palmer 1845:74).

Occasionally, Phoebe received what she thought might be divine messages in her dreams, and often she would open the Bible at random and take the first phrase her eyes rested upon to be divine guidance. On rare occasions, she reported that a soft voice communicated with her, but this could just be a turn of phrase describing her own thoughts, and vivid visions were simply not part of her spiritual repertoire. In any case, she never had the intense emotional and convincingly supernatural experience she had thought would mark sanctification. Then, after years of frustration and fervent Bible-reading, she concluded that such an experience was completely unnecessary.

Writing about herself in the third person, she later explained the logic that led to this leap of faith: "On looking at the requirements of the word of God, she beheld the command, 'Be ye holy.' She then began to say in her heart, 'Whatever my former deficiencies may have been, God requires that I should *now* be holy. Whether *convicted*, or otherwise, *duty is plain*. God requires *present* holiness.' On coming to this point, she at once apprehended a simple truth before unthought of, i.e., *Knowledge is conviction*. She well knew that, for a long time, she had been assured that God required holiness. But she had never deemed this knowledge a sufficient plea to take to God—and because of present need, to ask a present bestowment of the gift" (Palmer 1845:19).

The shortest way to holiness, indeed the only way, she now realized was simply to trust the Bible, and to realize that the biblical commandment to become holy was also a promise that the Lord would bestow holiness upon the faithful believer. Again, writing about herself as "she," Phoebe said, "And here most emphatically could she say, she was led by a 'way she knew not'; so simple, so clearly described, and urged by the word of the Lord, and yet so often overlooked, for want of that child-like simplicity which, without reasoning, takes God at his word. It was just while engaged in the act of preparing the way, as she deemed, to some great and undefinable exercise, that the Lord, through the medium of faith in his written word, led her astonished soul directly into the 'way of holiness,' where, with unutterable delight, she found the comprehensive desires of her soul blended and satisfied in the fulfillment of the command, 'Be ye holy' " (Palmer 1845:28).

Holiness had its obligations, so now that she was holy she was obliged to dedicate her life to helping everyone else achieve holiness. "She now saw that holiness, instead of being an attainment beyond her reach, was a state of grace in which every one of the Lord's redeemed ones should live—that the service was indeed a 'reasonable service,' inasmuch as the command, 'Be ye holy,' is founded upon the absolute right which God, as our Creator, Preserver, and Redeemer, has upon the *entire* service of his creatures" (Palmer 1845:33). "So reasonable did it appear, that all the Lord's ransomed ones, who had been so fully sanctified, set apart for holy service, as chosen vessels unto God, to bear his hallowed name before a gainsaying world, by having the seal legibly enstamped upon the forehead, proclaiming them as 'not of the world,' a 'peculiar people to show forth his praise'; that all the energies of her mind were now absorbed in the desire to communicate the living intensity of her soul on this subject to the heart of every professed disciple" (Palmer 1845:45–46).

Pheobe's sanctification came on July 26, 1837, and immediately she was speaking and writing actively for the holiness cause, staging massive camp meetings throughout the eastern United States and Canada, and working with individual disciples to help them achieve their own sanctification. Very quickly, she became one of the most influential religious figures in the nation. Although she never quite decided whether it was important for women to achieve formal ordination as clergy, in word and deed she advanced the feminist principle that women could transmit the good news of God and be every bit as effective evangelists as men. Although she remained a Methodist in good standing for the rest of her life, some Methodist leaders disagreed with her emphasis upon immediate sanctification, and others worried that her ideas about her own holiness boiled down the dangerous proposition that anyone who thought he or she was holy must indeed be so. She preached to persons of all Protestant denominations, and she frequently held her widely traveling crusade meetings outside churches, so that people of various denominations might feel comfortable in attending.

Especially during her four-year evangelizing tour of Britain, 1859–1863, Phoebe condemned ostentatious display of wealth, and her creed was well designed to offer efficacious specific compensators to poor people. Yet she and her close associates were rich, and she felt uncomfortable with the poor. Once her ministry was well established, she became an active supporter of various charitable attempts to help the poor, including the New York City Mission and Tract Society which is the subject of Chapter 12 of this book. Little did she imagine that her doctrine of entire sanctification would contribute greatly to the creation of numerous poor people's Holiness denominations, separate from the Methodist church. She criticized the tactlessness of Benjamin Titus Roberts who led an early Holiness schism, and she rejected the idea of Thomas C. Upham that a third work of grace might follow sanctification, making a person perfect and thus utterly incapable of sin (White 1986:42, 113). When she died in 1874, the Holiness movement within Methodism seemed solidly established. But in the decade following her death, an explosion of new Holiness sects began to burst out of the Methodist church, based in large part upon her transformation of traditional Wesleyan beliefs (Melton 1986:213).

Tension in Methodism

The hope that religion can save a person from the miseries of the world and the defects of his or her own character is a common motivation for faith in all major religious traditions. For example, in Chapter 7 we will read about the spiritual state of *satori* (or enlightenment) offered by Zen Buddhism. In Christianity, many different movements have sought salvation by different routes, and since the birth of the Protestant Reformation a furious debate has raged about the degree of salvation that can be achieved within this life. One form these disputes has taken is the somewhat simplistic contrast between two strategies: *works* and *faith*. The former emphasizes doing good works, which may include good deeds to strangers but emphasizes benevolent contributions to the community in general by being a good neighbor and citizen. Salvation by faith focuses not on the relation of the individual to the community, but on the inner condition of the person's soul. If the person fully accepts the Lord into his or her heart, and believes that Jesus Christ is his or her savior, then salvation is assured.

One of the ways in which this distinction between works and faith is simplistic is that it places the burden entirely upon the individual. Typically, religions hope that God will contribute to the process of salvation, perhaps unilaterally and totally. Then the question is how God does this. An answer that is frequently connected to salvation by works is *sacraments*. Holy rituals performed by clergy will help deliver God's benevolence to the person. This is a common combination in low-tension state churches. If people do what is required of them as good citizens and church members, the church will assist them in maintaining the proper relationship with God.

Often connected with salvation by faith is the concept of *grace*. For some Protestant movements, often called Calvinist whether or not they actually trace their lineage from theologian and reformer John Calvin, God has simply decided to confer grace upon some people, who are thereby saved, while withholding it from others. In other movements, a person may pray to receive grace and hope that by submitting to the will of God and achieving perfect faith within his or her heart, God will choose to reward this devotion with salvation.

There is much good sociology in this simple typology, works-sacraments versus faith-grace, although these are frankly rather vague concepts and reality is often exceedingly more complicated. Among the complicating factors is that believers themselves use these concepts, thereby placing extreme strain upon them in their desire to gain salvation. Sometime they place such a burden of hope on these or similar concepts that they bend them all out of shape, and the words a person uses to describe his or her own religious condition seem inappropriate to an outside observer such as a sociologist. Furthermore, these conceptual distinctions have become war cries in some of the religious battles of the past half millennium. At one level, works-sacraments was Catholic, and faith-grace was Protestant. But within Protestantism, works-sacraments was low-tension state churches, and faith-grace was high-tension sect movements.

Rather than devote many pages of sterile analysis to these concepts, seeking their purified root meanings, we should note that the confusions that surround them are not merely the intellectual muddles of scholars. Rather, millions of people have desperately longed for salvation and employed concepts such as these as guideposts for fervent spiritual quests. Any concept of salvation is ultimately unstable, because taken to the extreme it means achievement of the most valuable and general rewards here on earth, when religion can safely promise them only in a supernatural context such as Heaven. Put another way, salvation means not merely the redemption of a person's soul, but also redeeming the promises made by religious compensators, and this seems to happen rarely within mundane existence.

Phoebe Palmer's life illustrates both the source of the need for salvation, and of the difficulties that even the most religious people have deciding how near they have come to it. To be sure, each life contains its own special mixture of sorrows, but Phoebe's loss of three beloved babies is as pointed an example as one can find of the terrible costs we experience in this life. In the context of her religious beliefs, she pictured them living still in heaven, and she postulated that they had been taken away from her to teach her the lesson that they really belonged only to God. These self-centered words can easily be translated into a simple analysis of her psychology. In the wake of each death, she felt dreadful grief and possibly some guilt as well. If she really had complete faith in her religious beliefs, then she should have been literally happy to send her children to heaven, knowing that they could communicate by prayer until she joined them there. But no sane person really is serene over the death of a child, and indeed no sane religious movement expects them to be. Still, a common religious response to grief, guilt, and fear is a spiritual lunge toward faith. If only the person could wholeheartedly believe, then these awful feelings would be dissolved by blissful faith.

This emotional turmoil is very much focused in the present, but parallel to it are religious fears and longings aimed at the future. However horrible today may be, the person can hope that tomorrow, or in that distant day when the person enters the afterlife, all the promises will be redeemed in bliss. To be confident of that, the person must feel that the right things are happening today—whether in works, sacraments, faith, or grace—to ensure fulfillment of religion's promise at that future time. Phoebe had been raised in a tradition that expected two works of grace, although the second might not come until the end of life. She knew she had experienced the first work of grace, justification, and the combination of her manifestly unusual piety and the crying psychological need to overcome grief made her long to achieve the second, entire sanctification, immediately. But the overpowering emotional experience that many people associated with entire sanctification eluded her. Then came the rather intellectualized internal debate that eventually convinced her she had indeed achieved holiness, simply because the Bible said she would.

Each person seeking salvation has his or her distinctive thoughts and feelings, but Phoebe's case states the problem clearly, and it is not very different from that experienced by the founder of her Methodist religious tradition, John Wesley. It would take a lifetime to master the vast literature about this remarkable man, and the biographies alone might take a year to consume, so our chief source here will be the single monumental work by Henry D. Rack (1993), *Reasonable Enthusiast*. Professor Rack's title is an apt description of the book's subject, because John Wesley was intellectually a rationalist who nonetheless was impelled by vast emotions. Until recently, the word "enthusiast" was commonly used as a synonym for "religious fanatic." People read Wesley's life differently, depending upon their own religious standpoints, and I must stress that here we are looking merely for a few simple clues to help us with our sociological analysis of more recent religious movements in the Methodist tradition.

John Wesley was born in Epworth, England, in 1703 to Samuel and Susanna Wesley. Samuel was an Anglican clergyman who had switched to the conformist Church of England from the dissenting sects in which his father and grandfather had been ministers. Thus the family history already contained within it the struggle between established church and radical movement that was to tug John in both directions his entire life. Indeed, it seems that John was conceived immediately after his parents reconciled from a separation that was at least in part a religious disagreement. When John was a boy, their home caught on fire. At first John was trapped, and his despairing father resorted to prayer to save him. In later years, John's escape from the flames would seem providential, and he always liked to think of himself as "a brand plucked from the burning."

Following in their father's professional footsteps, not to mention those of their grandfather and great-grandfather, John and his brother Charles received the education required for the more erudite strata of the clergy. John read deeply in Christian literature at Oxford, graduated in 1724, became a priest in 1728, and did not leave Oxford for long until 1735. Late in 1729, John, Charles, and some like-minded friends began meeting regularly to study literature, both classical and sacred, and within a year this group was famous as Oxford's "Holy Club." John had earlier developed a personal religious discipline to guide his own education and spiritual development. The group's adoption of this systematic approach earned it the initially satirical name "Methodists." In 1735, John set out on a dismally unsuccessful attempt to take Christianity to the Native Americans of Georgia, and for two years he was largely confined to the tiny English colony of Savannah where he became embroiled in both romantic and religious disputes. On the voyage to Georgia, he was impressed at the calm demeanor during storms of a band of Moravian passengers, and he became fascinated by their radical salvationist Protestant religion, eventually visiting them in Germany.

Later, Wesley would criticize the Moravians for believing that justification would render a person free from doubt and fear (Rack 1994:184), but he shared with them the fervent hope that some such transformative experience was possible. "Wesley wanted to see the power of Christ living within us, the new man as a demonstrable effect, and he wanted actual dominion over sin" (Rack 1994:146). Like Phoebe Palmer a century later, however, he had difficulty gaining the full emotional impact of a transformatory experience. His brother Charles was more fortunate. While ill, Charles sensed someone come into his sick room and say, "In the Name of Jesus of Nazareth arise and believe, and thou shalt be healed of all thy infirmities" (Rack 1994:144). Despite the fact he was told that an ordinary person had done this, he became convinced Christ had spoken directly to him. On May 24, 1738, Wesley did achieve a spiritual breakthrough of some kind, although his biographers disagree over its magnitude and how much he was changed by it. For himself, Wesley clearly believed that an even greater transformatory experience was possible.

When a person is born again, in a profound religious experience, one would think that the individual's feelings and behavior would be vastly improved thereafter. Assured that one is saved, logically one should feel no nagging emotions like fear, embarrassment, or depression. One should never again need to sin against God or against other people. Wesley himself continually hoped that perfection would be the result of conversion. But he saw people who had undergone an apparent conversion continue to sin and suffer, and he himself felt far from perfect. One way to reconcile these uncomfortable facts would be to develop a more complex model of the process of conversion. The initial experience could be a moment of open communication with God who gives assurance of ultimate salvation. As Henry Rack (1994:156) explains, "Wesley did not abandon the doctrine of justification or the idea that it was normally received in a decisive experience of conversion and new birth. It remained the foundation of the holy life, but the picture he favored more and more was that it was the beginning of a process of sanctification, culminating in perfection—a perfection which could be received in a moment (exactly parallel to justification) but was also susceptible of further growth by faith and discipline."

An Evangelical revival swept Britain, with Wesley among its leaders. Most shocking to the Anglican establishment, "John Wesley and his followers preached a controversial doctrine of perfection as in some sense achievable in this life" (Rack 1994:168). Where the Church of England stressed proper morality, the revival asserted that the basis of good works must be "justification by grace through faith" (Rack 1994:167). Wesley not only built up his own portions of the movement, but he proved very skilled at gathering to himself portions initially started by other evangelists.

A pattern that would repeat again and again in the Methodist tradition allowed the revival to develop momentum before it faced the power of the established churches directly. People could meet in nonchurch settings, whether at public rallies or in small private groups like Wesley's Holy Club at Oxford, and conduct many of the activities of a religious service without defining themselves as a schism and often while maintaining membership in good standing of a conventional church. By trial and error, often taking suggestions from perceptive followers, Wesley built up a far-flung organization that consisted of local "societies" grouped into "circuits," and within each society there were "classes" of perhaps a dozen members each who met weekly under a leader (Rack 1994:237–238). Only once the Methodists had built up a counterorganization were they forced to break off from the old organization. And this is how the denomination of Methodism came into being, first as a revival movement within the Anglican Church, and then as a freestanding church of its own that combined many of the structures and symbols of Anglicanism with the fervor of evangelicalism. In practically every way imaginable, it was a union of opposites, hot and cold like that "reasonable enthusiast" Wesley himself, and this would give Methodism remarkable dynamism over the next two centuries, especially after it came to the United States.

Success and Schism in American Methodism

Max Weber (1958:95) noted that "Methodism, which first arose in the middle of the eighteenth century within the Established Church of England, was not, in the minds of its founders, intended to form a new Church, but only a new awakening of the ascetic spirit within the old. Only in the course of its development, especially in its extension to America, did it become separate from the Anglican Church." In 1784, at a decisive Christmas Conference in Baltimore, American Methodists formally established their movement as a denomination separate from the Church of England. It was a good time to declare independence, because the Americans had just won the Revolutionary War, and Anglican clergy were fleeing to Canada in droves accompanied by many of their Tory parishioners. Wesley himself deplored the Revolution, and he resisted ordaining clergy either for America or Britain itself, perhaps because ordination would have meant a final rupture with the Church of

England (Rack 1994: 377, 471–534). Thus he gave great emphasis to lay, itinerant preachers, a tactic that was to prove extremely effective in the new land, especially when these men gained ordination as clergy while retaining their aggressive, traveling evangelism.

At the moment of its birth, the Methodist Episcopal Church possessed only about 15,000 members. But sixty years later, they were the largest denomination in the United States with over a million members (Miyakawa 1964:45). Finke and Stark (1989:31) estimate that in 1776 the number of members of Methodist congregations within the Anglican denomination was 10,507, representing just 2.5 percent of all religious adherents. The 1850 census of the United States counted the number of seats in church as a measure of the religious facilities available to the American public. In an ingenious series of calculations, exploiting the fact that the 1890 census did the same thing but also counted actual church members, Finke and Stark (1986) were able to turn the 1850 census data into estimates of membership for the major denominations. On the basis of this analysis they concluded that the number of Methodists in 1850 was actually as high as 2,679,323, representing fully 34.2 percent of religious adherents (Finke and Stark 1989:31). From 1776 to 1850, the number of Methodist congregations grew from 65 to 13,302, which was a increase from 2.0 percent to 34.9 percent of the nation's churches (Stark and Finke 1988:49).

In the early decades in America, Methodism developed a remarkably effective system of evangelism that sent circuit riders through the small towns of the East, and through the new frontier lands of the South and Middle West. These itinerant preachers were often poorly educated and always poorly paid, but their dedication to the movement and their comradeship with each other were exceedingly strong. Finke and Stark (1989:35) note that Methodist clergy "were of the people. They had little education, received little if any pay, spoke in the vernacular, and preached from the heart." While the circuit riders traveled onward, the Methodist classes (local groups) they visited were led by lay preachers who possessed typically strong bonds of family, friendship, and economic exchange with the other members. Thus, Methodism arose to comprise a third of religious America by creating a network of relationships that were deeply rooted in local communities.

Whereas Wesley was an erudite scholar, the most prominent American leaders were relatively uncultivated, like the tremendously influential Francis Asbury who had completed only elementary school. In their limited education they were like the people they served, but they also shared the powerful ambition that motivated American pioneers and settlers. In a few short decades, this ambition, coupled with the riches of the land and the freedom of the political economy, brought prosperity to many Methodists, and this meant increased involvement in civic affairs and culture. As Finke and Stark (1989:36) note, "the Congregational, Episcopalian, and Presbyterian seminaries had educated over 6,000 ministers before a single student graduated from a Methodist seminary." And yet those three more established denominations frequently had trouble finding enough clergy, whereas the Methodists easily recruited plenty of ministers and backed them up with armies of lay preachers.

Advanced education of clergy is a very dangerous development for a religious movement, because it teaches them to respond to religion more intellectually than emotionally. They come under the influence of prevailing secular intellectual movements, and their own professors of theology teach them to analyze, to criticize, to consider alternatives, and thus to doubt. Their message becomes more worldly and they preach with less conviction (Hadden 1969; Stark et al. 1971; Stark and Bainbridge 1985, 1987; Finke and Stark 1992). Thus it was a change with tremendous implications when the Methodists began establishing colleges and seminaries in the middle of the nineteenth century. By 1880 they had eleven theological schools, forty-four colleges, and 130 women's seminaries. Soon, Finke and Stark (1992:158) report, "The traditions of Methodism were being challenged not by the laity but by the ordained intellectuals."

Miyakawa (1964:53) has noted that even during the first half of the nineteenth century "in rapidly becoming more prominent Methodism was repeating and strengthening a familiar Dissenting pattern, all the more quickly since the denomination had 'middle-class orientation' from the first. Wealth accumulates and educational and cultural standards rise, or the more wealthy and cultured join, the discipline weakens, and the sect increasingly resembles the society at large." Other measures of tension declined rapidly, such as the initial prohibition against marrying a non-Methodist (Miyakawa 1964:54). Finke and Stark (1992:163) summarize the entire nineteenth century for American Methodism: "Their clergy were increasingly willing to condone the pleasures of this world and to de-emphasize sin, hellfire, and damnation; this leniency struck highly responsive chords in an increasingly affluent, influential, and privileged membership."

Russell E. Richey (1991) has argued that early American Methodism used four different "languages" or ways of expressing what their religion was about, none of them particularly clear. First was the popular or evangelical language, that was affectionate and expressive; it focused on love feasts and camp meetings in which hearts melted together, stressing an egalitarian community of brothers and sisters defined in opposition to the surrounding society's structure of sex inequality, social class, and racism. Second was the Wesleyan language of the church publications that communicated the doctrines of the movement. Third was the Episcopal language taken from

Methodism's Anglican origins, complete with bishops and sacraments. Fourth, was the republican language, in part drawn from the brave new political culture of the postrevolutionary nation, that vested authority not in bishops but in mass conventions and in the good sense of all believers. The ambiguities in these languages allowed Methodism to contain within it several contradictory religious tendencies and to serve varied publics. These can be valuable qualities for a mass movement, allowing it to fulfill somewhat different functions for different people. A negative consequence of these alternative Methodist languages is that they made it easy for highly educated clergy to diverge significantly from their movement's traditions and the wishes of some members, without appearing to do so. They also permitted the development of religious movements within the denomination, stressing one or another aspect of the multifaceted tradition, that could organize just as Methodism did within Anglicanism, then burst forth in schisms.

The growth in the absolute number of Methodists in America continued throughout the nineteenth century, but if the estimates of Finke and Stark (1992) are correct, the Methodists lost "market share" after 1850. That is, even as their absolute numbers increased, their membership represented a declining percentage of all church members. The total population was increasing. In addition, the proportion of the population who belonged to any religious denomination increased, perhaps as a result of the economic and urbanization trends which made it easier for folk to get to church, and as religious movements mobilized an increasing proportion of the available population pools. The Baptists offered strenuous competition, and the Southern Baptist denomination escaped the over-intellectualization that was affecting Methodist clergy. But new and especially dangerous competition came from small schismatic movements that broke directly away from the Methodist Episcopal Church beginning in some numbers in the 1870s, many of them dedicated to holiness. And one of the chief casualties of the Methodist theology schools was John Wesley's original concern with the attainment of holy salvation within this life.

A series of American religious leaders sought to revive the original spirit of Methodism, and in so doing added their own creative developments. Phoebe Palmer's biographer (White 1986:232) has argued that the American Holiness movement adopted six of her modifications of Wesleyan Methodism: 1) identifying entire sanctification with the baptism of the Holy Spirit; 2) linking holiness with spiritual power; 3) stressing the instantaneous elements of sanctification to the exclusion of the gradual; 4) teaching that entire sanctification is not the goal of the Christian life but its beginning; 5) reducing the attainment of sanctification to a simple three-step process of entire consecration, faith, and testimony, and 6) holding that biblical texts provide all the assurance one needs of gaining entire sanctification. Several of these principles had been espoused by others, and we cannot say that Palmer was the founder of the Holiness Movement in the sense that Wesley was of Methodism. But she is a leading example of the kind of independent, serious, effective evangelist who launched a vast, continuing revival within American Methodism that eventually could not be contained inside any one denomination.

A large number of small movements burst out of Methodism in the 1890s, and several of them soon afterward came together into a tremendously successful denomination, the Nazarenes (Redford 1958). Especially notable was the ministry of Phineas Franklin Bresee, who had served for thirty-seven years as a minister of the Methodist Episcopal Church before becoming pastor of a mission in Los Angeles in 1894 (Melton 1986:40–41). The bishop did not appreciate the interdenominational, "center of holy fire" that Bresee created, so he was suspended. A night of prayer and weeping prepared Bresee to launch a tiny storefront church, which was so hugely successful that by 1907 it had grown into a denomination, called the Church of the Nazarene, with fifty-two churches and 3,827 members across the Pacific region of the United States.

A similar story took place slightly earlier in New England, where F. A. Hillery was expelled from the Methodist Episcopal Church for disobedience. In 1887, with about forty followers, he established the People's Evangelical Church in Providence, Rhode Island. Cooperation began with other breakaway evangelical churches, which led to Hillery's ordination in 1889 and the establishment of the Central Evangelical Holiness Association. In 1897, this organization was merged into the Association of Pentecostal Churches of America, which had emerged from the ministry of W. H. Hoople in Brooklyn, New York. By 1907, this denomination had forty-seven churches with 2,371 members. At a Chicago summit meeting in that year, with both Bresee and Hoople present, this group merged with the Nazarenes, under the combined name Pentecostal Church of the Nazarene.

In Tennessee in 1893, former Methodist R. L. Harris began holding holiness tent meetings, which led to the creation of the New Testament Church of Christ the following year. Despite Harris's untimely death, his congregation survived under the leadership of his wife who proved herself to be an able evangelist, establishing churches in seven other states. In 1905, this small Texas denomination joined with the Independent Holiness Church which had grown out of holiness revivals beginning about 1886. Under the name Holiness Church of Christ, this movement grew to ninety-two congregations with 2,307 members in 1908. It then merged with the Pentecostal Church of the Nazarene. Thus, out of individual ministries expelled or escaped from the Methodist Episcopal Church, three Holiness denominations had arisen in the West, East, and South, then merged with each other.

In 1898 in Nashville, Tennessee, a Cumberland Presbyterian minister, named J. O. McClurkan, created the Pentecostal Alliance, which initially was not intended to be a denomination, but a movement to promote holiness across several denominations. In 1906 in Glasgow, Scotland, a Methodist minister named George Sharpe who had spent several years in the United States was evicted from his church because of his Holiness persuasions, but eighty people marched out of the disorderly meeting with him to found the Pentecostal Church of Scotland. In Jamestown, North Dakota, in 1917, Methodist leader S. A. Danford organized the Laymen's Holiness Association, with no intention of starting a schism. The first two of these organizations soon merged with the Nazarenes, and many members of the Laymen's Holiness Association came over individually. In 1919, perhaps to distinguish itself from more radical Pentecostal sects, the combined movement renamed itself simply the Church of the Nazarene.

The Nazarenes have a very clear conceptualization of the religious territory they inhabit, one that is not very different from what a perceptive sociologist might use. First, they distinguish evangelical Christianity from sacramental Christianity (Redford 1958:33). Their own movement is evangelical, seeking to save individual souls through inspired ministry. In contrast, a sacramental church is one that relies upon ritual sacraments, expensive artworks and architecture, and the authority of priests. In the Nazarene view, the established churches are always in danger of losing "spiritual vitality" and falling into "lifeless sacramentalism," as they believe the Roman Catholic church had done, thus triggering the Protestant Reformation (Redford 1958:29).

Second, they divide the Holiness Movement itself into two large streams, which they call the right wing and the left wing. The right wing consists of the people who adhere strictly to Wesley's doctrine of entire sanctification but feel that the Methodist Church has abandoned it. In this wing were the groups that came together to form the Church of the Nazarene. The left wing believes that a person is not baptized in the Holy Spirit unless he or she has the experience of speaking in tongues, and in this wing are the groups that remained outside the Church of the Nazarene. Nazarene historian M. E. Redford (1958:11–12, cf. 42) says the left wing is "given to the ecstatic, handling fire and snakes, frequent trances, and other strange phenomena." To put this in sociological language, these independent Holiness groups stand in significantly higher tension with the surrounding sociocultural environment than does the Church of the Nazarene.

Given the significance of the sanctification experience, it is important to note that Nazarenes do not believe that it makes a person perfect, taking a position similar to that of Phoebe Palmer. The Nazarene *Manual* (quoted by Redford 1958:12) explains, "entire sanctification is that act of God, subsequent to regeneration [justification], by which believers are made free from original sin, or depravity, and brought into state of entire devotement to God, and the holy obedience of love made perfect." Although sanctification is holiness, the *Manual* explains, beyond it there remains room to grow: "There is a marked distinction between a perfect heart and a perfect character. The former is obtained in an instant, the result of entire sanctification, but the latter is the result of growth in grace" (quoted by Redford 1958:13).

The Holiness groups that joined to form the Church of the Nazarene were probably always a little lower in tension than most of the independent Holiness groups that did not join. One example is Christ's Sanctified Holy Church, of Perry, Georgia, founded by former Methodist preacher Joseph Lynch in 1887. Even today, this 1,500-member group regulates the style of clothing worn by members, avoids having professional clergy, resists participation in war, and rejects such rituals as communion (Melton 1993: 375–376). Another example is the 1,200-member Fire-Baptized Holiness Church which broke out of Methodism in 1890. The high tension of this group is indicated by its prohibitions against tobacco, alcohol, television, and jewelry (Melton 1993:381).

Today, the Nazarenes are a well-established national denomination with extensive international branches overseen by a progressively more elaborate bureaucracy (Nees 1991). Over the years of growth, it has reduced its tension somewhat. As with Methodism before it, this tension reduction made room for higher-tension sects to break away from it. Just before World War II, electronic engineers perfected television, and the end of the war permitted this new medium of communication to spread quickly into almost every home in the nation. But perhaps because it resembled the frivolous and potentially immoral theater, which conservative American Protestant groups had long opposed, television was not immediately accepted by high-tension sects. When the Church of the Nazarene accepted television in 1956, some members promptly broke away, founding the Voice of the Nazarene Association of Churches (Melton 1993:398).

One Nazarene preacher who vocally resisted the group's progressive accommodation with the world was Glenn Griffith. In 1956, the Bible Missionary Church coalesced around Griffith's message (Melton 1993:396). But in 1959 he accused it, in turn, of accommodating to the world by accepting divorced persons, and he launched the Wesleyan Holiness Association of Churches (Melton 1993:399). This group is the result of a long series of lower-tension accommodations and higher-tension schisms: Anglicanism, Methodism, Nazarenes, Bible Missionary, and finally Wesleyan Holiness. Clearly, we understand much already about this process of religious evolution, but it would be good to pause at this point and examine what we know in terms of a classical sociological theory.

Niebuhr's Theory of Tension-Reduction

In 1929, Helmut Richard Niebuhr published *The Social Sources of Denominationalism*, a book which quickly became tremendously influential both in sociology and in the Ecumenical Movement that sought to unify Christianity. Niebuhr strongly believed that fragmentation of Christianity into a motley assortment of sects and denominations was an extremely bad thing. He called denominationalism "an unacknowledged hypocrisy" and said it was "the accommodation of Christianity to the caste-system of human society" (Niebuhr 1929:6). Christ had preached the unity of all humanity, Niebuhr believed, and nothing less than the successful transcendence of all barriers of class and race would establish a truly Christian religion in America. Whatever one thinks of Niebuhr's prescription for Christianity, his analysis of the sources of denominationalism has much to recommend it.

Table 3.1 shows six factors that may reduce the tension of a religious movement, beginning with Niebuhr's ideas and adding those of other sociologists of religion. In the table I also suggest six parallel factors that maintain or increase tension, each one comparable to the tension-reduction factor with the same number. This set of twelve principles is not exhaustive, and the reader may be able to think of others. Also, I have made no attempt to fit them into a coherent intellectual structure, but merely present them as a list of mechanisms that probably play roles in shaping the fate of a high-tension religious movement.

Niebuhr (1929:19–20) begins his analysis of tension reduction by stating that the birth of children to members of a sect forces it to take on some of the qualities of an ecclesia or denomination, because it must develop regular methods to train them in the beliefs and practices, and they do not come to it with the powerful emotional needs of adult converts. Recall that both John Wesley and Phoebe Palmer had great difficulty achieving an intensely emotional salvation experience, because they were already so thoroughly socialized into their religious faith. Recall also that one of the defining characteristics of a sect (according to writers like Troeltsh, O'Dea, and Pope) is that its members are converted rather than born into the group.

Niebuhr's second point is that the very characteristics that make the sect more demanding than an ordinary denomination may ultimately reduce the member's needs for specific compensators. He say that "wealth frequently increases when the sect subjects itself to the discipline of asceticism in work and expenditure; with the increase of wealth the possibilities for culture also become more numerous and involvement in the economic life of the nation as a whole can less easily be limited. Compromise begins and the ethics of the sect approach the churchly type of morals" (Niebuhr 1929:20).

Niebuhr's third point is spread throughout his book, rather than being

Table 3.1: Factors that Affect Changes in the Level of Tension of a Sect

---

Factors that reduce tension:
1. Birth of a new generation of members who must be raised in the religion rather than converted to it.
2. Improvement in the economic level of members due to the ascetic values or other features of the sect.
3. Sociocultural assimilation of the ethnic group to which members belong.
4. Increase in the number of members, bringing the sect out of minority status.
5. Development of a stable leadership structure which builds a bureaucracy and emphasizes the needs of bureaucratic leaders.
6. Random processes, including regression toward the mean, that tend to reduce the deviance of individuals or groups.

Factors that maintain or increase tension:
1. A high level of recruitment of new members, which emphasizes their needs rather than those of members born into the group.
2. Failure of members to rise in the surrounding socioeconomic system, perhaps due to widespread economic depression and social chaos.
3. Rejection of members by powerful groups in society because they belong to a suppressed ethnic group.
4. Failure of a conversionist group to grow causes members to stress specific compensators in lieu of worldly evidence of success.
5. A sequence of charismatic leaders stages numerous revivals that pump up the tension.
6. Holy scriptures or other well-established traditions that anchor the group near a particular level of tension.

---

stated explicitly in the theoretical analysis of its first chapter. He devotes a considerable amount of space to the experience of immigrant ethnic groups, such as the Germans and Scandinavians who formed the original basis of the various Lutheran denominations. As immigrants assimilate into the wider culture, they no longer need their own distinctive churches, with sermons preached in the language of their home countries, and their increasing social relationship with persons of other ethnic origins ought to draw them together religiously. Bryan Wilson (1993:55) has criticized Niebuhr's theory of tension reduction, saying that he "was overly impressed by the special local conditions that prevailed in the United States" and failed "to see how American conditions specifically facilitated this process, and how some sects had persisted as such over several generations in Europe." Although Wilson does not specifically say so, the chief difference between the United States and Europe is the effect of massive immigration and cultural assimilation, which is largely lacking in twentieth-century Europe. However, Europe is currently experiencing a considerable degree of cultural unification, with religious consequences that are yet to be seen. In addition, a number of American sects have failed to reduce their tension over considerable periods of time, and religious differences between the two continents may have been exaggerated by the extreme political differences, which have now become muted.

The fourth point applies only to successful sectarian movements that grow in membership, but of course these will be the most influential ones, and movements that do not grow may fade into extinction rather than reducing their tension. When a high-tension religious group recruits successfully from the surrounding society, it grows in size and influence. This alone gives it a measure of respectability, and the power it gains allows it to negotiate some concessions from societal institutions. But once it enters into negotiations with institutions of the surrounding sociocultural environment, it adjusts to some extent to them. Thus its tension may decline both because it draws the society to some extent toward its own position, and because it moves toward the society. As it grows in size and thus in influence, it is likely to begin to recruit people who suffer less relative deprivation than did the founders, and these people will tend to reduce the group's tension slightly.

Point five appears in Niebuhr's analysis, but tangled up with the first two points from which it is logically distinct. Several factors, including simply the passage of time, permit a professional leadership to establish itself. Some religious professionals take on the task of socializing children born into the group. As the wealth of the members of a movement increases, so does their educational level, and both wealth and education lead to demands for a theologically trained, professional clergy. As we noted earlier in our discussion of the evolution of Methodism, this encourages the clergy to accommodate the group's beliefs and practices to the norms of the surrounding culture (Hadden 1969; Stark et al. 1971; Stark and Bainbridge 1985, 1987; Finke and Stark 1992).

The sixth point recognizes that chance greatly affects human life, and that random events often add up to meaningful processes. People who suffer a string of bad luck tend to wind up relatively deprived, and thus are suitable recruits to a religious movement that offers them specific compensators for the rewards they have lost. But luck changes, and a subsequent string of good luck may restore the lost rewards, thus reducing the value of membership in the movement. Indeed, this seesaw movement in the person's fate illustrates a principle called *regression toward the mean* (Stark and Bainbridge 1987:260–262). Individuals with extreme levels of reward at one point in time will tend to be nearer the average for the society at a subsequent point in time. And the children of highly deprived persons will tend to be less deprived than their parents were. Thus, both within a single generation, and across generations, random movement in the society's stratification system will tend to reduce the relative deprivation of a sect's members, and thus motivate them to reduce its tension.

Each of these six factors depends upon particular conditions. For example, the Shaker religious movement, described in Chapter 5, was celibate and did not bring children into the world, thus avoiding the first tension-reduction factor. The fourth factor assumes that the religious movement grows in size, but many sects in fact do not grow, perhaps because they start out at such high tension that they find it difficult to attract recruits (Stark and Bainbridge 1981). In addition, each of these six tension-reduction factors may be paired with an opposing tension-maintenance factor.

First, the tendency of children to reduce tension can be counteracted by a high rate of recruitment of adult converts who desire the specific compensators that only a high-tension movement can offer. Stark and Roberts (1982) note that in an actively recruiting movement it is entirely possible for recruits to outnumber members who were born into it. For example, they find that a recruitment rate of 10 percent per year is quite plausible, as is a fertility rate that gives each pair of parents four children. But the arithmetic of these assumptions means that converted members will outnumber members born into the group by a ratio of two to one. To understand what is happening in any particular movement, of course, one would need detailed statistics of the age at which converts are recruited and the patterns of defection of both converted and born-in members. In addition, one would have to know how strong the two competing effects are. Perhaps in their need-driven fervor, adult converts have a greater influence on the group. Or it could be that the parents of children born in the group are so strongly interested in their children's welfare that they actively change the nature of the movement to serve them. In any case, it should be clear that the arrival of a second generation may not be sufficient to reduce the tension of a religious movement.

The second factor the might prevent tension reduction is that socioeconomic conditions in the surrounding society may prevent members of the movement from gaining wealth and rising up in the stratification system. Perhaps the values of the sect do give its members the habit of working hard, but they may not get rewarded for their efforts. Perhaps labor unions or government regulations set standard wages with little opportunity for gaining more by greater effort. Or businesses may exploit laborers, forcing them to accept little pay while working them into exhaustion. Ascetic values, that prohibit spending money on luxuries, may encourage people to save and invest (Weber 1958). But stock-market crashes and inflation may eat up these investments. Indeed, the economy or other conditions of the society may worsen, thus giving the members of the sect all the more reason to accept specific compensators and strengthening the tension of the movement.

Third, members of an immigrant group may not be able to assimilate into the dominant culture if their ethnic group or race is rejected by the majority in the society or by a powerful elite. Thus, other things being equal, religious denominations populated by African Americans may tend to be slightly higher in tension, emphasizing the gifts of the spirit, than their European-American equivalents.

Fourth, a group that fails to recruit many new members, but is committed to doing so, may turn ever more strongly to compensators in response to this failure to gain the reward of membership growth. Chapter 7 reports that the Transcendental Meditation movement turned toward increased emphasis upon unusual supernatural compensators, thus increasing its tension, after recruitment of new members collapsed. Most dedicated members were teachers of the TM meditation technique, and their hopes for increased financial rewards and social status depended upon a steadily increasing flow of students. So when the students practically stopped coming, the movement grew in tension rather than in membership (Bainbridge and Jackson 1981).

Fifth, the leadership may more-or-less intentionally stage revivals and organizational revolutions that periodically increase the group's tension. A wise leader might be aware that tension reduction could ultimately endanger the movement. Or the leader could have exceptional personal needs for extreme compensators. Or battles within the movement's leadership could continually bring to the fore people whose policies or strategies increased tension. In Chapter 8 we will see that the leader of The Family (better known as the Children of God) launched a number of what he called "revolutions," once even dismissing the entire middle rank of leadership, that often increased the group's tension. And in Chapter 4 we will see that Jehovah's Witnesses had not one but two long-lived founders, one succeeding the other, each of whom kept rededicating the Witnesses to high-tension goals of recruitment and preparation for the end of the world.

It may not be immediately obvious why holy scriptures, the last of the factors preventing tension reduction, has anything to do with random processes, the last of the factors promoting reduction. The link is found in the mathematical theory of random processes, specifically in the concept of *absorbing state*. In random processes, an absorbing state is a situation that it is easy to get into but difficult to get out of. This is a very useful concept, but unfortunately is not a very familiar one. Therefore, we need a humble example. Imagine a marble rolling around in the bottom of a bathtub. Almost any place on the bottom of the tub, a slight push makes the marble move a considerable distance. However, if the marble falls into the drain, it is stuck there forever. The drain is an absorbing state.

There are several absorbing states in the sociology of religion. A religious seeker sets out on a quest to find a suitable religion to join; when he or she actually joins one, it is an absorbing state for the quest, and the person may stay in it forever. The afterlife is another absorbing state, from which few if any people return. A successful religious movement typically goes through a formative period, when it develops its distinctive doctrines and practices. If it writes these down into sacred books, or enshrines them in inflexible structures of social roles, then it will be unlikely to change them, short of a major internal revolution. Thus, fixed scriptures are an absorbing state that can prevent random movement away from high tension. The most prominent example, of course, is the great power of the New Testament to serve as the launch pad for an endless barrage of high-tension religious movements that seek to fulfill its world-transcending promise.

Social Status and Tension in the Holiness Tradition

To this point we have seen that sociological theory and qualitative historical evidence both suggest that Methodism is lower in tension than the Church of the Nazarene, which in turn may be lower in tension than the host of smaller Holiness groups. We can test these propositions with data from the General Social Survey, in the same manner as we compared sects with low-tension denominations in the previous chapter. Table 1.3 told us that the respondents to this national survey include 3,000 Methodists, 139 members of the Church of the Nazarene, and 213 members of miscellaneous Holiness groups. Some of the respondents labeled ordinary "Methodists" probably belong to small Wesleyan groups that are really independent Holiness sects, and most of those listed under the Church of God could be included in the Holiness Movement, as well. For sake of simplicity, we will compare just the three groups we have discussed.

Table 3.2 applies the measures used in Table 2.2, revealing that ordinary Methodists exhibit far weaker religious commitment, on average, than do Nazarenes or members of small Holiness groups. For each variable, the Nazarenes are slightly closer to the Methodists than are the Holiness respondents. However, the Nazarene and Holiness respondents are quite close to each other, never more than nine percentage points apart and as close as just one. Still the pattern fits the model. As groups that broke away from conventional Methodist, the Nazarenes and Holiness groups are more strongly committed to traditional religion, but the Nazarenes revel a slightly reduced commitment compared with the Holiness respondents.

Table 3.3 compares the degree of relative deprivation experienced by the three groups, employing some of the variables in Tables 2.3 and 2.4. Thirty-three percent of the members of Holiness churches are African Americans, compared with 12 percent among Methodists and only 6 percent among Nazarenes. Compared with the Methodists, members of the Nazarene and Holiness churches are more likely to have quit education before completing

Table 3.2: Religious Commitment in the Holiness Movement

	Methodists	Nazarenes	Holiness
Respondent is a strong member of his or her denomination.	33 (2,514)	55 (128)	61 (177)
Respondent belongs to a church affiliated group.	41 (1,878)	53 (93)	61 (127)
Respondent attends religious services weekly.	22 (2,983)	53 (139)	54 (213)
Respondent believes there is a life after death.	75 (1,909)	88 (89)	91 (155)
Respondent believes the Bible is the actual word of God and is to be taken literally.	33 (699)	61 (38)	62 (55)
Respondent says somebody who is against all churches should be allowed to speak.	61 (2,156)	56 (98)	45 (146)
Respondent approves of Supreme Court's ban on prayer in public schools.	33 (1,355)	22 (69)	18 (108)

high school, to have a low-prestige occupation, to report a below-average family income, and to be working or lower class. Here the differences between Nazarenes and the small Holiness groups are greater than those in Table 3.2. A plausible explanation is that the Nazarenes have been losing their relative deprivation more rapidly than their religious orthodoxy. Factors that maintain tension, such as those listed in Table 3.1, may be offsetting the improvement in the economic level of members, which would tend to reduce tension.

Questions about attitudes toward the future and social trust were included in several years of the General Social Survey, with just barely a sufficient number of Nazarene respondents that we can use these items to gauge the differences among the three groups. In a sense, these items are questions about the world, measuring the respondents' feelings about other people and the social system that surrounds them. Can people generally be trusted? Do people try to help each other, or to take advantage? Will the future be better than the present, or worse? As Table 3.4 shows, in each case there is a substantial difference between members of the

Table 3.3: Relative Deprivation in the Holiness Movement

	Methodists	Nazarenes	Holiness
Respondent did not finish high school.	26 (2,984)	41 (135)	51 (211)
Respondent's occupation has low prestige.	21 (2,764)	30 (127)	44 (176)
Respondents says his or her family income is below average.	26 (2,975)	29 (138)	42 (211)
Respondent says he or she is working class or lower class.	46 (2,803)	59 (126)	71 (193)

Church of the Nazarene and members of small Holiness groups, with the latter being more suspicious of the world. Only in the case of "Good Samaritan" helpfulness do the Nazarenes agree exactly with the Methodists, and for the other four items the Nazarenes are more suspicious of the world than are Methodists.

Conclusion: The Holiness System

Groups like those discussed in this chapter cannot be understood in isolation, but only in terms of their relationships with the secular world and with other religious groups to which they are related. The Methodist Episcopal Church—now called the United Methodist Church—broke away from the Church of England—also called the Anglican Church, or in America the Protestant Episcopal Church. The Church of England was "high church," emphasizing social hierarchy, formal rituals, and a highly educated clergy. Within the Church of England, clergy and lay leaders began to emphasize the experiential, transformational aspects of religion, in a Methodist movement led by John Wesley and others that was akin to a "dissenting church," but remained for decades within the Church of England. Eventually, the Methodists probably would have broken away from the Church of England, ordained their own clergy, and formalized the status of their proliferating houses of worship. But the American Revolution forced the decision. In 1776, something like an eighth of the Anglican congregations in America were already part of the Methodist Movement (Finke and Stark 1992:25).

Table 3.4: Holiness Attitudes Toward Other People and the Future

	Methodists	Nazarenes	Holiness
Most people can be trusted.	47 (2,022)	35 (86)	23 (138)
Most of the time people try to be helpful.	56 (2,099)	56 (93)	38 (148)
Most people would try to take advantage of me if they got a chance.	31 (2,098)	40 (93)	46 (148)
It is hardly fair to bring a child into the world with the way things look for the future.	37 (1,924)	48 (96)	56 (133)
The situation of the average man is getting worse, not better.	56 (1,925)	66 (97)	77 (133)

After the revolution, with the Church of England largely discredited and many of its clergy fled to Canada, the Methodists were able to pick up some of its pieces. And for the next seventy-five years, their relatively unschooled but energetic circuit riders were able to spread a brand of religion which was especially well-suited to the new nation.

As the nineteenth century wore on, many Methodists became prosperous and took positions of responsibility in their communities. Their educational level rose, as did that of their clergy. One result was that growth slowed, and another was that this reduction in tension with the sociocultural environment left many of the less fortunate Methodists dissatisfied with what their church had to offer them. Increasingly, throughout the second half of the century, individual pastors broke away under the influence of the Holiness Movement and founded independent churches. Emphasizing a strict, orthodox Protestantism that offered abundant specific compensators, these Holiness churches were especially appealing to people who suffered from relative deprivation. A few of these independent churches grew into tiny denominations, some of which merged into the highly successful Church of the Nazarene. Contemporary survey data confirm that members of both the Church of the Nazarene and members of smaller Holiness churches suffer greater deprivation than do Methodists, but the Nazarenes are not so severely deprived as their Holiness fellows and perhaps in consequence not quite so suspicious of the world. While still at relatively high religious tension, the Nazarenes are slightly more moderate than the other Holiness respondents.

New high-tension sects have broken away from the Church of the Nazarene, charging that it has lost some of its original religious purity. That is tantamount to saying that the Nazarenes have reduced their tension with the world. The same thing, incidentally, has happened with other substantial Holiness denominations that we have not analyzed here. For example, the Church of God (Guthrie, Oklahoma) broke away from The Church of God (Anderson, Indiana) in 1911, charging that the parent body had accommodated to the world (Melton 1993:297). The History of the Church of God, like that of the Methodist Church before it, illustrates the process of tension-reduction about which Niebuhr theorized. A host of factors can determine whether and at what rate a high-tension religious group moderates. Often the arrival of a second generation, amelioration of members' relative deprivation, and the development of an educated, professional clergy can erode the movement's dedication to intense forms of religion. When that happens, the way is cleared for a few disgruntled or inspired preachers to lead a sect movement into schism and renewed tension.

A comparison between the organizational histories of the Methodists and the Nazarenes is instructive. Methodism developed a substantial organization within the Church of England long before it became an independent denomination. Perhaps because its leaders were highly educated members of the religious elite who seemed to be merely reviving the religious spirit within Anglicanism, and because they assiduously avoided challenging the established church by ordaining clergy, they enjoyed decades of growth and development before they had to survive as an independent denomination. In contrast, practically every branch of the Holiness Movement about which I have any information was founded by a single highly effective preacher who took a single congregation, often just a part of one or individual members skimmed from several, into a tiny religious movement. The national Church of the Nazarene was created by the merger of no less than six of these churches, after each had grown by establishing new congregations into a tiny regional denomination.

The case of Phoebe Palmer reminds us that the Holiness Movement was launched in search of an experience of sanctification that many seekers hoped would free them from anxiety, guilt, and perhaps even from sin. Thus, the organizational dynamics of high-tension sects erupting from low-tension denominations, then sometimes losing some of that tension as they evolve into denominations themselves, is matched by a psychological dynamic. Impoverished people especially may wish to escape their deprivations and gain the rewards possessed by more affluent citizens, so they are frequently open to religious compensators that transvalue their condition and promise future rewards. The experience of sanctification eludes many of them, and others whose judgment is not clouded by intense emotions may observe that many people who claim to have achieved salvation continue to worry and to sin. Religious organizations based on the principle of salvation within this life are inherently unstable, although the factors that maintain high tension can sustain a sect's commitment to it for a long time. Individuals from any social stratum and with any level of talent can become obsessed with gaining salvation, and this fact provides much of the leadership for fresh outbreaks of the Holiness Movement.

Like the parent Methodist movement itself in the nineteenth century, however, Holiness denominations will have to cope with the constant elusiveness and disconfirming of salvation. The classic response is to reduce expectations for worldly sanctification, placing the greatest benefits on the supernatural plane where they cannot be proven false by human observation. This has the effect of reducing the emotionality of the movement, permitting it to accommodate further to the institutions of secular society, and lowering its sectarian tension. Then the combination of mass relative deprivation and individual longing for perfection can ignite the Holiness Movement afresh.

4

The Adventist Movement

Two of the world's most vigorous religious denominations, the Seventh-day Adventists and Jehovah's Witnesses, have their roots in a diffuse Adventist movement that arose in the early 1840s around a prophecy that the millennium was at hand. Sometimes these movements are called Second Adventist, because they anticipate the imminent Second Coming of Christ, and sometimes they are dubbed "millenarian" after the hoped-for thousand-year period that Satan will spend bound in the bottomless pit as Christ reigns on earth. Based in Protestant traditions, they give very special interpretations to the apocalyptic visions found in some books of the Bible, notably Revelation. These beliefs place Adventists in significant tension with the surrounding sociocultural environment. The task of this chapter will be to examine the origins and the logic of this movement, learning something about the remarkable individuals who were its founders, and questioning the extent to which a simple model of schism matches its social dynamic.

The Great Disappointment

William Miller, the man whose prediction of the end of the world launched Adventism, was born in 1782 in a log cabin on a farm near Hampton, New York, beside the Vermont border. His parents worked hard, and soon they had built a snug frame house, with a room for William where he could read books in the evening by candlelight. A bright child, he enjoyed writing and quickly surpassed his teachers in the district school. He hoped to attend one of the few colleges then in existence, but with fully sixteen children to worry about the family was not sufficiently prosperous to send him. In 1803, he married Lucy Smith and moved to her town, Poultney, just half a dozen miles into Vermont. There he made good use of the town library, did a little writing, and was appointed sheriff.

In 1810, Miller joined the Vermont militia, and he served honorably in the War of 1812, spending part of the time as a recruiter but also seeing action and achieving the rank of captain. On September 12, 1814, he wrote his wife about the terrible battle of Plattsburg the day before. "The British had thrown up a number of batteries on all sides of us. The next minute the canon began playing—spitting their fire in every quarter. What a scene! All was dreadful!—nothing but roaring and groaning, for about six or eight hours. I cannot describe to you our situation. The fort I was in was exposed to every shot. Bombs, rockets, and shrapnel shells, fell thick as hailstones. Three of my men were wounded, and one killed" (Bliss 1853:49–50). Miller entered the war as a skeptic with respect to religion, calling himself a Deist but somewhat perplexed concerning what exactly a Deist believed. He was dismayed by the vice he saw in the army—gambling, drinking, swearing, stealing—and by the chaotic way the war was fought. There seemed little to justify his idealism.

In the filthy conditions of army camps, he nearly died of disease, and when a sergeant named Spencer was carried off by the fever, he shared his feelings about the afterlife with his wife. "But a short time, and, like Spencer, I shall be no more. It is a solemn thought. Yet, could I be sure of one other life, there would be nothing terrific; but to go out like an extinguished taper, is insupportable—the thought is doleful. No! rather let me cling to that hope which warrants a never-ending existence; a future spring where troubles shall cease, and tears find no conveyance; where never-ending spring shall flourish, and love, pure as the driven snow, rest in every breast" (Bliss 1853:55). He concluded that Deism offers no hope because it implies humans are annihilated at death, so when he returned to civilian life as a farmer near his childhood home, he began reading the Bible extensively, seeking a consistent and compelling faith.

Often he would meditate in a beautiful grove a short distance west of his house, and he found it difficult to avoid war-stimulated brooding about death and damnation. "Annihilation was a cold and chilling thought, and accountability was sure destruction to all. The heavens were as brass over my head, and the earth as iron under my feet. Eternity—what was it? And death—why was it?" (Bliss 1853:65). On the anniversary of the Battle of Plattsburg in 1816 he could not get in the festive spirit of the celebration, and when asked to read in church he was overcome by emotion. From this desolation came conviction, but for Miller's rational mind it came almost as a deduction from logic. "I saw that the Bible did bring to view just such a Savior as I needed; and I was perplexed to find how an uninspired book should develop principles so perfectly adapted to the wants of a fallen world. I was constrained to admit that the Scriptures must be a revelation from God. They became my delight; and in Jesus I found a friend" (Bliss 1853:67). He professed his faith publicly, and became a lay preacher in the local Baptist church.

If logic had brought him to belief, what else could logic achieve when applied to the scriptures? For two years, in every spare moment, he analyzed the Bible following a systematic set of principles that assumed all the Bible was true, although some of it expressed the truth in parables and figures, and that the Bible itself contained all the clues needed for its own decipherment. For example, the concluding words of the vision in Daniel 8:14 say, "Unto two thousand and three hundred days; then shall the sanctuary be cleansed." Miller decided that the cleansing of the sanctuary must mean the second coming of Christ, and the beginning of the quotation appears to foretell when this momentous event was going to occur. But its meaning is not immediately clear, and Miller concluded, as many others have, that the key to this mystery is to be found in some other biblical passage that suggests what the word *day* might mean.

Eziekiel 4:6 says, "I have appointed thee each day for a year," and Numbers 14:34 agrees, "each day for a year." Therefore, Miller deduced, the 2,300 days really mean 2,300 years. The next task was to determine when this period of time began. Here Miller checked back and forth among several books of the Bible, also consulting secular historians about the dates when various ancient events occurred, arriving at 457 B.C. Subtracting that number from 2,300, he got the date of the second coming, 1843. Other calculations based on other passages seemed to give the same result. In 1822, he wrote out his twenty religious convictions, of which number fifteen said, "I believe that the second coming of Jesus Christ is near, even at the door, even within twenty-one years,—on or before 1843."

The next several years passed relatively uneventfully, while Miller established himself as a respected and even leading member of the community, despite the fact that he frequently shared his unusual prophecy with the people he met. In 1831, Miller began speaking publicly, saying it was his duty to spread the word as the fateful time approached, and the following year he began publishing articles. Within two years he could count eight ministers among his followers, all of them still in good standing with their denominations. As the decade before the predicted millennium passed, hundreds, and then thousands and possibly tens of thousands of ordinary Americans adopted his beliefs. They came largely from the Baptist, Methodist, and Presbyterian denominations, but also from other churches and even from the substantial numbers of citizens who initially considered themselves unbelievers. Some invested considerable energy and talent in spreading the word, through publications and mass meetings, notably Joshua V. Himes, a crusader who saw in the predicted date the fulfillment of the social progress he found so difficult to achieve through the various secular reform movements to which he had been devoting himself (Arthur 1987).

Miller staunchly denied being a "come-outer," someone who called people to come out of their churches and form a sect with him (Judd 1987). At first he spoke in many churches, but as his movement swelled it also gained opposition until his audiences were meeting in secular lecture halls and eventually in a great mobile tent that could hold three thousand listeners. Gradually, in many towns, groups began meeting informally outside the churches to discuss Millerism. Step by step and often unconscious of what they were doing, they slipped out of their denominations into something that looked more and more like a sect. But it was not born from the schism of any one denomination. Instead it peeled individuals, families, and friendship groups out of several denominations to assemble them in a new combination.

Miller's message affected people in a variety of ways. Skeptics scoffed. Many who accepted the good news of Christ's imminent return responded in joy. Others with depressive temperaments or deep-rooted feelings of inadequacy doubted that the savior would find them worthy. Twelve-year-old Ellen G. Harmon heard Miller speak in Portland, Maine, early in 1840, and was swept up in the revival fervor. "When sinners were invited forward to the anxious seat, hundreds responded to the call, and I, among the rest, pressed through the crowd and took my place with the seekers. But there was in my heart a feeling that I could never become worthy to be called a child of God. A lack of confidence in myself, and a conviction that it would be impossible to make any one understand my feelings, prevented me from seeking advice and aid from my Christian friends. Thus I wandered needlessly in darkness and despair, while they, not penetrating my reserve, were needlessly ignorant of my true state." Thus began a period of despondency that lasted more than two years and was not alleviated by hearing a second set of lectures from Miller (Olsen 1925:171). But eventually, Ellen had an intense prayer meeting experience when she broke through her timidity, spoke prayers with great vigor, and collapsed into a dead faint. Soon she was speaking at Millerite meetings, bringing her audiences to tears, and converting souls to the movement.

Except for the fact that he set a date for the second coming, Miller's ideas were relatively conventional. In Revelation and portions of other books, the Bible appears to prophesy a great future battle between good and evil, ending this world of pain and ushering in a perfect existence. However, many different interpretations can be placed on the passages. For example, one can place the second coming before the millennium, in which case some scholars would label one a "premillennialist," or afterward, in which case one would be a "postmillennialist." One way to tell premillennialists from postmillennialists is to learn how they feel about the present society. If they are premillennialists they are passive pessimists, because they believe the world will remain in a wretched state until Christ returns. Postmillennialists are active optimists, because they believe they can and must improve the world considerably before the return. In these terms, Miller was premillennialist, as are many small radical movements today, such as The Family (Children of God) we will consider in Chapter 8. But the distinction between premillennialists and postmillennialists really may not have been very clear during Miller's lifetime, and until challenged by his growing movement to work out their own ideas, the mainstream churches somewhat vaguely supported the idea of the second coming (Doan 1987a).

Miller's tremendous impact on America around 1840 depended upon the fact that he had set a date for the second coming, and yet the date itself was really secondary. Ruth Alden Doan (1987b:123) explains that "the date stood as a symbol for a set of assumptions rather than a literal test of faith." Millerites "shared a belief that Christianity was not a set of myths about spiritual forces, but a belief in the absolute reality of Christ, the urgent demands of God, and the immediate overturning of the existing order. For most Millerites, mention of 1843 served as a reminder of a supernatural order so real as to be almost palpably, physically present."

But as 1842 actually approached, and enthusiasm for Miller's prediction swept the northeast quadrant of the United States, people began asking him to set the exact day and hour. At first he held to "on or before 1843," and like many of his more moderate followers he resisted the call to be more precise. The first definite date that Miller anticipated was not the second advent itself, but a turn in world history that would be signified by the fall of the Turkish empire, predicted for August 11, 1840 (Anderson 1987). Turkey still stood on August 12, and as the news of the old world gradually seeped into America the Millerites attempted to see various political events as the beginning of the end for that empire. Under continuing pressure from his more radical followers, Miller announced that the great date would be some time in the next year by the Hebrew calendar, from March 21, 1843 to March 21, 1844.

Throughout this period Miller refused to set a day, although others often focused on this or that date. But it was difficult to ignore the passage of March 21, 1844. Shortly afterward, he wrote, "The time, as I have calculated it, is now filled up; and I expect every moment to see the Savior descend from heaven. I have now nothing to look for but this glorious hope." On May 2, he proclaimed, "I confess my error, and acknowledge my disappointment; yet I still believe that the day of the Lord is near, even at the door; and I exhort you, my brethren, to be watchful, and not let that day come upon you unawares" (Nichol 1944:169, 171).

Then an obscure Millerite preacher named Samuel S. Snow generated tremendous enthusiasm by predicting that the great moment would come on the Hebrew Day of Atonement, October 22, 1844. By this point, many of the more moderate members had been wrung out of the movement, and the remnant were ready for a confident prophecy of imminent glory. Some gave up their homes and businesses in anticipation they would shortly no longer need them. Henry B. Bear was a liquor distiller. When convinced the second coming was at hand he sold off his stock of alcohol at one-third its value, settled all his accounts, and invested the money in distributing Millerite publications (Bear 1987). A few others sold their farms, many became less diligent in planting and harvesting, and some discontinued their children's education. October 22, 1844, took their hopes to the pinnacle of emotional expectation, then dashed them into despair.

Hiram Edson, a farmer from western New York State, remembered that terrible night vividly. "We confidently expected to see Jesus Christ and all the holy angels with him; and that his voice would call up Abraham, Isaac, and Jacob, and all the ancient worthies, and near and dear friends which had been torn from us by death, and that our trials and sufferings with our earthly pilgrimage would close, and we should be caught up to meet our coming Lord to be forever with him to inhabit the bright golden mansions in the golden home city, prepared for the redeemed. Our expectations were raised high, and thus we looked for our coming Lord until the clock tolled 12 at midnight. The day had then passed and our disappointment became a certainty. Our fondest hopes and expectations were blasted, and such a spirit of weeping came over us as I never experienced before. It seemed that the loss of all earthly friends could have been no comparison. We wept, and wept, till the day dawn" (quoted in Numbers and Butler 1987:215).

The following day, Edson went walking with a companion to visit another group of disappointed Millerites, when he paused in thought while crossing a large field. At the peak of his distress, like a flash of light an inspiration came to him. The prophecy had indeed been fulfilled the day before, only Miller had misunderstood what that fulfillment meant. "Then shall the sanctuary be cleansed." Christ had entered the sanctuary, but that was in heaven, not on earth. After a brief preparation in the sanctuary, he would come to earth, so his second advent was still in the future, but very soon to come. Edson shared this insight with friends who included the editor of the local Millerite newspaper, and soon the word had gone out to all who were prepared to receive it. Building on an earlier idea of Miller himself, Apollos Hale and Joseph Turner added the claim that on October 22 the "door of mercy" had closed, so that only people who had awaited Christ on that day would be saved when he left his sanctuary to gather them (Numbers 1992:13–14). This combination of ideas was well-designed to console many of the Millerites who were not ready to give up, reinstating their prophecy and bestowing great sacred status upon them.

But the final great disappointment led most people who had been caught up in the movement to fall away from it. As M. Ellsworth Olsen (1925:160) has observed, the movement lacked a thorough organization to hold members. This had several causes. The movement had grown so rapidly it could not solidly incorporate all those attracted to it. With the end of the world in sight, there seemed little need to create organizational structures. Many of the recruits had been dissatisfied with the ecclesiastical power in their old denominations and did not want to replicate this oppressive authority structure in their movement. Miller and Himes forthrightly admitted their prediction had been wrong, which probably was not the right basis for a vigorous, supernaturally oriented movement.

In the wreckage of Millerism, various other leaders collected small groups of followers around reinterpretations like Edson's that denied the disappointment (Melton 1993:563). In Massachusetts, John T. Walsh preached that the millennium had occurred and the saints were waiting for Christ's imminent return. Jonathan Cummings preached that Miller had been wrong by a decade and Christ would return in 1854. George Storrs preached that the dead lay in their graves oblivious to everything until Christ would come and resurrect them, a doctrine contrary to common notions of the immortality of the soul that assumed the dead entered an afterlife soon after death. The groups led by Cummings and Storrs came together in the late 1840s, and after 1854 passed uneventfully the issue of immortality prevented them from gathering up many Adventists who had resisted date-setting. In 1855 they formed the Advent Christian Church based on Storrs' ideas but led by Cummings, and shortly Storrs became converted to Walsh's ideas and these two founded the Life and Advent Union in 1863. In 1964, the Life and Advent Union was absorbed into the Advent Christian Church, which in 1991 had about 27,590 members (Melton 1993).

The most significant denomination to come directly out of Millerism had a more modest beginning. A few weeks after the Great Disappointment, Ellen G. Harmon, now seventeen, led a prayer circle of girls seeking divine guidance, when she experienced a vision. The world around her vanished, and she was surrounded by light. Rising higher and higher into the air, she saw a straight and narrow path along which Adventists were moving toward New Jerusalem. In February 1845, she experienced a second vision. In another gathering, one of the girls expressed doubts about the assertion of Hale and Turner that the "door of mercy" had closed back in October, wondering why new converts could not still receive salvation. In agony, Ellen fell to the floor in a trance and received a message that indeed the door had shut, thus limiting divine favor to those who were already Adventists (Olsen 1925:171–175; Numbers 1992:14). Another vision, possibly influenced by contact with the Seventh Day Baptist Church, revealed that the Sabbath should be held not on Sunday but on Saturday.

In 1846, Ellen married James White, a Millerite preacher who had come to believe that her visions were entirely real contacts with the supernatural. The two made admirable partners, and James supplied a constant dedication and skill in communication that gradually built a movement around her visions. They published extensively, spreading their faith to the highly dispersed Millerite remnant, and after they abandoned the closed-door doctrine, they were able to recruit people who had not been caught up in Millerism. There may have been as few as 200 members of White's wing of the movement in 1850, but when they formally organized themselves as a denomination in 1863 they had about 3,500 members in 125 churches with twenty-two ordained ministers (Butler 1987:204).

Ellen had always been troubled by physical complaints, and her ministry began to stress new approaches to healing, including partial vegetarianism and abstinence from tobacco, liquor, coffee, and tea. She was strongly influenced by health reformers of her century, including Sylvester Graham of the graham cracker and Russell Trall who promoted water cures. In Battle Creek, Michigan, they established The Western Health Reform Institute which became the hub of a network of clinics that spread across the nation and the world. By 1987, the Seventh-day Adventist Church had grown to nearly 700,000 members in the United States and 5,000,000 worldwide (Melton 1993:758–759).

The Adventists never repudiated Miller, despite the great disappointment, and Ellen White (1888:317) called him "an American reformer" and "an upright, honest-hearted farmer." She explained, "Like the first disciples, William Miller and his associates did not, themselves, fully comprehend the import of the message which they bore. Errors that had been long established in the church prevented them from arriving at a correct interpretation of an important point in the prophecy. Therefore, though they proclaimed the message which God had committed to them to be given to the world, yet through a misapprehension of its meaning they suffered disappointment" (White 1888:351–352). Hiram Edson's insight that the sanctuary cleansed by Christ in 1844 might not have been the earth but a celestial place removed the prophecy from easy disconfirmation (White 1888:409–422). Ever since its formation, Ellen White's movement has resolutely avoided setting a date for the second coming, although believing the time is soon.

Jehovah's Witnesses

In 1870, seven years after the founding of the Seventh-day Adventist Church, eighteen-year-old Charles Taze Russell was walking through the dark streets of Allegheny, Pennsylvania, when the singing of a group of Adventists attracted him. He shortly began holding his own Bible study meetings. At this point, the diffuse Adventist movement was considerably larger than the small Saturday-observing denomination founded by Ellen and James White or the various Sunday-observing Advent Christian churches, and Russell could draw on interested Christians who had not been caught up in Miller's movement, which had run its course a generation earlier. Late in 1875 he read an issue of *Herald of the Morning*, a magazine published by Nelson H. Barbour who believed that Christ had returned invisibly the year before (Rogerson 1969:6–7). Immediately he entered into a partnership to publish the magazine and the first of many books, anticipating that Christ would fully reveal himself the allotted three-and-a-half years after 1874, that is in 1878. When nothing of the sort occurred, an argument with Barbour led to Russell going off on his own. In 1879 he printed the first issue of *Zion's Watch Tower and Herald of Christ's Presence* and began creating both a publishing empire and a fresh interpretation of the scriptures.

In several respects, Russell followed Miller closely, but with his own slight adjustments and additions (Rogerson 1969:191–192). Miller counted the beginning of the 2,300 years mentioned in Daniel 8:14 from 457 B.C. arriving at 1843 for the cleansing of the sanctuary. Russell started the count in 454 B.C. and concluded this would occur in 1846. Like the Seventh-day Adventists, he considered the sanctuary to be a supernatural place beyond the prying eyes of skeptics.

Other clues came from Daniel 12:11–12: "And from the time that the daily sacrifice shall be taken away, and the abomination that maketh desolate set up, there shall be a thousand two hundred and ninety days. Blessed is he that waiteth, and cometh to the thousand three hundred and five and thirty days." Thus, crucial events are prophesied to take place after 1,290 and 1,335 years. Because these counts are mentioned together, one can deduce that they are connected in some way. One approach at interpretation would be to add them, concluding that three events occur in sequence. The first takes place in ancient times. After 1,290 years another great event happens, and then the third occurs 1,335 years after that. But Russell concluded that the two periods should be counted forward from the same event, which he identified as the fall of the empire of the Ostrogoths in 539 A.D. This was the melancholy moment in history when the nominally Roman and Christian armies of Byzantine emperor Justinian retook Italy from the Ostrogoths at the cost of devastating the country, bankrupting the empire, and setting the stage for an uprising of the Goths that occurred two years later and required more than a decade of bloody fighting to suppress (Boak 1955:492). Counting 1,290 and 1,335 years separately after 539, Russell's two later events would take place in 1829 and 1874. This gives Russell three dates of biblical significance in his own century: 1829, 1846, and 1874. The first he said was the "separating work of the 'Miller movement,' " and the second was the cleansing of the heavenly sanctuary. This left 1874 for the Second Coming.

Russell became interested in a remarkable scholarly movement called pyramidology (Gardner 1957:173–185). Jeremiah 32:20 says that the Lord has "set signs and wonders in the land of Egypt, even unto this day," and among these may be the great pyramid of Cheops at Gizeh. In 1859, a London publisher named John Taylor argued that the architect for this ancient architectural wonder was a divinely inspired Hebrew, possibly Noah himself, who built into the pyramid mathematical truths of great sophistication. In 1864 the astronomer-royal of Scotland, Charles Piazzi Smyth, published a book reporting many remarkable conclusions along these lines, such as that the height of the structure is "exactly" one billionth of the distance to the sun. Most importantly, Smyth believed that the measurements of the pyramid's internal passages mapped out the great events of human history, past and future, if calculated in a unit called the "pyramid inch," only slightly different from the familiar British inch. For example, certain features of the Grand Gallery mark of the life of Jesus, one inch to a year, culminating in the Second Coming at a distance of 1882 or 1911 inches, depending on how the measurements are made.

Interpreting the reported measurements in his own way, Russell found that the dimensions of the pyramid supported his deduction from the scriptures that Christ's second coming occurred invisibly in 1874, and that the millennium would visibly begin forty years later in 1914. John and Morton Edgar, English brothers excited by Russell's theory, actually visited the pyramid to measure it, publishing a two-volume report that confirmed Russell's conjectures.

By 1880, thirty congregations ("ecclesias") of followers had formed out of the readership of the magazine, and the total number of followers may have reached 2,500 by 1899 (Rogerson 1969:15). The year 1914 came and went without a visible appearance of Christ, and the movement suffered another great and costly disappointment. Subsequently, the movement's leadership edited slightly one of Russell's books to tone down his prophecy, and they decided that the beginning of the First World War in 1914 was good confirmation it had been right after all (Curry 1992:183–185).

Russell died in 1916, and after a furious procedural and parliamentary battle, Joseph Franklin Rutherford emerged as his successor. Rutherford was in many ways Russell's equal, just as forceful in creating an efficient organization and developing strong doctrines. The following year the United States entered the First World War, and the Russellites' opposition to war and lack of national loyalty brought Rutherford into court where he and his closest associates were sentenced each to eighty years in prison by an unsympathetic judge. Less than a year later they were freed, after an appeals court ruled they had been wrongly convicted. This incident decimated the movement's membership but transformed the leaders into martyrs and confirmed that henceforth the movement need never compromise with secular authorities about matters of principle. Rutherford lasted until 1942, building a powerfully centralized "theocratic" organization that in principle was directed by Jesus Christ. Under Russell, the Elders had been elected, but now they were nominated for appointment by the top officials of the Watch Tower Society. Rutherford also jettisoned Russell's pyramid speculations and revised some of the millennial dating of the movement.

After Rutherford's death, his own voluminous writings went into the attic besides Russell's, and Jehovah's Witnesses do not currently reprint the works of either. But the nearly seventy years under the direction of these two very strong men created an immensely efficient and well-designed organization, less a church than a machine for distributing literature and proselytizing. In the Second World War many Witnesses were imprisoned in the United States, Canada, and Britain for refusing to bear arms, but this moderate persecution was nothing like the concentration-camp fate that met them in Germany. Sociologists who have written about Jehovah's Witnesses speculate that there is a high turnover in membership, although reliable statistics to test this hypothesis are unavailable. Despite this the movement has grown prodigiously. In 1991 there were nearly 900,000 active members in the United States and a total of 4,200,000 worldwide. Much of this growth was achieved by aggressive campaigns to bring the millennial message directly to people's homes.

Witness literature offers a fictionalized vignette to illustrate how door-to-door witnessing was supposed to work (Watch Tower Bible and Tract Society 1959). On a stormy night in the 1950s, Tom and Lois hear their door bell ring, and discover that their neighbors John and Maria have come over to answer questions about their Jehovah's Witness faith. John's first point is that their religious movement is older than all the Christian denominations, dating back nearly 6,000 years to Abel. Maria checks her King James Bible and finds proof in Hebrews 11:4, "By faith Abel offered unto God a more excellent sacrifice than Cain, by which he obtained witness that he was righteous, God testifying of his gifts: and by it he being dead yet speaketh." Note that the single word "witness" lets John claim Abel as the first member of his movement, but he has also dated Abel to a time just under 6,000 years ago, planting the hint that perhaps something spectacular is supposed to happen when the full 6,000 years have run out.

John points to a passage indicating Jesus was one of Jehovah's witnesses, and the four begin talking about the possibility of a Second Coming. Lois says that Matthew 28:20 implies that Jesus has not abandoned his disciples, and thus does not need to return because he never left. Maria is ready to respond to this question, and she pulls out her copy of the *New World Translation of the Christian Greek Scriptures*. This English-language version of the New Testament was prepared by scholars in Jehovah's Witnesses and uses the terminology of their religious movement, for example always referring to God as Jehovah. Maria reads, "Look! I am with you all the days until the consummation of the system of things!" The King James version, which the Witnesses say was inaccurate, implies a more dreadful conclusion than consummation of the system: "Lo, I am with you always, even unto the end of the world." Although "with" his disciples in a spiritual sense, Jesus would return more fully after some passage of time.

John says, "Your question, Lois, as to when and why Jesus would return, is one that has troubled some Bible students even from the days of the apostles. Some of the early Christians at Thessalonica were teaching that Christ had already returned in Paul's day, but he wrote them: 'Let no one seduce you in any manner; because it will not come unless the falling away comes first and the man of lawlessness gets revealed, the son of destruction.' " This is 2 Thessalonians 2:3, and the King James version refers to a "man of sin . . . the son of perdition." Next John turns to the discoveries of Charles Taze Russell who suggests that passage refers to the Roman Catholic Church and other false Christians. But in the early nineteenth century, freedom of thought made it possible for many people to begin an analytic study of the Bible to determine the truth about Christ's return, notably William Miller.

John explains that Miller was not the only one. "The German-Lutheran theologian Bengel set the date for 1836, whereas the Irvingites in England looked first to 1835, then 1838, 1864 and finally 1866, and then gave up. By this time several different Adventist groups had formed from Miller's movement. Still others, such as the Elliott and Cummings group, were looking for 1866. Brewer and Decker predicted 1867 and Seiss favored 1870. There was a Menonite group in Russia that put forth the date 1889." Then John and Maria take Tom and Lois on a journey through the life and thought of Charles Taze Russell, explaining that Christ's invisible presence in spirit for had begun in 1874, that kingdoms had indeed come to an end in 1914 as prophesied. After weeks of such visits from John and Maria, Tom and Lois are ready to become Witnesses themselves.

Being a witness is extremely demanding. Ideally, the role includes all of the following (Beckford 1975:70):

1) being a student of Watch Tower literature;
2) learning official doctrines;
3) showing willingness to proselytize actively;

4) undergoing baptism by total immersion into the Watch Tower faith as a symbol of "dedication to Jehovah God";
5) participating regularly in the congregation's meetings.

The meeting place for a congregation is called a Kingdom Hall, not a church or temple, and it may be either a rented space or an austere building belonging to the Witnesses themselves. Activities held in a Kingdom Hall include study of the *Watchtower* magazine, a public talk, a service meeting which instructs the witnesses in their preaching work, and a theocratic ministry school (Rogerson 1969:128). In return for their labors, Witnesses hoped to be among the "little flock" mentioned in Luke 12:32 who would receive "the kingdom." However, Revelation 14:3 speaks of "the hundred and forty and four thousand, which were redeemed from the earth." Presumably this little flock of 144,000 includes the departed disciples of Jesus and many other worthies throughout history who might be considered Witnesses, including Russell and Rutherford. So when the membership of Jehovah's Witnesses surpassed 144,000 it was clear that many members would not receive this direct heavenly resurrection. Instead, they are promised an earthly paradise of a thousand years (Watch Tower Bible and Tract Society 1952:279; Curry 1992:53). In 1920, Rutherford thought this might begin in 1925 and coined the powerful slogan: "Millions now living will never die."

In 1966, believing that Adam and Eve were created in 4026 B.C., Witnesses announced the Millennium would begin 6,000 years later, or in 1975 (Rogerson 1969:109). Where Miller had counted a day to a year, here they were counting a day to a thousand years. God created the world in six days, and then, Genesis 2:2 tells us, "on the seventh day God ended his work which he had made." The seventh day is the thousand-year millennium, so the six earlier days must be six thousand years of human history. Curry (1992:123–125) notes that the result of the 1975 prophecy was a big increase in proselytizing and baptisms right before the appointed date, and a marked decline afterward. For twenty years, the Witnesses have resisted setting a date, but this is so much an aspect of their heritage that it would not be surprising to see them do it again, restaging Miller's disappointment yet again more than a century and a half after he endured it.

The Personalities of Miller, White, and Russell

In the 1950s and 1960s, the theories of psychoanalysis and other forms of depth psychology were quite popular among sociologists, and scholars of many backgrounds applied its principles to practically every imaginable feature of society, including religion. Freud (1927, 1930) himself spent his last years writing about religion, analyzing it in the same terms he employed to dissect psychopathology. His disciple Geza Roheim (1955) considered religion to be nothing more than a shared psychosis, and Weston La Barre (1969, 1972) argued that every founder of a new religion is at the very least severely neurotic. Other members of the Psychoanalytic Movement reduced the religious innovations of Martin Luther and Mary Baker Eddy to neurotic manifestations (Erikson 1962; Zweig 1932). Scholars of religion currently find this approach far-less-convincing that some once did, but the popular press continues to brand "cult" founders madmen. Further, if applied undogmatically with full respect for historical facts, depth psychology can supplement sociological analyses to round out a balanced social psychology of religious innovation.

Belief in the imminent end of the world strikes many people as crazy, so they might be quick to call Miller, White, and Russell insane. Indeed, for two decades following 1844, occasional inmates of the nation's mental hospitals were diagnosed as victims of Miller-induced religious madness (Bainbridge 1984). Ronald and Janet Numbers (1987) have estimated that this happened to at least 170 persons, and they examined the hospital records of ninety-eight of them, concluding that most really did exhibit seriously pathological behavior rather than merely being labeled insane because of their unconventional religious views. None of the three Adventist leaders was in fact ever hospitalized for mental illness, although at the peak of his fame Miller had to endure occasional charges by opponents that he had gone crazy.

Once, when a doctor had come to treat his son, Miller asked the man to examine him to determine if he were a monomaniac. This is someone who is sane in all aspects of his life except one, and there he is an obsessed fanatic. For much of the nineteenth century, learned men debated whether monomania really existed and whether it could be used as a defense in criminal cases (Ray 1863, 1871; Dain 1964). The doctor discussed the Bible with Miller for two hours, at the end of which he pronounced him completely sane.

A second sanity investigation came when Miller was taken by a friend to visit a phrenologist in Boston (Bliss 1853:160–161). Phrenology was a popular pseudoscientific movement in mid-nineteenth-century America, bearing about the same relationship to psychology as astrology does to astronomy. Supposedly, the shape of a person's skull reveals the nature of his or her personality, because an overabundance of any character trait requires a greater size in one or another part of the brain, thus forcing the skull to bulge over that region. The phrenologist went to work without learning the name of the man whose head his fingers were running over, and he found Miller to have a large and well-balanced skull with no bulges. Still unaware of Miller's identity, the phrenologist happened to use the Millerite craze to explain his diagnosis. "Mr. Miller could not easily make a convert of this man to his hair-brained theory. He has too much good sense." Miller and his friend responded with interest to this statement, so the man continued excitedly, still unaware he was talking about the very man he was examining.

"O, how I should like to examine Mr. Miller's head! I would give it one squeezing." He placed his hand where phrenologists supposed the organ of marvelousness was located, saying, "There! I'll bet you anything that old Miller has got a bump on his head there as big as my fist." At the end of the examination, after pronouncing his client thoroughly normal, the phrenologist began filling out his report chart and asked the name of his client so he could write it down. When told that his client was the very same William Miller he had been disparaging, the phrenologist slumped in his chair, dazed and speechless.

Certainly this quack exam does not give us scientific proof that Miller was sane, but all the testimony of people who met Miller paints a picture of a very conventional, level-headed man respected by his community, completely lacking in eccentricities. His morose mood in the year following his military service is a reasonable response to the terrible lessons of the war, and his emotional investment in reading the Bible was standard behavior in nineteenth-century America.

Ellen White is a different story. She alone of the three great Adventist leaders experienced frequent "visions." Of course, if one believes in God, then one has to admit the possibility that sometimes the Deity will chose to communicate with individual humans. Furthermore, both the Old Testament and the New Testament describe visions, with those of Daniel and John of Patmos having the most immediate connection to Adventism. Perhaps a distinction should be made between orthodox visions and heterodox visions (cf. Ackerknecht 1943). It takes considerable tolerance to admit that visions radically at variance with the surrounding culture, and which are based on beliefs one does not personally subscribe to, could be other than psychopathological.

Ronald and Janet Numbers (1992), he a renegade Adventist historian and she a clinical psychologist, have argued that Ellen White suffered from "recurrent episodes of depression and anxiety to which she responded with somaticizing defenses and a histrionic personality style." The term "somaticizing defenses" refers to a tendency to transform emotional conflicts into physical complaints. A "histrionic personality style" (Shapiro 1965) means that a person has a tendency to be flamboyant or unusually dramatic, making herself the center of attention by grand emotional gestures. Another term for such as person is "hysteric." All her life, Ellen reported a "dazzling array of physical and psychological problems." One day when she was ten, Ellen was walking through a park with her sister Elizabeth and a friend when another child threw a rock at them, striking Ellen on the nose and knocking her unconscious. She did not regain full alertness for three weeks and claimed she could not breathe through her nose for two years. Clearly she suffered a traumatic injury in this incident, but it also focused her anxieties on her physical vulnerability, and for the remaining seventy-seven years of her life she constantly felt that death was near-at-hand.

In societies which believe that supernatural forces directly intervene in human affairs, such histrionics may take the form of spirit possession. A good example is the Zar religious movement of Ethopia, Somalia, and Sudan (Messing 1958; Kennedy 1967; Lewis 1971; Stark and Bainbridge 1987:163–165). This movement draws on popular beliefs that people can become possessed by supernatural beings called "abless," "afreet," or "shaytan." The victims are chiefly women who suffer terrible deprivation in a society that gives all power to their husbands, even excluding them from conventional religious organizations. The first symptoms are generalized physical complaints connected with restless anxiety, and as these symptoms persist the suspicion grows that an evil spirit may be at fault. The Zar healer comes and applies various diagnostic tests such as passing a lighted candle carefully under the lady's skirts to see if this triggers violent movement. If the woman is prepared to play the culturally scripted role of a possessed person, she is given an extravagant, often week-long curing ceremony, attended by other women who have already been cured, that showers attention on her, causes the spirit to dance, and leads to an accommodation between the woman and her spirit. Zar-possessed women can use their spirits "to extort economic sacrifices from their husbands by threatening a relapse when their demands are ignored" (Lewis 1971:79).

Such possession can be analyzed in terms of rewards, costs, and explanations. Men are far more powerful than women in these societies. This means that men can extract rewards from women at little cost to themselves. Women, in contrast, must endure great costs to gain even modest rewards. Indeed, because women are more plentiful than men in many regions, and men have great power in the culture, a husband could easily cast his wife aside and get a younger and more pliant woman. At worst, the costs outweigh the rewards for the women, and their desires are profoundly frustrated. This frustration might lead to aggression, but any direct action against the husband would only bring great costs down on the head of the woman. In her relationship with her husband, she has no recourse. But then a third party enters the picture, the spirit. The spirit appears to attack the woman, thus rousing the husband's sympathy and making him an ally with his wife against the spirit. The spirit appears to make demands on both the husband and wife, but these demands have the effect of improving the wife's situation. Thus the spirit is "really" the aggression and desires of the wife, but so long as the husband does not realize this the spirit can serve her needs, perhaps quite effectively.

The key, of course, is that both parties accept the widespread belief in their culture that spirits exist. The existence of a spirit world explains much to members of the culture, such as physical illness and the vagaries of a harsh natural environment. And the general religious culture to which the spirits belong provides a host of compensators, both general and specific. When a woman first becomes possessed, the spirit provides an explanation for her distress and extracts some rewarding nurturance from the husband. In the lavish Zar ceremony, she gains the reward of social attention from other women who have already come to terms with their Zar spirits, plus the compensator of a sense of wealth as they pile jewelry around her which is not hers to keep. And once the relationship with the spirit has stabilized, she gains both constant compensators for her low status in the form of periodic attention from the spirit and some measure of increased power in exchanges with her husband that reduce her costs and increase her rewards. If she is especially talented, in partnership with her spirit she will become a Zar healer, thus creatively sustaining the religious tradition to which Zar belongs.

This may seem very far from nineteenth-century America, but we chose the example because it illustrates with great vividness the social dynamics that may underlie especially intense communication with spirits (including sometimes angels, Jesus, or God). But notice, although the women may exhibit some symptoms of physical illness early in the possession, it is not really a case of mental illness. Rather, powerlessness within a cultural context that accepts the existence of spirits can lead to playing the role of a possessed person. In the middle of the twentieth century, when psychoanalytic ideas blurred the distinctions between real mental illness and the emotional extremes that may be experienced by completely normal people, scholars employed the language of psychopathology to describe every kind of human behavior under the sun. Sometimes, as in some discussions of religious behavior, they achieve some partial but very real insights, spoiling these insights by the use of inappropriate psychiatric language.

Ellen White was not mentally ill. She was an extremely effective person who had acquired a somewhat rare personality style early in life—I say *rare* not deviant or pathological—that emphasized a concern over health problems and gave her the ability to act out the belief current in her society that people could in rare moments communicate directly with the supernatural. In her teens and early adulthood, she would experience brief public episodes in which she became intensely aware of the spiritual realm. These were not hallucinations like those that sometimes afflict schizophrenics. It is possible that these experiences were simply real, and, as many Adventists believe, she really did enter into direct communication with the supernatural. Or these may have been intensely dramatic episodes in which she acted out the religious beliefs of her audience, applying all her creative intellect and imagination to religious questions so intensely that the results seemed fully real to her. Her followers defined the spiritual experiences as real, and they had the very real effect of providing the core of religious awareness around which the Seventh-day Adventist church could grow.

Russell is quite different from either Miller or White. He was not given to visions, but did have a will to dominate that Miller lacked. In the absence of good biographies or access to original documents such as letters, it is hard to get the measure of the man. Curry (1992) portrays him as an astute business man, who learned his skills in his father's retail-clothing chain and poured this expertise as well as much of his financial wealth into the movement. If anything, his successor Rutherford had an even stronger personality, tested in the furious competition for power that followed Russell's death, plus an equal measure of organizational and administrative ability. Traditionally, scholars have not thought of founders of religious movements as entrepreneurs, but in the free market of American religion they often need whatever personality characteristics favor success in any other entrepreneurial occupation (cf. Bainbridge and Stark, 1979). Ellen White's talents were more in the spiritual than entrepreneurial direction, but her husband provided whatever business sense she needed.

Sectarian Tension of the Millerites

From what we have read about sectarian movements in the past two chapters, we would expect that the Millerites were disproportionately poor and uneducated people who suffered relative deprivation. However, it is not certain that this is true. David Rowe (1987:2) has argued that "Miller's message was so orthodox that the movement achieved a comprehensiveness that sociologists usually ascribe to formal churches." Prior to the Great Disappointment, Millerism was not a separatist sect but a movement within and across the churches. Social movements of one kind or another are found in all corners of society, and some varieties of movement are even especially common among the rich, powerful, and highly educated (Bainbridge 1976). Miller did not originally seek to call people out of the standard denominations, but to fulfill the promise of the existing churches. Except for his conviction that the Second Coming was imminent and could be dated, there was nothing unorthodox about his teachings. Only later, as a series of organizations consolidated out of his diffuse movement would sect theory really apply.

We need to realize that no religious denomination perfectly meets the needs of its members. In particular, members of all denominations would like to experience the complete fulfillment of the promises of their faith right now in the material world. Put more formally, humans prefer rewards to compensators (Stark and Bainbridge 1987: 37). At any level of sectarian tension, if people are presented the opportunity to reach their religious goals immediately, and the opportunity is couched in terms of widely shared beliefs, then anyone might join the movement. But as the movement committed itself to a series of precise dates, and each led to disappointment, we can conjecture that relatively prosperous people may have been more ready to return to the conventional churches, whereas those who kept on with the Adventists may have been disproportionately people suffering relative deprivation. Thus one would expect the resulting Adventists to approximate more closely the standard picture of sectarians.

However, Malcolm Bull (1989:178) says that Adventism "is not, in Stark and Bainbridge's terms (1985), a sect—a high tension offspring of a single, usually low tension, parent body; nor is it a cult—an alien or highly innovative new religion." Essentially he is right, and the case of Adventism is one good reason for trying to get beyond sect-cult thinking in talking about religious movements. Certainly there are elements of both schism and independent innovation. Miller had not intended to lead multitudes out of the standard denominations, but this was the net effect of his movement. After they were out, the various branches of Adventism were able to collect some of these people. But perhaps because Adventist denominations arose out of this disorganized mass of potential believers, rather than breaking off directly from an existing organization, it was relatively free to innovate in terms of doctrine and practices.

Where on the scale of sectarian tension do the various Adventist groups stand? Several specific beliefs and practices originally set them apart from the rest of the nation, and many continue to do so. When "blue laws" used to distinguish Sunday officially as the day of rest, the fact that the Seventh-day Adventists held their sabbath on Saturday was a serious norm violation, but today there is little if any official distinction between Saturday and Sunday, so they are no longer deviant despite continuing the same behavior. James Beckford (1975:13) judges that Jehovah's Witnesses are culturally middle-class because their literature employs "closely reasoned arguments on obtuse theological and scriptural themes," and their gatherings lack religious emotionality. However, Witness groups never employ secular experts, cooperate with other denominations, or salute the flag of the country in which they live. In their dealings with medical professionals, they refuse to submit to blood transfusions. These facts, coupled with their aggressive dedication to proselytizing, prove they are in tension with the sociocultural environment.

From the beginning, the Seventh-day Adventists favored book learning, and today they value formal education, so one might expect that their tension with the surrounding sociocultural environment is only moderate. Like other conservative denominations, the Seventh-day Adventist Church has struggled to preserve its traditional beliefs and practices while confronting the challenges of a rapidly changing world (Pearson 1990). For example, religious penalties for divorce become very difficult when a substantial fraction of marriages fail, as is the case in modern America. Given their emphasis on education, Seventh-day Adventists have to confront seriously the challenges to cherished beliefs raised by historians within the church who examine the life of Ellen White (Butler 1992).

Beckford (1975) says that the highly centralized "theocratic" government of Jehovah's Witnesses has allowed this movement to resist significant reduction of tension with the surrounding sociocultural environment. Congregations are kept small, generally less than 200 members, and isolated from each other. This fact, coupled with the absence of any kind of representative government, prevents rival social organizations from arising within the movement that might try to change the level of tension or break off in major schisms.

A sufficient number of Seventh-day Adventists and Jehovah's Witnesses were polled by the General Social Survey to give us a picture of their religiosity and relative deprivation. In Table 4.1 we see that essentially the same proportion, 60 percent and 59 percent, consider themselves strong members of their denominations, compared with 43 percent among all Protestants (including themselves and all other high-tension groups). Seventh-day Adventists are slightly more likely than Jehovah's Witnesses to say they belong to a church-affiliated group, but this difference may be slightly misleading. The structure of activities in Jehovah's Witnesses gives a relatively greater emphasis to training in doctrines and missionary techniques than to a weekly religious service, but it does not usually spin these activities off into distinct church-related organizations.

Witnesses are more likely than Seventh-day Adventists to attend church weekly, 62 percent compared with 52 percent, although both show high levels of attendance. We have seen that Witnesses are expected to participate in many Watch Tower activities at church, rather than just coming to a religious service once a week, so we should compare the proportions in both groups who go to church "several times a week." Only 3 percent of Episcopalians attend church several times per week, and 11 percent of Baptists. As we might expect, Seventh-day Adventists have a slightly higher rate than Baptists, 15 percent, but fully 51 percent of Jehovah's Witnesses go to church several times a week.

The special traditions of Jehovah's Witnesses also show up in their response to the item about the afterlife. Among Seventh-day Adventists, 78 percent believe there is a life after death, but just 50 percent of Jehovah's Witnesses do. The official doctrine of Jehovah's Witnesses concerning death holds that the spirit of a dead person lies unconscious in the grave until Christ returns when it may experience resurrection. This is very different from the conventional

Table 4.1: Religious Commitment of Adventists and Jehovah's Witnesses—Percent

	Protestants	Adventists	Jehovah's Witnesses
Respondent is a strong member of his or her denomination.	43 (14,634)	60 (102)	59 (140)
Respondent belongs to a church affiliated group.	43 (11,008)	49 (76)	42 (108)
Respondent attends religious services weekly.	30 (17,087)	52 (116)	62 (156)
Respondent believes there is a life after death.	77 (11,302)	78 (77)	50 (118)
Respondent believes the Bible is the actual word of God and is to be taken literally.	43 (4,407)	50 (26)	62 (45)
Respondent says somebody who is against all churches should be allowed to speak.	62 (11,941)	64 (81)	71 (93)
Respondent approves Supreme Court's ban on prayer in public schools.	34 (8,051)	30 (47)	50 (66)

Christian view, and it is not what most people mean by "a life after death." Indeed, this particular question may not be valid for respondents who happen to be Jehovah's Witnesses, because they can answer "no" while remaining very devout believers if they interpret the item to mean a person goes immediately to heaven or hell after death. Or they could answer "yes" if they interpreted it to mean that some dead people sometime after death may live again.

The Witnesses are more likely than Adventists to believe the Bible is "the actual word of God and is to be taken literally," and Adventists are more likely to than the average Protestant. If we could rely upon this single item, and on the relatively small numbers of Adventists and Witnesses who were asked it, we would conclude that Witnesses are in higher tension than Adventists, although the differences are not huge. The two concluding items, concerning public speech against religion and prayer in the schools, reveal no difference between the Adventists and Protestants in general. Jehovah's Witnesses take civil liberties very seriously. A big majority, nearly three-quarters of them, support the right of a person to speak against religion, and half support a ban on prayer in school. Perhaps they remember that decades ago their children were expelled from public schools for refusing to pledge allegiance to the flag, and that in nation after nation their missionaries have been jailed for professing their beliefs in public.

We now see the reason why we did not include Jehovah's Witnesses in the "sect" category in the analysis of responses to the General Social Survey given in Chapter 2. For several questionnaire items, their responses are distinctly different from those of other high-tension Protestant groups. Despite holding sabbath services on Saturday and stemming from the same millenarian tradition as the Witnesses, the Seventh-day Adventists fit right into the standard Protestant tradition. To a significant degree, Jehovah's Witnesses are a new religious tradition. They do not go so far as to have wholly new sacred books, as the Mormons do, but their own translation of the Bible casts the traditional scriptures in their own terms. As we have just seen, they give markedly different meanings to some of the standard religious concepts.

Descriptions of the Seventh-day Adventists often remark upon their respect for education and suggest they have become solidly middle class, whereas descriptions of Jehovah's Witnesses still argue the membership is drawn from relatively deprived strata in the society (Beckford 1975; Pearson 1990). Thus we might expect to find a significant difference between respondents to the General Social Survey from these two groups. The proportion of African Americans is slightly higher among Jehovah's Witnesses than Seventh-day Adventists, 30 percent compared with 24. Table 4.2 shows the four measures of relative deprivation we employed in the two previous chapters. The differences are in the predicted direction, Adventists seeming to be better educated and more prosperous than Witnesses. However the differences are not large enough to achieve statistical significance with this relatively modest number of respondents, 246 to 274 depending on the questionnaire item. One possibility is that the two groups recruit from essentially the same strata in society, but the Adventists have a larger proportion of relatively well-educated people who were born into the church. The fact that the Seventh-day Adventist church has its own substantial institutions of higher learning, notably Loma Linda University, means that this denomination has a prosperous intelligentsia who naturally see their entire denomination in their own image and present that well-educated face to the world.

The Branch Davidian Catastrophe

Although the Seventh-day Adventists and Jehovah's Witnesses experience tension with the world, they do not by any means approach the extreme in high tension. That hazardous honor among groups in Miller's tradition goes to the Branch Davidians. The first seeds of this movement were sown in

Table 4.2: Relative Deprivation of Seventh-day Adventists and Jehovah's Witnesses—Percent

	Protestants	Adventists	Jehovah's Witnesses
Respondent did not finish high school.	32 (17,111)	37 (117)	43 (157)
Respondent's occupation has low prestige.	25 (15,796)	34 (106)	39 (140)
Respondents says his or her family income is below average.	29 (17,025)	37 (113)	44 (154)
Respondent says he or she is working class or lower class.	52 (16,107)	61 (107)	72 (147)

1929, when Bulgarian immigrant Victor Tasho Houteff began preaching within the Seventh-day Adventist community in Los Angeles (Melton 1993; Pitts 1994, 1995). In a typical sectarian argument, he proclaimed that the church had compromised with the world, and he called upon it to regain what he believed were its original principles. Christ would return as soon as Adventism could collect 144,000 followers "without fault before the throne of God." For six years Houteff and the Seventh-day Adventist church battled, until the break came in 1935 and he led a dozen followers to farmland near Waco, Texas, where he established a community called Mount Carmel.

Initially, Houteff hoped the second coming would occur within a few months, but soon, like the Shakers before them, his millenarians established a well-organized community that would be ready whenever the great event occurred. One sign of Mount Carmel's independence from the surrounding society was that it issued its own money, green-colored paper bills and cardboard coins carrying the image of the lion of Judah and a clock at the eleventh hour symbolizing the nearness of the endtime. Houteff's group printed a series of tracts, and he undertook to decipher the secret code in which he believed the holy scriptures had been written. When the Second World War began, he sought conscientious-objector exemption from military service for his men, and because he did not have the official recognition of the Seventh-day Adventist Church, he was forced to incorporate his group in 1943 as an independent church, calling it Davidian Seventh Day Adventists.

Houteff never set an exact date for the millennium, but his followers assumed that he personally would announce the coming of the messiah. Thus his death in 1955 was a severe disappointment to them. Against the advice of some advisors, his widow Florence announced that on April 22, 1959, God would remove both Jews and Arabs from Palestine and give the Holy Land to the Davidians. Nearly nine hundred Davidians across the country sold their property and converged on Waco, but after the appointed day passed without incident, the community at Mount Carmel dwindled to about fifty. Opposition to Mrs. Houteff's leadership, and the results of the disappointment, splintered the group into at least three tiny fragments: the Davidian Seventh-day Adventist Association (headquartered in Exeter, Missouri), the General Association of Davidian Seventh-day Adventists (in Salem, South Carolina), and the Branch Davidian Seventh-day Adventists (still near Waco).

Ben Roden took over the leadership of the Branch Davidians, and he continued to plan emigration to Israel. After his death, his wife Lois led the group until she died and her son George took over. A scripturally erudite member, Vernon Howell, led a tiny schism that was involved in a gun battle and complicated court maneuvers. Howell took over the splinter of a splinter group that remained at Mount Carmel and began moving the already sectarian millenarian message even further in the radical direction, focusing on the meaning of the seven seals described in Revelation 5–8 (Bromley and Silver 1995). Houteff had considered himself to be the biblical David, so when Howell assumed his mantle he, also, became David—David Koresh.

On February 28, 1993, a strike force of about eighty agents of the Bureau of Alcohol, Tobacco and Firearms (ATF) assaulted the Branch Davidian compound. Given their apocalyptic beliefs the Davidians may have expected an armed attack and had stockpiled weapons. In March, 1992, remarkably, members of the Los Angeles and other police departments had engaged in three days of target practice within earshot of Mount Carmel, which the Branch Davidians apparently took as a show of force meant to intimidate them or a warning of an assault to come (Sullivan 1993). Surviving Branch Davidians have claimed that most of the weapons were simply the merchandise of a member who happened to be a gun dealer. In any case, someone apparently tipped them off just before the AFT attacked and they were ready to defend themselves. Pictures broadcast on television news and plastered across the newspapers showed agents firing into the windows of the house, and then falling themselves in a hail of bullets from inside.

Everything about the ATF raid and the ensuing siege is controversial, and our aim here will be to tell just enough of the confirmed story to support a sociological analysis. Several critics have argued that the raid was unnecessary, and that it resulted from a combination of deliberate misinformation from opponents of new religious movements, accusations from disgruntled defectors, misunderstanding by officials, and possibly even a desire by ATF leaders to achieve a newsworthy success to defend their agency against budget cuts or a threatened elimination (Wright 1995). The Davidians possessed a considerable store of weapons, their leader had been involved in a gunfight before, and some of the weapons may have been illegally obtained. That would have been the one legitimate justification for an attack specifically by the ATF. Stories about child abuse, polygamy, and "cultism" aroused sentiments against the group, but they have subsequently been contested and such problems in any case are not the ATF's business.

When the raid was over, four agents had been killed, seventeen were wounded, Koresh himself was shot twice, and his little daughter and perhaps half a dozen other Davidians had been killed. No medical attention was available for the wounded, because despite the tremendous force it had assembled, the ATF had not brought so much as one medic. After the shooting subsided, the FBI took over from the ATF, ringed the Branch Davidian compound with its forces, and attempted to convince David Koresh and his followers to surrender. At some times negotiations seemed to be moving forward, and at other times the FBI inflicted psychological warfare tactics like blaring rock music on the Davidians. Periodically, people would leave the Davidian compound, and Koresh sought to get his religious message out. As the days of the siege wore on, the government officials in charge never sought advice from any of those social scientists who have invested years of research into new religious movements, although they consulted with psychiatrists and gave a little attention to scholars who had scholarly understandings of the scriptures, notably a church historian at Baylor University and a Virginia Pastor. Two biblical scholars, James D. Tabor and Phillip Arnold, gained limited involvement but apparently were unable to influence decisions of the authorities. Tabor and Arnold examined some of the statements made by David Koresh, and interviewed Livingston Fagan whom Koresh had sent out as his spokesman. First of all, the scholars quickly unraveled the meaning of the name Vernon Howell had taken.

"Koresh" is the Hebrew name for the Persian King Cyrus who defeated Babylon, and in Isaiah 45:1 Cyrus is referred to as anointed, the only time the Bible uses this term to refer to a gentile. Both "Messiah" and "Christ" refer to the anointed one, and the mass media quickly announced that David Koresh was claiming to be the Christ. However, high priests and kings of Israel were also anointed—as was the present Queen Elizabeth of England during her coronation—and the term may be broadly used for anyone who has been given a divine mission to perform. It appears that David Koresh took this name because he believed it was his mission to open the seven seals described in Revelation 5–8 that would destroy the Babylon that America had become (Tabor, 1994:13–14). Ominously, the Lamb who opens the seals in Revelation does so only after having been slain, which seems to be a reference to the crucifixion of Jesus but Koresh might believe was a prophecy that he would have to die to complete his mission. The Davidians believed they had reached the fifth seal, described in Revelation 6:9–11:

> And when he had opened the fifth seal, I saw under the altar the souls of them that were slain for the word of God, and for the testimony which they held:
> And they cried with a loud voice, saying, How long, O Lord, holy and true, dost thou not judge and avenge our blood on them that dwell on the earth?
> And white robes were given unto every one of them; and it was said unto them, that they should rest yet for a little season, until their fellow servants also and their brethren, that should be killed as they were, should be fulfilled.

Tabor and Arnold explained to the FBI that Koresh refused to come out of the compound because he believed God was telling him to wait "a little season," and that the prophecy plainly warned Koresh that he and his followers would be killed. The scholars were convinced that no amount of pressure from the FBI could force Koresh and his followers to come out, because to do so would be to disobey God (Arnold 1994; Tabor 1995). Hoping they could find a way to save the lives of the besieged Davidians, Tabor and Arnold went on a radio program they knew Koresh listened to and gave a different interpretation of the biblical passages, stressing the "little book" in Revelation 10, thus providing him a theological escape route. Two weeks later, Koresh sent out a letter to his attorney Dick DeGuerin, saying "I am presently being permitted to document in structured form the decoded messages of the *7 Seals*. Upon the completion of this task I will be freed of my 'waiting period.' I hope to finish this as soon as possible and to stand before man to answer any and all questions regarding my actions" (Facsimile of letter from David Koresh to Dick DeGuerin, April 14, 1993 in Scruggs et al. 1993).

Thus, Tabor and Arnold hoped that a few more weeks' patience would bring the Davidians out safely. On April 18 the authorities delivered writing materials to Koresh, and he began dictating his commentary on the first seal. However, apparently the leadership in the FBI and the Justice Department did not share the scholars' optimism, and several agents doubted that Koresh was capable of writing a book or even intended to. To them, it was just another delaying tactic, and they were not inclined to wait any longer. Early on the morning of April 19 they warned Koresh he must surrender immediately or the compounded would be flooded with tear gas.

When Koresh did not come out, the besieging forces began intermittently sending an armored vehicle up to the large wooden structure in which the Davidian men, women, and children huddled, breaking holes in the wall and squirting in "CS" gas. Tabor and Arnold guessed that this second violent attack confirmed the Davidians in their initial apocalyptic interpretation of what was happening. They understood the prophecy to say that the faithful would be slain in two phases, first some and then the others. The ATF assault was the first phase, and now the rest would die in the FBI attack. Somehow they endured the gas torture until fire broke out and quickly engulfed the highly flammable frame structure. When the flames had died away, seventy-five bodies were found in the ashes. The medical examiner reported that sixteen had been shot, including three children, apparent evidence of a wild murder-suicide in the last desperate minutes (Dennis 1993:28–29).

Analysis of Waco

The Branch Davidian calamity is so emotionally wrenching that it is difficult to gain perspective on it. Some writers even asserted that the whole government raid was intentionally designed to murder the Davidians, and unfortunately ideas like this have spread widely through radical groups of many kinds that are found across the United States. This may have been a factor in the mass-murder bombing in Oklahoma City on the second anniversary of the Waco fire. Many Americans, on the other hand, take the tragedy as further proof that novel religions are dangerous and should be tightly controlled if not eradicated. Sociologist James T. Richardson (1994:183) says, "We need to lower the level of hysteria about new and minority religions in this country, and increase the amount of understanding of religion among citizens and policy-makers. The ignorance shown by media and law enforcement about the Davidians was appalling, and contributed directly to the tragedy. Some major statements made since by national leaders perpetuates this ignorance and contributes to continued demonization of Koresh and his followers and, by implication, other minority religions."

James R. Lewis (1994) and Larry D. Shinn (1994) note that opinion polls revealed Americans overwhelmingly supported the federal agents who besieged Mount Carmel and blamed the Branch Davidians for the catastrophe. Lewis suggests that in part this near unanimity reflects a real and possibly growing hostility toward minority religions rooted in the need of American society to have an enemy. Common defense against an external threat can unify a people, support its norms and values, and provide a sense that the society's way of life is meaningful and virtuous. By 1993, the Soviet Union had disintegrated and for the time being, at least, America lacked a clearly defined external enemy, unless it had begun to assign this role to Islamic fundamentalism. Two decades of largely stagnant economic growth, and increasing but unrelieved social tensions affecting several segments of the population, magnify the need to find easily recognized signs of evil in the world, thus aggravating the hostility that Americans were prepared to direct against small, strange groups. Lewis's provocative thesis is rooted in much traditional sociological theory about collective behavior, so it is worth considering.

Political scientist Michael Barkun (1994:46) judges that the deaths of April 1993 could have been avoided: "Federal forces should have been rapidly drawn down to the lowest level necessary to prevent individuals from leaving the compound undetected. Those forces that remained should have been as inconspicuous as possible. The combination of a barely visible federal presence, together with a willingness to wait, would have accomplished two things: it would have avoided government actions that confirmed apocalyptic prophecies, and it would have deprived Koresh of his opportunity to validate his charismatic authority through the marathon negotiations that played as well-rehearsed millenarian theater." This plan would also have given Koresh a chance to write out his biblical interpretations, and thus test the theory of Tabor and Arnold that he would surrender immediately after. Over the passage of time, more individual members might have come out, either carrying messages for Koresh, in exchange for the materials he needed to complete his manuscript, or as defectors. On March 11, 1993, highly respected sociologist Dean M. Kelley, then serving as counselor on religious liberty of the National Council of Churches, and James Dunn of the Baptist Joint Committee urged President Clinton to demilitarize the siege.

In the investigations that followed the tragedy, Nancy T. Ammerman, then a visiting scholar in Princeton's Center for the Study of American Religion, concluded that the law-enforcement agencies had indeed neglected the advice of the best available experts, and she noted that even the FBI's own behavioral science team was overruled when the final assault was ordered. Ammerman (1993) argued that ten key insights could help prevent similar fatal errors in future, listed here in Table 4.3.

Ammerman believes that these ten points were not clear to the ATF and FBI, and their lack of awareness contributed to the tragedy. They had apparently learned the wrong lessons from the 1978 tragedy of the People's Temple, when Jim Jones led 918 people to their deaths (Reiterman, and Jacobs 1982; Hall 1987; Chidester 1988). In particular, many agents and officials connected with the siege simply considered Koresh to be insane or a con man, as they imagined Jim Jones had been, who possessed diabolical power over his brainwashed followers. They could not recognize that charisma and an alternative symbolic world can be created through intensive interactions among members, in which the leader plays a key role but is far from a dictator. Put another way, the law enforcement agencies never seriously recognized that religion was the motive behind the actions of the branch Davidians (Sullivan 1993; Ammerman 1995).

Table 4.3: Ammerman's Ten Points Concerning the Branch Davidians

---

1. Religious experimentation is a fundamental right deeply rooted in American history.
2. New religious groups are often millenarian.
3. Most new religious movements fade quietly out of existence.
4. New religious groups almost always provoke their neighbors.
5. Many new religious movements demand commitments that seem abnormal to outsiders.
6. Commitment to a new religious movement is generally voluntary.
7. A religious group can create an alternate symbolic world that is logical for members but may seem illogical to outsiders.
8. Charisma is not an individual trait, but emerges in the constantly evolving relationship between a leader and followers.
9. Tragedy can strike a volatile religious group, as the more than nine hundred deaths of the Peoples Temple in 1978 remind us.
10. Any group under siege is likely to turn inward, and pressure from the outside can strengthen the bonds between a leader and followers.

In November 1994, a computer disk containing the fragments of David Koresh's manuscript about the seven seals was released to the public and placed on the Internet from the University of Pennsylvania by James Tabor and Phillip Arnold, there for anyone in the world to read—unedited, a bit scattered, but filled with biblical citations and clearly a real attempt to uncover the meaning of the seven seals and answer the question, "Are we in the last days?"

Conclusion: The Adventist System

Adventist movements seem generally to begin not in the schism of a denomination into two or more parts, although that did occur in the recent history of the Branch Davidians, but in rather more subtle processes that take place within a diffuse Adventist cultural system. William Miller, we noted, was not a come-outer who led a dissident group out of his Baptist church to found a sect. Rather he thought his discoveries were compatible with existing denominations, and the first steps toward separation from the existing churches came as people interested in Miller's doctrine began to hold meetings that built links among like-minded people across denominations, thus weakening participant's bonds to their former congregations. The Seventh-day Adventists and the several small groups that ultimately became the Advent Christian Church emerged around strong leaders out of the remnants of Millerism, and Jehovah's Witnesses appear to have collected around Russell slightly later by a similar process. The story of the Branch Davidians, however, certainly

117

is one of schism upon schism that ejected a tiny religious movement to the deadly extreme in tension with the sociocultural environment.

Four highly successful novel religious denominations have arisen in American history: the Seventh-day Adventists, Jehovah's Witnesses, the Church of Jesus Christ of Latter-day Saints (Mormons), and Christian Scientists. Of these, the first three continue to gain ground rapidly, especially overseas, but the Christian Science denomination appears to have faltered. I suggest that one factor giving these religious movements great strength is precisely the ambiguity of their degree of tension with the sociocultural environment. In some ways they are in very high tension. They possess novel culture including books that are either presented as new holy scripture or the next thing to it. Their members are supposed to follow distinctive norms of behavior, both in religious contexts and in their daily lives. They consider their own brand of religion to be vastly better than that of conventional churches, and in varying degrees they accuse the ordinary Protestant denominations of falling away from the faith. But they also have low-tension features. For one thing, they emphasize education and have strongly intellectual orientations toward scripture. Their formal organizations are relatively centralized, rather than giving substantial autonomy to local congregations. In the main, their religious gatherings are emotionally restrained, and even some of the more passionate Seventh-day Adventist congregations would have difficulty competing with the Pentecostals or Holiness churches for emotionality. To the extent that these groups are in high tension, they have a strength of faith and purpose allowing them to recruit actively. To the extent they are in low tension, they are sober and respectable churches that can readily incorporate middle-class members. Thus their growth may rest upon the best features of both the high- and low-tension worlds.

However, the core assumption of the Adventist cultural system is the imminent Second Coming of Christ, and commitment to this belief limits the degree to which such groups can reduce their tension with the sociocultural environment. Their doctrines inescapably predict an end to the conventional society dominated by other groups, and their own ascendancy over nonbelievers. For their part, outsiders committed to continuance of the world as it is may feel they have ample reason to reject and distrust Adventists for their millenarianism. The Adventist cultural system marks out a distinct territory of beliefs and practices for its members, and some will inevitably wander into the extreme region occupied by the Branch Davidians. Despite lingering tension, the Seventh-day Adventists and Jehovah's Witnesses, however, have taken their place among major Protestant denominations.

5

American Religious Communes

Throughout American history, small bands of idealists have broken away from the larger society to establish religious utopian communes that sought to build ideal societies and achieve spiritual perfection. The earliest Christians may have lived communally, according to Acts 2:44–45: "And all that believed were together, and had all things common; and sold their possessions and goods, and parted them to all men, as every man had need." From those ancient days through the Middle Ages to today, the monastic tradition has stressed at least a measure of economic equality of members (Della Fave and Hillery 1980). Despite such deep roots in Christianity, however, utopian communes are in high tension with the surrounding sociocultural environment. They are socially separate from the world, hostile to its styles of life, antagonistic to its economic system, and dissatisfied with its failure to achieve spiritual perfection. For its part, the surrounding society responds with deep suspicion and sometimes harsh suppression to these deviant cultures in its midst. In this chapter we will examine five of the most famous nineteenth-century American religious communes: Oneida, Amana, Harmony, Zoar, and the largest of all, the Shakers.

The Shakers

Blood oozed from the pores of Ann Lee's skin, and her flesh withered until she was hardly more than a skeleton, in the dungeon where the respectable people of Manchester, England, had hurled her in rage over her religion. Through the keyhole of the prison door, her loyal Shaker followers poured milk punch and eggnog to sustain her. In darkness and agony, her spirit soared in the conviction that the prophecy of Revelation 12:1–2 referred to her: "And there appeared a great wonder in heaven; a woman clothed with the sun, and the moon under her feet, and upon her head a crown of twelve stars: And she being with child cried, travailing in birth, and pained to be delivered." A vision of Adam and Eve engaging in the first human sexual intercourse revealed to her that the knowledge responsible for their exile from the Garden of Eden was carnal knowledge, so only by abstaining from sex could weak mortals return to godliness (Eads 1884). And, the traditions of the Shakers say, she recognized that her own birth was the Second Advent, and that she herself was the new, female Christ (Bates 1849).

Ann never learned to read or write, so her own words were not committed to paper until a generation after she spoke them, and the memories of her listeners may have improved her deeds and maxims over the years. The earliest accounts of the Shakers, and some of the most vivid stories from the first half of the nineteenth century, were written by angry defectors who portray Ann as a harlot and witch, and the communes as concentration camps (Marshall 1847; cf. Anonymous 1846; Anonymous 1849). The sources most often cited by historians were pious Shaker writings that said she was a saint and glossed over the terrible conflicts that wracked the early communities (Robinson 1893; White and Taylor 1904; Melcher 1941; Andrews 1953). The truth may be somewhere in between.

Ann Lee or Ann Lees was the daughter of a blacksmith who lived on Toad Lane in Manchester, England. Born in 1742 on that most anomalous date, February 29, she was short, thickset but well proportioned, light in complexion with blue eyes. At the age of twenty, she married a blacksmith named Abraham Stanley or Standley or Standerin or Standerren or Standivin. The names of illiterate people exist for history only at the mercy of those able to write them down. Abraham was often drunk and unkind to Ann, so after she had given birth to four children who quickly died she had good reason to loathe relations with him. Soon she avoided her husband's bed "as if it had been made of embers" (Whitworth 1975; Stein 1992).

She joined a tiny, radical religious group led by James and Jane Wardley, possibly a schismatic offshoot of the Quakers, and, like them, employing vigorous bodily motions during group religious devotions: singing, dancing, shaking and shouting, speaking with new tongues, and prophesying. The Wardley's "Shaking Quakers" claimed to be the only true religion, led by revelations received by their prophet and prophetess, and by the summer of 1772 they had begun to have frequent quarrels with the authorities, which often resulted in Ann's arrest. Once, a mob tried to pull down the house of one of the other members, and another time the constables ripped open the Lee home on Toad Lane to apprehend a group of Shakers holed up there. At the end of May

1773, Ann served two days in jail for disturbing a conventional church service, and the same thing happened again at the end of July. Ranting against respectable religion had become one of the Shakers' chief ways of spreading their message, and Ann Lee was especially good at it.

The ranting sects of Manchester proclaimed the coming apocalypse, a harsh message that often expresses the resentment of the poor and down-trodden against citizens with property and position. In the Latter Days, the rich would be humbled and the poor raised up. Indeed, by asserting that they were the one true religion, the Shakers claimed moral and even intellectual superiority over the more moneyed and educated classes. Truth came to James and Jane Wardley in visions rather than universities. Although Ann could not read, legend says she had a gift far greater: she could converse on intimate terms with Jesus Christ.

Perhaps the continual prison terms exhausted her patience with England. Perhaps her heterodox visions caused a break with the Wardleys. In any case, a fresh vision told her to gather up a group of followers and do what many other dissatisfied or ambitious Britons were doing, emigrate to America. In May 1774, she left Liverpool on the square-rigged vessel Maria with eight followers, including her husband, brother William Lee, and a niece named Nancy. Almost immediately Ann's husband, Abraham, broke with her, according to one story because she refused to have sex with him, and he vanished from the pages of religious history. In New York the tiny band of Shakers struggled against the same poverty they had known in Manchester, and Ann supported herself as a washerwoman. A year after arriving in the new world, they moved to wooded land called Watervliet, near Niskeyuna, about seven miles northwest of Albany.

For five difficult years, they failed to gain converts, and few records remain of their doings except occasional documents written by defectors and enemies. In a sworn affidavit, Stephen and Martha Farnam stated that soon after coming to the United States, the "outlandish" Shakers tarried in Concord, New Hampshire, for a number of months (Marshall 1847:22–23). "Ann was short, and thickset; she wore a strap cap, and a large flat straw hat. William Lee was stout built, and of a sandy complexion. They proved themselves to be a people of the most vulgar sort; they lived near us, we often saw them, and were acquainted with much of their conduct. They pretended in telling fortunes—also, where stolen or lost goods were. They used ardent spirits to excess, frequented Samuel Farnam's house, a near neighbor, and at times staid all night; the family united with them in drinking, and the report from the family was, that Ann Lee lodged with Farnam, and William Lee with Farnam's wife. Their conduct left with Farnam and wife, a dirty complaint. From many circumstances, it is an undeniable fact, that those strangers were afflicted with, and doctored while here, for the venereal disease.

"Those foreigners appeared destitute of furniture—their lodging was boards nailed together for a large stead, on which lay straw, with their wearing clothes; this was said to be the lodging for all of them. They practiced singing, dancing, gambling with cards, gaming and lounging about. Ann told Samuel Farnam he had a pot of money hid under ground, and if he would give her and William each a suit of good clothes, she would tell where the money was. Farnam believed it, and got the clothes for them. Ann then pretended to tell where the money was. Farnam with others went to digging for the money, but found none. Ann found the inhabitants roused against them, borrowed some outside garments, pretending to go to a neighbor's, and that night fled. They were followed towards the state of New York in hopes of recompense, but none was obtained."

In later years, enemies of the Shakers would claim that Ann Lee was a prostitute in Manchester before she became the leader of her sect. Others said they saw her lurking around the American army during the revolution, a common camp follower selling sex and telling fortunes. She seemed the most unlikely messiah, but seen past the prejudice of prudish churches, her experience at fortune-telling and gratifying customers' emotional needs added to the informal theological education she had received with the Wardleys and sharpened further the skills needed to found a new religion. She had the gift to reach inside people and stimulate their hidden hungers, transforming lust and guilt into spiritual experiences with the proper supernatural incantations.

But this was not enough to produce a growing millenarian movement. Only when a wild religious revival swept the farms and towns around Watervliet, and dozens of people were hurled to the religious extremes by uncontrolled social explosions, did any suitable followers show up at the Shakers' doorstep. This was the chief secret of the Shaker success. They had created a community of millenarians, living a radical life that seemed drenched in sanctity when Ann learned to conceal parts of her real nature, within a nation that gave lip service to millenarianism. The religious dynamic in Protestant societies inevitably produces tiny splinter groups and hyper-enthusiastic individuals who try to fulfill the vision that the larger society has sought to pacify within the respectable churches. Only when they were able to garner these disaffected, disconnected people from the margins of Protestantism could the Shakers grow.

Ann Lee, her brother William, and James Whittaker who had come to America with them, led their small group in clearing the Watervliet land for farming and setting up a few simple buildings. From this base they traveled in 1781–1783 all over Massachusetts and Eastern Connecticut, evangelizing, suffering mob violence, and making themselves known to prospective converts by the hundreds. Ann had the gift of tongues, the ability to speak words of revelation in unknown languages. She claimed that she was judging the dead of all nations, as she was ready to judge the living world. She could heal, and she could discern the secrets hidden deep within a person's heart. She exploited many individuals' gnawing desire for escape from sin, and many came to her seeking righteousness.

Asa Pattee, who was a leader among the Shakers for several years, defected and described these wild scenes in a legal affidavit (Marshall 1847:27–28). "I have seen the Mother and the elders drink to great excess; and have myself, in obedience to the gift, drank to intoxication. I was dissatisfied, and told them, 'You make me drink too much.' They said, 'The liquor does not make you drunk; if you have faith, rum will not intoxicate you.' Elder Chauncey said, if I should see one of the elders drink a quart of rum at a time, and fall down and vomit, I should not say rum made him drunk. When they drank so as to vomit badly, they would call it *suffering for the sins of others*. I have seen Mother at Niskeyuna, in the state of New York, in times of her intoxication, come into a room where many were gathered for a meeting, and were, by her orders, stripped naked. I have seen her slap the men, rub her hands on all parts of their bodies. All the time she would be humming, and making an enchanting noise. We scarcely knew what we did. This was the woman whom we considered mediator between God and man.

"Once in a meeting in Petersham, Massachusetts, the Mother came in, leading with her a naked man, whom she committed to another, named Aaron Wood, saying, 'This man must go through the mill.' Aaron was stout; he whirled him round, threw him on the floor, hauled him round by the hair of his head, calling out, 'You bestial devil!' which caused the man to groan bitterly, and he appeared almost dead. After other indecent conduct, Mother told the women to dog him off, who clapped their hands, and cried out, Stu-boy! stu-boy! The man crawled away as well as he could. His own wife looked on and saw the whole ceremony.

"The next evening, some of the inhabitants came to mob the Shakers. The Mother sent Aaron to drive the mob off; but it was too hard for him, and he was wounded. As soon as the Mother heard of it, she ran down stairs, put her fist in the face of the man, saying, 'The churning of milk bringeth forth butter, and the wringing of the nose bringeth forth blood—and I will wring your nose for you.' Her violence drove back the mob.

"A man named Shepard constantly attended on Mother. This man, Elder Whittaker said, was born a eunuch, had no sinful nature and therefore we could not be suspicious. Shepard afterwards left the Shakers and became the father of several children." James Shepard defected, along with two other men who had come from England with Ann Lee, in a power struggle with Whittaker after Ann Lee had died.

Jonathan Symonds testified that Ann "would come to the men very lovingly, and endeavor to dupe them to adultery" and that Whittaker had tried the same trick with his wife, even though the married couple themselves were forbidden even to touch each others' hands (Marshall 1847:36–38). "They would frequently condemn people for their thoughts, for an unreconciled mind, for doubts of the way, or an unwillingness to obey. They had a cold spring, built up like a well, to receive persons in. When standing up the water came up to their waist—females would be stripped, a rope put around them below their arms, then they were placed in this water until they were near perishing. At other times, they would take all their clothes off, and expose them in a shameless manner in a room, where were assembled a number of people of both sexes, and there was no resistance. At times they dragged females and males around by the hair of their heads, and beat them cruelly in all parts of them. This was chastisement to save their souls."

Ann Lee's soul departed this earth on September 8, 1784, just seven weeks after the death of her brother William. Enemies of the Shakers charged that the two were murdered. A fellow named Hardy (Marshall 1847:42–44), who was with the Shakers at the time, told the story: "After Ann Lee and her elders returned from journeying, she had a gift for Whittaker to be next to her in authority; but her brother William was not willing to give up his station in command. Whittaker, Lee, and Ann quarreled continually about it, and she was severe against her brother William. At the time of their last fight, William Lee and some of the brethren had drank rum till it put them to sleep. When they awoke, Lee said, 'Now we'll rejoin in a dance.' Then they stripped naked, and began to dance. Ann came to the door, which she found fastened; she then went to the window, and commanded them to open the door. Lee told her he did not want her to come in—that he and the brethren wanted to praise God by themselves. Ann was enraged; she took a billet of wood, burst open the door, and fell upon William like a tiger.

"He begged her to let him alone, and tried to defend himself; but he was stupefied with drink, and the more he plead, the worse she abused him, uttering the most awful denunciations. The rest looked on—Whittaker would not allow anyone to interfere, saying, 'Who shall steady the ark of God? If any one touches Mother, he will be struck dead.' At last, seeing William was almost dead, he said, 'Come life or come death, I will part them.' He took Ann away; for which she was highly offended, and fell upon Whittaker, who left the house. Lee died immediately.

"Afterwards Ann renewed her quarrel with Whittaker, and they fought till she could not stand, and the blood ran out of her eyes, ears, nose, and mouth. She died, and was laid out and placed in a cellar of stone and line, with a stone bottom, to resemble a sepulcher, as the European Shakers said she would rise again the third day. The weather being warm, the body began to bloat, whereupon they strewed salt around it, and placed pewter platters upon it. On the third day, notwithstanding all these precautions, the body was putrefied."

Shaker tradition tells a very different story. Some wasting illness carried
both William and Ann away, each calm and filled with faith until the end
(Green and Wells 1823). In his last hours, William arose from his deathbed
and danced the Shaker dance once more, much to the surprise of his attendants who did not believe he could still move. Her burdens increased by the
loss of her brother, Ann told her followers, "Brother William is gone, and it
will soon be said of me, that I am gone too." To Job Bishop, she said, "I
shall soon be taken out of this body; but the gospel will never be taken away
from you, if you are faithful. Be not discouraged nor cast down: for God will
not leave his people without a leader. Elder James and Elder Joseph will be
left, and there will be a great increase of the gifts of God to all who are faithful and obedient." Moments before her death, she said, "I see brother
William coming in a glorious chariot to take me home." According to
Shaker historians Calvin Green and Seth Y. Wells, "Elder John Hocknell,
who was greatly gifted in visions, testified that when the breath left her
body, he saw in vision a golden chariot, drawn by four white horses, which
received and wafted her soul out of his sight."

James Whittaker succeeded Ann Lee as leader of the Shakers, tended her
far-flung flock of converts, and died in 1787 just when the first two colonies
of Watervliet and New Lebanon, New York, were gathered as religious communes. Joseph Meacham, an American recruit with experience in Baptist
movements, succeeded Whittaker and recognized Lucy Wright as his partner. From then forward, Shaker leadership would be shared equally between
males and females, thus consolidating the women's liberation begun by Ann
Lee. In 1790, other communities were established in Hancock and Pittsfield,
Massachusetts, and in Enfield, Connecticut. Before Meacham's death in
1796, eight others sprang up in Massachusetts, New Hampshire, and
Maine. A decade later, Lucy Wright launched a new wave of community
building chiefly in Kentucky and Ohio. When Charles Nordhoff visited
them in the early 1870s, the Shakers maintained eighteen societies strewn
across seven states, where celibates obeyed Ann Lee's commandment to "Put
your hands to work, and your hearts to God" (Anonymous 1888:208).

We may never know for sure whether the many affidavits written around
the year 1800 charging Ann Lee and her Shakers with lewd and violent behavior are truthful. But as historical records they seem to have the same
claim for belief as the saccharine Shaker accounts that most historians have
relied upon. Very recently, in a masterful study, Stephen J. Stein has revised
our picture of the Shakers considerably, revealing that their movement contained far more conflict throughout its existence than most earlier historians
were willing to admit. However, Stein does not accept the affidavits cited
here about Ann Lee's own character, perhaps because they were collected in
a very passionate book by Mary Marshall who fought unsuccessfully for

years to remove her children from the Shakers. But much of the content of Marshall's collection of anti-Shaker testimonies is supported by independent evidence, and certainly the Shakers themselves were not impartial witnesses. And I quote the sworn statements against the Shakers here deliberately for a scientific purpose.

Today the mass media spread many horrible stories about new religious groups. Some of these stories are true, some are false, and others are debatable interpretations of factual events. The negative stories about Ann Lee, above, are exactly the kind of thing one reads in the newspapers today about some "cult" founders. But by the middle of the nineteenth century, the Shakers had largely been accepted by Americans. In 1862, two Shaker leaders visited Abraham Lincoln to ask that their men not be conscripted into the Union Army in the Civil War, because their religion forbade them from killing. He agreed, and in 1864 he sent them a nice letter, thanking them for the "very comfortable chair" they had given him (Stein 201–202). Today, we remember the Shakers fondly, for their architecture, their furniture, their cuisine, and even their music (Miller and Fuller 1970; Shea 1971; Pearson and Neal 1974; Schiffer 1979; Reif 1981; Slesin 1981; Newman and Abell 1989). Recent television advertisements for the Oldsmobile Aurora automobile use their melody, "Simple Gifts." The General Motors executives may not have noticed the extreme irony that their capitalist corporation was selling cars by means of a communist tune.

Oneida and the German Communes

The founder of Oneida, John Humphrey Noyes (1870:614), claimed that his utopian experiment was "the only religious Community of American origins." In this he considered the Shakers to be an English import, ignored some American experiments which had expired before he wrote, and employed the term "Community" exclusively for socialist experiments. But, even if Noyes was prone to exaggeration, there is no denying that Oneida was a remarkable phenomenon, and he was a remarkable person.

At the Yale theological seminary in 1832, Noyes came under the influence of the Perfectionist Movement, which held it was possible to achieve a degree of holiness beyond the reaches of sin and attain perfect love with God. Soon after receiving his preacher's license he lost it again because he had begun to claim he already had achieved perfection and rejected the authority of the imperfect church. When he failed to gain recognition at a religious convention in New York, he suffered a bout of what many might call religious insanity. Sociologist Maren Lockwood Carden (1969:6) describes the episode: "Overcome with disappointment, tormented by religious questions, and alone, he sank into despair. For three weeks he wandered about the city, scarcely sleeping or eating. He drank in deliberate rebellion against the abstemious rules of the church. His mind preternaturally active, he struggled with the complexities and implications of Perfectionist thought. He preached Perfectionism to the poor and outcast of the city." An acquaintance spotted him in this desperate condition and alerted his brother, who brought him home to Putney, Vermont.

His religious excitement quieted and stabilized. Soon he was publishing his extreme views and gradually converting his brothers, sisters, and neighbors. Disappointed in love, he concluded that monogamous marriage stood in the way of perfection, and when he married he cautioned his wife that neither of them should enslave the other's heart. An opponent of the Millerites, he held that Christ had returned at the First-Century destruction of Jerusalem and that ever since then it had been possible to achieve true perfection if one took the correct religious path. He built a small but intensely committed group of followers that evolved into a commune. In 1846, he took Mrs. Mary Cragin as his sexual partner, letting her husband George experience his own wife, thus inaugurating the complex marriage system that would make his movement famous and incidentally arousing the ire of his neighbors who eventually chased him out of town for his adultery. In 1848, his group established the Oneida commune in the state of New York, dedicated to Perfectionism and Communalism.

Unlike Oneida, the communes of Amana, Harmony, and Zoar were not born in America but were brought here by immigrants. They had their historical roots in the powerful but diffuse Anabaptist movement of German-speaking Europe, and in comparable sectarian revolts against religious and secular authorities. The best-known Anabaptist groups in the United States are the noncommunal but culturally anachronistic Amish of Pennsylvania (Hostetler 1968). Others are the Mennonites and the Hutterites, of which only the last have communes (Hostetler 1974). Although they vary greatly, these groups tend to be high in tension with the surrounding society, and one indicator of this is the struggle the Amish have had over the years to protect their children from the influences of the public-school system (Keim 1975).

Amana, Harmony, and Zoar were already well-organized, cohesive communities before they arrived in America and settled down in their final locations. Nordhoff (1875:26) says the "Inspirationists" dated from at least as early as 1719, began assembling under the leadership of a carpenter named Christian Metz in 1825, came to the United States in 1842, and finally established their community in Amana, Iowa, in 1855. The "Harmonists" began to congregate in Würtemberg in 1787, crossed the ocean under the leadership of George Rapp in 1805, and finally settled in Economy, Pennsylvania in 1825. The "Separatists" were already a distinct religious community around Würtemberg before they began congregating ten or twelve years before coming to Ohio under the leadership of Joseph Bäumeler to establish Zoar (Nordhoff 1875:100; Dobbs 1947). Although each of the German immigrant colonies had a titular leader, their existence usually predated that person's tenure. They were well-organized communities, bound together by long-standing family, friendship, and work relationships, in which many individuals played influential roles.

The Harmonists may have adopted communism in the new country by consciously imitating the early Christians described in Acts. But the Inspirationists of Amana and the Separatists of Zoar pooled their resources merely to have enough capital to establish religious colonies in the United States. Shortly, however, their communism became so traditional with them that it began to seem sacred. In his *History of American Socialisms*, Noyes (1870) gives each of these groups a couple of pages, and Nordhoff (1875) devoted a chapter to each based on a personal visit. Thus these relatively traditional German religious communities became linked in American communal studies with the radical Shakers and Oneida as examples of communism. Alternatively, they could be considered as variations on the standard German peasant religious colony, of which a few happened to be economically communist but most were not. Thus we consider these groups together here not because they really are five examples of the same species, all fitting the same scientific definition of "utopian communal experiment." But, rather, we discuss them together because they have traditionally been grouped together by scholars, and because in their very diversity they suggest the wide range of communities that can be established in the name of religion.

Family in the Communes

Around 1860, the family of my great-grandmother, Lucy Seaman Bainbridge, developed a close friendship with the Shakers of North Union, Ohio, which later became the ordinary Cleveland suburb of Shaker Heights. Her father, John Seaman, owned a factory that provided shoes and boots for a wide range of people, from the miners up on Lake Superior to the Shakers. "They were among my father's customers, and would drive to town in cumbersome wagons to do their trading. Once, at my father's store, a young Shaker woman was taken ill, and in his big-hearted way, my father sent her to our home where my mother cared for her for several days. This led to an invitation being given us to visit them, and I was allowed to accept. It gave me an understanding of their queer customs and an intimate acquaintance with their scrupulously neat houses, the braided mats, also a good share of the good fare of the community table. The fertile land owned by the Shakers produced marvelous rye, wheat, and barley, while their cows gave richer cream and their gardens bigger strawberries than any other in the vicinity. They would often send my mother gifts of the most delicious butter and berries.

"The Shakers rigidly upheld the laws governing their religion. Their belief did not sanction marriage; the men and the women were supposed to have no interest whatever in each other; they had occupations apart, they did not sit together at meals, the brothers having one long table and the sisters another. Yet, within my recollection, romance somehow crept in between the rules. This same young sister who spent some days at our house was the community school-teacher. The duty of keeping the wood-box full was no doubt hard for her and a young brother offered to help. Then one dark night they ran away and were married, in spite of all the rules and commandments of the Shaker religion" (Bainbridge 1924:20–21).

Although the Shakers prevented members from forming families, and they abolished some aspects of the relations among members of families who joined, they nonetheless also supported other aspects of the family. Members of a family who joined would not be dispersed among several different colonies, but generally kept together. The chief residential unit in a Shaker colony was called the "Family," typically consisting of a couple of dozen people that might include several more-or-less intact biological families. Children typically slept in dormitory rooms, separated by sex, and the same was true for adult brethren and sisters. Affection was supposed to be shared widely with all members of a Shaker Family, not reserved for the few individuals with whom one happened to have a biological tie, and expressed in a restrained manner outside the rather ecstatic religious activities in which they shared bountiful love with God.

Oneida, as we have already seen, experimented with the exchange of spouses, and its family system could be described as a "group marriage" or "complex marriage" of all of the adults collectively married to each other (Muncy 1973; Foster 1981b). Carden (1969:26–35) argues that this was in great measure a reflection of the personality of John Humphrey Noyes. As a student at Yale and before, he "had been haunted by a sense of guilt and sinfulness." His doctrines were largely designed to assuage these painful feelings. "In preaching Perfectionism he had found a permanent means to ease, if not to cure, his own sense of guilt and sinfulness. In convincing others that he was perfect, he helped to convince himself." Throughout his life, however, he would fall into "neurotic fatigue" and "nervous physical disorders" which he once called "spiritual crucifixion" and which usually ended in "eternal spins" of hyperactivity and religious enthusiasm. Despite the commitment he demanded from others, he was never able to commit himself for very long to anything and anyone, and he frequently traveled away from Oneida leaving management of the everyday business of the place to others.

Having once been disappointed in love, he never again risked loving another individual. "He never established close ties with men or women. He insisted that everyone at Oneida should love *all* others, as he did, and transfer attention from one to another in a condition of 'perpetual courtship.' " His tendency to withdraw psychologically and to withhold himself from intimacy with others extended even to the act of sexual intercourse. He developed a technique, called *amative intercourse*, in which the man would control his arousal, avoid climax for a very long time, and then stop before the biological act had been completed (Noyes 1872). This fitted perfectly with the constant trading of sexual partners, because it guarded against unplanned pregnancy. Noyes controlled love affairs, always separating a couple if they became emotionally involved with each other, and often pairing a senior, experienced person (like himself) with a young and inexperienced person. The next logical step for Noyes was a system of controlled human breeding, which he called *spirpiculture*, in which children would be produced only by selected, religiously advanced couples (Noyes 1875). One consequence was that he fathered many more of the "stirp" children than did any other man at Oneida, and he also initiated many of the young women to sexuality, incidentally opening himself to criminal charges of statutory rape.

The children were raised communally, and although they were often cared for by their mothers, they were supposed to avoid becoming especially attached to them. Pierrepont Noyes (1937:66–67), one of John Humphrey Noyes's stirps, wrote that the afternoons spent with his mother, Harriet Worden, "meant a great deal to me." But if he showed the love too deeply, they would both suffer. One time a leader named Kelly disciplined him by forbidding his regular visit to his mother. "I promptly went berserk. Forgetting my Children's House training and my fear of its head, I raged; I howled, I kicked, I lay down on the sinkroom floor and exhausted my infantile vocabulary in vehement protestations and accusations. Whereupon Papa Kelly seized me and shook me and commanded in a voice charged with indignation and authority—just such a voice as I imagined Jesus Christ used when chasing out devils, 'Be still, Pip, be still!' Then, firmly, 'You have evidently got sticky to your mother. You may stay away from her another week.' The turbulence was mine, but the greater tragedy was my mother's."

Each of the German communes had its own distinctive orientation toward the family. Many of the original Harmonists were married, including George Rapp, their leader. But in 1807 a religious revival within the group persuaded them to live as closely as possible to the way they imagined the earliest Christians had done, and so they gave up marital relations. This provoked a small schism, and some members who refused to adopt celibacy left the group.

Again in 1831, a schism was provoked when a man calling himself Count Maximilian de Leon joined with a few followers, and carried off nearly a third of the total membership, some of whom later wound up at yet another German commune, Bethel, that did not require celibacy. A half century after the decision to abandon sexuality, a faithful member wrote, "Convinced of the truth and holiness of our purpose, we voluntarily and unanimously adopted celibacy, altogether from religious motives, in order to withdraw our love entirely from the lusts of the flesh, which, with the help of God and much prayer and spiritual warfare, we have succeeded well in doing now for fifty years" (quoted in Nordhoff 1875:73–74).

Both Amana and Zoar had ordinary families. Young adults entered into conventional marriages and bore their own children. Both groups were critical of marriage, however, and tended to view sexuality as disruptive and somewhat unhealthy. The formal principles of the Zoar Separatists state, "All intercourse of the sexes, except what is necessary to the perpetuation of the species, we hold to be sinful and contrary to the order and command of God. Complete virginity or entire cessation of sexual commerce is more commendable than marriage" (quoted in Nordhoff 1875:104). The Amana Inspirationists had their meals in common groups that were larger than nuclear families, and by pooling their material resources communally both groups minimized the economic importance of the family.

Work in the Communes

One way to get a picture of the lives of people in these communities is to look at the kinds of work they did. A good source of information is the old records of the United States census, the actual manuscripts on which the census takers wrote in longhand. They give occupations for most men but only some of the women, and Table 5.1 shows data for the men at five communities around 1860. Clearly, the communes were not primitive agricultural backwaters, and each of them engaged in a variety of work. They were more like small towns than rural districts, and several performed economic services for nonmember farmers who lived around them. The nineteenth-century census takers followed no standard set of occupational categories, but merely wrote down a word or two describing in ordinary language what a man did. Thus, the categories are rough groupings, but they do communicate the diversity of activities the men performed.

For example, the 534 Shaker agricultural workers of 1850 include 392 farmers, eighty gardeners, nine horticulturists, twenty-three herdsmen, and six shepherds. The twenty-one men in farm-product preparation were eight millers, one baker, six tanners, one currier, two extract preparers, one

Table 5.1: Occupations of Men in Five Communal Movements

Occupation	Amana 1870	Harmony 1850	Zoar 1860	Oneida 1870	Shakers 1850
Agriculture	113	44	16	20	534
Farm-product preparation	20	8	10	0	21
Construction	67	16	10	10	117
Laborers	114	0	1	1	83
Clothing and textiles	120	22	14	12	103
Metal and machines	44	12	12	20	64
Light manufacturing	10	10	1	4	81
Managerial	0	0	2	2	30
Commercial	16	5	4	16	10
Medical	5	0	0	3	12
Teachers	7	1	0	2	7
Publishers	6	0	2	11	2
Clergy	0	0	0	0	8
Other	3	0	8	3	20
Total	525	118	80	104	1,092

preparing herbs, one apothacarist, and one distiller—the last five of these clearly working in the profitable herbal medicine business the Shakers conducted. Obviously, one might want to code some of these under other categories—placing the tanners in clothing and textiles (with sixty shoemakers) or in light manufacture (with two harness makers), for example—but I think the scheme in Table 5.1 is good enough for present purposes. At Amana, 102 of the agricultural workers were farm laborers, so we might guess that many of Amana's numerous laborers were also farmers.

The 117 Shaker men in construction worked in a variety of fields that blend into each other. Forty-two carpenters probably did work that overlapped that of the sixteen joiners, six cabinet makers, and three chair makers. The twenty-two coopers practiced the highly skilled craft of barrel making, and might have been assigned to light manufacture, except that many others working in wood might also have been placed in that category had we possessed more information. Thus, it seemed reasonable to place most woodworkers in this general construction category, along with fourteen men who built with stone or brick. Blacksmiths were the largest subcategory under metal and machines. There were fifteen at Amana and thirty among the Shakers, but also common were mechanics, machinists, wagon makers, wheelwrights, and millwrights.

Occupational differences among the five communal movements reflect business ventures they founded, as well as ideological and organizational variations. Fully eighty-four of Amana's workers in clothing and textiles appear to have been employed in a woolen mill. The Shaker's thirty managerial workers were twenty-seven trustees and three elders, reflecting the formal system of governance of this society, and many other elders were counted under other occupations they also performed. Only the Shakers admitted to having any clergy, and John Humphrey Noyes may have avoided getting this label because he was away from Oneida when the census taker visited in 1870.

Four of the communities engaged in publishing, and one of Oneida's main activities was producing periodicals expressing Noyes's moral, religious, sociological, and socialist ideas. The eleven men in publishing at Oneida were eight printers, an author, a proof reader, and a shorthand reporter. A further eighteen women at Oneida also worked in publishing—a printer, two editors, and fifteen compositors. The Oneida silverware manufacture, still in business today, had not yet been established by the 1870 census, although three men worked in the important Oneida trap manufacture. Twenty women did silk manufacture, fourteen of them in the tedious job of silk spooler.

Records for the early decades of the nineteenth century give no information about the occupations of women. But at the 1880 census, when occupations for 1,123 Shakers were recorded, 659 of them were women. More than half (53.7 percent) of these were said to be keeping house, house employee, house girl, or domestic. Sixty-one Shakers were in various jobs having to do with food preparation, 87 percent of them female. Indeed, seven of the eight men in this group worked on extracts and may have been preparing medicinal products for sale, while no women did so. Clothing production was primarily a female occupation at this time, 85 percent of the 144 in this field being women. Seventeen of the twenty-two men producing clothing were shoemakers, a trade practiced by no women. The sexes were equally balanced among the eighteen doctors and dentists, whereas eighteen of the twenty-two schoolteachers were women.

In 1880, six Shaker occupations incorporating the word "farm" were exclusively male: farmer, farm assistant, farm hand, farm laborer, farm overseer, and farm work. Together these comprised 39.9 percent of the male workers. A further 11.6 percent of the men, but none of the women, were gardeners or held garden-related jobs. Thus, 51.1 percent of the men worked directly in agriculture in 1880, essentially identical to the 48.9 percent in 1850. Forty-nine of the men (10.6 percent), but no women, were laborers. A long list of light manufacturing trades also were exclusively male, comprising 12.7 percent of the male workers: basket maker, blacksmith, brick mason, machinist, mechanic, printer, saddler, tanner, and wood turner.

Much has been made of the supposed sexual equality of the nineteenth-century communes (Foster 1981a; Lauer and Lauer 1983). Early Shaker theologians had been forced to explain to an incredulous world how a woman had been selected as God's agent, and the special honor given Ann Lee was never matched by any of the male leaders who followed her (Green and Wells 1823; Eads 1884). By formal regulation, leadership positions were shared equally between men and women, two elders and two eldresses per colony. The very celibacy of both the Shakers and Harmonists was part of nineteenth-century women's liberation, because it freed women not only from the pains and dangers of continual childbirth, but also from sexual domination by men. Having few children, and raising these communally, Shakerism freed most female members from traditional maternal duties. But as we have just seen, a very traditional sex-based division of labor was maintained. Women's liberation is hard to discern at Amana or Zoar, and the academic debates about the real status of women at Oneida may never cease. Indeed, despite the fact that the fruits of their labors were shared communally, this quick look at the work done by the communists accentuates their continuity with the surrounding American society, not their distinctness from it.

Commitment Mechanisms

In his monumental sociological study of American communes, Oneidafounder John Humphrey Noyes (1870:57) attempted to explain the factors that gave strength to utopian communities: "Judging from all our experience and observation, we should say that the two most essential requisites for the formation of successful Communities, are *religious principle* and *previous acquaintance* of the members." For the next six hundred pages of his great volume, Noyes surveys all the American utopian experiments, finding that the secular socialist ones tended to die swiftly, whereas some of the religious experiments lasted several decades. He says, "It seems then to be a fair induction from the facts before us that earnest religion does in some way modify human depravity so as to make continuous Association possible, and insure to it great material success. Or if it is doubted whether it does essentially change human nature, it certainly improves in some way the *conditions* of human nature in socialistic experiments" (Noyes 1870:655).

From the standpoint of the individual, *religious principle* and *previous acquaintance* may be seen as two mutually reinforcing aspects of *commitment*. Each of them is probably a complex of factors, and much of this book is devoted to unraveling the several strands that make up religious commitment. Acquaintance, in the language of late twentieth-century sociology, is the social bond. If the people who found a commune are already solidly connected to each other by bonds of love and friendship, each individual in their cohesive social group will be held in by social bonds. Defecting from the commune is tantamount to abandoning one's friends and family, a step not lightly taken. The following chapter will stress the importance of social bonds in religious recruitment, and commitment is merely an advanced stage of recruitment.

A century after Noyes wrote, sociology finally returned to his important topic when Rosabeth Kanter (1972) developed a more complete theory of commitment and tested it on the same utopian communities Noyes had written about. The theory concerns six *commitment mechanisms*, specific ways that a group may be organized and defined, binding the individual to it. These mechanisms are not unique to religion or to communes, she says, but are exaggerated versions of processes that may be found in many kinds of group.

Kanter's six points are not steps that logically occur in a particular order, but six parallel processes that can simultaneously or in any combination commit an individual to the group. In a sense it is an eclectic model, because Kanter found essentially all of the steps in widely read sociology and other literature of the period in which she wrote. But it is not an arbitrary assemblage, because the six fit together in a logical structure. There are three pairs, each pair concerning a major dimension of commitment: rewards, social relationships, and personal identity. In each pair, one of the mechanisms asks the person to give something up, while the other gives the person something comparable in return. Table 5.2 lists the six commitment mechanisms, along with some of their subthemes.

Sacrifice requires people to give something up as the price of membership. Many of the most successful nineteenth-century American communes practiced a kind of sacrifice Kanter calls "abstinence"—giving up consumption of alcohol, tobacco, coffee, tea, rich foods, or meat and abstaining from sexual intercourse. They often led lives of "austerity," dwelling in plain buildings with few comforts or luxuries.

Now, we might think that commitment makes people willing to sacrifice. But Kanter means exactly the opposite. She says that sacrifice causes commitment. Because a person has sacrificed, he or she will be committed, to satisfy an innate human need for cognitive consistency. Here Kanter cites the cognitive dissonance theory of Leon Festinger (1957). In music, the word "dissonance" refers to tones that sound harsh when played simultaneously, and cognitive dissonance refers to contradictory beliefs that cause mental distress when a person believes them both. In the early 1960s this was one of the hottest new ideas in social psychology, but other theories explained the same data, and many sociologists doubt that people tend to be very consistent in their thoughts and behavior, unless the environment imposes consistency upon them. Thus the very first of Kanter's six commitment

Table 5.2: Kanter's Commitment Mechanisms

---

1. Sacrifice = Members feel membership is valuable because they had to give something up as the price of membership. Aspects: abstinence, austerity.

2. Investment = Members would find it costly to leave the group because they would lose the value of the labor and resources they contributed to it. Aspects: physical participation, financial investment, irreversibility.

3. Renunciation = Giving up social relationship that would be disruptive to the group reduces the forces that might pull the individual away from it. Aspects: outside world, couples, the family.

4. Communion = An emotionally satisfying bond to the group as a whole, connecting members equally to each other, holds a person within the group. Aspects: homogeneity, communal sharing, communal work, regularized group contact, ritual, a shared persecution experience.

5. Mortification = Stripping away a person's individual identity leaves him or her less able to resist the demands of the group. Aspects: confession and mutual criticism, sanctions, spiritual differentiation, de-individuating mechanisms.

6. Transcendence = The sense that the group is powerfully meaningful in a way that reaches beyond the mundane concerns of daily life. Aspects: institutionalized awe from ideology or from power and authority, mystery, guidance, ideological conversion, tradition.

---

mechanisms is highly controversial, and this unfortunately complicates our introduction of her model.

Festinger first presented his theory of cognitive dissonance, interestingly enough, in a study of a millenarian flying-saucer group that he and several associates studied by means of participant-observation field research (Festinger et al. 1956). Festinger called the leader of the group Mrs. Keech, but her real name was Dorothy Martin and her subsequent religious career was sufficiently successful to earn her an entry in J. Gordon Melton's *Encyclopedia of American Religions* (Melton 1993:728–729). Early in 1954 Mrs. Martin began receiving spiritual messages from the planets Clarion and Cerus, and she was telepathically guided by an advanced spiritual being named Sananda who was the personification of Jesus. One set of messages warned that a cataclysm would destroy much of the United States on December 21, 1954, but Sananda's followers would be saved by spaceships. When nothing happened on the appointed day, Festinger says, the tiny group around Mrs. Martin switched their proselytizing efforts into high gear, paradoxically spreading the message most aggressively right after it had been disproved. The explanation was that there was an uncomfortable mental conflict between believing in Mrs. Martin's prophecies and accepting the fact that neither the prophesied cataclysm nor the flying saucers had come. Believers resolved this cognitive dissonance by preaching their doctrine even more forcefully.

Soon after Festinger had published this study plus some theoretical works (Festinger 1957), and cognitive dissonance was sweeping the world of social psychology, Jane Allen Hardyck and Marcia Braden (1962) tried to replicate Festinger's results. They studied a millenarian religious group that expected a nuclear holocaust to occur and waited for it in an underground shelter. Eventually, individual members began giving up their seemingly endless vigil and coming out. Then the mass of remaining members returned to the world that had survived their prophecy. Festinger would have predicted that a campaign of aggressive proselytizing would follow this disconfirmation of a cherished belief, while members attempted to handle their cognitive dissonance. But nothing of the sort occurred. The group simply fitted back into the community they had left.

In fact, Festinger's own book really does not offer unambiguous evidence that Mrs. Martin's followers went on a preaching rampage after the world failed to end. Although they issued an upbeat proclamation, the news media were badgering them for some response to their failed prophecy, and there is real doubt how they would have behaved if left to their own devices. Indeed, through the entire period of field observation, Festinger's numerous covert researchers also stimulated the group sufficiently so there is no way of knowing what would have happened without them. The beginning of the book reviews some millenarian movements from history, implying that their reactions to disconfirmed prophecy also verified cognitive dissonance theory.

One case Festinger covered extensively, which we have also considered, is Millerism. It is not at all clear that Millerites proselytized more aggressively after the several disconfirmed prophecies. Most went through periods of depression, and many dropped out. If the movement as a whole seemed to get more radical as one prophecy after another was disconfirmed, this may only be the result of differential defection. When Miller's prophecy failed, the more moderate followers disproportionately dropped out, leaving the radicals. This is a process akin to evaporation. When a liquid evaporates, like wood alcohol on your skin, it cools because the hotter molecules evaporate more readily, leaving the cool ones behind (Stark and Bainbridge 1987:256–260). Social evaporation is any process in which differential defection by some kinds of members of a group changes the average character of the membership, even though no individuals may change their characters. But, even so, the Millerites do not seem to have proselytized more aggressively after the Great Disappointment. Rather, the remaining radicals detached themselves somewhat from the larger society and began creating the various Adventist sects, of which the most successful did not really get rolling until several years after Miller's death. Disconfirmation of world-end prophecies among Jehovah's Witnesses, including the most recent one in 1975, always seemed to result in depression and loss of commitment, rather than in increased proselytization.

To be sure, cognitive-consistency theories still have good standing within cognitive psychology, and some laboratory evidence suggests that cognitive dissonance may be a real phenomenon, if one of limited scope. Thus, we do not need to reject the first of Kanter's six commitment mechanisms, but merely mark it in our minds as doubtful. The second commitment mechanism stands on a far more solid scientific basis.

Investment commits members to the community by making them stay to receive the benefits of their hard work and financial contributions. They must participate in it physically, living in the commune rather than having a home of their own. They must invest all their financial resources and even all personal property. A good example is the Love Family Commune in Seattle in the late 1970s. A recruit who owned a house in Hawaii had to donate it, thus adding an Hawaiian branch to this religious group, and one communal garage was filled with the motorcycles and guitars which had been the chief possessions of many other recruits. These investments were irreversible, and when members did defect they could take little if any of their former possessions away.

In contrast to sacrifice, investment is a completely reasonable commitment mechanism. It could be stated simply in terms of rewards and compensators. People will remain in a group so long as they judge that the rewards outweigh the costs. Having invested heavily, a person will stay for the promise of a return on that investment. Promises are compensators. Often, promises are fulfilled and compensators are redeemed by rewards. In the case of a religious commune, some of the material promises may be kept, and the believer can always hope that the supernatural ones will be as well. Other things being equal, a person will not defect from a group unless enticed away by better rewards elsewhere, or if so many of the group's promises have been proven false that the rest of the promises lose their credibility. In any case, *sacrifice* and *investment* are a matched pair of concepts in Kanter's model. *Sacrifice* commits people because they have given up rewards. *Investment* commits people because they expect to gain rewards if they continue with the group.

"Renunciation" and "communion" are the second pair of commitment mechanisms. In renunciation, a person gives up social relationships that might be disruptive to the group. Social bonds with people in the outside world reduce the strength of the individual's attraction to the group, so commitment demands that the person renounce them. But some kinds of relationships within a group can also be disruptive, notably romantic and sexual couples. Kanter (1972:87) notes, "Successful nineteenth-century groups often discouraged couples in one of two extreme and experientially opposite ways—either through free love, including group marriage, in which every member was expected to have intimate sexual relations with all others, or through celibacy, in which no member could have sexual relations with any other." Oneida is the best-known example of the first strategy, and the second strategy was followed by Harmony and the Shakers. Also disruptive is the conventional family, and the greatest sorrow for Mary Marshall (1847) when she was living with the Shakers was they prevented her from being with her own children.

Communion provides a social bond to replace the ones lost in renunciation. This may be easier to achieve if members are homogeneous, such as from the same ethnic group. By sharing property and work equally with each other, by having regularized group contact at meals, by dwelling together, and by the symbolic unification of rituals the individuals are bound together. The experience of shared persecution could also build a sense of group membership. Kanter described communion in terms of psychological relationships to the group as a whole, whereas many sociologists would prefer to analyze communion in terms of the intensive structure of bonds linking individuals with each other. Communion thus means that the social network of the group is densely interconnected, with many interpersonal bonds tying individuals together. *Renunciation* means that few if any social bonds link members to outsiders. Renunciation plus communion implies a closed, cohesive social network that is a social world unto itself.

"Mortification" and "transcendence" are the final pair of commitment mechanisms, focusing on the identity of the person. Identity is a traditional sociological concept that has fallen into disuse in several influential schools of sociology, and has taken on different meanings in other schools. As Kanter employs the word, it refers to the self-image or self-concept of the person, which is presumed to be a powerful determinant of the individual's behavior. This conception of identity is rooted in Symbolic Interactionism, the sociological perspective or subdiscipline that focuses on the ways that human beings construct meanings by exchanging symbols (Denzin 1994). But the concept of identity would not be greatly distorted if translated carefully into the language of rewards and explanations (Stark and Bainbridge 1987:137–139). Mortification reduces a person's sense of individual identity, and transcendence allows the person to participate in the shared identity of the group. Thus, before this dual process, the individual seeks rewards according to explanations that focus on him or her as an individual exchange partner to whom God can give gifts. After the process, the explanations center on the group, trusting that the group will share God-given rewards with all good members.

Kanter derived the concept of *mortification* chiefly from the work of sociologist Erving Goffman (1961). A person entering a "total institution" such as an insane asylum, a military academy, or a monastic order submits to a degrading process in which elements of the person's individual identity are stripped away. The religious practice of confession requires people to reveal themselves psychologically naked to their confessor, and at Oneida members underwent mutual criticism sessions in which a person was forced to accept and respond thankfully to probing critiques by other members. Public denouncement and other sanctions designed to shame a person for deviating from group norms are not merely costs, from the symbolic interactionist point of view, but also diminish the person's sense of self-worth and independent powers of judgment. Kanter argues that spiritual differentiation, having a status system that gave high honor to members who more thoroughly accepted mortification, encouraged this practice. De-individuating mechanisms include abandonment of one's personal name, as is common in Catholic orders and was practiced by the Children of God (Chapter 8) and the Process (Chapter 9), and the wearing of uniforms that limit people's freedom to distinguish themselves by appearance.

For the concept of *transcendence*, Kanter turned explicitly to religion. Charismatic leaders, such as Ann Lee, George Rapp, and John Humphrey Noyes seemed to be able to see through and beyond each individual member of their groups, possessing the divine gift of charisma that allowed them to transcend the mundane boundaries of ordinary existence. Ideology and spiritually powerful leadership could inspire awe in the institution of the community, and uncanny feelings of mystery surrounded the more successful communities. Transcendence is supported by the often very detailed guidance given to members in their daily tasks, by the expectation that all had converted to the ideology of the group, and by the group's traditions.

Members feel that overpowering meaning inheres in a transcendent group. Like "identity," "meaning" is a word of some ambiguity for sociologists. Literally, what does "meaning" mean? In linguistics, meaning may simply refer to a translation function: *Deus* means "God." In the language of rewards and explanations, a meaningful object is something that plays a major role in many explanations concerning how to obtain valued rewards. In other words, something with great meaning is a key term in important general explanations. This definitely takes us to the border of religion, and perhaps carries us deep inside.

Kanter developed and tested her model of commitment mechanisms with data from thirty American utopian communes of the nineteenth century, nine of which she dubbed "successful" because each lasted at least thirty-three years. The five communes discussed at length in this chapter were among those nine. Kanter tabulated how many of the nine successful and twenty-one unsuccessful communes had each of the aspects of each commitment mechanism. The nine successful communes made great use of the commitment mechanisms, and the others generally did not. Thus, Kanter concluded, the model of six mechanisms provides a good theoretical explanation of commitment to utopian communities.

If Noyes were available to comment, he might compliment Kanter on having unraveled the mechanisms by which religion gives strength to the community, but he would stress that religion was the key (cf. Stephan and Stephan 1973; Bainbridge 1985b). Kanter (1972:136) noted in her book that all nine successful communes were religious, but she argued, "this was also true of a large number of the unsuccessful communities. . . . In general, the differences between the successful and unsuccessful communes was much broader than religion alone, so it does not seem that the presence of a religion or of religious origins made the difference between success and failure." However, religion is a very potent variable in her own data. The nine successful religious communes lasted an average of 74.3 years, compared with 7.3 years for the six unsuccessful religious communes. But the fifteen nonreligious communes lasted only 4.7 years on average. Furthermore, we could raise the same questions about renunciation and mortification that we did about sacrifice. Perhaps commitment comes from investment, communion, and transcendence—all of which involve rewards—and then commitment is the cause that makes people accept sacrifice, renunciation, and sacrifice. But whatever the directions of causation, the six factors identified by Kanter are clearly implicated in some way in the process of commitment to extreme religious movements, as exemplified by the successful utopian communities.

Questioning Commitment

Debates on the mechanisms of commitment are far from resolved in sociology. It may actually be possible to explain long-term affiliation with intense religious groups without the concept of commitment. John Finley Scott (1971) argued that people really do not internalize norms, values, and beliefs. Rather, human behavior is shaped by the immediate contingencies of rewards and costs in the environment. If people are rewarded for a certain behavior, they will perform it. But if the rewards cease, they will quickly fall away from that behavior. Thus, Scott would say that commitment does not exist. People will stay with a religious group so long as to do so is rewarding. Soon after the rewards stop flowing, or when the costs come to outweigh the rewards, they will defect.

Some apparent evidence for this radical idea comes from a study of sixty urban communes in the 1970s by Benjamin Zablocki (1980). Many of the commitment mechanisms operate over time. As the months and years pass, the individual's investment of time and effort increases. At least for the first several months, relationships with other members strengthen. Presumably it takes some time to adopt a new identity based on membership in the group. Therefore, we would predict that people who had already been members for a while were less likely to defect than newcomers would be. Old-timers must be committed to some extent, or they would not have hung around so long. Newcomers have not yet had time to become committed. However, contrary to these hypotheses Zablocki (1980:135) found that veteran members were just as likely as neophytes to defect.

Only a few of Zablocki's communes were religious, so this might be evidence that religion is required for commitment. Or, Zablocki's "communes" might not have been cohesive social units at all. Perhaps they were only chaotic temporary living situations for young adults who were not yet ready to commit themselves to anything but took pleasure in pretending to create communal utopias in the aftermath of the 1960s when such a dream was highly honored. But Zablocki's analysis presents a real challenge to commitment theory, because it seems to have been the first attempt to look at the question rigorously.

Data from the five Massachusetts Shaker colonies offer a good test, taken from the state census of 1855 and from the federal censuses of 1850 and 1860 (Bainbridge 1984a). We need to control for two variables known to influence defection possibilities greatly: age and sex. Pairs of Shakers were systematically sampled from the Massachusetts state 1855 census records, matched by year of birth and by gender. One person in each pair was a veteran of at least five years, having been a Shaker at the time of the 1850 United States census. The other member of the pair was a neophyte, not listed in 1850. To some extent, this procedure works against the theory that commitment increases over time, because many of the neophytes would have lived with the Shakers for a year or more, conceivably for nearly five years in some cases. Some people who vanished from the records between 1855 and 1860 would have died, rather than defected. The number of pairs was limited to ninety-seven (194 persons) by the fact that there are few veterans in the age and sex groups that suffer high rates of defection, and few neophytes in low-defection groups. These matched samples had a mean age of 29.6 years, and included forty-one male pairs and fifty-six female pairs.

After five years, according to the 1860 records, 55 percent of the 194 individuals were still Shakers. But among the veterans, the retention rate was 72 percent, compared with only 37 percent for those who had been neophytes in 1855. That is, a veteran was about twice as likely to remain a

Shaker as was a neophyte. This difference is statistically significant and represents strong disconfirmation of the random model of defection suggested by Zablocki. Apparently people do become committed, just as most social scientists always assumed they did. However they accomplished it, the communes of Oneida, Amana, Harmony, Zoar, and the Shakers were able to extract commitment from a significant fraction of their members for many years, before finally losing their grip, or in the case of Harmony and the Shakers, failing to recruit enough new committed members to survive.

Conclusion: Schism from the System

The five communal movements described in this chapter represent the ultimate in schism. They broke away as thoroughly as they could from the rest of humanity and sought to establish their own autonomous societies based in agriculture and simple industry. And yet they were inescapably part of a larger social system. Despite their relative self-sufficiency, all of them traded with the outside world. Okugawa (1983) has shown that there was extensive membership flow among nineteenth-century American communes that linked them into a social system with various subsystems. For example, members of Harmony and at least three Shaker colonies moved to Zoar, whereas some members of Zoar joined Amana. The German communes had gained their membership in the vast migration of people to North America in the nineteenth century, and both the Shakers and Oneida came into being by recruiting Americans. Like every sectarian movement, these separatist movements were really extensions of the surrounding society, although extreme ones.

In varying degrees, the communes attempted to create alternatives to the conventional family system. Amana and Zoar embedded ordinary nuclear families within an all-embracing larger socioeconomic unit. With a remarkable control over sexual intercourse, Oneida expanded the family unit to include all members of the community, thereby violating sexual norms of the surrounding society to an extreme degree. The Harmonists and Shakers suppressed sexuality and childbearing altogether, a choice which coupled with their failure to recruit many new members after 1850 lead to their extinction.

Among the Shakers, the sex ratio shifted remarkably, until there were hardly any men left. In 1840, 58 percent of Shakers were female, but by 1900 this had risen to 72 percent, and to 88 percent in 1936 (Bainbridge 1982:360). This was not simply because the group aged and men died at an earlier age. In fact, by the last quarter of the nineteenth century, the proportion female was as high among children as among adults (Nordhoff 1875: 256). A big part of the problem was the high rate of defection of boys and young men. In 1850, there were 470 girls aged ten to nineteen in all twenty-one colonies, but by 1860 only 39 percent of these individuals were still Shakers. In contrast, only 19 percent of the 436 boys in this age group were retained over the decade (Bainbridge 1984a). At the five Massachusetts colonies, the five-year retention rate from 1850 to 1855 was 47 percent for girls aged nineteen and under, and 32 percent for boys. From 1865 to 1870, the retention rate for girls had dropped slightly to 40 percent, but for boys the rate had plummeted to 14 percent.

The same was not true for Oneida and many of the German communes. We know that men at Oneida and Zoar were not significantly more likely than women to defect (Bainbridge 1992:119–120; Bainbridge and Stark 1996). Harmony died out from failure either to have children or to let the people who moved into the community become members themselves. When the Oneida, Zoar, and Amana communities ended their experiments with communism, they simply transformed themselves into ordinary American towns or neighborhoods (Carden 1969; Dobbs 1947; Barthel 1984). Oneida created a conventional silverware corporation, and the residents of Amana founded the Amana home-appliance company. It was not easy to untangle family relationships at Oneida, and Pierrepont Noyes recalled his childhood sorrow that when group marriage ended his mother had no one to marry (Noyes 1937), but most residents made the transition comfortably. When the communist experiments ended at Harmony and the various Shaker colonies, however, little was left but museum collections, because the members had died of old age without leaving children.

As alternatives to the prevailing economic system, the five communal movements discussed here appear to have been especially successful. Their standards of living compared favorably with those of ordinary Americans (Nordhoff 1875; Stark and Bainbridge 1996). There is some reason to believe that they were especially healthy. For example, a substantial body of evidence demonstrates that by-and-large the Shakers lived significantly longer than did average citizens in the surrounding society (Murray 1993). And the Shaker communities seemed to have been especially capable of recruiting new members when economic conditions in the surrounding society were bad (Murray 1995). In a myriad of small ways, the communes were economically more efficient than the typical ordinary household. For example, all the little children at Oneida could enjoy riding on a fine rocking horse named Shockey, and there was no need to buy one for each. But when the prosperity of the surrounding society increased to a certain level—buoyed by mass-production manufacturing, large-scale agriculture, and world-spanning trade—the communes lost their distinctive economic advantages. As Barthel (1984) explained, when the residents of Amana could borrow a car, drive to town, see a movie, and buy an ice cream cone, the end of the commune was at hand.

And yet, utopian communes are an eternal possibility on the extreme edges of religion in a free society. Many of the religious movements we shall consider in the following chapters are communal or had a communal phase in their history. By definition, a really high-tension religious movement would reject major societal institutions, like the family and the market, replacing them with some kind of radical alternative. And a thorough-going schism takes a cohesive small group not only out of their church but also out of its community.

No mortal society achieves perfection, and for all its successes industrial culture brings within it inevitable frustrations and disappointments. Religion promises to transport the believer to spiritual perfection, and it is perfectly natural for some participants in high-tension movements to believe they could bring heaven down to earth. The Holiness Movement tried to create a perfect believer, and Adventism longed for a perfect world. By seeking both, the Christian utopian communes took these twin American religious movements to their logical extreme.

The Dynamics of Innovation

6

Cultural Diffusion

Logically, we might want to describe religious innovation as a two-step process. First someone invents or discovers new religious culture, then it spreads to other people. But reality is not so simple. Indeed, many new religious beliefs and practices come into being as the result of the often accidental combination of new ideas spreading from different sources and bumping into each other. Traditionally, anthropologists and some sociologists of technology have used the term "diffusion" to name the myriad processes by which culture spreads from person to person, and from group to group (Rogers 1983). In religion, the conscious effort of missionary movements to propagate their faiths is a form of diffusion, as is the migration from one place to another of people holding a particular set of beliefs. This chapter will focus on the recruitment of individuals to new religious movements, which also is a form of cultural diffusion because it gives new religious culture to individuals who are likely to share it with still other individuals. Social scientists have developed a number of rigorous theoretical models of how recruitment works, so pedagogically this is a good place to start. But we will quickly discover a variety of mechanisms by which new religious culture is created, so recruitment is the intellectual door through which we can reach the foyer of diffusion and the parlor of invention.

Religious Movements on the World Wide Web

In the spring of 1995, "netsurfing" was the newest and quickest way to contact a large number of novel religious movements that employed high-tech means to spread their words and images. We wanted to explore this capacity, so, using a personal computer, we logged onto the Internet with a "web browser" software tool such as NCSA Mosaic or Netscape Navigator, and then cruised the nodes of the World Wide Web. The Web has been described as "the universe of network-accessible information, an embodiment of human knowledge" (Hayes 1994). Originally created at CERN, the high-energy physics laboratory in Geneva, Switzerland, the Web is a system that allows the user to jump easily from one computer to another, all around the globe, following a trail of meaningful connections in search of particular information. For example, we gave the software the following arcane address: http://akebono.stanford.edu/yahoo. (Fellow netsurfers: subsequently that address was changed to http://www.yahoo.com.) That got us into a computer at Stanford University with hot links to several computers in other cities and nations that maintain excellent indexes and search engines to find still other computers that have various kinds of information on them.

A search for "religion" quickly turns up scores of computers around the world that have one or another kind of religious culture available for the user to download. Much of the material is quite conventional, for example the King James translation of the Bible, which can be downloaded in a few minutes to the computer's hard disk. Also available are many other translations in a variety of languages, plus the Koran and the *Book of Mormon*. All of these are free of any cost, and they have several uses. For example, a minister preparing a sermon can search the Bible by means of a word processor for any word or phrase. Or someone unfamiliar with the *Book of Mormon* can browse it and perhaps print out a chapter for closer study. Thus, the Web is partly a medium for propagation of faith, and we should remember that all religious organizations are really movements. Each denomination believes the world should be transformed, at least to some degree in certain ways, and most want to share their message with nonbelievers.

Connect with a computer at a community college in upstate New York, and the photograph of a smiling man with a huge mustache and a garland of flowers appears on the screen, over the motto, "I have come not to teach but to awaken." We have found the World Wide Web home page for Meher Baba, Avatar of the Age. Below his portrait is a menu of seven, blue, italicized choices: 1) Who is Meher Baba?; 2) Images of the Avatar; 3) Books, videos, and music; 4) Centers and places of pilgrimage; 5) News and events; 6) Newsletters and journals; 7) Meher Baba groups.

Click your mouse on the first of these and you get a new picture of Meher Baba and another quotation, "I have come to sow the seed of love in your hearts so that in spite of all superficial diversity which your life in illusion must experience and endure, the feeling of Oneness through love is brought about amongst all nations, creeds, sects and castes of the world." One level deeper in the hypertext tree and you learn that the Avatar was born Merwan Sheriar

Irani in Poona, India, in 1894, of Persian parents who gave him a mixed Zoroastrian and Christian education. In 1913, he met a Perfect Master named Hazrat Babajan, a Mohammedan woman who gave him God-Realization, and from 1921 he attracted his own followers. With such a diverse religious training, it is not surprising that his movement seeks to embrace all previous major religious traditions while simultaneously transcending them.

In 1925 Meher Baba made a vow of silence, never again speaking until his death in 1969. Between 1931 and 1958, he visited America six times, teaching that humanity has always been deaf to the precepts of God, so now enlightenment must come without any words, not through saying the truth but by being it. Leaping across the hypertext links reveals pictures of the Avatar, some in color, a brief movie clip, a catalogue of publications, and information about meetings held in Britain, the United States, and India. A hot link takes you instantly to another computer in Norway that offers you kilobytes of Meher Baba literature you can download directly off Internet.

A World Wide Web search for Hare Krishna turns up electronic copies of the magazine *Back to Godhead*, complete with a pastel-colored masthead with the portrait of the guru, A. C. Bhaktivedanta Swami Prabhupada, gesturing a blessing. A brief biography explains that Bhaktivedanta was born in 1896 in Calcutta, India. His spiritual master, Srila Bhaktisiddanta Sarasvati Gosvami, whom he met in 1922, told him to teach Vedic knowledge in English, so he spent years learning the language and translating sacred scriptures into it. Arriving in New York in 1965 almost penniless, Bhaktivedanta was able to establish the International Society for Krishna Consciousness (ISKCON) in the dozen years of life remaining to him. One data file lists the addresses of all the centers around the world, including thirty-nine in the United States plus six farm communities and five restaurants. Other nations with five or more centers are Canada, the United Kingdom, Germany, Italy, Poland, Sweden, Switzerland, Croatia, Russia, Ukraine, Australia, New Zealand, Brazil, Peru, and India. Another data link takes us to a gallery of color paintings of scenes from the life of Krishna. And still another provides information about a campaign to promote vegetarian food, along with descriptions of such delicacies as puris, samosas, parkoras, and subjis, washed down with a glass of lassi. In addition, we can download several sacred texts, theological commentaries, and an application form to become life members of the Bhaktivedanta Book Trust.

Surfing the net further we come to Gainesville, Florida, where a computer sends us the picture of a man resting his head on his chin, saying "Welcome to Eckankar." This is Harold Klemp who continues the movement founded in 1965 by the late Paul Twitchell. The Vairagi ECK Masters trained Twitchell "to become the living ECK Master." Twitchell gathered the scattered high teachings of Light and Sound and began to hold Soul Travel workshops. Klemp became involved in the early days, and ascended to the level of Mahanta or Living ECK Master in 1981. He offers books, audiotapes, and videotapes, plus lecture courses to those fortunate enough to live near his center. To introduce Eckankar, Klemp gives the computer user a brief lesson on singing HU, one of the ancient names of God. "First get comfortable. Close your eyes, and take a few deep breaths. Next, gently put your attention on your inner visual screen, where daydreams and images come to you. With your eyes closed, sing HU (pronounced like the word "hue") as a song of love." In italicized capital letters, the computer informs us that Eckankar holds trademark rights on the words "ECK," "Mahanta," "Soul Travel," and "Vairagi."

On a San Francisco computer server belonging to the Whole Earth 'Lectronic Link, a remnant of the California counterculture of the 1960s, we find the Covenant of the Goddess (cf. Adler 1979). This group introduces itself as "one of the largest and oldest Wiccan religious organizations," explaining that "Wicca or Witchcraft is the most popular expression of the religious movement known as Neo-Paganism. . . . Witchcraft is a life-affirming, earth- and nature-oriented religion which sees all of life as sacred and interconnected, honors the natural world as the embodiment of divinity, immanent as well as transcendent, and experiences the divine as feminine and often as masculine, as well." The Covenant of the Goddess is not a denomination, because its congregations are autonomous and develop somewhat varied beliefs and practices, and it functions more as a communication medium than a source of authority (Griffin 1995). The local groups are covens, usually limited to thirteen members, and their monthly meeting is called "Esbat," usually held at full moon. Eight seasonal festivals or sabbats are distributed throughout the year: Samhain, Yule, Imbolc, Ostara, Beltane, Litha, Lughnasadh, and Mabon. After a few more screens full of definitions and doctrines, the computer disgorges page after page of addresses of Wiccan groups and businesses—such as Cheryl's Herbs, Realm of the Third Eye, The Crystal Portal, Jewels of the Moon, Earth World's Childe, and Woman of Wands. Information on requirements for membership, coven organization, and how to become a Priestess complete the introduction, and the computer then links to the Cambridge, Massachusetts, Community Center and the Horns and Crescent newsletter.

From Cambridge, we can jump back to Stanford, and from there it is a short hop to Hell. This is the name of the on-line guide to Satanism. Certainly there is good reason to doubt that Satanism really exists, because much of the "Satanism scare" that has swept the nation is the nightmare fantasy of police chiefs and individual teenagers who have no actual contact with Satanic groups (Richardson et al. 1991). Yet in Chapter 9 we will encounter a more-or-less Satanic church, and the World Wide Web offers considerable information about the Church of Satan and related groups. Anton Szandor La Vey, who founded the Church of Satan in 1966, glowers from an electronic portrait on the computer screen, a sinister symbol with Satan's face inscribed on a pentagram looming behind his shaven head (La Vey 1969; Alfred 1976).

Hypertext links lead to related organizations: Grotto ODM, The Grotto of the Wolf, Illuminati of Satan, The Infernal Garrison, The Luciferian Light Group, Order of the Evil Eye, Ordo Alogolis Interstellaris, Ordo Sinistra Vivendi, The Temple of Set, and The Worldwide Church of Satanic Liberation. In bombastic language marred by typographical errors, we can glean the outlines of Satanic theology. There are nine sins: stupidity, pretentiousness, solipsism, self-deceit, herd conformity, lack of perspective, forgetfulness of past orthodoxies, counterproductive pride, and lack of aesthetics. A Five Point Program urges: elitist stratification and an end to the myth of human equality, taxation of all churches, no toleration of religious excuses for behavior, development of artificial human companions, and the opportunity for anyone to live within a total environment of his or her choice. The section on Satanism from an army chaplains' manual legitimates its religious status, but the chief holiday is the member's own personal birthday, and one aphorism states, "No God shall come before the self, for we are the masters of our own destiny."

Not every group that we would consider a religion calls itself that, and to find Unarius we look under UFOs (unidentified flying objects or flying saucers). Dr. Ernest L. Norman, who founded Unarius in 1954 with his third wife, Ruth, is said to be a reincarnation of Pharaoh Amenhotep IV and of Jesus (Melton 1993:734). In the early 1940s, Ernest discovered he possessed clairvoyant talents, and after founding Unarius he employed this gift to search the previous incarnations of people who came to him for healing and to discover the prehistory of mankind on Earth and other planets in the galaxy. Together, the Normans wrote 125 books presenting these discoveries, several of which are advertised in the Internet service. Unarius New World Teaching Center offers classes in the Science of Life plus forms of spiritual therapy at its world headquarters in El Cajon, California, with other centers in North Carolina, Canada, and Nigeria. The Normans contacted a number of consciousnesses existing on higher frequency planes of being, notably the departed spirit of the brilliant scientist Nikola Tesla who died in 1943. A pioneer of electricity, Tesla invented the alternating current motor and experimented for many years with means to broadcast high-voltage electric power through the atmosphere. His biographies describe a person unlike any other, who needed to measure every morsel of food before eating it, who was terrified by round objects such as billiard balls and pearls, and who developed theories about the nature of energy that ordinary scientists still cannot comprehend (O'Neill 1944; Cheny 1981). In 1973, Ruth was able to affiliate the

Earth with the Intergalactic Confederation, so by becoming a student of Unarius one begins a journey that leads out into the infinite cosmos.

Coming at Unarius on the Web from a different direction, we discover a set of case histories of people who had suffered terrible psychological problems until past-life therapy cured them: "When Jonathan Hall (not his real name) first attended classes at the Unarius Academy of Science in El Cajon, California, he had been diagnosed by doctors as a schizophrenic. Jonathan seemed able to hold on to his sense of reality only a short period of months; then his behavior became very strange. He spoke in loud outbursts, reciting religious-sounding phrases. He paced and talked, or moved objects around the room, placing them in one position, then returning again in a few moments to move them. To some, his erratic behavior was a little frightening. His own parents had him incarcerated more than once in mental institutions because they knew of no other way to handle his loud and unpredictable outbursts."

A therapist at Unarius regressed Jonathan back into a previous life and made an amazing discovery. Four hundred years before, Jonathan had been tortured to death, and in his present life he periodically suffers reminiscences of that terrible episode. "The religious babble that came pouring forth from his mouth in a torrent of words was like an echo of the old priests and inquisitors enforcing their beliefs into their prisoner's mind." Now that he understands that his strange thoughts are simply real memories of a past life, he need not be so troubled by them and can go about the business of living his present life more effectively. Needless to say, most people outside Unarius do not believe a word of this, and nothing in the standard Judeo-Christian tradition supports the notion of past lives. But such concepts, and small movements based on them like Unarius, are no longer difficult to find in American society.

Although the World Wide Web spreads the novel beliefs of radically new religions like Unarius, it is not at all clear that this new communication medium actually garners a substantial number of recruits. As we shall see in this chapter, generally new religions grow as members develop strong personal relationships with prospective recruits, involve them in face-to-face activities, and thus personally bring them to become members of an intimate social group. Such things as magazine advertisements, radio broadcasts, and now Web home pages are called "disembodied appeals," and research on earlier varieties indicated that they are not an effective means of recruitment (Lofland 1966; Shupe 1976; Stark and Bainbridge 1980; Snow, Zurcher and Ekland-Olson 1980; Rochford 1982).

A possible exception is "televangelism," evangelistic programs on television (Hadden and Swann 1981; Hadden and Shupe 1988). Although many assume this practice is quite new, in fact a religious service was first broadcast by radio in 1919 and by television in 1940. Whereas such programs are fairly popular among people who are already religiously involved, there is some question whether they are capable of converting anyone. With their music, conversation, and action, religious television programs can arouse emotions and make some viewers develop affective bonds to the evangelists despite never meeting them in person. Conceivably, real-time communication via computers with members of a group might draw a person into it, but it is hard to believe that the relatively cool and impersonal magazine like medium of Web pages could accomplish this.

Certainly being on the Web confers prestige on a novel group, giving the impression that even very tiny religious movements have worldwide stature. Central organizations can use the Web to seem intimately involved with small branch organizations located far away. For example, both Sokka Gakkai and the Sri Chinmoy movement send out a daily poem or proverb for members to download and appreciate. And the extensive address lists maintained on the Web by several movements allow an isolated individual to make contact with the nearest outpost of a movement that might interest him or her, after which direct social interaction with members may complete the recruitment. If the future of novel religion is on the Web, then it is beyond our capacity to predict. But we have a considerable amount of information, and well-developed theories, about how people have been recruited to extremely novel religious movements in the past. And this chapter will use such relatively advanced technologies as multiple regression and computer simulation to explore this age-old topic.

Affiliation with Religious Movements

The process by which a person comes to belong to a new religious movement, profess its beliefs and engage in its practices is commonly called *conversion* (Lofland and Stark 1965:962; Snow and Machalek 1983, 1984; Malony and Southard 1992). However, this word implies that the person has been transformed in some essential sense, and this may not often be the case. To be sure, religious movements like to believe that they change people for the better, and every sinner wishes he or she were a saint. Thus, the concept of conversion is really a religious compensator. A person wants desperately to change in some profound way, and joining the new religious movement promises to accomplish this. Compensators are the valuable coinage of religion, but they are poorly suited to be concepts central to scientific analysis. Thus we should be cautious in using the term conversion here. Perhaps conversion in not entirely useless, as a concept, so long as we understand it to mean a profound personal metamorphosis that transforms one into a member of a religious group.

But many people seem to switch denominations or shift from being unchurched to belonging to a religious movement with little or no inner change. They are still the same folk they always used to be, except that now they are affiliated with a particular religious movement. Looked at from the standpoint of the person, this is a process of joining. From the standpoint of a group that actively seeks to make the person join, it is recruitment. The person joins the group, the group recruits the person, and we can call the complete, two-sided process *affiliation* (cf. Long and Hadden 1983).

Perhaps the most influential model of affiliation was developed by John Lofland and Rodney Stark (1965; Lofland 1966; cf. Judah 1974:159–181; Bainbridge 1978:11–13) through research on a group called the Unification Church, which we will examine in Chapter 7. The model consists of seven steps, shown here in Table 6.1, that are said to follow a "value-added" approach (cf. Smelser 1962). This concept from economics notes that each step in a manufacturing process adds value to the raw materials. A number of nations employ value-added taxes, for example taxing raw materials sold from a supplier to a manufacturer, rather than loading all the taxes up at the point of final sale to the customer. The value-added concept can be illustrated by the sequence of steps required to manufacture something. To make a steel car fender, a mining company digs iron ore from a mountain, a steel mill extracts the iron and produces sheets of steel, and the car company stamps one into the shape of a fender, attaches it to the car body, and finally paints it. These steps must be done in this particular sequence; it does no good to paint the mountain first. Similarly, the value-added models of affiliation with religious movements argue that the steps must be taken in roughly the order given.

The first step in the Lofland-Stark model asserts that prospective converts must experience acute tensions. "This tension is best characterized as a felt discrepancy between some imaginary, ideal state of affairs and the circumstances in which they actually saw themselves" (Lofland 1966:7). This tension might be called frustration, and frustration often drives people to acts of desperation (Dollard et al. 1939). The tension must have endured for some time, resisting all attempts to resolve it using ordinary means. Then the person has the motivation to accept a radical solution to the problem.

The second step, religious problem-solving perspective, probably should have been listed first, because people typically would have possessed a religious orientation toward life prior to the onset of the tension. The person was raised in a strong religious tradition, and nothing has happened to strip the person of religious faith. Stark and I have argued that religion arises in the human need to solve difficult problems, to find means for obtaining elusive rewards. Lofland suggested that people differ in their general responses to problems, some approaching them from a religious perspective. That is, some

Table 6.1: The Lofland-Stark Model of Conversion to the Unification Church

For conversion it is necessary that a person:
1. experience enduring, acutely felt tensions;
2. within a religious problem-solving perspective;
3. which lead to defining himself as a religious seeker;
4. encountering the cult at a turning point in his life;
5. wherein an affective bond to adherents is formed (or preexists);
6. where extra-cult attachments are low or neutralized;
7. and where, to become a "deployable agent," exposure to intensive interaction is accomplished.

people employ the following general explanation: when you cannot readily achieve a highly desired reward, you need a religious solution to this problem, and thus you should improve your relationship with God. The first thing such a person would do, when confronted with a seemingly intractable problem, is to go to their conventional church for help. But if the problem persists despite the ministrations of traditional clergy—if the tension endures—the only thing to do is seek a more effective form of religion.

Enduring tension within a religious problem-solving perspective makes one dissatisfied with one's current religious affiliation and thus open to a fresh one. The third step of the Lofland-Stark model says one becomes a religious seeker. This is a conscious sense that one needs a new religion, causing one to go on a quest. Perhaps the person visits various churches or consults with friends who belong to different churches. It is an open question how actively most people in this situation go out seeking a better church, and how many are merely passively open to fresh religious appeals. But as Lofland and Stark state this step in their model, the person redefines himself or herself as a seeker, and thus is fully aware that the enduring tension needs a fresh religious solution.

The fourth step, encountering the movement at a turning point, has several potential meanings. A turning point is a special moment in life when old lines of action have come to an end and some kind of fresh start is indicated. This step in the model may merely sum up the previous three; given enduring tension experienced within a religious problem-solving perspective, the person becomes a seeker. Or there could be a juncture in the general course of the person's life, such as completing school, losing or gaining a job, moving to a new town, or getting a divorce. As we shall see, the three concluding steps of the model concern social relationships, and the turning point could be a temporary weakness in social bonds that leaves the person open to new relationships. Whatever the nature of the turning point, it is essential to notice that this step of the model refers to an accident. By chance, a susceptible person encounters the particular religious movement at the right time. If the person encountered a different movement, he or she would join it instead. If no movement at all happened along while the person was at the turning point, then the person might remain forever in the old affiliation.

In step five, the person acquires affective, emotional bonds with members of the movement. This can be friendship, a romantic attachment, the feeling that a religious leader is like a parent, and so on. The Lofland-Stark model is highly social-psychological, talking about the person's thoughts and feelings. It begins with the emotion of tension, and here it adds the emotion of affection. Religious movements typically provide a range of settings and activities in which newcomers can develop emotional bonds with old-timers, including informal social occasions as well as group rituals and activities to promote the aims of the movement.

Some organizations consciously employ bond building as a recruitment tactic. The Unification Church applied "love bombing" to prospective recruits, showering them with affection and attention. The Process Church of the Final Judgement, discussed in Chapter 9, considered sexuality to be the glue that held members together, so recruiters flirted blatantly with newcomers. During the period when they were calling themselves the Family of Love, the Children of God discussed in Chapter 8 actually offered sexual intercourse to selected prospects, calling this tactic "flirty fishing" and considering it a legitimate religious ministry that offered God's love in the only way that some people could accept it. But more commonly, religious movements offer spiritualized emotional bonds and platonic friendships that seem more exalted and less precarious than those in ordinary life.

Step six suggests that a person is unlikely to join a new religious movement unless his or her attachments to people outside the movement are weak. There are two ways this can happen. First, the person can be low in attachments, having few friendship and family ties. Second, the person can have such ties but they are somehow rendered ineffective in preventing affiliation with the movement. Perhaps the person has moved away from his or her hometown, so all the friends and family are at a geographic distance that reduces their influence. In some cases, recruitment to the movement takes place in a manner that reduces the salience of existing social bonds. Many new religious movements have innocuous front organizations, such as classes or social events, that are not noticeable for their religious deviance, so the religious norms of friends and family may not apply until the person has already developed countervailing bonds with members of the movement. For many people in modern society, social bonds are severely segregated into different sectors of life. We see some friends exclusively at work, others in our residential neighborhood, and still others in clubs that meet only occasionally. We visit with family members only on particular days. This fragmentation of social life allows a person to spend several hours a week in a setting devoted to the religious movement, developing bonds with members, without any sense that the other relationships in his or her life are at all relevant.

Finally, step seven says that intensive interaction with members of the movement is required to make the person a "deployable agent," that is, a committed member who may now be sent out on the movement's business, including recruiting new members. This intensive interaction inculcates the doctrines, trains the person in how to observe the practices of the group, and instills commitment. Or, this intensive interaction can be described in terms of rewards and compensators. The person receives rewards from the members of the group with whom he or she develops strong relationships. These rewards can be social-psychological, such as affection, fun, pleasurable chats, and the music, art, and drama for which many religious traditions are justly famous. Also important can be material rewards, sometimes including base necessities such as food or clothing, or opportunities to find gainful employment. Social status within the group may also be important, including the sense that sheer membership in the group is more honorable than even high status in the surrounding secular society.

Here we reach the territory of compensators and return to the original enduring tensions that motivated the entire Lofland-Stark model. If lack of friendships was the cause of the tension, now the person has friends guaranteed by membership in the group. If low status was the source of the tension, now the person can gain self-esteem from recognition by fellow members and from the compensator that the movement is divinely inspired. Either by eradicating the causes of the original tension, or by compensating the person for whatever difficulties persist, affiliation with the new religious movement satisfies the acutely felt tension. The person continues to have a religious problem-solving perspective, but the problems have either been solved or encapsulated in a package of compensators. No longer low in social attachments, probably past the turning point, perhaps even prevented from encountering other religious movements, the person is now a committed member.

The Lofland-Stark model has been extremely influential in the sociology of religion, but researchers have not followed it slavishly. When James A. Beckford set out to develop a model of affiliation with the Watch Tower Movement of Jehovah's Witnesses, he had the Lofland-Stark model in mind but was chiefly guided by the data he collected on Witnesses in England. Table 6.2 outlines his five stages in the conversion process, each with several substages or examples, beginning with predisposing social conditions. Importantly, Beckford said that a person had to have been raised a Christian and still be a practicing Christian to join the Witnesses, and a profound emotional experience of conversion was not involved. Recruits tended to have marginal occupations, not because relative deprivation was a key part of Beckford's model, but because this meant they were not closely tied to

Table 6.2: The Beckford Model of Conversion to Jehovah's Witnesses

---

Stage 1: Predisposing Social Conditions
   a) Christian upbringing; church participation
   b) Marginal occupation
   c) Lack of intermediary associations and communal ties
   d) Young family of procreation
   e) Other family member in the Watch Tower movement
Stage 2: States of Suggestibility
   a) Perceived discrepancy between values and actuality
   b) Vestigial dogmatism
Stage 3: Critical Events
   a) Door-step sermon
   b) Incidental witnessing
   c) Active seeking
Stage 4: Affiliation
   a) Attendance at meetings and assemblies
   b) Friendship ties in congregation
   c) Participation in field-service
   d) Severance of "outside" social contacts
Stage 5: Retention
   a) Acquisition of Watch Tower *Weltanschauung*
   b) Continuing service work
   c) Extensive network of family and friendship ties in congregation
   d) Posts of responsibility in congregation

---

coworkers and had not invested all their hopes for their future in a job. Most recruits had young children ("family of procreation") and wanted to raise them religiously as they themselves had been raised. Often, members of their extended family were already Witnesses.

States of suggestibility were states of mind that prepared the recruits to accept the Watch Tower message. Future members had been raised to believe that the world was meaningfully based on a simple set of moral principles and that adherence to traditional norms was a virtue. But the modern society surrounding them seemed chaotic and had apparently rejected the principles they held dear. Their expectation that a single dogma could explain everything made them open to the dogmatic perspective offered by Watch Tower. Critical events consisted of encountering the movement, either because a missionary knocked on their door, because they met one by accident out in the world, or because the prospective member actually went in search of a religious movement to join. Stage four, affiliation, encompasses the last three steps of the Lofland-Stark model, building bonds with members through intensive interaction and severing bonds to outsiders. In the final stage, retention, the person fully accepts the *Weltanschauung* of the Witnesses—*Weltanschauung* is German for worldview—and becomes embedded in the Witness system of roles and social relationships.

Since Lofland and Stark wrote, more than thirty years ago, many sociologists of religion have developed variants of their model or have adopted individual concepts from it to explain recruitment to the particular religious movement they were studying (e.g. Richardson et al. 1979). Beckford's model could be described as *inductive*, developed empirically by looking at the process of affiliation as it takes place in a particular movement. The original Lofland-Stark model was developed during research on one group, but it is more deductive, trying to develop a logically structured set of theoretical principles that might be applied to any group. Such a general theory provides an excellent intellectual bridge from the specialized field of the sociology of religion to the general discipline of social psychology, and the broad concept of group solidarity.

Affiliation and Solidarity

A church congregation or the local branch of a religious movement is a social group, and much of the sociology of small groups is relevant to understanding its structure and dynamics. To my mind, the best framework for thinking about groups is the one proposed by Stephen Wilson (1978) that distinguishes six dimensions of group solidarity: 1) interaction; 2) norms; 3) status structure; 4) goals; 5) cohesiveness; and 6) awareness of membership. To the extent that a group functions as a unit, it has solidarity. The behavior of members is under considerable social control. Members are committed to the group. Forces outside the group will be relatively ineffective in shaping the thoughts, feelings, and behavior of members. Affiliation incorporates the new member within this solidarity. The opposite of solidarity is anomie.

The first dimension of solidarity, in Wilson's scheme, is interaction. Members of a high-solidarity group interact frequently with each other. Sociologists of different persuasions might emphasize different aspects of interaction. So-called Symbolic Interactionists focus on the symbolic messages that people express to each other, and the way that individual identities arise out of this give and take of concepts (Denzin 1994). Exchange theorists would focus on the rewards that people exchange (Homans 1950, 1974; Blau 1964). Stark and Bainbridge (1987) combine these two perspectives in their theory of religion. People seek rewards from each other, and they develop exchange relationships in which they repeatedly give and receive rewards with the same individuals. Among the most valuable rewards are explanations, which are information about how to obtain a variety of valuable other rewards, usually transmitted through words and other symbols. The defining feature of religious groups, in this theory, is that members constantly exchange supernaturally based compensators, symbolically encoded in sacred music, art, scriptures, sermons, and prayers. But theories aside, every successful church and religious movement is a hive of social interaction through innumerable group activities.

The second dimension of solidarity is *norms*. These are the rules defining proper behavior and the expectations members have for each other. In Chapter 10 and my recent book with Stark (1996), the reader will find extensive discussions of the ways that religious movements may reinforce or affect the norms of behavior in the larger society, a chief part of the *consequences* dimensions of religiousness identified by Glock and Stark. But the distinctive norms of a religious movement concern religious beliefs and practices themselves. It is true that the twentieth chapter of Exodus lists norms about secular life, telling us not to steal, kill, commit adultery, or bear false witness. But the Ten Commandments stress sacred norms: "Thou shalt have no other gods before me. . . . Thou shalt not take the name of the Lord thy God in vain. . . . Remember the sabbath day, to keep it holy." Furthermore, many other chapters of Exodus abound in detailed instructions about the proper way to prepare sacred implements and a place for worship. Indeed, it is hard to think of a sphere of life that is so completely drenched in norms as religion. Denominations differ, of course, in how much emphasis they place upon the precise details of liturgical ritual. But each of them extols its own set of norms for behavior in group gatherings and even for belief in the privacy of one's own mind.

Third, every solidary group possess a *status structure*. Religions generally distinguish clergy from laity. Even when some of the laity perform special sacred roles, generally they are lay preachers or others specifically identified as having special status among the laity. The very names of several popular denominations suggest their forms of governance and thus their status structures: Episcopal, Presbyterian, Congregationalist. The name of the Episcopal church refers to the fact that it is governed by bishops. A presbytery is a ruling body consisting of ministers and representative elders. In principle, a church organized along congregational lines places its final human authority in the assembly of the local congregations. The dynamics of religious movements often involve conflicts over status structure, as when schisms erupt to challenge the leadership of a denomination, or when a small group of people tries to create the new structure of statuses required to manage the far-flung branches of a rapidly growing, brand-new, novel religion.

The fourth feature of strong groups is a set of shared *goals*. Churches are infamous for having multiple goals, from finding marriage partners for local young adults to collecting donations for famine relief half way around the world. But the defining goals of a religion concern the sacred: worshipping the Lord and bringing His good news to the world. Social movements can be defined as more or less organized attempts by a number of people to cause or block changes in some significant aspect of society. Thus, movements of all kinds are especially goal-oriented. By definition, the goals of movements are always collective, requiring the concerted action of many people to achieve something that will affect all of them and perhaps many people outside the movement as well. The central goal of many movements discussed in this book is simply to transform nonmembers into members, often defined as involving sufficient change in the individual that it deserves to be called conversion. But commonly, religious movements also want to transform religion, sometimes operating within an existing denomination in an attempt to purify or reform beliefs and practices, but occasionally creating a new denomination. And some religious movements try to shape the secular world, such as the Pro-Life Movement mentioned in Chapter 10 that seeks to limit abortion. In the context of the present chapter, recruitment of new members is a widely shared goal of religious movements.

Fifth, *cohesiveness* holds the members of a group together, and it is chiefly defined as the network of interpersonal relations among members. The power of relationships to hold an individual is clearly expressed in the synonyms sociologists commonly employ: social bonds, social ties, and attachments. The Lofland-Stark model of affiliation stresses the development of strong social relationships with members, and a reduction of the strength of relationships to nonmembers, thus giving the individual an unopposed strong bond with the group. But this dynamic is not limited to the field of religion, and a highly fruitful line of research by Miller McPherson (McPherson et al. 1992) demonstrates its crucial importance for voluntary organizations of all kinds. In modern, pluralistic societies, the cohesiveness of many religious organizations is compromised by the fact that members may have little contact with each other outside of a few hours set aside for religious services and church social activities. Indeed, a person may belong to several nonoverlapping groups unconnected to church, each with a measure of solidarity, such as a work team, a sports club, and a residential neighborhood. A distinctive feature of many high-tension religious bodies is that members have relatively few social relationships with people outside the congregation. This means that ties with fellow members are both strong and numerous. In addition, within a high-solidarity congregation, one's friends tend to be friends of each other, and the highly interconnected, dense social network gives the group immense strength.

And finally, *awareness of membership* is the sixth dimension of solidarity. The better part of a century ago, social theorist Charles Cooley (1909) stressed the importance of a "we" feeling, the sense of group identity. A member of a high-solidarity group refers to himself or herself as a member, takes the gains or losses of the group personally, and derives some measure of esteem from identifying with the group. It is not surprising that essentially all religious denominations have a name for the group that is practically identical with the term for a member. A member of the Protestant Episcopal Church is an Episcopalian, and we commonly refer to fellow citizens as Catholics, Methodists, or Baptists. These names have meanings. By calling itself "Catholic" a denomination asserts that it is the church universal, directly descended from the original Christian church. "Methodist" and "Baptist" stress the importance of particular religious practices. Members of the Unification Church led by Reverend Sun Myung Moon do not like being called "Moonies," and some have launched a campaign to be called "Unificationists," implying that they are the central movement for the unification of world Christianity. One problem seems to be that the suffix "-ies" has connotations of disrespect (fans of *Star Trek* prefer to be called Trekkers rather than Trekkies). Certainly Lutherans do not appear to mind being named after an individual religious leader. Thus the words used to express membership are both rallying symbols that arouse positive feelings associated with group solidarity, and statements to the outside world about how the group wishes to be regarded.

These six dimensions of group solidarity are not really a theory, as such. Rather they are a list of broad areas in which theories can be constructed and an agenda for research. In a way, Wilson's dimensions are yet another scheme for classifying the ways in which a person can be religious, cross-cutting and supplementing those we introduced in Chapter 1. A researcher could examine each member of a religious group and ask: "Where does he or she stand in the status structure? To what extent does he or she work for the group goals?" Or one could classify the group itself in terms of where it stood on each of these six dimensions. Thus the list of six dimensions is partly a set of questions that could be asked about each member and each movement, that can be used to measure the extent that a person gains, possesses, or loses membership. But it is also a catalog of important features of high-solidarity groups of all kinds, based on a vast range of social-scientific research, that can be applied profitably in the sociology of religious movements.

Tension and Relative Deprivation

In earlier chapters we saw that many high-tension religious movements tend to recruit people from disadvantaged groups, but the evidence so far has chiefly concerned movements that are solidly within the standard religious tradition, such as the Holiness churches. Does the same principle apply to culturally novel religious movements? There is a good deal of evidence and logic that it may not (Stark and Bainbridge 1985, 1987). We already saw that there were modest ambiguities in the social class basis of Seventh-day

Adventists and Jehovah's Witnesses. Yes, they recruit people disproportionately from disadvantaged social class backgrounds, and yes, their culture is chiefly a mere intensification of ordinary Protestant beliefs and practices. But the founders and leadership were surprisingly intellectual, valuing education (at least within their own religious context) and spreading the word largely through writing. If Charles Taze Russell had not possessed a personal fortune, he could not have launched the Watch Tower Movement that developed into the Witnesses. And both of these groups added considerable culture to the old Protestant traditions.

People whose suffering comes simply from relative economic deprivation need the rewards that prosperous people in their society already possess. But they are forced to accept specific compensators instead. Those compensators will be most effective when they directly challenge the status of the upper classes, which they can most effectively do if they are deeply rooted in the same religious tradition that the prosperous people themselves accept. "Yes," such compensators say to rich folk, "you people have money, but your own religion tells you that this is not important. Far more important is being reborn in the Holy Spirit. Your own Bible tells you that it is difficult for a rich man to enter heaven." Thus, high-tension religious movements that are entirely within the standard tradition may offer the most effective specific compensators for economic deprivation.

The fact that Seventh-day Adventist and Jehovah's Witnesses do not perfectly fit this principle may tie in with their currently greater recruiting success outside the United States than inside. Beyond the borders of the society that spawned them, they may function primarily as effective Protestant missionary movements, and the exact details of doctrine may not matter for recruits who lack American Protestant backgrounds. Indeed, this advantage may apply to some extent to all American missionary movements that proselytize aggressively overseas. Outside their country of origin, the degree of their tension may be ambiguous. A Pentecostal group in Latin America, for example, may be at odds with the local Catholic Church, and thus in extremely high tension locally with the established church of the county. But it can project itself confidently as an expression of American Protestantism, the majority religious tradition of a major nation and thus not high in tension from world standards.

The people attracted to high-tension groups that are within the standard religious tradition are not only poor, but also tend to have received less formal education than the people who belong to low-tension denominations. In Chapter 2, low income and low education were simply alternative indicators of low social class. But with respect to novel religious movements, income and education may have different meanings. Experimentation with culturally novel religious movements may be but one aspect of experimentation with novel cultural and intellectual movements, and one might expect col-

165

lege-educated people to do more of this. Throughout the next several chapters we shall be alert to the cultural backgrounds and level of education of people who form and join novel religious movements. And we shall see several instances in which people from middle-class or even upper-class backgrounds are disproportionately drawn to distinctively new religions.

To be sure, there are exceptions, but they seem chiefly to involve members of ethnic groups that experience severe discrimination (Cantril 1941). Within each disadvantaged group there exist intelligent, highly motivated people who would have already attained high status in the larger society if they had been permitted to seek it. In the larger society, a small fraction of the elite are attracted to religious movements with highly novel beliefs and practices. So, too, a few members of disadvantaged groups have the same tendency to join or even create really novel religions. When they do so, however, crude sociological data will categorize the group as a sect of the disadvantaged, unable to detect the special qualities of the individual members who may be the elite of a disadvantaged group. In addition, when the society suppresses an ethnic or racial group, members of that group will look creatively in all directions for a way of overcoming this discrimination, and sometimes they will found a religious movement that is oriented toward eradicating the society's status differentials in a highly creative way.

In other words, the Lofland-Stark model is on uncertain ground when it says that recruits to novel religious movements have experienced enduring, acutely felt tension. If persons attracted to novel religions come from relatively advantaged backgrounds, then it is had to say that relative deprivation provides the motivation for their conversion. To be sure, it remains possible that especially dissatisfied members of the upper social class, people who suffer personal problems rather than class problems, may be attracted to such movements. This is an extremely contentious area for research, because opponents of such movements like to believe that only very unhappy (or stupid, or crazy) people would be so foolish as to join them. And it is not easy to carry out a definitive study of what brings people to join. All the great early studies, like the one done by Lofland and Stark themselves, were exploratory in nature, using relatively undemanding techniques of qualitative observational research to sketch out some theoretical ideas rather than to provide a rigorous test of a theoretical model.

In the absence of a series of definitive studies of the recruitment dynamics of particular religious movements, one of the feasible approaches is to examine the human ecology of participation in novel religious movements. One of the few such studies with at least moderate methodological sophistication was published in the *American Sociological Review* (Bainbridge, 1989a, cf. 1989b). This statistical study worked with data on four phenomena related to contemporary novel religious movements: *Fate* magazine, the *Spiritual*

Community Guide (Singh 1974), Transcendental Meditation, and Scientology. (We will say more about the first three of these in Chapter 13, and about all four in Chapter 14.) The data were all tabulated as rates for the seventy-five largest metropolitan areas outside New England where data on church membership do not geographically match the census areas. Since its beginning in 1948, *Fate* magazine has been a central publication of the American occult, advertising some new religious movements and publicizing others; the data were the number of residents in each metropolitan area who published letters in the magazine. The *Spiritual Community Guide* listed many New Age businesses, imported Asian religious centers, and spiritual development services in each city. Transcendental Meditation (see Chapter 7) and Scientology are especially successful new religious movements. The Transcendental Meditation Movement provided the number of people initiated into this practice in each urban area. And the public relations office of Scientology of Boston provided the number of members who had achieved the spiritual advanced state called *clear* for each three-digit postal zip code area. The raw data for these four variables were translated into rates per 100,000 population.

Two variables measuring different aspects of social class were taken from government census reports: the proportion of the population over age twenty-five who completed four or more years of college, and the per capita income. Both of these correlated strongly with each of the four new-religion rates. Relative deprivation theory would assert there should be powerful negative correlations, but in fact all the correlations are strongly positive. That is, each of these four new-religion phenomena is more fully developed in metropolitan areas where people are above average in education and income, rather than below average. The statistical technique called multiple regression was then used to look at the effect of several variables simultaneously. It did change the picture to introduce three control variables: the overall rate of church membership in the city, the rate of residential migration measured by the percent who had been living in a different house five years before, and the divorce rate. All of the income correlations went to zero, meaning that wealth and poverty, in themselves, do not affect recruitment to novel religious movements. College attendance went to zero for *Fate* magazine, but remained positive for the other three measures and was still statistically significant for the *Spiritual Community Guide* and Transcendental Meditation.

Although far from conclusive, these findings suggest we should not expect relative deprivation to explain affiliation with novel religious movements. Instead, it might be more profitable to emphasize other aspects of the models we have considered in this chapter. Membership in a new religion means developing social bonds that create solidarity, and the sociologist of religion might make more progress looking at the dynamic of social relationships rather than of relative deprivation (Stark and Bainbridge 1980).

The Concentration of Forces

Religious conversion is only partly a matter of faith; it is also a process of affiliation with a social group, and the history of a sect or other religious movements is greatly controlled by the rates of conversion and defection of individual members. Traditional theories of the growth of social movements emphasized deprivations, social strain, and similar special motivations (Cantril 1941; Smelser 1962; Toch 1965). Around twenty years ago, the resource mobilization approach added another dimension, the capacity of the movement to exploit resources in its environment (McCarthy and Zald 1973; Oberschall 1973; Bainbridge 1976; Tilly 1978; Bromley and Shupe 1980; Zald and McCarthy 1987). More recently, Finke and Stark (1988, 1989) proposed what amounted to a combination of these two approaches, arguing that denominations and sects compete in a kind of religious marketplace. Resources, including new converts, will flow to those religious movements that are most effective in serving the needs people have for socioemotional solutions to problems of both relative and absolute deprivation.

A very different approach is offered by theories of recruitment that emphasize the structure of social relations around a group. Quite apart from the needs of converts and the strategies of evangelists, the fate of a social movement is conditioned by the shape of the social network in which it is embedded. As we have just seen, Lofland and Stark (1965; Lofland 1966) attempted to combine network and deprivation theories in explaining recruitment to deviant religious groups. Stark and Bainbridge (1980, 1985, 1987) have suggested that processes of social bonding alone may be responsible for success or failure of religious movements. Research on voluntary organizations in general, including nonreligious as well as religious groups, confirms the importance of social bonds both in holding an individual in a group and drawing him or her out, perhaps to join a competing group (McPherson et al. 1992). A full analysis of recruitment should probably include the deprivations of recruits plus the resources and strategies employed by recruiters. But it is worth considering how much could be explained by the structure of social relations alone, setting aside other factors for the time being so that the possible effects of social networks can be considered clearly.

A good tool for doing this is computer simulation. Computer programs have been used to explore the logic of social interaction in several articles in major sociological journals (Macy 1990, 1991a, 1991b; Carley 1991), and there is no reason why this could not be done in the sociology of religion. Typically these studies evaluate the logical consequences of one or two theoretical assumptions, writing the key concepts into computer software and then running it to see if it produces the predicted outcomes.

Theory-based simulations are highly simplified models of reality, but this is also true of most laboratory experiments in social psychology. Like formal experiments, computer simulations can be powerful tools for evaluating and extending theories. Because sociologists of religion have not previously employed this technique, it would be premature to attempt to simulate complex theories, such as the entire seven-step, value-added model of conversion proposed by Lofland and Stark. In principle, every logically consistent formal theory can be written as a computer simulation, but it is wise to begin with very simple theories. Later, when many sociologists of religion are familiar with the approach, and a appropriate set of techniques for modeling religious behavior has been developed, simulations of more complex theories may be valuable.

A minimalist theory of recruitment through social networks will need to consider two factors: 1) the *traits* of individuals, in particular their religious identities, and 2) *bonds* connecting pairs of individuals. Such a theory was proposed by Bainbridge (1987), based on the root concepts of two traditional sociological theories: *differential association theory* (Sutherland and Cressey 1970; cf. Tarde 1903) and *balance theory* (Heider 1958). Combined, these theories can explain the consolidation of subcultures and their spread through a social network. These social processes are essential parts of any theory of the growth of religious movements.

Differential association theory is a classic, formal sociological statement of an idea familiar to everyone: people are influenced by their friends. In religious terms, people will tend to convert to a new religion if the majority of their friends already belong. The Lofland-Stark model of conversion includes elements of differential association theory. A potential convert develops affective bonds with current members of the group. His or her attachments to nonmembers are weak or somehow neutralized. Through intensive interaction the members of the group recruit the new convert and transform him into an effective agent for further conversion of other nonmembers.

Balance theory is a variant of cognitive consistency theory, asserting that people tend to adjust their attitudes and personal relationships to avoid mental contradictions. For example, if Adam and Eve are friends, and both are Methodists, then Adam and Eve experience no contradiction concerning religion. But if Adam joins a Holiness group, then there is an imbalance. It can be resolved by one of the two converting to the other's religion, which would be little different from differential association theory. But balance can also be achieved if Adam and Eve stop being friends. Conversely, two neighbors, in frequent contact with each other, may become friends if they already share the same religious faith.

From such simple beginnings, very complex theoretical models and computer simulations can be developed, so for sake of clarity we will focus here on a single line of analysis: the effect of concentrated social relationships on the growth or decline of a minority religious movement. We will set aside issues such as the deprivations that may motivate individuals to become religious seekers, the psychological power of charismatic leaders, and the appeals of various kinds of doctrine. In so doing, we examine the unique properties of social-network theories, the better to determine the roles they might play as part of more comprehensive explanations of religious behavior. The importance of bond density for collective action has recently been demonstrated analytically by Gould (1993; cf. Granovetter 1973), and by adding trait density we are able to investigate factors that shape the histories of small religious movements.

In a pluralistic society, it may be a great advantage if the members of a religious movement are socially concentrated. For one thing, the fact that they frequently interact with each other will sustain their faith in a world of unbelievers. In addition, members on the margin of such a social bloc may be sufficiently tied to fellow members that they will not be converted away, yet they may be able to build multiple bonds with a neighboring nonmember, and thus convert that person to membership. With balance theory operating, of course, sect members will quickly lose their ties to nonmembers, after which the sect will be unable to grow. This limitation can be overcome by *outreach*, the intentional building of social bonds to nonmembers in hopes that these bonds will convert them to membership.

A comparable phenomenon in military science, *concentration of forces*, has been subjected to mathematical analysis (Lanchester 1956). A numerically inferior army or fleet can triumph, if it maneuvers itself into local supremacy. The same can be true for religious movements. A concentrated minority can function locally as a majority, expanding in membership even until it outgrows objective minority status. Religious movements have often been compared with military campaigns, as we are reminded by familiar phrases like "Salvation Army" and "Onward, Christian Soldiers!"

To my knowledge, the earliest application to religion of the military idea of concentration of forces was made by my great-grandfather in his militaristically named study of Baptist missions, *Along the Lines at the Front*. In describing the need for more American missionaries in Burma, he drew an analogy to the tremendous battles of the Civil War which he had personally witnessed while serving in the Christian Commission: "Without thoroughly understanding the situation, it may seem strange that ninety-four missionaries—nearly all of them confined in their work to the lower half of the country—should not be deemed an adequate supply. Already it would appear that Burmah is three times as strongly occupied in proportion as India. But in every great warfare there are points of concentration. More soldiers were massed against Richmond than against Port Hudson or Atlanta" (Bainbridge 1882:164–165). He focused on the strategic importance of key targets for evangelization, rather than upon the role of concentration in social networks, but we can add that intriguing factor through a simple computer model.

A Computer Simulation

The computer simulation that explores the social network aspects of concentration asks us to imagine a community of 1,024 people, arranged for convenience in a square where each person has eight near neighbors with whom he or she might have a close friendship. There are four large religious denominations—call them "Alpha," "Beta," "Gamma," and "Delta"—each with 240 members. The remaining sixty-four people have just been converted to a new religious movement we can call "Epsilon." Denomination members are distributed at random across social space, but the members of the Epsilon movement are either distributed randomly or concentrated into a square bloc. This is a classic experimental design, in which the manipulated variable is concentration. We will do three experiments, each run under both concentrated and unconcentrated conditions.

In the first experiment, we let each person have a friendship bond with each of his or her eight near neighbors, and the number of reciprocal social bonds linking the 1,024 people is thus 4,096. We do not let people break off old friendships or form new ones. Thus, balance theory is not in effect, and we can examine the effect of concentration when differential association theory alone operates to change people's religious affiliations. An individual will change affiliation if the majority of his or her associates share a different affiliation. The simulation is run like a game, with a series of rounds on which the 1,024 people get a turn to play. When it is a particular individual's turn, the computer surveys the characteristics of his or her associates—those persons having social bonds with him or her—and determines if there is a plurality trait, held by more associates than any other trait. If so, the individual's characteristic is changed to that trait. For example, if the person is a Delta, but his or her associates tend to be Alphas, he will become an Alpha.

Each simulation run goes for 128 rounds, and sixteen runs were done under each of two experimental conditions: "no-bloc" in which the sect members were dispersed at random across the social network, and "bloc" in which they were concentrated. This adds up to 4,194,304 turns in the first experiment, for a total of 12,582,912 turns in all three experiments we shall describe. Thus it is impossible to play a theory game like this by hand, and a computer is essential. The program was written from scratch in Turbo Pascal, and run on a small Macintosh personal computer. Table 6.3 shows the average size of the religious movement over the series of rounds.

In the no-bloc condition of Experiment 1, the sect collapsed quickly, losing members to the larger denominations, the average size dropping in twelve rounds from sixty-four members to 3.1. What is happening? When members of a religious movement are dispersed throughout the social network, few of them will have other movement members for friends, so they

Table 6.3: Effect of Social Concentration in a Computer Simulation

| | Members of a Religious Movement over 128 Simulation Rounds | | | | | |
| | Experiment 1 | | Experiment 2 | | Experiment 3 | |
Rounds	No-bloc	Bloc	No-bloc	Bloc	No-Bloc	Bloc
0	64.0	64.0	64.0	64.0	64.0	64.0
4	6.6	81.9	41.2	116.3	20.9	88.8
8	3.4	83.9	59.5	160.6	16.4	105.1
12	3.1	83.9	76.1	208.0	17.5	120.9
16	3.1	83.9	91.8	259.4	18.5	133.3
20	3.1	83.9	106.1	310.2	20.8	146.7
24	3.1	83.9	117.4	364.2	21.9	158.9
28	3.1	83.9	129.3	421.8	24.8	172.3
32	3.1	83.9	139.3	476.3	27.8	181.9
48	3.1	83.9	171.0	705.3	32.7	228.4
64	3.1	83.9	204.3	844.0	37.0	266.1
80	3.1	83.9	232.2	913.3	42.6	209.3
96	3.1	83.9	265.9	951.3	46.9	348.5
112	3.1	83.9	289.3	954.5	52.0	391.0
128	3.1	83.9	306.2	954.5	57.9	429.5

In the no-bloc condition, members of the movement are initially spread out at random across a social network of 1,024 people. In the bloc condition, they start out concentrated together in that social network.

will be easily converted away from the movement if two or three of their friends happen to belong to a particular religious denomination. The four denominations will gobble up the movement members, and simultaneously compete with each other, until the pattern of religious affiliations across the network stabilizes. The only thing that can prevent the movement from going out of existence is when an occasional movement member, by pure chance, happens to start out with one or more close friends who also belong to the movement, who thus can form a tiny bloc that resists recruitment to one of the big denominations. This is more likely to happen along the line between two of the big denominations, where their competition with each other weakens the influence of both.

In contrast, in the bloc condition the average size of the religious movement grew from sixty-four to 83.9 members. This happened because the four larger denominations were not concentrated, so for a while the movement could recruit individuals around its periphery. But relatively quickly the numerous members of the four denominations created their own blocs spontaneously. Here is what would happen. In a particular region of the network there would happen to be more of one denomination, say Alpha, than of any other. Alphas who were friends with a non-Alpha would be more likely to recruit him or her to their faith than to be recruited away from it themselves. If this small knot of Alphas happened to be right next to another one, they would merge and begin recruiting others in their neighborhood. Thus the denominations exploited their general numerical superiority to build concentrations that eventually halted the expansion of the religious movement. Clearly, concentration of forces is a powerful factor, preventing collapse of a minority affiliation and even producing growth, but insufficient to make the movement surpass the denominations.

What factor could give a religious movement greater power to grow? To be sure, a charismatic leader or powerful ideology could do the trick, but here we are interested solely in social networks, so we want a factor that concerns social relationships. Innumerable ethnographic reports about religious movements indicate that they practice "outreach," intentionally building social relationships with nonmembers. So, our second simulation experiment adds outreach, giving members of the sect but not the denominations the capacity to build social bonds with people of different religious affiliation from their own. This recruitment tactic has meaning only if people lack some potential social relationship with their neighbors which the movement could create. Therefore, we start the simulation with only 2,048 social bonds linking near neighbors—half the total 4,096 that are possible—distributed at random across the social network. Now, as the fourth column of Table 6.3 shows, the bloc condition produces essentially endless growth, and the sect reaches an average size of 954.5 (out of 1,024) after 128 rounds.

The trend for the no-bloc condition is quite interesting. First the sect declines, but soon growth begins, and the final average size is 306.2. If we ran the simulation longer, the movement would continue to grow. What happened is that small blocs of movement members formed accidentally, then employed outreach to grow Because on average each person starts out with just four friends, instead of eight as in the first experiment, everything happens more slowly. But when two or three movement members happen to be near neighbors, they will develop friendships with each other, if they do not already have them. Then they will practice outreach, developing social ties to a nonmember, and effectively gang up on that individual to convert him or her. Soon sizable blocs of movement members have formed and are adding more and more members via outreach. Remember, this outreach consists simply of forming friendships with nonmembers. In this simulation game we have not given the religious movement any other advantages, such as an attractive leader or a heightened capacity to offer effective supernatural compensators.

The third experiment introduces balance theory, allowing members of the four denominations to break off bonds with members of the religious movement. The way this works is as follows. On each turn of an individual person, the computer randomly selects either differential association theory or balance theory. If it picks differential association, it takes a vote of the person's friends and then changes the person's religious affiliation to match that of the majority of these friends, if they are not already of the same denomination. If it picks balance theory, as it does at random half the time, it focuses instead on the social bonds. It checks whether there is a bond with each of the person's eight near neighbors. If there is no bond, but the two people are of the same denomination, a bond is formed between them. If a bond exists, but the person and the neighbor are of different denominations, the computer breaks off the friendship. Through outreach, the movement members may form these bonds again, and several ties to them may need to be in place before a member of a denomination will join the movement.

This third experiment shows very much the same pattern as the second experiment, but with far slower movement growth. Indeed, the population of sectarians in the no-bloc condition is just getting back to the initial size of sixty-four when the simulation ends. But in the bloc condition, about half way through the movement grows bigger than any of the original denominations that began with 240 members. Again, we see confirmation of the principle of concentration of forces. Concentration prevents collapse of a small subculture, and if other circumstances are favorable, it contributes to substantial growth. However, the fact that growth of the bloc stalled in the first experiment suggests that concentration is not sufficient for growth, and that some other advantage such as outreach must be combined with it. In addition, we have seen that random factors—pure, meaningless chance—also play a role.

Chaos and Unpredictability

Recently, there has been great interest in the role of chance in several of the sciences, and the concept of *deterministic chaos* has been the subject of many publications of both scholarly and popular kinds (Mandelbrot 1983; Hao 1984; Gleick 1987). Sociologist Barry Markovsky (1992) invoked chaos theory to describe patterns of results from running very different social network simulations from those reported here, in a study of exchange and social power.

Chaos theory in mathematics focuses on what are called recursive functions. These are mathematical formulas that are meant to be calculated again and again. Each time the results of the previous calculation form part of the input to the next calculation. A familiar example is compound interest. You deposit $100 in the bank at 5 percent interest compounded annually. At the end of the first year, your account contains the original $100, plus five dollars interest. You start off the second year with $105 dollars, so at the end of the second year you earn not five dollars interest but $5.25, which is 5 percent of $105. Therefore you start the third year with $110.25, and in the third year you earn $5.51, and so on. The compound interest formula is not chaotic, because the results are in no way unpredictable. By mathematical means such as calculus it is possible to work out an equation that will tell you how much interest you would earn in any particular year, without the necessity of actually doing all the calculations, year by year. A recursive mathematical function that produces results which cannot be calculated except by running through all the specific steps is *chaotic*.

An interesting feature of many chaotic functions is that even very slight differences in the numbers at one point in time can grow to huge differences later on, at least for some regions of the functions' domains. Any physical system that is based on natural laws incorporating chaotic functions will be very difficult to predict, and this apparently is the reason that meteorologists have been unable to predict specific weather patterns (other than gross seasonal changes) over more than a few days. If so, no improvement in data collection, theoretical understanding, or computation procedures will increase the accuracy of long-range weather prediction much over what it is today.

The analogy between meteorology and sociology is a close one. We often find it convenient to talk about storm fronts and religious movements as if they were bounded entities. But, really, the elements of the phenomena we study are individual air molecules and persons, or tiny movements of a molecule and actions of a person. Years ago, George Homans (1967) wrote about *divergent phenomena*, situations in which tiny changes today could result in vast, unpredictable differences tomorrow, and he asserted that many large-scale social phenomena—perhaps all—were of this unpredictable kind.

Our simple computer simulations gave highly chaotic results. For example, in five of the sixteen runs of the no-bloc condition of Experiment 1, no sect members remained at the end. More detailed printouts reveal that four runs ended with just a single member, located at the intersection of denominations and thus protected from conversion by the lack of a plurality among his associates. Three simulations ended with just two sectarians, and one each with eight, nine, ten, or twelve. The relatively large numbers in these last four outcomes were sustained by accidentally formed blocs of movement members.

The no-bloc condition of Experiment 2 produced an especially wide range of outcomes. Thirteen runs gave final sect memberships ranging from seventeen through 497, and the other three ended with 924, 981, and 1,024 sect members. This last run is especially interesting, because detailed examination revealed that sect membership collapsed in the beginning, dropping from sixty-four to only nineteen after four rounds (second-lowest at that point among the sixteen runs), before exploding and achieving complete conversion of the entire population immediately before 128 turns. At the terminations of the two other runs concluding with more than 900 members, the sect was still growing. Growth had stalled between twelve rounds and sixty rounds in the other thirteen runs.

We have not provided a proof that our simulation results are chaotic, in the strict mathematical sense, but for all practical purposes they appear to be (cf. Bak, Chen, and Creutz 1989). We are suggesting that events within a given set of simulation parameters are partly chaotic. But we are not saying that the chaos is complete. For example, we obtained very clear differences between the bloc and no-bloc conditions in each experiment, and the three experiments gave very different average outcomes from each other. This harmonizes well with the findings of empirical sociological studies. Social phenomena are a mixture of the predictable and the unpredictable.

Conclusion: Diffusion and Affiliation

Many sociologists and other scholars of religion have proposed models of how affiliation takes place, and thus how novel religious culture diffuses beyond the point where it was invented. These models typically consist of a series of steps a person goes through, taking him or her from outsider to insider, and they often combine four elements: deprivations, beliefs, accidents, and social interaction or social bonds. A person is unhappy, unsuccessful, poor, frustrated, deprived, and thus has a motivation to seek solutions to his or her problems, perhaps an entirely new way of life. The person already believes in the existence of the supernatural, perhaps socialized in childhood to a particular religious tradition, so he or she is primed to find the religious movement's ideology plausible. By accident, the person encounters a particular religious movement at a very susceptible moment in his or her life. He or she is weak in social bonds with nonmembers that might prevent joining, and intensive social interaction with members recruits the person and inculcates the specific beliefs of the group.

Although the Lofland-Stark model stresses that preexisting tensions are essential for a person to convert to a novel religious faith, subsequent work, including some crucial theoretical work by Stark himself, has brought this into question. Certainly, all human beings experience frustration with the conditions of our existence, and this fact is the taproot of religion. But decades ago the sociology of religion assumed that only the special and intense frustrations associated with extreme relative deprivation could motivate joining a high-tension group. Now, however, many social scientists suspect that relative deprivation may not be necessary at all for many religious movements that are culturally novel. It may be that in the past, novel religions were treated as so extremely deviant that only very unusual motivations were sufficient to make a person defy the will of the society and join or create one. In modern pluralistic society, where novelties of all kinds are attractive to diverse groups, there is relatively little penalty for joining a novel religion. Under cosmopolitan conditions such as these, tension and deprivation may be unimportant factors. If religious orthodoxy reasserts itself in future, however, and membership in new religious movements again becomes punished and therefore costly, only people in desperate need of exotic compensators may be attracted.

The importance of beliefs in religion cannot be denied, yet their role in recruitment to novel religions is unclear. Merely disseminating scripture over the World Wide Web may not be an effective way of transforming people into members. Yet the very essence of supernatural compensators, the defining feature of religion, is that they are explanations that require belief. For movements based chiefly in specific compensators for relative deprivation, the beliefs make possible the claim that members will receive greater rewards than nonmembers. Often such beliefs are transvaluational, asserting that the apparent rewards possessed by the rich and powerful are not actually of great value, compared with the sanctity offered by the movement. And for novel religious movements, a distinctive set of beliefs is a precondition for success. Whatever processes are involved in affiliation, they cannot operate without the excuse that the group has achieved a spiritual breakthrough described by the beliefs. To make any sense at all, these beliefs must connect to at least some familiar ideas, but they must be novel enough to confer the message that this movement is new, different, and better than all the others.

Traditional sociology is awkward in its treatment of accidents, hiding most of them in the "unexplained variance" of statistical analysis, but accident is a constant feature of human existence that deserves recognition for the role it plays in determining which of many competing religious movements will rise or fall. The concept of deterministic chaos is new to sociology, and our computer simulation results suggest that it may have an important role to play in helping us understand social phenomena. However, if collective behavior is truly chaotic, inescapable limits exist to sociological understanding. Members of religious movements will attribute their success to particular features of ideology and practice, to wise leaders, and to God. Sociologists must be careful to avoid similar fallacies of attribution when the real causes of success might be the structure of social relations around members and dumb luck.

The insight that interpersonal relationships are the one, essential element in all realistic models of religious recruitment and of cultural diffusion places the sociology of religion on a firm basis. As we shall see in the following chapter, Asian religions were imported effectively to the United States not in the form of books but of people, when gurus voyaged personally to our shores. Some forms of culture can certainly be transmitted in written form, and the materials disseminated over the World Wide Web are far from inconsequential. But the soul of a new religion can be transported from one place to another only in the vehicle of the human heart. And faith in a new creed can be given to a person only through the human voice and the human touch. When religion is transmitted from person to person, however, it can become changed, and religious innovation often reflects the fluctuating dynamics of social interaction. Thus, the story of religious innovation is a tale of people, of their movement from one society to another, and of their often trouble-filled dealings with one another.

7

Asian Imports

Among the chief processes that transforms religious culture is migration from one society to another. An immigrant religion may adopt beliefs, practices, or its management style from the dominant churches of its new home, and a self-conscious missionary movement may intentionally create a simplified form of its faith the better to penetrate the alien religious market. In addition, not all organizations in an existing religious system are equally prepared to send missionaries into other countries. When an imperial nation dominates another country, as was the case with the British Empire in India, it may invest significant resources in establishing branches of its most central denominations in the colonized land. But when colonialism is not involved, low-tension denominations may have little motivation to send out missionaries, and the task may be left to religious movements in rather high tension with their own societies. These are the movements with confidence, energy, and often a well-focused religious message that can convert people who lack the cultural assumptions that support low-tension denominations. Here we shall consider four Asian movements that established beachheads in the American religious market: Transcendental Meditation, the International Society for Krishna Consciousness, Zen Buddhism, and the Unification Church. We begin by recalling seventeen crucial days in religious history, when Asian faiths had their first substantial opportunity to present themselves to the American public as equals of Christianity and deserving of respect.

The World's Parliament of Religions

At noon on the fourth of July, 1893, flowers taken from the grave of Thomas Jefferson decorated the podium where speakers would salute the stars and stripes at the Chicago World's Fair commemorating the four-hundredth anniversary of the discovery of America by Christopher Columbus (Seager 1995:34–35). The centerpiece of this World's Columbian Exposition was the White City of buildings in monumental Greco-Roman style, including the Music Hall, The Palace of Agriculture, the Intermural Railway Station, and a pseudo-Egyptian obelisk. Tremendously impressive to the uncritical eye, these symbols of a nation's pride were constructed not of fine marble but crude plaster of Paris reinforced by horsehair and jute. To the west of the White City stretched the Midway, containing a simulated Mid-East bazaar populated by real hootchy-kootchy dancers and an ersatz mosque where exotic Hebrews as well as Moslems demonstrated their native rituals. Barges on Lake Michigan prepared to fire their cannon when the crowd of 25,000 sang the *Star Spangled Banner*. The replica Liberty Bell had not yet been delivered, but an electric switch would make it ring at its manufacturer's forge in far away Troy, New York. The inscription on the bell implied not only religious tolerance but also the superiority of Christianity: "A New Commandment I Give Unto You, That You Love One Another." Then the assembled notables discovered there had been an embarrassing oversight. No one had remembered to arrange for a Protestant clergyman to give the invocation and lead the doxology.

Jamal Effendi, imam of the simulated mosque, volunteered to save the event by filling in for his missing Christian colleague. In the words of the *Chicago Tribune*, Effendi "was attired in the full ceremonials of priesthood, a dark blue robe embroidered in gold bullion, and as he turned his face toward the East and raised his hands in supplication, a silence fell upon the crowd. He began chanting a prayer to Allah for his blessing on the United States, the flag above him, and the Exposition in Chicago. At every break in his prayer the Mohammedans united in a loud amen in old fashioned Methodist style."

Two months later, the Columbian Liberty Bell had finally arrived, and it rang ten times to open the fair-related World's Parliament of Religions and to count the ten greatest religions of the world: Christianity, Judaism, Islam, Buddhism, Confucianism, Hinduism, Jainism, Shintoism, Taoism, and Zoroastrianism. In the Hall of Columbus, sixty religious leaders prepared to open seventeen days of speeches and dinners devoted to celebrating the unity of all peoples under God. When the two huge, competing commemorative books were published later that year (Houghton 1893; Barrows 1893), both carried mottoes of religious unification: "With Gratitude to God for the Brotherhood of Man." "Have we not all one Father? Hath not one God created us?" But the form of unification desired by most participants and nearly all the audience was the peaceful submission of all other creeds to liberal Protestantism. Every other religion, the organizers of the Parliament believed, was a mistaken near-miss, and once the Catholics and Hindus recognized their honest but unfortunate errors, they would gratefully become Unitarians or Presbyterians. But that is not at all what happened.

The stars of the show turned out to be the delegates representing Asian religions. Especially celebrated were the Hindus, Protap Chunder Majumdar and Vivekananda, and the Jain, Virchand Gandhi, all from India, plus the Buddhist, Anagarika Dharmapala from Sri Lanka. A decade earlier, Majumdar had been the first Hindu teacher to speak on behalf of his religion in America, when he lectured in Concord, Massachusetts (Melton 1989). Links had formed between the Unitarian Movement in the United States and the Brahmo Samaj Movement in India, both of which sought to strip away the legends that centuries of superstition has encrusted over pure and sublime monotheism. If Christianity were freed from the Jesus myth, they thought, and Hinduism were freed from the myths of a thousand demigods, they would prove to be the same. Thus, Majumdar came to America not to submit to Christian dominance, but to rejoice with like-minded Americans in the revelation that underneath all the unnecessary cultural encrustations, Hinduism was identical with Christianity, and thus, its equal. Dharmapala proved to be a remarkably charismatic spokesman for Buddhism, but most impressive of all was Vivekananda.

Before this Hindu spoke, Anglican minister Alfred Momerie unintentionally set the stage for the triumph of Hinduism: "The fact is, all religions are fundamentally more or less true and all religions are superficially more or less false. And I suspect that the creed of the universal religion, the religion of the future, will be summed up pretty much in the words of Tennyson . . . 'the whole world is everywhere bound by gold chains about the feet of God.' "

Vivekananda rose to speak, resplendent in his ochre robes and turban, his solid form and dark, dramatic profile reminding some observers of a great actor playing Othello. "Sisters and brothers of America!" Vivekananda began, and applause burst from the audience that would not subside for several minutes. "It fills my heart with joy unspeakable to rise in response to the warm and cordial welcome which you have given us. I thank you in the name of the most ancient order of monks in the world; I thank you in the name of the mother of all religions, and I thank you in the name of the millions and millions of Hindu people of all classes and sects.

"My thanks, also, to some of the speakers on this platform who have told you that these men from far-off nations may well claim the honor of bearing to the different lands the idea of toleration. I am proud to belong to a religion which has taught the world both tolerance and universal acceptance. We believe not only in universal toleration, but we accept all religions to be true. I am proud to tell you that I belong to a religion into whose sacred language, Sanskrit, the word exclusion is untranslatable. I am proud to tell you that we have gathered into our bosom the purest remnant of the Israelites, a remnant which came to southern India and took refuge with us in the very year in which their holy Temple was shattered to pieces by Roman tyranny. I am proud to belong to the religion which has sheltered and is still fostering the remnant of the grand Zoroastrian nation. I will quote to you, brethren, a few lines from a hymn which I remember to have repeated from my earliest boyhood, which is every day repeated by millions of human beings: 'As the different streams having their sources in different places all mingle their water in the sea, so, O Lord, the different paths which men take through different tendencies, various though they appear, crooked or straight, all lead to thee.'

"The present Convention, which is one of the most august assemblies ever held, is in itself a vindication, a declaration to the world of the wonderful doctrine preached in the *Gita*: 'Whosoever comes to me, through whatsoever form I reach him, they are all struggling through paths that in the end always lead to me.' Sectarianism, bigotry and its horrible descendent, fanaticism, have possessed long this beautiful earth. It has filled the earth with violence, drenched it often and often with human blood, destroyed civilizations and sent whole nations to despair. Had it not been for this horrible demon, human society would be far more advanced than it is now. But its time has come, and I fervently hope that the bell that tolled this morning in honor of this Convention may be the death knell to all fanaticism, to all persecutions with the sword or the pen, and to all uncharitable feelings between persons wending their way to the same goal" (Barrows 1893:102; cf. Vivekananda 1953:183).

Many subsequent speakers imagined a future time when a single religion would embrace all humanity. In a talk entitled "Future of Religion," Roman Catholic delegate Merwin-Marie Snell modestly avoided naming that faith: "The religion of the future will be universal in every sense. It will embody all the thought and aspiration and virtue and emotion of all humanity; it will draw together all lands and peoples and kindreds and tongues, into a universal brotherhood of love and service; it will establish upon earth a heavenly order." In his address, "The Religion of the Future," John Talbot Gracy noted that Christianity already dominated half the earth and had developed a system of growth that would enable it to finish the job. The liberal rector of Catholic University, Bishop John Keane, was convinced that Christianity was "The Ultimate Religion" that would naturally sweep aside all the others. Several Protestants praised the missionary efforts that were, they believed, saving the souls of heathens and winning the world for Christ.

A British delegate with a remarkable last name, George Pentecost, was even less restrained, likening the Asian religions to the corrupt paganism of ancient Rome that deserved annihilation before the "fighting religion" of

Christianity. In particular, he charged that Hinduism fostered temple prostitution. This was too much for an Indian delegate, Virchand Gandhi, representing the Jain faith rather than the Hindu, who rose to the attack. "Some men in their ambition think that they are Pauls, and what they think they believe, and where should these new Pauls go to vent their platitudes but India? Yes, sir, they go to India to convert the heathen in a mass, but when they find their dreams melting away, as dreams always do, they return back to pass a whole life abusing the Hindu. Abuses are not arguments against any religion, nor self-adulation the proof of the truth of one's own. For such I have the greatest pity." Recognizing Gandhi's bravery, so far from his home, and the rudeness of Pentecost's attack, the audience applauded Gandhi's every word (Seager 1995:83).

Anagarika Dharmapala advised the Christians how to improve their work. "The platform you have built up must be entirely reconstructed if Christianity is to make progress in the East. You must send men full of unselfishness. They must have a spirit of self-sacrifice, a spirit of charity, a spirit of tolerance. . . . The missionaries sent to Ceylon, China or Burmah, as a rule, have not the tolerance that we need. The missionary is intolerant; he is selfish. . . . Who are his converts? They are all men of low type. Seeing the selfishness and intolerance of the missionary not an intelligent man will accept Christianity. Buddhism had its missionaries before Christianity was preached. It conquered all Asia and made the Mongolians mild. But the influence of western civilization is undoing their work. . . . I warn you that if you want to establish Christianity in the East it can only be done on the principles of Christ's love and meekness. Let the missionary study all the religions; let them be a type of meekness and lowliness and they will find a welcome in all lands" (Barrows 1893:1093).

In a polite but slightly haughty tone, Dharmapala (1893) noted that Buddha was born "five hundred and forty-three years before the birth of Christ" and created "a religious revolution, the greatest the world has ever seen." Among the successes of this revolution was overcoming the depraved forms of religion rampant in India at the time, "monotheism of the most crude type, from fetishism and animism and anthropomorphic deism to transcendental deism." Perhaps his Protestant listeners failed to note that logically their own creed might be placed within this spectrum of ignorance. Dharmapala said Buddhism contained "a comprehensive system of ethics, and a transcendental metaphysic embracing a sublime psychology. To the simple-minded it offers a code of morality, to the earnest student a system of pure thought."

The true Buddhist is an atheist who has given up belief in God as part of the renunciation of base emotions required before enlightenment can be attained. "Speaking of Deity in the sense of a Supreme Creator, Buddha says that there is no such thing. Accepting the doctrine of evolution as the only true one, with its corollary of cause and effect, he condemns the idea of a creator and strictly forbids inquiry into it as being useless." Dharmapala said that Buddhism was the religion most compatible with modern science, and he ignored any doubts his audience may have harbored when he claimed that Buddhism made no invidious distinctions by race, sex, or caste. "To be born as a human being is a glorious privilege. Man's dignity consists in his capability to reason and think and to live up to the highest ideal of pure life, of calm thought, of wisdom without extraneous intervention. . . . Buddha says that man can enjoy in this life a glorious existence, a life of individual freedom, of fearlessness and compassionateness. This dignified ideal of manhood may be attained by the humblest, and this consummation raises him above wealth and royalty."

Attainment of enlightenment is the essence of Buddhism, as Japanese holy man Banriu Yatsubuchi wrote (1893), "Buddha was a man, as we are, but he, apart from us, knew the truth or original body of the universe, and cultured the virtuous works, or, in other words, he worked thoroughly by his wisdom and mercy, so that he may be called our Savior. Buddha was not a creator, and he had no power to destroy the law of the universe, but he had the power of knowledge to know the origins, nature, and end of the universe, and cleared off the cravings and illusions of his mind until he had no higher grade of spiritual and moral faculties attainable. The truth or original body of the universe is absolute, infinite, eternity, and not material and not immaterial, and not existing and not unexisting. As every object of the universe is one part of the truth, of course it may become Buddha according to the natural reason." Another Japanese Buddhist, Horin Toki, commented that the rituals of religion were merely superficial human aids to enlightenment, "Prayer or worship is like a finger which points to the moon; when the round face of the moon is once seen there is no need of the finger" (Barrows 1893:547).

Vivekananda's (1893) essay on Hinduism expressed pride in his ancient, almost unimaginably diverse heritage. "Three religions stand now in the world which have come down to us from time pre-historic—Hinduism, Zoroastrianism, and Judaism. They all have received tremendous shocks and all of them prove by their survival their internal strength; but while Judaism failed to absorb Christianity, and was driven out of its place of birth by its all-conquering daughter, and a handful of Parsees are all that remains to tell the tale of this grand religion, sect after sect has arisen in India and seemed to shake the religion of the Vedas to its very foundation, but like the waters of the seashore in a tremendous earthquake, it receded only for a while, only to return in an all-absorbing flood, a thousand times more vigorous, and when the tumult of the rush was over, they have been all sucked in, absorbed and assimilated in the immense body of another faith."

The Vedas, he explained, are a book without beginning or end, or perhaps not a book at all. They are "the accumulated treasury of spiritual law discovered by different persons in different times. Just as the law of gravitation existed before its discovery, and would exist if all humanity forgot it, so with the laws that govern the spiritual world. The moral, ethical, and spiritual relation between soul and souls and between individual spirits and the Father of all spirits were there before their discovery and would remain even if we forgot them. The discoverers of these are called Rishis, and we honor them as perfected beings, and I am glad to tell this audience that some of the very best of them were women."

Vivekananda turned to the question of immortality, which for the Hindu implies reincarnation. "The body will die, but I will not die. Here am I in this body, and when it will fail, still I will go on living, and also I had a past. The soul was not created from nothing, for creation means a combination, and that means a certain future dissolution. If, then, the soul was created, it must die. Therefore it was not created. Some are born happy, enjoying perfect health, beautiful body, mental vigor, and with all wants supplied. Others are born miserable: some are without hands or feet, some idiots, and only drag on a miserable existence. Why, if they are all created, does a just and merciful God create one happy and the other unhappy—why is he so partial? Nor would it mend matters in the least by holding that those that are miserable in this life will be perfect in a future. Why should a man be miserable here in the reign of a just and merciful God? In the second place, it does not give us any cause, but simply a cruel act of an all-powerful being, and therefore unscientific. There must have been causes, then, to make a man miserable or happy before his birth, and those were his past actions."

He spoke to his Christian audience of Krishna, "God incarnate on earth," and he spoke sympathetically of idolatry, "the attempt of undeveloped minds to grasp high spiritual truths." Indeed, all the many religions of the world are different human visions of the same truth. "If there is to be ever a universal religion, it must be one which would hold no location in place or time, which would be infinite like the God it would preach, whose sun shines upon the followers of Krishna or Christ; saints or sinners alike; which would not be the Brahman or Buddhist, Christian of Mohammedan, but the sum total of all these, and still have infinite space for development; which in its catholicity would embrace in its infinite arms and formulate a place for every human being, from the lowest groveling man who is scarcely removed in intellectuality from the brute, to the highest mind, towering almost above humanity, and who makes society stand in awe and doubt his human nature." His listeners were left to contemplate the possibility that Hinduism was the basis for the future universal religion, because only it, of all great world faiths, made room for every other creed within it.

At the end of the Parliament, Vivekanada spoke again, directly defying the Protestant crusaders: "Much has been said of the common ground of re-

ligious unity. I am not going just now to venture my own theory. But if anyone here hopes that this unity would come by the triumph of any one of
these religions and the destruction of the others, to him I say, 'Brother, yours
is an impossible hope.' Do I wish that the Christian would become Hindu?
God forbid. Do I wish that the Hindu or Buddhist would become Christian?
God forbid." The audience always showed great interest in Vivekananda's
words, but now he could sense that they disapproved of what he was saying.

Aware he was attacking the very heart of the Christian missionary movement, he continued bravely: "If the Parliament of Religions has shown anything
to the world it is this: It has proved to the world that holiness, purity, and charity are not the exclusive possessions of any church in the world, and that every
system has produced men and women of the most exalted character."

"In the face of this evidence if anybody dreams of the exclusive survival
of his own and the destruction of the others, I pity him from the bottom of
my heart, and point out to him that upon the banner of every religion would
soon be written, in spite of their resistance: 'Help, and Not Fight,' 'Assimilation, and Not Destruction,' 'Harmony, and Peace, and Not Dissension.' "

Virchand Gandhi spoke next, telling a famous story: "Once upon a time
in a great city an elephant was brought with a circus. The people had never
seen an elephant before. There were seven blind men in the city who longed
to know what kind of an animal it was, so they all went together to the place
where the elephant was kept. One of them placed his hands on the ears, another on the legs, a third on the tail of the elephant, as so on. When they
were asked by the people what kind of an animal the elephant was one of
the blind men said, 'Oh, to be sure, the elephant is like a big winnowing fan.'
Another blind man said, 'No, my dear sir, you are wrong. The elephant is
more like a big, round post.' The third, 'You are quite mistaken; it is like a
tapering stick.' The rest of them gave also their different opinions. The pro-
prietor of the circus stepped forward and said: 'My friends, you are all mistaken. You have not examined the elephant from all sides. Had you done so
you would not have taken one-sided views.' Brothers and sisters, I entreat
you to hear the moral of this story and learn to examine the various religious
systems from all viewpoints" (Barrows 1893:170–171).

Charles Carroll Bonney, the attorney and Swedenborgian layman who
headed the committee of businessmen that created the Parliament, gave the
closing address. He did not comment that his own church was a novel religious
movement relatively high in tension with conventional Protestantism, but he
noted that experiences since childhood had familiarized him with the great religious systems of the world. "I was thus led to believe that if the great religious
faiths could be brought into relations of friendly intercourse, many points of
sympathy and union would be found, and the coming unity of mankind in love
of God and the service of man be greatly facilitated and advanced."

With distaste he recalled the moments when Protestant crusaders had criticized the Asian faiths or promoted the victory of Christianity over them. "If an unkind hand threw a firebrand into the assembly, let us be thankful that a kinder hand plunged it in the waters of forgiveness and quenched its flame. If some Western warrior, forgetting for the moment that this was a friendly conference, and not a battle field, uttered his war-cry, let us rejoice that our Oriental friends, with a kinder spirit, answered, 'Father, forgive them, for they know not what they say.' " After his farewell address, the conference closed with the Lord's Prayer and singing of *America* (Barrows 1893:185).

Very quickly after the Parliament ended, its dream of world religious unity vanished, and its participants would have grieved sorrowfully to see the century of intolerance, bigotry, and bloodshed that followed. However, the conference initiated a pluralistic opening of the spectrum of American religions that was not fully completed until sixty years later. The Asian delegates traveled extensively on speaking tours before leaving the country, taking their message to a wide audience. Majumdar went to Boston, Washington and New York, giving a total of three hundred addresses. Dharmapala went to New York, where he initiated his first American disciple, then went to San Francisco where a colleague launched American's first Buddhist journal. Vivekananda remained in Chicago for several months, then undertook a lecture tour of the East Coast before returning to India where he founded the Ramakrishna Mission Association that established the Vedanta religious movement in the United States. The Christian crusader delegates who had been excessively proud of their missionary movements to convert the heathen Asians would now have to contend with a small but significant missionary countermovement that would offer Hinduism, Buddhism, and other Asian faiths to Westerners.

Transcendental Meditation

The Asian religious movement that directly touched the lives of the largest number of Americans, Canadians, and western Europeans is probably Transcendental Meditation, also known as TM (Bainbridge and Jackson 1981). It is of sociological interest for three reasons. First, TM was a highly simplified form of Hinduism, adapted for Westerners who did not posses the cultural background to accept the full panoply of Hindu beliefs, symbols, and practices, thus illustrating how a missionary movement may seek to distill the essence of a religious tradition to make it more acceptable to nonbelievers. Second, to accomplish this, TM presented itself as a science rather than a religion, and the battle over how it was to be defined provides insights about the boundaries of religion. Third, in pursuit of worldly benefits by supposedly scientific means, TM offered specific compensators that were open to disconfirmation, and when the movement's growth stalled the members turned more resolutely to the supernatural general compensators of religion.

TM was the creation of Indian guru Maharishi Mahesh Yogi who visited the United States first in 1959 and again repeatedly in the 1960s. In 1965, his message caught fire among the students of the University of California at Los Angeles, leading to the foundation of the Students International Meditation Society (SIMS). In 1967, he spoke at UCLA, Berkeley, Harvard, and Yale. SIMS chapters were soon established near many major universities across the country. Similar growth took place in Canada, Germany, and Britain, and for a time the fabulously popular Beatles music quartet studied TM under the personal tutelage of the Maharishi, thus conferring a certain prestige upon him among young adults. Within a decade, nearly a million Americans and tens of thousands in other nations had learned how to practice TM, and extensive publicity had spread the concept of meditation into every nook and cranny of Western society.

Although meditation was simple, one had to learn it in a formal course taught at SIMS centers or by traveling TM teachers, costing as much as $165. Typically, the first step was to listen to lectures communicating a few simple principles and claiming that the technique would give a person peace of mind and increased energy. Then the student would receive individual instruction from the teacher. The student would bring fruit, flowers, and a clean handkerchief to the session. The teacher used them in a ceremony which was presented as expressing gratitude to the "tradition of knowledge" from which TM sprang, but was in essence a religious initiation ritual. The student was not expected to participate in this ritual, but merely to observe it, and many teachers interpreted it in philosophical or aesthetic terms. But, a training bulletin for teachers, "Explanations of the Invocation," draws the connection to Brahma, Lord of Creation: "The truth of Brahma, the Creator, born of the lotus, rooted in the eternal Being, is conventionally and traditionally depicted by a picture where Lord Narayana, lying in a restful pose, has the stem of a lotus emerging from his navel, and Brahma, the Creator, is seated on that lotus. So the wisdom of Transcendental Meditation, or the philosophy of the Absolute knowledge of integrated life came to the lotus-born Brahma from Lord Narayana."

Next, the teacher would briefly instruct the student in meditation and give him or her a mantra, a word supposedly selected to match the nervous system of the individual, but actually taken from a list of sixteen Sanskrit words on the basis of the person's age. During meditation, the person focused on the sound of the mantra to the exclusion of all thoughts. The next day, the student would be checked by the teacher, discussing how the meditations were going, and over the following years he or she might come in occasionally for further checks. Meditators who were especially attracted to the ideas or people of the movement might take one or more "residence courses" for teachers, thus becoming full-fledged members. Teachers generally worked from centers. They were required to keep accurate records of their new initiates and to send a percentage of the training fee to the central organization.

Data from TM's own computerized membership files show that about 1,000 Americans had learned to meditate by the end of 1966, then fairly steady growth continued through 1975, with modest dips in 1969 and 1974. By the end of 1975, fully 729,300 Americans had been initiated, 292,517 of them in that year alone. The peak month was November, 1975, when 39,535 learned the technique. Then there was a rapid decline in recruitment of new meditators. In 1976 the number added was 140,273, less than half the number in the previous year, and just 49,689 became meditators in 1977. In November 1977, only 2,735 were initiated, a drop of 93 percent over the period of two years. Most of the million people who had been initiated either ceased meditating or did so informally and irregularly without continuing connections to the TM movement. By October 1972, there were already 1,977 TM teachers in the United States, and by the beginning of 1977 fully 10,000 had been trained. The precipitous decline in growth was a severe challenge for the movement because teachers depended upon recruiting several new meditators a month to maintain the sense that their movement and their own contributions to it were successful.

Table 7.1 shows the rise and fall of initiations from 1970 through 1977 in fifteen "college towns" plus the United States as a whole. The fifteen were selected because at least 1000 people were initiated in each and the city or town is not so large as to swamp the influence of the university, as would be the case for UCLA in Los Angeles. Over the eight years, for example, a total of 2478 were initiated in Ann Arbor, Michigan, home of the University of Michigan. Of these, 167 (6.7 percent) were done in 1970, first year of the series. The peak came in 1975, when fully 595 (24.0 percent) were initiated. And in 1977, only 73 (2.9 percent) were initiated, a drop of 87.7 percent from the peak year of 1975. The next to last row of the table is an average of the preceding fifteen, making it easy to compare the college towns with the nation as a whole (including these towns). We can see that the TM movement gained initiates earlier in the college towns than in the nation as a whole, because the percentages are higher in the towns from 1970 through 1974, and lower from 1975 through 1977.

Undoubtedly, TM spread through a finite population of potential recruits who were centered around universities and thus had some degree of openness to new intellectual trends. The pool of prospective meditators was undoubtedly increased by the dual cultural tactic developed by TM. On the

Table 7.1: Rise and Fall of Transcendental Meditation in Selected "College Towns"

City, State	Percent of the Eight-Year Total Initiated in the Given Year								Total 1970–1977	Percent Drop 1975–1977
	1970	1971	1972	1973	1974	1975	1976	1977		
Ann Arbor, MI	6.7	7.7	12.8	19.9	14.3	24.0	11.7	2.9	2,478	87.7
Austin, TX	7.7	10.2	8.7	12.3	11.5	27.3	15.5	6.7	2,519	75.3
Berkeley, CA	8.6	13.9	16.7	21.8	14.8	15.0	6.3	3.0	3,823	79.7
Bloomington, IN	2.8	12.2	15.9	19.1	13.9	19.1	13.9	3.2	1,904	83.2
Boulder, CO	7.2	12.2	13.3	17.5	14.2	20.9	10.7	4.1	2,791	80.3
Cambridge, MA	8.7	10.1	16.4	17.4	14.6	17.9	10.3	4.7	2,421	73.7
Carbondale, IL	2.6	10.0	28.4	24.3	11.7	10.5	10.4	2.0	1,026	80.6
Chapel Hill, NC	4.0	10.6	10.4	21.7	14.2	23.6	11.6	3.9	1,000	83.5
Columbia, MO	3.4	8.6	18.5	16.1	13.0	18.0	17.1	5.3	1,149	70.5
Eugene, OR	12.9	9.9	9.3	12.0	13.7	23.0	13.5	5.7	1,661	75.1
Gainesville, FL	2.5	4.6	11.7	15.8	14.7	25.8	18.8	6.1	1,396	76.4
Ithaca, NY	1.8	4.7	9.7	21.3	20.8	22.9	13.3	5.5	1,570	75.8
Madison, WI	8.9	10.7	13.6	16.5	17.5	19.3	10.3	3.3	3,317	82.8
Palo Alto, CA	4.7	10.7	15.9	20.1	13.3	21.6	8.8	4.8	1,772	77.7
Tucson, AZ	4.7	9.0	10.2	15.0	13.0	28.3	16.2	3.7	2,721	87.0
Average of 15	5.8	9.7	14.1	18.1	14.4	21.2	12.6	4.3	—	79.3
USA Total	2.3	5.7	9.7	14.8	13.6	32.7	15.7	5.6	894,501	83.0

one hand, TM exploited a widespread India mystique in the counterculture of the late 1960s. But on the other hand it asserted that the technique was scientific and that the Maharishi had a background in scientific physics. Movement leader Robert Keith Wallace was able to publish favorable articles on the physiological effects of TM in the widely read and respected periodicals *Science* and *Scientific American* (Wallace 1970; Wallace and Benson 1972). Popular books told the general public they would benefit immensely from meditating (Forem 1973; Bloomfield et al. 1975; Denniston et al. 1975). At the time of its most rapid expansion, the movement purchased a defunct college in Iowa and founded Maharishi International University to educate meditation teachers in the Science of Creative Intelligence. But soon critics were charging that TM actually had no scientific basis and was really a religious movement (LaMore 1975; White 1976a, 1976b; Allen 1979). New Jersey courts determined that TM was essentially religious, and thus could not be taught in the public schools. The journal *Science* carried an article claiming that TM was nothing more than a nap in which meditators dozed on the margins of sleep (Pagano et al. 1976).

For the innermost members of the movement, TM's philosophy shaded over into religion, and advanced indoctrination included study of the *Bhagavad-Gita* and the *Rig Veda*. But the religious nature of the movement intensified immediately after the rapid decline of initiations that began in 1976. So long as the movement was growing, meditation teachers could imagine they had embarked on a new and profitable profession that would provide many rewards as they trained all Americans in a scientifically proven technique. That is, they had faith in the secular promise of TM, which was tantamount to believing in some specific compensators that were highly susceptible to disconfirmation. When initiations collapsed, the secular promise of TM died and thus the specific compensators were disproved. In mid-1977, well into the collapse, TM began offering teachers "a new breakthrough in human potential," the *siddhis*, which was a higher form of meditation that could give meditators paranormal mental powers including ultimately the capacity to levitate in mid air. Furthermore, if hundreds or thousands of them meditated simultaneously, the combined psychic influence could end wars, reduce crime, and stabilize a prosperous economy.

This response to failure exactly confirms the compensator theory of religion. As immediate attainment of worldly rewards proved impossible by scientific means, the promises of TM became simultaneously grander and more supernatural. Disconfirmation of magical compensators opened the door to full development of TM's religious potential. Finally, the hard core of meditation teachers formed an inward-looking religious movement, investing the bulk of its energies in the personal spiritual development of its relatively small band of dedicated members.

The International Society for Krishna Consciousness

Abhay Charan De was only four years old when the plague came to Calcutta in 1900, but he would always remember dancing through the streets with mobs of desperate people, singing for divine help against the infection: "Hare Krishna, Hare Krishna, Krishna Krishna, Hare Hare; Hare Rama, Hare Rama, Rama Rama, Hare Hare" (Gosvami 1980). The son of a Bengali cloth merchant who lived on Harrison Road in the capital of British India, he was raised both to have a personal, spiritual relationship with Krishna and to know the language and literature of the English. An education at Scottish Churches' College did not steal his Indian soul, but it gave him the words to communicate half a century later with Americans. His marriage was arranged for him by his family, and he was never very close to his wife emotionally or intellectually, despite their three children. He made his living by selling medicines, manufactured according to both traditional Indian and European recipes in little workshops he set up in this city or that as his fortunes rose or fell. The last of several business collapses in 1953 finally ended his pharmaceutical career, and shortly thereafter he left his family and began a life of poverty dedicated to religion.

In 1935 he had met Bhaktisiddhanta Sarasvati Gosvami, who became his spiritual master. In the Indian context, Bhaktisiddhanta was far from orthodox. He had initiated himself in 1918 into the sannyasa order with the help of nothing more than the mere portrait of his teacher. Thus, his Indian equivalent of apostolic succession was on shaky ground. In Western terms, Bhaktisiddhanta's religious movement was a high-tension sect, opposed by powerful leaders of the communities it swept through and offering a far more intense and emotional brand of religion than they preferred. In the Indian context, the movement was high in tension for opposing the caste system and proclaiming that anyone, no matter how low-born, could achieve spiritual perfection through chanting Hare Krishna.

Abhay saw Bhaktisiddhanta only a few times before the older man died in 1937, and it seems that Abhay was largely self-taught in religion, reading the vast corpus of Indian sacred texts by himself and writing his own scholarly commentaries on them. In 1944, he published a little magazine he called *Back to Godhead*, and furtive issues appeared every few years, whenever he could scrape together enough money for paper to print them on. Except for a brief attempt to launch a League of Devotees in the impoverished city of Jhansi in 1953, he was little involved in organized religion. In 1959 he decided to dedicate himself fully to a life of religious contemplation, but had difficulty finding any one to initiate him, until one of the splinter groups that had arisen out of Bhaktisiddhanta's movement was willing to do the job. With no material resources of his own whatsoever, he began a vast project to translate the *Srimad Bhagavatam* into English, with commentaries. Somehow he was able to publish three of the sixty projected volumes, without any support from an organized religious movement. Indeed, an optimistic estimate of the total number of followers he amassed in India was exactly one. In 1965, at the age of seventy, he arrived in New York with a shipment of books, eight dollars, and the imposing sacred name A. C. Bhaktivedanta Swami.

He stayed first with an immigrant in Butler, Pennsylvania, whose father wanted him to help Indian religious causes, then with Dr. Ramamurti Mishra who operated a hatha-yoga studio near Central Park in New York City (Gosvami 1980b). Theologically, the two Indian religious missionaries were entirely at odds. Dr. Mishra taught an impersonal vision of the deity, which asserted that all people and all gods are really manifestations of a single abstract and characterless Brahman. Thus he shared the liberal principles enunciated by Vivekananda. In contrast, Bhaktivedanta held that other deities, like Vishnu and Radha, were aspects of Krishna, that Krishna was a being of definite character, and that the ideal religious life depended upon having a strong personal relationship with Krishna. In some ways, Krishna could be compared with Christ. Krishna came to earth thousands of years ago in human form, experienced a terrestrial existence of many episodes and "pastimes," then withdrew to the spiritual plane but remained near enough to earth that followers could have the direct experience of contacting him. The Krishna movement has a fairly long history, reaching back at least to the radical ministry of Caitanya Mahaprabhu who may have been born in 1486, but it seems always to have existed in somewhat high tension with dominant forces in Indian culture. In its emotionality and personal relationship with the deity, Krishna worship contrasts greatly with the detached philosophical variants of Indian religion that reached the United States earlier, from Vivekananda to Mishra (Judah 1974).

Dr. Mishra was hospitable toward Bhaktivedanta, but prevented him from evangelizing among the yoga students, so Bhaktivedanta soon struck out on his own. He asked people back in India to send money to support his work, but they failed to do so. Within a few months, however, Bhaktivedanta had begun to find sympathetic Americans who helped him rent a two-room curiosity shop in the East Village, which became both his apartment and his temple. He incorporated his operation as the International Society for Krishna Consciousness (ISKCON). The first real recruit, Keith, had visited India and was already favorably disposed toward Bhaktivedanta's message. The rest came from the drug-using counterculture that was then expanding from Greenwich Village into the East Village. On September 9, 1966, Bhaktivedanta initiated his first nine disciples. Each received a set of beads on which to chant Hare Krishna 1728 times each day and a new name

193

(Hayagriva, Umapati, Ravindra Svarupa, Karlapati, Jagannatha, Mukunda, Janaki, Raya Rama, and Stryadhisa). With a small group of followers, an individual missionary became a movement. They made a terrific stir when they went throughout the East Village chanting Hare Krishna. In October they wowed the young people in Tompkins Square Park and landed in the pages of the *New York Times*.

The late 1960s was a time of tremendous cultural upheaval, and some sociologists argue that the conjunction of a controversial war, unprecedented prosperity, and erosion of traditional beliefs had brought America to a crisis of meaning that fueled participation in communal and religious experiments (Gardner 1978; Tipton 1982). Especially striking was the widespread use of so-called psychedelic or consciousness-expanding drugs to achieve radical visions (Benson and Smith 1967; Goode 1969; Leary 1983). The tiny Krishna movement intentionally targeted these young "hippie" drug-users, distributing handbills that proclaimed, "Stay High Forever! No more coming down. Practice Krishna Consciousness. Expand your consciousness by practicing the transcendental sound vibration, Hare Krishna." Devotees said that chanting Hare Krishna produced ecstasy, without any of the ill effects or legality concerns of drugs. It would be too reductive to say that the Hare Krishna movement was simply a therapy to help drug drop-outs find a viable, healthy way of life. The psychedelic ideology asserted that the drugs opened the doors to consciousness, and many experimented with these substances as part of a spiritual quest that might have brought them to some religious movement if not to Krishna. Indeed, scholar Larry D. Shinn warns that we will misunderstand the Krishna movement if we see it merely as an antidote or natural outcome of the drug counterculture. Rather, it is a genuine religious movement, stressing a powerful personal tie to the swami who in turn has a personal relationship with God (Shinn 1983, 1985; Gelberg 1989).

The early recruits to ISKCON were not given extensive training before initiation. They merely had to express an interest in it and promise to follow four ascetic rules: no meat-eating, no illicit sex, no intoxication, and no gambling. Immediately they could experience the divine bliss of chanting the Hare Krishna mantra. Later, after discarding their old identities and submitting to Bhaktivedanta's absolute authority, they could begin to learn some of the philosophy and even the language of Indian religion. Especially important were precise procedures for performing various ritual acts and exact methods for cooking traditional food. The small but rapidly growing group in the East Village were just beginning to learn these things, when Bhaktivedanta left them to struggle on their own as he visited a second ISKCON center that had been established in San Francisco by a couple he had recruited in New York. The East Coast center of the psychedelic counterculture was the East Village and the adjacent, established Bohemian section called Greenwich Village. The West-coast counterculture center was the Haight-Ashbury district of San Francisco, and logically enough that was also the site of the second ISKCON center. With the help of poet Allen Ginsberg, who had met and encouraged Bhaktivedanta back in New York, ISKCON became instantly famous throughout the California rock music and intellectual dissident scene. Grand public performances, in such places as the Avalon Ballroom and Golden Gate Park, spread the message among young hippies who flocked to join (Gosvami 1981).

Beginning in 1967 when he returned briefly to India, Bhaktivedanta traveled extensively, establishing new temples wherever he went. For a time the Beatles rock music group provided him a place to live in England, and Beatles-related publicity placed the Krishna movement near the heart of the counterculture of the late 1960s. In addition to quick recruitment of new devotees chanting the mantra, ISKCON stressed publications. These included *Back to Godhead* magazine, Bhaktivedanta's own translation of the *Bagavad Gita* which emphasized ISKCON's sectarian orientation, and a large number of other books and booklets. After Bhaktivedanta's death in 1977, his eleven anointed successors fought among themselves, and some of them exploited their positions for worldly gain (Rochford 1987; Shinn 1987; Gelberg 1987). Then literature distribution began to fail as the movement's economic basis, causing many members to take conventional jobs and forcing them to take responsibility for their children who had been living in special ISKCON boarding schools that folded (Rochford 1995). But the movement survived this dark period As we noted in Chapter 6 ISKCON's global constellation of centers now advertises itself on the World Wide Web.

J. Stillson Judah (1974:80–83) argued that six factors gave ISKCON the strength to endure as a religious movement, and the fact that it is still going strong more than two decades after Judah's analysis suggests his hypotheses have some validity. First, the movement has *unity of purpose*, in particular a devotion to experiencing and promoting Krishna Consciousness. Second, a *common discipline* unites the monastic communes, requiring total concentration on Krishna in all thoughts and deeds. Third, devotes share *similarity in age and background*, bringing to the group a relatively uniform set of values and attitudes that shaped their cohort during the counterculture of the 1960s. Fourth, a *common ritual* offers the possibility of shared religious experiences that validate the group's culture. Fifth, successful *business enterprises* offer financial stability. And sixth, despite its unitary discipline, authority, and purpose, ISKCON offers a *variety of alternative life-styles*, each best suiting some of the members. At the same time, the demise of the 1960s counterculture from which ISKCON drew its early membership may have signaled an end to rapid growth.

Zen Buddhism

At the World's Parliament of Religions, held in Chicago in 1893, Japanese Zen Buddhist priest Soyen Shaku spoke but discretely let others take center stage. Sixty years later, an intellectual Zen craze swept the American literati, especially their Bohemian wing. Existentialism was in the air, and Zen contributed to the widespread disaffection with aspects of mainstream American culture that led via the Beatnik movement to the counterculture of the 1960s. J. Gordon Melton (1987:54) says that Zen was the first form of Buddhism to achieve a measure of popularity in America, and it did so chiefly on the basis of the excellent literature that was made available in English. Zen is a form of Buddhism that offers sudden attainment of a state of enlightenment called *satori*, and the variety of Zen imported to the United States in a series of popular books seemed to imply that satori could be achieved in a flash of insight triggered by a paradoxical action, story, or question (Suzuki 1956).

Master Nan-in pours tea into a full cup to make the point that a seeker is not ready for Zen until he has emptied his mind of his own opinions. Master Mokurai commands his disciple to show him the sound of one hand clapping as a way to demonstrate that the individual does not exist in and for himself. Zen nun Chiyono achieves enlightenment when a pail of water accidentally breaks and its reflection of the moon disappears, thus illustrating that humans are too attached to their illusions. Or, perhaps, the interpretations of these three moments of insight are absolutely wrong, and each merely reminds us that the universe is a meaningless void. Except that to call it a void is merely another error of the same kind (Reps and Senzaki 1957:19, 41–42, 48–49).

Master Kyogen said, "Zen is like a man hanging in a tree by his teeth over a precipice. His hands grasp no branch, his feet rest on no limb, and under the tree another person asks him: 'Why did Bodidharma come to China from India?' If the man in the tree does not answer, he fails; and if he does answer, he falls and loses his life. Now what shall he do?" (Reps and Senzaki 1957:121). There are four valid answers to this question, each true for a different character in the drama.

First, there is the answer that belongs to Bodidharma himself. Although some scholars think Zen originated in China, an ancient legend says that Bodidharma brought its rudiments from India to China around the year 520 (Suzuki 1956:61; Watts 1957:84–86), and subsequent masters brought it to Japan. Bodidharma's long journey must have been exceedingly difficult, so we would ordinarily expect Bodidharma to have an unusually intense motivation to undertake it, such as fanaticism to promulgate his religion. However, Buddhism teaches detachment from the desires of the world, so if Bodidharma was truly enlightened he should not have felt this or any other driving emotion.

Therefore, superficially it would appear that the nature of his religion would have prevented him from taking the arduous voyage to China. However, Buddhism does not in fact prevent people from taking action, and Zen especially stresses that after enlightenment a person will act in many respects the same as before, but with a spirit of transcendence. Buddha is said to be compassionate, not in the sense of moaning over another person's pain and doing everything possible to alleviate it, but rather in the far-more-fundamental sense of offering enlightenment that will incidentally allow the person to transcend the pain. Having already transcended pain himself, Bodidharma was quite ready for the voyage, and despite lacking a powerful personal desire to go, his Buddha-nature took him from India to China.

Second, there is the answer for the man hanging for his life by his teeth. His human desire is to continue living, so he wants to bite all the harder. If he is unenlightened, he does not know the answer to the question, and even if he knew the words of the answer (without fully understanding them), as an unenlightened person he would feel no compulsion to speak them at the cost of his life. But an enlightened person is a Buddha and thus has the duty to communicate the truth. So it seems the man should speak and thus lose his bite on the limb. But there is no point answering the question if the person who asked is not ready to understand it. A student of Zen must meditate often for many years before being ready for the flash of insight triggered by a few words of his master. A student who was perfectly prepared would instantly recognize the answer, without having to hear it, if he saw this man hanging by his teeth over the precipice. Thus, under all these different conditions, the right response to the question is to remain silent and continue to bite the limb, but a Buddha would do so in a mood of perfect serenity.

Third, there is the answer for the reader of the story. The man hanging from the limb by his teeth symbolizes the reader's own essential condition. The reader lives for a short time, precariously, knowing that when his or her grip on life loosens, a swift plummet into annihilation will follow immediately. But there is a double illusion here. First, because the man exists only in a story, it is entirely possible for him to open his mouth without falling, and remain levitating in the air. The reader need only imagine that this is what happens, and for the fictitious man, it will be true. Second, the reader only imagines that he or she must hold a tight grip on life in order to survive. Like the man in the story, if the reader loosens his or her obsessive, emotional grip, perhaps life will continue unaffected. Thus, it is an illusion to believe that existence will cease without a constant, exhausting act of will. Another way to put this is to note that the man in the story does not really exist, and the man symbolizes the reader. Thus, the reader does not really exist, if by existence is meant an individualistic self-willing into being.

Fourth, there is the answer for the story's author. Tradition holds that

Master Kyogen told the story originally, but it was translated from Japanese into English (as from India to China) by Nyogen Senzaki and Paul Reps, and finally, I myself have copied it into this book and provided the interpretations. Kyogen was a liar. It is impossible to translate anything accurately from Japanese into English, so Senzaki and Reps failed utterly to capture the sense of the story in their words. In terms of Zen, I am not enlightened, so everything I have written about the story is a gross misunderstanding.

There would be a fifth and ultimately authoritative answer, the answer belonging to God, except Zen Buddhism has no God.

In many respects, Zen is an Eastern form of psychotherapy that counteracts anxiety and excessive self-consciousness (Suzuki, Fromm, and De Martino 1960). Or, it is a spiritual discipline that facilitates performance of very difficult tasks with "artless art" and unconscious skill. Eugen Herrigel's famous book, *Zen in the Art of Archery*, describes the six-year course of training the author received from a Japanese master of archery, that concentrated on gaining the right spiritual immersion in the act of shooting rather than on practice hitting the target. The first year was devoted simply to learning to breathe properly and to draw the bow without its arrow. Learning how to let the arrow fly without jerking took longer. The aim was to develop an un-self-conscious flow of drawing and shooting, without intentional aiming, in which the action became a spiritually oriented ritual rather than an obsessive attempt to hit the target. After Herrigel had made some progress, the teacher said, "You know already that you should not grieve over bad shots; learn now not to rejoice over the good ones. You must free yourself from the buffetings of pleasure and pain, and learn to rise above them in easy equanimity, to rejoice as though not you but another had shot well" (Herrigel 1953:87–88). Only if one is unburdened of the need to succeed, can one fully succeed. To prove his point, the master fires two arrows effortlessly into the nighttime darkness. The first hits the center of the target; the second splits the first.

A chief character in all of these stories is the Zen Master, a person who has achieved satori and spends his life leading disciples to their own moments of sudden insight. In Japan and China, the masters and their disciples tended to live in monasteries or to travel, supported by gifts from ordinary people. Even in the variants of Zen most totally dedicated to sudden enlightenment, in practice years of spiritual preparation were often required. Thus when Zen came to America chiefly in the pages of books, rather than carried by latter-day Bodidharmas, we can wonder whether it could be successfully transplanted without the monastic system and supportive surrounding culture it enjoyed in Japan. The real test of Zen's translatability occurred when a small number of Zen masters settled in the United States.

In 1893, Soyen Shaku had returned to Japan, reportedly convinced that his monks were totally wrong when they said, "The land of white barbarians is beneath the dignity of a Zen master" (Tworkov 1994: 3). The first two Zen masters to stay for an extended time in the United States were his students Daisetz Teitaro Suzuki, whose books and lecture tours from 1897 onward did much to familiarize the American intelligentsia with Zen, and Nyogen Senzaki, a modest monk who touched the mind of only a few Americans, but did so with great effectiveness. When Soyen Shaku crossed the wide ocean to the United States again in 1905, he composed a poem that expressed his hopes (quoted in Seager 1995:158):

> Mountains join into mountains.
> Where is the center of water?
> Where is the destination of clouds?
> I do not know!
> My heart tells me there is a happy field in the American land.
> I presume myself as a follower of old Columbus.

Helen Tworkov, who has written an excellent study of Zen in America based on extended interviews with the leading American-born Zen masters, notes that Soyen Shaku and the other Zen masters who brought their movement to the United States were unconventional by Japanese standards: "His teacher, Kosen, was the first in Japanese history to combine academic studies with monastic training, thus releasing Zen from its hermetic heritage and paving the way for its move to the West" (Tworkov 1994:4). Kosen also accepted lay students, and neither Suzuki nor Senzaki had received "dharma transmission" that would fully qualify them as "lineage holders" and thus Zen authorities. Robert Aitken, an influential American Zen teacher, received dharma transmission from Yamada Koun, but this Japanese master had just founded a new sect that diverged even further from the monastic tradition (Tworkov 1994:26). Major metropolitan areas now possess Zen centers where Americans may study meditation, and in a few cases, tiny communal movements have arisen around particular masters. However deviant by Japanese standards, the growing number of American-born Zen teachers testify that this challenging form of Buddhism has been successfully transplanted to the United States.

The Unification Church

The Holy Spirit Association for the Unification of World Christianity, also known as the Unification Church, was founded in Korea in 1954 by Reverend Sun Myung Moon, and subsequently spread by his disciples to Japan, the United States and many other nations. It could be described as an echo of the extensive missionary effort invested in Korea by American and European missionary movements, and it offers a transformed Christianity with discernible Asian qualities. For some reason, Korea proved a far more fruitful field for Christian missions than did other Asian countries. Certainly, American Baptists and others invested tremendous energy and the blood of martyrs in Burma, to very little effect (Anderson 1956; Trager 1966). Perhaps it was the national character of Koreans, who seemed more individualistic than the people of other great Asian nations. Or it could have been the fact that Koreans did not experience colonial domination by Christians, and instead found Christianity an effective countermovement against imperial domination by Japan, and potentially by China. Alternatively, the success of Christianity in Korea may reflect the strategy by which much of the missionary work was carried out, the so-called "Nevius plan."

John Livingston Nevius was an American Presbyterian missionary who had decades of experience in China (J. Nevius 1869; H. Nevius 1869, 1895). A tremendously inventive man, he had improved the fruit of the Chinese pear by grafting, and he had redesigned the passenger-carrying Chinese wheelbarrow for use on his frequent missionary tours of the countryside. In 1879 he mailed a remarkable questionnaire about spirit possession to all the Protestant clergy in China for a book he wrote on the subject (Nevius 1896). In 1890 Nevius visited Seoul, Korea, and his radical ideas had gone before him. He argued that foreign missionaries should do little more than teach native Christian missionaries, who should be the instruments for converting the people. Native Christians and their churches should be self-supporting, should recruit new members through active participation in the community, and should limit construction of church buildings to structures of native architecture they could afford without American contributions (Paik 1970). In its early years, at least, the Unification Church proved that it had learned these lessons well.

We do not have an authoritative biography of Reverend Moon, but reportedly he was born January 6, 1920 in the village of Junj ju (or Cheongju), northern Korea, when the entire peninsula was under harsh Japanese occupation (Anonymous 1990:26). When he was ten years old, his family converted to Presbyterianism (Barker 1984:16). On Easter Day, 1936 he was praying on a mountainside, when Jesus appeared. According to a brief Unification Church description, "Jesus told him to complete the task of establishing God's Kingdom on earth and bring His peace at last to mankind" (Anonymous 1990:31). For nine years, Moon studied his Bible to discern the way he would accomplish this, and he simultaneously studied electrical engineering at Waseda University in Japan. According to one story, activism to free Korea brought him four months of torture by the Japanese.

Soon after the war ended, he began his own religious ministry, outside of any existing organization, and he received a vision to go north to Pyongyang. This was the heart of communist North Korea. He was repeatedly arrested and eventually sentenced to five years imprisonment in the Hung-nam labor camp, where he might have died if another war had not saved him. North Korea launched a surprise attack on South Korea, June 25, 1950, and allied forces were driven south almost into the sea. A brilliant amphibious landing at Inchon, designed by General Douglas MacArthur, incidentally liberated the prison camp the day before Moon was scheduled for execution. A highly revered photograph, on display at the Washington, D.C., Unification Church, shows Reverend Moon carrying on his back a disciple whose leg had been broken, and they trudged south like thousands of other refugees.

Detailed analysis of Unificationist theology, examining its origins and evolution, has not yet been done, and one complicating factor will be that the literature was apparently written by several different followers under varying degrees of guidance from Reverend Moon, rather than by him. (Of course, the same is true for Jesus and Socrates.) Unificationism is not simply an echo of western Protestantism, because it incorporates distinctive Korean elements along with the fresh revelations of Reverend Moon. For example, each being, from God to each individual human to each plant and animal, is said to have a dual nature: internal character and external form, or in Korean, Sung Sang and Hyung Sang. On another level, Unificationists refer to positive and negative, or *yang-un* (Korean for the Chinese duality, "yang-yin"), which do not mean good and bad, but rather male-female, subject-object, or indeed the two electrical polarities which Moon knew so well from his profession as an electrical engineer. Unificationist theology sometimes illustrates this with the symbol of the yin-yang monad disk, found on the South Korean flag, divided by arcs into light and dark halves. At other times, it uses structural diagrams showing how Sung Sang divides into positive and negative aspects, as does Hyung Sang (Kwak 1980; Lofland 1977:15).

Moon's interpretation of the Bible begins with the same revelation on which Ann Lee based Shaker celibacy: the tree of knowledge in the Garden of Eden represented carnal knowledge. It was sexual intercourse, first between Eve and the serpent and then between her and Adam, that got Adam and Eve banished. Moon was convinced that God intended Adam and Eve to gain sexual knowledge, but not until after they had achieved full maturity. Had the first human couple waited until they were spiritually ready, they would have been able to create a world full of children, living in harmony and revering them as the True Parents. Instead, many centuries of human misery would be required to pay indemnity for this original sin. Four thousand years later, Jesus was supposed to be the second Adam, marrying the second Eve and establishing the harmonious world family that should have been founded at the beginning. He failed, or humanity prevented him from

201

succeeding by crucifying him. Nearly another two thousand years would pass before the Lord of the Second Advent, the third Adam, would give the world another chance for peace.

Like William Miller, Reverend Moon believed it was possible to calculate the date of the second coming, but Moon gave greater emphasis to important dates he identified in the history of Christianity, and less emphasis to deciphering any particular biblical passage. Certain events in Old Testament history come at intervals of 400, 400, 120, 400, 210, and 400 years, and Moon found comparable events in the history of Christianity ending in 1930, the year that he and his family were converted to Christianity (Anonymous 1973; Lofland 1977:21). For many years, Unificationists were reluctant to admit to outsiders that they believed Moon was the Lord of the Second Advent, but they have now acknowledged this to be true. Outsiders often associate stunning supernatural events with the Second Coming, but (at least at present), Unificationists do not. The goal of the third Adam is not to open the sky and carry Christians up to heaven. Far from it. His goal is to marry and with his Eve fulfill the duty of being True Parents to the world, uniting all nations into one, extended family that will live on earth in peace, harmony, and love. Thus, Unificationists have good reason to equivocate when outsiders ask if they believe Moon is the messiah. They do believe this, but they have a very different image of what the messiah is supposed to do from that presumably held by the outsider, and they know that the outsider is likely to heap ridicule on them because of his or her ignorance of Unification theology.

A committee of theologians advising the National Council of Churches has concluded that Unificationism is not in fact Christian (Cunningham et al. 1978). Among the theological points they argue set Unificationism apart from Christianity are dualism (the *yang-un* principle that even God has a dual nature) and materialism (that a perfect life can be achieved here on earth). Of course, since ancient times the orthodox Christian tradition has battled against avowedly dualist religious movements with exotic names like Manichaean, Bogomil, Albigensian, and Cathar. More often victims of fire and the sword than defeated in theological debate, many of these groups are better described as Christian heretics than as non-Christians (Runciman 1947). Ultimately, of course, Unificationists disagree with other Christian groups because they believe that Jesus failed in his mission, and the successful Christ will be Reverend Moon.

Unificationism was brought to the United States in 1959 by Dr. Young Oon Kim, who enrolled in the University of Oregon in Eugene and began recruiting students for the theology. She had been a professor of New Testament and Comparative Religions at a Methodist university in Korea until being expelled in 1955 for refusing to leave the Unification Church (Barker 1984:44). Sociologist John Lofland studied her tiny movement after it moved to Oakland, California, and research he carried out in partnership with Rodney Stark led to the influential Lofland-Stark model of recruitment we considered in the previous chapter (Lofland 1966, 1977; Lofland and Stark 1965).

The small group of Americans who clustered around Kim were economically unsuccessful, often pathetic people, thus giving Lofland and Stark good reason to begin their model with "enduring, acutely-felt tension." However, the picture Lofland paints of these people includes controversial hues, because he automatically dismissed any religious experiences as hallucinations. In addition, he invests many pages of his book somewhat scornfully describing their many different failed attempts to recruit members, without quite noticing the positive features of their admittedly amateur evangelism that gave some hint of future success. First of all, in the Nevius tradition they were self-reliant, not depending upon financial help or close direction from Korea. Second, they kept trying, and, as Lofland analyzed in depth, they possessed a number of ideological tactics for explaining away failure. Third, they experimented with alternative approaches, thus increasing the chance that eventually they would find a pool of potential recruits and the means to garner them.

Kim explained to her followers that the original sin of Adam and Eve was premature sexual intercourse, so Reverend Moon could restore humanity's relationship with God only by marrying at the correct moment, which for numerological reasons was when he was forty years old. In 1960 he married Hak Ja Han, a seventeen-year old follower, and this couple would gradually be revealed to the world as the True Parents that Adam and Eve should have been. Not only have they produced thirteen children of their own, but they have made it their mission to unite thousands of couples from different nations, sometimes helping to select mates. The aim, Lofland (1977:25) reported, "was to restore man symbolically at the tribal, national, and international levels. Thirty-six Korean couples were matched and married in 1961 in order to effect the symbolic tribal restoration. Seventy-two simultaneous marriages in 1962 accomplished national restoration. International restoration would require 144 couples drawn from twelve nations and was to occur sometime before 1967." Subsequently, the church explained that Kim was mistaken to think that the millennium would be ushered in by 1967. Since then, further periodic mass blessings of ever-larger numbers of couples have raised the hopes of Unificationists that the New Age was just around the corner.

Although Kim gained a small group of recruits, the American branch of Moon's movement was the work of subsequent Korean missionaries and the influx of money from highly successful Korean and Japanese operations. John Lofland believes the American membership of the Unification Church reached a peak of about 2,000 in about 1974. Like other new religious movements of that decade, it may have gained a number of recruits from the wreckage of the counterculture of the 1960s, people alienated from conventional religion but filled with idealism. Contrary to the self-reliance principle of the Nevius plan, the church sent money to America from lucrative Asian businesses and perhaps from individual wealthy patrons who wished to influence American politics, to stage elaborate conferences and to acquire valuable assets, of which ultimately the *Washington Times* newspaper was the most costly but also most influential.

The prominence of Moon's movement in the 1970s brought trouble. Parents who had lost children to Unificationism organized with other opponents to form an "anti-cult movement" that constantly attacked it (Bromley and Shupe 1979; Shupe and Bromley 1980). A Senate committee chaired by Robert Dole investigated the movement, urging the Internal Revenue Service to scrutinize Reverend Moon's tax returns (Anonymous 1990:72). Congressional hearings on possible illegal influence of the Korean government in America alleged that the Unification Church might be a tool of the Korean Central Intelligence Agency (Ad Hoc Committee 1979). As a result, Moon was indicted for evading income taxes. Despite supportive *amicus curiae* testimony from many major religious denominations and civil-liberties organizations, Moon was sentenced to prison at the federal facility in Danbury, Connecticut (Anonymous 1985; Sherwood 1991). It is widely believed among sociologists of religion that many conventional religious leaders have the same difficulty as Moon in distinguishing their personal financial accounts from those of their organization, and that Moon was prosecuted only because of the controversial nature of his movement. Given his international organization and the fact that he was overseas for part of his prosecution, it seems likely that Moon could have avoided imprisonment, but he chose instead to go to Danbury as an act of sacrifice comparable to Jesus going to the cross.

After serving a year, Moon returned to active leadership of his movement, launching vigorous new campaigns in Russia and other communist nations that were then entering their periods of dramatic transformation. In the early 1990s a series of new challenges burdened Unificationism. Much of the rhetoric, and even a good deal of the millenarian theology, saw the latter days as a death struggle against Communism, but then the Soviet Union collapsed, rendering this key part of the beliefs irrelevant. We do not have the results of a careful study to rely upon, but it appears that this was followed by a loss of support from anti-communist patrons in both Korea and Japan. Again and again Moon pronounced that a great breakthrough had been achieved, for example at the mass-marriage blessings, yet the golden age of the one-world family was as elusive as ever. Church-related public events had often fallen short of expectations, but with money the appearance of ever greater success could be achieved. For example, in 1992, Hak Ja Han Moon traveled the globe, speaking at lavish conventions for a new church-related but superficially independent organization, the Women's Federation for World Peace.

In the summer of 1995, when the church sought to stage a worldwide blessing of 360,000 couples, the only way it could hope to achieve even the semblance of this figure was by encouraging already married couples who were not members of the movement to take this as a beautiful occasion to renew the sacredness of their marriage vows. Members of the movement told me they no longer thought it was realistic to hope that their movement would gain control of an entire nation, as they had once thought, or even to gain enough members worldwide to conduct such a blessing without nonmember help. The death of a charismatic leader is always traumatic for a religious movement, but the demise of Reverend Moon (which members anticipate in the near future despite his apparent vigor in public speeches) could be devastating because the prophecies implied the New Age were supposed to be visibly inaugurated by a living Lord of the Second Advent. Precisely because Unificationists have placed such stock in their worldly successes, a worldly failure could be catastrophic for the movement. However, many hundreds of international couples have indeed been brought together by the movement. Among my own neighbors I count a Senegalese-Singaporan couple and a Dutch-Japanese couple, who in their own households are building the one-world family, thanks to the Unificationist movement.

Conclusion: Asia in America

On June 5, 1993, the ambassador of India, Siddhartha Shankar Ray, gave the keynote address at a festival commemorating the appearance of Vivekanada at the World's Parliament of Religions a century earlier. Two other ambassadors also spoke, Ananda W. P. Guruge from Sri Lanka and Yog Prasad Upadhayay from Nepal. The location was the Self-Revelation Church of Absolute Monism, in Washington, founded by Paramahansa Yogananda in 1927 and turned over to Swami Premananda the following year (Premananda 1960). The current minister, and director of the associated Gandhi Memorial Center, is a woman of European ancestry named Srimati Kamala. The approximately three hundred guests, who enjoyed Indian music and cuisine as well as uplifting speeches, were about equally divided between people of European descent and immigrants from India. The front wall of the temple carries symbols of the major world religions, and the central principle of the church is that the Hindu religious tradition is ideally designed to bring together the other faiths of the world in recognition of their essential oneness under the superficial differences of belief and practice. Thus, like similar independent philosophically oriented Hindu centers around the country, the Self-Revelation Church of Absolute Monism is an imported missionary movement dedicated to converting Americans to a diluted form of Hinduism.

On Sunday, July 9, 1995, more than 2,000 Hindus from all over the East Coast of America converged on Lanham, a Washington suburb, to join seven priests from Kerala, India, in consecrating a new wing of Sri Siva Vishnu Temple (Arden-Smith 1995). Built at a cost of three million dollars from gleaming white stone, fully paid for without mortgage, the temple covers twelve thousand square feet and is believed to be the largest of its type in North America. Unlike ordinary Christian churches, it does not have a definite membership, but it serves and is supported by the estimated 80,000 Hindus who live in the Washington area. Thus, the Sri Siva Vishnu Temple is a very different organization from the Self-Revelation Church of Absolute Monism. It serves ethnic Hindus, and any conversion of people from other traditions is entirely incidental. Thus, the two Washington-area Hindu temples represent utterly different forms of religious import. The Self-Revelation Church of Absolute Monism offers a simplified version of Hinduism intended to attract recruits from ordinary American society. Therefore, a significant degree of cultural transformation was required to adapt Monism to this mission. In contrast, the Sri Siva Vishnu Temple offers traditional religion to immigrants from India, in all its cultural richness. It remains to be seen which approach will have the greater impact on American society.

Each of the Asian-imported religious we have considered in this chapter presented a highly attenuated form of its cultural traditions to its alien American converts. Transcendental Meditation reduced Hinduism to simplified meditation, with some additional myth and philosophy available for the few participants who became dedicated teachers. ISKCON offered a very personal relationship with Krishna, achievable simply by chanting and acceptance of an ascetic lifestyle, with instruction in some elements of Indian culture coming later. Zen Buddhism similarly introduced a few ideas to American intellectual life without communicating the full system of Japanese religion. The Unification Church smuggled a few Asian concepts in with an apparently Christian missionary faith. In three of these four cases, the particular variant of imported religion was in somewhat high tension with its culture of origin, and Transcendental Meditation was such an extreme dilution of Hinduism that it is hard to compare it within standard Indian worship.

After the great success the Asian representatives enjoyed at the World's Parliament of Religions, one might have thought that religious movements carrying their messages would have swept the country. A very few religious teachers entered the United States early in the twentieth century, against considerable anti-Asian sentiment, but federal legislation in 1917 and 1921 effectively barred Asian immigration, holding it at very low levels until 1965 when the Immigration Act was amended to permit more Asians to enter. J. Gordon Melton (1989:90–91) says that a "new era of American Hinduism" began in that year. "Between 1871 and 1965, only 16,013 Indians had been admitted to the United States. Between 1965 and 1975, more than 96,000 were admitted, and the 1980 Census reported 387,223 Indians in the United States, the largest community (84,000) being in the New York City metropolitan area. Over fifty Hindu congregations serving first-generation Indian immigrants can currently be found in Chicago."

However they arrive, whether in books, the speeches of missionaries, or immigrant communities, Asian faiths have begun to establish a firm footing in the United States, Canada, and western Europe. For centuries, the only non-Christian faith recognized as legitimate in these countries was Judaism, and the addition of Islam keeps the religious marketplace still within a single, major world-monotheistic tradition. Diffusion of Hinduism and Buddhism, accomplished by recruitment and immigration, greatly expands the religious marketplace. Many cultural innovations arise when elements from previously separate cultures are brought together, so the importation of Asian faiths into western nations is likely to set the stage for religious innovations that will increase the diversity of faiths even beyond that created by the importation directly. Still, the first century after the great Parliament in Chicago has seen only very modest growth of Eastern religion in the West, and the potential of exotic faiths to penetrate Christendom remains unproved.

8

The Family (Children of God)

Among the most famous American new religions of the period around 1970 was The Children of God. Part of the Jesus People Movement that emerged from the counterculture of the 1960s, this group vanished from American consciousness by the mid-1970s, and some scholars wondered what had become of it. Then, around 1990, bands of members came in from all around the world, under the new name, The Family. During their overseas sojourn, they had created an enduring communal way of life and an attractive expressive culture. Now, back in the States and around the world, they found new friends as well as old enemies, challenging the world's one remaining superpower to recognize the depths of its own weakness and prepare for the end-time prophesied by the Bible. We begin our examination of this fascinating millenarian movement with the conversion stories of eight men and women who joined The Family in its first dozen years, based on interviews.

Gathering the Children

Raised in Miami, Florida, Serina was sixteen when she met The Family in 1966. The group then consisted just of David Brandt Berg, his wife, and their teenage children. David was an ordained minister, leading his family around the country on an evangelical tour, but the key work of spreading the message was performed by the children. Serina recalls, "They were singing in the beaches, at hamburger stands, wherever there were teenagers. When they would go into a city, they would meet with the different church people of the area and work with their youth to try to get them to go out to evangelize the other youth of their community. My mother had heard about these singers, and they were going to be at a full gospel businessmen's dinner, and she wanted to take me."

Serina had received Jesus into her heart when she was twelve, and she would have done so much earlier if her mother had not felt it was premature. When she was six or seven, at a Billy Graham crusade her mother said she was too young to go forward to receive Jesus, but she crawled on her knees under the chairs in an attempt to reach Jesus anyway. Every summer, she visited her grandparents, and she would go to a little church near their home, ring the bell to be let in, and pray to become a missionary. Serina used to wake up with a clock radio, and because her brothers fiddled with the dials, providentially she once woke up to a program broadcast by evangelist Virginia Brandt Berg. "Most teenagers wouldn't listen to that, but somehow it just drew me, so every Sunday morning I would turn that radio program on and listen, not knowing, when I met the group, that was their grandmother!"

"I was at a turning point in my life, because I began to feel that Christianity was Churchianity." She had become dissatisfied with the spiritless organizations that defined respectable religion. "I began reading books on Eastern religion, searching." Her family was very religious, used to attend church three or four times a week, and refused to let Serina wear a bathing suit or go mixed bathing. "But I became quite disillusioned with my faith, and the churches I saw were the Hypocrisy. Plus as a teenager you are very idealistic; you expect everybody to be perfect. In the society we grew up in there were home, school and church, and they were three different worlds. You have to be a different person in each of those worlds, and sometimes they really are in conflict." Recurrent mononucleosis kept her at home for a long time. None of the people she thought were friends bothered to visit her, and her supposed best friend took this opportunity to steal her boyfriend. During these months of social isolation, she began thinking what she would do with her life. "I felt like I was in a fairground, but I had only been on the merry-go-round, so I wanted to try the roller-coaster. I wanted to see what there was [in life], because I was going to make a decision. Whatever I was going to do, I was going to do with my whole heart. And that was also with Jesus. Either he was real, and he could answer my questions and prayers, and I would give him my whole life. Or he wasn't."

The next year she started going with "the wrong crowd." They smoked, drank, and indulged in vandalism, such as lighting fires on the highway. They tormented one girl by toiletpapering her house and putting seaweed all over her new car. The next day, Serina and her gang heard on the radio that the girl had just died, perhaps a suicide. They began laughing gleefully, when Serina, in deep shock, asked, "How can we laugh? We did that to her!" Later, after one of her parents' frequent arguments, Serina attempted suicide herself by consuming bottles of aspirin, hoping to reach Jesus. Her brothers were also deeply troubled, one using heroin, and the other stealing cars. By that point, the family had been ostracized by her church, so she began searching for religious help by joining a series of Bible-study groups, and she attended a Christian and Missionary Alliance church that she later learned had been established by Virginia Berg. Her mother had dragged her to many different religions, from the holy rollers to the Roman Catholics, but nothing helped until they heard the Berg family sing at a local restaurant.

At the door she met Hosea, one of the Berg sons, and Caleb, the group's first real recruit, who were passing out literature. In the ladies' room she met Faithy, a Berg daughter, who showed great maturity and deep interest in Serina. At the dinner meeting, the Berg children sang and gave testimony. "They're on fire, and they're happy, and they're teenagers!" After the performance, Faithy asked her if she wanted to serve the Lord. Serina replied that she was only in her last year of high school, and did not have the college education she needed to become a missionary. Faithy replied, "Your best ability is availability. If you just make yourself available to God, he's going to use you."

Faithy gave Serina a tract, and she staid up all night studying the Bible verses cited in it. She wanted to find the group again, but the tract had no address on it. "Lord, I believe this is what I want, that they will have some answers or some way to help me. Help me meet them!" The next day Serina was astonished to find the Bergs performing in her Sunday-school class. Faithy and Caleb lived in Serina's home for a couple of weeks and involved her in all their activities. Serina found a missionary purpose in evangelizing to the young people of the nation, and with her mother's permission she joined, becoming the first female recruit. She traveled the country as one of the family in a motor home called "The Arc," and when they settled for a time in California at Virginia Berg's home, she helped the Berg children recruit dozens of young hippies and other youth who had embarked on the spiritual quests that were so common at the end of the 1960s.

Peter grew up in Michigan City, Indiana, was raised Roman Catholic, and lived in the same house for his first nineteen years. Typical teenage problems, including being dumped by girlfriends, brought him to desperation. He had completed his first year at Purdue University, studying engineering. In retrospect, it seemed the wrong choice of major, and music or art might have been better. He had smoked marijuana regularly for a couple of years, and on rare occasions tried LSD or another psychedelic drug, but he did not consider himself a hippie. In the summer of 1972 he gained a great girlfriend, whom he was very proud to be with. He was deeply impressed when her aunt, who was a charismatic Catholic, told him, "I believe the end of the world is going to happen by the end of this century." He had never heard such words before, and they kept repeating in his mind. He began telling his friends and parents about the end of the world, and they accused him of having lost his mind. Peter went to the charismatic meetings at a Catholic church, and there he found out about receiving Jesus into his heart. "I prayed to receive Jesus in my heart, and from that moment I knew something had happened different in my life. There was an awareness that God was real." His concerned parents suggested he take a year off from Purdue and visit his brother who was a physics teaching assistant at the University of Oregon.

He began thinking he would like to do something with music for God. He imagined living in the country somewhere, with like-minded people, similar to Jesus with his disciples. "During this time I was really searching, thinking 'What am I going to do? Where am I going to find something like this?' " For a couple of weeks in Eugene, Oregon, he went on the rooftop every day to read his Bible, but did not understand it. He couldn't find work of any kind. "I had a future of food stamps and no job and living off my brother's good will." One day he ran out of cigarettes, and having no money he decided it was time to quit smoking. He rode his brother's bicycle up a nearby mountain, and sat down at an overlook totally exhausted, thinking "What am I going to do with my life?"

Along came a casually dressed man with a Bible in his hand, who looked very different from all the students, perhaps because his hair was short while theirs was long. Peter was terrified that the man would speak with him, but when he did Peter became fascinated and they conversed for three hours. Finally they got hungry, but Peter said he had no money to buy food. The man said, "That's okay. The Lord will supply." To Peter's absolute astonishment, the man easily garnered a donation of hamburgers and french fries for both of them. The man moved in with Peter and his brother, and witnessed to them both. It turned out that he was a member of The Family who had not fit well, and the group had suggested that he go on a trip to let the Lord test his faith. This was the seventh time this had happened for the fellow, who may have been too much of an oddball to fit into The Family well, but each time he went out he would win someone. "Then he would come in for a month or so while that person got adjusted to being in the home, and then he'd get the boot again." In October, Peter and his brother moved into The Family commune in Portland.

April also had been raised in a strong religious tradition, but Judaism, not Christianity. She recalled, "I think I spent more time in Hebrew School than in public school." Quite religious as a girl, she was deeply shocked upon entering her teens to discover how much evil and suffering existed in the world. Disillusioned from faith in God, she resolved to change the world herself. At age fifteen, at the very end of the 1960s, she began using drugs and joined the tail end of the Hippie Movement. She also started going to protest demonstrations and immersed herself in the extensive political activism of the Boston area. But her idealism drowned in the hypocrisy and hedonism that swirled around her. "I just ended up a drug addict." One time all her drug-supplying friends got busted, and when she came down from her last drugs she realized that her life was really a mess. "I met a friend who had been through a similar experience, and who had wanted to get back into religion. I got into meditation, Yoga, the whole Eastern religion trip. I visited the Hare Krishna. I went to churches." When she sought spiritual guidance from a Jesuit priest, she was dismayed that he wanted her to teach him about drugs. "Finally, I felt there's no answer. There's no God. There's nothing. And then I met The Family."

Some recruits came from secular households. Tim's father was a superstar chemist whose discoveries had made him vice president of a major chemical corporation, and his family lived in fashionable Scarsdale, New York. It was "a household where materialism was the religion." His parents were both Presbyterian, but almost never took their five children to church. "We never talked about God at home. I felt a real vacuum for spiritual things, especially when I got to college and realized I didn't know exactly what I wanted to do. Both my parents had become alcoholics. It was an unhappy home life. So the five of us kids went off in all different directions." One brother became a computer whiz with a major electronic corporation. Tim went to the University of Rochester to major in engineering. "I really wanted to do something with my life. But I had no idea what it was. I had no spiritual upbringing, so this led to my being a searching hippie. So in college I read a lot of books on mysticism, and I experimented with drugs. And I started going around to a lot of people who were committed to faiths, learning what their solutions to the world's problems were. I was looking for a total solution." After wandering from major to major, he concentrated in Eastern religions, then left before completing a degree.

Traveling in California around 1971, he heard the theory that nuclear tests in the Aleutian islands might cause the entire Pacific Coast to split off, so he and the man he was traveling with headed for high ground. During college breaks Tim used to visit Colorado, to meditate surrounded by the majesty of nature, so that is where they went. On the way they explored the possibility of singing for their food, and they dreamed of providing free food for multitudes of hungry people. They sought "some kind of humanitarian life that would support itself." Tim carried a backpack of religious and spiritual books, and the only one he never consulted was the Bible at the bottom of the pile. "I knew that there was a spirit world. I knew there was more than just this physical life." But Tim disliked mainstream Christianity for what he saw as its obvious hypocrisy and lack of warmth. He had long hair, and redneck Christians had insulted him for it. He sensed that the world could not remain as it was much longer, and in each of the world's religions he found the message of a coming New Age.

In a Denver park they met members of The Family who invited them to a donated ranch on top of a mountain. "Out the front door was Pike's Peak. Out the back door was the Continental Divide. Breathtaking! It was a traveler's dream." It was packed with about two hundred members and fellow spiritual travelers. "All kinds of people, ex-hippies, ex-bankers, there was even a guy who had come down by helicopter to visit the place and ended up staying." The group included a prominent New Left radical, a television actor, and ex-marines from Vietnam. Tim was amazed to find so many "people who were sincerely searching, people who had gone to extremes." No drugs were allowed, and much effort was devoted to Bible study, yet warmth and spirituality prevailed. "That is what struck me. I woke up the next morning, and the people were so happy. And they were all quoting the Bible at each other, rehearsing their verses." A group starting playing amazing music. "They were singing beautiful songs about the Lord. There was rock music about the Time of the End. It was all meaningful. And there were gypsy songs. But they acted normal, and they smiled." The musicians were completely free of the arrogance that marked all commercial performers, and they humbly communicated their spiritual message direct from the heart. "Their eyes had such sincerity and such light." Although radiating warmth, The Family spoke with great authority that Tim found utterly genuine.

Some young people joined as couples, rather than individuals. Phil was raised in Chicago, as a devout Roman Catholic, but reading the Bible had never been part of his training, and upon reaching adulthood he felt dissatisfied with the Catholic Church. One of his brothers got within two months of ordination as a priest, then totally rejected it all, spun downward into a breakdown, and ended up an unfulfilled employee of the post office. Phil says, "I was always searching for the light. I used to take a lot of drugs. And it came to a point where my friends didn't even want to be around me, because all my conversations would turn to God." Prior to that he was very popular, but everybody "got tired of me being a fanatic, as far as searching for inner peace, and trying to find God." He explored various spiritual alternatives, including an ashram of the teenage guru Maharaji Ji. He met Sandy at a hippie party and she began living with him. They sought help unsuccessfully from many sources, until they met The Family in Tucson in March, 1972. Despite their religious backgrounds, neither of them had any concept of Christ's second coming, and the teachings about the endtime excited them. As soon as they arrived at The Family, their cigarettes were taken away and they were admonished to avoid sex because they were not legally married. They separated for two years, going to different communes, until finally they reunited and were married.

Others joined through kin connections. Marc was raised in the Missouri Synod Lutheran Church, and when he left his home to become a Los Angeles musician, his mother gave him a Bible hoping it might keep him from harm. One night in 1971, his sister, Lydia, took the psychedelic drug LSD with a boyfriend who had recently left The Family, and while they were high he told her all about salvation through receiving Jesus Christ as her personal savior. Amazed, at that moment she dedicated herself to Jesus Christ and was never the same again. The boyfriend was also surprised, because he had no intention of recruiting her to a religious group. Despite all the entreaties of her parents, Lydia immediately quit high school, just two months before she was to graduate, joined The Family and married a member she met in the Texas commune.

Life was not going very well for Marc in Los Angeles, although he was able to support himself playing electric bass and guitar in night clubs, doing some studio work, and playing for cocktail parties in Beverly Hills. He knew there was more to life than what he was experiencing. One day Marc opened the Bible at random, not really expecting to find guidance but with his mind open to some alternative to his unsatisfactory existence. His eye glanced upon Luke 11:13: "If ye, then, being evil, know how to give good gifts unto your children: how much more shall your heavenly Father give the Holy Spirit to them that ask him?" Struck by this passage, he bowed his head and prayed God to fill him with the Holy Spirit. The next day, he discovered he could no longer continue with his habitual routine. "Even the colors and everything were completely different from what I had experienced the day before. . . . I realized this was an inflowing of the Holy Spirit. It was manifested in me in a way that I felt no impatience anymore. It was like I was in a euphoric state. For those days I took no drugs or drank. I was so completely happy, which was completely contrary to the way I had been before." He began reading his Bible much of time, and bought stacks of books at Christian bookstores, but he found all the literature confusing because every author seemed to have a different interpretation of scripture.

Lydia and her husband, Titus, came to visit, and they brought some Family publications. "What they showed me was a lot of Father David's writing about the eventual fall of America, the degradation of the society here, the end of the world and all. And I wasn't really into that." So at first Marc resisted the message. But when his sister went out witnessing, he found himself reading some of the literature they had left behind, and quickly decided that it clearly was the answer after all. "I would come home at three in the morning from a night club, not in real good shape, and they'd wake up and cook me something." His brother-in-law often excitedly shared scripture with Marc. "They never pushed it on me, but they were really samples of the Lord's love." After a month, Lydia and Titus left to join a Family home. "When they left, it was like the light had gone out, and I knew that they had something that I wanted. I knew that was I was doing was not making me happy. They left me a stack of a salvation letter that Father David had written, and every day I would go out on the street and pass them out. I didn't really know how to witness yet, but I knew I had to preach the Word somehow, and these tracts enabled me to do that." In a few days he called the Family home where his sister had gone, and was immediately invited over. "As soon as I came through the door, everybody was hugging me and asking how I was. It was the warmest feeling I had ever had." A few weeks later he made the decision to forsake all, sold all his possessions, paid all his bills, and joined.

After recruiting many young people who belonged to the youth counterculture of the late 1960s and early 1970s, plus individuals who had embarked on their own, private religious quests, most of the Family left America to evangelize across the world. Claire was born in Canada to nonreligious parents, and in her teens she turned her back on the rather weak Christian identity she had received from the society around her. She was a superb student, and at age sixteen she won a scholarship to attend school in Brazil for a year, where she was very happy. But after she returned home, she became very unhappy. Shy and introverted, she missed close communication with other young people. She worked hard on her studies, including English literature and concert piano, but this only estranged her from the other teenagers who would not accept her industriousness and success. Claire received college scholarships and was admitted to several Canadian universities. But she finished high school early and figured she had time before she needed to go to college. "When I went back to Canada, I was really searching for answers, just wasn't satisfied with my life." Having loved her year in Brazil, she decided to return for a while in 1978.

Waiting in a Brazilian airport, she met members of The Family, who gave her literature and talked with her for a long time. "They were concerned about me because I was going through a hard time at that moment." When she reached the town where the school she had attended was situated, a friend looked at the literature Claire had received and said, "These are the people they're talking about on TV. They rape people, and they steal children, and they murder people!" Claire watched one of a series of television programs against The Family and found the charges to be ludicrous. She simply did not believe that the horrible things reported on the program could be true of the sweet people who had shown such concern for her at the airport. Paradoxically, the television program attacking The Family convinced her that she needed to see what these people were really like.

Claire endured a fifteen-hour bus ride to Rio de Janeiro. "I went to the community, and as soon as I walked through the door, I felt I was home. It was just so beautiful. Everybody was so sweet and so caring. I felt real happy there. And I decided to stay, even though I didn't at all understand what was going on. I didn't really understand a whole lot of it. I didn't really know what their vision was, I just knew I liked it." The community was

215

right across from the beach, a spacious house with a back yard. Claire's background was very conservative, and she had never taken drugs. Still, she was not put off by the commune's hippie style. "Everybody was very sweet and concerned. When I came through the door, nobody knew me, but everybody cared about me."

About two weeks later, the police came and placed everybody under arrest, confining some to the home and locking others in jail. Because Claire was just eighteen and new to the group, they took her to a high police official in hopes he could extract from her the truth about The Family, which he assumed was horrible. He asked her about free sex in the group and its reported campaign to win the support of outsiders by offering them sex. There was nothing she could tell him, never having seen anything about these matters. All the long-time members of the commune were deported from Brazil, but Claire was released through the intercession of an influential person who had known her in school days.

Claire returned to the now empty commune, and did the business necessary to close it. Then she sat on the front porch, thinking. She knew that the authorities were completely wrong about the group, but now that it had been expelled from the country she did not know what to do next. At that moment, by chance a Brazilian member showed up, thus giving her contact again. He took her to a commune in São Paulo, which had not been raided, where she re-joined. There she met an Argentinean man, whom she later married. Harried by the continuing persecution, they next went into the interior of the country, then to Paraguay, and thence to Argentina, where a group was cautiously operating under the shadow of the military dictatorship.

From the very beginning, Claire was fully aware of the negative portrayal of the group in the mass media, and she immediately saw firsthand the official persecution from which it suffered. To her, the group seemed a perfect sample of Christian love, and from the very beginning of her contact with it her life changed for the better. Within it, she felt happy, and loved. "I was a witness of what God's love within The Family was doing. I knew what the cost was. But I also knew that what I was seeing was true and sincere and honest. It was the first time I had seen something like that in my life. It was the first time I had seen people who were really willing to forsake their own lives and dedicate themselves to this truth they'd found, and to giving it to other people." Despite the potential pain (and the two episodes of religious persecution she would later experience in wretched Argentine prisons would certainly prove painful), she consciously reckoned that the rewards of membership were well worth the costs.

Roy Wallis (1987:84–85) says that The Family is a prime example of world-rejecting movements. "They are born characteristically from the anxiety, despair, and deprivation of those who find themselves socially marginalized. The world-rejecting movements of the 1960s, however, did not draw upon the poor and dispossessed but upon a constituency that had turned against the materialism and impersonality of corporate capitalist society and that had migrated to its margins and interstices in rebellion or indifference. There they had sought to change society or to found an alternative way of life." Certainly, the recruits we have just described fit many of the steps of the Lofland-Stark model, introduced in Chapter 6, including enduring, acutely felt tensions, frequently a religious problem-solving perspective, and a turning point. But beyond the personal troubles and spiritual seekership that motivated them, they represented a widespread youth culture in rebellion against American materialism. Combined with the evangelical, Holiness tradition, this counterculture created a new religious movement that challenged practically every aspect of conventional society.

A Brief Organizational History

David Brandt Berg, the founder of The Family, was a third-generation evangelist. His grandfather, John Lincoln Brandt, preached that Christians have an urgent duty to win souls for Christ: "Haste is essential, because men are under the sentence of death. Haste is essential, because our children are forming habits that are determining their character and destiny. Haste is essential because the devil is never idle. Haste is essential because our day is fast passing away, and we must sound the trumpet so that the blood of no man be upon our heads. Haste is essential because the day of judgment draweth nigh, when we shall be called upon to answer before the judgment seat of Christ for the deeds done in the body. Haste is essential because Jesus declares His Father's business comes first" (Brandt 1926:18–19).

A pre-publication draft of an official Family biography of David Berg reports that his grandfather was a Methodist circuit rider before becoming a leader of the Campbellite movement of the Disciples of Christ. Brandt's daughter, Virginia, is said to have fallen away from faith before experiencing a miraculous healing. Her husband, Hjalmer Berg, was a preacher in the Disciples of Christ, but the two were expelled in connection with her claims of divine healing. The two then joined the Christian and Missionary Alliance, and despite constant friction with this high-tension denomination she was a very successful radio evangelist and he taught Bible for many years in the Miami area.

The Christian and Missionary Alliance emerged from the religious quest of Albert Benjamin Simpson. Born on Canada's Prince Edward Island in 1843, as a boy Simpson experienced a precipitous drop in socioeconomic status when his father's previously prosperous business failed. Raised a Pres-

217

byterian, he worked his way through Knox College and was ordained a Presbyterian clergyman. From 1873 to 1880, he ministered to a congregation in Louisville, Kentucky, where he became involved in the Holiness Movement. While running a Presbyterian church in New York City, he began to avow Holiness principles, and a miraculous cure he experienced at the Maine resort town of Old Orchard made him an advocate of faith healing. Unable to continue in the conservative Presbyterian denomination, he and a group of associates formed their own church and founded missions for the poor, orphans, sailors, and prostitutes. Soon a pair of movements oriented toward missionary work outside the confines of ordinary churches were formed, the Christian Alliance and the Missionary Alliance. These merged in 1887 as the Christian and Missionary Alliance. For more than three-quarters of a century, this movement resisted becoming just another Protestant denomination, but it steadily evolved in that direction, and in 1974 reorganized as a standard if somewhat high-tension church (Melton 1986:260–261, 1993:374–375).

Thus, when David Brandt Berg became a minister of the Christian and Missionary Alliance, and then experienced numerous disagreements with its leadership, he was following exactly in the footsteps of his parents, grandfather, and the founder of his denomination. In 1944 he married Jane Miller, and they raised their four children to be fourth-generation preachers of the Word. For a time David held a pastorate in the town of Valley Farms, Arizona, but the congregation was split by racial hostilities, and his conflict with the denominational hierarchy steadily increased. In 1954 he came into contact with Fred Jordan's Soul Clinic in Los Angeles, and shortly he was operating a branch of this evangelical missionary organization in Miami. Having frequently traveled with his mother on evangelizing tours, he was well prepared to take his family on the road, to preach while surviving on the donations given them by the many friendly strangers they would met on their way. As the children grew, they became progressively more involved in the family ministry, eventually taking center stage as evangelical singers called Teens for Christ (Wallis 1976a; Van Zandt 1991).

In 1965 David was stationed at Jordan's Soul Clinic Ranch West of Forth Worth, Texas, when his visiting mother received the Warning Prophecy: "Even now, the skies are RED, RED with WARNING, and BLACK, BLACK with clouds gathering for the GREAT CONFUSION which is ALMOST UPON YOU!" David studied the books of Daniel and Revelation, the parts of the Bible that described the endtime that would usher in the millennium, and their traveling ministry set out to proclaim this apocalyptic vision. The endtime must be close, because never before had mankind possessed the means to destroy itself. Two years later they joined David's mother at her small home at Huntington Beach, just south of Los Angeles, where David's children began operating the Light House coffee house that had been set up by David Wilkerson's Teen Challenge organization.

Numerous novel religious groups had already targeted the hippie psychedelic drug counterculture for converts. In the previous chapter we saw that the Hare Krishna movement had already achieved considerable success with hippies in New York's East Village and in Los Angeles. Various Christian groups were trying the same thing, recruiting "Jesus Freaks" from among the hippies as part of a larger, diffuse countercultural Jesus People movement. Thus, to this point David Berg had operated on the fringes of a system of denominations and evangelical organizations, and now he was at the moment in time where the Holiness Movement encountered the Psychedelic Movement. With his guidance, his children began ministering to the hippies along the beach, recruiting many of them to a growing drug-free commune, living off donations and surplus food they could scavenge, or as they called it, "provision."

Parallel to the Hippie Movement was the New Left, a movement of political radicals opposed to the Vietnam War in particular and to capitalism in general (Kenniston 1968; Lipset 1971). Unlike other Jesus People ministries that tried to turn hippies into ordinary evangelical Protestants, Berg's group adopted much of the hippie style and the anti-establishment stance of the larger youth rebellion of which it was a part. They disrupted the sober services of ordinary churches with emotional outbursts of religious exaltation and proclamations attacking the evil system that surrounded them. They couched the counterculture's hostility to America in terms of an imminent Armageddon.

David's daughter Deborah remembered the powerfully dramatic effect of the most elaborate public demonstrations: "We planned the vigils in great detail. One of our buses would deliver the disciples to a predetermined location. Then we would march single file in perfect unison (after hours of practice) to the actual site of the protest. The seven-foot wooden staves we carried—representing God's righteous rod of judgment—would strike the ground simultaneously, creating a noise like thunder. People would turn to see what was causing this frightening sound and be awestruck to see seventy-five to a hundred red-robed prophets walking silently down the street with stern countenances, large wooden yokes about their necks, and ashes smeared on their foreheads. The long robes symbolized mourning for the nation, and the red sackcloth (burlap) was an ominous sign of the blood that would be shed in the coming destruction. The yokes represented the bondage that was to befall America, paralleling the bondage of the Israelites under the Babylonians" (Davis 1984:73).

A journalist referred to Berg's group as the Children of God, and for a number of years it was happy to be known to the public by this name, while often referring to itself internally simply as the Family, an extension of the family ministry with which it had begun. David Berg took the public name Moses David, although he was called Father David or simply Dad by members. For a time he and most followers were located at Fred Jordan's Texas ranch, but a final disagreement with Jordan brought this relationship to an end. Dividing into subgroups, the Children of God traveled across the United States and Canada, gathering recruits as they went.

In Chapter 3 we saw that six Holiness groups combined to form the Church of the Nazarene, and new religious organizations often combine with others that have arisen from similar cultural roots. Thus it was not unusual in 1971 when two other small Jesus People groups merged with the Children of God (Davis and Richardson 1976). One was the Jesus People Army of Seattle, Washington, and Vancouver, British Columbia, led by Linda Miessner. The other was David Hoyt's House of Judah in Atlanta, Georgia. In 1972, small groups began establishing colonies in Europe and subsequently in Latin America and Asia. By the middle of the 1970s most members had left the United States to evangelize the world. At this point there were just over two thousand Children of God, and the population trends along with key events in the history are given in Table 8.1.

As The Family fanned out across the world, Father David kept in touch with members by mail, and his letters became the chief medium of communication, called Mo (Moses) Letters. They were also an important source of funds, as members gave them out on the streets in return for donations. Through the Mo Letters, David Van Zandt (1991) explains, Father David was able to assert charismatic leadership. There is considerable disagreement among sociologists about the nature of charisma, and even over whether this concept is scientifically useful. The classic sociological statement, by Max Weber (1968), contrasts "charismatic authority" with two other kinds, "traditional authority" and "bureaucratic authority." Although we commonly speak of religious leaders as possessing charisma, Weber's theory was not really about the characteristics of individuals. Rather, he was interested in contrasting various kinds of argument one might make or rhetoric one might use to legitimate the authority of a leader. The traditional grounds for authority are that a particular person fulfills the customary requirements for leadership, such as being the son of the king, enshrined in the customs of the tribe. Bureaucratic grounds for authority consist of saying that the proper procedures were followed (such as majority-rule voting) to confer authority upon a particular leader.

Weber said that charismatic grounds for authority assert that there is, indeed, something very special about the person who is the leader, allowing him to sweep aside all traditions and bureaucratic rules. In religious terms, charisma is a divine gift, typically for Christians meaning that the person has

Table 8.1: The History of The Family (Children of God)

Year	Homes	Live-In Members	Live-Out Members	TS Members	Events
1994	265	8,648	314	3,922	Father David's Passing
1993	231	8,986	351	3,274	France, Argentina Persecutions, the PER
1992	231	9,002	279	3,073	Australia Persecution
1991	219	9,014	285	2,891	
1990	247	10,213	398	1,727	Spain Persecution, Push Into Eastern Europe
1989	324	10,244	785	1,390	DO Standards Tightened, TS Begun
1988	670	11,541	900	0	School Vision
1987	673	11,349	710	0	FFing Abolished, Philippines Persecution
1986	713	10,713	543	0	
1985	769	9,626	611	0	
1984	982	9,793	603	0	
1983	1,438	10,020	581	0	Return to Cooperative Living
1982	1,754	9,333	611	0	
1981	2,007	9,019	668	0	Fellowship Revolution
1980	1,973	7,865	251	0	Music With Meaning
1979	1,323	5,937	368	0	FFing Ministry, Security Reorganization
1978	862	5,062	0	0	Reorganization Nationalization Revolution
1977	741	5,101	0	0	
1976	736	4,823	0	0	
1975	679	4,215	0	0	
1974	228	3,031	0	0	Flirty Fishing Experiments in Tenerife
1973	180	2,244	0	0	
1972	130	2,080	0	0	Great Escape from the United States
1971	69	1,475	0	0	
1970	2	300	0	0	Community at Texas Soul Clinic
1969	1	100	0	0	
1968	0	50	0	0	Light Club in Huntington Beach, California

Data provided by Peter Amsterdam of The Family.

received supernatural power from the Holy Spirit, or that the Holy Spirit actually dwells within the individual. Father David revealed to his followers that he received divine messages, from several supernatural intermediaries, and thus was speaking for God. William Friedland (1964) has argued that charisma is not a special property of the leader, but arises in the needs of a group of people to find a voice for their dissatisfactions where it is hazardous to express them. Someone who successfully expresses the message that these people intensely wish to communicate will be treated by them as charismatic. Apart from the practical guidance, spiritual ennobling, and frequent entertaining humor that they contain, the Mo Letters are emotionally powerful accusations against conventional society. Their style is conversational, often employing slang and colloquial exclamations, sometimes intensely sexual or dreamlike, and frequently chastising the sociocultural "system" from which The Family had escaped. Thus, through his letters, Father David gave a powerful voice to the deepest feelings of the members, thereby becoming charismatic.

This charismatic leadership developed in tandem with an extensive bureaucracy, however. In 1976, scholars Rex Davis and James T. Richardson described the complex formal structure of the Children of God that had developed to that point. Individual "colonies," as the communal homes were then called, belonged to a "district," and districts belonged to a "region." Each unit at each of these three levels of aggregation was administered by a "shepherd." Regions belonged to "bishoprics," and bishoprics belonged to "archbishoprics," with the attendant "bishops" and "archbishops." Above that were "ministries" directed by "ministers," and six "prime ministries" with "prime ministers." At the time, these large areas were North America, Latin America, Southeast Asia with the Pacific, Southern Europe, Northern Europe, and Scandinavia.

In 1978, Father David launched the Reorganization Nationalization Revolution (RNR), dismissing more than 300 leaders and stripping away almost the entire bureaucracy. Sociologist Roy Wallis (1981) has summarized the RNR changes and their probable causes, listed here in Table 8.2. As Table 8.1 shows, in 1979 a new category of members appears, those living outside a communal home. Also, from 1978 to 1979, the average number of members drops from 5.9 per home to 4.5, thus reducing the communal aspects of the movement. Although no substantial drop in total membership shows up in Table 8.1, The Family estimates that about 2,600 members departed during this period, offset by an influx of recruits who were native to the nations in which the homes were placed (the nationalization part of the revolution) and by the birth of babies. Wallis's list of causes of the RNR misses the chief explanation given by the Family itself, which is Father David's discovery that the bureaucracy had begun exploiting the rank-and-file, sometimes demanding more than a simple tithe from the homes and using the money to support a comfortable lifestyle rather than to build the movement. Among those we have interviewed, Peter told us he was one of the lower-level leaders dismissed at this time, that indeed the bureaucracy was exploiting the rank-and-file, and that after a period outside The Family he had chosen to return as an ordinary member.

Starting around 1974, chiefly on the island of Tenerife, Father David experimented with a radical new form of ministry that would build emotional channels of communication with outsiders by offering them erotic experiences up to and including sexual intercourse (Millikan 1994). After the RNR, this practice gradually spread to the far-flung homes of The Family,

Table 8.2: Roy Wallis's Description of the Reorganization Nationalization Revolution

Changes:
1. The effective disappearance of leadership between the local unit and the movement's prophet, i.e., from a tightly integrated authority structure to leadership via the mail.
2. The rapprochement of substantial sectors of the movement with a society and social institutions formerly regarded with intense hostility.
3. The effective disappearance of a communal life-style.
4. A differentiation in levels of commitment among those attached to the movement.

Causes:
1. The disappearance of the movement's original recruitment base.
2. The rising age of the members which created a desire to settle down, to have a more predictable and secure mode of life, particularly among those who had produced a substantial number of dependent children.
3. The difficulties occasioned by growing "anticult" feeling, particularly in the public response to the Jonestown deaths, which encouraged a less visible ministry.
4. The internal dynamic of the movement's view of history—the proximity of the endtime.

and Father David issued a number of letters that provided the ideological justification. Jesus was a fisher of men, and this new method of fishing employed flirting, so it came to be called "Flirty Fishing" or "FFing." Until its abolition in 1987, caused by concern over sexually transmitted diseases and the harsh reaction of prudish forces in the surrounding societies, The Family estimates that FFing reached a total of 1,010,171 people (mostly men) and gave 223,989 of them full physical love. Outside of the Judeo-Christian-Islamic tradition, sexuality has often taken religious forms (Davis 1937), and The Family was merely bringing the sexual revolution taking place in the larger society into the realm of religion.

The Jesus Movement of the 1960s and early 1970s bore many similarities with the wider tradition of American Protestant fundamentalism, but it tended to focus almost exclusively upon a personal relationship with Jesus and placed a greater emphasis upon the spiritual experiences resulting from involvement than upon the beliefs or practices. Richardson and Davis (1983) suggest that this experiential orientation is one of the reasons that many members of The Family were ready to engage in FFing. The counterculture of the 1960s, which gave birth to the Jesus Movement, also prepared members of The Family for this erotic ministry. "People in the counterculture wanted to love one another, and they did, often using sex as a vehicle of love's expression. And the COG [Children of God] have developed that willingness to express love through sexual behavior" (Richardson and Davis

223

1983:421). Quite apart from the love they received in FFing, flirty fishers were culturally prepared to respect the fish's need for sexual love. Similarly, sexual *sharing* was endorsed within a home where some adults might not have marriage partners to serve their sexual needs.

On top of the RNR and FFing, the Family underwent many other changes. It dropped the name Children of God in favor of Family of Love. Partly stimulated by the horrendous public reaction against novel religious groups touched off by the mass murder-suicide of the Peoples Temple in Guyana (Hall 1987; Chidester 1988), the Family instituted a Security Reorganization to protect its homes. A radio and audio cassette ministry called Music with Meaning began in 1980. The following year, greater emphasis was placed on fellowship meetings to bring members living in a region together. Soon after that, members began moving back into cooperative living settings, and the homes grew again. By 1989, the average home had 31.6 members, and some were far larger than that. The standards were strengthened for home membership (Disciples Only, or DO), leading to formal recognition of a new category of tithing but noncommunal member, the TRF Supporters or TS members. Throughout the 1980s and 1990s, ever-increasing emphasis was given to the education of children, which was done by creating schools within the homes, often sharing a school across two or more nearby homes.

From the very beginning, The Family had experienced minor acts of persecution from individuals or from the authorities of the nations in which they lived. But in the late 1980s, stimulated by an international "anti-cult" movement, they were the victims of several massive police assaults that took away their children and placed some of the adults in prison on charges of child abuse and morals violations. Approximately 600 children were seized by the authorities and examined for possible abuse. Eventually all were returned to their parents, and the charges of child abuse were dropped or thrown out of court. In addition a number of behavioral scientists have reported favorably on the mental health and abilities of second and now even third generation members of The Family (Palmer 1994; Lilliston and Shepherd 1994; Shepherd and Lilliston 1994).

In the early autumn of 1994, Father David passed away. Wallis (1987:89) predicted that the death of Father David would be an unusually acute crisis for the Family, throwing the group "into chaos and uncertainty." His reasoning was that Father David had been able to sustain his charismatic leadership, reviving it by announcing periodic revolutions, and that this prevented the development of stable institutional structures that could survive the demise of any individual leader. In this prediction, Wallis is simply applying traditional Weberian charisma theory to public information available to him about the group, and by the time of Father David's actual passing Wallis' assumptions were wrong.

In fact, over the years before his death, Father David had assembled a talented and highly experienced leadership around him. In the years after Wallis made his gloomy pronouncement, Father David's companion, Maria, had become an active participant in generating the torrent of Mo Letters that provided constant inspiration and guidance to the homes, and words explicitly attributed to her became important in these publications. In addition, rank-and-file members recognized that she was the leader of the various stages of the youth revolution taking place in The Family, first taking a major responsibility for creating the educational programs needed by the children, then acting as their spokesperson in negotiating their relationship with their elders as they grew into young adults. Invisible to most people was the emergence of Peter Amsterdam (a different person from the Peter mentioned above) and Gary as first lieutenants and then most recently as practically a triumvirate with Maria at the pinnacle of leadership. For those sociologists who like to see evidence of bureaucratization in religious movements, it is worth noting that Amsterdam has served for years as The Family's chief statistician in charge of collecting and analyzing quantitative data submitted regularly by the homes.

During Father David's last months on Earth, a team carefully evaluated all the rules of Family life and compiled a substantial document called *The Love Charter* that stated the responsibilities and rights of Family members, along with bureaucratic procedures for handling a variety of situations. *The Love Charter* goes into great detail about the conditions of membership, including procedures for sharing the financial obligations of a home and for allowing an individual to move from one to another. This document appears to rest on a considerable body of practical experience handling past problems, and it is evidence that The Family has a achieved a considerable degree of institutionalization.

At the same time, charisma has by no means been abandoned. Immediately after Father David's death, World Services, the communication center of the Family, reported that many members had achieved visions of him in Heaven and announced that henceforth Maria would be the chief channel for revelations. In this she is assisted by Amsterdam, and so far their pronouncements have been somewhat minor in nature, perhaps the most significant one merely reaffirming the policy against artificial birth control. As in the days of Father David, directives from the central leadership produce sudden changes that reassert charisma and reduce bureaucracy. One has been a directive to change the size of the homes, reducing the maximum to thirty-five members. Another action stripped away the middle level of management, those roughly 100 functionaries who stood in the hierarchy between the homes and the continental leaders. Whether the leadership structure becomes more bureaucratic, or remains charismatic, the real strength of The Family has been in the local communal homes, and both recruitment and commitment have come through the network of intimate relationships linking members with each other.

The Family's Musical Culture

For sociologists, among the most intriguing questions about The Family is how its far-flung homes manage to remain culturally unified, despite the tremendous distances between them and the diversity of nations in which they are situated. Insights into this issue come from examining a key example of Family culture, its music. From the very earliest days, when David Berg traveled the country with his singing children, music was a central medium of communication. As soon as the Children of God coalesced around Teens for Christ, recruits began writing new music which is now remembered as "the songs that made the revolution." Samples of some of their lyrics are given in Table 8.3.

Early songwriters are widely revered, including Singin' Sam (Aminadab), Jerry Paladino, Michael Fogarty (Martin), and Jonas. A quarter century after The Family's founding, a new generation of songwriters joined them. Gideon was four when his parents joined The Family, and not long afterward his dad began to teach him how to play the guitar. By the age of ten, he was singing with his dad as they went witnessing on the streets of Sweden, and today he is one of the musicians and composers who are creating the new generation's music. "I Will Go There" is his favorite song, among those he has written himself. "I got that song at a time when we were first starting to work here in the D.C. area. Financially we were having a lot of difficulties, and I was feeling a lot of pressure because I was in a position of leadership at the time, and it was a high-stress situation. So the message of the song is to pull out of that mundane, material plane and look to Jesus and find relief from that stress, to go to the Lord in prayer and find freedom. That's really the message, about looking forward to Heaven, where we won't have all the problems of this life." The word "there" in the title means not just the afterlife, however. "It also is referring to that place of peace, the Heaven in your heart, where you cast your burdens on the Lord and you let go of the stress and you no longer let it affect you, where you find peace in your soul."

"Another song I wrote which is probably much more popular with everyone else is the PER song. It's a very up-beat, exciting song, so it's a fun song to sing together. The initials for the PER are the Personal Encouragement Revolution. Part of it is encouraging the young people to take leadership. And another part of it is learning to have more love and affection in

Table 8.3: The Songs That Made the Revolution

California's Going Down

Yes, America, you're going down, because you've lost your foundation.
Don't you know Christ is the only firm ground in which to base a nation?
Many other nations have forgotten Him, and that is why they fell.
Yes, America, you better turn from your sin or you shall be turned into hell.

The Beavers

The beavers, the beavers, they climb around the logs.
America, you've destroyed your beaver population.
Jesus, Jesus, He died for you and me, He died for you and me.
America, you've destroyed your Jesus population.

The Crash

I can remember when I thought I had bad times, but the times they weren't so bad at all.
This time the 30's look like good times and 'cause the whole world is headed for a fall.
You say it might be time for revolution but I've seen a lot of puppets bought and sold.
I'm not trying to tell you there's no solution, but it's in your heart, you'll never buy it with
      your gold.
It won't be long till the money won't do you no good. You'll have to live on Love.

You Gotta Be a Baby

Suffer little children to come unto me for of such is the kingdom of Heaven.
Suffer little children to come unto me for of such is the kingdom of Heaven.
You gotta be a baby, you gotta be a baby. You gotta be a baby to go to Heaven.
You gotta be a baby, you gotta be a baby. You gotta be a baby to go to Heaven.

Mountain Man

Something deep inside of me kept me moving endlessly.
I could never really be free as a valley man.
I traveled 'round, I tried to be somebody else, but never me.
But then Jesus set me free, and now I'm a Mountain Man.
Mountain Man, Mountain Man,
We're going to walk hand in hand way up here where the air is fresh and clean.
Mountain Man, Mountain Man,
I'm going to win every soul that I can.
I'm just a proud, unworthy, but happy Mountain Man.

The Revolutionary Children of God

The revolutionary children of God have been around a long time, from Abel to the
      prophets,
the revolutionary children of God have been around a long time, from Abel to the
      prophets.
Against the rotten, decadent, decrepit, hypocritical, self-righteous, inflexible, affluent,
self-satisfied, proud, stubborn, disobedient, blind, bloodthirsty, godless, dead selfish,
churchy, unchangeable, older generation of their day.

---

our homes. The words of the song are: 'Jesus will never forsake you, to Heaven will take you!' " Gideon says he usually gets a melody first, then he writes words to fit the impression he has in connection with the melody. Then the words are submitted to a central review counsel at The Family's media center, Creations. "They check the words and see how they may be changed that will make them more relatable to The Family as a whole, or more usable as a witnessing song or for a certain project. They see the whole globe, because The Family is in fifty different countries with all kinds of different cultures, and what may be acceptable in one country may not be acceptable in another country." Gideon says that his own lyrics have frequently been improved artistically through this communal process of criticism.

Music links the far-flung Family homes, and songs written in one place can travel either via cassette tapes or in the minds of traveling musicians. Gideon judges that a song spreads quickest on tapes that are distributed to many homes, and that the movement of musicians from home to home is slow enough that only the oldest songs have really had time to spread in this way. Music videos are produced at The Family's studio in Japan, and all around the world young members of The Family will learn the songs and the dance moves by watching and imitating these tapes. Gideon reports that a large body of excellent Spanish-language and Portuguese-language songs exists among the Latin American homes, and that Australian homes have produced excellent songs as well, but few of them have been heard by members from other parts of the world, unless they actually traveled through these regions.

Local homes can create their own music centers, as the Washington, D.C. home has done. This home has taken on a special mission to communicate to receptive leaders outside The Family, and two of the senior members, Marc and Claire, frequently attend conferences of religious scholars and provide information concerning religious freedom issues to Congress. Fourteen younger members have created the Show Troupe, including two with special talents brought for this purpose from homes on the other side of the world. It has sung in the White House and the Special Olympics, and performed song and dance in malls, hotels, and other locations around the nation's capital. In the basement of their home, Daniel, John, Gideon and other young people have created a recording studio, by soundproofing a tiny room. They started with an ordinary four-track recorder, then requested support from the central leadership of World Services, who gave them a grant to get some more serious equipment: an eight-channel recorder, a couple of synthesizers, a drum machine, and one good microphone.

In the same home, Joy and Jonathan have been compiling lyrics and chord progressions for a grand Family songbook that already contains

Table 8.4: Family Songs Popular in 1995

"The PER"

Lonely brothers and sisters around
Need a lot of love and affection.
So let the hugs and kisses abound
With the Encouragement Revolution.
Your words can lift up or knock down,
It's up to your decision.
So listen to the uplifting sound,
And keep up the Heavenly vision.
Jesus will never forsake you, to Heaven He'll take you and He'll make you a son of
    God.
You'll be purring like a kitten, so forget about quitting,
'Cause we're getting all together now on the job.

Get It Together

We won't give up, you know we'll never give in,
We're not walking by sight, we're just trusting in Him,
If you see your brother fall, pick him up and start all over again.
We've got to get it together, step down off of your pride,
We've got to get it together, let Jesus know we're alive

We'll Still Have Jesus

Just one touch from His loving hands,
Is more than enough, and gives me strength to stand.
Ooo oo oo ooo!
Just one glimpse of His tender face
Gives me the grace and helps me run the race.
Ooo oo oo ooo!
We'll still have Jesus, when all else fails,
His loving hands will mend our sails,
Ooo oo oo ooo!
We'll sail out again, on raging seas, knowing that Jesus clearly sees the waves ahead!

Just Fall in Love with Jesus

Just fall in love with Jesus,
He'll take you as you are.
He's altogether lovely,
The bright and morning star.
He never will forsake you;
He'll save you from your sin,
And take you Home to Heaven.
Just fall in love with Him.

(continued)

Table 8.4: (continued)

"Home of Hearts"

Giving your heart to another is making it a home,
Where the heart can rest in safety with no more need to roam,
It's making the best from nothing, two independent souls
Yield to the Holy Spirit and make a three-fold chord.
Building a home of hearts, my love,
Is what we've got to do,
Making a peaceful haven, to shelter others too,
Bearing each other's burdens, and sharing the heavy load,
Yoked to the Master's service, and walk a single road.

1,700 items but is not yet finished. Excerpts from the lyrics of five of these, beginning with Gideon's "The PER," are given in Table 8.4. Although the endtime remains very present in people's minds, and the young people enjoy hearing the historic music of their elders, the most popular songs focus on their life together and their abiding relationship with Jesus.

Three of the fifteen songs on The Family's 1992 video, *New Worlds to Discover*, tell the story of the endtime, with powerful rock music, flashing colored lights, and exuberant performers. "We're living in the time of the end!" shouts Gideon, singing the prophecies of Daniel 12:4, "many shall run to and fro, and knowledge shall be increased." This passage foretells the revolutions of transportation and communication wrought by science in the twentieth century. Dressed black below the waist, with bands of black, blue, red, and yellow above, the dancers move violently, leaping and striking at each other, spinning in confusion, and bowing in agony. Then the dancers begin to march like robots, jerking in their steps yet driven forcefully, their arms moving like hinged rods of metal, and their faces frozen. Miguel sings, "In a vision of the future, I saw in a vivid dream that the hour is coming when men will become machines. A new one-world order will rise and then demand that all the world's people receive the scientific brand." In the background, a quartet of women urges, "Don't sell your soul." Finally, the dancers are transformed, their Antichrist uniforms replaced by casual slacks, dresses and colorful shirts, looking like clean-cut American youth of the 1950s. Their faces lit by gleaming smiles, they prance vigorously like horses leaping high in the air, as Jennifer sings of the salvation invasion of Jesus and his celestial cavalry. "No earthly battalions can stop these stallions as they descend from above. No nuclear weapon directed at heaven can stop this great army of love. We'll ride across the sky! On white horses we're going to fly!"

Language

Religious language is a well-recognized field of linguistics (Sawyer 1994; Soskice 1994). Several major world religions keep alive otherwise dead ancient languages, such as Latin and Sanskrit. In contrast, new religious movements almost invariably develop novel terminology of their own (Bainbridge 1994b). In some cases, the movement develops a very large lexicon of distinctive words and phrases and may even publish its own dictionary (Horner and Ridolphi 1972; Hubbard 1975). The Family has produced a moderate number of new terms, generating them by a variety of mechanisms, so it is a good example for linguistic analysis of new religious movements. This section is based on interviews with leaders, observation of speech in gatherings, and samples of the literature including *The Love Charter* which includes definitions of some terms relating to formal rules and the movement's organizational structure.

A standard mechanism by which many languages construct new terms is by stringing a set of familiar words in a row. A "church-bell fund" is a collection of money to buy or maintain a bell belonging to a church, probably the bell or bells hanging in a "bell tower" and used to announce a "church service" or the time of day. Each of these three terms ("church-bell fund," "bell tower," "church service") is a noun phrase. When a word is used often, people may abbreviate it to save time and effort. But there is a limited number of possible short combinations of letters and sounds. Also, words that are very similar may easily be confused with each other. Therefore, there are good reasons to keep many words rather long, most reasonably those not used often. The Family has followed standard English practice in coining noun phrases and then shortening them.

Much of the work of Family members consists of distributing printed literature. Thus, they abbreviated "literature" to "lit" and "publications" to "pubs." They refer to their public proselytizing as "witnessing," and they put "lit" and "witnessing" together to form the compound word "litnessing," meaning public evangelization through distributing literature. A common method for abbreviating a phrase is to take just the initial letters of key words. Thus, in Family talk, "YA" means Young Adult and is pronounced as two syllables, "wye ay" not "yah."

When a string of initials is pronounced as a word which the letters spell, then we have an acronym. A Family member aged twelve through thirteen is called a "JETT" (pronounced "jet") from Junior End Time Teen. A "CRO" (pronounced "crow") is a "Continental Reports Officer," currently the one layer of administrators between World Services and the individual homes. Tithing members in good standing who live outside communal homes are called "TRF Supporters" (pronounced "turf") because they regularly submit a Tithers' Report Form. These words happen to sound the same as common English words (that is they are homonyms with "jet," "crow," and "turf") but the acronyms do not carry any of the meanings of these words for members of the Family. "PER" ("the Personal Encouragement Revolution") is pronounced "purr," and Gideon's song about the PER puns "purring like a kitten," quoted in Table 8.4.

"TRF Supporter" is also an example of the ways in which figures of speech can help produce new language. Here a person (the supporter) is identified by something associated with a person in that category (the report form). This is a case of metonymy, using the name of one thing for that of another with which it is associated. In some cases, The Family employs metonymy to change the meaning of an ordinary term. A "teamwork" is a team, such as the elected committee that runs a home, who cooperate to get a job done. In ordinary English, "teamwork" refers to the work itself or to a team-oriented philosophy of work, but for The Family it identifies the group that does this work and that follows the philosophy. Each member of a teamwork is called a "teamworker."

Often the novel usage of a word is sufficiently close to the common one that its meaning is immediately obvious. Members of the Family use the word "sample," where others might say "example," when referring to a member representing or channeling God's love. *The Love Charter* contains these instances: "Help us, Lord, to be a good sample of You and Your Love." "We want to be a sample of His Love to others." "Lord, if we're not taking proper care and education of our children, we're not a very good sample or example to others." "You must be a sample, not only a sermon."

People often try to avoid a particular common word because of its negative connotations, and they employ a euphemism instead. Members of the Family must strive to overcome their personal weaknesses, but they avoid accusing the person by euphemistically calling such a problem an "NWO," which stands for "Needs Work On." At other times, a strong connotation is needed. A new commune member needs to remain very conscious of his or her neophyte status, for example, and therefore is called a "babe." The term "babe" comes from the simile, "A new member is like a baby," expressed in the song, "You Gotta Be a Baby," quoted in Table 8.3.

A simile is a figure of speech asserting that two different things are really similar. Of course, it is a matter of opinion how different or similar two things are, especially in language and literature where the precision of scientific measurement is difficult to apply. Consider the Family's use of the word "tool." *The Love Charter* says, "Mass Distribution Outreach Tools" are "publications, either written, audio (cassette or CD), or video, intended for distribution to the general public." Elsewhere, it says, "If anyone wishes to locally create a tool, whether it be a pub, video, audio tape, CD, etc., which will be used for GP mass distribution, they must receive approval from World Services before doing so." Thus, tools are the literature and other communication media distributed to the "general public" ("GP"), often in return for donations. They are tools in the sense that they are the instruments by which witnessers spread the message of The Family and obtain financial support. Thus, the term seems based on a simile: "Publications are like tools." But one could equally well argue that they really are tools, and the term comes merely from emphasizing the instrumental aspect of the publications.

Related to tools is the metaphor of "seed corn." *The Love Charter* defines this as the "fixed amount of money (the cost of each tool) which you should set aside from the gifts you receive when you distribute tools, to use to purchase new tools." That is, if a witnessing team distributes literature that cost $100 to obtain, it must set aside $100 from the proceeds to buy more literature. This money is like the fraction of an agricultural grain crop that must be set aside at harvest time as seed for the next year's planting. A comparable metaphor produced the term "common pot," which refers to a financial account into which two or more individual homes put some money for collective needs or projects.

Some similes come from physical imagery. A "blob," for example, is an overly large communal home, currently any home with more than thirty-five members. Other similes draw a parallel between The Family and the early Christian communes described in Acts or in popular histories of the church. Early Christians are reputed to have hidden from persecution in the catacombs beneath the city of Rome. With this image in mind, the Family uses the term "catacomber" to refer to members who are unable to join or form communal homes, due to special circumstances such as being too young or being in military service.

A mysterious biblical term, found in Habakkuk and Psalms, is *selah*, which the Family pronounces "say-lah." Conventional dictionaries somewhat uncertainly suggest that this might be an exclamation (Wow!), or a liturgical or musical instruction, perhaps telling the reader to raise his voice or to pause. The Family understands this biblical word to be an instruction to pause and reflect, as it were to take special care or to realize that something has a hidden meaning. Thus *selah* is the term applied to information and materials that must be handled with extra care so that they do not fall into the hands of people who would misuse or misunderstand them. *The Love Charter* emphasizes, "Selah trash is to be burned safely or shredded regularly, recommended daily. . . . Be very sure that no confidential materials or papers or identifying envelopes, etc., bearing names, addresses, or other selah information are ever placed in trash containers which are emptied by the System! Burn or destroy these separately in your own wood stove or fireplace." An entire Family home can be selah if it is forced to keep its existence secret and its members are prevented from witnessing, as might be the case in a "sensitive country," that is, a nation where political or religious conditions cause great danger. Possession of special language marks a group as a subculture, and the word selah evokes the tension between The Family and the surrounding sociocultural environment.

Enemies and Allies

In July 1971, Ted Patrick's fourteen-year-old son, Michael, came into contact with the Children of God on Mission Beach in San Diego, and the elder Patrick soon discovered that a number of parents were concerned about their own children who had gone so far as to join the group. By August he had created an organization called "FreeCOG" ("Free the Children of God") to pay him to bring young people out of the group by force if necessary. Patrick told a group of parents, "We have to be willing to do whatever is necessary to rescue your children. The cult operates illegally under legal sanctions. We have to do the same thing. There's no other way to fight them. Hopefully, in the long run, as a result of what we're doing, the laws will be changed. Until then, we do what we have to do" (Patrick and Dulack 1976:64–65; cf. Charity Frauds Bureau 1974).

As he himself described them, Ted Patrick's methods involved bodily abduction of the children from the communes they were living in. Supposedly these children were all under-age, but this claim is open to dispute, and Patrick's methods did not begin with attempts to get the children through the legal system. Patrick claimed these members of the Children of God had been "programmed" by the religious group, essentially turned into zombies by sleep deprivation and hypnotism, and thus lacked free will. Therefore, there was no need to pay attention to what they said they wanted. Instead, they would be physically seized, taken a distance from the commune, placed under confinement, and subjected to intense badgering which Patrick called "deprogramming."

Patrick's first attempt to seize a member of the Children of God failed, when the private detective his client had hired refused to enter the commune's property without the owner's permission. In the second attempt, nine "trusted helpers" were used instead of licensed detectives, and they successfully seized a woman member with the help of her mother. The woman was taken across state lines against her will, confined to a motel room, subjected to two days of biblical argument from Patrick, and made to "snap." This was Patrick's first deprogramming success, and it led to many more requests for similar help from distraught parents. When Patrick published a book about his exploits five years later (Patrick and Dulack 1976), he included a sequence of photographs showing another member of the Children of God being seized and deprogrammed during three-and-a-half days of enforced confinement.

Patrick asserted that he did not "brainwash" his subjects, using this popular term derived from the Chinese practice of forcible indoctrination, but proponents of deprogramming frequently asserted that the subjects had been brainwashed by the group from which they were rescued. As soon as deprogramming became widely publicized, social and behavioral scientists began criticizing its scientific premises as well as its ethical propriety. Bromley and Shupe (1981:211) observe, "The centerpiece of the anticultists' allegations is that cults brainwash their members through some combination of drugging, hypnosis, self-hypnosis, chanting or lecturing, and deprivation of food, sleep, and freedom of thought. If this argument were true, the new religions would not have such a sorry recruitment record, the defection rate among those who do join would not be as high as it is, individual members could not be counted upon to work with the zeal they do, and ex-members would not be able to recall in such exquisite detail how they were brainwashed. Social scientists have largely repudiated the concept of brainwashing as the anticultists have used it. Certainly it is possible to break people down physically and psychologically through coercive techniques. But there is no evidence that people so abused will show the kind of positive motivation and commitment that converts to the new religions manifest."

There are at least seven major flaws with the *programming* or *brainwashing* perspective. First, it is not clear that effective non-biological techniques for controlling a person's mind exist at all, and the chief classic case of alleged *brainwashing* of American prisoners in the Korean War resulted in few if any successes (Schein et al. 1961). Second, a very high proportion of people who attend some activities at new religious movements fail to join (Barker 1984). Third, substantial numbers of long-term members of new religious movements leave of their own volition (Bainbridge 1982, 1984a; Wright 1983). Fourth, many researchers have carried out long-term observational research inside a variety of new religious movements, including all those frequently accused of brainwashing, and their reports do not fit the brainwashing model (Bainbridge 1978; Taylor 1983). Fifth, sociologists have developed some highly plausible theoretical models of how people join new religious movements, and they all combine several factors, notably the motivations of the individual and the structure of social relations around the individual (see Chapter 6), so there seems no need for the brainwashing hypothesis. Sixth, the concept of brainwashing seems designed as a rhetoric to discredit new religious movements and to excuse the individual of any responsibility for joining them. Thus it has the effect of legitimating action against the group or individual that in any other context would be considered a violation of civil rights (Bromley 1983; Kelley 1983). Seventh, the brainwashing rhetoric is "anticollectivistic and antitotalistic" (Richardson and Kilbourne 1983), assuming that a mentally healthy person must be autonomous and failing to recognize the importance of religion and community in human society (Hargrove 1983).

Legal difficulties soon forced Patrick out of the deprogramming business, but from this dramatic beginning a widespread movement arose to combat novel religions, drawing much of its energy from the concerns of parents of converts, generally called the "anti-cult movement" ("ACM"). The Children of God had the unpleasant distinction of being the very first group targeted by the ACM (Shupe and Bromley 1980:88). In the United States a pair of related organizations currently stand at the center of this movement, the Cult Awareness Network (CAN), and the American Family Foundation (Langone 1993:24). Spokespersons for CAN deny that coercion is currently employed to deal with members of religious movements, and they do not describe what they do as deprogramming. Clearly, a major function of CAN and similar organizations around the world is to identify "cults" to the authorities and urge actions against them.

The Family believes that agitation against them by the worldwide anti-cult movement has triggered the seizures of more than 600 Family children that occurred in the early 1990s in France, Spain, Australia, and Argentina. Family member Claire Borowick (1994) has described vividly the brutality of the raids on Argentina communes that took place in the rainy night of September 1, 1993. For three-and-a-half months, she was imprisoned under horrible conditions, as her son was confined to a rotting institution for juveniles with no schooling, wretched lack of sanitation, and the expressed threat that his mother would never be released. In some of these seizures, parents were not allowed to see their small children for extended periods, and the children were subjected to intrusive physical and psychological examinations with little attention to their privacy or concern about the impact that such assaults would have upon them.

Even under conditions The Family considered to be extreme persecution, as in Argentina in 1993, it has enjoyed the support of friends, some of them influential. Many ordinary people have offered help whenever persecution has struck, but two categories deserve analysis, attorneys and scholars. The Family draws an analogy with Gamaliel, the doctor of the law who defends the apostles from being slain in Acts 5:34–40. So far as we know, he never became a Christian, but he was knowledgeable about new religious movements, and without his stalwart defense, the Christian religion might never have survived. Attorneys and judges were ultimately able to get most legal charges against The Family dismissed. Scholars and social scientists of religion have frequently refuted brainwashing and child-abuse claims when their research indicated they were false (Lewis and Melton 1994).

Recently, The Family has begun to make common cause with other novel religious movements that face similar challenges in fending off the ACM and dealing with other practical problems. It has been difficult for The Family, as it has been for scholars of religion, to know what to make of radical religious movements like the Branch Davidians and Aum Shinrikyo that have come into violent conflict with the governments of the societies surrounding them. During the FBI siege, Father David prayed to the Lord to deliver the Branch Davidians from harm. He said The Family should not stockpile weapons, as the Davidians had done, but the government assault showed that in the Last Days the forces of the Antichrist would not hesitate to kill anyone who resisted them. The mass media had lied so often about The Family, Father David observed, that it was easy to believe they were lying about the Branch Davidians, as well. Two years later, when the nerve gas attack on the Tokyo subway was attributed to Aum Shinrikyo, Family leaders in Japan wrote their brethren around the world with agonized concern that the episode might be a case of religious persecution, but they wisely cautioned against publicly supporting Aum Shinrikyo until more facts were known.

With their different backgrounds and skills, novel religious movements often have valuable practical experience to share with each other, and on occasion they can join together for a common effort. During the hearings on Waco held by the U.S. House of Representatives in July, 1995, emissaries from The Family, Scientology, the Unification Church, and the scholars of new religions met to plan a response to the poor coverage of deeper religious issues in the hearings. The Family has communicated extensively with unconventional Protestant groups on such important practical issues as home schooling of children and how to deal with state licensing of religious organizations. Unlike the members of the National Council of Churches, these novel groups do not share roughly the same set of religious beliefs and practices. But their common situation in society draws them together and may eventually create a new kind of organization, call it the World Council of Novel Religious Movements.

Conclusion: Challenging the System

A year after the death of David Brandt Berg, The Family launched a well-designed information service on the World Wide Web, thus making its message available to every high-tech member of the system. The introduction is a photo tour of The Family, showing members around the world, looking healthy, happy, and friendly. A set of detailed policy statements begins with

237

a thirteen-part exposition of The Family's "Christ-Centered Bible-Based Education." The titles of several of these essays explain why The Family educates its children within the homes and uses a carefully designed curriculum: "Our children have a right to be brought up in the faith in which they were born. The Bible is central to our children's education. . . . Commitment to God is not an option but a commandment. The highest form of training that we can give our children is to train them for a life of service to God. A God-centered education requires a godly, Word-centered learning environment, separate from unbelievers. Secular educational objectives are often contrary to our fundamental beliefs, values and goals. Our children receive a scholastic education in addition to their spiritual training. . . . Unique learning opportunities are available to our children." Other policy statements concern The Family's origins, its opposition to physical violence, the key elements of its faith, and the home life of its children.

Referring to the Family of Love era, the Web service says, "In the latter part of the '70s and early '80s, Father David, responding in part to the sexual liberality of that time period, presented the possibility of trying out a more personal and intimate form of witnessing which became known as 'Flirty Fishing' or 'FFing.' In his Letters at that time, he offered the challenging proposal that since 'God is Love' (1 John 4:8), and His Son, Jesus, is the physical manifestation and embodiment of God's Love for humanity, then we as Christian recipients of that Love are in turn responsible to be living samples to others of God's great all-encompassing Love. Taking the Apostle Paul's writings literally, that saved Christians are 'dead to the Law [of Moses]' (Romans 7:4), through faith in Jesus, Father David arrived at the rather shocking conclusion that Christians were therefore free through God's grace to go to great lengths to show the Love of God to others, even as far as meeting their sexual needs." The Web user who clicks on the two biblical citations will get the chapters of the Bible that contain them, thus linking The Family's doctrine through advanced materialistic technology to ancient religious traditions.

Among contemporary Western religious movements, the Family is almost unique in its sacralization of sexuality. But, as the Web pages indicate, this cultural innovation is in great measure a combination of the sensual ideals of post-1960s secular America combined with the sublime passion that can be found in many passages of the Bible. At present, The Family prohibits sexual relations with persons outside a member's commune, and some of the young adults are reluctant to engage in the sexual sharing that helps to bind the older members together. If The Family can overcome the twin threats of sexually transmitted diseases and public condemnation, it may be able to teach the surrounding society new ways of integrating sexual communication into lives of holiness.

The Web service is also quite explicit about the endtime, explaining the doctrine in essays and illustrating it in a series of brilliantly colored poster pictures. One of these, titled "Watch out for 666!" is divided into three parts. At the top, guards stand over a multitude of suppliants who bow before the Great Beast, a massive robot and supercomputer that has taken power over the entire world. In the lower left, a young man is having a computer chip inserted in his forehead, and in the lower right, a young woman buys groceries by placing her hand, which contains a similar chip, over a scanning device. The computer chip is the "mark of the beast" described in Revelation 13:16–17: "And he causeth all, both small and great, rich and poor, free and bond, to receive a mark in their right hand, or in their foreheads. And that no man may buy or sell, save he that had the mark, or the name of the beast, or the number of his name." In these computer-transmitted images, The Family links the threat and the promise of advanced technology to age-old prophecies.

It may seem ironic that a high-tension religious group which believes Satan will briefly rule the world through the medium of a universal computer system employs just such a system to transmit its message. Yet, as in its sacralization of sexuality, by adopting advanced communication technology The Family believes it can turn the tools of the satanic System to the purposes of God. Almost all Family homes around the world are hidden, in that they are not listed in the phone book, and only their friends can easily find them. But anyone can make contact by phoning 1-800-4-A-FAMIL[Y] (1-800-423-2645) or by sending an e-mail message to family@thefamily.org. Some homes have recently gotten on Internet, but for years they have been communicating by fax and modem. Their music has been broadcast on radio and television in many countries, and among the witnessing tools are audio cassettes, video cassettes, and compact laser disks. When Family member Regina comes to my house to babysit my daughters, she brings her laptop computer. For more than three-quarters of a century, sociologists have suspected that human history was the plaything of technological development (Ogburn 1922), but no one has figured out how to ensure that technology will be the servant of humanity rather than its master. By basing its use of technology in powerful religious communities, The Family offers the world one model of how this might be accomplished.

The culture of The Family is American secular culture reborn. Except possibly for the striking wholesomeness of its performers, the songs might be counterculture music of the 1960s, laced with white folk music and pop from earlier decades. Born in a dramatic exodus from the system, The Family is nonetheless part of a larger cultural system, that contains them both. Perhaps more directly than any other group, The Family forces Christianity to confront the technological and sexual realities of modern society. The

239

Family has shown a remarkable capacity to survive persecution and diaspora. The question now is whether the Family can resist the temptation to compromise with the surrounding sociocultural environment. Some social scientists and religious scholars have advised it to do so. But to have a significant impact on the religious life of the future, the Family must maintain relatively high tension, perhaps for several generations, while growing in membership and spreading its message around the world.

9

The Process Church of the Final Judgement

On the fringes of Western religion, a very large number of tiny groups have come into existence, most of them unnoticed by scholars, that seek to establish novel religious traditions. Some cloak their essentially supernatural concerns in the disguise of psychotherapy, whereas others masquerade as fraternal or cultural organizations. A couple of hundred such groups have incorporated as religions and thus appear in Melton's (1993) great encyclopedia. And when the millenarian Solar Temple ended in a fiery murder-suicide in Canada and Switzerland, a European scholar of new religious movements estimated that 100 groups existed in its narrow Neo-Templar tradition alone (Introvigne 1994). We have no exact censuses, but the numbers of individuals involved must be small, perhaps as few as 50,000 in the United States. However, these groups are important because their very high levels of cultural change afford scholars the opportunity to observe religious innovation as it occurs, and out of the myriad such groups a handful may develop highly effective new approaches to the sacred and grow into substantial denominations. Here we will examine the Process Church of the Final Judgement (Bainbridge 1978; 1991), one of the more creative small religious movements, to understand better the sociocultural dynamics of religious innovation.

An Encounter with Jehovah

Thirty people sat in a circle, meditating in a Bahama garden, one warm evening in July 1966. They were Processeans, remarkably creative young English adults who had developed a novel kind of psychotherapy that had impelled them on a quest for a door out of this world to a superhuman level of existence. Among them and deeply immersed in the same intense spiritual experiences were their therapists, Robert and Mary Ann de Grimston. When the newspapers had begun to pry, and audiences heckled their harangues, they had decided London was a miasma and had departed to find a tropical island paradise where they could found a new civilization. For a time they took ordinary jobs in Nassau, a couple of them helping to design a police station, but they knew they had to move on if they were to escape the swamp of mundane reality. And so they meditated, waiting for a sign.

Their meditation circle was like a magnetic compass, and the subconscious influences turned the arrow of their attention first this direction then that. For a time it pointed south toward Caracas, Venezuela, but then it turned decisively west toward Mexico City. When they reached the Mexican capital some days later it was clear that this was not their destination, and they meditated onward following signs and portents. Soon they were in Sisal, a little fishing village on the north coast of the Yucatán not far from Merida, meditating in a mood of some desperation. Visions floated into their minds. They told each other what they saw, assembling the fragmented images like the pieces of a jigsaw puzzle. One saw ruins near the sea. Others mentally picked up a verdant location, like an oasis. A man with a stick and a dog would mark the spot, said another. They should walk along the beach, but they were not sure whether to go east or west. The daughter of Michael Ventris, an architect who was famous for deciphering the Linear B ancient Greek script, felt west was the right direction. Everyone else disagreed.

Early the next morning, they began walking eastward beside the Caribbean, singing. As the heat rose, their spirits sank. Finally late in the afternoon they were falling into despair when they rounded a point of land, encountered a man with a stick and a dog, and rushed past him into exactly the marvelous place their visions had foretold. It was a ruined coconut plantation, abandoned and overgrown. All around them were palm trees bursting with coconuts. There was a reasonably intact house with a tile roof, and some other buildings in greater states of disrepair. They asked what the name of the place was, and had some difficulty understanding what the local people told them. Perhaps it was the Place of the Little She-Rabbit. Perhaps it was The End or Terminus. In any case, the locals called it something like "Xtul," a Mayan word pronounced "schtool." In future song and story, Xtul would be the Eden of Process legends:

> Come to Xtul, cries the voice of angels in the wind.
> Come to Xtul, where the wonders of this world begin.
> For you the glory of Xtul!
> For you the glory of Xtul!

They wrote to the owner in Mexico City, explaining how they had found Xtul and asking to rent the place. He responded, "I understand completely that you were led to my property by 'voices.' There is, however, one thing that slightly worries me. What if the voices tell you not to pay the rent?" Money reassured the owner, and the wanderers settled in, sleeping in hammocks or on straw mats, most of them out of doors. They ate coconuts plucked off the trees, prickly pear cactus that was delicious but had to be eaten carefully to avoid a tongue full of prickles, fish fresh out of the water, and beans they bought in the village. Kenneth, an Australian with an advanced degree in fluid dynamics, rigged up a water supply.

Kenneth was fascinated by the "iguanas, like prehistoric monsters in miniature. They would lie in the sun all day. And then when our dogs got near them, they would look around, and with their legs out sideways they would run off as fast as they could, and get up a tree before the dogs could get to them. We had wild horses as well, grey and white and black and tan, grazing, nomadic, and free. And pelicans would fly overhead in formation, going who knows where on some migration. We also had snakes, some big ones something like a boa. We had vipers in the water and coral snakes, pink and writhing in the grass. Scorpions—very scary—but nobody ever got hurt, fortunately. Jumping spiders as well, and fish, lots of fish. They used to jump around while we swam in the waters of the Gulf. Beautiful place! One day, I remember the birds danced outside the window while we watched them. It was a real magic. A place called Xtul."

Gradually, their mysticism, aesthetics, and psychotherapy drew them into religion. Robert had been writing essays on human psychology called "Logics," finishing one on ambivalence titled "Intention and Counter-Intention" while in Nassau. Now in discussions with the others he developed a series of seven *Xtul Dialogues* that began to speak of God. The last of these states that the factor preventing full success in their psychotherapeutic explorations was "ignorance of all things spiritual." They had been trying to vanquish the subconscious, because it consisted of debilitating compulsions and contradictions, but now he realized, "the subconscious is there to replace GOD, and is therefore in competition with GOD. . . . It is so much weaker basically than GOD that it must build a positive arsenal of weapons and a fortress of barriers and barricades, even to stay in the game." Thus, successful psychotherapy would open a gateway to divinity.

For most Processeans, however, it was not intellectual speculation that brought them to God, but the direct, powerful sensation of being immersed in nature. They lived well off the land, without benefit of insurance policies, flush toilets, or electric toasters. They could sleep comfortably on the beach, the stars spread out above them and their dreams expanding across the universe. In this fresh environment, they felt that they had achieved the goal of their wanderings, radical transformation of themselves. Some began adopting new names, often selected from the Bible, like Dominic and Micah. In this Garden of Eden, they were being born again.

About a month after their arrival, a British consul named Macmillan unexpectedly showed up at Xtul, warning them a terrible hurricane was brewing and urging them to come with him to safety in Merida. They refused, and immediately started preparing for the storm. They took the tiles from the roof of the main house, so the wind would not rip them off, and the five architects in the group analyzed how best to make a shelter for themselves. One of the ruined buildings consisted of masonry walls more than a foot thick, and the fact that it lacked a roof meant there would be nothing to fall on their heads. It had seemed like a monastery to them, and now they made it into their fortress. The architects constructed a sturdy shelter by leaning old doors against the inside of the north wall and bracing them with beams and stone blocks. When the sky darkened, they crawled inside, huddling together in excited anticipation.

The churning sea dug away the beach just a few yards from them, and the salt spray mingled with rain as the wind blew ever faster. A wing of the main house disintegrated, and its boards tumbled away like leaves in the breeze. Horrified, the Processeans watched the massive masonry walls of the monastery bend as if they had been made of bread, and the south wall suddenly crashed inward. Realizing that the north wall might tumble down and kill them in an instant, they scrambled outside directly into the full force of the hurricane. Palm branches lashed at them as they ran, and coconuts shot through the air like cannonballs. The day sky was dark as night, and the wind gusted far above a hundred miles an hour. Each person vainly sought shelter under a tree, one was nearly killed by a heavy branch that fell inches away, and they wrapped soaking wet blankets around themselves to cut the terrible chill. For two whole days they experienced the wild wrath of the hurricane completely unprotected. Nearly three hundred people were killed by that storm, but all the Processeans survived despite their unimaginable suffering.

Mary Ann knew that they had experienced both aspects of Jehovah, the God of nature, both creation and destruction. She had always felt a special bond with the ancient Hebrews, and when she teamed up with Robert she made him wear a ring shaped in a star of David, even though the points cut into his finger. Now she interpreted their experiences in biblical terms. Before the hurricane they had discovered the bounty of nature, thus understanding the Garden of Eden for the first time. Now they had felt the wrath of Jehovah, who could destroy any living thing in an instant.

Robert was uncomfortable with Mary Ann's image of God, so stern and demanding like she was herself. The second Xtul Dialogue said, "There are many Gods, but only One True GOD who embodies all of them. . . . Jehovah for example is the Knowledge of the Physical Universe." Listening to Joshua sing Process songs, he began thinking about an alternative God of love and acceptance he would later call Lucifer. In retrospect the Processeans would realize, "Xtul was the place where we met God face to face. It was the experience that led to the establishment of The Church. In terms of commitment, it was the point of no return where each one of us, plucked by fate out of a workaday world, found that we had a God-vocation."

Within four years, The Process would have chapters in London, Toronto, Boston, Chicago and New Orleans. Wearing stunning cloaked uniforms, Processeans stormed through North America and Western Europe, spreading a doctrine that the universe had been created when God split into four competing gods: Jehovah, Lucifer, Christ, and Satan. Humanity was like a shattered mirror, they said, with each splinter of personality reflecting one god or another. Now, the great Game of the Gods was concluding, and the world was approaching an end and a new beginning. Jehovah and Lucifer, who between them had fought the conflict of the mind, were joined in union. At the final reckoning, the Processean Sabbath Assembly announced, "Through Love, Christ and Satan have destroyed their enmity and come together for the End, Christ to judge, Satan to execute the judgement. . . . Christ and Satan joined, the Lamb and the Goat, pure Love descended from the pinnacle of Heaven, united with pure Hatred raised from the depths of Hell . . . . The End is now. The New Beginning is to come."

Roots in an Earlier Movement

Robert and Mary Ann developed a partnership and a powerful emotional relationship around 1960 while both were in training to become therapist-clergy at the London branch of a movement that has elements of both psychotherapy and religion. The group still exists, and I think it would not enjoy being linked to The Process, so I will not reveal its name or many of its characteristics here. Let us call the founder of this movement Gordon Rogers. Because a chief aim of this chapter is to chart the ways that new religions arise on the basis of existing beliefs and practices, we will suggest a few possible sources of some aspects of Rogers's movement and give their correct names. However the movement itself may be quite right when it asserts that the chief source is Rogers's own research discoveries. The root idea is that people would naturally have the powers and wisdom of gods if these qualities had not been damaged or stolen during periods of unconsciousness, perhaps including the intermissions between their several past lives. The right spiritual technology, consisting largely of therapeutic psychological exercises, can restore the person.

Rogers acknowledged intellectual debts to the creators of two earlier mental sciences (or pseudosciences, if you prefer), Sigmund Freud (Freud 1924; Brown 1967) and Alfred Korzybski (1948, 1950; Gardner 1957; Bainbridge 1994a), although he also argued that these men had missed key insights. Like Freud's psychoanalysis, Rogers's techniques employed verbal interactions between a client and a highly trained therapist. Like Korzybski's general semantics, they aimed to take a normal person up to superior levels of functioning. Rogers had personal connections to both the psychoanalytic and semantic movements. He had learned about psychoanalysis from a mysterious naval doctor nicknamed "Snake" who always wore a kelly green scarf decorated with a snake pin, a remarkable adventurer who had spent nearly two years as a spy for the United States inside the Japanese Empire (Seoane 1960). Rogers's friend, A. E. van Vogt, was deeply involved in general semantics and had written a popular novel based on it (van Vogt 1948).

Whatever cultural influences contributed to the richness of Rogers's church, Robert and Mary Ann brought some ideas to the training that were not part of it. Notably, they shared an interest in the theories of Alfred Adler (1927, 1928), the first of psychoanalyst Sigmund Freud's disciples to break with him. Adler believed that each individual has an unrecognized goal and unconsciously builds a worldview or cosmic picture to match it. Thus, each of us experiences the world in terms of our hidden goal, but usually in a distorted manner, and all our actions are shaped by these perceptions. Ideally, some variety of psychoanalysis could help a person discover this hidden goal, resolve the compulsive habits he or she had acquired in the uncomprehending attempt to pursue it, and finally achieve that goal utterly. To Robert and Mary Ann this idea was extremely attractive, and in Rogers's system they believed they had found techniques capable of realizing it.

In her training, Mary Ann practiced a psychoanalysis-like technique on Robert, causing him to relive emotionally charged experiences from his past, and he practiced the technique on other students. One result was that Robert developed an immensely powerful emotional attachment to Mary Ann, as clients in psychoanalysis often do to their doctors. Another was that Mary Ann saw the possibility of teaming up with him to explore the depths of the psyche and develop new techniques of her own. When they began experimenting on other clients, understandably the leadership of the center got rather disturbed. From their perspective, this religious technology was sacred and should not be tampered with, and they had a reasonable concern that such powerful techniques could harm people if used incorrectly.

This dispute caused Robert and Mary Ann to leave Rogers's movement. It is hard to call this a schism, because they took no followers with them, but their departure is an example of a common process in the origins of novel religious groups. Very often, perhaps universally, the founder of one novel religious group has first been an active member of an earlier one. Often the future founder is a lieutenant to the leader of that earlier group, or at least has a position of some responsibility. The point is that founding a new religion is very difficult business that relies upon specialized skills, cultural tools, and considerable practical experience running such a group. Therefore, the prospective founder must first serve an *apprenticeship* in a thriving religion, preferably one that already is somewhat novel. Robert and Mary Ann served their apprenticeship under the students of Gordon Rogers.

With no thought of creating a new religion, they started a psychotherapy service, called Compulsions Analysis, based on Adlerian notions of subconscious goals and the technology Rogers had developed. Here is another important point that will resurface in Chapter 13 when we consider the New Age movement: the cultural territory around religion contains a number of organizations and diffuse phenomena that are very similar to religion but do not fully qualify as religious. Psychoanalysis is the next best thing to religion, and many of the more recent brands of psychotherapy also address problems of the human spirit following theories that have little connection to rigorous, scientific research (Rachman 1971; Salter 1972; Tennov 1975). Some brands of mental treatment have greater potential to blossom into fully religious disciplines, notably the tradition established by Freud's renegade disciple, Carl Jung (Fodor 1971). But all the approaches that take the "subconscious" seriously, or otherwise pay close attention to what people say when encouraged to share their deepest thoughts and feelings, are capable of being drawn in a spiritual direction. Rogers had already asserted his system had religious qualities, so when Robert and Mary Ann founded Compulsions Analysis as a secular therapy they were already not far from the territory of religion, and it would not take much to move them across the line.

Their first client was an old boyfriend of Mary Ann who wanted to get back into her good graces, but when that did not work, he vanished. From then on the clients all came from Robert's friendship network. He had attended architecture school, and several of his friends were highly creative architects or artists, ready to devote their talent and energy to a new cause. Each of them initially tried Compulsions Analysis because their trusted friend, Robert, said its techniques might free them from harmful and unnecessary psychological contradictions and allow them to pursue their unrecognized life's goals more effectively. There was no thought they were joining a religion, nor any sense that they were engaging in any kind of deviant behavior that might elicit derision or punishment from their uninvolved family and work associates. Each individual client submitted to psychoanalysis-like sessions, run by either Robert or Mary Ann, that laid bare their inner feelings and built powerful bonds of intimacy linking each of them with the pair of therapists. Group sessions were added, in which the clients performed supposedly therapeutic psychological exercises with each other, thus building strong bonds among them. The result was a social implosion.

In a social implosion, part of an extended social network collapses as social ties within it strengthen and, reciprocally, those to persons outside it weaken (Bainbridge 1978:51–52). Figure 9.1 outlines what implosion looks like, although we would need a motion picture to convey the idea perfectly, and it is impossible to map social relationships accurately on a two-dimensional book page. We see three diagrams, showing the process at beginning, middle, and end. Each dot represents a person, and a line connecting two dots means that an intense positive emotional bond links the two people. Mary Ann and Robert are the two dots at the center of each diagram. Initially she is connected only to Robert, but he is also connected to his close friends who are embedded in an extended social network that reaches far beyond the page to encompass the entire middle-class population of London.

Robert convinces his best friends to try Compulsions Analysis, and they enter into therapy relationships with him and Mary Ann, and into group sessions with each other. They in turn convince some of their friends to try the therapy also, and we get the picture shown in the middle diagram. The people immediately around Robert in his social network have come closer together and developed a larger number of ties with each other. As the weeks pass, more people were added to the clientele of Compulsions Analysis, until Robert and Mary Ann reached the limit in how many therapy clients they can handle. They began training some of Robert's friends to be therapists, but not quickly enough. Participants become totally involved in the process and in each other, losing their ties to outsiders and thus ending the recruitment of new people. At the end of the social implosion, the situation is as shown in the bottom diagram. A closely knit, highly interconnected small group has broken away from the extended social network. Now its members are no longer under the social control that enforces conformity to the norms of the larger society (Faris and Dunham 1939; Hirschi 1969), and they are especially free to deviate in developing new beliefs and practices.

At the beginning of 1966 they leased a large stone row house at 2 Balfour Place, tall and narrow but rather elegant in the fashionable Mayfair section of London, and many of the thirty members moved in to live communally. Robert had started writing essays, developing new theories of human psychology, and he came to be called The Teacher. Mary Ann's leadership was equally strong, but on a more emotional or spiritual plane, and she became The Oracle. Conscious they had gone far beyond a mere therapy business, they became dissatisfied with the name Compulsions Analysis, so they started an informal contest to find a replacement. They had been calling the various rigorous psychological exercises "processes," and they decided that

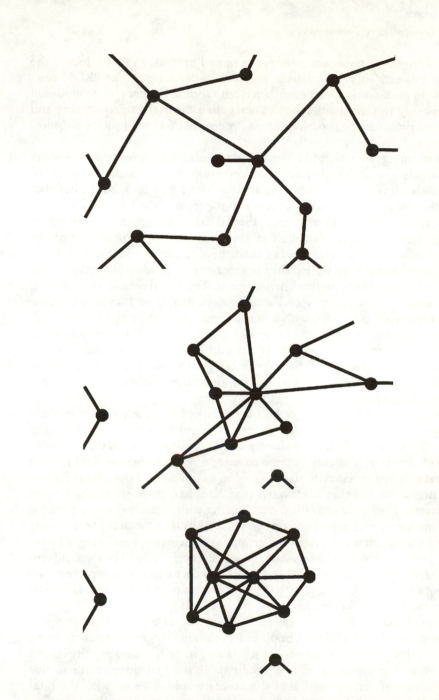

Figure 9.1 The Social Implosion of the Group that Formed the Process (Each dot is a person, and each line is a relationship linking two people)

their entire enterprise was a change-oriented process, so they adopted the name Process. They pronounced this word with a long O (like PROH-cess) in the English fashion, and even American Gordon Rogers had pronounced it this way in recorded lectures. They called themselves Processeans and dubbed their theatrical performances Processcenes. One of their chief mottoes was, "Process means change."

A stunning movement like The Process needs a logo, they felt, so one day the artists and architects all began sketching various candidate symbols. Mercedes invented the best one, an intersection of four bold lines that looked like a Nazi swastika but was a monogram of the letter P. With their increasingly radical ideas which they tried to communicate in public speeches, and their new symbolism, they began to make an impact on the London scene. The newspapers called them "Mindbenders of Mayfair," and after recruitment stalled they began to feel considerable tension with the surrounding sociocultural environment. Their final recruits tended to be very weak in restraining social attachments, including Joshua who came from Scotland to London with a music group that broke up, and Kenneth who came from Australia to undertake graduate studies in chemical engineering at London University. At the end of the social implosion, Processeans found themselves estranged from conventional society, and ready to abandon it to build a new civilization in a tropical island paradise. That took them to Xtul.

Eventually they would have become tired of Xtul, but before this could happen parents of three underage members sent an agent to Xtul to drag them back to London. Immediately the Processeans meditated to find a course of action, and they decided to leave a few members at Xtul to hold the fort while the rest returned to London to rescue the young trio. Back in the British capital they discovered that Xtul had given them remarkable charisma. They were confident, overflowing with creativity, and capable of making a powerful impression on everyone they met. One of the three young members, Christian, rejoined the group, and the newspapers chewed over the episode. Robert and Mary Ann, now collectively called The Omega (pronounced OH-ma-ga, not oh-MAY-ga), toured the eastern Mediterranean, arriving in Athens the day before the military coup and departing Israel the hour the Six Day War broke out.

Near Izmir, Turkey, Robert began writing *The Tide of the End*, an apocalyptic sequel to the biblical Book of Revelation. The first part introduced the watchwords of the Process, "As It Is . . . So Be It." In every ritual, and whenever Processeans met, one would speak the first three words of this "exchange of acceptance," and the others would respond with the final three. The truth that required absolute acceptance was in fact the immanent end of the world:

1. a) Humanity is doomed.

   b) If we are part of humanity, identified with humanity, in sympathy with humanity, we are doomed.

   c) If we attempt to save humanity from its doom, we shall fail, because humanity has chosen its doom and has shown its unwillingness to reverse its course.

   d) Our only valid course of action is to detach from humanity, climb out of the quagmire of its lies, its hypocrisy, its blind desire for its own destruction, find our own truth and create our own destiny. . . .

2. a) And there is not much time. The distant rumblings that are heralds of the End have become a mighty roar closing in about us, piercing our eardrums and causing the very Earth to quake beneath our feet; so that very soon even the blindest numbest, most oblivious of us will no longer be able to shut out the sound of it.

   b) By then the whole world will be stricken by the sound of its own approaching doom. Every man will gaze in horror at his fellow man, and see his own fear reflected back to him.

   c) And by then we must be free—if we are ever to be free. By then the bonds that bound us must be broken, and we must stand above the terror of the End, aloof, detached, a part of something new.

   d) For with every end there is a new beginning, and if we are not of the End, then we shall be of the New Beginning.

Fueled by their remarkable, rapidly accumulating experiences, the Process had become a *culture engine*. This term recognizes that occasionally in human society a special configuration of social relationships, motives, native talent, and ideas can generate culture at an extremely rapid rate.

Perhaps it is most surprising that humans generally are not very creative. Look out on a neighborhood, some day, and try to imagine realistically what creative acts are being performed in it at that very moment. Perhaps in one of the garages, teenagers are jamming on their electric guitars, imagining their music is fresh and new, and in the privacy of her own room another teenager is writing poetry. An adult's attempt to fix a broken household appliance may approach invention, and another's struggle to make dinner out of leftovers might produce a new family recipe. But usually, these acts of creation have no lasting result, and the heavily promoted culture mass-produced in Hollywood, New York, and industrial laboratories across the country utterly swamps the feeble attempts at creativity of the vast majority of citizens. In many respects, this is tragic. For example, if it were no longer possible to record or broadcast music electronically, the small number of current music world-superstars would be replaced by tens of thousands of local musicians beloved and supported by their own communities, and music would regain a human voice. Today, many decades into the numbing massification of culture, creativity needs a special environment to survive. The Processeans had been at least mildly rewarded for creativity in the art, music, and architecture schools they had attended, but to sustain this creative excitement in the "real world" they needed to build a special, dynamic subculture.

Any social-psychological situation that automatically and perpetually generates new elements of culture is a "culture engine" (Bainbridge 1978:180). The Processeans had convinced themselves it was possible to achieve a surreal level of existence, far more fulfilling than conventional life. At first they believed that a therapy based on novel techniques could liberate the individual from crushing inhibitions and allow him or her to achieve grand subconscious goals. They then applied their talent and training to create a new civilization, and incidentally a new religion. Next they went on a search for the miraculous, seeking whatever exciting elements of culture they could find from whatever source. For example, they scoured libraries and toured the world for information about the rituals and symbols of earlier esoteric religious movements, notably the Rosicrucians (McIntosh 1980, 1992) and the renegade Golden Dawn movement of Aleister Crowley (Crowley 1969; Symonds 1958). Among the most striking religious results was a new psychological theology.

The Gods and Their People

In the middle of the twentieth century, scholars offered several competing systems of personality theory that divided people into ideal-typical groups. Psychiatrists liked to categorize neurotics as either hysterics or obsessive-compulsives (White 1964). Some anthropologists preferred the distinction between Dionysians and Apollonians (Benedict 1934), based on Greek myths about the gods Dionysus and Apollo (Nietzsche 1872). The Process developed a similar system, speaking of Luciferians instead of hysterics or Dionysians, and Jehovians instead of obsessive-compulsives or Apollonians. Naturally, the separate categorization schemes were not identical to each other, but they reflected the standard habits of European languages to describe things in terms of pairs of opposites, or "dichotomies." We imagine that some people are emotionally warm, whereas others are cold, for example.

Robert was the chief theologian of The Process, as he was the chief psychologist, and he wrote extensive analyses of human compulsions and the gods that represent alternative life strategies. The opposition between Jehovah and Lucifer was "the conflict of the mind," and bringing the two together to transcend their differences was "the Union." If Jehovah and Lucifer were alternative ways of being neurotic, then Satan represented psychosis. As the archetypical psychotic, Satan had a split personality, two deities in one, as it were. One half of Satan was withdrawn, spiritual, catatonic. The other was assaultive, carnal, homicidally maniac.

The theological system of The Process was constantly changing. By the end of the 1960s, they had identified these three gods (Jehovah, Lucifer, and Satan) but were beginning to recognize Christ as a fourth principle, not yet a god, that sought to unify the others. According to de Grimston (1970a), the three great gods of the universe represented "three basic patterns of human reality." Each was a type of personality that an individual might have, or a set of desires that could sweep over any individual at a particular moment:

> JEHOVAH, the wrathful God of vengeance and retribution, demands discipline, courage and ruthlessness, and a single-minded dedication to duty, purity, and self-denial.
> LUCIFER, the Light Bearer, urges us to enjoy life to the full, to value success in human terms, to be gentle and kind and loving, and to live in peace and harmony with one another.
> SATAN, the receiver of transcendent souls and corrupted bodies, instills in us two directly opposite qualities; at one end an urge to rise above all human and physical needs and appetites, to become all soul and no body, all spirit and no mind, and at the other end a desire to sink beneath all human values, all standards of morality, all ethics, all human codes of behaviour, and to wallow in a morass of violence, lunacy, and excessive physical indulgence.

At this point, Christ was the "emissary of the gods," whose job it was to bring people to recognize their connections to the deities, and to act as a go-between communicating among the three gods and gradually reconciling them with each other. As the theology evolved, Christ then entered into a partnership with Satan and became a coequal god for Processeans. Immediately after Christ had been redefined as a god on equal footing with the other three, The Process published a magazine dedicated to the theme of love, defining this emotion in terms of people who reflected the essence of each deity:

> To the Jehovian LOVE means strong, courageous, enduring loyalty and self-sacrifice.
> To the Luciferian LOVE means a soft, gentle, understanding warmth and tenderness.
> To the Satanist, at one end, LOVE means a mystical, magical, unearthly spirituality and transcendence, and at the other end it means an earthy, lustful, sensual, abandonment and physical involvement.

To the Christian LOVE means a universal, all-embracing, all-forgiving acceptance and conciliation.

The "golden rule" in standard Christian religion is, "Do unto others as you would have them do unto you." This is a moral precept. The Process stated what it called "the universal law," which was, "As you give, so shall you receive." This is not so much a moral law as a description of how the universe supposedly works. Satan was the principle of separation. Applied to the mind, Satan thus separated Jehovah from Lucifer, producing the conflict of the gods. But because Satan separated them, by the universal law Satan also became separated into the upper (spiritual) and lower (sensual) aspects. Christ was the unifier, working for Unity with Satan.

On the level of human psychology, this theology became a complicated system for categorizing people, moods and actions. By 1972, each Processean was considered close to either Jehovah or Lucifer, and to either Christ or Satan. This meant there were four god patterns: Jehovian Christian, Jehovian Satanic, Luciferian Christian, and Luciferian Satanic. When talking among themselves, Processean usually just spoke the abbreviations: JC, JS, LC, LS. Robert de Grimston himself was a Luciferian Christian, whereas Mary Ann was a Jehovian Satanic personality. Perhaps reflecting the genders of Robert and Mary Ann themselves, Lucifer was usually described as male, whereas Jehovah was often female. Processeans actually did interpret people's behavior in terms of these categories. If somebody were depressed in a very demanding way and complaining about how much he or she suffered on behalf of others, someone else might exclaim, "What typical JC behavior!"

On the level of the cosmos, the theology asserted that originally there had been only God. But then in order to have a universe, God separated into the four gods and the numerous splinters that were lesser spirits and human beings. In ordinary life, people did not perceive any aspect of God, but dumbly played "the human game." By uniting with the Process and experiencing its spiritual techniques, a person could become aware of the higher-level "game of the gods." Ultimately, by serving the gods and assisting Christ in his task of reunification, Processeans would escape the crumbling world of humanity and join into the reassembly of God.

Status and Ritual

A few months after many Processeans had left Xtul and astonished London, most of them headed back again toward Xtul, intending to rejoin the small band that had been left there to hold the fort. They stopped in New Orleans, where they experienced such a positive response that they stayed for an extended period and eventually abandoned Xtul altogether. They began soliciting donations on the street, and this brought trouble from the police. But they discovered they could solve this problem by registering as a religious organization. Thus, for very practical reasons, The Process became a church in New Orleans.

Partly because they were having trouble with the immigration authorities who wanted to kick them out of the country, they began traveling, some going at various times to San Francisco, Los Angeles, and New York. Several Americans were attracted to the group, but at first the original Processeans did not imagine they could become full members, because they had not had the transforming experience of Xtul. But, gradually, this handful of Americans became second-class members, called "messengers." As messengers of The Process, they were at first not exactly Processeans themselves.

Unable to stay in the United States legally, the Processeans headed home, taking a score of new messengers with them, but the British authorities would not let the Americans into their country. Robert and his chief advisors found a strategy to deal with this challenge in the tenth chapter of Matthew, where Jesus sends his disciples out into the world to preach, to heal the sick, and to live off the kindness of the people they meet. So the new American members, with a few of the Britishers, wandered in pairs throughout Germany, having neither money nor cars nor places to sleep. They survived, experienced the whole affair as an adventure as well as a testing challenge, and developed powerful social bonds among themselves. Thus for the Americans, the "Matthew 10" trip was equivalent to the Xtul implosion for the original members.

Finally immigration problems were sorted out, and The Process took root back in the United States and Canada. Other ranks evolved above messenger: prophet, superior or priest, and master. The masters formed a council that managed the affairs of the group, under the leadership of the Omega. Below messenger came the ranks of disciple, initiate, and acolyte. Everyone of messenger rank or above lived in one or another commune and subsisted on donations chiefly acquired through street begging. Lower-ranked members might hold ordinary jobs and live in conventional apartments. In what may have been the fatal mistake of The Process, after Xtul the leadership never reinstituted the therapy service that had brought in the original members, thus losing an effective way of earning both money and talented converts. But now The Process was fully a religious movement, that sought salvation not so much in a spiritual technology but by marching in the army of God.

An individual rose from one status to the next in a ritual called a "baptism," at each point receiving something. Going from acolyte to initiate, a person received a simple cross representing Christ, purchased in quantity from an ordinary church-supply house. From initiate to messenger, a person received a triangular Mendes Goat badge representing Satan—or in later years a larger silver-colored cross bearing a red serpent—plus a new name and the right to be called Brother or Sister. Anyone might be present during baptism to initiate status, but baptisms to higher status were open only to members who already had that status plus the candidate for advancement. Thus in the ritual the candidate joined the elite circle of those who already held the rank. Baptism required one priest, called the "sacrifist," and two assistants, called "servers," who would move solemnly at certain points to bring the ritual objects required by the sacrifist. We will illustrate baptism with the ritual for prophet rank, which could be performed only on someone who was already a messenger.

The *alpha* ritual room would be arranged as for a Sabbath Assembly, with a circular altar in the middle of the room and two stands on either side of it, one supporting a bowl of water, and the other, a bowl of fire. The sacrifist would sit on a carved chair facing the altar, garbed in black robes over which hung a purple tabard marked with the Sign of Union, a symbol composed of the nested Greek letters alpha and omega representing the sexual union of the god Lucifer with the goddess Jehovah. On cushions in a circle around the altar sat members of prophet, superior, and master rank, along with the candidate. They would begin by chanting.

Some chants consisted of single phrases repeated over and over in a numbing rhythm: "Living death, living death, living death. . . ." "Death, death, death, punishment and doom. . . ." "Glory to the Gods, glory to the gods. . . ." Some, like the Chant of Testing, sang a challenge to the candidate for advancement through the ranks:

> Are you strong, will you give all?
> Are you strong, will you not fall?
> For the Gods, will you stand tall?
> Will you serve the Will of GOD!

When the proper mood had been established, the gong would sound. The candidate would stand, move clockwise around the altar, and kneel before the sacrifist. The two servers would take their bowls and stand facing each other on either side of the sacrifist and candidate, offering the fire and water in their outstretched arms. In a dramatic voice, the sacrifist would recite, "You who have been chosen to be Baptised as a Prophet: In the Name of the Lord Christ. . . ." The sacrifist touches the first two fingers of his or her left hand in the water and draws a cross on the forehead of the candidate. ". . . And in the Name of the Lord Satan. . . ." The sacrifist passes two fingers of the right hand through the flame and draws an inverted cross. "I Baptise you as a Prophet of The Process—Church of the Final Judgement. From henceforward you shall be entitled to wear upon your robe the Symbol of The Process and upon the first finger of your left hand the Prophet's Ring. And you shall be entitled to receive into the Church all those who wish to receive the Blessing of Christ and the Gods."

Immediately, music begins for the Consecration Chant. The servers replace the fire and water bowls, and one sits down. The remaining server brings the "consecration plate," carrying a badge and ring, and stands to the left of the sacrifist. The three-inch circular badge is black with The Process symbol in silver, and it has velcro on the back so it will hold when the sacrifist presses it onto the candidate's robe above the heart. Then the sacrifist places the silver ring, also carrying The Process symbol, on the index finger of the candidate's left hand. The candidate moves clockwise around the altar again, and sits, as does the server. All the while the participants sing:

May the Water give me life,
Purify me with the Fire . . .
Lord Christ, please receive me to Your warm heart, Your strong Heart.
May the Water give me life,
Lord Christ, tell me how I can serve You. Deserve You.
May the Water give me life,
Purify me with the Fire . . .
Satan, test me in Your Pit of Fire, desire.
Purify me with the Fire,
Tell me how to give my life to You.
May the Water give me life,
Purify me with the Fire.

The sacrifist commands, "Prophets of The Process—Church of the Final Judgement, repeat after me the Prophecy." All the prophets in the room including the new one repeat each line the sacrifist recites:

The Gods are with us.
    The Gods are with us.
Christ is among us.
    Christ is among us.
The Time of the End is now.
    The Time of the End is now.
As herald of the Time,
    As herald of the Time,
a wave of pain and suffering sweeps the world from end to end.

a wave of pain and suffering sweeps the world from end to end.
And fear is growing in the hearts of men.
And fear is growing in the hearts of men.
And we shall conquer fear with love.
And we shall conquer fear with love.
And love shall triumph.
And love shall triumph.
And the world shall be reborn in love.
And the world shall be reborn in love.
As it is . . .
. . . so be it.

The candidate now has joined the ranks of the prophets, ready to lead groups of messengers on missions, to perform a variety of responsibilities for the IP commune where the Inside Processeans of higher rank live, and to teach doctrinal seminars for initiates. The baptism ends with a hymn:

Cleanse us in the water of Life,
Purify our Souls in Your Fire . . .
Holy Lord Jehovah,
Holy Lord Lucifer,
Holy Father, Holy Mother,
Christ and Satan, Unity and Love,
God and Goddess, Salvation to our GOD.

For about seven years after Xtul, the Process developed this elaborate, bizarre but very aesthetic small religious movement. But the promised rewards always seemed just out of their grasp. From the heights of ecstatic adventures they would tumble periodically into the pits of despair. One explanation of what happened next is simply that they became tired of the struggle. For a time they loved being the most famous band of Satanists on the planet, but then journalists linked them inaccurately to Charles Manson and his murderous gang (Lyons 1970; Sanders 1971; Bugliosi and Gentry 1974). In the face of public outrage, they had to clean up their image, so they switched from gloriously sinister black uniforms to dowdy bland grey ones that made them look like flight attendants from a third-rate airline. Messengers and prophets broke their hearts begging endless hours on the streets to support the higher ranked members who puttered with publications and rituals back at the chapter house. As they pulled in their Satanic horns, their tension with the surrounding sociocultural environment reduced, but at the cost of weakening still further the value for members of the compensators.

After this decline came the fall. In an attempt to revive the movement, the council of masters expelled Robert de Grimston and his theology. With bell, book, and candle they went through the rooms of their chapter houses, exorcising all the gods except Jehovah. For a time they became the Foundation Church of the Millennium, wearing blue uniforms, running a kind of psychic carnival, and preaching that the Messiah was about to come for the first time (Blau 1974). The switch from Process to Foundation was a remarkable transformation, and it revived their energies for a few years. But eventually they abandoned their splendid headquarters in New York to try once again in Utah and Texas. Although The Process never found stable success, in their wild adventure they explored many of the mechanisms by which human beings can create new religious culture.

Cultural Transformation Mechanisms

Invention usually does not require the discovery of wholly new facts or concepts; far more often, inventors assemble existing components into new configurations (Bainbridge 1985a). Technological invention sometimes exploits fresh scientific discoveries, completely new elements of culture. Religious innovation sometimes exploits new secular cultural fads. In our own era many of the most influential social developments stem from scientific and technological innovations, so it is not surprising that scientific metaphors have shown up in new religious movements such as Transcendental Meditation. Some older groups seem far less scientific but take their name from science, including Christian Science, Divine Science, and Religious Science. Novel religious movements offer new configurations of familiar elements taken piecemeal from other religious organizations, from secular institutions, and from the petty details of modern daily life.

Founders of The Process privately referred to their work as "religious engineering," the conscious design of aspects of a new religion to perform valuable functions. Such innovation involves finding attractive elements in the cultural environment, adding them to an existing religious core, subtracting parts that interfere with more valuable parts, and transforming elements to make them fit into their places in the compensator package. Most religious leaders want to satisfy the needs and desires of the membership, so they have a natural motivation to adjust the doctrines and practices to maximize satisfaction. Large, well-established churches are locked into particular structures and ways of doing things, whereas small and new groups still have the flexibility to innovate.

"Addition" is the simplest mechanism for creating a new culture. A better technical term might be "insertion," because a new element of religious

259

culture must be fitted into a suitable place in the existing structure of beliefs and practices, not merely piled on top. Throughout their working lives, founders of new religions cannot resist appropriating new ideas and activities from their competitors. We do not think it strange that car or computer manufacturers continually monitor their competition and adopt any innovations that seem good for business. Perhaps the otherworldly rhetoric of religion impedes our ability to see the same process at work in sacred affairs. Religions are supposed to be God-given, and God is no tinkerer. But hardly a modern religion can be named that did not add elements from other sources as it grew. Of course, novel religions often hide their borrowings to emphasize the unique quality of their message. The Process did not start out as a group of "Satan worshippers." Satan appeared in Process doctrine in 1967, four years after the beginning of the group and just after its leaders had seen the successes of Anton La Vey's Church of Satan in San Francisco (La Vey 1969; Alfred 1976).

Back in London, Processean "religious engineers" trying to create a rich religious symbolism for their new church ransacked the library for evocative images. Apparently in obscure Rosicrucian or occult texts, they found pictures of an intriguing set of ritual furniture, a circular altar carrying a mystical symbol flanked by two columns, one belching fire and the other gushing water (Hall 1945; King 1975). Originally, the columns represented the two brass pillars made by Solomon for his great temple, named Jachin ("He shall establish") and Boaz ("It is strength") described in the Bible (Spence 1960). It was a short step to put their own symbol on the circular altar, interpreting the water and fire as Christ and Satan, and to contain them in silver bowls.

Often a new religious movement prospects for new additions, just as one might prospect for gold across a wild terrain. In June 1972, the leaders of The Process quested for "the healing power." They left their home in Toronto and flew across to Vancouver, then went down to Seattle to hear the famous faith healer, Kathryn Kuhlman. Later in Florida, they visited many local faith healers and designed new rituals to incorporate healing into their practices. The modification to adapt healing prayers and the laying on of hands was slight—invoking the power of four gods rather than just one.

The Process adapted many other traditional practices with only such transformations as absolutely required by existing cult doctrines. Some conventionally religious persons try to find guidance in "bibliomancy," which means opening the Bible at random, selecting a passage unseen, then reading personal meaning into the verses. The Process adopted bibliomancy and merely substituted its own holy book for the Bible. Later, it consulted with independent psychics and occult lecturers, learning from them such skills as aura reading and astrology.

The opposite of addition is "subtraction" (or "deletion"). Novel religions, like the more established denominations, have a tendency to preserve whatever culture was ever part of their repertoire, even if it may languish unused for many years. Yet when a dormant element of culture interferes with a new, vital element, it may be discarded. In general, costly unprofitable elements will be jettisoned most readily. When The Process expelled its founder, Robert de Grimston, at a time of extreme stress, it reduced the old pantheon of four gods down to one, Jehovah. This was a case of drastic cultural deletion. The Process had already quit applying any psychotherapy techniques to inner members. Too much deletion will leave a group without enough beliefs and practices to function. Often, therefore, subtraction and addition go together.

Frequently a group will add and subtract culture in order to differentiate itself from another group that owns the original culture. Sometimes, as in the case of The Process right after its schism, it may furiously drop and add to cut itself off from an unsuccessful past. This is "substitution."

When the main body of The Process expelled de Grimston at a time of extreme organizational crisis, it felt the need to kick the dust of the past from its sandals and start anew. But many of the old concepts and behaviors were absolutely necessary for day-to-day functioning. To balance change and stability, the group substituted many elements by the simple expedient of renaming them—old wine in new bottles. For example, the group's bookkeepers used a financial indicator of how much business was done by a branch. In the Process years, it was called "DJ" for "Dow-Jones," the conventional stock-market indicator. Under the Foundation, it was "JF," which stood for "Jehovah's Finances." Some other substitutions, most of which were made in one cataclysmic week, are shown in Table 9.1.

Cultural substitution in the form of renaming has been practiced by other groups, including the Family discussed in the previous chapter. When Father David, The Family's leader, launched the Reorganization Nationalization Revolution in 1978, that transformed his groups' leadership structure, he also renamed several crucial things. The group itself ceased being the "Children of God" and became the "Family of Love." Leaders formerly called "shepherds" were now "servants," and the communes were no longer "colonies" but "homes." As we stressed in Chapter 8, language is a crucial element of the culture of new religious movements. Social scientists should give it greater attention, because it frequently reveals much about conditions and changes in all aspects of the members' lives.

The "P-Sign" symbol was an extremely important emblem in The Process, stamped on every publication, embroidered into priests' robes, cast into the silver rings worn by member of Prophet rank and above, and carved into the altar. Obviously, the instant the Foundation came into being, the P-Sign

Table 9.1: Foundation Substitutes for Process Terms

Process Terminology	Foundation Terminology	Meaning
Ritual Terms:		
Alpha	Sanctum	the main ritual room
Altar	Shrine	the ritual table
Assembly	Celebration	a group ritual
Sacrifist	Celebrant	presiding priest in a ritual
Evangelist	Herald	priest who gives the sermon
Servers	Bearers	ritual assistants
Membership ranks:		
Master	Luminary	top leader
Provisional Master	Minor Luminary	lieutenant leader
Superior	Celebrant	junior Mother or Father
Prophet	Mentor	senior Sister or Brother
IP Messenger	Covenantor	lowest rank minister
OP Messenger	Witness	student minister
Disciple	Lay Founder	tithing lay member
Initiate	Aspirant	new member
General:		
The Process	The Foundation	name of the group
Processeans	Founders	members
Chapters	Foundations	branches of the group
IP	Elect	core members, ministers
Donating	Funding	street begging
Baptize	Consecrate	initiate to a new status
The Cavern	The Garden	the coffee house

had to be done away with. But the members had come to rely upon this visual symbol of their group identity, so the leaders immediately had to come up with a substitute. The P-Sign had originally been created out of the letter P for Process, so they made the new symbol out of F and J for Foundation and Jehovah. Anthropologist Franz Boas (1908) suggested long ago that a culture may retain underlying concepts of proper form, even while changing the superficial shapes of important cultural objects. Both the old symbol and the new one were block-letter monograms, based on the name of the group. As the background for their new monogram, the Founders chose the six-pointed Star of David, which they felt was a traditional symbol for their one remaining god, Jehovah.

For a time, the members of Jewish origin had disproportionate influence in the Foundation, because they were thought to understand Jehovah better. But when the group continued to suffer great difficulties, despite the fresh cultural start, Jewish elements were downplayed and a new move toward Jesus took place. The symbol was changed again to reflect this shift. The group was then calling itself the Foundation Faith, so the monogram could be interpreted as two letters F, one of them upside down, but the Old Testament emphasis in the surrounding star had to be altered. It was redrawn with elegant curves to look like a six-petaled flower rather than a star, perhaps an Easter lily. For a while some Jewish members started an offshoot group in Arizona, Jewish Crusade for Jesus, using the six-petal flower but with their own JCJ monogram in the center. Notice that the evolutions of the P-Sign communicate both radical changes in the groups' orientation and a sense of underlying continuity.

In one of our early collaborative publications, Stark and I described such innovations in terms of competition in the religious marketplace, using the now-abandoned world "cult" to mean a culturally novel religious movement:

> We suggest that cult entrepreneurs will imitate those features of other successful cults which seem to them most responsible for success. They will innovate either in nonessential areas or in areas where they believe they can increase the salability of the product. In establishing their own cult business they must innovate at least superficially. They cannot seize a significant part of the market unless they achieve product differentiation. Otherwise they will be at a great disadvantage in direct competition with the older, more prosperous cult on which theirs is patterned. The apparent novelty of a cult's compensator-package may be a sales advantage when the public has not yet discovered the limitations of the rewards that members actually will receive in the new cult and when older compensator-packages have been discredited to some extent (Bainbridge and Stark, 1979:290–291).

What economists call "product differentiation," geneticists call "character displacement." Both mean the development of differences to distinguish oneself effectively from the competition. In the sociology of religion, under whatever name, this is not a new idea. Long ago, H. Richard Niebuhr (1929: 220) noted that the churches of immigrants to the United States "were transplanted into a common social environment but at the same time they were set into the midst of a competitive system of denominationalism." Initially, the linguistic and national divisions between them assured each of a laity to support its existence. But as the ethnic groups became more assimilated, the possibility that many denominations might die as their members were attracted to others prompted a defensive tactic of doctrinal differentiation. When ethnic markers no longer serve to protect the uniqueness of the group, it accentuates its "theological or liturgical peculiarities." Niebuhr insightfully noted, "The influence of competition on doctrinal differentiation is, of course, not confined to the foreign-language churches. Whenever rivalry has arisen between culturally similar groups, the doctrinal strategy has usually been adopted" (Niebuhr 1929: 229–230).

Apparently independently of Niebuhr's work, John A. Hostetler (1968:35–36) discovered two general principles of differentiation in his research on Amish groups: "A sectarian movement must establish an ideology different from that of the parent group in order to break off relations with it. A sect must establish cultural separatism, involving symbolic and often material as well as ideological differences, from those of the parent group."

Conclusion: Evolution in a Cultural System

At the latest report, a small remnant of The Process exists in the American Southwest, greatly transformed and hardly recognizable. Although several individual members attempted to start their own movements, we do not have information about any that succeeded. Thus, The Process would appear to be a monumental failure, despite the richness of their culture and the great vitality the members showed for a decade. Success might have been within their grasp, for example if they had continued to recruit talented new members through the arts and through a psychotherapy service. But the fact is that most new religious movements fail. A fair proportion persist for decades and do not become entirely extinct until all members of the first generation have died. But very few grow to even a thousand members and establish an organization that lasts beyond the first generation.

Perhaps that is to be expected, especially if we look at novel religions in terms of a theory of evolution by spontaneous mutation and natural selection. In the animal kingdom, evolution takes place most rapidly among small creatures, with quick breeding cycles and large numbers of short-lived individuals inhabiting a complex environment. Under such circumstances, even very unlikely mutations and combinations of mutations can occur, and if they are advantageous they will spread and may form the basis on a successful new species.

Presumably, a really successful new religious tradition requires its inventors to get several separate things right simultaneously—several new beliefs, some rituals and other practices that reinforce them, and perhaps entirely new recruitment techniques that tap just the right population pools of prospective recruits. It is unlikely that any one tiny movement can succeed in doing all these things. But a group that gets a few of them right may be successful enough to spawn several other tiny movements, whether by ordinary schism, or more likely through individual leaders like Robert and Mary Ann who serve an apprenticeship in the group before leaving to found their own. One or two of these offshoot groups will innovate in the right direction, perhaps by chance, and they will survive long enough to have their own offspring, one or two of which will move even closer to an effective new tradition. This evolutionary perspective focuses not so much on the individual group, as upon the system of groups that share the same family heritage.

The published literature on innovative tiny groups tends to ignore this evolutionary perspective, although a few writers have pointed out the importance of these families of religions (Wallis 1985; Bainbridge 1985a; Melton 1993). The reason may be simply that it is such a tough job to study one new movement, that the researcher simply cannot devote much attention to anything beyond it. In addition, founders tend to obscure the origins of their ideas and their own life histories. In the case of The Process, the group had attracted the attention of newspaper reporters quite early in its history, thus leaving a paper trail that linked it back to Rogers's movement. In addition, the field research on this group was rather more extensive than the usual such project, following the group on and off for more than five years and culminating in a week when Robert de Grimston lived with the researcher in a two-room apartment, actually wrote scripture before the researcher's fascinated eyes, and provided the researcher with a detailed oral history of his wanderings. A final piece of good luck was the fact that the researcher had just completed six months of ethnography inside Rogers's movement, and he quickly spotted the connections.

The Process culture was a distinctive amalgam of elements from several sources. The names of the deities, at least, came from standard Christian traditions, and some of the ritual actions were reminiscent of the Anglican church services which many of the founders had attended in childhood. The personalities of the gods, and many features of the psychotherapy came from the leaders' own lives. In their self-conscious religious engineering, the designers of the Process took elements from books about Rosicrucians, from styles of music that were popular at the time, and from other religious movements they encountered in their travels. And, of course, the initial impetus had been the spiritual techniques developed by Gordon Rogers and the sectarian psychoanalysis of Alfred Adler. Rampant eclecticism built The Process, and if it borrowed culture and invented it at an unusually high rate, still the same social processes operate at a slower pace in other small novel religious movements.

The Process was part of a vast sociocultural system that extended from psychoanalysis to Rosicrucianism, from general semantics to Rogers's movement. But it was also a system unto itself. Although Robert was presented to the public as the group's charismatic leader, and his Christ-like visage gazed out from the inside covers of many Process publications, the novel culture was really a group product. Robert and Mary Ann played the central roles, but their artistically creative lieutenants were also crucial. After the social implosion that ejected the group from London middle-class society, the dynamics of interpersonal relationships within the group became the paramount social reality. Thus, The Process and every comparable small religious movement is a marriage of two sociocultural systems, one internal to the group and one external. At rare moments in the history of religion, such systems become an engine of cultural transformation generating a new tradition that may persist for centuries and influence the spiritual lives of millions of people.

The Dynamics of Transformation

10

Morality

In previous chapters, we have examined variability in religious beliefs and practices, caused by religious movements and by the social pressures that give them strength. Here, and in subsequent chapters, we will add the consequences dimension of religiosity. When and how, we will ask, does religion possess the power to make people behave morally? Part of the answer, we will find, is that individual faith can gain great influence over a person's life when he or she operates within the sustaining environment of a religious community or a religious movement. To the extent that movements seek to enact policies and transform behavior in accordance with a distinct set of values, it becomes important to learn whether scientific research endorses the folk concept of values. It is possible that human behavior is shaped primarily by the constant, day-to-day exchanges that a person has with his or her friends, workmates, and relatives. Outside of that context, values may be nothing more than rhetorical hot air having little capacity to move people. Current political leaders constantly say that American society has lost its values, and many hint that a return to tradition religion might help us locate them. We can wonder, however, whether values have any reality, unless wedded with a vigorous religious movement.

Watergate

On June 17, 1972, five men were arrested inside the Watergate complex a dozen blocks west of the White House, while they were burglarizing the headquarters of the Democratic National Committee. Their leader initially gave a false name but was soon identified as James W. McCord, Jr., a former CIA agent who was then employed by the Committee to Re-elect the President ("CREEP"). The other four were Cubans who had CIA connections and carried forty-five serially numbered $100 bills plus a check signed by E. Howard Hunt who was connected with the Republican effort to re-elect President Nixon (Ervin 1980:153). Soon Hunt had been arrested, along with G. Gordon Liddy who had been hired by CREEP to spy on the Democratic presidential campaign and disrupt it. The chief aim of this inept break-in, it was later learned, was to replace electronic listening devices that had been installed in an earlier burglary.

Two years later, Richard M. Nixon resigned from the presidency. The man who had been elected his vice president, Spiro Agnew, had already been hounded from office for corruption when he had been governor of Maryland. Nixon had nominated Congressman Gerald Ford as Agnew's successor, so Ford replaced Nixon on August 9. A month later, Ford granted Nixon a presidential pardon for any crime he committed while in office. Ford selected former New York governor Nelson Rockefeller to be his vice president, and the nation found itself governed by two men who had not been elected to the positions they held. The United States came to this unexpected situation after two agonizing years during which Nixon's presidency was at first defended but ultimately destroyed by a top-level attempt to cover up the full implications of the Watergate burglary.

Despite a vast number of books about Watergate, many of them written by participants and eyewitnesses to the drama, some details remain unclear or disputed. However, responsibility for the original crime went at least as high as the U.S. Attorney General, John Mitchell The cover-up was carried out with the encouragement of the president, and with direct involvement by his two chief political and domestic policy advisors, H. R. Haldeman and John Erlichman. A pivotal actor, first in creating the cover-up and then in destroying it, was John W. Dean, counsel to the president. Two other key players were Charles W. Colson, special counsel to the president and White House overseer of the 1972 campaign, and Jeb Stuart Magruder, aide to Haldeman and deputy director of the re-election committee.

Colson and Magruder are especially interesting for the sociology of religion, because both subsequently devoted their lives to religious endeavors after having intense conversion experiences. We can wonder whether the Watergate break-in and cover-up would have occurred, if the president and his advisors had been guided by religion. In fact, at least two of them, Haldeman and Erlichman, were devout Christian Scientists who neither smoked or drank. Other members of the White House team found them rather puritanical. Theodore H. White (1975:412, cf. 129) says they "were true believers in the purpose of America, as they saw it, and sought nothing for themselves."

At first, members of Nixon's staff apparently did not consider their actions to be crimes, but merely standard behavior in the tough battle of a presidential election campaign. The previous president, Lyndon Johnson, launched an espionage campaign against Republican candidate Barry Goldwater in 1964, and against Nixon himself in 1968, that may have involved illegal acts (White 1975:131–132). John Kennedy's triumph over Nixon in the 1960 presidential race may have been the result of election fraud (White 1975:96).

Nixon's aides had started bugging telephones soon after his 1968 election in order to stop leaks of secret information that imperiled negotiations to end the Vietnam War, as well as to gain political advantage over their Democratic opponents, and they may not have drawn a clear distinction between their communist and Democratic enemies. Convinced that only Nixon could bring the Vietnam War to an acceptable conclusion, they feared that victory by the liberal wing of the Democratic party would expand the youth counterculture which promoted drugs, free sex, and communes. These beliefs and motivations did not excuse their actions, when they faced the bar of justice, but they do partially explain their behavior (White 1975:241, 417–422).

Irving Janis (1982:174–175) has analyzed Watergate in terms of his theory of "groupthink." This is an eight-part shared delusion of members of a highly cohesive social group, leading them to fiasco and disaster. First, the group has an illusion of invulnerability that encourages it to take great risks. Second, unquestioned belief in its own morality makes the group ignore ethical consequences. Third, rationalizations prevent the group from heeding warnings about the course they are taking. Fourth, members hold such intensely negative stereotypes of enemy leaders that they never consider negotiating. Fifth, members impose self-censorship on any deviations from group consensus. Sixth, a shared illusion of unanimity prevents each member from expressing his or her own personal doubts. Seventh, group loyalty requires members to avoid arguing with any of their shared stereotypes, illusions, or commitments. And eighth, some members become "mindguards," protecting the group against any information that might undercut the shared assumptions. Janis found evidence of seven of these eight in the documents, testimony, and tape-recorded conversations from the Watergate cover-up. Only unquestioned belief in the group's inherent morality seemed to be missing, and conceivably religion could have supplied it. Indeed, some facets of groupthink can be found in many religious movements, so it is far from clear that religion would have prevented the Watergate cover-up, rather than supporting it.

Immediately after the burglary, Hunt and Liddy destroyed incriminating physical evidence and documents. Magruder burned the files containing transcripts of telephone conversations from the bugs in the Democrats' Watergate offices. Dean seized the contents of Hunt's safe, giving some especially incriminating documents to L. Patrick Gray, acting director of the FBI, who later burned them. Nixon told Haldeman and Erlichman to use the CIA to limit the investigation of Watergate by the FBI. Nixon and many of the men around him participated in a scheme to buy the false testimony of the Watergate burglars. As soon as investigators begin digging into the scandal, many members of the team made false statements, thus committing the crime of perjury (Ervin 1980:130–132; Janis 1982:204–208; Schudson 1992:37–40).

The cover-up unraveled, not primarily as a result of investigative journalism or ethical second thoughts on the part of conspirators, but simply because some of the jailed men directly involved with the break-in were unwilling to pay the full price for their deeds. On December 7, 1992, Hunt's wife was killed in a plane crash, while carrying $10,000 of the hush money. Thoroughly distraught, Hunt secretly demanded great sums of money to provide for his now motherless children and his attorneys' fees (Ervin 1980:39). With the awareness of Mitchell and Nixon, the conspirators for a time tried to give him the cash he wanted. Every dollar deepened their criminal guilt, because these payments were a clear obstruction of justice. In March, 1993, just when Judge Sirica was about to sentence him, McCord wrote a letter to him saying he was prepared to implicate others in the conspiracy, hoping for a reduced sentence (Ervin 1980:59). Liddy kept silent, and his perversely stoic acceptance of prison may have contributed to the mystique that years later made him one of the most influential radio commentators in the nation. But the other conspirators were sorely tempted to confess. At the end of June, 1973, John Dean stunned the nation in his testimony to the Select Committee on Presidential Campaign Activities, chaired by Senator Sam Ervin of North Carolina, which traced the cover-up all the way to the president .

Colson and Magruder were deeply involved in the cover-up, and Magruder was also implicated in the burglary itself (Ervin 1980:95). No involvement by Colson in the burglary was ever proven, but he had urged Magruder to be aggressive in gaining information about what the Democrats were doing. Dean (1976:90) has called Colson "crazy" for the lack of restraint with which he promoted politically dangerous actions, and said he "was about as subtle in pursuing political intelligence as a pig hunting truffles." Dean, Colson, Erlichman, Mitchell, and even Nixon were attorneys, so they might have been expected to understand the illegality of the cover-up. Magruder, by contrast, had a background in marketing (Magruder 1978:61; Dean 1976:249). It would be too harsh to say that lawyers, like marketers, are trained to serve the interests of their clients in an adversarial system that gives no role to the public welfare. But little in the professional background of these two men prepared them to assign truth and justice higher priority than loyalty to their president.

The routes by which Magruder and Colson found their ways to Jesus were very similar. For both the turning point came when they had begun to reveal what they knew to prosecutors, and thus when they could no longer share their thoughts and feelings with their former friends, the other conspirators. Magruder, especially, felt safe in confiding in a clergyman, because the conversation was sure to remain confidential. The strain of these months was terrible. Each felt that other Watergate conspirators were telling lies about them. Many of the conspirators hoped that the prosecutors would be understanding and treat them with compassion, but in fact the prosecutors pulled no punches—threatening, insulting, and perhaps even tricking them. Over all hung the twin dangers of prison and professional disgrace.

Magruder and Colson both sought help from a high-status person involved in religion, in Magruder's case a clergyman, and in Colson's case a businessman involved in the Evangelical Movement. Magruder was a fairly regular churchgoer, and early in 1973 he bypassed the local church where his children were in Sunday school to hear the new minister of National Presbyterian Church, Louis H. Evans. It had been difficult for Magruder to continue attending church, because he felt the other parishioners were watching him scornfully. He even felt that God might scorn him. But Evans' sermon amazed him with the hope, understanding, and compassion that the preacher offered. Months later, after Magruder had testified before the Senate Watergate Committee, he was surprised to receive a cordial letter from Evans and his wife. A little later, when the emotional stress was especially acute, Magruder went to see Evans. Evans did not force Christianity upon Magruder, nor was he judgmental. Instead, he offered unconditional friendship.

Colson had known Tom Phillips, the president of Raytheon, for several years as he had represented the company both before joining Nixon's staff and after leaving it. But when he visited the corporate offices during the summer of 1973, he was surprised to discover that Phillips had experienced a religious transformation. Colson did not know what to say when the man told him, "I have accepted Jesus Christ. I have committed my life to Him and it has been the most marvelous experience of my whole life" (Colson 1976:192). Five months later, when Colson was in the depths of despair, he drove to Phillips' home to seek his guidance. The business executive spoke of having found success to be hollow, and having stepped forward at a Billy Graham crusade to ask Christ to come into his life. Then with remarkable clarity he dissected Watergate. "Chuck, I hate to say this, but you guys brought it on yourselves. If you had put your faith in God, and if your cause were just, He would have guided you. And His help would have been a thousand times more powerful than all your phony ads and shady schemes put together" (Colson 1976:237). After an emotion-provoking conversation, Colson drove home, then parked for a long time in the darkness outside his home, praying.

While they were not exactly intellectuals, Magruder and Colson had professional careers in which both reading and writing were of paramount importance. Thus it is not surprising that religious books played a significant role in the conversion of each. Evans suggested several books to Magruder, and Phillips gave Colson a copy of *Mere Christianity* by C. S. Lewis, a compilation of three of Lewis's short books providing an intellectual basis for faith. Perhaps more important, the two Watergate conspirators' spiritual guides brought them into contact with Christian groups where they could find acceptance and fellowship.

Magruder had earlier met Doug Coe, who had organized weekly prayer breakfasts for government employees, but he had not gotten involved in them. Now he learned about Coe's more extensive work at Fellowship House with small groups of Christian seekers. There came to be two kinds of people in his life, the prosecutors and the Christians: "To the prosecutors I was dirt, and everything I told them increased their contempt for me. They seemed to make themselves my moral judges and passed sentence on my wrongdoings every day. But my Christian friends made me feel that I was important to them as a person. They didn't condone any of the wrong I had done, but they were concerned about the pain I was experiencing as I faced up to it" (Magruder 1978:69). Magruder joined a fellowship group led by Evans, and one cold night sitting in the minister's Toyota the two of them prayed for Christ to remove Magruder's fears and doubts. At that moment, Magruder gave his life to Jesus.

While sitting alone at the seashore in Maine, after studying the Bible and pondering his life, Colson found himself speaking aloud: "Lord Jesus, I believe you. I accept you. Please come into my life. I commit it to you" (Colson 1976:278). Back in Washington Doug Coe visited Colson at Phillips' request. Remarkably, Coe insisted that Colson meet Senator Harold Hughes, a vehement opponent of the Nixon administration and of all that Colson had stood for. When he told Hughes and a roomful of other Christians his story, he was amazed that they accepted him. After praying together on their knees, Hughes embraced Colson, and for the first time Colson knew the meaning of fellowship.

These conversion experiences were only the beginning of a long journey for both men, that would extend through and far beyond the seven months that each spent in prison. For Magruder it was a shock to discover that other conspirators had tape-recorded phone conversations with him in which they slyly attempted to get him to admit his guilt while they pretended not to have been involved, themselves. This brought home the enormity of the crime involved in bugging the Democratic National Headquarters, because now he had been the victim of hostile bugging himself. For Colson, a moment of dedication came immediately after the death of his father, when rummaging through his dad's effects he discovered that his father had taken great interest in prison reform back in the 1930s and had invested great effort in trying to help convicts find a new life.

For a time, Colson, Magruder, and Dean were kept together at Fort Holabird prison near Baltimore, chiefly used to house Mafia witnesses where they would be conveniently located to give testimony in federal cases but could be protected from killers hired to keep them from telling what they knew about organized crime. Colson (1976:573) says about Dean, "I discovered that he had once worked on a graduate-school project for a modern revision of the Bible, and had read it thoroughly. Furthermore, his belief in God had been strengthened by the tumultuous experiences he was now going through." Dean (1976, 1982), however, does not report that he experienced any heightened religiosity as a result of Watergate.

Dean does recall that Colson had begun informal evangelizing, the first step toward full-time commitment to prison religious work. One night he overheard Colson telling a guard, " 'I used to have trouble reading the Scriptures, too. But I found something that helped me. Start with John in the New Testament. Don't start with Genesis. And get yourself a modern version. It's hard to get started. It took me forty years. I'll tell you what, though. You can come down to my room and read with me any time you want. Be glad to have you.' " (Dean 1976:368–369).

After prison, Colson published a book about his conversion, titled *Born Again*, which sold 340,000 copies and was subsequently made into a movie (Schudson 1992:133). At a Hollywood party staged by the producer of this movie, surrounded by born-again Christians sipping nonalcoholic fruit punch, hard-drinking John Dean (1982: 221–224) was offended by the aggressive manner in which Colson tried to press Christianity upon him. Dean (1982:130) cynically imagined Colson as a Hare Krishna, complete with shaven head and saffron robes, chanting in front of the White House and distributing the *Bhagavad Gita*. Magruder earned a divinity degree from Princeton, and served for a time as an assistant pastor in the First Presbyterian Church of Burlingame, California. Later, he became minister of a church in Columbus, Ohio, and headed the city's Commission on Values and Ethics (Schudson 1992:130). Even Dean, the cynic, who did not experience religious conversion after Watergate, ultimately recognized that Colson and Magruder had indeed gained new lives through it:

> Chuck Colson and Jeb Magruder have committed their lives to Christ: Chuck with his prison ministry, and Jeb as an ordained Presbyterian minister. As 'born again' Christians, these two men have very successfully replaced disgrace with grace. Their conversions are heartfelt, sincere, and proof positive that a soiled identity can be cleansed by the greatest of powers.

275

In many ways I feel envy over the way Chuck and Jeb have made themselves better persons from their mistakes. At the same time I feel happy for
them, that from the low points of their lives they could discover a calling
that exemplifies all that is best in life. I have read what they have written
about finding their way to God; I've talked with them both, and I know
it's no publicity stunt. (Dean 1982:356–357)

Religion and Morality

The power of religious movements to change society depends very much
upon the general capacity of religion to shape individual human behavior,
and sociological research has found that this capacity is extremely variable.
For example, perhaps the most perplexing issue facing the sociology of religion in recent decades has been the question of whether religious faith and
churchgoing prevent teenagers from engaging in delinquency. An influential
study done in the 1920s found no tendency of Sunday school students to be
more honest than other children (Hartshorne and May, 1928; cf. Robison
1960). Several writers wondered if religion might have lost its historical
power to uphold morality under the conditions of modern, secularized society, but were unable to answer this question with the unsatisfactory data
available to them (Tappan, 1949; Kvaraceus 1954; Neumeyer, 1955; Fitzpatrick, 1967; Schafer and Knudten, 1970).

Perhaps the most influential single study was "Hellfire and Delinquency"
(Hirschi and Stark 1969; cf. Hirschi 1969), employing an excellent survey of
northern California high school students to examine the possible effects of
religion on delinquency. The data showed that religious teenagers were no
less likely than irreligious ones to steal or to commit comparable acts of
delinquency. This was true whether religiousness was defined as believing
that hell awaits sinners, as attending church and Sunday school regularly, or
even as having churchgoing parents. A similar study of teenagers in the Pacific Northwest also discovered no tendency of religion to deter theft (Burkett and White 1974). Just as this negative finding was becoming enshrined
as common wisdom among criminologists, other studies came to a different
conclusion. A survey of teenagers in Atlanta, Georgia, revealed strong negative correlations between church attendance and delinquency (Higgins and
Albrecht 1977), and similar findings came from a study of several Mormon
communities (Albrecht et al. 1977).

Working with his graduate students, Rodney Stark from the original Hellfire team was able to resolve the striking disagreement between these studies. The negative findings had come from West Coast areas where rates of
church membership were unusually low, whereas the positive findings had

come from other areas of the country with higher church-member rates (Stark et al. 1982). This observation was supported by the finding in other research that the rate of church membership for different geographical areas has strong negative correlations with rates of larceny based on crimes known to the police (Stark et al. 1980). A comprehensive recent examination of several datasets shows clearly that religion can deter juvenile delinquency unless the rate of church membership is especially low (Stark and Bainbridge 1996). Because Rodney Stark discovered this principle, I call it the "Stark effect." The biblical commandment says, "Thou shalt not steal," but in highly secular communities, religious children are no less likely than their irreligious peers to commit theft.

There are two kinds of exception to the Stark effect, both involving acts of deviant behavior rather different from stealing. Statistical studies of homicide and church membership rates across major metropolitan areas indicates that religion has no power to deter murder, despite the biblical commandment against it (Bainbridge 1989a). Naturally, questionnaire studies do not provide information about homicides, so we do not at present have a wealth of research on this point. But, apparently religion lacks the power to prevent killing even in highly religious communities.

The other exception is the consistent finding that religion deters illegal drug use, heavy alcohol drinking, promiscuous sexuality, and other hedonistic acts regardless of the rate of church membership in the community (Wuthnow 1978; Hadaway, Elifson and Petersen 1984). Thus, surprisingly, surveys done in areas of low church membership show that religion can deter hedonistic deviance at the same time it fails to deter larceny in the same group of respondents (Burkett and White 1974; Stark and Bainbridge 1996).

To recapitulate, research on larceny-like delinquency has consistently found no relationship between religiousness and delinquency, at the individual level in communities where organized religion is weak, for example as measured by the church-member rate. But, equally consistently, studies performed where organized religion is relatively strong have shown that churchgoing and believing individuals were far less likely to be delinquent than their irreligious peers. However, the religion of an individual lacks the capacity to prevent homicide regardless of the religiousness of the community. And in all environments, religious individuals are less likely to indulge in drugs and alcohol, making allowances for denominational differences on alcohol. How can we explain this perplexing but vitally important complexity?

Our analysis of recruitment and commitment to religion stresses the importance of social bonds. Individuals are drawn into new churches by social relationships with people who are already members, and members with the strongest intragroup bonds will be most orthodox in belief and behavior. Impressed by the success of both differential association theory and control theory in criminology (Sutherland and Cressey 1974; Hirschi 1969), I believe the influence of friends is also important in determining whether young people will commit acts of deviance or not.

Religious beliefs are not automatically salient for behavior, but must be made salient through some social process. A survey study of college students, done in Seattle, Washington, where the church-member rate is extremely low, examined the extent of agreement between members of 424 pairs of close friends (Bainbridge and Stark 1981b). If one friend attended church often, the other tended to as well. If one friend's religious beliefs were important to him or her, the same tended to be true for the other. But this religious similarity among friends turned out the be largely the result of the Born-Again Movement that had just swept the campus. A quarter of the respondents answered yes, when asked: "Would you say that you have been 'born again' or have had a 'born again' experience—that is, a turning point in your life when you committed yourself to Christ?" When born agains were removed from the analysis, the remaining 219 pairs of friends no longer showed any tendency to share religious orientation.

There was no significant tendency for pairs of friends to have similar rates of church attendance, after born-agains had been removed from the analysis. Similarly, the importance of one friend's religious beliefs said nothing about the importance of the other's. When born-agains were left in the analysis, friends tended to share attitudes toward the following beliefs: "I definitely believe in God." "God or some other supernatural force has a very strong influence on my life." "Suffering often comes about because people don't obey God." "Miracles actually happened just as the Bible says they did." And when one friend liked "religious books and articles" or " hymns and spirituals," the other tended to as well. But when the effect of the Born-Again Movement was removed from the analysis, all of these religious agreements between friends vanished. These findings illustrate the capacity of a powerful religious movement to shape beliefs, attitudes, and behavior, even in communities where organized low-tension religion is weak.

A few families in any community may be so involved in extreme religious groups that religion is salient for all aspects of their lives, but the typical teenager from a moderately religious family will not be constantly reminded of religious commandments, especially in those settings far from parental influence where most delinquency occurs. Thus, the crucial factor is whether religion is brought into the private lives of teenagers by the youth themselves. If a majority of a juvenile's friends are religious, then religion will become a part of their shared experience and will deter delinquency. But if a majority are not religious, then the personal beliefs of the individual will not be rendered salient, and religious individuals will be as likely as others to commit delinquent acts.

Crimes of passion, notably homicide, are not undertaken rationally with the wishes of one's peers in mind, and thus they will not be affected by religion. However passionate, many hedonistic acts are not performed on impulse, but represent long processes of learning and adaptation, and thus might be deterred by religion. Thus, religion may deter illegal drug use, heavy alcohol drinking, promiscuous sexuality, and other hedonistic acts, while failing to deter violent crimes such as homicide.

The fact that religion deters hedonistic deviance, even in areas of low church membership, suggests that one potential criticism of the delinquency research is incorrect. It might be claimed that in religious areas individual irreligiousness is simply one more kind of deviance, thus correlating with other kinds of deviance, while in areas of weak organized religion, it is not deviant at all and thus should not correlate with deviance. But it is difficult to square this idea that irreligiousness is merely a contingent marker for general deviance with the consistent finding that some religion-deviance correlations survive in areas of low church membership, despite the collapse of others.

An approach toward understanding is to compare the two categories of delinquency, the larceny-type with the hedonistic-type. One distinction is that the former are crimes with victims, while the latter are "victimless" crimes (Burkett and White 1974: 456). It may be that religion has the power to deter individuals from committing acts that would be to their obvious advantage (assuming they were not caught and punished), for example by instilling a strict moral code or humane sympathy for the feelings of potential victims—but only when religion spreads its message powerfully through influential social networks. This power would collapse where the church-member rate was low.

However, religion may also have an *advisory function*, helping an individual decide what to do in ambiguous circumstances where each available course seems to have advantages and disadvantages. Thus, even when not sustained by a social majority, religious socialization may convincingly warn young people that they themselves will be hurt if they indulge in drugs, excessive alcohol, and uncontrolled sex. This analysis springs from the Stark-Bainbridge theory of religion, sketched in Chapter 1, which derives religion from the human need to gain rewards and avoid costs. From that perspective, religious beliefs are *explanations*, guides for personal decision making about dangerous, ambiguous, but potentially rewarding matters.

One may also begin an analysis with the different social bases of the two types of deviance. While larceny may be performed either by individuals or gangs, and the degree to which larceny is a collective crime has long been debated, the hedonistic acts are clearly social. Young deviants take drugs supplied through an elaborate social network and drink alcohol often obtained and imbibed in groups. The social nature of sexual intercourse is undeniable. Thus, in areas where organized religion is weak, congregations may function as subcultures in competition with the deviant subcultures of drugs, alcohol, and sex. By the principles of differential association, individuals will be pulled more toward one subculture or another, toward church or toward drugs, and a negative correlation between religion and deviant hedonism will result. Alternately, those who become members of hedonistic subcultures may feel themselves estranged from religion. They may be rejected in turn by the churches, because their particular brand of deviant behavior is difficult to hide, while occasional larcenies go unnoticed by the church.

Two early studies that found a deterrence effect on hedonism but not on larceny noted that religion and secular culture were in agreement that larceny was wrong, but differed with respect to hedonism (Burkett and White 1974; cf. Batson et al. 1993:335). The authors felt that if religion merely added a supernatural assent to secular norms, it could not be responsible for much variation in behavior. This explanation fails in the light of the abundant subsequent evidence that religion can powerfully deter larceny in communities with high rates of church membership. Its flaw is the failure to note that the salience of religious prohibitions depends upon the structure of social relations in which the individual is embedded.

Research in this exciting area is still quite new, and it is possible that future studies will complete a very different picture of the variable power of religion to shape moral behavior. But the image we have just sketched has immediate implications for research on religious movements. First, the Stark effect reinforces that religion is part of a larger sociocultural system, and the success or failure of a religious movement will depend on the characteristics of that larger system, as well as upon the actions of members. Second, the inability of religion to control impulsive violence suggests that limits of several kinds may exist to the power of religion, even when it is reinforced by a favorable social environment. We can wonder, for example, whether religion's impotence to control homicide extends as well to killing in war, and thus vitiates religiously oriented peace movements. Third, the capacity of religion to control hedonistic acts, even when unaided by the surrounding community, suggests that some kinds of religious movements may be highly effective regardless of the sociocultural environment in which they find themselves.

Religious movements that seek to change society are of many kinds, and some would seem to fall under each of these hypotheses. Thus the very complexity of findings about religion and individual deviance predicts a matching complexity in the patterns of success and failure experienced by religious movements whose goal is the transformation of public morality.

The Question of Values

In 1870, John Humphrey Noyes found religion to be one of two factors that explained the success of experimental communes, and thus by extension religion was a key factor committing individuals to the norms of any kind of community. Significantly, the other factor was the strength of social bonds between individuals. From Emile Durkheim (1897) to the present, one of the most challenging questions has been whether the influence of religion can be reduced simply to the action of social bonds, or whether religion may have distinctive modes of influence.

A contemporary of Noyes, social theorist George Harris (1873: 87), suggested that religion had three modes of influence. First, religion raises the minds of believers to a higher standard of dignity. For Durkheim (1961: 103–104), this means orienting the individual to "supraindividual ends," thus committing the individual to serve the needs of the society (Durkheim 1915). And from a more individualist point of view (Stark and Bainbridge 1987), the pride in being allied with God may seem more rewarding than acts of petty deviance.

Second, according to Harris, religion instills into believers' minds "the consciousness of a constant observer of all their actions, to whom they are accountable for every deed." This can be taken as simple utilitarian theory, holding that those who fear divine punishment will avoid acts they believe will incur it, but it also can be interpreted in terms of social attachments. Modern *control theory* asserts individuals commit deviant acts when their social bonds are weak, and Travis Hirschi (1960: 90) has noted that a juvenile is deterred from delinquency not merely by the actual presence of his parents, but also by the extent to which "he perceives them as part of his social and psychological field." A God allied with the parents and supporting their norms may help strengthen their influence by making it psychologically omnipresent.

Third, for believers religion establishes "a strict and unerring rule of the highest authority for the direction of their conduct on all occasions." A single, authoritative standard of behavior resists erosion because the boundaries it sets on virtuous behavior are clear, and by being sacred they are not open to human amendment (cf. Durkheim 1915, 1961). This sounds like the concept of societal values, which was so popular in sociology in the middle of the twentieth century, and Harris's first point might be subsumed under values, as well.

Clyde Kluckhohn defined "value" as "a conception, explicit or implicit, distinctive of an individual or characteristic of a group, of the desirable which influences the selection from available modes, means, and ends of action" (Kluckhohn 1951:395). Thus, values are the legitimate goals of human action, enshrined as the central axioms of a culture and inculcated into the society's members through socialization. The concept of values assumes that each human being and each coherent social group is rather like a philosopher possessing a logically coherent world view or value orientation. Kluckhohn claimed, "There is a 'philosophy' behind the way of life of every individual and of every relatively homogeneous group at any given point in their histories" (Kluckhohn 1951:409). Lofland and Stark (1965:862) put the proposition this way: "All men and all human groups have ultimate values, a world view, or a perspective furnishing them a more or less orderly and comprehensible picture of the world."

Sociologists at mid-century distinguished values from norms and beliefs. Values are overarching, general conceptions of what is desirable, whereas norms are specific prescriptions for proper behavior in particular kinds of situation. In principle, the norms of a stable culture are integrated with the values, and a person who follows the legitimate means for attaining the values stands a good chance of success (Merton 1968). Beliefs are assumptions of fact, and do not contain the evaluative component shared by norms and values. Ordinary people, not to mention politicians, frequently refer to an individual's or community's value system, yet in recent decades sociologists have tended to reject or ignore this entire conceptualization.

For one thing, the concept of values is connected to the notion that society is highly unified, and from the 1960s onward many schools of sociology have viewed society as a free-for-all contest among social groups or individuals, lacking any clear unifying philosophy. For another thing, empirical sociology has tended to move away from abstract concepts like values to give greater emphasis to concrete factors in a person's life, such as the socioeconomic status of the individual or location in a social network. Once upon a time, sociologists used to explain behavior as the natural expression of an individual's attitudes, but then researchers found many instances in which words and deeds diverge, and verbally expressed attitudes no longer seemed so sociologically relevant (LaPierre 1934; Deutscher 1973; Liska 1974; Schuman and Johnson 1976; Schuman and Presser 1980). Attitudes and values may be important, but it was no longer appropriate for sociologists to assume so without direct evidence in the particular situation under study, and it often proved difficult to measure their influence in particular studies.

Many social scientists have found the distinctions among values, beliefs, and norms less than compelling. William McCready and Andrew Greeley (1976) identified five alternative ultimate values of American society: pessimism, diffusion, hopefulness, secular optimism, and religious optimism. Each of these is a way of understanding what humans can expect from the world, and thus they mingle values with beliefs. In more recent work, Greeley (1989, 1990) builds on the classical work of Durkheim and Weber to argue that Protestants and Catholics possess distinctive ethics and worldviews. Protestants stress individualism and a dialectical imagination that views the world as inherently evil. In contrast, Catholics are communitarian and have an anaological imagination that sees God's hand at work in all aspects of the world.

The term "meaning system" is frequently used to describe an orientation to the world so global that it encompasses both ultimate values and basic beliefs. Expressing the traditional sociological viewpoint, Robert Wuthnow asserted, "Societies are organized with reference to systems of ultimate meaning" (Wuthnow 1976:vii) and "people adopt relatively comprehensive or transcendent, but nonetheless identifiable, understandings of life which inform their attitudes and actions under a wide variety of conditions" (Wuthnow 1976:2). He defines these meaning systems as "overarching symbolic frames of reference . . . by which people come to grips with the broader meaning and purpose of their lives" (Wuthnow 1976:2–3). Wuthnow speculated that new meaning systems had emerged in American culture that were not based in traditional religion, calling them individualism, social science, and mysticism. However, two major survey data sets failed to confirm the existence of effective secular-meaning systems while demonstrating again that traditional religion can provide the overarching interpretation of life to which Wuthnow refers (Bainbridge and Stark 1981a). Exactly how influential this interpretation is in shaping people's behavior is another question.

Robert K. Merton (1968:186–187) defined values as "culturally defined goals, purposes and interests, held out as legitimate objectives for all or for diversely located members of the society," and he said they were the things people feel are "worth striving for." In contrast, norms define "the acceptable modes of reaching out for these goals." Although this conceptualization has been tremendously influential in sociology since Merton first enunciated it in the 1930s, the fact that values have practically vanished in recent years from the pages of the most prestigious sociology journals suggests that there is something wrong in the formulation. The first flaw is that it is difficult to draw a line between values and norms. Values are said to be very general in nature, stating what a person is supposed to seek as a grand goal of life. Norms are supposed to be very specific, setting limits to human behavior in narrowly defined situations. Thus, both values and norms are rules governing behavior, and the difference between them is that values have greater scope than norms. It is as if we had two different terms for weight, one for heavy objects and one for light ones. This would make it difficult to speak about objects of medium weight, and it would obscure the physical laws of mass that dealt with variations in weight.

In addition, Merton and others of his generation asserted that societies have great latitude in the values they can choose to honor, as if "culture" were a totally independent force in human life having nothing to do with the physical conditions of the natural environment, the level of technological development of the society, and the universal laws of human nature. To be sure, culture is of some importance, and it comprises all the accidents of history and innovation that have brought the society to a particular point. An individual or small group can occasionally decide some very general issues on behalf of the entire society, as when Thomas Jefferson writes the *Declaration of Independence,* or a small social movement of visionary engineers creates modern spaceflight (Bainbridge 1976). But if such sweeping innovations are out of tune with conditions of the times, they will not be accepted by the society. And outside of very special examples such as these, there is no reason to believe that the principle of a culture will be coherent, integrated, or even readily intelligible.

The Stark-Bainbridge theory of religion suggests that people need rules for behavior in order to cope with a complex environment in satisfying their basic needs. The only fundamental values are those built into human beings by biology, and here we would count also the rudimentary social experiences of infancy that must have existed long before the human species separated from other primates, because chimpanzees are as good parents of their dependent babies as we are of ours. All the nonprimate behaviors we engage in, from agriculture to reading books, are learned techniques for gaining primary rewards more-or-less indirectly. This learning, and indeed the development of culture over the millennia, has taken place not on the overarching level of Mertonian values, but on the tiny level of everyday situations and small challenges, an even lower level than Mertonian norms.

In pursuit of rewards, humans seek explanations of how the world works and what actions will succeed. Culture is, in the first instance, the accumulated set of explanations a society possesses on how to obtain particular rewards and avoid costs. Here, sociologists should learn from our colleagues, the archaeologists who make such a fuss over arrowheads and shards of pottery. Of vast importance are the technical rules of how to hunt, how to exploit edible and technologically useful plants, and how to protect ourselves against the elements and our enemies. By largely ignoring these recipes for accomplishing practical tasks, sociologists (outside the narrow discipline of science and technology studies) have missed some of the most important kinds of human interaction, because we learn these methods from each other. This ignorance, in turn, leads to the mystification of norms and values. Norms are simply specific explanations having to do with social situations, and values are general explanations having to do with social situations. To limit these terms to "social situations" is not to say much, because purely technical actions readily shade over into social activities, for example when building a house requires one not only to know how to pound nails, but also how to deal with plumbers and electricians.

Merton and others of his school seem to treat values as primary, and all the other features of culture as secondary. But it is a mystery to me how values could come first. Rather, it appears far more likely that human culture arose in millions of tiny innovations, most of them at the absolute lowest level of abstraction. Only when many effective specific explanations had been discovered in a particular area was it possible to induce moderately general explanations. The Stark-Bainbridge theory explains that very general explanations were achieved more readily in the sphere of religion than in areas directed toward mastering the physical and social worlds, because it is difficult to subject supernatural explanations to empirical tests (Stark and Bainbridge 1987). Thus, values, to the extent that this concept means anything at all, are likely to be religious in nature.

Ironically, the concept of value may be primarily a compensator. Recall that compensators are postulations of reward according to explanations that are not readily susceptible to unambiguous evaluation. Sociologists traditionally assumed that values were potent determinants of human behavior; they did not come to this conclusion on the basis of careful scientific tests. At best they deduced values from the regularities they observed in the social world, but they did not consider alternative explanations. Sociologists did not really invent the concept in the first place, drawing upon popular notions of why people behaved. Notice how the concept of values allows us to be optimistic about obtaining rewards from other human beings. If a society is based on a coherent set of values, then social life is comfortably predictable. If a particular person has internalized these values, then we can trust him or her.

An alternate view is that human beings exhibit stable patterns of behavior only because they are rewarded for doing so and are punished when they diverge from the patterns of behavior that other people desire them to follow (Scott 1971; Homans 1974). This means that a society can achieve coherence and predictability only by having strong institutions and social networks that hold individuals accountable for their behavior. Certainly the general explanations of religion—the beliefs and the practices that impinge upon daily life—have *some* power of their own. But that power may be greatly amplified by being promoted by vigorous social movements and through them enshrined into laws and stable social structures. We will examine that possibility shortly, but first we must digress briefly to consider whether it really is possible for human society to exist without values.

The Problem of Social Order

Social scientists and philosophers of many schools of thought have long wondered how it is that society could achieve some measure of stability. For the individual, this becomes the question of why individuals typically behave properly, according to the desires of their fellows. Certainly, it is possible that overarching philosophical concepts (call them values if you wish) might be part of the answer. We are not trying to deny that possibility here, merely to raise the question whether values are absolutely necessary and whether they in themselves are an adequate answer to the problem of social order. Traditional sociologists, with the notable exception of George C. Homans (1974), tended to doubt that society could really be based simply on the self-interest of the individuals that comprised it. In particular, they doubted that cooperation could have evolved without values to guide it.

Speculation along these lines should have been chastened by the fact that many animals possess societies, not humans alone. Everybody has seen an ant colony and realized that the individual ants cooperated with each other, presumably because some kind of biological mechanism caused them to do so (Wilson 1971, 1975). If mere bugs could accomplish this without benefit of values and religion, then perhaps humans could as well.

The most extreme challenge to traditional value-oriented social thought is a perspective known as game theory, practiced by several specialists in psychology, economics, political science, and sociology. Game theory views individuals as strategic players in the game of life, constantly calculating their individual best interests in their exchanges with other players. Some people dislike game theory because it seems pessimistic and reductionist. Certainly, the kind of human being described by game theory is not very nice, and we might prefer to think of ourselves as rather more exalted and spiritual beings. But precisely because game theory is a radical denial of much that humans hope and believe about themselves, it can be a sensitive tool for examining the irreducible minimum conditions required for the emergence of human society.

The most effective intellectual tool for game-theoretical analysis of cooperation is a strange little parable called "the prisoner's dilemma." Imagine this:

Two men are suspected of committed a crime together. They are placed in separate cells, and each is informed separately that he may choose to confess or not, subject to the following stipulations: (1) If both independently choose not to confess, they will receive only moderate punishment. (2) On the other hand, if one chooses not to confess and the other simultaneously confesses, the confessor will receive the minimal sentence while his partner will be given the maximal sentence. (3) If both choose to confess, they will both be given heavy sentences. (Gergen 1969:54).

This situation is ironic and tragic. Each prisoner will think to himself as follows. "What if my partner confesses? If I keep silent, then I will get a worse sentence than if I confess, too. So, it that case, I would be better off confessing. What if he does not confess? Then I can get a very light sentence if I do confess. So I should confess, no matter what."

This logic will convince both of the men to confess. But if both prisoners confess, they will get harsher sentences than if they both keep silent. This gives the seeming paradox that men acting logically in pursuit of their own personal interests will harm themselves. Indeed, even if they have read about the prisoner's dilemma and know the tragic implications of their situation, they will find it hard to trust the other to keep silent and thus will confess despite the ultimate harm it does them.

The concepts of the prisoner's dilemma have been applied to many situations far more realistic than the strange choice the jailers offer these two imaginary captives. For example, Raymond Boudon (1981:21) has analyzed the relations between Britain and Germany leading up to the First World War in these terms.

Are there any conditions under which the prisoners could escape their dilemma? A standard answer from outside game theory is that they can escape the dilemma if they accept some higher law than mere self-interest. For example, the prisoners could be freedom fighters caught by the secret police. If so, they may have been trained to follow the norm, "Thou shalt not rat on thy comrades." Under the influence of this norm, they will not calculate what to do, but will automatically keep silent. This example stresses the belief that society rests upon certain norms and values that transcend or even oppose narrow, rational self-interest.

Game theory has another answer, however. It notes that the situation of the prisoners is extremely unusual, in that it describes what may be the last decision that the men have to make about each other. Ordinarily, in human life, we interact with the same people, day in and day out. What we do on this occasion is likely to affect what the other person does next time. People may constantly act to maximize their own self-interest, but they do so in an enlightened manner, taking account of future rewards and costs as well as the ones that may result from the immediate situation.

Political scientist Robert Axelrod (1984) held a contest in the computer magazines, soliciting computer programs that would play repeated prisoner's dilemma games against each other. The idea was to see what strategies could do best in a competition where self-interest over the long run was the only determinant of success. And in most of the games, the strategies that did best were ones that encouraged cooperation. Subsequently, sociologists got into the act, publishing software that allowed students to do these experiments themselves (Bainbridge 1987) and exploring factors that encouraged or discouraged the learning of cooperation (Macy 1990, 1991a, 1991b; cf. Deutsch and Krauss 1960).

Game theory has certainly not proven that values do not exist, or if they do exist that they are ineffective in shaping human behavior. However, the game-theoretical experiments have shown that cooperation can evolve without culturally defined values, or without exalted human sensitivities of any kind. Certainly the simulated prisoners in Axelrod's computer program lack both religion and immortal souls. The point is that we cannot assume that cultural values are necessary for human cooperation, and thus that religion is necessary for society. This may be the case, but we would need good empirical evidence and perhaps a very different theoretical argument before we would be sure that it is so.

Secularization and Suicide

If the thought that values might not exist is a chilling idea, there is a slightly less pessimistic possibility. Perhaps strong, shared values can guide the citizens of a society, but they have a precarious hold on existence and might be destroyed by secularization or social disintegration. As pioneer sociologist Emile Durkheim (1897) asserted, societies may fall into a state of anomie in which previously effective values lost their capacity to sustain morale and morality. Rather than merely contemplate this dismal possibility, we should find a way to examine it empirically. Durkheim's tactic is still effective: examine the social and religious factors that shape the different rates of suicide across communities.

Social scientists long before Durkheim had discovered that the rates of suicide were much higher in Protestant parts of Germany than in Catholic parts (Wagner 1864). Reflecting on this fact, Morselli (1879) called "the influences of religion" among "the strongest motive powers which act on the will of man." Durkheim asserted that the Protestant-Catholic difference was not limited to Germany but was found across all of Europe. Modern re-examination of the data suggests that Durkheim was wrong, and for reasons that are still unclear Europe as a whole does not show the same denominational effect on suicide as Germany and perhaps also Denmark (Pope 1976; Stark and Bainbridge 1996). In addition, suicide data from the United States at several points in time fail to show a Protestant-Catholic difference (Stark, Doyle and Rushing 1983; Bainbridge and Stark 1981c). However, the modern studies do indicate that religion in general, whether Protestant or

Catholic, has the power to deter suicide. Across the United States, communities with high rates of church membership have low suicide rates, whereas places where the churches are weak experience high levels of self-murder.

Durkheim explained the high rates of suicide he attributed to Protestant communities as the result of *egoism*, which he said was excessive individualism and a lack of social integration. In modern terms, egoism is the condition of a society whose social network is sparse and fragmentary, or in which individuals tend to lack strong social bonds with each other. In other chapters of his influential book, but not in connection with religion, Durkheim discussed *anomie*, a state of normlessness akin to the loss of values. As many twentieth-century commentators on Durkheim have noticed, he did not distinguish egoism from anomie clearly. But it is very useful for clear theorizing to separate them, and the distinction has been used by many authors, before Durkheim as well as after. Recall again that John Humphrey Noyes (1870:57) said, "the two most essential requisites for the formation of successful Communities, are *religious principle* and *previous acquaintance* of the members." Previous acquaintance means strong social bonds, or the opposite of egoism. Religious principle means a strong set of norms, beliefs and values, or the opposite of anomie.

Over a century ago and well before Durkheim wrote, Thomas Masaryk (1881) argued that increasing suicide rates over the nineteenth century were the result of weakening religious faith. Some recent authors have speculated that the power of religion to deter suicide might have continued to decline through the twentieth century (Stack 1983; Breault 1986). In some respects religion has steadily strengthened over the decades, for example as measured by the increasing proportion of the American population who formally belong to churches (Finke and Stark 1992). Therefore, we cannot simply assume that the authority of religion has declined. In addition, it is worth recalling from Chapter 1 that religion has many dimensions, some of which might have strengthened while others weakened. Furthermore, there are several different sets of data that could be examined in several different ways, so the very brief analysis we offer here must be very far from definitive.

In 1926, the Bureau of the Census surveyed 232,154 individual churches all across the nation belonging to 212 denominations with a total of 54,576,346 members (Bureau of the Census 1930). Suicide rates were also available for major cities, and these were much higher in communities where the church member rates were low (Bainbridge and Stark 1981c). From the work of Durkheim to the present, one of the most challenging questions has been whether the influence of religion can be reduced simply to the action of social bonds. That is, strong religion may merely be a reflection of the solidarity of a stable community with a cohesive social network. In that case, the values promulgated by religion are superficial and lack any distinctive power of their own, apart from the cohesion of the community. It is possible to explore this empirically by measuring community cohesion, for example as reflected in low rates of residential migration, and statistically controlling for the effect of cohesion on the relationship between suicide and religion. When this was done in the 1926 data, the church-member rate proved to be a robust predictor of the suicide rate, not reducible to social bonds.

Another study (Bainbridge 1989a) replicated the same analysis with data from 1980, finding a very different picture. First of all, the power of religion to deter suicide appears smaller in 1980 than in 1926, even before applying any statistical controls. Correlations are stronger for big cities than for smaller ones, and the cities grew from 1926 to 1980, so one would also like to control for city size in comparing the two years. I have employed a statistical method called "moving correlations" (Isaac and Griffin 1989) to correct for this city-size problem, and I found that the religion-suicide correlation dropped to just exactly one-half of its former value over the space of fifty-four years. Statisticians often like to square correlation coefficients to get the percent of variance explained by the relationship, and in those terms the apparent power of religion has dropped to one-fourth its earlier strength. Furthermore, controlling for plausible measures of social integration erased the religion-suicide link altogether.

Table 10.1 presents some of the results in a manner that should be clear even to readers who have not studied statistics. The data cover the 120 metropolitan areas outside New England with populations over 300,000 in 1980. It was impossible to include the cites of New England in this particular analysis, because the measure of church membership is based on a census of church members by county (Quinn et al. 1982), but in defining metropolitan areas the Census Bureau did not follow county boundaries in New England as it did in the rest of the country.

The table separates the 120 metropolitan areas into three equal groups of forty each, in terms of their rates of church membership. On average, just 39.0 percent of the residents of the forty low-church-membership cities belong to religious denominations. In the forty medium-church-membership metropolitan areas, an average of 54.1 percent belong. And in the forty areas where organized religion is strongest, on average 66.9 percent belong to religious denominations. To estimate the full potential effect of secularization, we also will imagine a hypothetical city without churches, where the membership rate is 0.0 percent. At the opposite extreme, 100 percent of the residents of a hypothetical fully churched city would be members.

There are many variables that measure egoism or social integration, some more directly than others. One of the best available in the census reports is the proportion of people who were living in a different house five years before. As the second row of Table 10.3 shows, the groups of cities do vary in

Table 10.1: Church Membership and Suicide, 1980

| | Hypothetical City Without Churches | 120 American Metropolitan Areas with Church Membership: | | | Hypothetical Fully Churched City |
		40 Low	40 Medium	40 High	
Percent Church Members	0.0	39.0	54.1	66.9	100.0
Percent living in a different house five years earlier	68.8	54.9	46.4	43.2	32.3
Suicide rate per 100,000	17.2	13.9	12.0	11.4	8.3
Suicide rate controlling for percent living in a different house	12.7	12.5	12.4	12.3	12.2

the proportion who have moved in the past five years. In the forty metropolitan areas with relatively low church membership, 54.9 percent of residents were living in a different house five years earlier. By contrast, only 43.2 percent of residents in cities with high rates of church membership had moved. A technique knows as linear regression allows us to estimate the figures for hypothetical cities with 0 percent or 100 percent church membership. Essentially, regression is like drawing a graph of the two variables (church-member rate and five-year moving rate), getting a scatter of 120 points across a page. Then regression in essence draws a line through the points that captures the general direction the points are running. Then we read off the graph the points on the line at 0 and 100 percent church membership, to see what levels of five-year moving they represent.

Naturally, the process is really far more exact than that. The result of the regression analysis is that 68.8 percent of the people in a city with zero church membership are predicted to have moved in the past five years, compared with only 32.3 percent in a hypothetical city where everyone belongs to a church. Why should these variables be connected like this? Most probably, high rates of moving tear apart the social relationships that comprise church congregations, and newcomers to town do not yet have the social bonds that would connect them to particular local churches (Bainbridge 1990). At the same time, instability in social relationships should be a major cause of suicide. People who fall into deep depression, for whatever reason, may be prevented from killing themselves by the emotional support and physical surveillance of friends. Conversely, socially isolated individuals may be more prey to depression.

The third row of the table shows us that in 1980 there was a tendency for the suicide rate to be higher than average where the church-member rate was low, and lower than average where it was high. In the forty metropolitan areas with low church-member rates, 13.9 out of every 100,000 people killed themselves in 1980, compared with 11.4 in cities where the churches were stronger. This is a difference of 2.5 deaths per 100,000 that year. Of course, the contrast between the two hypothetical cities is greater. A city where nobody belonged to any church might expect to have 17.2 suicides per year per 100,000 population. In contrast, a city where everybody belonged to a church would have less than half as high a rate, just 8.3 per 100,000. So church membership appears to make a difference. But could this apparent relationship really be the spurious result of variations in social integration?

The final row of figures in the table uses multiple regression statistical techniques to estimate the suicide rates when the effect of residential migration is removed. Naturally the original journal article offers a technically more compelling statistical analysis, but here in a far simpler version of that analysis we see at a glance the very small effect that might really be attributed to religion. The cities with weak churches have an average suicide rate only 0.2 per 100,000 higher than the cities with strong churches. The most that church membership can accomplish, after the effect of the residential migration variable is controlled, is to reduce the suicide rate from 12.7 per 100,000 to 12.2. As the journal article explains, the effect is not only small but statistically insignificant. That is, the apparent residue of religion's former power might be nothing but a tiny random fluctuation in the numbers.

I must stress that this analysis is not conclusive. Although I used very standard techniques of quantitative sociological analysis, there are always several ways of approaching the numbers. It also is possible that there are unrecognized flaws in the 1980 data set, not possessed by the data from earlier years. Soon, I hope, someone will publish an analysis for the data that were collected in 1990, and perhaps comparable religion data will be collected at the time of the 2000 census. The comparison of data from 1926 with those from 1980, however, indicates that the power of religion to deter suicide may have lessened over the years. The absolute rate of church membership has not declined during these fifty-four years, so there must have been a weakening in some particular aspect of religion.

We cannot be sure about any of this, but one striking possibility is that American society has cut itself adrift from the complex of values and beliefs that would allow religion to be the regulator of collective action. As we have seen, surveys indicate that religion retains some power to deter some kinds of deviant behavior but not others. Just as support from the community was required for religion to have the power to deter larceny by juveniles, perhaps religion has become utterly dependent upon community stability to deter suicide. In both of these cases, religion may gain power when it is packaged within living social structures. This observation suggests that one major way that religion can affect society is when it expresses itself through well-organized social movements. A familiar recent example is the so-called right-to-life movement, which may in part express the differing values that religious and nonreligious groups possess in the realm of sexuality.

Sexual Morality

Throughout history, religions have promulgated rules and attitudes concerning sexuality, and the assumption was that they actually were effective in shaping behavior. Sexual desires are a strong biological drive, so presumably only powerful forces can channel or suppress them. In part, religion may merely codify the norms inherent in the society's kinship structure or in other parts of the secular culture, but religion may also promote more demanding sexual standards. This may occur particularly if recruitment of clergy tends to garner persons with somewhat unusual orientations or if the realities of the priestly profession shape the sexuality of clergy. Ancient religious traditions tend to promote views of sexuality consistent with conditions of ancient society, rather than reflecting modern trends, and the religious legacy of Western societies appears largely hostile toward sex (Schulz, Bohrnstedt, Borgatta and Evans 1977; Kelley 1978; Richardson and Weatherby 1983; Shea 1992).

In contrast with classical paganism and perhaps with Hinduism, the Judeo-Christian-Islamic tradition has tended to be somewhat puritanical, at least in its official pronouncements. In particular, puritanism is generally associated with Protestantism. When capitalized, the word "Puritan" refers to a Protestant sect that sought to purify Christianity of Roman Catholic influences. Weber (1958) wrote about the worldly asceticism of several Protestant groups, and some authorities trace puritanism back to medieval monasticism and even to the medieval Cathar (Albigensian) heresy that had an extremely negative attitude toward sexuality (Ferm 1945:628; Runciman 1947; Onions 1966:725).

We cannot hope to undertake a sociology of religion and sexuality here, because that is a vast topic worthy of its own, large book. Rather we should keep our focus on religious movements and the way they exist as part of a larger cultural and social system. Some social movements related to sexuality have their basis in traditional religious orientations to life, whereas movements opposing them are favored by people with more secular orientations. Thus, when we consider the sexual attitudes typical in different religious traditions, we should treat them as evidence about the kinds of people likely to

293

support, join, or even lead social movements oriented toward changing societal norms about sex.

Over the years, the General Social Survey has repeatedly included items measuring the respondent's attitudes toward sexuality and other kinds of sensuality such as marijuana use. Table 10.2 employs data from the General Social Survey to see how members of different denominations respond to such attitude questions. This table and the following one compare six denominational groups: No religion, Jewish, Catholic, Mainline Protestant (Methodist, Lutheran, Presbyterian, Episcopal, United Church of Christ, Unitarian, Reformed, and Quaker), Baptist, and Sects (Holiness, Pentecostal, Adventist, Church of Christ, Assemblies of God, Church of the Nazarene, Church of God, and Jehovah's Witness).

Our chief focus here is sexuality, so I have included the question about legalizing marijuana only to provide comparison with a nonsexual issue that also relates to hedonistic pleasure. Sexuality appears throughout the Bible, but marijuana is not even mentioned. There is a commandment about not committing adultery, but none about not smoking "pot." Thus, religion should affect attitudes about marijuana not through specific religious regulations, but through more general values, such as the virtue of being ascetic versus hedonistic, or obeying the law. The pattern of responses is very clear. More than half of those with no religious affiliation favor legalizing marijuana, compared with one out of nine among sect members.

The next three items all concern sexual relations outside "straight" heterosexual marriage: premarital sex, extramarital sex, and homosexuality. Across the board, respondents are more tolerant of premarital sex than of the two other kinds. But for each questionnaire item, the members of sectarian movements show much greater opposition than do members in all the other groups. The three concluding items concern "sexually explicit materials" (literature, pictures, movies) often condemned as "pornography." The item actually using the word "pornography" refers to the age of the person receiving and using the materials so that people will not answer merely in terms of whether sexually explicit materials should be available to children. A majority of sect members believe that such materials should be forbidden even to adults. "Sexual materials lead to breakdown of morals" is a theory that conceivably could be proposed by a sociologist and tested through scientific studies. But here it is a way of exploring the unscientific thoughts (pro or con) that various people may have about the relationship between availability of sexual materials and public morality. The final item actually concerns the respondent's behavior, and we see that people with no religion are more than twice as likely as sect members to have seen an X-rated (sexual) movie in the past year.

The obvious conclusion of the data in this table is that religious groups

Table 10.2: Attitudes toward Marijuana Use and Sexuality—Percent

	No Religion	Jewish	Catholic	Protestants: Mainline	Baptist	Sects
MARIJUANA:						
The use of marijuana should be made legal.	51.5 (1,216)	41.7 (343)	21.5 (4,230)	19.3 (4,594)	15.9 (3,460)	11.4 (1,188)
SEXUAL RELATIONS OUTSIDE STRAIGHT MARRIAGE:						
Always wrong for a man and woman to have sex before marriage.	7.6 (1,218)	12.0 (400)	24.2 (4,358)	26.2 (4,812)	39.0 (3,477)	57.1 (1,119)
Always wrong for a married person to have sex with someone other than the marriage partner.	45.6 (1,170)	50.3 (356)	72.8 (4,333)	73.1 (4,738)	80.1 (3,538)	87.5 (1,153)
Sexual relations between two adults of the same sex are always wrong.	41.9 (1,126)	35.3 (337)	70.9 (4,163)	73.4 (4,518)	85.9 (3,463)	93.1 (1,135)
PORNOGRAPHY:						
There should be laws against the distribution of pornography whatever the age of the person.	19.1 (1,261)	21.5 (349)	39.7 (4,344)	42.3 (4,702)	45.2 (3,501)	59.1 (1,184)
Sexual materials lead to breakdown of morals.	34.0 (1,207)	36.7 (332)	61.6 (4,132)	63.3 (4,463)	67.9 (3,299)	78.1 (1,143)
Respondent has seen an x-rated movie in the last year.	35.4 (1,281)	33.0 (357)	22.7 (4,373)	18.9 (4,750)	20.9 (3,540)	15.5 (1,208)

differ greatly in their propensity to accept the ideals of a variety of sex-related social movements that are in fact active today in American society. The movement to legalize marijuana may have practically vanished from sight, but substantial gay-liberation and gay-pride movements exist and command great public attention. Movements related to sexual literature, pictures, and movies rise and fall over the years, sometime blazing brilliantly, and sometimes fading from sight. But at a peak period for this issue, it is not uncommon to see two diametrically opposed social movements battling each other in the public arena: an antipornography movement versus a free-speech movement. Other things being equal, we can predict that members of sectarian movements are more likely to take part in movements opposing liberal sexual norms, than in ones favoring them.

The most visible religiously charged such debate today concerns abortion, with the "pro-life" movement opposing abortion under most circumstances, and the "pro-choice" movement battling against it (Wuthnow 1988; Tribe 1990). The General Social Survey has included a battery of questions, beginning with this introduction: "Please tell me whether or not you think it should be possible for a pregnant woman to obtain a legal abortion if. . . ." Table 10.3 lists the alternatives and again reveals that sect members are more likely than others to take what might be described as a puritanical attitude. The last of the seven items concerns the legality of abortion, if "the woman wants it for any reason." All six other items include something that might be considered an extenuating circumstance that would legitimize abortion. Three such circumstances get majority support for abortion in all groups: serious defect in the baby, danger to the woman's health, and rape. But on the four items lacking such strong justifications, the contrasts across the religious groups are really quite striking.

Incidentally, the official and unequivocal opposition to abortion of the Roman Catholic Church might lead us to expect that Catholics are more fervently against abortion than are Protestants. This is true if we compare Catholics with the relatively liberal "Mainline" Protestant denominations. But in Table 10.3 Catholics are really not distinguishable from Baptists, and members of Protestant sects are far more strongly opposed to abortion than either Catholics or Baptists. If we were to combine all the Protestants, there would be little overall difference between them and the Catholics. Of course, there are great differences within Catholicism, just as there are within Protestantism, but it is harder to find them in questionnaire surveys. Although a few relatively small Catholic sects exist, Catholicism does not have all the various larger denominations that Protestantism does, and there are no easy questions to ask Catholics that divide them into religious groups, as denominational membership does so effectively for Protestants.

So far, we have established that substantial pools exist of supporters for pro-life movements among higher-tension religious groups, and of supporters for pro-choice movements among low-tension or secularized groups. But as we have seen in earlier chapters, effective movements need to mobilize individuals into organizations. John McCarthy and Mayer Zald have examined how this occurred in the abortion struggle (McCarthy 1987; Zald and McCarthy 1987).

Although about equal number of Protestants and Catholics oppose legal-

Table 10.3: Attitudes: Abortion Should be Legal . . .—Percent

	No Religion (1,639)	Jewish (518)	Catholic (5,989)	Protestants: Mainline (6,674)	Baptist (4,848)	Sects (1,546)
If there is a strong chance of serious defect in the baby.	91.2	95.2	74.0	87.8	74.0	62.6
If she is married and does not want any more children.	71.7	81.5	35.6	49.7	33.4	18.3
If the woman's own health is seriously endangered by the pregnancy.	94.8	97.3	83.0	93.1	86.0	76.2
If the family has a very low income and cannot afford any more children.	73.9	84.9	40.4	55.5	38.0	24.7
If she became pregnant as a result of rape.	91.1	96.3	75.2	87.8	74.6	59.6
If she is not married and does not want to marry the man.	71.6	85.1	36.9	51.8	33.0	21.2
The woman wants it for any reason.	66.7	75.0	31.9	43.2	28.7	15.6

izing abortion (outside of cases with clear extenuating circumstances), Catholics were far more active than Protestants in the early days of the pro-life movement. Table 1.3 showed that about 25 percent of the population identifies with the Roman Catholic Church, but surveys of the membership of pro-life organizations done around 1980 reveal a proportion Catholic between 70 percent and 85 percent (McCarthy 1987:53–54). The reason is that the extensive, nationwide network of existing Catholic organizations unrelated to the abortion issue served as a very effective scaffolding upon which antiabortion groups could form.

Catholics with antiabortion sentiments would meet at church and in other Catholic organizations to which they belonged and share their feelings about abortion. It has long been known that social movements can grow more rapidly if they can spread through existing social networks, than if they have to build such a network from scratch, relationship by relationship

(Granovetter 1973). Furthermore, existing organizations have a variety of resources that can be transferred to new organizations, including skills, mailing lists, and in the case of the Roman Catholic Church and the pro-life movement, semi-official endorsement. Protestant sects also put themselves on record against abortion, but the fragmentation inherent in high-tension Protestantism delayed their mobilization of anti-abortion sentiments. At the same time, the pro-life movement was unable to exploit existing religious infrastructures, and thus was forced to rely upon technological substitutes, such as media advertising and mass mailings.

Conclusion: The Enigma of Religious Morality

Religion used to mean regulation. That is, religion traditionally was believed to provide the moral center for a society, controlling the behavior of individuals so that cooperation was possible (Parsons 1964). In today's secularized world, there is some question whether society actually has a center, or whether a moral center could be reconstructed in the face of the tremendous disagreements that divide citizens of modern societies (Neuhaus 1984). Ironically, the Watergate conspirators apparently believed they were defending traditional sociocultural values against the forces of chaos and revolution, even as they committed crimes that weakened the traditional political system.

This chapter has shown that religion has the capacity to shape individual behavior, but this power is highly variable. It is not enough for an individual to possess private faith in God. Only if this faith is embedded in a network of community ties will it deter theft and suicide. Although individual religiousness shapes ascetic or hedonistic behavior, involvement in a religiously inspired social movement magnifies this influence. Indeed, religion is sustained by movements and affects the world most decisively through the medium of movements.

In the three following chapters, we will examine the ways that religious movements serve as the highways along which influence between religion and the world travels. Chapter 11 examines the New York City Mission society, a prominent charity and personal renewal movement that sought to change the lives of people living under dreadful material conditions. Chapter 12 addresses how religion and democracy strengthen or weaken each other, an issue of tremendous current policy significance worldwide, which also illuminates profound theoretical questions. In Chapter 13, we see the quasi-religious New Age Movement, that may be eroding the fringes of traditional religion, or represents a religious response to the depredations of secularism. In each of these three topics, we see examples of the ways that religion shapes society, and is shaped in return.

When Colson and Magruder were born again, in a sense they merely regained the respectable status they had lost by their involvement in Watergate. Before the cover-up, they were trusted members of the team that ruled America. Through convictions and prison sentences they lost their honor, and they needed a transformation of identity that would restore honor, both in their own minds and in the eyes of the general public. Being born again and gaining a special status within a religious movement is a powerful means for cleansing a soiled reputation and being re-labeled respectable (Trice and Roman 1970). These two men dedicated themselves to religious careers, so conversion did have a clear effect on their subsequent actions. But the issue of when religion does or does not influence individual behavior is a crucial and complex issue for the scientific study of religious movements and for the sociology of religion in general.

11

The New York City Mission Society

Many religious movements concern themselves with alleviating the ills of society, and such reform or social service movements often exist in rather complex relationships to religious denominations. This chapter will focus on the example of one of the oldest such movements in the United States, the New York City Mission Society, emphasizing the "Gay Nineties" a century ago, when it was playing an important role in acculturation of immigrants. Much of the following is taken from the pages of the *City Mission Monthly*, its annual reports, and miscellaneous ephemeral publications. These can be found only in the New York City Public Library and the storeroom of the Mission Society itself, so I have not wasted space providing detailed references.

The Great Panic of '93

In a mood of great satisfaction, the New York City Mission and Tract Society celebrated its seventieth anniversary on December 14, 1892, in the affluent Fifth Avenue Presbyterian Church. Originally founded simply "to seek the sinner in his lurking place, to awaken his conscience and to speak to him until he is placed within the sound of the gospel," the Society had evolved into a complex multifunction organization (Miller and Miller 1962:45). The 1865 state charter said, "The objects of this corporation are to promote morality and religion among the poor and destitute of the city of New York, by the employment of missionaries, by the diffusion of evangelical reading and the sacred Scriptures, by the establishment of Sabbath-

Schools, mission stations and chapels, for the preaching of the Gospel and for other ordinances of Divine worship." But by the close of the nineteenth century, the Society had taken on many social-service functions and aimed chiefly to use religion to uplift the poor and help immigrants adjust to the new country.

The master of ceremonies of the anniversary festivity was philanthropist Morris K. Jesup, railroad financial magnate, who served as the Society's president when he wasn't busy managing the American Museum of Natural History and other causes dear to his heart. Sixty city missionaries, about three-fourths of them women, sat in dignified poses on the stage as a train of speakers recounted the challenges and accomplishments of the past year.

The pastors of the Society's three churches took their turns (Miller and Miller 1962:112–114). Reverend Alexander H. McKinney of Olivet Church announced that 821 persons had attended his Sunday school that week. Reverend William T. Elsing of the De Witt Memorial Church, which Jesup had built a decade earlier in memory of his wife's clergyman father, found lessons of faith in stories of his rowdy, egg-throwing parishioners. Reverend Theo Leonhardt joked he was the left arm of McKinney and Elsing, because he preached the German-language services at both their churches. Reverend Charles H. Tyndall, resident pastor of the Broome Street Tabernacle recounted his battles with the thirteen liquor saloons in his neighborhood "that are fighting the Gospel as hard as they can." These churches did not serve the patrons and contributors to the Society, who preferred the more fashionable midtown temples of worship. Rather they opened their doors to the masses of immigrants and native-born poor who swarmed below Fourteenth Street, where the Jews and Catholics each outnumbered the Protestants three to one, and the social problems of industrial society cried out for mercy.

The reporter for the *Mail and Express* was enchanted by Lucy Bainbridge's "commanding personal appearance, sweet voice, and charming countenance," when she introduced the forty-five ladies who worked full-time for her Woman's Branch. The twenty-seven Bible-reading missionaries stood as she described the gifts of comfort and hope they brought to poor mothers. Then the eight trained nurses stood, as she told of their medical service among the children and elderly. Finally the eight students stood, the hope of the future. Others who spoke were Hermann Warszawiak, a flamboyant convert who delighted in debating theology with his fellow Jewish immigrants, and Alexander F. Irvine, a dedicated religious social worker with the lodging-house bums.

The superintendent of the Society, Dr. Schauffler, decried the fact that twenty-one churches had left the Society's area of the city in the past twenty years, leaving the 542,000 residents with few sources of Protestant religion.

This observation brought him to the bottom line, an appeal for money. It is hard to translate the dollars of 1892 into the coinage of a century later, but the entire vast operation of the Mission Society could get by on just $100,000 for the following year. "Two thousand five hundred dollars will support one of our English pastors for a whole year, and through him preach 104 sermons, take care of about 500 meetings, visit the sick and the godless and minister in a thousand ways to those who are in dire need of such service. . . . One thousand dollars will pay for the whole outlay of one of our free reading rooms and circulating libraries for a year. This means about 44,000 readers who are thus furnished with a comfortable place in which to read and with wholesome reading matter. The numbers of the young who are thus kept off the streets is very great. It helps them and prepares them for larger usefulness in life."

For forty years, the Mission Society had its offices in Bible House on Astor Place, but early in the new year it moved to the fourth floor of the brand-new United Charities Building at the corner of Fourth Avenue and Twenty-second Street, donated by John Stewart Kennedy. Three other organizations shared the building rent-free with the Mission Society: the Charity Organization Society, the Association for the Improving of the Condition of the Poor, and the Children's Aid Society. Seven stories high and sixty by 150 feet, the building had so much space they were able to lease some out, and for the rest of the decade the Mission Society received about two thousand dollars rent each year. The owner of the building was a special United Charities corporation, directed by a board of nine managers consisting of Kennedy plus two representatives from each of the four organizations. To preserve the corporation's nonsectarian charter, a further provision stipulated that a majority of its managers should never belong to the same religious denomination.

The United Charities Building was created by the wealth of a single man, but it expressed the vast financial power of one of the world's greatest cities at a time of strong economic growth. Railroad financier that he was, Mission Society president Jesup must have worried about the bankruptcy of the Philadelphia and Reading Railway Corporation on February 20, just when his organization was beginning to pack up at Bible House for the move to its splendid new offices. On April 22 the federal gold reserves dipped below a hundred million dollars for the first time since 1879, a more subtle sign of trouble but an equally worrisome one. Prices of wheat and iron declined, signaling weak markets, and the rate of business failures increased. On May 3, the stock market dropped precipitously, with many industrial companies losing as much as 15 percent of their value. The following day, three Wall Street brokerage companies failed. The Great Panic of 1893 had begun, a worldwide economic depression that would not be equaled in severity until the 1930s (Hoffman 1970). The stock market crashed. Banks failed in unprecedented numbers across the country, and in July the reserves of New York banks fell below the legally required minimums. That month the Erie railroad failed. Unemployment soared, not only because workers lost their jobs at companies that failed or retrenched, but also because many people lived by doing odd jobs, from individual seamstresses who repaired or made clothing by hand to carpenters, delivery men, ditch diggers, and all-purpose workers who lived off a series of short-term employments. Many of these independent laborers lived just above the ranks of the already numerous paupers, and they quickly fell into this destitute population.

In July 1893, Lucy asked the readers of the *City Mission Monthly* to help increase the number of social workers. "Several young women, well fitted for our work, are asking to be received. We hesitate, seeing the treasury running low. Who will pledge the support of one—five hundred dollars a year? There are heavy financial clouds overhead. Shall our force of missionaries be reduced when the work is increasing and the workers are ready? Why not send to this treasury a thank-offering to-day? Banks may fail, stocks may go down, but God's dividends are sure."

In September, Schauffler expressed the "fear that, for the poor, the coming winter will be a very trying one," and he said the city's population of beggars was temporarily reduced by the fact that many had gone out to Chicago to beg at the World's Fair. In the summers, the rich patrons of the Mission Society took long vacations in the country, and every year the treasury got low without their constant contributions. But now the need was extreme, and Lucy herself began begging in her magazine articles:

"A few days ago a brawny woman accosted me on the street with these words, "If you please, ma'am, could ye tell me of anybody as would give me a day's scrubbin' or washin'. I'm no beggar woman, ma'am,' and her face glowed with honest pride, 'but me man's place is shut down, and there's five little 'uns to feed and the rent. May the Lord pity us, if the rich folks don't come from the country soon, to give us work.'

"At the office there sat waiting a frail young widow with a baby on her lap. It was a sad story, and the tears ran down her cheeks as she told of her husband's death and the struggle for bread. 'The landlord says just this to me now, 'give me money or give me my rooms.'

"Another caller, a feeble white-haired woman, whose face showed the refinement of better days, 'Could you kindly give me a little plain sewing?' she said. 'My eyes are rather poor but I'll do my best; fifty cents worth a week, even, would be a great blessing now.'

"Down town, bread, by the wagon load, has been given out to the hungry. Provisions have been sent from the West to the poor of our city. There are many generous efforts, official and private, for the feeding of the thousands of the unemployed, and surely there is no city in all the world quite equal to New York for generous giving. But shall we let our self-respecting poor depend on this charity?

"Can we not help some of our poor women by letting them try to help themselves? There are those who will quickly reply, 'Send them into domestic service; there the supply does not equal the demand.' True, but can you find homes where untrained women, with little clinging children, are accepted as kitchen or nursery maids? I often wish the overworked factory girls could realize the comfort, health and real privileges which the house maids enjoy. But will you not make it possible for the Woman's Branch to give some employment to special women at special times?

"We know of tenements where the wife and mother is not able to scrub and wash, and so the bedding and clothes are waiting for soap and water over long for health and decency.

"There are rooms cared for by aged women or young girls, where an occasional day of washing or scrubbing would give new courage and brightness, and our spiritual work would be quickened.

"Then there are many too feeble to wash or scrub. Have you ever been to the office on a Monday morning? You have then seen the company of 'rheumaticy' coughing women bringing and carrying bundles. Dorcas [the charity clothing office] gives these feeble sisters a little very plain sewing, such as skirts and aprons, which a missionary gives to the convict women when they leave prison life. Do you say, 'Dorcas pays these women—where does Dorcas get her money?' The bills for sewing and materials used for these convict women are paid for by one generous friend. But for all the rest we look to you, and must frankly say your Dorcas has been running into debt.

"The generous friends of the Woman's Branch used to slip into the hands of [my predecessor] Mrs. A. R. Brown sums of money, for her use in charity. At her death there was found of such undesignated funds, $743.27. This amount we have long since expended, through our missionaries and nurses, together with all the donations sent us, from time to time for nurses relief, special coal, etc, and have used as was right and then borrowed from our Easter Fund for such charitable relief. But now we must stop short. Charity is bankrupt! Yet a distressing winter for the sick poor is just ahead of us."

Visiting college student Gertrude Burrage was profoundly shocked by what she saw while making the rounds with a Mission Society lady. "Oh, the poverty and destitution of lower New York this fall! How many, many times did I hear wives and mothers of little children say, 'My husband has been able to get no work during the summer,' or 'My husband died several years ago and this summer I have been able to earn only two or three dollars a week.' One of the missionaries went out one evening to carry flowers and reading matter to a poor family in which she was interested. Although the gifts were received thankfully yet she soon found that they were only a hollow mockery, for the family was starving."

On Cherry Street, Gertrude saw an intact but destitute family. "My companion and I stumbled through the dark hallway, up the back staircase, and found ourselves in a good-sized room which seemed all the larger on account of the scarcity of furniture. Let those people who live in luxury homes listen while I tell what that room contained: A bed on which lay a woman, her baby two days old, and her three-year-old boy; her husband was bending over the stove heating some water, a chair was visible in one dark corner, a stool in another; a table, a trunk and a few dishes completed the furniture of the room and the *home*. The husband was very kind and polite that night, but I found out afterward that it was his terrible appetite for strong drink that had brought his family to that condition. It is only God who can forgive a man for dragging down into hopeless misery not only himself but his wife and innocent children."

They then went in search of four-year-old Katie, to whom the missionary had given a small doll with plain dress that the child loved dearly. "We found her, poor little thing, locked out on the street, sick with the whooping cough. The neighbors told us that when the terrible paroxysms of coughing came on, all the strength left the little body and she could scarcely stand." A few days later, Gertrude learned that Katie had died. Her mother placed the doll under a glass globe, surrounded with artificial flowers, to remember her lost darling. The missionary found solace in religious faith and the hope that her work with Katie would give her family a lasting connection with God: "Katie's mission was ended; but that which could only have been begun through her is going on, and some day mother, teacher, and child will meet again where there shall be no more tears."

Shortly before Thanksgiving, when the winter chill was only just beginning, a reporter from the *Mail and Express* followed Mission Society nurse J. M. Glasgow on her morning rounds, beginning with the moment she awakened in the five-story home on East Tenth Street where most of the ladies of the Woman's Branch lived. "A pretty white and gold room, with windows looking out over St. Mark's churchyard. A dainty white bed occupies one corner and a dressing case another. In still another corner stands a small bookcase and a glance at the back of the books in it shows that the owner is of more than the average culture. One of the most noticeable things in the room is a nurse's graduation certificate from Mount Sinai Hospital hanging over the bookcase."

Shortly after seven, Miss Glasgow steps down stairs toward the day's activities. "On the way down she greets many other women, always with a gentle smile and a kind inquiry after this or that one's health, and they go into the large study next to the dining room and offer up a prayer for help in their day's work. Then comes breakfast. The dining room contains three long tables, each of which seats fourteen. It would be hard to find more attractive women than these forty-two who are seated at the long tables. In age they range from 24 to 40. There are only two or three older. . . . After breakfast is eaten they all gather in the study and discuss their different plans for the day. Each of the missionaries has her own district and work for each particular day. The nurses' working day is about six hours long and the missionaries devote seven hours to their labor, but there are many extra calls beside their visiting ones, and after a day spent with them one realizes that a city missionary works as hard as a laboring man or woman and that nothing but Christianity and a real love of doing good enables them to stand it."

Miss Glasgow begins her rounds. "She carries a black satchel of medium size. The satchel contains milk tickets [which will allow poor mothers to get milk for their babies], several instruments, bandages and medicines appropriate to the cases she is to visit, and a couple of paper parcels." The first stop is the Virginia Day Nursery, where mothers in especially difficult situations may leave their children while they work. She has a special responsibility for the health of the children there and in the Society's two other daycare centers, the Jewell Day Nursery and the Baby Fold.

Then she heads "into the heart of the most densely populated district in all the crowded East side. Here she stops before a dilapidated building. She has a patient in a rookery back of the tumble down building, which is not visible from the street. Down a narrow, noisome hallway in the front structure she gropes through darkness so black she cannot see her hand before her face. Some would-be cleanly soul had recently flooded the hall, and the nurse wades through a river of water until she comes into a small court which answers for a yard. The rear house is even worse than the front. She goes up two flights of stairs and into a stuffy little room.

"This is where the patient is with a two day's old baby and a pair of other half starved mites of children. The nurse goes there every day to wash and dress the baby and make the mother as comfortable as her surroundings will permit until she is well. She also looks after the other children, tidies up the house and prepares the food. The father of this unfortunate family was killed three months ago, and now that the mother is ill all the care these helpless ones have is from the missionaries.

"The next call is several blocks away, at the very top of a tenement house that contains a good sized colony in itself. Here she goes to see little Eddie, who has spinal disease and whose poor little body is wrapped round and round with plaster of Paris. He is really 5 years old, but is so stunted that he doesn't look more than 2. Some children race up stairs ahead to say, 'Eddie's lady is coming,' and Eddie toddles to the door and his poor pinched little face grows quite pretty in his delight. He stands beside the woman holding her hand and smoothing her dress as she talks to his mother and then you discover that one of the paper bundles in the nurse's hand contains fruit for the little sufferer and she tells him that she has some nice little dresses for him that she will bring some day.

"The husband and father (there are five children) has had no steady employment all summer and they are looking toward the cold weather in dread. Down the long flights of stairs, out into the streets, and then to several other families, whose misery makes the heart ache. The missionary has been doing this work for more than three years and although she acknowledges to being almost disheartened sometimes over the vast amount of wretchedness that she sees, she still goes on working hopefully and even cheerfully."

At 12:30 Miss Glasgow takes the reporter back to the missionary home for lunch. "Here you find most of the workers, although some have not been able to get back yet. They exchange experiences. They look bright and cheerful. Some of the younger ones ask advice. Mrs. Bainbridge is at the table, and listens to all their tales of woe, gives them advice, comforts and encourages them and directs their plans. With all her gentle sweetness the superintendent is a woman of action. She takes complete possession of those who meet her and explains the work in a manner that shows what a thoroughly practical knowledge she has of it. Her office is in the United Charities building at Twenty-second street and Fourth avenue. There she is to be found every day except Saturday both in the morning and afternoon. She receives donations there and generally directs the movements of woman's work."

After lunch, Lucy puts the reporter into the hands of the Italian missionary, Lydia Tealdo, "a pretty little woman considerably under 30, and is one of the beauties of the house. She has big, dark eyes and a thoroughly Italian type of face. She speaks English fluently and is intensely interested in her work." On Mulberry street Lydia has rented a pair of rooms for a satellite mission. There she teaches English and Bible to little children during the day, and older people at night, assisted by Anna Rau, a Swiss who also speaks Italian. "Very few of the women [in the neighborhood] speak English, but the men and children do after visiting the mission rooms. The missionary calls on some very poor and sick people. Everywhere she is greeted with smiles. The little children are glad to see her and follow her from house to house.

"In Mulberry Bend she takes you into several places where the halls are pitch dark and the stairs are rickety. In one building there is a barber shop back in an alley. After going through the alley you come out in a filthy yard, then go up a flight of steps built on the outside of a wooden shanty and a long dilapidated platform that creaks and threatens to give way. In one little room live the barber, his wife and five children. The woman is ill and the father lazy, therefore the youngsters have a hard time of it. The missionary knows just what to say to these people. She talks to them in their own tongue, scolds the man for being lazy, sympathizes with the woman and praises the children when they are good. When the man is scolded the shameless creature laughs."

On Mulberry Street, they pass some children playing with a live mouse with a string tied to its tail. Lydia tells them they should not be so cruel, but then turns to the reporter and says, "They have so little amusement." Both of them were exhausted when they reached the missionary home at six for dinner, but there was a full evening of classes to attend at mission churches, where girls were taught sewing, mothers were taught how to make the most of the poor foodstuffs they could afford, and everyone who would listen was told about Jesus.

The winter of 1893–1894 was to be an especially cold one. A modest attempt by the city government to provide coal for the poor fell far short of need, and sometimes their pathetic wooden furniture found its way into the stove to provide one glorious evening of warmth. We cannot pretend that the Mission Society and the other charitable organizations of New York were equal to the challenge of the Great Panic. But they did their best to raise money and dispense help in this most difficult period. By one estimate, across the whole city only two-and-a-half million dollars were available for relief during the winter of 1893–1894, and even if one grossly underestimates the number of the needy, less than fifty dollars was available for each destitute family or individual (Hoffman 1970:68). The Mission Society's records show that they received more that twice as much in bequests from dying supporters in 1893 than in any other year of the nineteenth century, $67,796 compared with $28,000 in 1897, the second-highest year.

Industrial production fell until around June 1894, then very sluggish growth followed, and the depression would not fully end for another three years. But for the Mission Society the toll in visible human agony was far more impressive than the economic statistics. In August 1894 Lucy wrote, "Close by, in the very shadow of the wolf of hunger, crouches the wolf of disease. Destitution and distress of the winter are being followed by the long-continued summer heat; tenements are like bakers' ovens. Sickness and death are in many of the homes; feeble children and overworked mothers and aged folks cannot endure the strain if August is like July."

The People of the Society

A religious charity like the Mission Society is an organization composed of individual people who have a variety of needs to be met and roles to be played. Any categorization of people is bound to oversimplify, but we can discern five major groups of participants in the Mission Society social system: 1) patrons, 2) leaders, 3) workers, 4) contributors, and 5) clients. Patrons are super-rich individuals with the resources to make things happen on a large scale. Leaders are the functionaries of the Society, including the superintendents of the men's and women's branches, and the clergy who manage the Society's own church missions. The workers are the rank and file employees of the Society, chiefly the fifty nurses and missionaries of the Woman's Branch. Contributors are ordinary churchgoers who donate a few dollars when the plate is passed for a special collection, or individual professionals or business people who contribute a little of their time and expertise. Finally come the clients, most numerous of all, the people helped by the Society who may grow to become contributors if the Society's aid helps them get on their feet. Each of these categories receives somewhat distinctive rewards from participation in the charity, and the life stories that brought them to it are highly varied.

During the 1890s, the chief *patron* and president of the Society was Morris K. Jesup, who was born into a rich and religiously strict family in 1830. The great financial panic of 1837 wiped out the family's wealth, and his father died soon after, leaving his mother struggling to raise eight children. In time, tuberculosis killed all but two of the little ones, and poverty forced Morris to drop out of school after the sixth grade. He became a messenger boy in a locomotive factory run by one of his father's old friends, and he quickly learned the railway business. At the age of twenty-two, he formed a partnership with a bookkeeper and started buying and selling railway equipment. Before long he had become an investment banker, buying and selling entire railroads. Despite his limited formal education, he was an active supporter of science and helped to found the American Museum of Natural History in 1869. In 1880, the museum was on the brink of financial collapse, but Jesup took over its presidency and built it into one of the world's premier scientific and educational institutions, personally launching many of its great expeditions to amass scientific collections (Preston 1986).

In American culture, "rags to riches" is a favorite story, spreading the message that anybody can make it in our society if he or she tries hard enough. But Jesup's life history is actually rather common, riches to rags to riches, or put more generally: a person from an advantaged background is beaten down by bad circumstances then struggles to regain all that was lost. (Many will recognize this as the story of Scarlet O'Hara in *Gone with the Wind*.) "Rags to riches" parallels the myth of religious conversion; an unworthy person accepts Jesus and in consequence is raised up. Stories like Jesup's may not often be told because they do not fit American populist mythology. But they do fit the influential theory of human capital for which economist-sociologist Gary S. Becker (1993) won the Nobel Prize.

The term *human capital* refers to the nonmaterial resources of a person that allow him or her to participate more effectively in the socioeconomic system. The example that springs to mind most quickly is the valuable skills and knowledge a person may gain through education, but there are many other kinds of human capital. Sociologists have expanded the concept to include all those acquirable resources (other than financial capital) that affect the individual's capacity for status attainment. Among these are social capital, which may be defined as the value of the individual's social network and ascribed statuses such as race or gender (Coleman 1988). Jesup must have learned some effective behavior patterns from his father, before losing him, and from all of his family he learned valuable lessons about how to speak, plan, and dedicate himself to challenging goals. His first employer had been a friend of his dad, so even though the job was tough and paid poorly, it signaled that Jesup still had some contact with the valuable social network of his father. Given the right combination of motivation and opportunity, even if a person is beaten down by misfortunes, he or she had the chance to exploit this human capital and become prosperous again.

The *leader* responsible for day-to-day operation of the Mission Society was its vice president, Adolph Frederick Schauffler, the son of American missionaries to Turkey who had been raised near Constantinople (A. Schauffler 1919; R. Schauffler 1951). He knew five languages, graduated from Williams College in 1867 and the Andover Theological Seminary in 1871, then served as pastor of the Society's Olivet Church from 1873 until 1887 when he became vice president. He married Julia Baker, daughter of a wealthy family, and her sister married John Stewart Kennedy who also was financially successful. Neither couple had any children, and they lived together, making the Mission Society the center of their lives.

Schauffler's story reminds us that religious leaders are professionals, and that professions traditionally have been handed down from father to son. All the excitement about conversion in the sociology of religion has obscured the fact that most participants in religious organizations were not converted at all. They were born into their religion, and those of them who become leaders often learned their leadership skills from members of their own family. Indeed, much of the strength of really successful religious organizations is the extent to which they are based in families and networks of families. Morris K. Jesup could have devoted himself entirely to the American Museum, but the fact that his wife was the daughter of Thomas De Witt, president of the Mission Society from 1846 to 1873, gave him a deep family commitment to the Society. In 1881, when Morris became president of the Society, his wife succeeded her own mother to became First Directress of the Woman's Branch, a position she held until 1915. Thus, leadership positions can also be handed down from mother to daughter as well as from father to son.

Schauffler's partner beginning in 1891 was Lucy Seaman Bainbridge who directed the Woman's Branch. Born in Cleveland in 1842, she had been a nurse with the United States Sanitary Commission in the Civil War, a volunteer medical corps that Abraham Lincoln scornfully called the army's "fifth wheel" but which made up for his administration's failure to provide adequate medical aid for sick and wounded soldiers (Maxwell 1956). On a Virginia battlefield she met her future husband, William Folwell Bainbridge, who was a minister with the Christian Commission, an organization of volunteer religious workers informally attached to the Chaplains Corps that gave the soldiers some material aid but chiefly handed out tracts and urged the men to pray. In 1886, William became the director of the relatively small Brooklyn City Mission Society, and Lucy founded its women's auxiliary. Having published three books seeking to establish missionary work on a "scientific" footing, he became obsessed by a grand scientific project to trace the original meaning of every place and tribe name in the Bible in the appropriate ancient languages, so he quit regular work and abandoned family responsibilities. When, as she believed, the Holy Spirit gave Lucy the Mission Society job, it kept her and her two children out of poverty while recovering the honor she had lost with her husband.

We know the stories of only a few of the hundreds of lady *workers* who served over the years as missionaries or nurses, but the information we do have suggests that they were not former clients who were plucked from poverty to minister to the neighborhoods from which they had come. Rather, they appear to have come from established middle-class families, discovered they had a special vocation for service, then received extensive formal instruction in the Training School of the Woman's Branch before being sent below Fourteenth Street to work with clients who were very different from themselves. In a number of cases some life misfortune may have precipitated joining the Mission, and like Lucy herself around six workers at any given time in the 1890s were called "Mrs." despite the apparent lack of a husband. But for these ladies the Mission Society may have been a means of keeping from falling down out of the middle class, rather than a route up into it.

Despite the fact that many clients were Italian immigrants, for a time only one of the missionaries could speak their language, Lydia L. Tealdo, who had been born in Milan (Tealdo 1928). But her story was very different from those of her clients. Her father had been a Protestant minister trying to convert Italy away from Catholicism, and she was raised for some kind of religious vocation. She had just reached young adulthood when her parents died. A school friend of hers had recently married a minister and was working in America for the evangelization of Italy. This contact put her in communication with the Woman's Branch, and in 1888 she applied for admission to its training school. Very soon she was working under the direction of Antonio Arrighi, pastor of the Italian Church on Worth street, who was operating the Italian Evangelical Mission located at the Five Points House of Industry, a work institution for the destitute poor with appalling conditions. Lydia never married, and the story was that she found the unmarried Italian men she met in her work so impoverished or degraded that none were acceptable to her.

Lydia's description of the conditions in which her clients lived, when she was first working under Lucy's predecessor, Mrs. A. R. Brown, indicates the gulf she felt between them and herself: "What I saw were filthy streets, filthy old rookeries, windowless rooms—dark, airless, and unfit to live in—but crowded with adults and children and shared with cats, dogs, chickens, pigeons, and all sorts of other animals both visible and invisible. These 'homes' were also used as barber shops, clothing factories, laundries, and storage rooms for unsold vegetables and fruit. Once, while visiting a sick man, I saw hundreds of worms crawling out from under the bed where he had stored unsold chestnuts. I wanted to run away and take the first boat back to Italy; but Mrs. Brown, then the Superintendent of the Woman's Branch, persuaded me to stay. She told me that if I was afraid the bugs would crawl on me while I was kneeling in prayer, I could pray standing up!" (quoted in Miller and Miller 1962:180–181).

Many of the missionaries and nurses entered service directly from education. Miss Adelia Hitchcock had taught classical Greek in college and been the principal of the Warsaw, Indiana, high school before "she heard the call of God for missionary service among the poor and neglected, and came to New York in 1878." After the Training School for Christian Workers opened in 1885 with four students, many of the ladies of the Woman's Branch entered through it. In its first two decades, a total of 149 women completed the one-year course, and sixty-one one of them actually worked for the Woman's Branch (Bainbridge 1904). Most others took careers in some phase of religious work.

The gentlemen of the Mission Society were far less numerous than the ladies, and much of the male effort went into running the three churches. The few nonclergy male workers did tend to have colorful stories. Alexander Irving was an Irish Protestant, the son of a shoemaker father and alcoholic mother, who joined the Royal Marines and saw service in the tardy 1885 relief expedition that failed to save major-general Charles "Chinese" Gordon at the siege of Khartoom in the Sudan by the forces of Mohammed Ahmed, a self-proclaimed messiah seeking to expel foreign forces (Churchill 1899; Miller and Miller 1962:122–124). When he came to America, Irving struggled to survive in a series of hard, low-pay jobs until he was hired to work on the new edition of *Webster's Dictionary*. The editors had planned merely to polish up the old 1859 edition by cribbing material from other publications, but Irving convinced them to invest in considerable new scholarship, and soon they were paying him the princely sum of $100 a month. But with his combination of fine mind, extensive world experience, and sensitivity to the conditions of the poor, he was not satisfied simply to develop his own career. At that time, seventy cheap lodging houses had grown up on a street called the Bowery and around Chatham Square. A few of them were charity dormitories but most were absolutely the most wretched sleeping-places for unemployed men. Schauffler recruited Irving to be the missionary to the Bowery, which had become the nation's most famous "skid row" before Seattle's Skid Road had popularized that term. Irving's was a challenging job if ever there was one.

During his early years in the Bowery, Irvine recruited two men to the staff of the Mission Society, Dave Ranney, to be described later, and Edward Dowling. Like Irving, Dowling had served with the British military, getting caught up in the bloody Indian Sepoy rebellion of 1857 in which Hindus and Moslems made common cause against their Christian overlords (Holmes 1888; Miller and Miller 1962:125–126; Pemble 1977). He and two other soldiers looted a rajah's palace and concealed masses of gems inside hollow bamboo canes. In escaping without their loot, one of the men was shot dead and the other disappeared, so for years Dowling suspected that the third man came back for the treasure. Fleeing to the United States, Dowling became a tract colporteur, trying to make a living selling religious literature door to door in upstate New York. Somewhere along life's difficult course he had lost an eye, and for years he supported himself as a traveling tinker, mending umbrellas and similar humble items. When Irving discovered him he was lying on a cot in the lodging house, reading the *Life of Buffalo Bill*. At first he refused to attend the Mission Society's religious meetings, with the excuse that he was an Episcopalian, but before long he was a trusted worker in the Church of the Sea and Land. Shortly before his death, by chance he encountered his lost partner from the looting of the rajah's palace, and each was overjoyed to learn that the other had not in fact retrieved the treasure. When he died, the government of India had just sent him five hundred dollars to come and dig it up for them, so possibly the jewelry is still there, hidden in rotten canes under the ground, waiting for someone to rediscover it.

It is easy enough to ascribe motives to the patrons, leaders, and workers, but difficult to determine the precise balance of rewards and compensators that committed them to the Mission Society. Some would say the rich were merely trying to buy their way into heaven, citing John D. Rockefeller as a churchgoing robber baron who must have know his wealth was ill-gotten (Flynn 1932). But this is far too simple an explanation. Many of the rich undoubtedly did not think of themselves as sinners any more than the ordinary middle-class person might. For fine men like Morris K. Jesup and John Stewart Kennedy, giving their efforts as well as their money to charities was simply a way of living a full and religious life. And we can see a religious quality in the specifics of some of their good deeds. In 1891, Kennedy's sweet young niece, Emma Stewart Baker, died. Nothing could be done to save her, yet his instinct to help and to express his love for this child found an outlet. He endowed a free bed for fifteen years in the Presbyterian Hospital, for any patients the Mission Society could help. Some of the money of Jay Gould, robber baron par excellence, found its way into the Society, but not because he tried to buy salvation. Rather, his daughter Helen had become a friend of Lucy and devoted a considerable amount of her own energy and inherited resources into the people and causes that appealed to her sensitive nature (Hoyt 1969).

In Chapter 10 we noted that a growing body of research indicates that the power of religion to sustain morality is limited and variable. Logically, the same should be true of religion's capacity to encourage voluntary giving. Wilson and Janoski (1995) found very complex relationships linking religiosity variables to the extent of giving, varying markedly across denominations, in data from a large questionnaire survey. Clearly, many nonreligious people do good deeds, and several very different motives for altruism appear to exist.

The December 1994 issue of *Review of Religious Research* is devoted to a scientific examination of the factors that shape patterns of giving among church members, and a few general principles seem to arise out of the vast complexity of the topic (Hoge 1994). Twenty percent of the members of a congregation tend to be responsible for 75 to 80 percent of the financial contributions. Not surprisingly, the more religious a person is, the more he or she tends to give. The larger the person's disposable income the more he or she tends to give in terms of dollars, but the less in terms of proportion of income. Other things being equal, smaller congregations seem to extract more per capita from their members than large ones, perhaps because they are better able to apply informal social pressures to keep their members from becoming "free riders" who obtain the benefits of membership without contributing much. An alternate explanation for this congregation-size effect is that in any congregation there is a small, cohesive group of patrons and leaders, and this group has a natural upper limit to its size regardless how numerous the rank-and-file members of the congregation are. This last explanation seems to fit the Mission Society especially well, because it possessed a highly cohesive small group at its core. Despite tremendous visibility in New York social life, it was never able to grow after about the time of the Civil War, perhaps because its core group of patrons and leaders had already reached the optimal size for intensive, constant interaction among its elite members.

Robert Wuthnow (1991:58) has suggested that four distinct concepts of motivation shape the way Americans think about apparently altruistic giving: biblical tradition, nature, utilitarianism, and voluntarism. According to the first, the Judeo-Christian religious tradition instills in many Americans the value of mercy, compassion, and being a good Samaritan. Alternatively, some degree of altruism may be an integral part of human nature, perhaps instilled in us by biological evolution and developed or suppressed to a greater or lesser degree in different individuals. From the utilitarian perspective, giving to others is a rational strategy that ultimately serves our own enlightened self-interest. And finally, many people simply believe they desire to help others, as an act of free, voluntary will, possibly as a way of achieving a sense of efficacy that they have the power to reshape the world (Schervish 1990).

Wuthnow presents these as rhetorics that Americans commonly use to discuss their giving, rather than as formal explanations, but we have certainly seen some evidence of both religious tradition and utilitarianism in the likely motivations of Mission Society patrons and supporters. The third explanation, that it is human nature to help others, may connect to the family aspect of Mission Society charity. From the Jesups and Kennedys on down, people gave as families more than as individuals. If nature breeds altruism it does so most strongly within the family, and the Mission Society was in a very real sense the extended family of the chief givers.

The utilitarian explanation is not necessarily demeaning, because it does not reduce everything to money. Rather, it notes that people take pleasure in many kinds of social action, and they will engage in costly actions to obtain great psychic rewards. Philanthropy is, after all, a kind of love, and giving to the object of one's love is intrinsically rewarding. The religious context adds supernatural compensators that promise great future rewards, although it is impossible at this distance from the 1890s to know the precise mixture of rewards and compensators that motivated the people of the Society.

In 1896, Schauffler wrote, "Altruism . . . is a somewhat new word. It denotes the opposite of egotism. In these days we hear a good deal about altruistic philosophy, and much is said about it, which seems to indicate that its advocates think it a new thing. But new it certainly is not. Altruism is as old as the law of God. True altruism is nothing more or less than Christianity. The greatest Altruist in the universe is God Himself, and this is proved by John 3.16. ("For God so loved the world, that he gave his only begotten Son, that whosoever believeth in him should not perish, but have everlasting life.") The Bible is saturated with this truth, and wherever the Church is living up to the measure of its privilege, there one may see altruism exemplified. Of this altruism our City Mission tries to be a faithful exponent."

Gertrude Burrage, the college student who had visited the Mission Society in 1893, believed the ladies of the Woman's Branch were amply rewarded for their devotion. "They are not looking forward to the next world for their reward, for they have a part of it every day of their lives. They are rewarded by the love of the children over whose faces a happy smile breaks when they meet the ladies on the street. They are rewarded by the reclaimed drunkards' homes, by the wives and mothers who have been led to Christ in the church or the Mothers' Meeting, by the stalwart young men who have left the street and the saloon to have a part in the Lord's work. I never met happier women, or those whom it was a greater joy to know than those I met in the Christian Workers' Home."

Contributors

The biggest donations, such as money to build the United Charities Building and the De Witt Memorial Church, came from super-rich patrons like Kennedy and Jesup. But the day-to-day running expenses were chiefly paid by individual contributors giving less than a thousand dollars, and by special collections at a set of churches belonging to two denominations. Table 11.1 shows the income of the Woman's Branch for 1893, a total of $25,264. Contributions from individuals totaled $10,133, and collections from the Presbyterian and Reformed churches totaled $15,131. In addition to these contributions for the general running expenses of the Woman's Branch, there were a number of special accounts: relief fund ($2,430), aged pilgrim's fund ($623), fresh air fund ($819), Easter fund ($752), Thanksgiving fund ($559), Christmas fund ($562), Italian work fund ($145), Baby-fold fund ($1,354), and special contributions ($107). There is a sociological law of charity donations which says: within limits, the greater the number of different funds being solicited for, the larger the total amount of money that can be collected. People will give something to each fund appeal made at their church. They will feel more righteous the larger number of good deeds they do, and given that the minimum cost of each good deed is low (a one-dollar bill or a five-dollar bill in the collection plate) or ill-defined (a check of some denomination written out to the fund), prosperous families can afford several good deeds above the basic cost of supporting the church where they worship. But repeated appeals for the same fund may quickly run into resistance, as the donators feel they have already purchased credit in heaven for contributing to it.

An annual income of $25,264 does not seem much in terms of the money

Table 11.1: Income of the Woman's Branch, December 1, 1892—November 20, 1893

INDIVIDUAL DONORS:	
Wealthy donors supporting a worker for at least part of year	$9,477
Other individuals	$656
	$10,133
CHURCHES:	
Fifth Avenue Presbyterian Church	$7,695
Madison Square Presbyterian Church	$1,672
West Presbyterian Church	$1,072
University Place Presbyterian Church	$919
Collegiate Reformed Church, Fifth Avenue and 48th Street	$894
Collegiate Reformed Church, Fifth Avenue and 29th Street	$751
Englewood Presbyterian Church	$600
Brick Presbyterian Church	$590
Broadway Tabernacle	$317
Central Presbyterian Church	$210
Madison Avenue Presbyterian Church	$161
Fourth Presbyterian Church, 34th Street	$110
South Reformed Church	$105
West End Presbyterian Church	$25
Second Collegiate Reformed Church, Harlem	$10
	$15,131

of a century later, but the largest cost, the salaries and expenses of all the workers, totaled just $21,538. Ten months' rent for Tealdo's two Italian rooms was just $143. Despite all the correspondence, postage cost just $63, enough to send 2,100 letters at the full first-class rate, which was only three cents in those days. A separate account shown in Table 11.2 explains the income and expenses for the Christian Worker's Home, where the missionaries and nurses lived. The workers had to pay board (food, utilities, etc.) from their modest salaries (all under $350 for the year), but they did not need to pay rent as such because the building had been a gift from Mr. and Mrs. Jesup. Note that there was no electric bill. The ice, delivered by the "ice man," had been cut in giant blocks from lakes the previous winter, and kept frozen by sawdust insulation in huge warehouses throughout the year. The coal must have been for heating and cooking, and the gas for lighting. Less than $5,000 was needed for provisions to feed three dozen missionaries. Aside from bread and butter, essentially all of the food would have been in its natural state, without the elaborate packaging and factory preparation we take for granted today.

In addition to the donations of money, people often gave things or labor.

Table 11.2: Accounts of the Christian Worker's
Home, 1893

RECEIPTS:	
Board money from workers	$7,705
Individual donors	$800
Student's fund	$500
Total income	$9,005
DISBURSEMENTS:	
Salaries and wages	$1,467
Matron's memoranda	$222
Provisions	$4,909
Milk	$491
Ice	$99
Gas	$367
Coal and wood	$342
House furnishings and hardware	$375
Repairs	$341
Rent of room	$20
Water tax	$21
House tax	$313
Total expenses	$8,967

Table 11.3 lists the nonmonetary donations to the Woman's Branch for a single month, August, 1893. Note that three ladies of the Olyphant family gave boxes of cut flowers, a reminder that contributors, like patrons, often operated as families. Many of the donated garments were new, and those given to the Baby Fold this month had been sewn by ladies and girls who donated both the materials and their amateur labor. We can imagine that much of the used children's clothing had been outgrown by the sons and daughters of prosperous contributors, but often a child died from one of the many as yet unconquered infectious diseases, and giving the little one's clothing to the Mission Society helped the parents deal with their grief.

Systematic records were not kept of the highly skilled labor donated to the Society by individuals with professional training, but one possibly extreme, well-documented example will illustrate how free giving could actually be rewarding. Lucy's son, Will, graduated at the top of his class from the medical school at Columbia University, completed his residency in a couple of the best New York hospitals, donated much time to the care of Mission Society workers and clients, and exploited his mother's contacts to embark on a splendid career. Her friends gave him a good footing in the tremendously influential religious and cultural Chautauqua movement (Vincent

Table 11.3: Non-Monetary Donations to the Woman's Branch, August 1893

VIRGINIA DAY NURSERY:
Mrs. Robert Olyphant, box of cut flowers
Mrs. C. B. Wheeler, basket of peaches
Members of the "Lend a Hand" class, of the Second Street Working Girl's Club, two
    scrap books, six babies' flannel jackets

JEWELL DAY NURSERY:
Miss Sophia V. Olyphant, box of cut flowers
Miss Annabella S. Olyphant, box of cut flowers
Through City Mission, 8 tickets for mothers' excursion to Coney Island

BABY FOLD:
Garments: 12 children's dresses, 11 infants' dresses, 3 flannel wrappers, 3 flannel
    sacques, 7 shirts, 22 diapers, 5 coverlets, 8 pin cushions, 2 clothes bags, 2 pair
    worsted slippers

DORCAS ROOM:
Mrs. Webb, 21 magazines
Mrs. J. V. Reed, 37 partly worn garments, dolls, and clothes
Mrs. Leggett, 10 magazines, books, and papers
Mrs. J. T. Terry, 88 new garments
Miss R. M. Heiser, per Miss Clatworthy, Mantoloking, N. J., 2 garments, doll for
    sick child
From two little brothers, shells and starfish for the "city children"
Circle Earnest Workers, First Collegiate Reformed Church, 11 new garments, papers
    and partly worn garments

CHRISTIAN WORKERS' HOME:
Flowers from Riveredge, N. J., flowers from Flower Mission

1885; Morrison 1974). In 1892 Will played the dashing role of Christopher Columbus in Chautauqua's celebration of the four-hundredth anniversary of his voyage, and by the end of the decade, he was among the most successful doctors tending the thousands who came to Chautauqua every summer for education and vacation. When wealthy Mission Society director John Sinclair went violently insane, Will became his personal physician, taking him to every leading medical center of Europe, where Will was able to study the most advanced techniques of the world's best surgeons. This tremendous experience, plus the immensely valuable contacts he had made throughout the Mission Society and Chautauqua social networks, allowed Will to set up a highly successful practice in fashionable Gramercy Park, just three blocks from the United Charities Building, and to become one of the world's most prominent medical figures, shuttling almost annually between New York and the capitals of Europe (De Forest 1950). He gave free medical care to the family of Reverend Alexander H. McKinney of Olivet Church, later Schauffler's successor as superintendent of the Society, and in return McKinney wrote the first biography of his mother (McKinney 1932).

Among others who received obvious benefit from donating their labor were students at the Union Theological Seminary who gained practical experience to supplement their theological studies, working at the Mission Society and other institutions under Schauffler's direction. Today as in the Gay Nineties, such intern programs are a formal part of training to become clergy. Ministers, like physicians and other professionals, could benefit from the valuable social contacts offered by the Society and the network of elite organizations to which it was connected. Likewise, businessmen find clients by participation in religious charities, and their reputations may gain luster from involvement in such altruistic and benevolent activities. But, at the same time, participation allows them and their families to express on a wider scale the honest feelings of nurturance generated in happy families, and to gain the personal satisfaction of being a good person. Thus, although the motives behind religious giving can be expressed in terms of rewards and compensators, it should not be assumed that the rewards are always mercenary.

The Clients: Rescue versus Salvation

The official aims of the Woman's Branch, given here in Table 11.4, begin with a pledge "to carry the Gospel of Christ to all homes in the lower part of the city, even the most degraded." A chief goal of the Mission Society had always been converting people to Protestant Christianity. But it is not clear that it often achieved this goal. Instead, it helped good people through bad times, and assisted hard-working immigrants in becoming Americans. If in Protestant terminology "salvation" implies religious conversion—saving sinners—then the Mission Society failed to achieve salvation. Instead it *rescued* people, often folk who had once been respectable members of the middle class but had met with accidental misfortune.

For example, consider one of the Mission Society's "aged pilgrims." In a cold room under the roof of a tenement, windowless except for a dirty skylight, a Society nurse found an elderly lady named Mrs. Marion McDermott. Seventy years earlier, she had been the blessed daughter of a prosperous doctor. But he was killed in an accident, and her mother did not survive the shock. There was no extended family to turn to, so Marion and her sister were left in the care of a friend of their parents, who raised them well and gave her happy memories of singing in the choir of the Methodist church. At eighteen she married a Methodist preacher, and they moved to Westchester

Table 11.4: Official Aims of the Woman's Branch, New York City Mission Society

1. To carry the Gospel of Christ to all homes in the lower part of the city, even the most degraded.

2. To elevate in their homes the families, by teaching the wives, mothers, and sisters those things that will be for their physical, moral, and spiritual advantage and prepare them better to fulfill their duties.

3. To reach the children, and by planting early seeds of industry, honesty, temperance, and truth, cheat the tares of a harvest and help the children to become good men and women.

4. To minister to the sick poor, providing things necessary for their recovery in their homes, or removing them to hospitals if necessary.

Charitable societies search out the worthy, we the unworthy, in the full belief that the blood of Jesus will cleanse the foulest and the Holy Spirit teach and sanctify the most ignorant and degraded.

Source: Seventieth Annual Report of the Woman's Branch of the New York City Mission and Tract Society, February 20, 1893.

County where she gave birth to four children before her husband died. Strong and full of hope, she took up the challenge of raising her four babies alone. But soon death stole her two daughters in a single week, and afterward one of her sons. Her remaining son survived until the Civil War, when he marched off to battle and never returned.

Marion struggled on, bereft of hopes, the results of all her efforts gone. For sixteen years, she lived in the House of Industry, a kind of poor house that required its inmates to labor for their lives, where she sewed with her ever stiffer fingers. And for the past nine years, she had huddled in this attic, sewing in the near darkness for her food, and at times singing to herself the old Methodist hymns she had loved so many years before. When the nurse found her, she had been seized by influenza, and was in great misery. She said, "Not a cent do I owe; I am no beggar and only want to be able to work again." The Mission Society found her a place in the Presbyterian Hospital, but when she regained a fragile health, it was obvious her eyesight was too poor for her ever to sew again. So impressed by her dignity and her life's struggle, the ladies of the society could not abandon her to the abysmal degradation of the lowest poorhouse, so they persuaded a respectable rest home to take her in. A photograph in the Mission Society's monthly magazine shows this "attic saint" sitting, her sightless eyes closed, waiting for her Maker to take her away from all the world's suffering.

Assisting the dying was considered to be a noble success. The religious faith of the Society's workers postulated these stories had happy endings, although none could be seen directly by human eye. The case of poor Fanny illustrates the tragic choices that faced the impoverished mentally ill or retarded. For twenty years, Fanny had lived in one corner of her mother's room, seldom going outdoors and judged too "idiotic" for work or education. The only alternative was to send her to the snake-pit institutions of Blackwell's Island, and the phrase "the island" struck terror into the hearts of poor New Yorkers. Lucy used to visit forty-year-old Fanny and marvel at this wretched loss of a life: "Do you wonder at the wasted form and wild stare of the poor creature housed year after year amidst such dreadful surroundings?" Her aged mother's only comfort was the missionary's visits. "The old, wrinkled face would light up as she talked about Christ, and the future life. 'I could die if only Fanny was cared for. I am getting so old and tired I'd be glad to be at rest.' " Then, "the old woman dropped dead in the hallway, and no one could understand the sorrow of the poor, half-witted daughter as the coffin that contained her best earthly friend was carried out. Since then she has been dreadfully neglected; her drunken stepfather did not want any one to do anything for her. 'She'll have to get out now,' he said. Fanny must go to the island.

"It was all arranged, and I visited her the evening before she was to go. As I opened the kitchen door, the room was so full of smoke that I did not notice the men at the table gambling, until a gruff voice said, 'She's in there.' I looked into the darkness of the little den, and found Fanny crouched in the corner on a heap of old bedding and rags, with some food on a chair beside her, and fearing that some one would come to take her away. 'Oh, won't you help me!' she pleaded. 'Get me a place to work. I'll do anything, only don't let them take me away!' She became more quiet as I told her she should not be treated cruelly, and I would come to see her. 'Fanny, can you understand,' I said; 'tell me, do you trust Jesus? Your mother loved him.' 'Yes,' she said, in a sort of dazed way, 'Yes, mother did.' " The next day when they came to take her away, they discovered that Fanny had died. Several times during Lucy's long career of service, someone whom she was trying to help out of a desperate situation died, and she always interpreted the death as a blessing and a perfect solution to the person's problems. "Suddenly she exchanged the dark hovel for a glorious mansion of the Father's house."

The ladies of the Woman's Branch invested vast time and energy in their work, and Table 11.5 does not exaggerate when it tabulates a year's labors. "In such work as ours," Lucy wrote in 1891, "we cannot expect to see the results of our labor as in many other forms of Christian service. To us is given the duty of seed sowing, and largely among the stones and rocks of intemperance and godlessness, and amidst the briars and thorns of poverty and misery. The dews fall, the winds blow, the sun shines, and the seed of truth germinates in the heart, and appears in the outward life. We can only gather out the stones, and break away some of the briars and tend the frail little plants of divine life for a time, then, more often, just as they blossom into beauty, they are translated into better soil in some church garden of upper New York or Brooklyn." With these garden metaphors, she makes two points. First, the work of the missionaries is only one factor that may help many people a little bit, and then it is the forces of nature (God, perhaps) that determine more completely whether this or that client is able to climb out of poverty and degradation. Second, those who escape poverty also escape lower Manhattan, moving to more respectable parts of the city where they are no longer seen by the Mission Society which thus cannot know about their successes.

Help for children was temporary, and Society workers seldom saw them grow to adulthood, but even their mere survival would seem like success. If anyone wanted to know how the babies came to be in the Baby Fold, Miss Glasgow was quick to tell them. The first baby, admitted in November, 1892, "was a little three-weeks-old Italian boy whose mother was insane. It was hoped she might improve, but reason remained dethroned until her death, which occurred a few days ago [in the madhouse] on Blackwell's Island." Baby Julia's "mother is a deserted wife, and had two other children to support. She has a position as a wet nurse up the Hudson." This means, of course, that Julia's mother gives the very milk from her breasts to a rich child whose own mother is unable or unwilling to provide it. "Next comes little Louise, seven months old, whose mother is also a wet nurse and has five children, two in the 'Home of the Friendless," one in the hospital on Randall's Island, one in the country and one with a friend. This poor woman was found by one of our missionaries, sick and deserted, left to starve with all those children." Fifteen-year-old Margaret's mother died of pneumonia soon after giving birth to a baby girl. Now Margaret must support both herself and her sister, and while she is working she fortunately can leave the tiny one at the Baby Fold.

On the premise that "an ounce of mother is worth a pound of priest," the Woman's Branch sought every possible way to strengthen the religious faith and homemaking competence of the mothers beneath Fourteenth Street. Hundreds of women and girls learned to sew, cook, and clean in evening classes at the Society's three churches. Sometimes the help was extremely mundane, as when Miss Fletcher got a glass eye for the father of little crippled Willie so he could get a respectable job and feed the boy. The nearest thing to a systematic survey of Woman's Branch successes was a book detailing fourteen cases (Bainbridge 1917), outlined here in Table 11.6. In the book's introduction, Schauffler stresses the spiritual quality of each of the stories, yet not one of them describes religious conversion or spiritual regeneration. Instead, material reward comes to a virtuous person who is the victim of circumstances, deceit, or a parent's wickedness.

Table 11.5: Work of the Woman's Branch, December 1, 1892—November 20, 1893

NURSES' WORK:

Number of new cases	1,043
Total cases attended	1,727
Number patients sent to hospitals	149
Number patients died	79
Garments given	2,497
Articles lent	127
Tracts given	1,265
Bible or parts given	61
Number of visits made by nurses	10,179
Average number of hours work per day	7:02
Average number of nurses reporting each month	7.5

MISSIONARIES' WORK:

Tracts and papers distributed	22,053
Bible and parts distributed	251
Volumes loaned	350
Children gathered into Sunday school	203
Children gathered into Day school	46
Adults gathered into Bible classes	75
Prayer meetings conducted	284
Women's and children's meetings conducted	678
Women's and children's sewing meetings conducted	238
Total meetings attended	6,645
Total meetings assisted in	2,296
Total missionary visits made and received	22,056
Average hours of work per day	7:22
Garments given out	2,933
Average number missionaries reporting each month	21.75

OFFICE WORK:

Estimated number of visitors at office	5,000
Estimated number of letters sent out	3,000
Estimated number of reports, appeals, etc., sent out	2,700

Source: Seventy-First Annual Report of the Woman's Branch of the New York City Mission and Tract Society, February 1894.

A standard Mission Society scenario is the reclamation of a formerly respectable family that had lost status to drink, but in the hundreds of cases described in Mission Society literature the reclamation part actually seems quite rare. In 1893, Reverend William T. Elsing told a story that fits this model: "In one of those great tenement houses in which more than a thousand people live, I found the family of a man who had at one time been a fine steel en-

Table 11.6: Successes of the Woman's Branch

	Problem	Solution
1.	English couple impoverished by accident; wife is pregnant, and husband is unemployed	Returned to England where their kin help them start over
2.	Young woman comes from small town, answering marriage ad from man who turns out to be vile	She is returned home and marries nice widower with a motherless baby
3.	Girl is abused by religious fanatic mother, who fills her mouth with ashes and threatens her with knife	Lives with Lucy for a year, then is placed with a kindly, trustworthy uncle
4.	Mother with little girl loses husband to tuberculosis; widower father seeks help with his two little girls	First he hires her to take care of his girls, then he marries her
5.	Girl abandoned by drunken parents	Adopted by a nice farm family
6.	Young Ohio woman comes to New York, tricked to think a house of prostitution is a music academy	Hired to take care of crippled rich boy then marries his good uncle
7.	Little girl's mother dies, father vanishes	Adopted by a nice farm family
8.	German girl tricked to join religious cult that may be a house of prostitution	Returned to her father in Germany, marries wealthy childhood sweetheart
9.	Orphan girl neglected by pauper stepmother	Adopted by small-town family
10.	Home of honest but poor family is a mess	The missionaries clean it up as surprise, leaving fine dinner and Bible for family
11.	Poor elderly couple loses their bank book	Missionary helps them find it, rent farm
12.	Good poor boy of drunken parents faces bullies' demand he take off "Christian Endeavor" badge	Prep school boys donate rent for his family; he becomes rich businessman
13.	During economic panic man pawns last belonging, runs away in shame, leaving family destitute	Missionaries take care of family and eventually bring man back; he prospers
14.	Elderly widow who lost husband in the Civil War can no longer support her intelligent granddaughter	Wealthy Helen Gould gives the girl a boarding school scholarship

graver. Intemperance and neglect of God had reduced his family to the verge of starvation. I have sometimes entered the home and have seen the little children rush at the food we brought like hungry dogs at a morsel of meat. There was not a decent piece of furniture in the house, not even a chair on which it was safe to sit. After many visits and much earnest conversation I found an entrance into that man's heart. He came to the church, stopped his drinking, gave up his evil ways and became an earnest Christian man; gradually the home began to improve; one piece of furniture after another was introduced, until the place began to look like home. After a while the family moved out of the monster tenement house and found a home in Brooklyn. Finally they moved to one of the pretty little villages in New Jersey within an hour's ride of New York. A few months ago I called on them. I saw the man's children in the woods filling a bag with dried autumn leaves, and said, 'What are you going to do with all those leaves?' They answered, 'We have a cow now, and we are taking the leaves to our barn to make a bed for our cow.' These children who had actually suffered hunger in the past, who formerly looked so pale and starved that they made my heart sick, were now looking rosy and fat, and not only lived in their own house, surrounded with a little garden, but actually drank all the fresh milk they wanted morning and evening. When I entered the house the mother, with beaming face, said, 'We owe it all to our Savior. If it had not been for our blessed Lord we would still have been it that big tenement house and we might have starved to death by this time.' "

Alexander Irvine, lodging-house missionary to the Bowery, had the daunting assignment of saving men who had fallen to the absolute depths of depravity. Two photographs of the same person, taken thirty-seven years apart, hung on the wall of his office in the Broome Street Tabernacle. One showed a healthy two-year-old boy wearing his first pair of pants. Irving said it was "as pretty a picture of childhood as heart could desire." The other picture was "a wretched tramp covered with dirt and filthy rags. The bloated face and unkempt hair betoken a life of sin and debauchery. It is revolting to look into that pinched face, every lineament of which is traced with misery." Just a week before the bum's death, Irvine had converted him to Christianity, and his family gave Irvine the baby picture when they came to pick up the body. Of course, had the bum lived he might have fallen quickly back into the dissolute street life from which Irving had plucked him.

Another failure was a man Irvine called "C," whom he found in 1890 in a seven-cent lodging house, "in which humanity can be seen at its lowest. There were about one hundred men there that afternoon and a junkman would not have given five dollars for their entire clothing. Filth abounded in a degree highly revolting and the sounds gave one the impression of hell upon earth." Irvine picked C for special attention, because, when he shook hands with the men, tears were running down C's cheeks. "For about three weeks I made him my companion, ate in five-cent restaurants with him, sat for hours with him in the lodging house, and walked miles with him in order to walk off the craving for liquor." This siege led to C's apparent conversion, and he took on the job of cleaning up the lodging house, which to him greatly meant physically "chucking out" disorderly men. After a year, he began drinking again, and Irvine invested more terrible days sharing the same room and even bed with the man, to prevent him from drinking. Another brief period of sobriety, while he worked at Coney Island, and then back into the grip of liquor and Irving was again drawn into the man's wild torments. Leaving him asleep in the gymnasium of the Broome Street Tabernacle one day, Irving went out to work in the lodging houses. When he returned he discovered that C had stolen his Imperial Dictionary, which had cost Irving two years' savings, to trade for booze. Neither Irvine's superhuman efforts, nor the supernatural intervention of Christ seemed to avail anything. Yet Irving would not admit defeat. "I have never had the faintest shadow of a doubt but that *this man shall be saved*, but he will verily be a brand plucked from the burning."

Irvine's clearest success was the salvation of Dave Ranney in 1892. Ranney had been born in Dutch Row, a tough neighborhood in Hudson, New Jersey, to a loving mother and a brutal, hard-drinking father. He learned to drink, himself, while still a small boy, stealing sips from the ale bucket he frequently carried to his grandfather. When he came home dead drunk, his mother exclaimed, "Oh! My God, my boy, my only son, oh! What happened to you?" All night she knelt beside his bed praying, but her prayers availed little. Bad companions and his own daring taught him to steal during his teens, and when he lost his job he stole all his sister's savings and ran off to become a professional thief. After nine months in prison, he married a decent girl named Mary, but he could not keep a job, and she wound up giving birth to their son in the notorious "Hell's Kitchen" slum. He abandoned his wife, wandered, and returned to his mother just as she was dying. With her last breath she begged him to make two promises, to stay sober until after her burial and to meet her later in heaven. He broke the first promise immediately, and there seemed no likelihood he would keep the second.

After another prison term, he found himself on the Bowery, penniless, looking for someone to rob for drinking money. He was about to clobber Irvine, but lost his nerve at the last instant. Irvine politely gave him fifty cents and told him to come to the Broome Street Tabernacle the next day. There Ranney received a bath and clean clothes, while Irving explained, "God is waiting for the chance to help you!"

Ranney began working at the Tabernacle, and two months later he was one of several poor people hired to deliver Thanksgiving dinners to other needy folk. Seeing he had no overcoat to protect him against the cold, Lucy Bainbridge was about to give him one from the Mission Society's "Dorcas Room" where donated clothing was kept, but sensing that the man was receptive, she decided to try a commitment tactic instead. She sent him to one of the finest clothing stores with a note telling the clerk to provide him with a high-quality coat. When Ranney incredulously protested her generosity, she told him, "David, that coat is for you, but listen, David; that coat is mine. Now I wouldn't go into a saloon, and I want you to promise me that you will never enter a saloon while you wear it." He never did, and when Dave Ranney (1910) published his autobiography years later, he could look back on nearly two decades of sober service as a missionary himself. Presumably he is now in heaven with his mother, but he became such a famous person with a best-selling book precisely because his case was so rare. Although Edward Dowling had been found in a lodging house, he was neither a drunk nor a thief, and all the other reliable workers of the Mission Society appear to have been effective individuals before they joined.

The Sociocultural Context

The Mission Society had a vast network of relationships with other organizations. One hint of this can be seen in the positions held by some graduates of the Training School of the Woman's Branch who did not become workers of the Mission Society itself. A total of twenty-seven worked for other American mission societies, five of them for the Presbyterian Home Board. Nine others took positions with the Presbyterian and Reformed churches that helped support the Mission Society in New York City. At least twenty-two entered foreign missions in India (five ladies), Japan (four), China (four), Africa (three), Italy (three), Mexico (one), Spain (one) and Macedonia (one). Naturally many of the others married—and it is hard to think of a better place for a pious young gentleman to seek a bride than at the Mission Society—at least eight of them becoming clergymen's wives and thus forging a link with their husband's churches. Mary Barnard became assistant matron of a girl's school in Cambridge, Massachusetts. Ida Hubbard became principal of a "colored" (African-American) school in Knoxville, Tennessee, where she was assisted by fellow Training School graduate, Lena Kalbfleisch. Alice Lathrop and Jennie Meier taught in a "blind asylum" in Hartford, Connecticut, whereas Katheryn McLeod directed the Kawaiahao Seminary in Honolulu, Hawaii.

In the latter half of the nineteenth century, a chief recruiting ground for women missionaries was the growing number of girl's boarding schools, often then called seminaries, that ranged from the high school through the college academic level. Successful women missionaries often visited these schools to lecture, all these schools taught Bible classes as well as secular subjects, and there frequently was a small mission society in the school that collected money and made clothing to donate to a particular adult missionary cause. Among the young ladies' institutions most closely connected to the Mission Society were Mrs. Life's Seminary at Rye, Miss Lockwood's School at Mt. Vernon, and Misses Masters' School at Dobbs Ferry.

We have already seen that a vast network of contributors supported the Society financially, but many other organizations cooperated or competed with the Society. By one estimate there were between six and seven hundred separate organizations in some way dedicated to helping the needy throughout New York City in the 1890s, and the Mission Society was merely one of the most prominent. Since colonial days, the states had provided some financial relief to those individuals officially inscribed on the lists of paupers. In 1860, essentially every town in Massachusetts possessed a poor house, about 220 of them, although they were designed for poor natives of the town and would not let an immigrant stay beyond a single week. Such secular institutions gave no spiritual encouragement and only the most primitive support, often not enough even to stay alive. The welfare programs of the twentieth century had not yet been created, and in the vast metropolis the old institutions were designed for small-town society.

The workers of the Mission Society were middle-class, refined ladies and gentlemen, passing material benefits down to degraded citizens and poor immigrants, but they were quite aware that there were alternative approaches. In December, 1892, Lucy contrasted how things were done in the Salvation Army: "The women of the so-called 'Slum Brigade' endeavor to live just as do the poor people they are trying to help. They wear the badge of service; they eat and sleep and dress in the most economical way, without regard to comfort; they visit among the tenements of the very poor, and scrub and wash and cook and nurse the sick, and talk of the Master's love which prompts their kind action.

"Our city missionary workers are given a comfortable and healthful home within easy access of the tenement people. They are enabled to dress simply and neatly, as becomes the Christian woman of average life. From this home, with its refining and spiritual associations, they go forth to their ministry among the poor. From cellar to attic they visit for hours nearly every day. Like their army sisters they wash the babies, prepare food for the sick, make up the bed, sweep and dust, read the Bible and pray; but it is our plan to try to teach the mother how to cook, and clean and sew, rather than do it for her. A missionary caring for a sick and miserable family will often help another poor woman, who is in distress for food and rent, by hiring her to wash and patch for the sick mother. Thus, during the days of the cholera scare, our 'relief funds' were heavily taxed, because we gave work to poor emigrants wherever we found in a home of poverty and sickness piles of rags and soiled clothing."

In November 1896, Schauffler noted that the Episcopal church had grown more rapidly than the Presbyterian denomination that contributed so heavily to the Mission Society, and this was doubly disturbing to him because he did not consider Episcopalians to be evangelicals, as he did consider Presbyterians to be. In 1865, 15,000 New Yorkers had been members of

Presbyterian churches, compared with just 12,000 Episcopalian church members. But by 1895, there were nearly twice as many Episcopalians, 43,000 to 22,000. The chief explanation, he concluded, was material rather than spiritual: "One of the reasons why Episcopalians are making such rapid headway in our city, is to be found in the fact of the tremendous power exerted by Trinity Church corporation. Our readers know that this church's large revenue is derived from the real estate which it holds. These funds, which are over and above the contributions in the churches, are used for the advancement of denominational work on this island." This was the period that Kit and Frederica Konolige (1978:204) have called the "Episcocratic consolidation," when the nearest thing America has ever had to a national upper class emerged, centered on Episcopal churches, prep schools, private clubs, and family connections. The New York Episcopalians supported a number of organizations in competition with the Mission Society, including missions to sailors, Italians, Spanish, and Germans, plus a temperance society despite the widespread acceptance of alcohol among the wealthy.

In the early 1890s, the men of the Mission Society wasted much of their energy and resources in an ill-advised attempt to convert the 200,000 Jews of lower New York. A remarkable conversion frenzy began when the Society encountered an extremely talented but also troubled Jewish convert named Hermann Warszawiak. Every Saturday, Warszawiak addressed large groups of Jewish men in the Society's DeWitt Memorial Church, and on Wednesdays he held a discussion meeting for them. Members of the audience would write challenging questions on numbered cards, and Warszawiak would answer them (brilliantly, his supporters judged). Why do Christians not keep the commandments of Moses? How could Jesus be the Messiah when the prophesies said that war would cease upon the Messiah's appearance? How could God have a son? Why does Jesus crucified on the cross call out to God, instead of calling for his Father; indeed, if Jesus is God, why does he call out at all? This might lead to a discussion of the Trinity, about which Warszawiak had written a pamphlet, and he was ready to hand out Hebrew translations of the New Testament from a stock of 20,000 copies his Christian patrons had provided. Soon he opened a Home for Persecuted Christian Jews and Enquirers in a four-story building at 65 Avenue D, filling its four apartments and nine beds with followers and designing a new symbol for his satellite movement, consisting of a cross embraced by a star of David.

In their belief that the Jews ought to be ripe for conversion, the men of the Society interpreted Warszawiak's life as a religious quest. Born in Warsaw in 1865, the son of a wealthy merchant and grandson of a rabbi, he studied the Talmud as a boy, but his father urged him to delve deeply into Leviticus, and this triggered an intense debate between them over sacrifice and forgiveness of sin. Sent to his rabbi uncle for more advanced Jewish studies, Warszawiak descended into a guilt-ridden struggle to find atonement, racked by the conviction he was a lost sinner. He began preaching in a family synagogue but soon was accused of apostasy because of his preoccupation with the messiah and with gaining salvation. A Hebrew edition of the New Testament came into his hands, and shortly he found himself in Edinburgh, Scotland, where the Jewish Committee of the Free Church labored for six months to complete his conversion to Christianity. The instant he arrived in New York, he began working for the Mission Society.

In their enthusiasm, the men of the Mission Society ignored the warning signs in Warszawiak's life. His religious quest went hand-in-hand with emotional trouble and inability to bear his family responsibilities, and he ran away from his rich, young wife and their children. He was prey to bouts of depression, having accepted baptism only after an emotional collapse brought on by remorse at abandoning his family, who continually tried to bring him back to home and sanity. More recently, he had contemplated jumping into the sea while crossing the Atlantic. Even after becoming the Society's missionary to the Jews, Warszawiak exhibited a mercurial temperament, rushing back to his family, dragging his wife and children to New York to be converted, and shortly vanishing from missionary work altogether, allowing his fragile movement to collapse without evidence that a single person had actually been converted, least of all himself (Miller and Miller 1962:73).

Conclusion: A System of Charity

You have found my own great-grandmother, Lucy Bainbridge, in these pages. Religious movements touch many members of all our families, and she illustrates the fact that sociology is in great measure the study of ourselves. I hope you occasionally contemplate the connections linking your own family to various religious movements. But Lucy and the Woman's Branch of the Mission Society which she led serve another sociological purpose. They remind us of the tremendously important and often distinctive role that women play in religion, not merely as exceptional individuals such as Phoebe Palmer and Ann Lee, but also as rank-and-file members of women's movements.

The New York City Mission and Tract Society initially set out to save souls, assuming that the practical problems suffered by the poor would be overcome by God's aid and by the transformation of their own characters. Indeed, the Society did save thousands of people over the decades, but seldom by reforming character. Instead, some poor people of "good character" were helped through temporary material problems, after which they regained their economic balance. Many immigrants were taught the ways of the new country and given a boost toward becoming citizens. Wives of dissolute husbands and children of dissolute parents were often helped toward a better life for themselves. The evangelical religious faith of the Society undoubtedly comforted the dying and gave the mission workers themselves greater courage than they might otherwise have possessed. But it failed to convert the poor.

The barriers to conversion were many. Over the decades of the nineteenth century, the denominations that supported the society lost some of their evangelical fervor, just as the Methodists did. Essentially all of the patrons, workers, and contributors to the Mission Society were solidly middle-class or even upper-class, and there was no room in their own churches for their working-class clients. Although the missionaries frequently caused clients to develop powerful emotional attachments to them, these were dependency relationships, rather than the coequal friendships that could be the social bonds needed to recruit a client to the movement.

Despite aid to thousands of needy people, the Mission Society did not solve the problems of poverty, alcoholism, and ill health that dragged so many of their clients down. Later generations decided that America owed a decent life to its poor, and social reformers of the twentieth century would say that an individual's poverty was frequently the result of societal factors entirely beyond his or her control. After the bitter lessons of the Great Depression of the 1930s, an economic crisis even deeper that the Panic of 1893, government regulation guarded against another depression. In retrospect, for much of the twentieth century the approach of the Mission Society seemed naive and self-serving. But a century after the Panic, a political movement swept the nation that looked back to the "Victorian Era" of the 1890s with nostalgia, and sought to dismantle the welfare system and other innovations that separated the 1990s from the 1890s. If the reforms of the twentieth century were intended to give a better life to the poor, then it is debatable whether they succeeded. But, frankly, the most wretched conditions of today's poor, with all their potential for drug death and family disintegration, cannot be compared with the vastly worse, subhuman conditions suffered by New York's poor a century ago.

The women and men of the Mission Society did the best they could to help their fellow human beings under desperate conditions. As short-term aid for the swarms of immigrants and temporarily impoverished respectable citizens, their work was exceedingly valuable. The fact that they could not solve the great social problems of their society is not to their discredit, because a century of effort has failed to solve those problems. Perhaps we will do better in the twenty-first century, possibly by a combination of government programs and religious evangelism.

12

Democratization Movements

Many chapters of this book have touched upon sensitive matters, but this chapter promises to be the touchiest of all. A proverb says that one should never discuss religion or politics in a polite gathering, yet here we plan to discuss both sensitive topics together. To make matters worse, the research on the role of religion in promoting or retarding democracy is still quite meager, so we will seldom be on solid scientific ground in the following pages. However, the spectacular transformation of the political, economic, and cultural systems of so many nations around the world demands attention in a book about religious movements. The reader's tolerance will be appreciated, if at some points we stray into contentious territory. We begin with a pair of examples that remind us the process of social development is incomplete even in the United States.

Father Divine and Martin Luther King, Jr.

The life of Father Divine is a story of a man so severely damaged by an oppressive society that his original identity was destroyed, but of a man so creative that he constructed a fresh identity for himself and went on the lead a religious movement that elevated his people without alienating his oppressors (Divine 1982; Weisbrot 1983). Major J. Divine may have been born in 1877, or 1883, or some other year someplace in the deep South, perhaps North Carolina or Georgia. He denied persistent rumors that his real name was George Baker, but it may be that he was the shadowy figure called The Messenger who went from place to place preaching early in this century.

Calling himself the Son of Righteousness, he may have done hard labor on a chain gang in Georgia, and whatever the details of his history, he certainly experienced all the worst persecutions of African Americans in the decades after the Civil War. In 1936, a woman named Elizabeth Maysfield claimed that he was her son, Frederick, but this was dismissed as the scheming of an opportunist until a quarter century later when half-conscious in a hospital Divine said his name was Frederick.

In 1906, while he was earning a living as a hedge-cutter in Baltimore, George Baker met self-anointed black preacher Samuel Morris and his disciple John Hickerson. I Corinthians 3:16 says, "Know ye that ye are the temple of God, and that the Spirit of God dwelleth in you?" Morris took this verse personally, and he toured black churches proclaiming, "I am the Father Eternal!" moments before he was invariably thrown out. Morris adopted the spiritual name, Father Jehovia, whereupon Baker became The Messenger, and Hickerson became Reverend St. John Divine Bishop. Whereas Father Jehovia applied the Corinthians verse only to himself, Reverend St. John Divine Bishop decided that all human beings were temples for the holy spirit, and in 1912 both disciples set out on their own. The Messenger arrived in New York City around 1915, assembled a congregation, and four years later was able to purchase a large home in Sayville on the southern shore of Long Island under his new name, Major J. Divine.

Many of his followers were servants of prosperous white residents of Sayville, able to contribute something from their reliable wages, and soon Father Divine was staging banquets every week for his growing band of followers, which began to include a few whites as well as the black people who formed the heart of the congregation. With the onset of the Great Depression, his fortunes seemed to increase, as more and more desperate people turned to him for hope. Many Sayville residents resented a black household in their midst, and the ever-increased waves of visitors magnified their ire. The county district attorney sent two female undercover agents into the church, to search out any corruption that could be the pretext for a purge, but they could not find any.

Near the end of 1931, a small army of police, firefighters, and politicians raided Father Divine's home by night. An assistant district attorney was punched unconscious after he broke through the back door, and Divine was arrested with seventy-eight disciples. The following May, with what an appeals court would later call gross judicial prejudice, Judge Lewis J. Smith rejected a jury's recommendation of leniency and sentenced Divine to a year in jail for being a menace to society. Divine weathered the circus atmosphere of the trial with great dignity, and calmly went off to prison. Some of his followers loudly predicted that God would strike Judge Smith down dead, and to the surprise of everyone else, Smith indeed did die unexpectedly in perfect health just three days after pronouncing sentence. When Father Divine heard of Smith's sudden demise, he coolly commented, "I hated to do it." Released shortly on bail, Divine basked in tremendous publicity and soon won total victory in an appeals court. Among the most famous people in America, he spread his growing movement and business enterprises across the land.

Fully committed followers of Father Divine turned over all of their property to his Peace Mission. They were supposed to be industrious, honest, thrifty, temperate, celibate, and peace loving. "They are real Americans in that they are people of different racial, national, religious and social backgrounds. They believe in the Brotherhood of Man under the Fatherhood of God and never use terms that separate or designate one from another in a discriminating way." Many members lived communally, brothers and sisters housed in separate buildings or separate floors of one building, practicing racial integration. In 1936, six thousand followers flocked to Harlem to hear Father Divine urge humanity to "make it a crime to discriminate on account of race, creed or color in any public place; for landlords to refuse tenants, or for employers to discharge workers for this reason; also to discriminate in hiring practices or withhold any classification of work from qualified civil servants. Segregation in neighborhoods, schools and colleges, churches, theaters, public conveyances, etcetera, to be abolished."

At the end of the 1930s, psychologists Hadley Cantril and Muzafer Sherif (1941) called Divine's church escapist. "It is not difficult to see why Father Divine should flourish in Harlem, famous for its congestion, poverty, high rents, and general squalor. Bewildered and hopeless souls, living under these conditions, readily surrender to a God who literally provides them what they have always craved—food, shelter, peace, security." For those who already possessed these material benefits, the Peace Mission provided "an escape from a tortuous mental confusion caused by complex, conflicting circumstances. He gives meaning to the individual life and to the world." In addition, Divine offered social status and honor to black people who lacked respect in a white world, no matter how much education, money, or good character they were able to achieve. Only decades later would scholars, like Father Divine's academic biographer Robert Weisbrot (1983), recognize that the racial equality he taught was not a fantasy but a glimpse of the future. Far from being a cultic escape from reality, the Peace Mission was a rational challenge to a reality that needed to be changed.

There is no mystery about the identity of Martin Luther King, Jr., although there is a story to tell about his name. He was born January 15, 1929, in Atlanta, the second child of Alberta and Michael King. Alberta's father, A. D. Williams, was pastor of the Ebenezer Baptist Church; his father had been a lay preacher to his fellow slaves, so Christianity ran deep in the family tradition. A year after his son was born, Michael graduated from

Morehouse College, and the following year he succeeded to the pulpit at Ebenezer upon the death of Williams. When Michael was born, back in 1899, his parents had disagreed over what to call him. His father, James, wanted to give him the names of his two brothers, Martin and Luther, but his mother, Delia, wanted him named after the archangel Michael. Delia won, but thirty-four years later, practically on his deathbed, James prevailed upon Michael to change his name to Martin Luther King, and at the age of five his son became Martin Luther King, Jr. Whether named after a biblical angel, or after a great European religious reformer, the boy was destined for the church (Baldwin 1991:101–102).

Despite growing up during the Great Depression, Martin Luther King, Jr., enjoyed a secure life with some comfort. But he experienced painfully all the harm to dignity and freedom that segregation could impose. At Morehouse College, he studied sociology with Walter Chivers, who had done research on lynchings. Chivers taught him that racial injustice could not be separated from economic injustice, a lesson that would later make King a spokesman for all the poor, not just for African Americans (Ansbro 1982:76; Baldwin 1991:26). Next, King attended Crozier Theological Seminary, a small, pre-dominantly white Baptist school in Pennsylvania. For a course on great theologians he read a book by Walter Rauschenbusch that introduced him to the doctrines of the Social Gospel Movement. It was not enough, this school of American Christian thought asserted, to seek one's own salvation through prayer, scripture reading, and worship in a church congregation. In addition, the Social Gospel preached good works for one's fellow humans through self-sacrifice to achieve social reform (Ansbro 1982:163–197). After Crozier, King went north for his doctorate to Boston University, an intellectual center of the Social Gospel Movement. Thus, King's later career as a leader of the Civil Right Movement was a fulfillment of the Christian education he had received. In 1953, he married Coretta Scott, a student at the New England Conservatory of Music. Over the objections of his wife and father, King chose to take a church in the deep South, in Montgomery, Alabama, where he felt he could perform the greatest service for his people.

On December 1, 1955, a black woman named Mrs. Rosa Parks refused to give up her seat on a Montgomery bus so that a white man could sit. At the time, city regulations and local white custom required blacks to sit in the back of the bus, never to sit in the same row of seats as a white, and to relinquish their right to sit if the rows reserved for whites became full. In fact, there was a free seat next to Mrs. Parks in which the man could sit, but that would have forced him to acknowledge her equal status by sitting in the same row as she. The bus driver called the police, who promptly arrested Mrs. Parks. This news quickly reached E. D. Nixon, a local black activist and former president of the city's chapter of the National Association for the

Advancement of Colored People. Nixon enlisted the aid of Clifford Durr, a white lawyer and racial liberal, and together they sought the permission of Mrs. Parks to use her case to change the city's unfair bus regulations.

As soon as Mrs. Parks agreed, Nixon began contacting black clergy, beginning with Ralph D. Abernathy, secretary of the Baptist Ministers' Alliance. Abernathy recommended that they hold a meeting, and suggested calling the young pastor of Dexter Avenue Baptist Church, M. L. King, along with several other clergy. At first King hesitated, concerned about his family and the time such an effort might take from his ordinary ministerial duties, but then he assented. The meeting launched a bus-system boycott with great fanfare, and shortly the clergy and activists had formed a new organization, the Montgomery Improvement Association, to direct the boycott. Everybody assumed that one of the well-established leaders of the community would be chosen president of the group, but to everybody's surprise one of the chief candidates nominated King, and it seems that almost by accident the social dynamic of the meeting gave him the job.

The effort had two thrusts. One was the legal drive to get local laws overturned by higher courts, employing the case of Mrs. Parks and then the case of King himself when he was convicted of leading an illegal boycott. The other thrust was the boycott itself, which initially aimed merely to soften the bus-seating rules while still keeping blacks in the rear, and whites in the front. In the beginning, there was little thought that the boycott would last beyond a single day, let alone weeks and months. But the black community of Montgomery showed remarkable enterprise and organizational skill in being able to create, instantly and with hardly any resources, a substitute transportation system so that their people could avoid the city-licensed bus system with its oppressive rules. The end came on December 20, when the final decree of the U.S. Supreme Court reached Montgomery, ending the bus-system segregation. Leaders of the boycott called upon members of their movement to resume using the busses, doing so with "loving dignity" and not intentionally sitting next to a white person unless there was no other seat available. King said it was time to "move from protest to reconciliation" (Garrow 1986:82).

Throughout the boycott, King's followers practiced strict nonviolence. Not so, some of their opponents. King began receiving obscene and threatening telephone calls. After his first brief experience of being thrown in jail, King pondered the danger that surrounded himself and his family, brooding late into the night until a religious experience clarified his mind and gave him courage: "And it seemed at that moment that I could hear an inner voice saying to me, 'Martin Luther, stand up for righteousness. Stand up for justice. Stand up for truth. And lo I will be with you, even until the end of the world' " (Garrow 1986:58). During the boycott, someone hurled a bomb at King's house, exploding a hole in the cement floor of the porch, and afterward someone fired a shotgun through the front door.

Much has been made of the fact that King had read extensively about Mohandas Karamchand Gandhi, who had used nonviolent methods to free India from British rule, and it has often been said that King applied Gandhi's methods to America. King himself said, "I have been a keen student of Gandhi for many years. However, this business of passive resistance and nonviolence is the gospel of Jesus. I went to Gandhi through Jesus" (Garrow 1986:75). Indeed, although Gandhi's nonviolence expressed the Hindu religious principle of *ahimsa*, the doctrine that one should never harm any form of life, in an important sense his campaign for Indian independence was Christian. Gandhi's campaign aimed to convince the British to withdraw from India voluntarily, and to do so it had to play upon the highest principles of British culture, which, after all included the values of self-determination and democracy, and most importantly were rooted in merciful Christian religion. Gandhi's nonviolent campaign would not have worked if his opponents had been Nazis; they would simply have killed him at the first sign that he was gathering any followers. Similarly, King's nonviolence depended upon the fact that most white Southerners thought of themselves as law-abiding, God-fearing Christian people, with some measure of good will toward their black neighbors. This would not prevent some individuals from taking up guns or dynamite against the Civil Rights Movement. But it did mean that many whites, perhaps most of them, were prepared to search their own souls when they were forcefully but nonviolently shown the suffering of African Americans and their dignity in that suffering.

On August 28, 1963, King stood before the Lincoln Memorial to give the keynote address of the Civil Rights March on Washington. The words he used were simultaneously American and Christian, speaking phrases that were already planted deep in the American consciousness. "Fivescore years ago, a great American, in whose symbolic shadow we stand today, signed the Emancipation Proclamation. . . . But one hundred years later, the Negro still is not free." "Continue to work with the faith that unearned suffering is redemptive." "I still have a dream. It is a dream deeply rooted in the American dream that one day this nation will rise up and live out the true meaning of its creed—we hold these truths to be self evident, that all men are created equal." "And when we allow freedom to ring . . . we will be able to speed up that day when all of God's children—black men and white men, Jews and Gentiles, Catholics and Protestants—will be able to join hands and to sing in the words of the old Negro spiritual, 'Free at last, free at last: thank God Almighty, we are free at last' " (King 1986:217–220).

Five years later, on the balcony of a motel room in Memphis, Tennessee, Martin Luther King, Jr., met freedom in the form of an assassin's bullet that released him from the bonds of this cruel world. The Montgomery bus boy-cott had catapulted him to national fame. His intelligence and dedication had made him a leader of the Civil Right Movement. His deep religious faith and theological scholarship had prepared him to join Lincoln in martyrdom.

Democracy and Religious Heritage

In Chapter 1 we were able to define religion, a difficult enough task, but here we find that defining democracy may be beyond our grasp. Indeed, one's definition is likely to be shaped by one's personal political orientation, liberals defining democracy in terms of equality, and conservatives defining it terms of liberty. In an essay on democracy's connection to religion, Lonnie Kliever (1987) identifies three fundamental principles of democracy. The first is the equality of all persons, in that each person is recognized for his or her humanness, and that competition between individuals should take place in a fair environment where no one is denied opportunities because of the group into which he or she was born. The second is the principle of the au-tonomy of each self: "In democracies, social consensus is fashioned from be-low out of discussion and compromise rather than being imposed from above by entitlement and force" (Kliever 1987:42). And third, ruling elites must be open in the sense that it is always possible for an individual to work his or her way into the elite, and also in the sense that the elites are answer-able to the mass of citizens. These principles may seem to contradict each other, for example individual autonomy may create inequality, and equality can be achieved only at the expense of autonomy (Kliever 1991). Thus, democracy is a dynamic concept, describing a political system that possesses considerable openness and flexibility, but that may emphasize one or an-other set of principles at different times in its history.

In Chapter 10 we noted that both religion and morality have several di-mensions, and thus we could not expect to find a simple relationship be-tween them. The same is true for the connection between religion and democracy. Religion—or different kinds of religion—may favor different as-pects or varieties of democracy. Among other things, this means that one's judgment about whether religion promotes or retards democracy will de-pend both upon which facets of democracy one holds most dear, and which forms of religion one is contemplating at the moment. Furthermore, imme-diate personal needs and political commitments will shape one's theory.

For example, among the grandest essays ever to address the relationship between religion and democracy is *Christian Life and Character of the Civil Institutions of the United States* by B. F. Morris (1864). This ponderous vol-ume primarily consists of quotations from famous Americans asserting that

American democracy rests upon Christianity. Two quotes printed on the title page might seem sufficient: "True religion affords to Government its surest support" (George Washington). "The highest glory of the American Revolution was this: it connected in one indissoluble bond the principles of civil government with the principles of Christianity" (John Quincy Adams). Morris felt the need, however, to go on for 831 pages in the same vein, ending up with many proclamations by and for Abraham Lincoln. Apparently, this book was Morris's contribution to the Union side in the Civil War, providing a wealth of propaganda that the institutions of the North were either divinely inspired or guided by the true religion.

There are at least three ways in which religion might contribute to democratization of a society. First, as we noted in Chapter 10, social scientists traditionally believed that religion was an essential basis for the moral order, and a moral consensus would seem especially important in a democratic system where by definition the state is very limited in the degree to which it can coerce obedience from citizens by force. There are many variants of this thesis. For example, John Attarian (1995) argues that secularization has caused the American government to lose control of its spending, and thus approaches fiscal crisis. This is true, Attarian believes, because people's fears and desires grow in the absence of religious belief: "Life in an indifferent, inexplicable universe is an insupportable psychological burden. Modern secularized people are caught in a terrible trap—more aware of their mortality and vulnerability to suffering than ever before but no longer reconciled to it. They are, have been, or will be afraid for their prospects in the all-important material world. They regard that fear as natural rather than shameful, and they indulge it rather than strive to override it" (Attarian 1995:299). Lacking faith in God, they demand that government protect them from economic fluctuations, from ill-health, and from old age. At the same time, they demand the freedom and resources to indulge their desires, because they think that existence and thus the opportunity to gain rewards ends with death. The result is that they demand the impossible of government, and the costs escalate without limit. When the government becomes insolvent, democracy will drown in red ink, ultimately because of a loss of faith in supernatural compensators.

Second, democracy may succeed best in differentiated societies where power is already distributed among a number of distinct groups or classes, so that none can rule over all, and every group must negotiate with others to advance its interests. One way in which a society can be differentiated is if it contains a significant number of religious denominations. Each denomination provides social organization for a segment of the public, which can be the basis of political organization. If there are enough denominations, overlapping in their population pools, then the society will not be so thoroughly fragmented along class or ethnic lines so as to descend into violent chaos.

Third, a particular religious tradition may possess beliefs and institutions that are especially conducive to democracy. In his presidential address to the American Sociological Association, Seymour Martin Lipset counted religion among the most influential factors determining whether a society will develop democratic political institutions: "Historically, there have been negative relationships between democracy and Catholicism, Orthodox Christianity, Islam, and Confucianism. These differences have been explained by (1) the much greater emphasis on individualism in Protestantism and (2) the traditionally close links between religion and the state in the other four religions" (Lipset 1994:5). Comparisons between Protestantism and Catholicism can be found in many classics of sociology. In 1879, Henry Morselli noted the tendency of Protestantism toward "encouraging free enquiry into dogmas and creeds" (Morselli 1879: 125). Emile Durkheim accepted Morselli's judgment, saying that Protestantism encouraged "a spirit of free inquiry" and the "overthrow of traditional beliefs" (Durkheim 1897: 158).

This view has been contested. Andrew Greeley (1989, 1990) argues that Catholicism provides better support for democracy than Protestantism does. In a competitive economic system the very individualism of Protestantism can encourage elitism in which a few very successful individuals become the lords over everybody else. Through its emphasis on the spiritual health and social integrity of the local community, Catholicism may encourage grassroots organization and a populism that stresses the democratic value of equality. *Mutatis mutandis*, this debate can be translated to Asia. Buddhism has been called "the light of Asia," but it might as well be called the Protestantism of Asia because it tends to splinter into sects and places great emphasis on the spiritual enlightenment of the individual. In this analogy, Confucianism might take the role played by Catholicism in the West.

When Lipset refers to "Confucianism," he means the influence of Chinese Confucian thought throughout East Asia, rather than just the cultural structure at the center of Chinese society itself. Martin Whyte has suggested that the ethical-political system of pre-Maoist China was "proto-totalitarian" and thus not conducive to the development of democratic institutions: "For example, in state Confucianism, a single set of orthodox ideas was supposed to bind the entire society together under a moral consensus, and numerous indoctrination procedures were carried out among the populace to foster this 'one-mindedness.' Ideas and groups that seemed to elites to threaten this moral consensus were branded heterodox and suppressed" (Whyte 1992:60). He also noted that China lacked a separate church hierarchy which could have been the beginning of a pluralistic system of power-sharing, and thus a step toward democratization.

341

The problem for the sociology of religion is to understand the distinctive role of Confucianism, as a religion. This is doubly difficult to do, first because it is hard to separate Confucian culture from the bureaucracy that existed in a symbiotic relationship with it, and second because we can doubt whether Confucianism is in the Western sense of the term, a religion. My aunt, Elizabeth Bainbridge, who happens to be the daughter of a high-ranked pre-revolutionary Chinese diplomat, was raised in the Confucian tradition at the very center of Chinese society. She asserts that the Confucianism of her family was an ethical and philosophical discipline, with none of the supernatural elements that would distinguish religious faith. In this she may merely be expressing the attenuated faith of a highly secularized elite that denies the supernatural elements of its tradition, a reaction certainly familiar enough among Christians. But there is also a sense in which the religious structure of Asian cultures is far different from that found in Christian or Islamic societies. A welter of religious faiths and magical practices exist beside each other, and any individual may draw upon several, going to each at a different time for different rewards and compensators. China was not merely Confucian, but also Buddhist, Taoist, and animist. Given the corruption and chaos of the final imperial regime, Confucianism had little opportunity to demonstrate its capacity to promote development of democratic institutions (O'Connor 1973). One would think that Confucian emphasis upon moderation and upon fulfillment of public responsibilities would be assets for a democracy.

Ultimately, the argument that Protestantism is more conducive to democracy than Catholicism and the other faiths rests on the historical fact that democracy has suffered endless difficulties outside the English-speaking nations and a handful of others in northern and western Europe. The democratic tide rises and falls in Latin America, and across much of Asia and the Islamic world, democratic ideas are taking root for the first time. One could just as well argue that democracy developed in league with science and technology, in a small set of nations in one corner of the globe, and many of the cultural features associated with democracy are simply the accidental characteristics that those nations happened to possess.

If religion does unilaterally affect the political culture of a nation, there are several ways in which it might do this. Lipset's argument appears to rest on a traditional concept of values, with only Protestantism asserting the individualistic values upon which democratic institutions supposedly rest. But in Chapter 10 we saw there is some question whether the concept of values can bear the weight that sociology traditionally placed upon it. Even when religion preaches a particular set of norms, it may have little capacity actually to shape behavior unless other aspects of the society are conducive. The secret of Protestantism may be simply that it is fragmented. Thus, Hinduism may be equally conducive to democracy, because it lacks unity and shows tremendous geographic and socioeconomic variation. The difficulty with Catholicism and Confucianism may be that each holds a monopoly in one or more societies. Perhaps any religious tradition can support democratic institutions, if the society lacks a single monopoly denomination in alliance with the state. And any tradition could support tyranny if it lacked significant opposition and saw its own interests served by a strong state.

An alternative way in which a religion might be conducive or hostile to democracy is if a substantial body of sacred law defines proper relations between people and institutions. All major world traditions have their legalistic sides, although Westerners tend to be most familiar with the various regulations in the Bible, some of which are quite specific. But in the context of contemporary democratization debates, the focus tends to be on Islam and on the rules concerning treatment of women in the Koran and in the traditions associated with it.

Women's Rights in Islam

Islam, a religious tradition comprising a billion believers, is a tremendously complex phenomenon that cannot be reduced to any simple formula. Thus, we cannot properly speak of "the status of women in Islamic society" or "women's rights under Islamic law." Furthermore, a person needs tremendous linguistic as well as cultural erudition to claim expertise on the subject of Islamic law, and the author of this book certainly lacks these prerequisites for a profound analysis. However, we would be derelict in our scholarly duty if we ignored the chief contemporary example of an apparent contradiction between religion and democracy, especially as such a large number of influential religious movements are oriented toward it. With the collapse of the Soviet Union, some irresponsible writers have begun to assert that the chief enemy of Western civilization is now Islam, and that Islam is by nature anti-democratic. In fact there are many features of Islamic traditions that are conducive to democratization, and especially to the development of flourishing market economies upon which democracy can rest. But democracy without women's rights is not democracy, and here Islam faces a special challenge (*The Economist* 1994).

One way to document the status of women in Islamic societies is by means of a checklist of seven legal reforms developed by the scholar Elizabeth H. White (1978). A society like Turkey that had enacted all these reforms would be considered highly reformed, whereas a society like Saudi Arabia that had enacted none of them, is unreformed. First, White says, women's equality requires a law setting the minimum age at which a girl

343

may be married, or else many girls will marry when they just reach puberty, thereby missing out on an education and the chance to choose their roles in life. The second reform requires civil registration of marriages, providing a basis for the wife to assert her rights in any later disputes with her husband. Third is a provision that gives the wife the right to divorce, comparable to the right of the husband. Fourth is inheritance law reform; by one widely applied traditional standard, women's inheritance shares were half as large as those of men. Fifth is an end to a man's right to take as many as four wives, often without even the requirement of consulting his current wives before acquiring another one. The sixth reform would abolish a husband's traditional right to divorce his wife provisionally by merely saying the word *talaq* before witnesses, and to effect a permanent divorce by doing this on three separate occasions. And seventh, religious law would be abolished and replaced with a secular legal code created by popularly-elected representatives. In addition to these legal changes, White says, full emancipation requires equal education for women and an end to the customs of veiling Islamic women's faces and restricting them to their homes.

Under Islamic law, the Koran established the general values to guide Islamic society, as well as stating some specific norms of behavior. Much of the work of Islamic legal scholars centers on determining exactly what the Koran said on a particular matter, including careful interpretation of the meaning of specific passages. This should not seem very strange to Americans, who commonly refer to a two-century-old document, the Constitution of the United States, for fundamental principles. However, the Constitution may be amended, and the first ten amendments are the Bill of Rights that establish the legal basis for much of American's political freedoms. Although the Koran cannot be amended, it has been supplemented by much other ancient material, and there are several schools of thought on how it should be interpreted.

John Esposito (1982) has sketched a useful outline of the structure of Islamic legal interpretation. He says there are really four sources of Islamic law, of which the first is the Koran, a holy book said to be divine revelations that were given to Mohammed around the year 600 A.D. The second source is the *Sunnah* of the Prophet, the sayings and deeds of Mohammed as recorded in stories (*hadith*) by people who knew him or claimed to have good secondary evidence. There is great debate over the authenticity of these hadiths, and some modernist legal scholars would like to set all of them aside and rely strictly upon the Koran, but they continue to be tremendously influential. Third is the use of analogy (*qiyas*), not reading one's own meanings into the *Koran* and *Sunnah*, but with devout care applying the ancient wisdom to new contexts by reasoning about similarities. Fourth comes *ijma*, the unanimous agreement of Islamic legal scholars on a particular issue. This is not the same thing as voting by a legislature, although the concept of *ijma* may sometimes be stretched to justify legislative democracy. Rather, the idea is that the total community of Islamic legal scholars could not be in error, and *ijma* applies only when there is a very high degree of consensus.

The first point to note about the Koran's orientation to women is that it apparently instituted a number of reforms that raised the status of women above what they had been before. Coulson and Hinchcliffe (1978:37) summarize the situation: "Under the customary tribal law existing in Arabia at the advent of Islam, women as a general rule had virtually no legal status. They were sold into marriage by their guardians for a price paid to the guardian, the husband could terminate the union at will, and women had little or no property or succession rights." The Koran confers specific rights to women, and several strong female characters in the Koran could serve as role models for their modern liberated sisters. Stowasser (1994) notes that Mary (mother of Jesus) is depicted as having the gift of prophecy, thus providing a basis for women to seek religious careers in Islam, and Bilqis (Queen of Sheba) is a model of a competent woman political leader and executive.

Some passages of the Koran, however, appear to set limits to gender equality, notably verse 34 of chapter 4 ("Women"). Table 12.1 gives this verse in four different translations, the first three downloaded from the World Wide Web service of the Islamic Society of the University of Essex, and the fourth quoted from an analysis of the passage (Engineer 1992:49). This verse is commonly taken to mean that men are superior to women and have the right to beat them. But the translations differ greatly. The last one, by a modernist translator, makes good women obedient to God, rather than to men, and manages to omit the reference about beating them. Thus, there are many ways to interpret Islamic traditions, and each potentially may be the ideological starting point for a religious movement oriented to promote or to block changes in women's status.

The limits placed on women in traditional Mid-Eastern Islamic societies cross-cut the status of non-Islamic groups. Historically, Islam considered Christians and Jews to be "people of the book" (Bible) who had failed to recognize that Islam was the fulfillment of their faith, but who none-the-less deserved tolerance. At some times this meant that Christian and Jewish communities could follow their own laws, so long as Muslims were not involved in the particular case. This special recognition was not accorded to other groups. A Muslim man could marry a Christian or Jewish woman, but a Muslim woman was not allowed to marry a Christian or Jewish man. Extreme penalties could be levied against those who converted from Islam to another religion, death in the case of a man and life imprisonment in the case of a woman. This set of rules has the effect of blocking women from us-

Table 12.1: Alternative Translations of Chapter 4 ("Women"), Verse 34 of the Koran

Abdullah Yusufali's translation:

Men are the protectors and maintainers of women, because God has given the one more (strength) than the other, and because they support them from their means. Therefore the righteous women are devoutly obedient, and guard in (the husband's) absence what God would have them guard. As to those women on whose part ye fear disloyalty and ill-conduct, admonish them (first), (next), refuse to share their beds, (and last) beat them (lightly); but if they return to obedience, seek not against them Means (of annoyance): For God is Most High, great (above you all).

M. H. Shakir's translation:

Men are the maintainers of women because Allah has made some of them to excel others and because they spend out of their property; the good women are therefore obedient, guarding the unseen as Allah has guarded; and (as to) those on whose part you fear desertion, admonish them, and leave them alone in the sleeping-places and beat them; then if they obey you, do not seek a way against them; surely Allah is High, Great.

Mohammed Marmaduke Pickthall's translation:

Men are in charge of women, because Allah hath made the one of them to excel the other, and because they spend of their property (for the support of women). So good women are the obedient, guarding in secret that which Allah hath guarded. As for those from whom ye fear rebellion, admonish them and banish them to beds apart, and scourge them. Then if they obey you, seek not a way against them. Lo! Allah is ever High, Exalted, Great.

Ahmed Ali's translation:

Men are the guardians of women as God has favored some with more than others, and because they spend of their wealth (to provide for them). So women who are virtuous are obedient to God and guard the hidden as God has guarded it. As for women you fear are averse, talk to them persuasively; then leave them alone in bed (without molesting them) and go to bed with them (when they are willing). If they open out to you, do not seek an excuse for blaming them. Surely, God is sublime and majestic.

---

ing conversion to another faith as a means to escape the restrictions placed on them by Islam (Mayer 1991:141–161; Nasir 1990:27–42).

Stowasser identifies three competing kinds of movements seeking to clarify the status of women within Islam: modernists, conservatives, and fundamentalists. The modernists are not secularists, really, although many of them would be content to live in a pluralist society with separation between the state and religion. Rather, they are Muslims who believe that much of the female oppression traditionally associated with Islam was historically added in the centuries following Mohammed, and that a true return to the Koran would accomplish women's liberation. Conservatives, Stowasser (1994:6) says, "view Islam as an inherited, balanced system of faith and action based on, and sanctioned by, scripture and its interpretation through the verifying authority of community consensus." They attempt to preserve their traditions against the corrosive force of westernization, and this means keeping women in a subordinate status. Fundamentalists agree with modernists on one point, that Islam should return to the purity of the Koran. But in their holy book they find ammunition to fight against non-Islamic Western ideas, and they are likely to insist upon traditional women's subordination. In the terms of early chapters in this book, the modernists seek to reduce the tension of Islam with the surrounding sociocultural environment of science and social development, whereas the fundamentalists seek to increase that tension.

Melford Spiro (1979) examined the changing status of women in Israeli kibbutz communities, developing a conceptual approach that could be used to analyze conditions beyond Israel's borders. He had performed field research inside one of these communes in 1951, then returned a generation later in 1975 to see how it had changed. In its earliest years, the kibbutz had attempted to achieve absolute sexual equality by such means as relieving mothers of the duties of child-rearing and giving women the same jobs as men, including physically demanding agricultural labor. Over the first generation, there was a partial evolution away from this stringent standard of equality toward a slightly more traditional system in which men and women, on average, tended to have somewhat different roles but the community accorded these roles equal status. Spiro says that the kibbutz started with an "identity" definition of equality, in which sexual equality required the sexes to perform the same roles. As the years passed, it moved toward an "equivalence" definition, in which the sexes played different but equally rewarded roles. In terms of Islam, modernists probably waver between identity and equivalence definitions of women's equality, whereas conservatives and fundamentalists either hold an equivalence definition or reject equality altogether.

Spiro's theoretical distinction, between identity and equivalence definitions of equality, is a real issue for all societies, including the United States and Islamic nations, as well as for Israel. Prior to the 1954 U.S. Supreme Court decision, *Brown versus the Board of Education*, many American communities segregated the races and claimed to give their children *separate but equal* educations. But this equivalence definition of racial equality turned out to be a sham, because minorities in fact did not receive equal educations or equal treatment in many public facilities and private businesses. With respect to gender, the United States has moved far in the direction of an identity definition of equality, but has not achieved it. Many Americans would prefer some kind of equivalence definition, although they undoubtedly disagree with each other about the precise roles that the two sexes should play and how we could enforce equality of reward between them. In a way, the identity definition of equality is conceptually easier to handle, because it sets a clear standard against which to measure success. Tremendous opportunities for argument arise when a society sets an equivalence standard. No standard measurement unit can be applied to all the settings where gender roles differ in order to asses how equal or unequal the rewards are, because money is not the only reward. Islamic societies implicitly apply an equivalence definition, asserting that their legal system and traditional customs benefit women as well as men, while expecting them to play very different roles in society.

Under colonialism and the paternalistic influence of Europe and America that followed it, many Middle Eastern nations experienced "modernization" that moved some of the states away from religious law toward secular law, thereby changing the status of women. Turkey, which had been an empire rather than a colony, adopted European secular politics wholesale, whereas some other nations, notably Tunisia, were able to adopt liberal gender-related laws within an Islamic religious context. In many nations, however, a so-called "Islamic resurgence" began about the time of the 1967 Arab-Israeli war (Mayer 1991:1). Westerners who object to "Islamic Fundamentalism" should recognize that it is in great measure a reaction to the arrogance of the European colonial powers and of the United States, and also to the tremendous social disruptions brought on by economic and technological development. Traditional church-sect theory can be expanded to explain the emergence of Islamic states more-or-less hostile to the West. Europe and the American superpower are the sociocultural environment in which these states experience tension born of relative deprivation. Like other sectarian movements, they seek to regain the honor and the power of ancient religious forms.

At the same time, we have to recognize that Islam has always contained fundamentalist movements, just as Christianity has, and they exhibit tremendous variety (Arjomand 1995). The social, economic, and technological changes occurring in Islamic societies challenge traditional cultural assumptions and place people under significant stress, both of which may stimulate a fundamentalist reaction. But it is possible that "modernization" has an even greater effect by providing new channels of communication and supporting the emergence of extensive new social structures. Thus we cannot expect Islamic fundamentalism to wither away when modernization is complete, just as Protestant fundamentalism has not withered away in technologically advanced Western nations. As is true for Christianity, we would expect Islam to receive continual renewal from fundamentalist movements, and to produce ever new fundamentalist movements whenever old ones become secularized and exhausted.

In Chapter 10 we doubted that religion possesses great power to determine behavior, unless it allies itself with other social forces. Thus, it is possible for a society to remain true to the general tenets of its religion, while modifying or ignoring a few selected elements of it. For example, Islam is certainly not the only religion that had made divorce far easier for a man than for a woman. Deuteronomy 24:1 says, "When a man hath taken a wife, and married her, and it come to pass that she find no favor in his eyes, because he hath found some uncleanness in her: then let him write her a bill of divorcement, and give it in her hand, and send her out of his house." This biblical verse says nothing about what favor he has in her eyes, or how she might send him out of her house. And it also says little about the actual conditions of marriage or divorce in many nations ostensibly based on this religious tradition, from Israel to Italy and all across Western civilization. All the great world religions carry forward to this day maxims based on the social conditions and cultural assumptions of long-bygone days. For each religion, the process of translating ancient traditions into viable modern lifestyles is very difficult, and in a sense unending. The debate among modernists, conservatives, and fundamentalists in Islam is comparable to the eternal church-sect battle in Christendom. The chief difference is that few of the Islamic nations possess the secular institutions that would be compatible with religious pluralism and with political democracy.

It is certainly possible to argue that Islamic law sets strict limits on the development of democracy. But the only way to determine if this theory is true is to watch the events of the next decades, to see if many Islamic nations make stable transitions to representative forms of government. Given that Islam is a living religion in the hearts of the people of these nations, the only way they can approach democracy is by building upon the conducive elements within Islam itself. The signs concerning the future status of women are not clear at the present time. However, we should note that after forty-two presidencies, the United States has still not had a female chief executive. In contrast, at the moment two of the major Islamic nations have women prime ministers, Turkey (Tansu Ciller) and Pakistan (Benazir Bhutto). When Bhutto was being considered for the chief executive position in Pakistan, a disputed *hadith* decrying female rulership was used by conservatives against her, but they did not prevail (Engineer 1992:17). The road ahead of Islamic women may be a difficult one, but it is not for us to say where it will lead.

Moroccan feminist sociologist, Fatima Mernissi, advocates the separation of mosque and state, and establishment of secular governments like that of Turkey across the Islamic world. She accuses the fundamentalists, paradoxically, of losing faith in their own religion, because they seem to believe that people would turn away from Islam unless coerced to follow it. She theorizes, "As both Christianity and Judaism have done, Islam can not only survive but thrive in a secular state. Once dissociated from coercive power, it will witness a renewal of spirituality. Christianity and Judaism strongly rooted in people's hearts are what I have seen in the United States, France, and Germany. In those countries the secular state has not killed religion; rather, it has put a brake on the state's manipulation of religion" (Mernissi 1992:65). Thus she is optimistic not only that Islam can foster democracy, but that democracy would stimulate the growth of Islam. This brings us to the crucial general question of whether freedom of religion strengthens or weakens faith.

The Free Market of Religion

One of the liveliest current debates in the sociology of religion centers on two opposing arguments about the relationship between religious pluralism and commitment (Warner 1993). In a series of publications, Roger Finke and Rodney Stark (1988, 1989, 1992; Finke 1989; Stark 1994) have pictured religion as a market economy in which denominations compete with each other for members. Different individuals and groups in society have different needs, cultures, and nonreligious affiliations, so therefore religious pluralism should increase commitment by offering each person the style of religion that suits him or her best. In their empirical work, Finke and Stark have tried to show that rates of church membership in areas of the United States are higher where there are more denominations in the religious marketplace.

Figure 12.2 shows Stark's (1994) simplified version of this theory, in four definitions and four propositions. Notice that Stark calls religious denominations "firms" by analogy with commercial and industrial corporations. When he refers to the "religious economy," he does not mean merely the flow of money into collection plates, but the entire social system of congregations and denominations in competition with each other for members who are conceived of as customers. "Market segments" are subgroups in the population who would prefer different kinds of religion, for example the upper classes who might like low-tension religion, and relatively deprived people who might prefer a high-tension faith. If many market segments exist, then people would be most satisfied and therefore participate at the highest rate in religion, if there were also many different firms. This means that religious pluralism, which Stark sees as the natural result of real religious freedom, will generate the highest rate of church membership.

In contrast, other researchers have argued that religious pluralism has a

Table 12.2: The Finke-Stark Theory of Religious Pluralism

Definition 1: *Religious firms* are social enterprises whose primary purpose is to create, maintain, and supply religion to some set of individuals.

Definition 2: The *religious economy* consists of all the religious activity going on in any society.

Definition 3: *Pluralistic* refers to the number of firms active in the economy; the more firms having a significant market-share, the greater the degree of pluralism.

Definition 4: To *specialize*, a firm caters to the special needs and tastes of specific market segments.

Proposition 1: The capacity of a single religious firm to monopolize a religious economy depends upon the degree to which the state uses coercive force to regulate the religious economy.

Proposition 2: To the degree that a religious economy is unregulated, it will tend to be very pluralistic.

Proposition 3: To the degree that a religious economy is pluralistic, firms will specialize.

Proposition 4: To the degree that a religious economy is competitive and pluralistic, overall levels of religious participation will tend to be high. Conversely, to the degree that a religious economy is monopolized by one or two state-supported firms, overall levels of participation will tend to be low.

negative effect on church membership, or no effect (Breault 1989; Land, Deane and Blau 1991; Blau, Land and Redding 1992; Blau, Redding and Land 1993; cf. Christiano 1987). Religious monopoly might be associated with higher rates of religious involvement, if individual affiliations are chiefly the result of social influence, and if social influence is most effective when it is monolithic. My own view differs from both groups of authors, holding that American data on church membership are not ideal for testing these two theories, and that both theories are probably right (Bainbridge 1995).

Thus we have two competing models of religious mobilization, the diversity theory and the monopoly theory. Both, as it happens, are rooted in the Stark-Bainbridge general theory of religion. In any scientific collaboration, people bring different knowledge and orientations to the work. On balance, Stark has been more interested in religious revival, whereas I have been more interested in religious innovation. Revival invokes church-sect theory and the ways that religion may compensate people for their relative material deprivations. Thus Stark has been prepared to contribute to the relatively new rational choice perspective within sociology, which is often couched in economic terms. Innovation, in contrast, links more directly to the generation and transmission of novel beliefs and practices, which brings in communication research, social networks, and cognitive science. Thus, I have collaborated with Michael Macy and John Skvoretz (Bainbridge et al. 1994; cf. Macy 1990, 1991b; Skvoretz and Fararo 1995), whose work in learning theory is a direct challenge to rational choice theory. Learning theory views human behavior as primarily conditioned by past histories of rewards and costs, whereas rational choice theory emphasizes rational calculation of future rewards and costs—not much of a difference, admittedly, but enough to energize some sociological debates. In going our separate roads, Stark and I have merely emphasized different parts of our shared theory.

Table 12.3 lists seven propositions and a definition from the Stark-Bainbridge theory, sketching one way that the monopoly-mobilization theory could be derived (Stark and Bainbridge 1987:89–96). To the extent that denominations differ in doctrine or practice, a person socially connected to two or more will experience lowered faith, compared to someone living in a religiously monolithic society where there are no religious disagreements. Thus, consensus should strengthen religion. The key point is proposition 67, which is derived from the other propositions, and follows from the general theory of rewards and compensators.

The fact that both the diversity-mobilization and monopoly-mobilization theories are rooted in the same general theory of religion does not mean the underlying theory is contradictory. Rather, the Stark-Bainbridge theory often describes situations in which opposing forces are at work. This means that one needs to have a fair amount of information about a concrete social situation before one can make a confident prediction about it. And we would expect the tug-of-war between diversity and monopoly to have different outcomes under different circumstances. In all communities, both diversity of need and faith through consensus are important factors, but their relative strengths may vary. The nature of the religious tradition matters, as well. If all of the religious organizations in a community are of the same tradition, Protestant for example, then they will agree on many of the same general compensators, such as the divinity of Jesus and the efficacy of prayer. This means that a measure of consensus can exist even in diversity.

It is difficult to know how much diversity is enough, and how much is too much. We do not have good ways of measuring how many market segments potentially exist in a given population, a problem touched on already in the section of Chapter 2 about relative deprivation. The definition of "firm" is also somewhat shaky. Industrial sociologists, actually, are of two minds whether to study the dynamics of major industries at the level of corpora-

Table 12.3: Religious Monopoly-Mobilization in the Stark-Bainbridge Theory

Proposition 13: The more valued or general a reward, the more difficult will be evaluation of explanations about how to obtain it.

Proposition 62: No human being can personally evaluate all the explanations he uses, including verifiable ones.

Proposition 63: The value an individual places on an explanation is often set by the values placed on it by others and communicated to him through exchanges.

Proposition 64: In the absence of a more compelling standard, the value an individual places on a reward is set by the market value of that reward established through exchanges by other persons.

Proposition 65: The value an individual places on a general compensator is set through exchanges with other persons.

Proposition 66: When there is disagreement over the value of an explanation, the individual will tend to set a value that is a direct averaging function of the values set by others and communicated to him through exchanges, weighted by the value placed on such exchanges with each partner.

Proposition 67: The more cosmopolitan a society with respect to religious culture, the lower the market value of any given general compensator.

Definition 36: *Cosmopolitan* refers to the existence of plural cultures within a society.

---

tions or at the level of individual factories, several of which may belong to the same corporation. Similarly, although published studies consider denominations to be firms, perhaps because appropriate data exist at the denominational level, we could just as well argue that each congregation is a firm. Like chains of fast-food franchises and grocery stories, religious denominations often go to great lengths to mitigate the fact their individual churches in an area are in competition with each other, but the fact is that they do compete. Many denominations give congregations considerable latitude in their degree of tension with the sociocultural environment. Thus, for example, the Southern Baptist church at one end of town may be a very dignified place that offers low-tension religion to its middle-class members, whereas the poor Southern Baptist church at the other end of town holds emotional services worthy of holy rollers. Existing studies entirely miss this kind of diversity, and it would be very costly to obtain good data about intra-denominational diversity in a large enough number of communities for statistical analysis. A long list of problems like this gives me little confidence that readily available American data allow us to evaluate the two competing theories, and thus I am not surprised that published studies disagree (Bainbridge 1995).

In a way, the theories apply better outside the free religious market of the United States. In western European nations where there was a long-standing alliance between the state and a single denomination (ecclesia), the diversity-mobilization theory predicts that disestablishment of that denomination and achievement of a free religious market would result not only in a great increase in the number of denominations, but also in the proportion of the population that participated actively in religion. Even more spectacularly, religious freedom in a nation where all religions had been suppressed should produce an explosion of religious movements, and an upsurge in participation by individuals. A decade ago, Stark and I (1985:522–530) noted the survival of religion under atheistic Communism that first sought to destroy it, and then to contain and co-opt it. Not in our wildest dreams did we imagine that the Soviet Union was on the verge of collapse when we wrote, or that an excellent field for testing our theories would be the flowering of religious movements in the vast liberated territory from Germany eastward to the Pacific.

Writing about recent events in the former Soviet Union can be hazardous. It is not merely that any moment the situation might change, rendering published judgments obsolete, but new information may come out that sets past events in an entirely different context. In the case of religious movements, we can gain proper perspective on the great current turmoil only after conditions have settled down, and we can see who were the winners, and who, the losers.

Consider the case of Ukraine. A nation the size of France, with vast agricultural potential, Ukraine inherited nuclear weapons and the engineers needed to operate them, at the breakup of the Soviet Union. It also inherited much land that was radioactively contaminated by the explosion of the nuclear power plant at Chernobyl. One thing the Ukraine does not possess is sufficiently developed energy resources, so it remains energy dependent upon Russia, which no longer wishes to provide the oil at Soviet-subsidized rates. Establishment of an independent Ukrainian currency, separate from the Russian ruble, was exceedingly difficult, and economic reform has been practically nonexistent. I recently heard a representative of the Ukrainian embassy say that economic and health conditions for families were so dreadful that hardly any children were being born. The nominal borders of Ukraine contain a large number of Russian-speaking people, many of whom would prefer to be Russian citizens. Two early bones of contention with Russia were possession of the Black Sea fleet and of Crimea, both of which were within Ukrainian borders but seemed to many Russians to belong to them. The remarkable thing is that the Ukraine has gone so long without outright catastrophe.

Under such conditions of culture shock, economic collapse, and social disorganization, we would expect many people to turn to religion for help and comfort. Ukraine possesses rich religious traditions, including such architectural treasures as the eleventh-century St. Sophia Cathedral in the capital city, Kiev. The immediate question is who owns them. Those religious resources that were not seized by the state have been in the custody of the Ukrainian branch of the Russian Orthodox Church, directed from Moscow. When the Soviet Union disintegrated in 1991, Patriarch Volodymyr declared the independence of the Ukrainian Orthodox Church, began gaining support among Ukrainian nationalists, and laid claim to the church's possessions within the new nation. To complicate matters further, there had long existed a Ukrainian Orthodox Church in exile, headquartered in New Jersey, which continues to assert that it is the real national church. In 1995 Patriarch Volodymyr died, and a bizarre incident cast into stark relief the chaotic religious and political situation in this major nation.

The patriarch's supporters requested permission to bury him at St. Sofia Cathedral. All three competing denominations claim this architectural masterpiece, which the Soviets had turned into a museum that is now operated by the Ukrainian government. Former president Leonid Kravchuck supported this request. The administration of his rival, President Leonid Kuchma, refused, realizing that Patriarch Volodymyr's burial at the cathedral would allow his followers to claim both the cathedral and preeminence among the rival denominations. In response, Volodymyr's Ukrainian Orthodox Church staged a funeral march down a main street of Kiev to the walls of the cathedral, in the company of new allies, the anti-Russian paramilitary right-wing Ukrainian People's Self-Defense. When they reached the cathedral gate, the paramilitary marchers broke through police lines, used metal poles to dig a big hole in the sidewalk, and placed the patriarch's body in this improvised grave next to the holy ground. The clerics just had time to pronounce a burial service when riot police attacked with tear gas and truncheons, injuring seventy people, including priests as well as paramilitary. As is the habit among modern nations, the entire debacle was broadcast on television for everyone to see. A few days later, a great cortege of clergy led by Metropolitan Filaret, the church's leading living figure, conducted a memorial service on the spot, under guard by their paramilitary allies. To put it mildly, the religious situation in Ukraine remains fluid (Rupert 1995a, 1995b).

Two years earlier Kiev had been the scene of a similarly wild altercation, involving not rival orthodox churches, but a radical millenarian religious movement. It started when Marina Tsvigun, a mother and journalist, came into contact with a psychologist named Yurii Krivonogov who had founded a small movement called Institute of the Soul: Atma. Soon Mrs. Tsvigun had metamorphosed into the living god Maria Devi Khristos. Posters, showing her looking like a cross between a nun and a pharaoh, with two fingers of her right hand raised to heaven and an emblematic shepherd's crook clutched in her left, were plastered all over Russia and Ukraine. Some time in November 1993 she was supposed to enter Kiev at the head of the White Brotherhood, be crucified, be resurrected, and usher in the millennium. Tormented by visions of thousands of marching cultists, the Ukrainian government made preparations, and arrested her just as she reached St. Sophia cathedral (Kipp 1994). It will be interesting, to say the least, to follow the histories of the new religious movements of Ukraine, liberated by the wave of democratization that toppled the Soviet Union.

Freedom of New Religions

Not long ago I had the opportunity to meet a Croatian who was involved in the effort of his newly independent nation to write a law setting the conditions that a religious organization had to meet before it could be officially registered with the government. At first, the framers of this legislation thought this would be a simple matter, and they proposed to register only those denominations that had at least 50,000 members. Then a leading Jewish citizen of Croatia spoke up, pointing out that his religion was certainly respectable and well established, yet it had fewer than 50,000 members. Indeed, a recent count indicated there were just 633 Jews in the country. So the current plan is to register only those denominations which have 50,000 members or have been active in Croatia for more than fifty years.

All across Europe, from France to Russia, throughout Latin America, and in Japan, religious leaders and government officials have been discussing plans like this. Some of these nations recognize that small groups of immigrants to their country bring their own religions with them, so there is good reason to let them register even if they fall below this standard of 50,000 members or fifty years. Thus, the French, for example, have been considering how a standing government committee might be able to examine small, new religious groups to determine whether they were valid or not. To citizens of English-speaking countries, these ideas seem exceedingly strange, and the American tolerance for new religions is nearly matched by that found in Britain, Canada, Australia, New Zealand, and South Africa. In rebuttal, my Croatian visitor reported that his people resent the invasion of well-funded foreign missionary movements, and wish to be left to their own traditions. However, Croatia is ready to register both the Seventh-day Adventists and Jehovah's Witnesses, because they meet the fifty-year criterion.

The meaning of regulations concerning religion varies across nations and decades. Even in politically democratic nations, an unregistered religion may be denied tax exemptions, the license to build a house of worship or a school, recognition of the validity of marriages performed, or access to the mass media. Lack of registration leaves a religious movement open to both official and unofficial harassment, such as police officials looking for an opportunity to arrest its leaders on whatever charge they can find, the press feeling it can profit from exposés based on only flimsy information, and local rowdies feeling encouraged to desecrate its shrines and beat up its members. A member of the Unification Church from Singapore, who had been a police officer in that country, told me that he had been explicitly urged by his superiors to quit the church, because his membership endangered his career and would prevent promotion. That is, a person whose religion is not registered does not have full protection of civil rights regulations, and may be discriminated against legally on the basis of his or her religion, to a greater or lesser degree depending upon the country.

Discriminating against a religious group because it is new or small may seem unfair to most readers. A far more contentious question concerns how to handle religious groups that violate minor laws or regulations of the society, and do so as a matter of faith. Over many years the Amish ("Pennsylvania Dutch") struggled to keep their children out of public schools so they would not be contaminated by secular culture (Keim 1975). Today education at home rather than in state schools is favored by many religious groups, including The Family discussed in Chapter 8. The society has an interest in the well-being of all its children, and compulsory school attendance laws inevitably require a definition of what is a proper school and what credentials a teacher must have to teach. At present, the home-schooling movement is growing, especially among conservative Protestant groups. Therefore, conflict over appropriate standards for educating the children of religious minorities will continue to rage for years to come.

I do not want to mention the names of particular religious groups in connection with the commission of crimes, even minor ones, but the following are real examples from my research. One novel religion believed that once a person had been born again, he or she would no longer have a definite age, but would be timeless. Getting a driver's license required proof of age, so as an act of religious devotion members regularly drove cars without licenses. Members of several international religious movements have on occasion entered a nation without official permission to do so, or have stayed in a nation beyond the period of a visitor's visa, believing that God's commandment to spread the word takes precedence over immigration laws. Some groups that get most of their money through donations from the general public refuse to register with the local government, thus violating laws regulating charities, and they often employ means of solicitation that run afoul of regulations concerning both businesses and nonprofit organizations. Urban communal groups frequently find it difficult to find suitable housing to rent, because zoning or health regulations limit the number of people who can live in a given space, so they often misrepresent the number of members to landlords and violate numerous ordinances simply by living together in a modest home. Especially in communal groups, or in others that devote much of their time to proselytizing and lack conventional wage-paying jobs, there is a tendency to avoid paying income tax. Indeed, it is very difficult for a member of such groups to figure out what his or her income is, especially if the religious movement is not registered and does not keep detailed financial records that distinguish clearly between individual property and the property of the movement.

Those are all situations where thoughtful people may disagree about whether members of radical religious movements should be held to the same strict accounting as other citizens. But the cases that are etched in the public memory concern really egregious behavior of a very small number of infamous "cults." For many folk, the archetypal violent "cult" was the Peoples Temple (Reiterman and Jacobs 1982; Hall 1987; Chidester 1988). Jim Jones founded his independent movement in Indianapolis in 1956, after having been a pastor of the Assemblies of God. In 1960 Jones was able to affiliate his church with a moderate Protestant denomination, the Disciples of Christ, and at that point his church technically would have met the 50,000 members or fifty-years test, and did not appear to a casual observer to be a religious cult. While preaching a religious message of racial tolerance, Jones was privately a Marxist who expected a final war between the United States and the Soviet Union, in which would be rooting for the Soviets. In 1965, he led about 140 members to Ukiah in California's Redwood Valley, where he proceeded to build a small empire of nursing homes and ingratiate himself into San Francisco political circles. He never had to face a court of justice, but the charges leveled against him include a myriad of financial frauds, numerous sexual improprieties, and harsh child abuse. Attracted by the Marxist regime in Guyana, Jones sent followers to the South American jungle in 1974 to create a utopian settlement. There, on November 18, 1978, members of the Peoples Temple murdered American congressman Leo Ryan who had come to investigate the commune, along with some of his party. Then followed the dreadful murder-suicide of 914 members including 276 children and Jones himself.

Although there have been other fatal tragedies involving new religious groups, across the Western world their rate is very low, perhaps one every three or four years out of thousands of religious groups and nearly a billion population. The overwhelming majority of new religious movements never experience unusual violence. In contrast, Marxist groups have often engaged in wanton killing, with the Pol Pot regime in Cambodia being only the most extreme case. If we take the self-professed Marxism of Jim Jones seriously, then it seems unfair to religious movements to call the Peoples Temple a church. In modern times, the death rate from political movements is vastly higher than that from religious movements, and there is always some risk that any kind of collective behavior might lead to unintended disaster.

Scholars of new religious movements have not had very great success developing a scientific model to predict which religious movements might turn to violence. Some say the best recipe for holocaust is to have a radical, separatist, millenarian sect get attacked by the government, essentially what happened to the Branch Davidians at Waco. But when the government has chosen to move cautiously against a millenarian religious movement, and not storm in with guns drawn, the result has almost invariably been peaceful. For example, the substantial Rajneesh community in Oregon melted away under pressure, despite being well-armed. Scholars of new religious movements are aware of many similar examples, none of which are familiar to the general public. Thus it would distort reality to base a policy concerning new religious movements on the desire to prevent future catastrophes like the Peoples Temple. Nonetheless, society has the right to take some precautions against religious extremism, and it will be next to impossible to find a perfect balance between religious freedom and responsible citizenship.

To this point we have contemplated the uneasy status of new religious movements within democratic societies. One would think that less democratic societies would be even more hostile to new religions, but in fact the situation is unclear. A distinction used to be made between right-wing authoritarian regimes, like the Franco government in Spain, and left-wing totalitarian regimes, like the Soviet Union. It appeared that authoritarian regimes permitted considerable freedom in economic and cultural matters, merely suppressing political opposition, thus leaving themselves room to evolve peacefully into democratic societies. In contrast, totalitarian regimes sought to dominate all aspects of their people's thought and behavior, and thus could never become democratic. This theory is now less plausible, since the world's most powerful totalitarian state simply fell apart revealing a great diversity of attitudes and behavior patterns among its populace. However, one point remains valid. Moderately dictatorial regimes of the kind usually called right-wing can in fact be fertile ground for the emergence and survival of new religious movements.

A good example is the history of The Family (Children of God) in the Philippines. In 1985 a number of experienced Family leaders went to the

Philippines to assist the struggling homes there. Both Father David and Maria became directly involved in the operation of local communes, as they had not been for several years, and they took up incognito residence there. The Philippines became a major center of Family activity, and the group received exceedingly favorable treatment from the military and from the Marcos regime which the military supported. FFing was part of the Philippine ministry, but the attractiveness of Family women was far from the only feature that endeared the group to the regime. Despite its communal lifestyle, the Family was resolutely anti-Marxist, and like more conventional Protestant missionary groups, it seemed a likely ally in the regime's dispute with the Roman Catholic Church.

However hospitable it seemed, Philippine society was torn by intense social conflicts. In 1969, the Communist Party of the Philippines, following the example of Chinese revolutionary Mao Tse Tung, had created the New People's Army to oppose the regime through guerrilla military action. Separate from the Maoists, but responding to some of the same social pressures, were the Roman Catholic Base Communities, associated with Liberation Theology. This is an international democratization movement among Roman Catholics that identifies with the poor, seeks to represent them within church and state, and attempts to create a new form of grass-root community. In 1970 in Brazil, the Roman Catholic bishops themselves began to criticize the oppressive military government then in power, and considerable sympathy has existed throughout the Latin American church hierarchy for movements that challenge similar regimes. A base community is a network of two or three dozen religiously devout but politically conscious Catholics in a local area. By the late 1980s there were as many as 80,000 of these organizations in Brazil alone, with substantial numbers in other Latin countries (McGuire 1992:239–245). This movement spread to the Philippines, and soon constituted a considerable fraction of the peaceful opposition to the Marcos regime. Violence against them soon drove some into outright insurgency, notably when a Catholic leader named Conrado Balweg organized the Coreillera People's Liberation Army, and some fifty priests actually joined the New People's Army (Kowalewski 1991).

Without embracing armed struggle, the central leadership of the Roman Catholic Church continued to criticize the Marcos regime, and chief prelate Cardinal Jaime Sin used radio effectively to build sentiment for a new government. In 1986, Marcos left the country and Corazon Aquino, widow of an assassinated political opposition leader, became president. It is not our task here to judge the sequence of regimes that have governed the Philippines, but Aquino came to power with great hopes among many Philippine citizens and the moral support of many Americans. For The Family, however, this great change in the surrounding political system created a very difficult problem. It was not merely that their friendship with the Marcos government left them open to the charge of being Marcos supporters and thus subject to punishment and repression. In addition, The Family is always vulnerable to religiously motivated suppression as heretics and violators of the conventional sexual mores. This vulnerability, church-sect theory would predict, is greatest in nations where one religious denomination approaches the status of ecclesia, as had been true for the Roman Catholic Church in several nations where The Family has experienced persecution: Argentina, Brazil, France, Mexico, Spain and the Philippines.

It is not that the official organs of the church directly attacked The Family. Rather, public officials and media executives who fancy themselves to be defenders of conventional morality and of the one, true religion launch campaigns against The Family. It is possible that their real motive is often simply personal career advancement, and they judge that the religious consensus existing in their society will permit them to gain substantially by attacking a tiny religious minority that has no constituency. In the Philippines, the departure of the Marcos regime led rather swiftly to a newspaper campaign against The Family. Evangelical Protestant forces, usually opponents of the Catholics, joined the campaign excoriating The Family as a "sex cult" corrupting the morals of children and adults alike. Father David and a council of Family leaders quickly decided that the Philippine environment was no longer hospitable, and within months 600 members had left for other areas of the world including the United States, leaving a small cadre of Philippine national members behind.

Conclusion: Religious Political Economy

In 1995, more than three decades after Martin Luther King, Jr., stood before the Lincoln Memorial and spoke about the American dream, an estimated 400,000 African-American men marched behind Reverend Louis Farrakhan on the same ground. For many of these men, King's dream had not been fulfilled, and the "Million Man March" had an ambiguous relationship to it. Many call Farrakhan's Nation of Islam a separatist movement that has given up on achieving an integrated society. Others see in it a way that black men may fulfill American values through self-control and self-reliance. Wherever this radical religious movement goes, it reminds us both that the United States has not met the challenge of its own democratic principles, and religion is a prime force holding it to account.

Popular mythology holds that new religious movements are autocratic, and therefore that they detract from democracy rather than contributing to it. Certainly we have seen religious movements that were directed by a single individual, from Russell's and Rutherford's Jehovah's Witnesses to The Family under Father David. Yet, usually, power is shared among a variety of individuals around the anointed leader, and members of many such groups do not perceive themselves to be oppressed. Few nonmembers would like to see a radical faith become the established church of their society, and that is not the proper place of such movements. Innovative groups like Jehovah's Witnesses and The Family exist and play positive roles as part of a wider religious system that includes highly secularized low-tension denominations and competing high-tension sects.

This complex story of The Family in the Philippines points out that conventional church-sect theory was designed to fit relatively stable societies, where a long-standing alliance between the state and a single religious denomination stably defines religious and political orthodoxy. Under revolutionary conditions, whether during the creation of democracy or its destruction, this simple theory may no longer hold. Leaders will form fluid alliances with other leaders, sometimes bringing their organizations into strange coalitions in a free-for-all battle for power. The largest religious denomination may find itself at war with the civil government, and a previously outcast sect may suddenly take up a position at the very center of authority. We shall return to these questions in Chapter 14, but for the moment it is worth noting that democracy is inexorably connected to religious freedom, but novel religious movements sometimes find authoritarian regimes or general chaos to be more favorable for growth and survival.

At the end of successful democratization, a society will possess a relatively unregulated economy, a political system that distributes power widely, and a free system of several religious denominations and movements. It is not certain whether this can be stably achieved in societies in which a single denomination, usually the former ecclesia, is the religion of the overwhelming majority of citizens. The chief familiar example is France, although the road to democracy was difficult and traveled at the cost of considerable anti-clericalism and secularization. Among the most controversial developments in modern religion is the Protestant invasion of Latin America, and it remains to be seen whether this will strengthen the renewed democracies of that quadrant of the world. Sociologists of religion are few in number and hardly any of them are trained to do research outside their own society. Thus it is with great awe and a sense of scientific helplessness, that we watch the stupendous democratization dramas of the former Soviet Union and Islam.

13

The New Age

The New Age Movement is a strange potpourri of myths and rituals drawn from Asian religion, European legends, and the imaginations of its practitioners. Much of it claims to be science, history, or the arts, rather than religion, but at every turn an explorer of the New Age will confront supernatural forces. Although it does not yet seem to possess much influence, the New Age movement permeates Western culture. For example, three bookstore chains have outlets in the complex of buildings that houses the National Science Foundation, the premiere U.S. government agency that supports fundamental scientific research. Each bookstore has a New Age section, containing an average of ninety-three different titles on such topics as alien abduction, astrology, biorhythms, channeling, dream interpretation, healing crystals, near-death experiences, Nostradamus prophecies, palm reading, past lives, ritual magick [sic], spiritualism, werewolves, and Wicca (witchcraft). One of these stores also sells two sets of tarot cards, an astrology kit, and a bone oracle kit. At one level, all this seems quite trivial. But when we find these topics showing up frequently in movies and television dramas, and when a president of the United States is revealed to have regularly consulted an astrologer, the possibility arises that we are witnessing a gradual but significant cultural change that might result in repaganization of Judeo-Christian civilization.

The Glastonbury Mythic System

The singers of the 1960s rock musical *Hair* proclaimed, "This is the dawning of the Age of Aquarius." The astrological New Age millennium can be seen nowhere more clearly than in the English town of Glastonbury, a town of fewer than 10,000 people, about 120 miles west of London. A short distance down the redundantly named avenue, Street Road, is the town of Street, headquarters of the Clark shoe company, and a considerable portion of the population works in small factories and has no particular appreciation for astrology. Amply supplied with conventional Christian churches, the majority of residents are probably not New Agers, but a substantial minority are involved in such groups, and a series of myths connects conventional religion with highly unconventional religious and quasi-religious movements. To the international occult subculture, Glastonbury is "a major acupuncture point of the Earth body" and "one of the most powerful centers on the planet" (Singh 1981:36).

Legends surround Glastonbury Abbey, which was sacked by the Protestants in 1539 and reduced to ruins by the villagers who stole its stones over the centuries for their shops and homes. A tall, plain, wooden cross, donated by the Queen, identifies the place as a Christian shrine, but there is no suggestion which denomination it belongs to. Above one remaining doorway are carvings of biblical scenes, and they show the three kings dressed in full suits of medieval armor. This anachronism reminds us that religions commonly interpret their ancient traditions in terms familiar from believers' own lives.

On one of the great walls are dimly legible the much eroded names JESUS and MARIA. Said to date from the thirteenth century, this inscription may merely mark one of the stations visited by pilgrims of the period. But the inscription is widely believed also to commemorate the historical fact that Jesus and Mary came to Glastonbury, in the years before he took up his mission. Supposedly, they journeyed with Joseph of Arimathea, said to be a tin merchant, on a commercial visit to the tin-mining area near the town. After the crucifixion, Joseph returned to Glastonbury with the two cruets containing the blood and sweat shed by Christ on the cross, where he established the world's first above-ground Christian church (Capt 1983). St. John's Church, in the middle of town, has a stained glass portrait of Joseph, flanked by the cruets, and its former vicar published a scholarly defense of the legend (Lewis 1922).

The official tourist guidebook to the abbey (Radford 1973) and a guide to the town published by local businessmen (Glastonbury Advertising Association n.d.) note the legend and leave it to the reader to decide how much stock to place in it. The abbey displays a thorn tree said to be descended from the staff of Joseph, which blossomed when he thrust it into the soil of England. Surely there are many theories about where Jesus traveled in his youth, and thus this legend is considered an optional, plausible belief among Anglicans. In a beloved old hymn, poet William Blake (1946:412) asked,

> And did those feet in ancient time
> Walk upon England's mountains green?
> And was the holy Lamb of God
> On England's pleasant pastures seen?

Within the roofless arches of the abbey, framed by soft, green grass, a cement rectangle marks the supposed location of King Arthur's tomb, which was found by the monks in the year 1191. Skeptics suspect that the discovery was a hoax perpetrated by the abbot who needed tourist business to rebuild the abbey after its destruction by fire in 1184. But a recent archaeological excavation did find an ancient grave apparently belonging to a prominent person. The old stories tell that Arthur went to the Isle of Avalon to die, and Glastonbury is not an island. However it may have been one long ago. Surrounded by low and sometimes marshy land today, the hills of the town were apparently circled by swamp in earlier times, and archaeological remains of a lake settlement have been found.

Further, the nearby hamlet of Cadbury has long been a claimant to be Arthur's fabled Camelot, and surprising archaeological excavations carried out around 1970 revealed a massive, walled town of just the right period, much more impressive than the competing Camelots (Alcock 1971; Ashton 1974). This legend is important for many tiny unusual religious or mystical movements of the area, but there is nothing deviant about believing in the reality of Arthur, and the idea that he was buried at Glastonbury does not strain credibility greatly (Ashe 1971).

Rising above a sheep meadow beside the town is a pointed hill called the Tor, which figures prominently in neopagan and New Age mythology. On top stands a ruined church, only the tower still standing, and modern pagans claim the old deities rose up and destroyed the Christian temple with a bolt of lightning, leaving only the phallic tower. Snaking around the sides of the Tor are terraces believed to date from Neolithic times, perhaps tracing a ritual pagan maze (Ashe 1979). Proof that the Tor was a center of ancient worship for the same people who created Stonehenge is lacking, but the terraces seem ancient and appear unsuited for agriculture or military defense. One writer reports that the Tor "has been called a magic mountain, the fairies' glass mountain, a spiral castle, a Grail castle, the Land of the Dead, Hades, a Druid initiation centre, an Arthurian hill-fort, a magnetic power-point, a ley-line crossroads, a centre for the Great Goddess fertility rituals and celebrations, and a converging point for flying saucers" (Howard-Gordon 1982:1). According to one modern pagan, "Atlantean geomancers . . . sculpted its upper contours into the shape of a seated Lion" back in the age of Leo, around 11,000 B.C. (Roberts 1984:9).

Nestled beside the Tor is Chalice Hill, named for the Holy Grail, and at its base an ancient spring is believed to have healing properties (Hardcastle 1982). The well is operated by a small religious center founded by Wellesley Tudor Pole, a businessman and author of numerous essays that mix Christian with spiritualist and theosophical ideas (Villiers 1977; Pole 1983a, 1983b, 1983d). Pole believed that a vast, secret hierarchy of spiritually advanced beings rises from our level to that of God, and he wrote about Elders of the Race and of The Blended Ray which has been secretly "brought into being by the joint efforts of Great Masters and Initiates gathered together as a Hierarchy, under divine guidance, for this very purpose" (Pole 1983c:4). This hermetic organization is preparing the way for a spiritual revolution, a Second Coming to be experienced within each spiritually advanced person, focused on Glastonbury's Chalice Well.

On the other side of Chalice Hill is a second modest religious group, the Ramala Society, founded in 1972 by David and Ann Jevons, consisting of a fine, square building with a swimming pool, an annex of comfortable bedrooms, a complex of gardens, and a small wooden meditation building. David Jevons was a transoceanic airline pilot who has a talent as a trance medium, which he practices in healing sessions with clients and in receiving teachings that have been issued in several languages. Like Pole's writings, *The Revelation of Ramala* (Jevons and Jevons 1978) is a vague amalgam of Christian, Eastern, and contemporary occult ideas. In a multi-media presentation offered to guests at its bed-and-breakfast, Ramala endorses all the myths about Glastonbury and suggests that the return of Christ, to herald in the Age of Aquarius, will shortly occur at this "center of great power" and "chakra" of "cosmic energy."

If one stands atop the Tor, and gazes down at the landscape, one sees a maze of hedges, walls, roads, and an occasional stream. Like a Rorschach ink-blot, or the clouds in which madness-feigning Hamlet professed to see the forms of animals, this scene can suggest meaningful shapes to the eye. One of the most widely discussed myths of Glastonbury says that the features actually do draw a picture, a ten-mile wide sketch of the zodiac. Katherine Maltwood, an artist then scrutinizing maps of the area to help her illustrate the legend of the Grail, "discovered" the Glastonbury Zodiac around 1925. Maltwood and her disciples asserted that the twelve signs of the zodiac could be seen in maps and aerial photographs, saying they really were there on the land, not fancifully imagined (Maltwood 1964; Caine 1978).

Aquarius is drawn by certain features of Glastonbury itself, including the Tor, but instead of being a water-carrier, it is a Phoenix bird with outstretched wings, symbolizing "the coming Aquarian Age when mankind must rise from the ashes of his past stupidities, and all things will be made anew" (Bord and Bord 1974:225). Sagittarius depicts King Arthur in the act of falling from his horse, and other signs represent Lancelot, Guinevere,

Mordred, and Percival from the legends of Arthur and the Holy Grail. Indeed, the Glastonbury Zodiac is said to be the Round Table, and also the Grail itself.

According to the Maltwoodians, the legends we know of Arthur and the Grail are relatively recent adaptations of very ancient truths expressed in the gigantic drawings. Maltwood said the zodiac was about 5,000 years old, built by the same people who constructed Stonehenge and the Avebury monuments, about forty miles due east. Some of her disciples believe instead that the zodiac was drawn by the cosmic forces that created the world. For many enthusiasts, modern Glastonbury is but a transition from the ancient Isle of Avalon to the New Jerusalem that is to come. For them, the Glastonbury Zodiac is the "geomythic" unifier of the various traditions and forces that flow through the town (Roberts 1978:10–12). To Robert Coon, "a poet and magickian [sic] currently focused in the Glastonbury area," the Zodiac is "an instrument for the Building of New Jerusalem" (Coon 1984), and to further this end, Coon has founded The Omega Point Foundation.

Many small New Age businesses have sprung up in the town, including two astrological services. The Glastonbury Experience is an occult shopping center including Broiderwise wool products, Sunrise Wholefoods, Manu Solis Craft Gallery, Candle Workshop, Courtyard Restaurant, and Helios Books. The associated Natural Health Clinic has practitioners in many pseudomedical fields: acupuncture, the Alexander technique, family therapy, herbalism, massage, music therapy, nutritional guidance combined with shiatsu and acupressure, osteopathy, reflexology and metamorphic technique, and yoga. Further up the main commercial street is Gothic Image, a countercultural store that conducts "mystical tours of Glastonbury," and Rainbow's End Wholefood Cafe, which serves organic vegetarian meals and advertises Sufi meetings.

Glastonbury could not support such a range of cults and cultic businesses, if it were not for the tourists drawn in by the web of myths surrounding the place. But one can imagine a future time when paganization had progressed to the point that a far greater number of places could support a similar occult subculture. Already, quite a list of American towns benefit from occult tourism, from Salem, Massachusetts, to Shasta, California. Given half a chance, Devil's Tower, Wyoming, and other currently unpopulated mystic sites could develop cultic villages. By its very definition, paganism is spotty, a patchwork quilt of myriads of small cults, locally based and blending into general mythologies providing cultural support for groups of them. Ancient pagan shrines also served tourists, it must be remembered.

Among the most instructive features of Glastonbury cultism is the way that flamingly deviant beliefs shade over into optional opinions that link them to established faiths. There is nothing strange for an Englishman to believe that both Jesus and Arthur existed and that both came to Glastonbury, yet an Anglican is not required by his church to believe the story of Christ's teenage sojourn in England. The Tor may indeed have been a major pagan religious center, and much merit may be found in the Oriental traditions upon which both the Chalice Well and Ramala movements draw. The wildest part of the whole mythos is undoubtedly the ten-mile zodiac, yet it features prominently in tourist advertisements and it links together into one great cycle all the myths, both conventional and unconventional.

Degrees of Organization

The New Age movement is an exceedingly diffuse phenomenon, bringing together many beliefs and practices that seem to have little to do with each other and having no clear boundaries. Other terms have been used for roughly the same thing, notably the "occult milieu." Parts of it are sometimes called "pseudoscience" by detractors. For our purposes the interesting aspects of this manifold, multidimensional fabric of myths and magic are those that impinge upon religion, in particular upon those well-organized little religious movements that operate as novel denominations. But the New Age also influences the widespread crazy quilt that we call modern culture in general, thus shaping the background against which religious denominations exist. Thus it is worth beginning our analysis with a review of how movements compare with other social phenomena of greater or lesser degrees of organization. We shall do so with a hypothetical example that is outside the sphere of religion.

Imagine a town in a country ravaged by famine. Some citizens have food; others do not. At night, starving individuals sneak into their neighbors' houses to steal a crust of bread or a scrap of meat. They have not conspired together to plan these raids, and some are not even aware that many other people are also nocturnal thieves. Each person is doing the same thing for the same reason, but each is doing it alone. This is called *parallel behavior*. Although it takes place in a social context, it is not socially organized.

Now suppose that a number of hungry people collect in the town square and mill about in front of the food warehouse. After a few have gathered, word spreads: "There's a hungry crowd in the town square!" Others come to see what all the fuss is about. Folks urge each other, "Come to the square!" They argue excitedly about the famine for a while, then they start demanding that someone give them bread. Finally, they break down the doors of the warehouse and take everything that is inside. An unplanned gathering of hungry people has turned into a food riot. People facing a common problem or opportunity tend to communicate informally and influence each other's actions so that they end up doing similar things in a somewhat unified way. Interaction among people reveals to them their common concerns and turns parallel behavior into *collective behavior*.

Now that the famine has become a public issue, and starving people have shared the social experience of breaking into the warehouse, they start discussing their mutual problem at length in order to find a more fundamental solution. First in little groups and then in well-advertised mass meetings, they plan and organize. After several meetings, they set up an organization called "Food for All," dedicated to making the town government solve the crisis. They elect leaders and write a statement of purpose. Many people are working together toward a specific goal through concerted action. Continued, focused interaction has transformed collective behavior into a *social movement*.

In response to the growing strength of the movement, the town council appoints the leaders of Food for All to head a new government agency, the Department of Food. New laws empower the Secretary of Food to distribute bread to the needy and to set up a grain reserve for the next famine. Bureaucrats now occupy set positions in a hierarchy, perform standard roles, and work together according to established procedures. Social movement agitation in this crisis has led to the establishment of a *social institution*.

These four degrees of social organization are really areas of a spectrum rather than separately delineated categories. Parallel behavior blends imperceptibly into collective behavior which shades into social movements which carry over into societal institutions. Social institutions derive their status from the fact that they are recognized by other institutions of the society, a kind of mutual admiration society. But in a very real sense institutions are merely slow movements. In turn, movements are well-organized instances of collective behavior, and collective behavior is simply parallel behavior augmented by communication.

Food for All and its successor the Department of Food provide a humble metaphor that may useful for this chapter. In pluralistic modern societies, the religious system is like a pot of stew. The big potatoes, carrots, and chunks of beef are the major mainstream denominations. Each one has clear edges. The liquid surrounding them is the general cultural residue of faith, such things as belief in God and familiarity with the concept of messiah, which permeate the denominations but also exists outside them. The celery and onions, which have fallen to pieces in the cooking, are alternative religious traditions that are represented by a number of small organizations and have contributed their distinctive flavors to the juice. The tomatoes are practically dissolved into the liquid, so they must represent forms of collective behavior that are poorly organized but add substantially to the entire recipe; they are the New Age.

Using the common language employed by its adherents, we have called the New Age a movement, but really it is a loosely defined set of collective behavior phenomena. Sociologists frequently study three kinds of collective behavior: panics (in which people rush away from something they fear), riots (in which they rush against something they hate), and crazes (in which they rush toward something they love). In this terminology, the New Age is a set of crazes, although the word seems rather too negative in connotation. The other available words are no more flattering: fad, infatuation, and mania. But the generic term has a neutral connotation. Collective behavior is unusual action taken by a number of people who influence each other informally but are not members of a well-defined organization. In contrast, social movements are relatively organized groups of people dedicated to causing or preventing change in some significant aspect of life. For religious movements, that aspect is somehow connected to religious beliefs and practices.

Another rubric for categorizing the degree and form of organization of semi-religious phenomena was derived from the empirical study of the New Age itself. Apart from the well-organized novel religious organizations, researchers noticed that there were individual professionals who offered quasi-religious services to clients, for example astrologers who cast horoscopes in return for money. In addition, there are individuals who write books or give lectures for pay, without developing direct business relationships with their readers and listeners. And when the rank-and-file participants in the New Age are not busy receiving all that these organizations and practitioners have to offer, they sometimes engage in semi-religious activities or have experiences in private. In an early theoretical formulation, we distinguished three degrees of organization in the New Age: "audience cults," "client cults," and "cult movements" (Bainbridge and Stark 1980a). Today, we would drop the pejorative term, cult, and add a fourth "private" degree at the lowest level of organization, comparable to parallel behavior.

Private New Age or occult phenomena are chiefly experiences that individuals and very small groups may have, without a leader or professional practitioner, and without any large-scale communication or organization. *Audience* phenomena display little or no formal organization, and their modern audiences typically partake of them through the media, including television programs, magazines, and books. Audiences typically are interested in several different such phenomena, although a given person selects to some degree among the ones available. *Client* services involve an exchange relationship between a practitioner and a customer, usually well defined and based on some special qualities or professional training possessed by the practitioner. Involvement with a particular practitioner generally prevents the individual client from simultaneously seeking the same service from other practitioners, but it does not prevent participation in audiences of all kinds, involvement with practitioners who offer distinctly different services, or even membership in a religious movement, so long as the movement itself does not reject the particular client service. Full *religious movements* are the topic of this entire book and need not be given special attention here.

Analysis in terms of rewards and compensators is useful here. A religious movement chiefly offers general compensators, but a client service offers specific compensators. An astrologer at best gives limited knowledge of some portions of the future. Many client practitioners offer the cure of a particular disease or emotional complaint, what would be a specific reward if successfully delivered. Certainly, many New Age services do provide rewards, but often they provide only compensators for the specific rewards sought. In other words, they provide magic. "*Magic* refers to specific compensators that promise to provide desired rewards without regard for evidence concerning the designated means" (Stark and Bainbridge 1987:105).

The compensators offered by the creators of audience phenomena are not usually specific; indeed they are often quite general. The claim that flying saucers really exist does not help you commute to work tomorrow, but it presents a vague image of unlimited future possibilities if ever the saucers decide to share their secrets with us. However, audience compensators are seldom very valuable. At most they offer a diffuse hope that the universe contains more than meets the eye, the hint that cracks in the laws of causality allow spirit to escape the prison of mundane reality. This sense of expanded possibility can come also from experience of private spiritual phenomena, but the creators of audience phenomena know how to package it, give it an appealing superstructure, and distribute it to the mass of people who seldom have paranormal experiences of their own.

With our rough classificatory rubrics to guide us, and the theory of rewards and compensators ready at hand when we need it, we can survey the private, audience and client aspects of the New Age. The aim of this overview, of course, is to understand the diffuse and changing cultural system that surrounds new religious movements and gives some promise of shaping the religious consciousness of the future.

Private Phenomena

Human experiences do not come with labels attached. Everything we perceive must be interpreted to some extent before it is meaningful. Interpretation shapes memories, and recollections of unusual experiences are usually recast in terms of an ideology, a system of beliefs, or widely shared but incoherent cultural notions. People who are solidly integrated into the moral and social community which surrounds them will tend to interpret their experiences in conventional terms, employing standard psychological, religious, or other frameworks. But people who are detached from the community, who belong to ideologically distinct subcultures, or who stand at the confluence of two or more competing cultures, are thereby given great latitude in how they make sense of extraordinary experiences.

Michael Carroll (1983, 1985) has studied the process by which apparitions of the Virgin Mary are constructed. First, an individual member of a strongly Catholic community has an unusual experience, perhaps a confused vision of an unidentified person. He or she then shares the experience somewhat incoherently with members of the community who want it to be a vision of the Virgin. An implicit and even unconscious negotiation ensues between the community and the person who reported having the experience. This reshapes the story until it conforms to standard religious expectations, and an apparition of the Virgin is announced. What the person really saw, if anything, has been lost in the social construction of a proof of faith. In its raw form, the experience was puzzling, but now it has become a compensator embedded in a religious system, and thus of great value to the experiencer and to the community. In particular, the community rewards the experiencer for having brought further evidence of the truth of its system of general compensators.

Carroll's model applies when the surrounding society already possesses a well-articulated religious faith into which anomalous experiences can be fitted. But a similar if lengthier and less predictable process can presumably create a particular new religious movement from scratch, or might even underlie the general phenomenon of religion. James McClenon (1994) has observed a variety of "wondrous events" in different cultures around the world, including: déjà vu experiences, extrasensory perception, contact with departed spirits of the dead, out-of-body experiences or astral projection, poltergeists, and spiritual resistance to pain. Setting aside the question of whether any of these are "real," he argues that such events occur in all societies at a significant rate and that they provide the raw material for religious faith.

Many people in our society report having had such experiences. Perhaps you have. With your permission, I will share four of my own experiences. First, one afternoon at summer camp, when I was eleven, a fellow camper challenged me to guess a two-digit number, and to his genuine or feigned surprise, I succeeded. I wanted to believe this was a real case of mind-reading, but I decided he was probably inflicting a prank on me. Second, a couple of years later, I gazed out my window over the cove and saw a silvery disk that looked for all the world like the popular image of a flying saucer. I assumed it was a weather balloon catching the reflection of the sun off the water. Third, in my late teens, I awakened with the sensation of being swallowed by death, with eerie music in the background, learning a few moments later by telephone that my dear grandfather had died at apparently the exact moment of my dream. Later, when I inherited his record collection, I heard for what may have been the first time his favorite piece of music, *Death and Transfiguration* by Richard Strauss, which was exactly what I heard in my dream. The event had such emotional power that it deeply affected me, but on balance I decided it was the result of coincidence and of reshaped memories in a context of extreme grief. Finally, about a week after the death of my chief sociological mentor, George Caspar Homans, George appeared to me in a dream. He did not seem aware of his own demise, so I made him promise he would return to speak with me whenever I needed his scientific advice. So far, I have not attempted to conjure up his departed spirit, but some day I will try, and until then the tiny suspicion that I might succeed lurks in one of the least critical corners of my mind.

This is a fair sampling of the kinds of paranormal experiences that many people have. I suppose we could all dredge up from our memories instances when something happened that we felt sure was going to happen, without good evidence that it would. The sense of knowing what somebody else was thinking is extremely common. If taken seriously, these are examples of "extra-sensory perception" or "ESP." Inexplicable knowledge of an event before it happens is called "precognition." Reading the thoughts of another person is "telepathy." Related to these two is "clairvoyance," perceiving something at a physical distance. A related "wild talent" is "telekinesis" or "psychokinesis," moving a physical object at a distance by means of pure mental power. The most incredible variety of telekinesis is "teleportation," sending an object or even a person to a great distance without traversing the space between.

Belief in ESP is extremely widespread. In a survey of 1000 San Francisco residents, 90 percent of people aged sixteen through thirty who had heard of ESP, and 87 percent of older respondents, thought it "probably" exists (Wuthnow 1978:63). When the British weekly science magazine *New Scientist* polled its readers, 25 percent were convinced ESP was "an established fact," and a further 42 percent considered it a "likely possibility" (Bainbridge 1976:187). In 1979 I asked more than 1400 students at the University of Washington their opinion, in a survey successfully testing other hypotheses in the sociology of religion (Bainbridge and Stark 1981a, 1981b). As shown in Table 13.1, a majority of both men and women think ESP "probably" or "definitely" exists, and differences between the sexes are insignificant (Bainbridge 1986a:163, 1986b:12).

Within the diffuse New Age culture, for more than a century a small army of scholars and self-proclaimed scientists has studied ESP and comparable experiences under the related rubrics of "psychical research" and "parapsychology." Although some of these researchers derive support for existing re-

Table 13.1: Belief in ESP Among University Students—Percent

Opinion on ESP	Male Students	Female Students	All Students
Definitely exists	22.6	22.9	22.7
Probably exists	33.6	35.6	34.6
Possibly exists	38.4	36.8	37.6
Does not exist	5.4	4.7	5.1
Total percent	100.0	100.0	100.0
Number of students	735	677	1,412

ligious beliefs from the deduction that these experiences prove the existence of the human soul, in general the thrust of this movement has been to place the phenomena in a rational, scientific context.

The founder of American scientific psychology is generally considered to be William James, and the fifteen-story building that houses the Psychology and Sociology departments of Harvard University is named William James Hall. But an entire thick volume of his collected works (James 1986), published by Harvard University Press, is devoted to his essays on psychical research, the first of which dates from 1869. In the twentieth century, academic psychology and psychical research separated, and modern psychology textbooks tend to ignore or disparage parapsychology (Kalat 1986:40–47; cf. Burtt 1967). In 1930, another Harvard psychologist, William McDougall, assisted Joseph B. Rhine in setting up a laboratory at Duke University for the systematic study of ESP (Rhine 1934, 1937).

Rhine and his associates did a great quantity of parapsychological research that appeared to demonstrate the existence of ESP. They employed a variety of methods, but most famous are the card-guessing experiments. A Duke colleague of Rhine, Karl E. Zener, developed a special set of cards with abstract symbols on them, such as a square, circle, or wavy lines. I once published a computerized system for doing such experiments employing the four suits of playing cards, so I will describe that one, and it is easy enough to employ a regular set of cards.

In my computerized system, two people would sit on opposite sides of a table, with the computer between them (Bainbridge 1986b:11–21). The computer has to be the common type, in which the monitor screen is separate from the keyboard. Let's say that John and Sally are doing an experiment, in which John attempts to receive telepathic messages from Sally. She gets to look at the screen, but it is turned so that John cannot see it. He has the keyboard instead. The session starts. A picture of a card appears on the screen; say it is hearts. Sally looks at it and silently tries to send the mental message "Hearts, hearts, hearts. . . ." John opens his mind and tries to receive her message via extrasensory perception. After a moment, he presses a key, C, D, H, or S for clubs, diamonds, hearts, or spades. If he presses H, he may simply have guessed correctly, and there is one chance in four that he will get a right answer by pure chance. In each round of the experiment, they try twelve times. The computer keeps track of the guesses, and the software includes a simple method for determining whether John guessed correctly more often than would be expected by chance.

There are many possible sources of error in ESP experiments, and several possible ways that fraud can be perpetrated, especially so because the evidence for ESP usually consists of very slight but statistically significant divergences from random performance. Consider fraud. John may see the computer screen reflected in a window, a picture on the wall, Sally's eyeglasses, or even in her eyeballs. Or Sally may say that John's performance was better than chance even if it wasn't.

Properly designed computer systems can reduce the chances for unintentional error, but there are so many potential sources it is hard to exclude them all. In the old days, experimenters used to record the card guesses by hand. Suppose there is one chance in four of getting a card right, purely by chance, and the experimenter writes W for a wrong guess, and R for a Right one. Suppose on average every 100 guesses the experimenter puts down the incorrect letter, with no bias toward either W or R. Because wrong guesses are three times as common as right guesses, this random error will artificially increase the number of correct scores, making it 25.5 percent rather than the expected 25.0 percent.

Another problem is that the arrangement of the cards may not be perfectly random, whether they are physical cards shuffled by hand or computer images of cards determined by supposedly random numbers. Perhaps a given research subject tends to guess more red cards early in a run, then more black ones later on, and a faulty randomization of the cards produces the same imbalance. Then there will be more correct guesses than statistical calculations of randomness would predict.

In some versions of the experiment, the person receiving the telepathic messages may get clues on whether the first guesses were right or wrong. This could happen entirely unconsciously if the telepathic sender hears the guesses and slightly smiles or frowns upon hearing them. This can give the receiver information that can slightly improve the guesses later in the experimental run.

Psychologist C. E. M. Hansel (1966) argues that the apparent evidence for

ESP found in Rhine's work and other classical parapsychology is really the result of fraud on the part of some research subjects and parapsychologists, and credulity on the part of the remaining parapsychologists who happen to be honest. In response to methodological criticisms, parapsychologists have labored to improve their techniques (Morris 1978). A vast number of studies have now been published, usually not in conventional psychology journals but in such places as *The Journal of Parapsychology* and the *Journal of the American Society for Psychical Research* (Palmer 1978).

It is not so easy to meet the accusations of deliberate deception, and exposés have rendered parapsychology notorious for fraud, as when Rhine's successor at his institute resigned after admitting he had falsified data (*Time* 1974). Logically, experiments could be replicated by researchers who do not personally believe in ESP, and such attempts generally produce no evidence that it exists. However, parapsychologists can reply that of course the experiments don't work when done by skeptical experimenters, because the experimenters' own telepathy blocks the ESP.

Among the complaints against parapsychology is that it has made no progress whatsoever determining how the alleged phenomena operate. If ESP is something like radio, then electronic devices should have detected it by now. If it is a form of radiation, then it should weaken with distance, perhaps inversely as the square of that distance. K. Ramakrishna Rao has discussed a number of the nonreligious models proposed by his fellow parapsychologists, and finds they do not harmonize well with the explanatory frameworks commonly employed in the physical sciences: "Sooner or later, science will have to face the parapsychological facts, for it cannot shut its eyes forever, however compelling the reason for doing so may be" (Rao 1978:246).

So far there is no sign of this happening, but for the purposes of this book it is more pertinent to wonder about the extent to which parapsychology promotes religious conceptions of reality, especially ones that are outside of the standard religious traditions. Jesus used to preach to his disciples in the ordinary way through his mouth, remember, and despite all the miracles he did not apparently broadcast his message via telepathy.

Audience Phenomena

At a first approximation, there are two kinds of New Age audience phenomena, admittedly fictional ones and supposedly factual ones, but the line of demarcation is blurred. The gods of yesteryear, in which bygone people actually believed, now strut their roles on the grand opera stage before audiences that do not believe, and stride through the pages of novels like paper-thin ghosts. Since the first hours of the Renaissance, ancient pagan religion has infiltrated the official high culture of Christendom, offering a constant reminder that radically non-Christian religious alternatives exist. Many Renaissance paintings depict Christian religious subjects, when they are not portraits, landscapes, or historical scenes. But on occasion great Renaissance painters illustrated pagan myths as well. *The Birth of Venus* by Sandro Botticelli shows the naked pagan goddess arising from the sea on a scallop shell, and Raphael depicted Galatea riding across the waves on a similar shell, drawn by a team of dolphins.

Some grand operas focus on pagan religion without assuming that its gods actually exist. *Norma*, composed by Vincenzo Bellini in 1831, concerns a priestess of ancient European Druidism. Giuseppe Verdi's blockbuster success, *Aïda*, first performed in 1871 at Cairo to celebrate the completion of the Suez Canal, depicts ancient Egyptian religion with great reverence but no belief. However, other operas pretend that the pagan gods are real. Indeed, grand opera really began in the year 1600 with a setting of the classic myth of Orpheus's descent to Hades to rescue Eurydice, by Giulio Caccini and Jacopo Peri. In 1607, the first real masterwork of the genre, *l'Orfeo* by Claudio Monteverdi, was composed on the same pagan mythological subject. Subsequently, the myth resurfaced repeatedly, notably in the very popular operas by Christoph Willibald von Glück and Jacques Offenbach. The vast, four-part music drama by Richard Wagner, *The Ring of the Niebelungen*, presents the Norse gods as real beings, with no concessions to the dominant Christian religious culture whatsoever. Somewhat more ambivalent is Mozart's *Magic Flute*, which traces the initiation of a rather timid young fellow into a Masonic cult, complete with an actual encounter with the Queen of the Night.

The appearances of pagan deities and occult themes in literature are so numerous it is impossible even to hint at their extent. In shaping people's perceptions of the supernatural, presumably children's stories are especially influential. Although it is hard to find examples of pagan deities outside the special genre of children's anthropology, there are thousands of stories containing magic. Especially notable is the Oz series by L. Frank Baum and his successors. The 1939 Judy Garland movie is only the most memorable of the many visual versions (McClelland 1989), and the most challenging may be the Nintendo video game (Seta 1993), which after two-dozen hours I was able to win only by cracking the secret password code rather than by actually playing through all the levels. The eponymous wizard himself turns out to be a carnival humbug, but both the Wicked Witch of the West and Glinda, the Witch of the South, possess real, effective magic. The revolutionary fact about Glinda, of course, is that she was a good witch: "She was both beautiful and young to their eyes. Her hair was a rich red in color and fell in flowing ringlets over her shoulders. Her dress was pure white; but her eyes were blue, and they looked kindly upon the little girl" (Baum 1900: 211–213). The popular movie actually increased Glinda's role in Dorothy's Odyssey, while presenting her as pure benevolence incarnate, rather a direct challenge to conventional Christianity, if for a moment one takes the story seriously.

At the end of the second Christian millennium, the branch of popular culture containing the richest and most varied forms of magic and alternative religion is science fiction. Some of the most popular "sci-fi" movies involving contact with alien intelligence depict the extraterrestrials as so technologically advanced that their capabilities seem like magic to mere humans, and so philosophically elevated that they act like angels, as in *Close Encounters of the Third Kind* (Spielberg 1978), or like gods, as in *2001: A Space Odyssey* (Clarke 1968; Agel 1968). As we shall demonstrate at the beginning of Chapter 14, the Jedi knights of the *Star War* trilogy are a military religious order, rather like Zen Buddhist Templars, and the doctrine of the Force expounded by Jedi masters is explicitly labeled religious (Lucas 1977). The movies reach a far-wider audience than the novels and specialty magazines, but science-fiction literature has the capacity to develop alternative conceptions of reality and insinuate them into the minds of individuals who will play crucial roles in science-related professions and in creating the cultural movements of the future.

Science fiction is a highly effective "cultural redoubt" for "deviant knowledge." A redoubt is a safe refuge or secure retreat into which one may flee from destruction. And re-doubting can refer to doubting one's own doubts. That is, we may wonder whether ideas the society has rejected actually might be of great value. Science fiction contains many seemingly impossible notions: time travel, travel faster than the speed of light, reincarnation, levitation, telepathy, evolution into a superhuman being, intelligent machines with self-awareness, and conspiracies that span the far reaches of time and space. "Deviant knowledge," from the standpoint of the sociology of knowledge, is a collection of beliefs capable of being considered true by some people but rejected as false by the majority or by culturally dominant groups.

A questionnaire study has identified four dimensions of science-fiction ideology (Bainbridge 1986a). Participants at a world "SF" convention in Phoenix, Arizona, filled out a survey that chiefly asked them to rate 140 authors and sixty-two kinds of literature on a preference scale, in terms of how much they liked each one. A factor analysis of the correlations among the best-known authors showed that there were four dimensions of variation, and correlating the factor scores with the types of literature defined what each dimension means. Table 13.2 names the four dimensions and lists the questionnaire items that best describe each one.

Table 13.2: The Four Dimensions of Science Fiction

Dimension	Attributes
1. Hard-science SF	Fiction based on the physical sciences Stories about new technology Factual science articles Stories which take current knowledge from one of the sciences and logically extrapolate what might be the next steps taken in that science Stories in which there is a rational explanation for everything Factual reports on the space program and spaceflight
2. New Wave SF	Avant-garde fiction which experiments with new styles Fiction based on the social sciences Fiction that is critical of our society Fiction which deeply probes personal relationships and feelings Feminist literature Stories in which the main character is sensitive and introspective Fiction concerned with harmful effects of scientific progress
3. Fantasy Cluster	Sword and sorcery Science-fantasy Stories about magic Myths and legends Sagas and epics Stories set in a universe where the laws of nature are very different from those found on our world Tales of the supernatural Horror-and-weird Stories about barbarians Ghost stories Occult literature
4. SF History	Classic science fiction from the early days of SF Golden Age science fiction Science fiction of the 1920s and 1930s Science fiction of the 1940s and 1950s

The first three dimensions can be defined in terms of three contrasting intellectual disciplines: the physical sciences, the social sciences, and magic. Symbolically enough, the fourth dimension is time, defined by the classic literature that created science fiction, such as *The Time Machine* by H. G. Wells. The first three dimensions can also be described in terms of what they say about the future of science and society. Hard-science SF asserts that continued development in the physical sciences and technology will improve human life and lead to exciting new possibilities for future adventures. The new wave is extremely skeptical about the utopian visions of hard science, and it places more confidence in the social sciences and in literary sensitivity to unravel the problems of the present. Fantasy is a cluster of subgenres (Sword-and-sorcery, Science-fantasy, Horror-and-weird, etc.) that postulate a world dominated by supernatural forces, essentially none of which have anything to do with conventional Judeo-Christian traditions.

Interestingly, the two forms of literature out of sixty-two in the survey that were rated the lowest were "the Holy Bible" and "Occult literature." By all accounts, members of the organized science-fiction subculture are highly irreligious. However, occult and pseudoscientific speculations permeate the literature, not merely the Fantasy Cluster but other types as well (Farmer 1977; Ash 1977). Stories by hard-science writers such as A. E. van Vogt (1940) and Robert A. Heinlein (1942) postulate that psychic powers may be natural attributes of the superior species to evolve out of human beings in the near future. Two intriguing novels by Alfred Bester (1952; 1956) analyze the parallels between psychoanalysis and parapsychology. *The Demolished Man* combines Sigmund Freud's theories with telepathy, and *The Stars My Destination* combines Alfred Adler's theories with teleportation.

Many of the supposedly factual New Age audience phenomena are only a short step from science fiction. For example, not only did the flying-saucer craze employ SF concepts such as interstellar space ships and extraterrestrial civilizations, but much of the early publicity was provided by an editor of SF magazines, Ray Palmer, who had been involved in a series of occult crazes and who launched the central periodical of the American occult, *Fate*. Several small religious movements have arisen in the United States and Western Europe based on the notion of contact with extraterrestrial beings, including Aetherius, The Cosmic Circle of Fellowship, Mark-Age, Star Light Fellowship, Unarius, and the group founded by Dorothy Martin and described in Chapter 5 (Melton 1993:727–736).

Among the most successful pure audience crazes related to extraterrestrials is the series of books by Erich von Däniken (1971, 1972, 1974, 1975a, 1975b), beginning with *Chariots of the Gods*. According to von Däniken, astronauts from an advanced extraterrestrial civilization visited the earth in ancient times, giving our ancestors the rudiments of civilization. His evidence consists chiefly of radical reinterpretations of ancient carvings from the Mayan and other civilizations. Where archaeologists saw traditional royal or religious symbolism, he sees spaceships and astronauts. A veritable army of authors has debunked these notions (Wilson 1970, 1975; Lunan 1974; Omohundro 1976; Story 1977), but for a decade or more the books sold very well, and in the absence of a client service or fully religious movement they exemplify New Age audience phenomena.

The fact that I frequently used to teach a large course in the sociology of deviance allowed me to explore the factors that promote or prevent acceptance of such myths, so I administered surveys to the willing students in two such classes, with 114 and 121 respondents (Bainbridge 1981b). To be sure, these respondents were far from a random sample, but because the course carried college-distribution credit it attracted undergraduates with a wide range of interests and orientations. The day before administering the survey, I showed the class the film *In Search of Ancient Astronauts*, which presents von Däniken's basic ideas in a clear and vivid manner.

The questionnaires were designed to test the comparative success of four types of sociological deviance theory in explaining acceptance of von Däniken's space-age mythology: strain theory, control theory, cultural-deviance theory, and trait theory (Stark 1975). Travis Hirschi has described the first three concisely: "According to *strain* or motivational theories, legitimate desires that conformity cannot satisfy force a person into deviance. According to *control* or bond theories, a person is free to commit delinquent acts because his ties to the conventional order have somehow been broken. According to *cultural-deviance* theories, the deviant conforms to a set of standards not accepted by a larger or more powerful society" (Hirschi 1969:3). "Trait" theory holds that persons deviate from conventional standards because of their individual characteristics, whether innate or acquired.

Many of the questions concerned attitudes, so I was worried that any statistical regularities in the data might merely reflect the tendency of some students to agree with anything ("yea-saying") and of others to disagree with anything ("nay-saying"). Therefore I used two diametrically opposite items to assess acceptance of ancient astronauts: "Von Däniken's theory is true." "Von Däniken's theory is false." Other items were varied, some stated in positive and others in negative terms. Naturally, a small study such as this cannot explore all the possible variants of the theories, and unfortunately very few sociologists have attempted studies like this, so the findings are only a hint of what remains to be discovered.

Strain theory did poorly. There appeared to be very slight tendencies for believers in von Däniken to be dissatisfied "with the future facing you and your family" and to say, "I am often bothered by the feeling of loneliness." But the correlations were very weak and far from statistical significance. And the following items did not correlate at all with belief: "I am fairly satisfied with the progress I am making at college." "I often wonder about the meaning and purpose of life." "I am a basically happy person." Strain theory expects people who accept deviant beliefs to be frustrated with their lives, reaching out for a radical alternative, suffering at least in a mild degree from the tension of the Lofland-Stark model of recruitment. But there was little evidence in favor of this proposition.

There are many versions of control theory, and the one I tested focused on the intellectual environment in which the students found themselves. Hypothetically, students who have received more education in relevant fields like astronomy and anthropology should have been socialized to the norms of those fields, thus under conventional intellectual control and prevented from accepting von Däniken. But it did not matter whether students had taken courses in astronomy, anthropology, ancient history, social sciences, or physical sciences. Freshmen did not differ from seniors. The questionnaire included a short astronomy quiz, and scores did not predict acceptance or rejection of von Däniken. Believers did not seem to reject the intellectual discipline of the university, because there was no tendency for them to feel "a college education is pretty much a waste of time." Finally, believers showed the same distribution as nonbelievers in attitudes toward science and technology.

The questionnaire was not prepared to distinguish cultural-deviance theory from trait theory, because to do so it would have to chart the social influences that gave individuals their attitudes. But the evidence was very strong that some combination of the two offer the best explanation, because people who accepted von Däniken were especially likely also to say: "Extrasensory perception probably exists." "I myself have had an experience which I thought might be an example of extrasensory perception." "Some Eastern practices, such as Yoga, Zen, or Transcendental Meditation, are probably of great value." "There is much truth in astrology." Thus, this modest pilot study did not find good evidence that people who accept von Däniken's theories are more frustrated (strain theory) or less well restrained by forces of intellectual conformity (control theory). They do tend to accept a variety of other New Age notions (subculture-deviance theory and trait theory), reinforcing our observation that the New Age is a somewhat coherent example of collective behavior, if not a well-organized movement.

Client Services

The extent, variety, and public visibility of New Age and occult services continues to increase. A few years ago, this sort of business was limited to a few locally known astrologers and other fortune-tellers, and an occasional bookstore or front office of a new religious movement that sold mystical products. Then Asian-oriented services, specialized food stores, and restaurants proliferated in some number. Now the services are spreading out through the electronic communication media. More than two dozen services offer psychic readings over long distance telephone at the present time, some connected with the names of celebrities such as La Toya Jackson and Margot Hemingway. Typical fees are $3.99 per minute if the client dials a 1–900 number for which the phone company does the billing, or $2.99 per minute for a 1–800 number for which the client pays via credit card number. In addition, astrology and biorhythm services have now appeared on the Word Wide Web.

Of all the professions of the New Age, astrology lays the most valid claim to antiquity (McIntosh 1969). The astrology columns in newspapers and in the most widely read magazine, *TV Guide*, are merely material for audiences. But for thousands of years astrology has been a professional client service, in which an expert astrologer casts horoscopes for nonexpert customers. The zodiac was probably a Babylonian invention, and astrology was widely practiced by the Greco-Roman Civilization. In the centuries after the fall of Rome, heretics like the Gnostics were attracted to astrology, and the Catholic church opposed it with varying success. The Arabs preserved astrological knowledge while it went into eclipse within western Christendom, but by the year 1186 it had become sufficiently popular again that many Europeans expected terrible windstorms when the planets congregated in the wind-sign constellation of Libra. For the record, the storms never came.

The most highly regarded English writer before Shakespeare, Geoffrey Chaucer, combined astrology with apocalypse to produce farce in his fourteenth-century "Miller's Tale." This is one of the *Canturbury Tales*, in which a group of travelers entertains itself by taking turns telling stories. The knight had just finished reciting a very long, elegant romance when the crude, half-drunk Miller demanded the floor. "Once upon a time," he said, "a rich guy named John was living in Oxford, a carpenter by craft, who kept boarders in his home." Living with John was a poor scholar, named Nicholas, who was deep into astrology and other black arts. John had recently married a beautiful wife much younger than he, Alison, whom he guarded jealously. Secretly, Nicholas and Alison developed a mutual passion, but they could not find an opportunity to indulge it. To complicate this romantic triangle still further, a parish clerk named Absolon started chasing after Alison.

Saying he must have Alison or die, Nicholas developed a scheme to spend the night with her in the carpenter's bed. First Nicholas locked himself in his room for many hours, until John because curious and entered. As if sharing a confidence unwillingly, Nicholas told John that his astrological research, combined with a message straight from Jesus, had revealed to him that a great deluge was coming the next night, to rival Noah's flood, and they would all be killed unless they prepared themselves. Totally convinced, John followed Nicholas's instructions to the letter. He hung three big tubs up under the roof, each provisioned with food, drink, and an ax to sever the ropes and allow the improvised arks to float free. At nightfall, John, Alison, and Nicholas climbed three ladders into the three tubs, said their prayers, and prepared to sleep until awakened by the rushing waters. Soon snores told Alison and Nicholas it was safe to climb down, and they leapt into John's snug bed to have sex while the bed's owner was uncomfortably asleep in his tub up under the roof.

Meanwhile, Absolon the parish clerk happened to hear that John had not been seen around town since Saturday and leapt to the false conclusion that he was away on a carpentry business trip. Thinking this was his chance to plight his lusty troth with Alison, he rushed to her bedroom window and begged her to kiss him. What follows is obscene, so we will not report it here, but the result was that Absolon rushed off angrily to a blacksmith who happened to be working late at his forge, and borrowed a red-hot poker. Back under Alison's window, he begged another kiss, promising her a gold ring his mother had given him. Again, an obscene altercation ensued, which terminated when Absolon wounded Nicholas in a vulnerable spot with the poker.

In gut curdling agony, Nicholas shouted "Help! Water! Water! For the love of God!" At this, carpenter John awoke, sure that Noah's flood was upon him, as Nicholas had foretold. He swung his ax, breaking the ropes that held the tubs. Carpenter, ladders, tubs, bread, and wine crashed to the floor breaking John's arm. The naked lovers ran into the street screaming, and the dazed carpenter raved to the townsfolk about the flood and sleeping in a tub. Before long everybody in the county knew of the quartet's disgrace. John was proven a fool and had a broken arm to worry about. Alison had lost every shred of reputation and had to deal with three very angry men. Absolon faced the wrath of Nicholas and the ruin of his career as trusted parish clerk. And poor Nicholas had paid for his hour of joy by the scalding, which had wrecked him; indeed, given the lack of modern medicine, this catastrophe may have been his bitter end (three puns intended).

In a sense, "The Miller's Tale" is an early classic in the sociology of knowledge (Mannheim 1936; Berger and Luckmann 1966) because it shows how an intellectual's ideology can be shaped by self-interest. The same lesson actually is taught in "The Clouds" by Aristophanes, nearly two-thousand-years older, which depicts Socrates suspended in a basket amid the clouds, operating a school that teaches young philosophers how to cheat people. "The Miller's Tale" also shows the potential of private magic to evolve into a client service. Nicholas studied astrology avidly in the privacy of his room, apparently believing it in. But when his desires for Alison became overpowering, he faked an astrological prediction to gain a few minutes of her amorous attentions. But this does not prove that every professional astrologer is a conscious fake. On the contrary, many may be firm believers as Nicholas was, only rarely tempted to exploit their clients. Like other professionals, they think it only right that they get paid for their work.

Early in the twentieth century, Sigmund Freud's good friend, Wilhelm Fliess invented a starless astrology called "biorhythms" (Thommen 1973; O'Neil and Phillips 1975; Cohen 1976; Dale 1976; Smith 1976; cf. Fodor 1971). Supposedly, at birth three powerful rhythms start that dominate a person's changing strengths and weaknesses: the twenty-three-day physical cycle, the twenty-eight-day emotional cycle, and the thirty-three-day intellectual cycle. Each day, a person should consult his or her biorhythms to learn whether this was a particularly propitious or dangerous day, for example one of extreme emotional and intellectual weakness. Sports stars are supposed to win when the cycles are high, and to lose when they are low. Accidents happen at critical days, when a rhythm is passing the zero line between high and low. Locally organized biorhythm institutes began teaching courses about the method, and professional biorhythm consultants applied it in advising their clients. Soon after the books became popular, a number of companies began selling devices to facilitate calculating the rhythms, including an electronic "biolator" calculator from the Casio company, and programs for doing this on computers were quickly written (Fox and Fox 1976).

Because biorhythm theory makes very explicit predictions about the performance of sports stars, about whom vast troves of data exist, it was easy for careful researchers to demonstrate that it was false (Fix 1976; Bainbridge 1981a; Hines 1981). However, many people feel that their own biorhythm calculations accurately describe how they are feeling on a particular day and provide valuable clues about what may happen to them. How can the results of systematic research and personal feelings be so contradictory?

In one of my large sociology classes, I asked each student to tell me his or her birth date (Bainbridge 1981a). Some days later, I lectured on biorhythm theory, just as if it were a standard sociological theory of human behavior. Then I distributed a questionnaire, each one individualized with a student's name. I explained that I had used a biolator to calculate both the day of the week on which they were born, an interesting tidbit of information that people tend not to know about themselves, plus the state of their three biorhythms (high or low) for the day of the questionnaire. The birthdays were correct, and distracted the students from the possibility that the biorhythms had really been selected at random, which was in fact the case. Students were asked (yes or no) whether each of the three biorhythm calculations was correct. By chance, they would average 1.5 yes answers per student, but they averaged 2.24. Only 5.6 percent of the 108 respondents rejected all three rhythms, whereas 45.4 percent accepted all three. Students were about as likely to accept high rhythms as low ones.

These results suggest that people do not carry accurate scales of their conditions in their heads. They do not have a well-calibrated "average" against which to compare statements about whether they are currently above or below average. Thus, they are susceptible to suggestions when asked to make such judgments (Bachrach and Pattishall 1960; Schachter and Singer 1962). One of the questionnaire items asked students to estimate the probability biorhythm theory was true, among a list of various theories, and thinking it was true predicted accepting one's own biorhythms. The students did not get to see their own biorhythms until after filling out most of the questionnaire, so we know that their ratings of the theory were not determined by the accuracy of their rhythm calculations for that day.

This study links back to the modest project mentioned earlier that examined von Däniken's theories about ancient astronauts (Bainbridge 1981b). The questionnaire revealed not only that students who accepted their own fake biorhythms were likely to say "Biorhythm theory is true." They also tended to agree that "von Däniken's theory is true" and "extrasensory perception exists." Thus, biorhythms are part of the same New Age subculture that includes the other topics, although the subculture is sufficiently diffuse that individuals may easily accept some parts of it while rejecting others.

Religious Implications of the New Age

The forms of religious movement most closely associated with the New Age are occult, neopagan, and Asian. The connection between Asian and occult groups has existed for more than a century. In Chapter 7 we noted that Charles Carroll Bonney, the organizer of the 1893 World's Parliament of Religions, was a member of a Swedenborgian church. The founder, Emmanuel Swedenborg (1688–1774) was a medium who contacted the departed spirits of famous people and traveled through the spirit world by astral projection, thus marking his movement as among the very first occult religions in America. On the connection to Asian imports, J. Gordon Melton says, "The first Hindu and Buddhist groups which broke out of their ethnic ghettos found their following among people already open to alternative perspectives from their prior participation in occult activities. When the new generation of Eastern adepts swept across American, they found fertile ground previously prepared by the large occult community. Occult magazines announced the coming of each new guru or swami. Occult organizations invited them to address their audiences, and occult bookstores marketed their publications" (Melton 1985:279–280).

Back in Chapter 6 we mentioned what was perhaps the most comprehensive guide to the New Age, the *Spiritual Community Guide* (Singh 1974,

1978, cf. 1981). It was edited by an American originally called Howard Weiss but who became involved in Asian religion and took the name Parmatma Singh. It is a classified directory giving the locations of a large number of New Age organizations and businesses, including many branches of Asian religious movements such as Yogi Bhajan's Healthy Happy Holy organization. Also included are many independent ashrams and spiritual retreats, New Age communes, occult bookstores, restaurants specializing in vegetarian and macrobiotic meals, and "natural" food stores. Similar guidebooks cover particular dimensions of the New Age. *The Organic Traveler* (Davis and Tetrault 1975) covers organic, vegetarian, and health-food restaurants. The *International Psychic Register* (McQuaid 1979) and *Who's Who in the Psychic World* (Finch and Finch 1971) cover psychic and metaphysical practitioners. Another source of data is the listings of professional astrologers in the nation's telephone books. The geographic distributions of the entries in these guidebooks are very similar, suggesting that they appeal to the same population pool (Bainbridge and Stark 1980a).

If these guidebooks cover the client services and fully religious movements of the New Age, then the best single source of information about private and audience New Age phenomena is the occult monthly magazine, *Fate*, also described back in Chapter 6. For decades, it has carried two sections of little personal experience stories submitted by readers, "True Mystic Experiences" and "My Proof of Survival," giving the town in which the author lives. For example, the August, 1995 issue contains six mystic experiences. Three are prophetic dreams. Edith Dean dreams that her picket fence is strewn all over her lawn, and the next day a speeding car makes it so. Susan Minarik dreamed of a naked woman dancing with a sun lamp, which turns out to be a friend two thousand miles away who was having trouble finding the right posture to apply the heat of such a lamp to herself. Sheila O'Connor dreams her cat's missing vaccination certificate is in a magazine, and the veterinarian calls to say they just found it in one. Three mystic experiences are spirit voices or apparitions. Running in the darkness, John Wasylenko hears a voice telling him to stop just before he falls over a cliff. While watching his wife peel potatoes, Martin Jensen's grandfather sees a man dressed in dark clothes, who speaks incoherently and then vanishes. In 1907, a departed spirit tells a woman not to have an abortion for the child she is carrying, and the result is the birth of Genevieve Nichols who tells *Fate* about it eighty-eight years later. The stories have clearly been rewritten by the editors for literary impact, but the many photographs of authors and their addresses are genuine. Data on the numbers of *Fate* subscribers in each state are available from the publishers. These geographic distributions are practically the same as those for the guidebooks, and all are very similar to the pattern for initiates to Transcendental Meditation, the religious group described in Chapter 7 that served as a mere meditation training service for most people who came into contact with it (Stark and Bainbridge 1985).

In Chapter 14 we will analyze some of these geographic data on the basis of cities and metropolitan areas, to understand the religious factor that makes some areas of the country more receptive to the New Age and to novel religious movements. But here a brief description of how the gross regions of the country differ will convey the general picture. By far the strongest concentrations of these phenomena are along the Pacific coast, not merely in southern California, but all the way up through British Columbia into Alaska. The Mountain region, from Arizona and New Mexico to Montana and Alberta, tends to be above average in New Age phenomena, although weaker than the adjoining Pacific region. At the opposite extreme, the East South Central region (Kentucky, Tennessee, Alabama, and Mississippi) is hardly touched by the New Age. The rest of the country shows moderate rates on all these variables. The South Atlantic region's rates would be lower than average if it were not for the vigorous New Age activity in Florida and in the Washington, D.C., metropolitan area. By some measures, chiefly the *Spiritual Community Guide* and Transcendental Meditation, New England is above average but still considerably weaker than the far West. By some measures, the Pacific region has more than twenty times the rate for the Each South Central region, and the geographic variation in the strength of the New Age subculture is really quite substantial.

Given that the strength of the New Age varies from place to place, we can wonder how it varies from person to person. Because it presents a direct spiritual challenge to traditional Christianity, we can guess that conventional religion, especially the more intense, evangelical varieties, opposes it (Lewis 1966; Hague 1993). If so, the New Age should appeal most to people who are not involved in more traditional religious movements. Evidence on this point comes from the survey of University of Washington students that provided information about belief in ESP given in Table 13.1. One of the questionnaire items asked, "Would you say that you have been 'born again' or have had a 'born again' experience—that is, a turning point in your life when you committed yourself to Christ?" A total of 345 respondents said "yes" and also responded to another item by saying their religious beliefs were "very important" to them. These Born-Again Christians can be compared, in Table 13.3, with the 241 who had no religion, and the 251 ordinary Catholics and 319 ordinary Protestants (Bainbridge and Stark 1981d).

Seven other items concern New Age topics: Eastern practices like yoga, UFOs, extra-sensory perception, occult practices, occult literature, and the respondent's horoscope. For every one, the respondents with no religion are

Table 13.3: Attitudes toward New Age Phenomena among University Students

	Percent Giving the Indicated Response			
	241 with no Religion	Ordinary Christians		345 Born-Again Christians
		251 Catholics	319 Protestants	
Agrees: "Some Eastern practices such as Yoga, Zen, and Transcendental Meditation, are probably of great value."	73	66	60	28
Agrees: "UFOs are probably real spaceships from other worlds."	67	66	60	43
Agrees: "Some occult practices, such as Tarot reading, seances, and psychic healing, are probably of great value."	16	22	12	6
Agrees: "I myself have had an experience that I thought might be an example of extra-sensory perception."	59	57	55	44
Respondent thinks that ESP "definitely exists."	26	29	17	17
Respondent very strongly dislikes "occult literature."	38	34	36	65
Respondent very strongly dislikes "your horoscope."	29	24	23	53

far more accepting of the New Age than are Born-Again Christians, and the ordinary Christians generally fall between them. The weakest of the variables is the one about whether the respondent thinks ESP exists, and such items often fail to show interesting correlations in survey data, perhaps because sociocultural variables in fact explain little about variation in feelings about such a private matter as ESP. But Table 13.3 clearly shows that the New Age movement and the Born-Again Christian Movement are antagonistic to each other. It also is worth noting that this survey was done in an area of the country with very low church membership, so the evidence also bears on the Stark Effect mentioned in Chapter 10, which argued that an individual's religion loses some but not all of its powers to deter deviance in communities where the churches are weak. Apparently, conventional religion retains the power to deter involvement in the New Age, even where the churches are weak, operating through early socialization to religious doctrines and current involvement in traditional religious movements.

Conclusion

The New Age phenomenon surrounds conventional religion like a cultural fog bank, almost completely lacking in large-scale formal organization but giving the fringes of faith a mysterious appearance. It provides paranormal and supernatural explanations that individuals may draw upon to understand their private spiritual experiences. It entertains vast audiences with fantasy and science-fiction stories, some presented as fiction and some as fact. It also provides the cultural justifications for a number of client services, such as astrology. And out of this thin epistemological soup, occasional new religious movements may solidify, a very few of which will be substantial denominations of the future.

Early in this century, Charles Fort (1941) published a library of books cataloging a large number of strange and unexplained events, the sort of thing that shows up regularly in *Fate* magazine today. Consequently, some scholars refer to all inexplicable marvels that exist outside standard religion as *Fortean phenomena*, and a Fortean Society exists to cultivate awareness of them, complete with its own service on the World Wide Web. Stories of Fortean phenomena are audience products that encourage the suspension of disbelief concerning marvels in general. They are myths conveying the vague general compensator that reality is far more extensive than the material world that confronts us every day, and thus potentially more rewarding.

Each popular myth has a life of its own, attracting authors, readers, clients, and movements, generation after generation. This is true not only for major traditions, like astrology, that have histories going back hundreds or even thousands of years. The principle also applies to lesser traditions like the legend that human culture was a gift from ancient astronauts, popularized by Erich von Däniken. Others presented the idea much earlier; it has survived in numerous variants within the cultural redoubt of science fiction (Clarke 1968), and a fresh generation of authors has just begun to exploit it (Hancock 1995). But we have seen that these myths knit together in a larger cultural fabric—as each devotee of one myth is relatively receptive to others—a loose network of symbols and concepts that form a non-Christian cultural system.

The various fortune-telling and spiritual-healing client services build upon the private experiences of clients and upon the cultural system of the New Age. Frequently these client services are entry points to more coherent religious organizations. People attracted to astrology could receive services from The Rosicrucian Fellowship of Oceanside, California, and take the next step to membership in a communal religion by staying for a time in its hotel. An emotionally disturbed person who did not find satisfaction in the demeaning ministrations of psychiatrists, could respond more positively to the past-lives therapy of Unarius, and begin contributing to it on a long-term basis as a member of this tiny extraterrestrial religion. The high-tension Christian hostility to the New Age presents this non-Christian alternative with tremendous challenges that must be met before it can spawn really successful formal organizations. However, with its ties to pseudoscience and Asian religion, the New Age is clearly the most formidable thorough-going religious counterculture that currently exists in modern society.

Conclusion

14

The Perpetual System

The thesis of this concluding chapter is that religion will constantly renew itself through religious movements, indefinitely into the far-distant future. To this point in the book, every story that introduced a chapter has been true, but here our challenge is to imagine the future of religion, so history may be of little help. Therefore we begin with one of the most familiar science-fiction stories, the three-part *Star Wars* saga, treating these popular movies as if they were true (Lucas 1977, 1980, 1983; Titelman 1977; Call 1980; Attis and Smith 1980; Pollock 1983). Amazingly, this is a religious trilogy, postulating a religious movement totally independent from the Judeo-Christian-Islamic tradition and situated in a highly advanced technological society. Perhaps George Lucas, the creator of *Star Wars*, will forgive us for finding our own meanings in these films, and we shall avoid dipping into all the ancillary novels and television productions, to concentrate just on the information in the three original movies. Those familiar with the saga will recognize that we leave out much of the adventure, concentrating instead on the religious significance. Those who are not especially fond of science fiction should ask themselves the penetrating question of what religion really will be like, four thousand years from now.

May the Force Be with You!

A long time ahead, across the galaxy, the evil officers who command the Death Star meet in consultation. Their immense battle station is finally operational. The size of a small moon, it has been artificially constructed as a single machine that combines the features of a weapon and a city. Their only concern is that rebel spies were able to steal a set of plans to this mighty machine, and if they could deliver this information to their hidden base they might be able to find a weak point that would permit them to defend against it. But those plans may nearly be back in the hands of their owners, because a small space ship has just been captured in the skies over the planet Tatooine, that was carrying Princess Leia Organa, most likely the espionage courier. She now suffers in the detention center, undergoing torture designed to make her reveal the location of the hidden rebel base. Now, finally, the Death Star officers have the power to crush the rebellion and deliver dominion over the entire universe to their master, the mysterious Emperor.

It is a time of disorder among the star systems. A former galactic republic has fallen, and the last vestige of its representative government, the Senate, is being dissolved by the Emperor. For a thousand generations the old republic was defended by a priesthood of Jedi Knights, but they were eradicated in the Clone Wars that ushered in the Dark Time. Presumably, the clones of the Clone Wars were biologically mass produced soldiers who overwhelmed the Jedi with their very numbers. The Jedi were warrior monks who followed a transcendental spiritual discipline. Thus, the clone victory represented the triumph of materialistic technology over spiritual religion.

The chief principle of Jedi philosophy was called the Force, an energy field that permeates all existence and binds the galaxy together. It has no personality of its own, although sensitive humans can communicate through it, and thus it is not a god. Indeed, outside the ranks of the Jedi, belief in the existence of the Force was sparse and possessed none of the organization and practices that would allow it to be called a religion. Even before the forces of the Emperor crushed the Jedi, therefore, the galaxy lacked wide-ranging religious denominations, much less an established ecclesia. Two factors seem likely to have created this situation. First, the galactic civilization was an amalgam of many highly diverse societies created by almost as many independently evolved intelligent species, so there may not have existed the common assumptions and institutions that could have been the basis of a universal religion. Second, the progress of science and technology, which had advanced furthest in areas that emphasized power and control, had driven traditional religions out of the thoroughly secularized interstellar society, to survive precariously only in isolated pockets of cultural rebellion in remote regions of backwater planets.

The victory of the clones over the Jedi was not merely a triumph of science over religion, however, because the Emperor had been aided by treachery within the ranks of the Jedi, themselves. A talented young Jedi named Darth Vader, student of two prominent Jedi Masters named Yoda and Obi-

Wan Kenobi, allowed himself to be seduced by the dark side of the Force. The Jedi believed that the Force was at their disposal to accomplish miracles, but this could be done safely only if they suspended their own desires and adopted a spiritual state of philosophical detachment. If a trained Jedi approached the Force with feelings such as fear, longing, or anger, the result could be catastrophic even if the Jedi's intentions were benevolent. For a highly adept Jedi to use the Force to satisfy his own personal lusts, the result would be disastrous in the extreme. At least this was the Jedi belief. All we initially know about the defeat of the Jedi, however, is that Darth Vader betrayed his fellow knights to the Emperor, and the only sign that the Force could be any more than a primitive superstition is some vestigial power, possibly only psychological, that Vader appears to possess.

Governor Grand Moff Tarkin presides over the war council in the Death Star conference room, as Darth Vader stands ominously to one side. Vader's grotesque respirator mask, part of the life-support system he has needed ever since some misadventure years before, gives him the appearance of a great sinister beetle. Admiral Motti boasts about his Death Star, "This station is now the ultimate power in the universe."

Vader disputes this, saying, "The ability to destroy a planet is insignificant next to the power of the Force."

Motti scorns Vader's "sad devotion to that ancient religion," but suddenly he finds he cannot breathe, because Vader has slyly used his paranormal powers at a distance of several meters to choke the admiral's windpipe. After teaching Motti a lesson, Vader releases his spell.

Meanwhile many parsecs away, a motley assortment of adventurers is streaking toward the planet Alderaan on a smuggler's spaceship named the Millennium Falcon. The pilot is cocksure Han Solo, happy enough to get away from Tatooine where there is a price on his head. His co-pilot and partner is a tall, hairy Wookiee named Chewbacca, who speaks in grunts and roars. C-3PO is a gold-colored protocol android whose chief function is to interpret between all galactic languages. Perhaps because his communication function requires great tact and familiarity with many primitive cultures, he is the only character in the trilogy to refer to God, once at a moment of great relief exclaiming, "Thank the Maker!" R2-D2 is another robot, unlike C-3PO shaped more like a washtub than a human being, into whose memory banks Princess Leia Organa was able to place the Death Star plans before her capture. The real hero of the story, R2-D2 brought the other passengers together by fulfilling Leia's instructions to take the plans to General Obi-Wan Kenobi.

For many years, Kenobi had lived a solitary existence, withdrawn from the conflicts that raged across the galaxy. He had served honorably under the command of Leia's father in the Clone Wars, but about the time that

Darth Vader betrayed the Jedi he entered anonymous exile in the Dune Sea of Tatooine. There R2-D2 found him. He has not lost all the powers of a Jedi knight and is still capable of clouding the minds of imperial stormtroopers, but he seems a very powerless old man. Han Solo calls Kenobi's spiritual discipline a "hokey religion," even as the elder seeks to train young Luke Skywalker in the ways of the Force.

Luke is a teenage orphan who had been enduring the difficult existence of a desert farmer with his uncle and aunt, until R2-D2 found him. Only when he met Kenobi did Luke discover that his father, whom he does not recall, had been a Jedi as well. On the trail of the robots, stormtroopers murdered Luke's uncle and aunt, destroyed the farm, and left him with no reason to stay on desolate Tatooine. Having been fascinated by a holographic motion picture of Princess Leia, projected by R2-D2, Luke has joined Kenobi and the robot on a wild mission to Alderaan, so the rebels on that prosperous planet can find means for defeating the Death Star.

Kenobi is training Luke to use his father's weapon, an elegant sword consisting of a beam of light, when he suddenly sits down, as if in a faint. "I felt a great disturbance in the Force," he says, "as if millions of voices suddenly cried out in terror and were suddenly silenced. I fear something terrible has happened." Recovering his balance, Kenobi tries to explain to Luke that "a Jedi can feel the Force flowing through him" and use it to guide his aim in battle. A few moments later, the Millennium Falcon comes out of hyperspace at the location of Alderaan to find the planet gone, entirely blasted to meteoroids by a demonstration shot of the Death Star.

The Death Star seizes the Millennium Falcon in its tractor beam and pulls it into a hangar, so stormtroopers can capture the crew. But Han Solo has hidden himself and all the others in a smuggling compartment, and Kenobi's mental powers dull the suspicions of the guards. One of Obi-Wan's ancient enemies is sensitive to his presence, however. In the conference room, Darth Vader tells Governor Tarkin that he has sensed "a tremor in the Force" telling him Obi-Wan Kenobi has entered the Death Star. Tarkin is incredulous, convinced that Kenobi is long dead, but Vader insists he must not underestimate the power of the Force. Tarkin replies, "The Jedi are extinct, their fire has gone out of the universe. You, my friend, are all that's left of their religion."

At that very moment, Kenobi is disabling the tractor beam while Han and Luke rescue the princess. Stormtroopers surround the heroes in the hangar, but Kenobi is able to distract them by engaging Vader in a lightsaber duel. Vader boasts that now he is the master, while his former teacher's powers have weakened with age. Kenobi replies that in death he will become more powerful than Vader could possibly imagine. After a violent struggle, punctuated by the hiss and zap of lightsabers striking, Vader cuts Kenobi cleanly through. Instead of dying visibly, the old man simply vanishes, his worn, brown cloak dropping empty to the floor. He has left the world of the living to join the Force, and he has given the others time to escape.

Hotly pursued, the Millennium Falcon reaches the rebel base on a moon of the planet Yavin, where they quickly analyze the plans that Leia had concealed in R2-D2, finding that it might just be possible to destroy the Death Star by firing a proton torpedo through a small exhaust port to the main reactor. As the Death Star itself bears down on them, they hurriedly prepare a desperate attack using small fighter spacecraft that might be able to penetrate the battle station's unwieldy defense system. A terrible struggle ensues, and most of the small spacecraft are destroyed before one is able to fire the first torpedo toward the exhaust port. Despite advanced computer targeting, it misses. With little hope left, Luke Skywalker begins his own attack run, supported by two other rebel spacecraft, one piloted by Biggs, his boyhood pal from Tatooine. Flying low over the surface of the Death Star, in a vast trench that shields them from many of the battle stations' turbo-laser guns, Luke and his companions are almost ready to fire, when Darth Vader zooms toward them in his own fighter craft and blasts Biggs' ship to atoms. Torn by shock at his friend's death, Luke hears the voice of deceased Obi-Wan Kenobi telling him to trust the Force. Luke switches off his targeting computer, reaches his feelings out to the force, and at the moment his intuition tells him, presses the firing button. A few moments later, the Death Star disintegrates with the force of a supernova.

The Empire, of course, remains strong, and after a brief celebration, the rebels escape to Hoth, an ice planet where they hope the Emperor's forces cannot find them. But Darth Vader survived the destruction of the Death Star, and his scouts soon locate the rebel base. Battling their way out through an imperial blockade, the rebels escape and head in various directions to rendezvous later at a designated point outside the galaxy. Flying his small fighter craft, Luke heads for the Dagobah system, because in a vision he heard the apparition of Obi-Wan Kenobi tell him to go there to seek Yoda, a Jedi master.

Yoda proves to be a deceptively tiny creature who has the spiritual power to levitate Luke's spacecraft. In the weeks that follow, he gradually teaches Luke how to levitate objects, as well, and instills in him the first rudiments of Jedi philosophy. "For the Jedi it is time to eat as well." This means that, like Zen Buddhist masters, the Jedi must live in a natural manner, attending to the ordinary tasks of life like eating and sleeping as well as occasionally performing miracles. A Jedi must have deep commitment and a serious mind, never craving excitement and adventure, even though he will be surrounded by them. "A Jedi's strength flows from the Force. But beware of the dark side. Anger . . . fear . . . aggression. The dark side of the Force are they.

Easily they flow, quick to join you in a fight. If once you start down the dark path, forever will it dominate your destiny." A Jedi should use the Force for knowledge and defense, not for attack, and should remain serene. Strong emotions lead to the dark side of the Force, so the Jedi must seek peace.

After preliminary instruction, Yoda brings Luke to a gloomy, damp cave, a place where the dark side of the Force is strong, where he must confront the evil that is within him. Deeper and deeper Luke presses into the darkness, his lightsaber drawn and ready. With a sudden hiss, Darth Vader leaps at him, and Luke desperately swings his sword, decapitating his nemesis. The severed head rolls until Luke can see the face, and he discovers that it is his own. Only when Vader fades away does Luke realize it was a vision, created by his own, tormented mind.

A passionate young man of action, Luke must unlearn everything he has learned, if he is to make the Force his ally. "And a powerful ally it is. Life creates it, makes it grow. Its energy surrounds us and binds us. Luminous beings are we, not this crude matter. You must feel the Force around you. Here, between you . . . me . . . the tree . . . the rock . . . everywhere!" Luke admits he cannot believe, and Yoda explains that this is the reason he fails many of the tests Yoda sets him. It is not so much that the Force requires faith as that any nagging emotion like doubt will be a distraction undermining the Jedi's needed serene concentration. In a state of perfect calm, the Jedi's mind can see the past or the future. From the past a Jedi can draw strength and wisdom, as both Yoda and Luke do from the departed spirit of Obi-Wan Kenobi. It is difficult to control or even predict the future, because it is in constant motion, but during one training session Luke suddenly realizes that his friends are in grave danger. In a cloud city across the galaxy, Darth Vader has seized Han, Leia, Chewbacca, and the two robots. There he is torturing Han, knowing that the pain will travel through the Force until it reaches Luke. Yoda protests that Luke must complete his training before he confronts Vader, but Luke is consumed by the need to save his friends, despite the risk that this emotion may seduce him to the dark side of the Force.

Soon, Luke and Vader face each other in the cloud city's carbon-freezing chamber, their lightsabres drawn. Their duel sweeps back and forth, neither gaining a lasting advantage over the other, until Vader begins to bait Luke to rile up his emotions. "Obi-Wan has taught you well. You have controlled your fear . . . now release your anger. Only your hatred can destroy me." They battle into the reactor room, with ever increasing fury, then onto a reactor shaft overlooking a chasm descending hundreds of meters. Vader distracts Luke and severs his right hand with a vicious sweep of his lightsabre. Because he ignored the chief principle of the Jedi and allowed himself to be consumed by emotion, he has lost the battle and now faces the loss of his life.

Remarkably, Vader does not kill him, but offers to complete Luke's training so they can together defeat the emperor and rule the galaxy in his place. Luke resists, but Vader reminds him that Kenobi never fully explained what happened to Luke's father. With his hand outstretched to aid him, Vader proclaims, "I am your father." In his heart, Luke realizes that this is true. He also realizes that Vader's offer would require him to accept the dark side of the Force. With an expression of grim resolution, Luke turns away from Vader and steps off the platform over the abyss to almost certain death.

The calmness that washed over Luke as he made that fateful step restored his connection with the Force, and by what otherwise would have been an impossible accident he was able to halt his fall where his escaped friends aboard the Millennium Falcon rescue him. Outside the galaxy, rebel surgeons gave him a prosthetic robot arm to replace the one severed by his father. After a series of dangers and difficulties, Luke returned to Dagobah to complete his training with Yoda. He arrives just in time to be with the nine-hundred-year-old Jedi master as he dies. In his last words, Yoda tells Luke to beware the power of the Emperor.

Word reaches the rebels that a second Death Star is being assembled in orbit around the Moon of Endor and protected by a force shield on the ground below it. They have no choice but to attack before it is completed, and a volunteer squad must reach the surface of Endor to disable the force shield. Luke, Han, Chewbacca, Leia, and the two robots volunteer for this risky assignment. After wild escapades eluding imperial scouts, this company is captured by the Ewoks. These are short, hairy humanoid creatures who would seem cute if they were not so ready to kill Luke and his companions.

When the Ewoks see gold-plated C-3PO, they prostrate themselves on the ground in adoration. Apparently he resembles the image of God of their primitive religion. Under the direction of their witch doctor, the Ewoks prepare to sacrifice the humans as offerings to the deified C-3PO. Despite being trussed up like a roast ready for the barbecue, Luke draws upon the Force to levitate C-3PO, thus discrediting the witch doctor and causing the Ewoks to release their captives. Translating with difficulty into the unfamiliar Ewok language, C-3PO is now able to enlist these furry warriors into their attack on the force shield protecting the Death Star. Luke allows himself to be captured by imperial forces, manipulating them to be brought to Dark Vader in hopes of convincing his father to relinquish the dark side of the Force. But instead his father takes him into a vast throne room built into the Death Star to submit to the Emperor.

The Emperor is not an imposing figure, as he sits on a ordinary swivel chair gazing out into the blackness of space. He is a small, old man, bent and shriveled, hardly the image of power. Within a few moments, however, he reveals to Luke that he has anticipated every aspect of the rebel attack. The field generator on Endor, which protects the new Death Star, is itself defended by a legion of crack troops. The rebel fleet appears, but finds itself met by withering fire, because the apparently incomplete battle station is in fact fully armed and operational. Everything has been a ruse to draw the rebels into an ambush and to lure Luke into the Emperor's clutches.

With greedy anticipation, the Emperor says to Luke, "I'm looking forward to completing your training. In time you will call me Master." He taunts Luke, knowing that frustration, fear, and anger will turn the young Jedi toward the dark side of the Force. He offers Luke a lightsabre with which to strike. Luke seizes it, strikes, but meets Vader's ready blade of light. Luke and Vader duel furiously, as the team on Endor struggles with the unanticipated help of the Ewoks to overcome the defenders of the field generator and give the rebel fleet a chance to destroy the Death Star.

In this duel, unlike their earlier one, Luke senses that Vader is reluctant to kill him. After an especially violent exchange of blows, Luke succeeds in severing Vader's right arm, just as Vader had earlier done to him. Sensing the immense power of the Force concentrated in Luke, the Emperor urges him to kill Vader and serve him in his stead. Poised to end Vader's life, he halts, then casts his lightsabre aside. "Never! I'll never turn to the dark side. You've failed, Your Highness. I am a Jedi, like my father before me."

Enraged, the Emperor reaches out his arms, and great bolts of lightening leap from his finger tips, slamming Luke like electric sledgehammers. "Young fool . . . only now, at the end, do you understand." Vader stands supportively beside his Emperor. The truth has indeed now dawned. The Emperor, himself, is a Jedi, perhaps the greatest of them all. From the dark side of the Force he has drawn the power to destroy the earlier republic, to turn Darth Vader to the dark side when he was an idealistic young Jedi, and to assemble the legions of stormtroopers that created his empire.

Although the Force can affect physical objects, it is primarily spiritual in nature. It arises from all the limited life forces of the intelligent beings across the galaxy, and it allows a Jedi to influence the thoughts of weaker beings. In the hands of an evil genius like the Emperor, who has turned to the dark side, it becomes ultimate charisma. Without even knowing that they are led, millions of people go where the Emperor desires them to go, do what he wishes done, and submit utterly to his will. Just as the Force binds the galaxy together, transformed into charisma it binds the people of the galaxy together in slavery to their evil master.

Luke writhes in pain, but he forces his agonized body to speak to Darth Vader: "Father, please. Help me." Unexpectedly, Vader turns, seizes the Emperor in his good left hand, holds him high in the air, then as the Emperor's lightning bolts cascade down Vader's body, hurls him into a bottomless shaft where the sparks trigger a devastating explosion. Somehow, deep within the half robot shell of the dark monster, a spark of goodness remained. Whether from the honor of a Jedi, or the love of a father, Darth Vader could not see Luke die. And so, at the last moment before redemption became impossible, it was he who ended the Emperor's evil reign and sacrificed himself for freedom.

Vader is mortally wounded. Removing the respirator that has made his father appear like a demon for so many years, Luke finds a gentle, pathetically scarred human face. Dragging his father toward an escape rocket, he promises to save him. Darth Vader says, "You already have, Luke," a moment before succumbing to his wounds. And within the religion of the Jedi, this is true. Luke has accomplished the impossible, returning a Jedi from the dark side. This, indeed, is salvation.

Then the joyful triumph of the Ewoks demolishing the shield generator, and the destruction of the second Death Star by the rebel fleet, seem anticlimactic. A few hours later, as the first night of freedom falls on Endor, Luke stands beside the celebrating Ewoks smiling at his friends, Leia, Han, Chewbacca, and the two robots. But he looks beyond them, into the Force. And there he sees his father, Yoda, and Obi-Wan Kenobi, smiling at him. He alone of the celebrants has the capacity to see them, but they truly exist, on a higher plane of being. The three Jedi are the only figures Luke perceives in this vision of the afterlife. He does not see his Uncle Owen or Aunt Beru, who were slaughtered by the stormtroopers back on Tatooine, nor does he see the many fellow rebels like Biggs who died in the battle on Hoth or the assaults on the two death stars. Like the Norse Valhalla, this is an elite heaven, where only the most transcendent heroes may go.

The *Star Wars* myth states a very clear conception of the religion of the far future. The Force is not a god, although it clearly is supernatural. The Ewoks worshipped a God, and mistook C-3PO for that golden deity, because they were primitives. Religion had expired in the civilized parts of the galaxy, persisting only among savages, and only a real miracle could bring it back. This is the most challenging claim of *Star Wars*, by far. In advanced technological societies, religion will die, unless its beliefs are literally true. Only actual intervention by the supernatural can save religion from science. At least this is the implication of the *Star Wars* stories.

Secularization, Revival, Innovation

A strange, halting intellectual debate has limped forward over the decades concerning the future of religion. Sociology has long acted as if religion were dying and deserved little notice. In contrast, adherents of various religious faiths never seemed to contemplate the chilling possibility that their own denomination might someday vanish. At rare moments, a scholar would address the issue directly. For example, in 1966 prominent anthropologist, Anthony F. C. Wallace, predicted that the future of religion is extinction:

> Belief in supernatural beings and in supernatural forces that affect nature without obeying nature's laws will erode and become only an interesting historical memory. To be sure, this event is not likely to occur in the next hundred years, and there will always remain individuals, or even occasional small cult groups, who respond to hallucination, trance, and obsession with a supernatural interpretation. But as a cultural trait, belief in supernatural powers is doomed to die out, all over the world, as a result of the increasing adequacy and diffusion of scientific knowledge and the realization by secular faiths that supernatural belief is not necessary to the effective use of ritual. The question of whether such a denouement will be good or bad for humanity is irrelevant to the prediction; the process is inevitable. (Wallace 1966:265)

Other scholars have agreed that religion faces doom (Freud 1927; Fenn 1978; Wilson 1979), and that science-driven secularization gnaws steadily at the roots of faith. However, anyone who glances in a newspaper sees that religion continues to affect deeply a wide range of human activities, and it is hard to discern extinction in a phenomenon as varied and vigorous as faith. Stephen Warner (1993) announces that a contrasting New Paradigm has arisen in the sociological study of religion, denying that secularization is killing faith, and clearly the Stark-Bainbridge theory is a central part of this paradigm. As a human phenomenon, religion arises through social exchanges in which individuals seek rewards and attempt to avoid costs. Although science supports highly rewarding technologies—ignore for the moment the costs and dangers of technology—it has come nowhere near solving the chief problems of human existence. Until that inconceivable day when science and technology transform humans into gods, people will postulate supernatural exchange partners from whom to obtain the most general and valuable rewards. Thus, although individual religions are constantly born, change, and die, religion in general is eternal.

In earlier chapters, we saw that religious organizations often gradually reduce their tension with the surrounding sociocultural environment. For the particular organizations involved, this is tantamount to secularization, the gradual accommodation to secular standards of belief and behavior. However, this process calls forth a countervailing process of religious revival and innovation. According to Daniel Bell (1971:474), "when theology erodes and organization crumbles, when the institutional framework of religion begins to break up, the search for a direct experience which people can feel to be religious facilitates the rise of cults."

Stark and I have not limited the response to deviant "cults," instead recognizing that new religious movements are highly varied in nature: "Religions that abandon powerful, specific supernatural claims thereby lose their ability to serve many people's religious needs. More youthful and vigorous religions, that promise rewards and confidently explain the costs humans endure, will win converts at the expense of the more fully evolved religious organizations" (Stark and Bainbridge 1987:117; Iannaccone 1994).

In Chapter 3 we saw that Methodism arose as a response to secularization in the Church of England, but then began to accommodate to the secular world, itself. This secularization within Methodism led to the eruption of the Holiness Movement which included the Church of the Nazarene. And modest secularization within this denomination also led to the eruption of sects. In principle, this cycle could continue forever, constantly renewing Protestantism with vigorous, new movements that gradually ossify, only to be replaced in turn by their more vigorous offspring. This is a picture of Christianity running in place, as it were. The movements within Christianity move, but Christianity as a whole does not.

This model of the circulation of sects and denominations says that secularization is self-limiting, calling forth revivals that restore the existing religious tradition. Yet, we know that throughout history entirely new religious traditions have arisen. One model of how this could happen is that entire religious traditions might become secularized, leaving a gap into which fresh religions can expand (Stark and Bainbridge 1985). But Anthony F. C. Wallace argues that faith in all religions, not just a particular one, would be eroded by secularization. Empirically, we know that communities vary in the strength of their churches, and this fact can be exploited to test the competing theories of secularization. The old secularization paradigm of Wallace and company predicts that all religions weaken together, and thus that communities that are weak in traditional religion will also be weak in new religions. In contrast, the new paradigm to which Stark and I have contributed, predicts that communities that are weak in traditional religious denominations will be strong in new religious movements.

With its large number of cities and its geographic diversity, the United States is an excellent laboratory in which to evaluate these competing predictions. In 1980, a survey of denominations tabulated the number of members each possessed in every country of the United States (Quinn et al. 1982), making it possible to calculate rates of church membership for all metropolitan areas outside New England. Unfortunately, the metropolitan areas defined by the Census Bureau for New England do not coincide with counties, so they cannot be included in this particular analysis. A journal ar-

Conclusion

Table 14.1: Church Membership and Novel Religious Movements, ca. 1980

| | Hypothetical City Without Churches | 120 American Metropolitan Areas with Church Membership: | | | Hypothetical Fully Churched City |
		40 Low	40 Medium	40 High	
Percent Church Members	0.0	39.0	54.1	66.9	100.0
Scientology Clears per 100,000	15.0	7.5	1.4	1.1	0.0
Fate Letter Writers per 100,000	2.3	1.3	0.8	0.7	0.0
Spiritual Guide Listings per 100,000	3.3	1.8	0.8	0.7	0.0
TM Meditators per 100,000	1,021.4	608.7	417.8	349.3	0.0

ticle has analyzed these data using sophisticated statistical techniques (Bainbridge 1989a), but here we will employ a simpler approach. In Table 14.1 we will deal with the 120 largest metropolitan areas (outside New England), all those with populations above 300,000. As we did back in Table 10.1, we have divided them into three groups of forty, in terms of their church-member rates, and we use statistical regression techniques to estimate the characteristics of hypothetical cities with church-member rates of 0 percent and 100 percent. The 120 real cities span a wide range of secularization, and we are prepared to estimate what might happen at the logical extremes. Next we need measures of novel religious innovation.

The real religious movement that in many ways fulfills best the image of future religion presented in *Star Wars* is Scientology, a tremendously creative movement founded by a science-fiction author named L. Ron Hubbard. Scientologists believe that each individual has latent godlike powers that can be liberated by its training and spiritual-development techniques. After considerable "processing" and "auditing," a scientologist reaches the honored status known as "clear," and the geographic distribution of "clears" is a good measure of the degree to which Scientology has advanced further in some regions of the country than in others. Clears are the elite of the church, so the total number of Scientologists in a particular town will be substantially larger than the number of clears. I requested national data on clears from the public-relations office of Scientology of Boston, and it in turn requested the data from the Los Angeles organization which had an address file for clears. The data proved to have great scientific value, and thus I deeply thank both Scientology organizations for the confidence they showed in giving me a tabulation of the number of clears for each three-digit zip code as of November 1985. These, then, were turned into rates per 100,000 for each metropolitan area.

In the forty cities with high rates of church membership, on average there were only 1.1 Scientology clears per 100,000 population. The rate was somewhat higher, 1.4 per 100,000, in the forty cities having medium levels of church membership. But the rate is substantially higher, 7.5 per 100,000 in the forty cities with low church membership. Thus, data on the most obviously futuristic religion, Scientology, confirms that novel religions are most successful where traditional religions are weakest. This supports the new paradigm of secularization, not the old paradigm.

A commonly used statistical technique called linear regression allows us to predict what would happen in cities with church-member rates of 0 percent or 100 percent. Naturally, such estimates are on shaky ground, but the results are sufficiently interesting to report them here. In a city with no church members, the regression analysis predicts there will be fifteen clears per 100,000 residents. And in a city where everybody belongs to conventional churches, there will be no Scientology clears at all.

We can replicate these results with data on three aspects of the New Age. In the previous chapter, we described *Fate* magazine and the *Spiritual Community Guide*. And in Chapter 7 we introduced the Transcendental Meditation movement. The data reported here are based on the addresses of people who published letters to the editor in *Fate*, listings in the *Guide*, and the number of persons initiated into TM from each of 3,200 urban areas in the country, all combined into the appropriate metropolitan areas. For each of these, Table 14.1 shows the same pattern as it did for Scientology. Cities with low rates of church membership have relatively high rates for these measures, whereas cities with high rates of church membership have low rates of novel religious movement. Again, with three fresh, independent measures of receptivity to new religions, the new paradigm wins, and the old one loses. A weakening of traditional religion does appear to stimulate the growth of novel religions.

Table 14.2 looks back to the middle of the roaring twenties and provides four more measures of novel religion. In Chapter 10 we mentioned the splendid survey of churches done back in 1926 by the Bureau of the Census, which collected information about 212 denominations (Bureau of the Census 1930; Bainbridge and Stark 1981c). Five of these qualify as novel religious movements and provided apparently valid data: Christian Science,

Table 14.2: Church Membership and Novel Religious Movements, 1926

	Hypothetical City Without Churches	285 American Cities with Church Membership:			Hypothetical Fully Churched City
		95 Low	95 Medium	95 High	
Percent Church Members	0.0	41.4	56.6	74.7	100.0
Christian Scientists per 100,000	455.8	331.6	203.0	181.7	78.9
Theosophists per 100,000	28.8	18.9	9.3	7.2	0.0
Three Small Groups* per 100,000	19.6	10.8	2.8	2.6	0.0

*Combining Baha'i, Divine Science, and the Liberal Catholic Church

Theosophy, Baha'i, Divine Science, and the Liberal Catholic Church (Stark and Bainbridge 1985:234–262). This time we have data on the 285 largest American cities, including New England, which we can divide into three groups of ninety-five in terms of their church-member rates.

Christian Science was founded in 1879 in Boston by Mary Baker G. Eddy and focuses on religious healing (England, 1954). By 1926, there were 140,081 members of 1,913 congregations across the nation. Theosophy is a Western religious movement founded by Helena Petrovna Blavatsky, greatly influenced by Hindu traditions, and it was very active in the 1893 World's Parliament of Religions in Chicago. The 1926 religious census found 223 congregations with 6,780 members. Divine Science is an American movement very similar to Christian Science; Baha'i is an imported religious movement of Persian Sufi origins, and the Liberal Catholic Church combines elements of Theosophy with Christianity. All three of these were rather small and lacked congregations in a number of cities, so in Table 14.2 we combine them. There were 3,466 Divine Scientists, 1,247 members of Baha'i, and 1,799 Liberal Catholics. The numbers of congregations were twenty-two, forty-four, and thirty-nine, respectively.

Again we find evidence in favor of the new paradigm. Where the conventional churches are strong, these new religious movements are weak. But where the churches are weak, the novel movements are most strong. A linear-regression analysis predicts that there would be no members of Theosophy or of the three small groups in a fully churched city, but it predicts there will still be 78.9 Christian Scientists per 100,000. This is not surprising, because Christian Science had many of the qualities of an ordinary Protestant denomination and contributed appreciably to the rate of church membership itself. The four other groups, each far smaller than Christian Science, had not achieved anything like the public acceptance of Christian Science and remained pure measures of a community's receptivity to novel religion.

For those readers familiar with linear-regression techniques I should say a little more about the analyses in tables 14.1 and 14.2. It is not a coincidence that statistical analysis predicts exactly zero rates for the six novel religious movements. In fact, each analysis predicts that the movement's rate would reach zero well before the church-member rated reached 100 percent. This makes substantive sense. When even 90 percent are members of conventional churches, the remaining 10 percent may not include enough with identical needs or shared social bonds to sustain alternative religions. When an overwhelming majority belong to conventional churches, the religious norms of the community will be very strict, and any individual will be under tremendous pressure to conform. But there is also a statistical explanation. We do not have a sufficient number of cases to determine the precise mathematical function that describes the relationship between church membership and participation in novel religious movements. In fact, the relationship may be curvilinear, and thus the predictions for a hypothetical city with zero church-member rate may be gross underestimates. These observations do not undercut the data in the tables from real cities, of course, but merely underscore the provisional nature of hypothetical estimates.

If the estimates for a hypothetical city without conventional churches are at all accurate, however, they seem to show that these relatively successful novel religious movements would be incapable of filling the gap left by the retreat of traditional denominations. Thus, although there definitely is a tendency for novel religions to flourish where conventional churches are weak, none of them seem to be ready to supplant the formerly dominant religions. Therefore it is worth examining the features that a novel religious movement must possess if it is to succeed spectacularly, and the conditions in the surrounding environment that will be conducive to the rise of a new religion.

Success of New Religious Movements

In an influential essay summing up a variety of research and theoretical work, Rodney Stark (1987) has listed eight factors that contribute to the success of a new religious movement, here quoted in Table 14.3. I have listed Stark's eight points in the order he gives them, but I think it is useful for this discussion to rearrange them into two groups. Five points concern the internal structure and functioning of the religious movement itself, and while they certainly are worth mentioning, it is hard to find a basis for disagreement. These points are numbers 3, 4, 6, 7, and 8. They all concern building a church that has a broad base in the community and strong internal organization. Effective mobilization means that most members are powerfully committed to the aims of the group and can be induced to contribute their energy and resources. A dense network of internal relationships binds the individuals to each other, thus constituting a goodly portion of the necessary commitment, but the movement must be capable of reaching out an incorporating new recruits. Chapter 6 said much that relates to these two issues. A normal age and sex structure is necessary if the group is to form a complete community that can reproduce its membership through fertility rather than recruitment. Socializing the young is necessary for them to remain members. Resisting secularization sustains the religious fervor essential to grow.

The three remaining points concern the relationship between the group and the surrounding sociocultural environment: 1) cultural continuity; 2) medium tension; and 5) favorable ecology. The last of these is really three points, or possibly two if deregulation of the religious economy is inevitably connected to weakening of conventional faiths. And there is considerable room for controversy in discussing this group of ideas.

It is a fact that the most successful new religious movements do tend to exhibit continuity with the existing religious culture. That is, they maintain some of the fundamental concepts, symbols, and practices of the religious tradition that already is popular, merely adding modifications or extensions of their own. Christianity drew upon Judaism, and Islam drew upon them both. The particular order in which Christians arrange the books of the Old Testament emphasizes their claim that the ministry of Jesus was a fulfillment of ancient Hebrew prophecy, and many Christian editions of the New Testament are replete with footnotes connecting passages back to others in the Old Testament. The story of Buddhism is slightly different. Buddhism did have considerable cultural continuity with Hinduism, and may be seen as a purification of it. But after getting a good start in India, Buddhism practically died out there, and achieved its great success in China and other parts of east Asia as an imported faith. Presumably, however, Buddhism would not have had the chance to expand outside India if it had not achieved substantial strength there first, and that apparently required cultural continuity with Hinduism.

Certainly the Holiness sects had great cultural continuity with Methodism, and there is some merit to their claim that they preserved the traditions of John Wesley as the Methodist church weakened them. Adventism was a

Table 14.3: The Stark Model: Success of New Religious Movements

New religious movements are likely to succeed to the extent that they:

1. Retain *cultural continuity* with the conventional faiths of the societies in which they appear or originate.

2. Maintain a *medium* level of *tension* with their surrounding environment; are deviant, but not too deviant.

3. Achieve *effective mobilization*: strong governance and a high level of individual commitment.

4. Can attract and maintain a *normal age and sex* structure.

5. Occur within a *favorable ecology*, which exists when:
   a. the religious economy is *relatively unregulated*;
   b. conventional faiths are *weakened* by secularization or social disruption
   c. it is possible to achieve at least *local success* within a *generation*.

6. Maintain *dense* internal network relations without becoming isolated.

7. Resist *secularization*.

8. Adequately *socialize* the young so as to:
   a. limit pressures toward secularization;
   b. limit defection.

---

departure of some significance from the existing denominations, but it convincingly rooted itself deeply in the Bible and offered Protestants much that was familiar to them, as well as something new. Certainly, all four of the really successful distinctly novel American movements remain Christian: Seventh-day Adventism, Jehovah's Witnesses, the Church of Jesus Christ of Latter-Day Saints (Mormons), and Christian Science.

Roy Wallis (1987) has suggested that a new religious movement might be utterly different from the traditional religions of a society, yet possess continuity with some other important aspects of the culture. His example is Scientology, which has no discernible connection to Christianity but draws its symbolism from science, which pervades the culture. One problem about being a scientific religion, Wallis notes, is that by its very nature science constantly changes, so there is the danger of becoming obsolete. Naturally, this danger vanishes when scientific progress ceases, or when the progress is so arcane that the ordinary person cannot understand it. Furthermore, a single religious organization may not be the best means for transforming religious culture. More effective would be a new tradition sustained by a host of competing organizations, effectively an independent religious economy with its own process for constantly generating new sects fired up with fresh religious visions. Even as some denominations in this alternative religious tradition fell by the wayside because their science became obsolete, new ones would stay out in front of changes in scientific culture. Such a situation does not yet exist, so this possibility remains speculative.

A novel religious movement that lacks cultural continuity demands that recruits learn an entirely new set of beliefs and practices, which at the very least requires a substantial amount of education and indoctrination. In contrast, a movement that has continuity can present itself as the fulfillment of the faith the recruit already possesses, and it demands far less labor to learn. Furthermore, a movement that departs greatly from the religious traditions of the society will *ipso facto* stand in high tension with its sociocultural environment, which invokes the next of Stark's points.

Stark argues that a religious movement in exceptionally low tension will be unable to provide the motivation necessary for successful conversion. He assumes that low-tension denominations already exist, and that there may be little to recommend joining yet another low-tension denomination if it appears. This is the case in Western societies, but may not be true throughout the former communist nations and in a variety of other societies where a fundamentalist religious movement has forged a temporary alliance with the state. In those societies, religious movements comparable to low-tension American denominations have practically been eradicated, and once the repressive state loses power there may be substantial opportunities for low-tension movements. The fact that very few low-tension church movements appear in the literature of the sociology of religion may merely reflect the fact that most studies employing modern methods of analysis have been done in the United States.

Stark also states that a movement in exceptionally high tension will be unable to build bonds with potential recruits because it is stigmatized and excluded by the conventional community, although he cites the early Christian church as a potential counterexample. Thus, under some circumstances, extreme high tension may be an advantage for a religious movement, at least for a portion of its existence. If tension is high for a number of years after the movement has gained at least a few thousand members, then the struggle of fending off a hostile environment may give the movement great strength which it can exploit later when conditions become more permissive. The question of the optimal level of tension may have a different answer depending upon the kind of success one wants to explain. Medium tension certainly seems to give a new group the best chance of evolving into a relatively large, stable denomination. But this is success of a very limited kind. Higher tension may be necessary for the emergence of a group than not only achieves tremendous membership growth but results in a denomination that represents a real cultural alternative to the existing ones. The Mormon experience in Illinois was one of rather high tension, as is attested by the murder of their leader and the departure of a substantial fraction of the membership to go into the wilderness and create a new society.

Tension is a two-way street, depending not only upon the nature of the religious movement, but also upon that of the surrounding sociocultural environment. Therefore, a favorable ecology dovetails with the degree of tension. Stark suggests that a movement will succeed, other things being equal, when the religious economy is relatively unregulated. For a religious economy to be strictly regulated means that an oppressive state has granted a monopoly to one ecclesia or a near-monopoly to a handful of denominations, and that new religious movements are so severely punished that they can hardly survive. Thus, a relatively unregulated religious economy permits the movement to be in low or medium tension, whereas in a monopolistic religious economy, every movement is by definition high in tension.

As we saw earlier in this chapter, weakness of standard denominations gives new movements an opportunity to grow, and below we will return to the issues of secularization and social disruption. However, it is possible that an utterly unregulated religious economy will be so fluid and chaotic that even an otherwise potent new religious movement will be incapable of making any progress. This may be one of the reasons that new religions are more successful in the Pacific region of the United States and Canada, and yet have failed to grow into substantial movements there. The rates of geographic migration are so high that people are constantly being torn away from every religious congregation. Although medium-tension movements may have a religious advantage over low-tension denominations, because they offer more efficacious compensators, they may suffer equally from some of the social factors that erode congregations of any kind, notably high rates of social, economic, and geographic mobility. Thus it may be that very low regulation of the religious economy, and very low levels of social stability, are not conducive to movement success. If so, we would have to say that movements succeed best under conditions of medium regulation and medium social disruption, just as Stark says they do with medium tension.

Stark's point 5c, about achieving local success within a generation, considers the factors likely to sustain morale in a religious movement. If the criterion of success is the number of members, even high rates of growth take several years to make a movement a major player on the national religious scene. It may be easier to achieve apparent recruitment success locally than nationally, and many objectively small religious sects have a sense of recruitment success because they concentrated their efforts locally or in one region, and were able to make their mark on the local religious economy. Other criteria of success are possible, especially for high-tension religious movements, and so the maintenance of morale without very rapid membership growth tends to return us to the issues of tension level and regulation of the religious economy. The fact that many tiny high-tension sects do persist for many years despite lack of growth suggests that its members have found compensatory criteria of success, notably feeling they are the true religious elite.

With Stark's full model in mind, we then can return to his first crucial point, cultural continuity. The problem here is that a movement with high cultural continuity is thus one that offers little if any innovation. It is a sect within the standard religious tradition. It may very well succeed in becoming a major denomination of the future, but it is not prepared to transform the religious culture in any essential sense. Thus, if one merely wants to explain how it is that some religious movements grow, and others decline, the model seems very close to being correct. But if one wants to explain those rare occasions when an utterly new religious tradition arises, then the model may not be helpful. On the other hand, the model may really contain the seeds of a full explanation. Perhaps under ordinary conditions, such as those in Western countries today, a really new religious tradition simply cannot become established. Only under really extreme conditions of secularization or social disruption may this be possible.

Religions of the Future

How, then, can really novel new religious movements, ones that constitute entirely new traditions, rise to significance within modern society? One answer, to be sure, is for them to take advantage of the weakness of conventional denominations in particular geographic areas. But that does not seem sufficient to create major new denominations with novel beliefs and practices. As we saw, in areas of low church membership, the novel movements have not in fact grown to fill up the gap; if they had, church membership would not vary geographically.

Careful analysis of data over several decades does not support the naive view that novel religions have recently increased in number (Finke and Stark, 1992). This would seem to contradict the prediction Stark and I made a decade ago that they would eventually rise to replace many current conventional denominations. However, among the most rapidly growing large religious groups are some that began with a significant degree of religious deviance and retain much innovative culture. In the nine years between 1971 and 1980, the Mormons grew by 26 percent, and the Seventh-day Adventists by 25 percent, for example (Johnson et al. 1974; Quinn *et al.* 1982). And from 1980 to 1990, they grew by 32 percent and 35 percent, respectively, reaching American memberships of 3,540,820 and 903,062 (Bradley et al. 1992). Thus, these two vigorous religious movements have maintained high rates of growth even after becoming substantial denominations.

Our theory of secularization and innovation is meant to explain processes that span centuries, and our analyses are certainly not precise enough to predict trends over a few decades, let alone over just one. Our colleagues may complain that our theory is not designed for quick and conclusive testing, but this, of course, is also true for many of the leading theories in the physical sciences. Astronomers say that the planet Pluto will circle the solar system in 248 years, and our solar system will circle the galaxy in about 200,000,000. We would like to stay around to check both of these predictions out, but we will not hold the astronomers responsible for our inability to do so.

While we have no quantitative techniques that can let us see into the future, imagination permits qualitative exploration of two scenarios, both of which may come to reality. First, the emergence of many small innovative movements coupled with increased toleration for alternative supernatural beliefs may achieve a kind of re-paganization of society, as hinted in Chapter 13. Second, conditions may exist under which novel religious movements can become institutionalized as major denominations that through schism and further innovation will create entire new religious traditions comparable in strength and variety to the great world religions of today.

Let us consider the first scenario, paganization. The term "pagan" commonly means "heathen." Where once it might have described any non-Christian, it has been narrowed in our more cosmopolitan times to mean anyone who does not belong to one of the great monotheistic faiths, perhaps leaving open the question of which Asian faiths qualify. Derived from *pagus* "rural district," for Tertullian the word *paganus* had a connotation of "civilian" in contrast to the soldiers of Christ, thus meaning someone who had not enlisted in the Christian movement. I like the rural connotation, because paganism, whether classical or contemporary, is homespun religion. Paganism is local and self-created. Thus, a re-paganization of society would mean the eruption of thousands of freshly created religious movements, each one being of very little significance with membership limited to a small area or small segment of the population. Paganization does not mean an end to conventional churches, merely the growth of a significant and highly diverse milieu of new religious movements that is no longer in very high tension with the surrounding sociocultural environment. Walk through Glastonbury, England, or Rosicrucian Park in San Jose, California, and you get the picture.

The second scenario, institutionalization, is rather more challenging. When people think about religions of the future, they generally imagine something more solidly organized than the diffuse paganism described above. In particular, they foresee one or more major denominations coming into existence, complete with substantial church buildings, hundreds of thousands or even millions of adherents, and formal authority structures. Distinctively new denominations have emerged already in America, notably The Church of Jesus Christ of Latter-Day Saints (Mormons), Christian Science, Jehovah's Witnesses, and Seventh-day Adventism. Each of these, of course, is largely Christian in nature, and might be considered merely another Protestant denomination if it did not possess a substantial body of novel culture.

Additional hybrid religions, half Christian and half something else, are to be expected in the future. Some will be amalgams of Christianity with non-Western cultures, adding whatever twist the founders contributed. Hybrids with Asian traditions already exist, notably the Unification Church from Korea and the Local Church (founded by Watchman Nee) from China. Hybridization is apparently an effective strategy for creating a new religion, capitalizing on the familiarity and cultural plausibility of an existing tradition while claiming to have overcome all its bad points and added many wonderful novelties.

Exotic, imported religions have had a difficult time in Western Europe and North America. Given the tremendous intellectual stir Zen Buddhism caused in the 1950s, the high prestige of Japanese society, and Zen's inherent attractiveness, one would have thought that Zen would have become a major force in the West, after fully forty years of growth. Yet the number of Zen adherents is so small as to be undetectable in major surveys. Hinduism, whether in its original forms or greatly modified as in Theosophy, has done hardly better. An entire book could be filled with the stories of imported Asian religious movements that gained considerable attention in American mass media, only to shrink to a few dozen adherents and fall into public obscurity. The present cultural climate gives us little reason to believe that purely Asian religious movements will gain greater significance in the near future, but the economic and industrial importance of the western Pacific rim may give some of them the needed boost.

Opportunities exist for Islamic and other Near-Eastern movements. While far from popular, Sufism keeps resurfacing on the fringes of American religion, often attracting relatively well-educated recruits. Islamic groups appealing to Americans of African descent already exist in some numbers. The tremendous international significance of Islam, which has been steadily increasing, is not likely to diminish in our lifetimes. The liberation of Muslim portions of the former Soviet Union is of absolutely first-rate importance, as was the brief but bloody war between Russia and the Chechen Moslems. Travelers from neighboring Dagestan report a revival of Islamic traditions, including the partial seclusion of women. It is beyond our capacity to imagine what variants or hybrids of Islam might eventually become major forces in Western religious life.

Other new religions are truly fresh departures. This is one reason for my enduring interest in Scientology. It is hard to know how many Scientologists there are, but Roy Wallis's (1986) estimate of 4,000,000 American Scientologists is not remotely credible. A good 1990 estimate based on a telephone survey of 113,000 Americans is 45,000 (Finke and Stark, 1992:242). The 1985 printout of Scientology clears by zip-code area, which we used briefly earlier in this chapter, indicates 8,600 clears in 288 metropolitan areas, and 9,117 nationwide. It is entirely plausible that one-fifth of dedicated Scientologists are clears, which extrapolates to just over 45,000 total American membership. Certainly the confidence interval around this estimate is narrower than an order of magnitude. While well-established, Scientology has not yet achieved the level of success necessary to make it a socially powerful new religious tradition. But, then, Christianity needed three centuries of growth to achieve dominance, and Scientology has not quite reached the half-century mark.

In *The Future of Religion*, Stark and I discussed the fact that entire religious traditions have vanished in the past. No one today worships Osiris, Odin, or Zeus. We suggested that some existing religious traditions would collapse in the future, and be replaced by fresh ones. In part, evolutionary processes may be at work, and in *A Theory of Religion* we argued that a gradual reduction in the number of gods should be expected over the centuries in any initially polytheistic tradition. Thus, a polytheistic religion might gain few adherents today. The gods of ancient Greece were certainly not very attractive characters; Zeus was an unreliable bully and a philanderer. Christianity provided a far more appealing God and a more optimistic view of existence. Thus, superior religions may replace inferior ones. But often the contest between major religions is between somewhat different mixes of virtues, and a clear winner cannot be identified until events give victory to one faith or the other (cf. Ulansey, 1989).

In some ways, a religion can be rendered anachronistic by the passage of events. To be sure, a religion can gain strength from holding a very different set of norms and beliefs from that of the surrounding society. It is remotely conceivable that a time will come when the advancing march of science, coupled with radical transformations in the nature of society, undercuts the plausibility and the emotional appeal of the entire Judeo-Christian-Islamic tradition, based as it was on the perspectives of an initially nomadic herding society that became rooted in the pre-industrial cities of the Roman Empire. But new religions are constantly arising, and some will rest on assumptions more in tune with science and providing comfort more satisfactory for inhabitants of advanced industrial societies. Thus, admittedly without great confidence, one can imagine a future time when the central religious denominations were scientistic in character, rather than biblical.

Conclusion

Two factors may facilitate replacement of one religious tradition by another: a cultural shift that discredits the assumptions of the old religion and a social collapse that renders the society vulnerable to new movements. Our discussion cannot be very precise, and historical analogies are not very compelling, but these factors might render modern Western society very much like the ancient Roman Empire: a drifting, sinking hulk ready to be overwhelmed by new religious waves.

First, significant parts of modern culture seem to have moved rather far from the assumptions of the Judeo-Christian-Islamic tradition. Most obviously, science contradicts specific statements in the Bible, and promulgates a set of assumptions at variance with basic beliefs. However, we are not at all sure that science directly shapes the thinking of very many citizens, even today. McClosky (1983) reviewed a number of studies that revealed few people understand even the most elementary principles of Newtonian physics. Lightman, Miller, and Leadbeater (1987) surveyed Americans concerning astronomy, finding that they knew very little about it and tended to reject some of the most basic discoveries of the twentieth century, such as the expansion of the universe. Certainly, many scientists profess religion, especially if their work is in practical or narrow fields and does not require them to take a stand on fundamental questions about human existence.

Second, major religious traditions do not wink out of existence in an instant. While a new religious movement can achieve a substantial growth rate and sustain it for decades, this is not enough to create the flourishing range of denominations at various levels of tension that constitutes a completely new religious economy. Thus, an essential condition for the rapid rise to dominance of an entirely novel religion might be catastrophic social conditions that practically destroyed the society that supported the old religion. The nearest thing in the twentieth century is the rise of Marxism, which succeeded only after Russia was essentially defeated in World War I and China suffered a series of revolutions culminating in what amounted to defeat by the Japanese. The formal fall of Rome occurred only after Christianity supplanted paganism as the official religion, but Mediterranean society had lost its cultural vitality and had entered an eventually fatal slide which the early Church was able to exploit.

Perhaps we should re-examine the classic work of Pitirim Sorokin on social and cultural dynamics, which to a great extent is a theory of secularization (Sorokin, 1937). For reasons which escape me, Sorokin is almost completely ignored by sociologists today; for example, his theories of society get no mention in Jonathan Turner's influential theory textbooks (Turner 1986; Turner, Beeghley and Powers 1989). Sorokin's major work is wordy, nearly three thousand pages long, and it is subtle, thus defying brief synopsis. However, the following rough ideas from Sorokin's thought bear

418

on the conditions under which totally new religious movements may gain prominence.

Sorokin believed that smoothly functioning societies tend to have rather coherent systems of beliefs and values, which can be analyzed in terms of a set of ideal types. Most important are the "ideational" and "sensate" categories, each being a different conception of truth with its own particular cultural style and orientation toward religion. Over historical time, societies tend to swing from one extreme to another, and the movement from ideational to sensate is practically equivalent to secularization.

Ideational culture believes that reality is nonmaterial, and it strives to achieve goals that are primarily spiritual (Sorokin, 1937: I:72–74). In contrast, sensate culture does not believe in any supersensory reality, places all its conviction in the world of the senses, and seeks satisfaction of sensual desires. In the context of modern society, religion is ideational, while science is sensate. The fall of Rome and the rise of Christianity marked an exceedingly painful transition from a sensate to an ideational form (Sorokin, 1937: II:78–79), while the transformation back to sensate culture was more gradual and is only now being completed. Extreme sensate society is Epicurean, in the classical meaning of the term, marked by pessimism as well as sensuousness, leading to a collapse of values that prepares the way for emergence of a new ideational phase.

Writing over half a century ago, Sorokin said the sensate collapse was already well-advanced. If he were alive today, he would be warning that chaos was just around the corner, but in historical terms a corner may take a century or two to turn. He wrote, "Neither the decay of the Western society and culture, nor their death, is predicted by my thesis. What it does assert . . . is simply that one of the most important phases of their life history, the Sensate, is now ending and that we are turning toward its opposite through a period of transition. Such a period is always disquieting, grim, cruel, bloody, and painful" (Sorokin, 1937: III: 537). In the extreme social disorganization and cultural anomie of this great crisis, entirely new religions could gain a foothold, grow to prominence, and proliferate a full range of denominations and sects.

Sorokin wrote in the aftermath of the First World War, aware that the shadows of a second great conflagration were lengthening across the globe. A sense of doom pervades much European art, philosophy, and even music of the first two-thirds of the twentieth century, and one wonders if this was more a result of the two world wars than of inexorable cultural collapse. As I write these words, there is every hope that the great clouds that have darkened the world for nearly a century have finally parted, and there seems every reason to believe that Western Civilization has a long and brilliant future ahead of it. However, some regions seem locked in local versions of the cultural collapse Sorokin predicted, and they may be fertile fields for the emergence of radical new religious movements.

As we saw in Chapter 12, reports from Russia and Eastern Europe indicate substantial magical and religious revivals in progress. Writers have tended to misperceive this, however, as an upsurge of anti-scientism (Kapitza 1991). To be sure, Marxism pretended to be scientific, and its collapse may discredit real science in some people's minds. Furthermore, the abysmal environmental record of the former Soviet bloc may convince some residents that science-based industrialization was at fault for polluting nature. But we think the flowering of magical client services and religious movements in Russia has far deeper roots than a mere reaction against Marxist technocracy.

In *The Future of Religion*, Stark and I discussed the failure of the Soviet Union to eradicate religion, and the growing religious movements that already a decade ago were pressing hard against the walls of their prison. We predicted that religion would leap again to prominence if ever the tyrannical state were destroyed, and that is what is happening. We wish we had possessed the powers of prophecy to imagine that the Soviet regime could have so swiftly and so completely collapsed. And I wonder what new surprises will occur between the day I write these lines and the day the reader sees them. But a liberated Marxist society is one perfectly designed to generate new religious movements.

All people need more than life offers them, and thus every society is a fertile ground for religions. Soviet despotism at first sought to eradicate religion, then merely to contain and control it. Generations of Russians were raised without religious socialization. Now, millions of them hunger for some kind of faith, yet their longings are not contained within Russian Orthodoxy. Some are quickly regaining the lost faith of their grandfathers, but others are ready to follow new messiahs. Consider the conditions under which more than 300,000,000 million people live: extreme economic distress, social disorganization, cultural collapse, and potentially bloody ethnic rivalries. Add to this the fact that many are well-educated and live in cosmopolitan, industrial societies, and you have a recipe for the explosion of novel faiths. Some new religions being born right now in St. Petersburg or Kiev may prove exportable, spreading throughout the world.

Conclusion: The Human System

"And this, too, shall pass away." These famous words were spoken by Abraham Lincoln in a speech to Wisconsin farmers in 1859. He told a fable about an Eastern monarch who had commanded his wise men to discover a sentence that would always be appropriate, and this melancholy idea was the result. Lincoln hoped that the United States might prove an exception to this universal maxim, and we are sure he would have wanted to exempt Christianity, as well. Yet the great faiths of the classical world have vanished, and there is every reason to believe that every particular religious tradition would eventually meet the same fate, whether through total collapse or through such radical transformation that it was no longer recognizable.

Yet religion in general will survive the demise of any particular religious organization or tradition. New religions are constantly emerging. Only a tiny fraction will grow to prominence, but out of these will develop flourishing new traditions complete with their own sets of denominations of both low and high tension. Furthermore, the great world religions seem unlikely to die in the foreseeable future. They possess such tremendous cultural and human resources and have shown themselves so adaptable in the past, that it would be foolhardy to predict anything but continued health well beyond the lifetime of the author and reader of this book. However, some very important religions have faced the very real danger of extinction within our lifetimes.

We must not forget for a moment that sinister and powerful forces did their best to eradicate Judaism in the early 1940s, and this danger has not entirely passed. Too little attention is given to the current sorry condition of Taoism and Confucianism, which still suffer repression. The fact that they have almost completely been limited to one nation does not brand them insignificant; with a fifth of the human population, China is a world unto itself. A few years ago, when there was great credibility to the "domino theory" that Marxism could easily spread to all of Asia, even Buddhism was in danger, and it certainly has been severely damaged by the communists. Our theory says little about the murder of a religion, however, focusing more on what might be called death by natural causes.

The present great world faiths arose within or at the peripheries of traditional agricultural empires, so we might wonder what validity the thoughts of their ancient authors might still hold in a postindustrial world society. In each culture, the holy books of these religions are typically the oldest books still read by substantial numbers of people. Perhaps, therefore, these faiths are permanent features of humanity, because they enshrine the most fundamental wisdom of our species, established at the very dawn of history. If there exist any eternal verities, they are to be found in the Bible and the other ancient religious scriptures.

Given the variety of religions around the globe, and the very limited successes achieved by foreign missionary movements in societies that already possessed major religions, it is difficult to foresee the triumph of one major faith over all the others. The vision of Vivekananda at the 1893 World's Parliament of Religions seems destined to triumph: the world will always be home to many great religions, not just one. And in that great assembly of faiths, surely there is room for yet-unborn religious traditions.

More than four thousand years ago, men and women whose names have long since been forgotten built circles of great stones at sacred spots across France and England, that today bear names like Carnac, Avebury, and Stonehenge. We do not know a word of their language. We do not know what stories they told to explain the vast world around them, or the prayers they spoke to comfort the parents of a dying child. From their monuments we infer that their gods dwelled in the sky, perhaps in the sun, moon and stars. Able to climb no higher than the branches of a hilltop tree, their perspective on the universe must have been limited. And yet they dreamed cosmic dreams, and their desire-driven imagination postulated the existence of forces beyond their comprehension.

We, who have touched the face of the moon and sent robot probes beyond all planets of the solar system, understand that our entire world is but a tiny speck of dust lost in an immense vastness. Many of us believe that God, the master of the universe, loves us despite our sins and our physical insignificance. What will be the future of our faith, more than four thousand years ahead? The images of carolers singing Christmas songs under the hurtling moons of Mars, and of a priest hearing confession on an outer satellite of Saturn, are faintly ridiculous. And yet, if humanity does move outward toward the stars, it will take its familiar religions with it. The line from Stonehenge to here extends onward to infinity, and the religious movement that quarried those stones, then dragged them miles to the site, will be born again on other worlds. Religion is a prime component of the system of human life, that moves across all time and links the ancient past with the unimaginable future. Religion will undergo schism, innovation, and transformation, sending echoes throughout human society, unto the end of time.

In describing his own impending death, whether in the Glastonbury zodiac or elsewhere, King Arthur gave us words to understand the constant renewal of faith through religious movements: "The old order changeth, yielding place to new; and God fulfills himself in many ways."

Bibliography

Axelrod, Robert
  1984 *The Evolution of Cooperation*. New York: Basic Books.
Ackerknecht, Erwin H.
  1943 "Psychopathology, Primitive Medicine and Primitive Culture,"
  Bulletin of the History of Medicine 14:30–67.
Ad Hoc Committee of Members of the Unification Church
  1979 *Our Response to the Report of October 31, 1978 on the Investigation of Korean-American Relations*. New York: Holy Spirit Association for the Unification of World Christianity.
Adler, Alfred
  1927 *Understanding Human Nature*. Greenwich, Connecticut: Fawcett,
  [1954].
  1928 *Individual Psychology*. Totowa, New Jersey: Littlefield, Adams
  and Company, [1968].
Adler, Margot
  1979 *Drawing Down the Moon: Witches, Pagans, Druids, Goddess-
  Worshippers and other Pagans in America Today*. Boston: Beacon
  Press.
Agel, Jerome (ed.)
  1968 *The Making of Kubrick's 2001*. New York: New American Library.
Albrecht, Stan L., Bruce A. Chadwick, and David S. Alcorn
  1977 "Religiosity and Deviance: Application of an Attitude-Behavior
  Contingent Consistency Model," *Journal for the Scientific Study of Religion* 16:263–274.
Alcock, Leslie
  1971 *Arthur's Britain*. Harmondsworth, England: Penguin.

Alfred, Randall H.
  1976   "The Church of Satan." In *The New Religious Consciousness*, edited by Charles Y. Glock and Robert N. Bellah. Berkeley: University of California Press. 180–202.
Allen, Don
  1979   "TM at Folsom Prison: A Critique of Abrams and Siegel," *Criminal Justice and Behavior*, 6(1):9–12.
Ammerman, Nancy T.
  1993   "Report to the Justice and Treasury Departments." Letter reprinted in *Recommendations of Experts for Improvement in Federal Law Enforcement After Waco*. Washington, D.C.: Department of Justice and Department of the Treasury.
  1995 "Waco, Federal Law Enforcement, and Scholars of Religion." In *Armageddon in Waco*, edited by Stuart A. Wright. Chicago: University of Chicago Press. 282–296.
Andelson, Jonathan G.
  1985   "The Gift to be Single: Celibacy and Religious Enthusiasm In the Community of True Inspiration," *Communal Societies* 5:1–32.
Anderson, Courtney
  1956   To The Golden Shore: The Life of Adoniram Judson. Boston: Little, Brown.
Anderson, Eric
  1987   "The Millerite Use of Prophecy: A Case Study of a 'Striking Fulfillment.' " In *The Disappointed: Millerism and Millenarianism in the Nineteenth Century*, edited by Ronald L. Numbers and Jonathan M. Butler. Bloomington: Indiana University Press. 78–91.
Andrews, Edward Deming
  1953   *The People Called Shakers*. New York: Oxford University Press.
Anonymous
  1846   *Investigator, or a Defense of the Order, Government and Economy of the United Society Called Shakers against Sundry Charges and Legislative Proceedings*. New York: Egbert, Hovey and King. Reprint of 1828 edition.
Anonymous
  1849   *Report of the Examination of the Shakers of Canterbury and Enfield before New-Hampshire Legislature at the November Session, 1846*. Concord, New Hampshire: Ervin B. Tripp.
Anonymous
  1888   *Testimonies of the Life, Character, Revelations and Doctrines of Mother Ann Lee and the Elders with Her*. Albany, New York: Weed, Parsons.
Anonymous
  1973   *Divine Principle*. New York: Holy Spirit Association for the Unification of World Christianity.

Anonymous
  1985 *Constitutional Issues in the Case of Reverend Moon: Amicus Briefs Presented to the United States Supreme Court*. New York: Edwin Mellen Press.
Anonymous
  1990 *Reverend Sun Myung Moon*. (Book in Russian and English). McLean, Virginia: International Peace Foundation
Ansbro, John J.
  1982 *Martin Luther King, Jr.: The Making of a Mind*. Maryknoll, New York: Orbis.
Arden-Smith, Tara H.
  1995 "Hindus Consecrate a Sacred Symbol of Their Ties to India," *Washington Post* (July 10):C1, C4.
Arjomand, Said Amir
  1995 "Unity and Diversity in Islamic Fundamentalism." In *Fundamentalisms Comprehended*, edited by Martin E. Marty and R. Scott Appleby. Chicago: University of Chicago Press. 179–198.
Arnold, J. Phillip
  1994 "The Davidian Dilemma—To Obey God or Man?" In *From the Ashes: Making Sense of Waco*, edited by James R. Lewis. Lanham, Maryland: Roman and Littlefield. 23–31.
Arthur, David T.
  1987 "Josua V. Himes and the Cause of Adventism." In *The Disappointed: Millerism and Millenarianism in the Nineteenth Century*, edited by Ronald L. Numbers and Jonathan M. Butler. Bloomington: Indiana University Press. 36–58.
Ash, Brian
  1977 "Fringe Cults." In *The Visual Encyclopedia of Science Fiction*, edited by Brian Ash. New York: Harmony. 333–342.
Ashe, Geoffrey
  1968 (ed.) *The Quest for Arthur's Britain*. London: Paladin.
  1979 *The Glastonbury Tor Maze*. Glastonbury, England: Gothic Image.
Ashton, Graham
  1974 *The Realm of King Arthur*. Newport, Isle of Wight: Dixon.
Attarian, John
  1995 "The Fiscal Crisis of the Secular Age," *The World and I*, 10 (November):297–311.
Attis, Diana and Lindsay Smith (ed.)
  1980 *The Empire Strikes Back Notebook*. New York: Ballantine.
Bachrach, Arthur J., and Evan G. Pattishall
  1960 "An Experiment in Universal and Personal Validation," *Psychiatry* 23: 267–270.

Bibliography

Bainbridge, Lucy Seaman
  1904   "Woman's Branch," *New York City Mission and Tract Society Monthly* 16: 13–28.
  1906   *Eighty-Third Annual Report of the Woman's Branch of the New York City Mission and Tract Society*. New York: New York City Mission Society.
  1917   *Helping the Helpless in Lower New York*. New York: Fleming H. Revell.
  1924   *Yesterdays*. New York: Fleming H. Revell.
Bainbridge, William Folwell
  1882   *Along the Lines at the Front: A General Survey of Baptist Home and Foreign Missions*. Philadelphia: American Baptist Publication Society.
Bainbridge, William Sims
  1976   *The Spaceflight Revolution*. New York: Wiley-Interscience.
  1978   *Satan's Power: A Deviant Psychotherapy Cult*. Berkeley: University of California Press.
  1981a   "Biorhythms: Evaluating a Pseudoscience." In *Paranormal Borderlands of Science*, edited by Kendrick Frazer. Buffalo, New York: Prometheus. 191–207.
  1981b   "Chariots of the Gullible." In *Paranormal Borderlands of Science*, edited by Kendrick Frazer. Buffalo, New York: Prometheus. 332–347.
  1982   "Shaker Demographics 1840–1900: An Example of the Use of Census Enumeration Schedules," *Journal for the Scientific Study of Religion* 21:352–365.
  1984a   "The Decline of the Shakers: Evidence from the United States Census," *Communal Societies* 4:19–34.
  1984b   "Religious Insanity in America: The Official Nineteenth-Century Theory," *Sociological Analysis* 45:223–240.
  1985a   "Cultural Genetics." In Rodney Stark ed. *Religious Movements: Genesis, Exodus, and Numbers*. New York: Rose of Sharon. 157–198.
  1985b   "Utopian Communities: Theoretical Issues." In *The Sacred in a Secular Age*, edited by Phillip E. Hammond. Berkeley: University of California Press. 21–35.
  1986a   *Dimensions of Science Fiction*. Cambridge: Harvard University Press.
  1986b   *Experiments in Psychology*. Belmont, California: Wadsworth.
  1987   *Sociology Laboratory*. Belmont, California: Wadsworth.
  1989a   "Religious Ecology of Deviance," *American Sociological Review* 54:288–295.
  1989b   "Wandering Souls: Mobility and Unorthodoxy." In *Exploring the Paranormal*, edited by George K. Zollschan, John F. Schumaker, and Greg F. Walsh. Bridport, Dorset, England: Prism. 237–249.
  1990   "Explaining the Church Membership Rate," *Social Forces* 68: 1287–1296.

1991   "Social Construction from Within: Satan's Process." In *The Satanism Scare*, edited by James T. Richardson and David G. Bromley. New York: Aldine de Gruyter. 297–310.

1992a   *Social Research Methods and Statistics*. Belmont, California: Wadsworth.

1992b   "The Sociology of Conversion." In *Handbook of Religious Conversion*, edited by H. Newton Malony and Samuel Southard. Birmingham, Alabama: Religious Education Press. 178–191.

1994a   "General Semantics." In *The Encyclopedia of Language and Linguistics*. Oxford: Pergamon. 1361.

1994b   "New Religious Movements," In *The Encyclopedia of Language and Linguistics*. Oxford: Pergamon. 2791–2793.

1995   "Social Influence and Religious Pluralism." *Group Processes* 12:1– 18.

Bainbridge, William Sims, Edward E. Brent, Kathleen M. Carley, David R. Heise, Michael W. Macy, Barry Markovsky, and John Skvoretz

1994   "Artificial Social Intelligence," *Annual Review of Sociology* 20:407–436.

Bainbridge, William Sims, and Daniel H. Jackson

1981 "The Rise and Decline of Transcendental Meditation." In *The Social Impact of New Religious Movements*, edited by Bryan Wilson. New York: Rose of Sharon Press. 135–158.

Bainbridge, William Sims, and Rodney Stark

1979   "Cult Formation: Three Compatible Models," *Sociological Analysis* 40:283–295.

1980a   "Client and Audience Cults in America," *Sociological Analysis* 41:199–214.

1980b   "Sectarian Tension," *Review of Religious Research* 2:105–124.

1981a   "The 'Consciousness Reformation' Reconsidered," *Journal for the Scientific Study of Religion* 20:1–16.

1981b   "Friendship, Religion and the Occult," *Review of Religious Research* 22:313– 327.

1981c   "Suicide, Homicide, and Religion: Durkheim Reassessed," *Annual Review of the Social Sciences of Religion* 5:33–56.

1981d   "Superstitions: Old and New." In *Paranormal Borderlands of Science*, edited by Kendrick Frazer. Buffalo, New York: Prometheus. 46–59.

Bak, Per, Kan Chen, and Michael Creutz

1989   "Self-Organized Criticality in the 'Game of Life,'" *Nature* 342:780–782.

Baldwin, Lewis V.

1991   *There Is a Balm in Gilead: The Cultural Roots of Martin Luther King, Jr.* Minneapolis: Fortress.

Barker, Eileen
  1984 *The Making of a Moonie: Choice or Brainwashing?* New York: Basil Blackwell.
Barrows, John Henry
  1893 *The World's Parliament of Religions.* Chicago: Parliament Publishing Company.
Barthel, Diane L.
  1984 *Amana: From Pietist Sect to American Community.* Lincoln: University of Nebraska Press.
Bates, Paulina
  1849 *The Divine Book of Holy and Eternal Wisdom.* Canterbury, New Hampshire: Shakers.
Batson, C. Daniel, Patricia Schoenrade, and W. Larry Ventis
  1993 *Religion and the Individual.* New York: Oxford University Press.
Baum, L. Frank
  1900 *The Wonderful Wizard of Oz.* New York: Ballantine [1979].
Beal, Fred E.
  1937 *Proletarian Journey.* New York: Da Capo [1971].
Bear, Henry B.
  1987 "Henry Bear's Advent Experiences." In *The Disappointed: Millerism and Millenarianism in the Nineteenth Century*, edited by Ronald L. Numbers and Jonathan M. Butler. Bloomington: Indiana University Press. 217–226. Reprint of an undated mid-nineteenth-century pamphlet published by the Shakers of Whitewater, Ohio.
Becker, Gary S.
  1993 *Human Capital.* Chicago: University of Chicago Press.
Beckford, James A.
  1975 *The Trumpet of Prophecy: A Sociological Study of Jehovah's Witnesses.* New York: John Wiley and Sons.
Bell, Daniel
  1971 "Religion in the Sixties," *Social Research* 38:447–497.
Benedict, Ruth
  1934 *Patterns of Culture.* Boston: Houghton Mifflin.
Benson, J. Kenneth and James Otis Smith
  1967 "The Harvard Drug Controversy: A Case Study of Subject Manipulation and Social Structure." In *Ethics, Politics, and Social Research*, edited by Gideon Sjoberg. New York: Schenkman.
Berger, Peter L., and Thomas Luckmann
  1966 *The Social Construction of Reality.* Garden City, New York: Doubleday.
Bester, Alfred
  1952 *The Demolished Man. Galaxy* 3 (January):4–66; (February):101–158; (March):101–158.
  1956 *The Stars My Destination (Tiger, Tiger!). Galaxy* 12 (Octo-

ber):8–58; *Galaxy* 13 (November):88–143; (December):88–142; (January 1957):98–142.

Blake, William
1946 *The Portable Blake*. New York:Viking.

Blau, Eleanor
1974 "Young Sect No Longer Hails Devil," *New York Times* (December 1):53.

Blau, Judith R., Kenneth C. Land, and Kent Redding
1992 "The Expansion of Religious Affiliation: An Explanation of the Growth of Church Participation in the United States, 1850–1930," *Social Science Research* 21:329–352.

Blau, Judith R., Kent Redding, and Kenneth C. Land
1993 "Ethnocultural Cleavages and the Growth of Church Membership in the United States, 1860–1930," *Sociological Forum* 8:609–637.

Blau, Peter
1964 Exchange and Power in Social Life. New York: Wiley.

Bliss, Sylvester
1853 *Memoirs of William Miller*. Boston: Joshua V. Himes.

Bloomfield, Harold H., Michael Petter Cain, Dennis T. Jaffe, and Robert E. Korey
1975 *TM—Discovering Inner Energy and Overcoming Stress*. New York: Dell.

Boak, Arthur E. R.
1955 *A History of Rome to 565 A.D.* New York: Macmillan.

Boas, Franz
1908 "Decorative Designs of Alaskan Needlecases." In *Race, Language, and Culture* by Franz Boas. New York: Free Press [1966].

Bord, Janet, and Colin Bord
1974 *Mysterious Britain*. St. Albans, England: Granada.

Borowick, Susan Claire
1994 "Falsely Accused and Jailed in Argentina," *Persecution Endtime News* 3:1–8, 4:1–12.

Boudon, Raymond
1981 *The Logic of Social Action*. London: Routlege and Kegan Paul.

Bradley, Martin B., Norman M. Green, Jr., Dale E. Jones, Mac Lynn, and Lou McNeil
1992 *Churches and Church Membership in the United States, 1990.* Atlanta, Georgia: Glenmary Research Center.

Brandt, John L.
1926 *Great Bible Questions: Twenty Sermons on Interrogatory Texts*. New York: Fleming H. Revell.

Braude, Ann
1989 *Radical Spirits*. Boston: Beacon Press.

Breault, Kevin D.
    1989   "New Evidence on Religious Pluralism, Urbanism, and Religious Participation," *American Sociological Review* 54:1048–1053.
Bromley, David G.
    1983   "Conservatorships and Deprogramming: Legal and Political Prospects." In *The Brainwashing/Deprogramming Controversy: Sociological, Psychological, Legal and Historical Perspectives*, edited by David G. Bromley and James T. Richardson. New York: Edwin Mellen. 267–293.
Bromley, David G. and Anson D. Shupe, Jr.
    1979   *"Moonies" in America: Cult, Church, and Crusade.* Beverly Hills, California: Sage.
    1980   "Financing the New Religions: A Resource Mobilization Perspective," *Journal for the Scientific Study of Religion* 19:3.
    1981   *Strange Gods: The Great American Cult Scare.* Boston: Beacon.
Bromley, David G. and Edward D. Silver
    1995   "The Davidian Tradition." In *Armageddon in Waco*, edited by Stuart A. Wright. Chicago: University of Chicago Press. 43–72.
Brown, J. A. C.
    1967   *Freud and the Post-Freudians.* Baltimore: Penguin.
Bugliosi, Vincent, and Curt Gentry
    1974   *Helter Skelter: The True Story of the Manson Murders.* New York: Norton.
Bull, Malcolm
    1989   "The Seventh-Day Adventists: Heretics of American Civil Religion," *Sociological Analysis* 50:177–187.
Bureau of the Census
    1930   *Religious Bodies: 1926.* Washington, D.C.: U.S. Government Printing Office.
Burkett, Steven R., and Mervin White
    1974   "Hellfire and Delinquency: Another Look," *Journal for the Scientific Study of Religion* 13:455–462.
Burtt, Cyril
    1967   "Psychology and Parapsychology." In *Science and ESP*, edited by J. R. Smythies. New York: Routledge and Kegan Paul. 61–141.
Butler, Jonathan M.
    1987   "The Making of a New Order: Millerism and the Origins of Seventh-day Adventism." In *The Disappointed: Millerism and Millenarianism in the Nineteenth Century*, edited by Ronald L. Numbers and Jonathan M. Butler. Bloomington: Indiana University Press. 189–208.
    1992   "The Historian as Heretic." In *Prophetess of Health: Ellen G. White and the Origins of Seventh-day Adventist Health Reform* by Ronald L. Numbers, Knoxville: University of Tennessee Press. xxv–lxviii.

Caine, Mary
  1978   *The Glastonbury Zodiac*. Ashford, England: Flexishape.
Call, Deborah (ed.)
  1980   *The Art of the Empire Strikes Back*. New York: Ballantine.
Cantril, Hadley
  1941   *The Psychology of Social Movements*. New York: Wiley.
Cantril, Hadley and Muzafer Sherif
  1941 "The Kingdom of Father Divine." In *The Psychology of Social Movements* by Hadley Cantril. New York: John Wiley. 123–143.
Capt, E. Raymond
  1983   *The Traditions of Glastonbury*. Thousand Oaks, California: Artisan.
Carden, Maren Lockwood
  1969   *Oneida: Utopian Community to Modern Corporation*. Baltimore: Johns Hopkins University Press.
Carley, Kathleen
  1991   "A Theory of Group Stability," *American Sociological Review* 56:331–354.
Carroll, Michael P.
  1983   "Visions of the Virgin Mary: The Effect of Family Structures on Marian Apparitions," *Journal for the Scientific Study of Religion* 22:205–221.
  1985 "The Virgin Mary at LaSalette and Lourdes: Whom Did the Children See?" *Journal for the Scientific Study of Religion* 24:56–74.
Charity Frauds Bureau
  1974   "Final Report on the Activities of the Children of God," report delivered to Louis J. Lefkowitz, Attorney General of the State of New York.
Cheney, Margaret
  1981   *Tesla: Man Out of Time*. New York: Dell.
Chidester, David
  1988   *Salvation and Suicide: An Interpretation of Jim Jones, the Peoples Temple, and Jonestown*. Bloomington: Indiana University Press.
  1990   *Patterns of Transcendence: Religion, Death, and Dying*. Belmont, California: Wadsworth.
Christiano, Kevin J.
  1987   *Religious Diversity and Social Change*. New York: Cambridge University Press.
Churchill, Winson Spencer
  1899   *The River War: An Historical Account of the Reconquest of the Sudan*. New York: Longmans, Green.
Clark, Elmer T.
  1937   *The Small Sects in America*. Nashville, Tennessee: Cokesbury.
Clark, Samuel Delbert
  1948   *Church and Sect in Canada*. Toronto: University of Toronto Press.

Bibliography

Clarke, Arthur C.
    1968   *2001: A Space Odyssey*. New York: New American Library.
Coffin, William Sloane
    1927   "Historical Address at the Centennial of the New York City Mission Society." New York: New York City Mission Society.
Cohen, Daniel
    1976   *Biorhythms in Your Life*. Greenwich, Connecticut: Fawcett.
Cohn, Norman
    1961   *The Pursuit of the Millennium*. New York: Harper.
Coleman, James
    1988   "Social Capital in the Creation of Human Capital," *American Journal of Sociology* 94(supplement):95–120.
Colson, Charles W.
    1976   *Born Again*. (Large type edition) Boston: G. K. Hall.
Cooley, Charles H.
    1909   *Social Organization*. New York: Scribner's.
Coon, Robert
    1984   *Elliptical Navigations through the Multitudinous Aethyrs of Avalon*. Street, England: Excalibur.
Coulson, Noel and Doreen Hinchcliffe
    1978   "Women and Law Reform in Contemporary Islam." In *Women in the Muslim World*, edited by Lois Beck and Nikki Keddie. Cambridge: Harvard University Press. 37–51.
Crowley, Aleister
    1969   *The Confessions of Aleister Crowley*. Edited by John Symonds and Kenneth Grant. New York: Hill and Wang.
Cunningham, Agnes, J. Robert Nelson, William L. Hendricks, and Jorge Lara-Braud
    1978   "Critique of the Theology of the Unification Church as Set Forth in *Divine Principle*." In *Science, Sin, and Scholarship*, edited by Irving Louis Horowitz. Cambridge, Massachusetts: MIT Press. 103–118.
Curry, Melvin D.
    1992   *Jehovah's Witnesses: The Millenarian World of the Watch Tower*. New York: Garland.
Dain, Norman
    1964   *Concepts of Insanity in the United States, 1789–1865*. New Brunswick, New Jersey: Rutgers University Press.
Dale, Arbie
    1976   *Biorhythm*. New York: Pocket Books.
Däniken, Erich von
    1971   *Chariots of the Gods?* New York: Bantam.
    1972   *Gods from Outer Space*. New York: Bantam.
    1974   *The Gold of the Gods*. New York: Bantam.

432

1975a   *Meine Welt in Bildern*. Munich: Knaur.

1975b   *Miracles of the Gods*. New York: Dell.

Darnton, Robert

1970   *Mesmerism and the End of the Enlightenment in France*. New York: Schocken.

Davies, James C.

1962   "Toward a General Theory of Revolution," *American Sociological Review* 27:5–19.

Davis, Deborah

1984   *The Children of God: The Inside Story*. Grand Rapids, Michigan: Zondervan.

Davis, James A., and Tom W. Smith

1991   *General Social Surveys, 1972–1991: Cumulative Codebook*. Chicago: National Opinion Research Center.

Davis, Kingsley

1937   "The Sociology of Prostitution," *American Sociological Review* 2:744–755.

Davis, Maxine W., and Gregory J. Tetrault

1975   *The Organic Traveller*. New York: Grasshopper Press.

Davis, Rex and James T. Richardson

1976   "The Organization and Functioning of the Children of God," *Sociological Analysis* 37:321–339.

Dean, John W.

1976   *Blind Ambition*. New York: Simon and Schuster.

1982   *Lost Honor*. Los Angeles: Stratford.

De Forest, Louis Effingham

1950   *Ancestry of William Seaman Bainbridge*. Oxford: The Scrivener Press.

De Grimston, Robert

1970a   *The Gods and Their People*. London: The Process.

1970b   *The Gods on War*. Chicago: The Process.

Della Fave, L. Richard, and George A. Hillery

1980   "Status Inequality in a Religious Community," *Social Forces* 59:62–84.

Demerath, Nicholas J.

1965   *Social Class in American Protestantism*. Chicago: Rand McNally.

Dennis, Edward S. G.

1993   *Evaluation of the Handling of the Branch Davidian Stand-off in Waco, Texas, February 28 to Appril 19, 1993*. Washington, D. C. Department of Justice.

Denniston, Denise, Peter McWilliams, and Barry Geller

1975   *The TM Book—How to Enjoy the Rest of Your Life*. New York: Warner.

Denzin, Norman K.
  1994   "Symbolic Interactionism." In *The Encyclopedia of Language and Linguistics*. Oxford: Pergamon. 4449–4452.
Desroche, Henri
  1971   *The American Shakers*. Amherst: The University of Massachusetts Press.
Deutsch, Morton, and Robert M. Krauss
  1960   "The Effect of Threat upon Interpersonal Bargaining," *Journal of Abnormal and Social Psychology* 61:181–189.
Deutscher, Irwin
  1973   *What We Say/What We Do*. Glenview, Illinois: Scott Foresman.
Dharmapala, Anagarika
  1893   "The World's Debt to Buddha." In *The World's Parliament of Religions*, edited by John Henry Barrows. Chicago: Parliament Publishing Company. 862–880.
Dittes, James E.
  1971   "Typing the Typologies: Some Parallels in the Career of Church-Sect and Intrinsic-Extrinsic," *Journal for the Scientific Study of Religion* 10:375–383.
Divine, Mother (Edna Divine)
  1982   *The Peace Mission Movement*. Philadelphia: Imperial Press.
Doan, Ruth Alden
  1987a   *The Miller Heresy, Millennialism, and American Culture*. Philadelphia: Temple University Press.
  1987b   "Millerism and Evangelical Culture." In *The Disappointed: Millerism and Millenarianism in the Nineteenth Century*, edited by Ronald L. Numbers and Jonathan M. Butler. Bloomington: Indiana University Press. 118–138.
Dobbs, Catherine R.
  1947   *Freedom's Will, the Society of Separatists of Zoar*. New York: William Frederick Press.
Doherty, Robert W.
  1967   *The Hicksite Separation*. New Brunswick, New Jersey: Rutgers University Press.
Dollard, John, Neil E. Miller, Leonard W. Doob, O. H. Mowrer, and Robert R. Sears
  1939   *Frustration and Aggression*. New Haven: Yale University Press.
Durkheim, Emile
  1897   *Suicide*. New York: Free Press [1951].
Eads, Hervey L.
  1884   *Shaker Sermons*. South Union, Kentucky: United Society of Believers.

Earle, John R., Dean D. Knudsen and Donald W. Shriver, Jr.
1976   *Spindles and Spires: A Re-Study of Religion and Social Change in Gastonia.* Atlanta, Georgia: John Knox Press.
Economist, The
1994   "Islam and the West," *The Economist* (August 6):3–18.
Eister, Allan W.
1967   "Toward a Radical Critique of Church-Sect Typologizing," *Journal for the Scientific Study of Religion* 6:85–90.
Ellis, Timothy Craig, and Rebecca Smith Hasty
1995   *A History of Loray Baptist Church, Gastonia, North Carolina.* Gastonia, North Carolina: Loray Baptist Church
Engineer, Asghar Ali
1992   *The Rights of Women in Islam.* New York: St. Martin's.
England, R. W.
1954   "Some Aspects of Christian Science as Reflected in Letters of Testimony," *American Journal of Sociology* 59:448-453.
Erikson, Erik H.
1962   *Young Man Luther.* New York: Norton.
Ervin, Sam J., Jr.
1980   *The Whole Truth: The Watergate Conspiracy.* New York: Random House.
Esposito, John L.
1982   *Women in Muslim Family Law.* Syracuse, New York: Syracuse University Press.
Faris, Robert E. L., and H. Warren Dunham
1939   *Mental Disorders in Urban Areas.* Chicago: University of Chicago Press [1967].
Farmer, Philip Jose
1977   "Religion and Myths." In *The Visual Encyclopedia of Science Fiction*, edited by Brian Ash. New York: Harmony. 222–236.
Fenn, Richard K.
1978   *Toward a Theory of Secularization.* Ellington, Connecticut: Society for the Scientific Study of Religion.
Ferm, Vergilius
1945   *An Encyclopedia of Religion.* New York: Philosophical Library.
Festinger, Leon
1957   *A Theory of Cognitive Dissonance.* Stanford, California: Stanford University Press.
Festinger, Leon, Henry W. Riecken, and Stanley Schachter
1956   *When Prophecy Fails.* New York: Harper and Row, 1956.
Finch, William J., and Elizabeth Finch
1971   *Who's Who in the Psychic World.* Phoenix, Arizona: Psychic Register International.

Finke, Roger
    1989   "Demographics of Religious Participation: An Ecological Approach, 1850 1980," *Journal for the Scientific Study of Religion* 28:45–58.

Finke, Roger, and Rodney Stark
    1986   "Turning Pews Into People: Estimating 19th Century Church Membership," *Journal for the Scientific Study of Religion* 25:180–192.
    1988   "Religious Economies and Sacred Canopies: Religious Mobilization in American Cities, 1906," *American Sociological Review* 53:41–49.
    1989   "How the Upstart Sects Won America: 1776–1850," *Journal for the Scientific Study of Religion* 28:27–44.
    1992   *The Churching of America 1776–1990*. New Brunswick, New Jersey, 1992.

Fitzpatrick, Joseph P.
    1967   "The Role of Religion in Programs for the Prevention and Correction of Crime and Delinquency." In *Juvenile Delinquency and Youth Crime*, Task force on Juvenile Delinquency, The President's Commission on Law Enforcement and Administration of Justice. Washington, D.C.: U.S. Government Printing Office. 317–330.

Fix, A. James
    1976   "Biorhythms and Sports Performance," *The Zetetic* 1:1 (Fall/Winter):53–57.

Flynn, John T.
    1932   *God's Gold: The Story of Rockefeller and His Times*. New York: Harcourt, Brace and Company.

Fodor, Nandor
    1971   *Freud, Jung and Occultism*. New Hyde Park, New York: University Books.

Forem, Jack
    1973   *Transcendental Meditation*. New York: Dutton.

Fort, Charles
    1941   *Lo!* New York: Garland [1975].

Foster, Lawrence
    1981a   "Free Love and Feminism: John Humphrey Noyes and the Oneida Community," *Journal of the Early Republic* 1:165–183.
    1981b   *Religion and Sexuality*. New York: Oxford University Press.

Fox, Joy, and Richard Fox
    1976   "Biorhythms for Computers," *Byte* (April):20–23.

Freud, Sigmund
    1924   *A General Introduction to Psychoanalysis*. New York: Washington Square Press.

1927   *The Future of an Illusion.* Garden City, New York: Doubleday [1961].

1930   Civilization and Its Discontents. New York: North [1961].

1939   *Moses and Monotheism.* Letchworth, England: Hogarth.

Friedland, William H.

1964   "For a Sociological Concept of Charisma," *Social Forces* 43:18–26.

Gardner, Hugh

1978   *The Children of Prosperity.* New York: St. Martin's Press.

Gardner, Martin

1957   *Fads and Fallacies in the Name of Science.* New York: Dover.

Garrow, David J.

1986   *Bearing the Cross: Martin Luther King, Jr., and the Southern Christian Leadership Conference.* New York: Vintage [1988].

Gelberg, Steven J.

1987   "The Future of Krishna Consciousness in the West: An Insider's Perspective." In *The Future of New Religious Movements*, edited by David G. Bromley and Phillip E. Hammond. Macon, Georgia: Mercer University Press. 187–209.

1989   "Exploring an Alternative Reality: Spiritual Life in ISKCON." In *Krishna Consciousness in the West*, edited by David G. Bromley and Larry D. Shinn. Lewisburg: Bucknell University Press. 135–162.

Gergen, Kenneth J.

1969   *The Psychology of Behavior Exchange.* Reading, Massachusetts: Addison Wesley.

Glastonbury Advertising Association

n.d.   *The Glastonbury Guide.* Glastonbury, England: Glastonbury Advertising Association.

Gleick, James

1987   *Chaos.* New York: Penguin.

Glock, Charles Y., and Rodney Stark

1965   *Religion and Society in Tension.* Chicago:Rand McNally.

Goffman, Erving

1961   *Asylums.* Garden City, New York: Doubleday.

Goode, Erich

1967   "Some Critical Observations on the Church-Sect Dimension," *Journal for the Scientific Study of Religion* 6:69–77.

1969   "Marijuana and the Politics of Reality," *The Journal of Health and Social Behavior.* 10:83–94.

Gosvami, Satsvarupa Dasa

1980a   *A Lifetime in Preparation.* Los Angeles: Bhaktivedanta Book Trust.

1980b   *Planting the Seed.* Los Angeles: Bhaktivedanta Book Trust.

437

1981   *Only He Could Lead Them*. Los Angeles: Bhaktivedanta Book
        Trust.

1982   *In Every Town and Village*. Los Angeles: Bhaktivedanta Book
        Trust.

Gould, Roger V.

1993   "Collective Action and Network Structure," *American Sociolog-
        ical Review* 58:182 196.

Granovetter, Mark

1973   "The Strength of Weak Ties," *American Journal of Sociology*
        78:1360–1380.

Greeley, Andrew

1989   "Protestant and Catholic: Is the Analogical Imagination Extinct?"
        American Sociological Review 54:485–502.

1990   *The Catholic Myth: The Behavior and Beliefs of American
        Catholics*. New York: Charles Scribner's Sons.

Green, Calvin and Seth Y. Wells

1823   *A Summary View of the Millennial Church, or United Society of
        Believers*. Albany, New York:Packard and Van Benthuysen.

Griffin, Wendy

1995   "The Embodied Goddess: Feminist Witchcraft and Female Divin-
        ity," *Sociology of Religion* 56:35–48.

Gurr, Ted Robert

1970   *Why Men Rebel*. Princeton, New Jersey: Princeton University Press.

Gustafson, Paul

1967   "UO-US-PS-PO: A Restatement of Troeltsch's Church-Sect Ty-
        pology," *Journal for the Scientific Study of Religion* 6:64–68.

Hadaway, C. Kirk, Kirk W. Elifson, and David M. Petersen

1984   "Religious Involvement and Drug Use among Urban Adoles-
        cents," *Journal for the Scientific Study of Religion* 23:109–128.

Hadden, Jeffrey K.

1969   *The Gathering Storm in the Churches*. Garden City, New York:
        Doubleday.

Hadden Jeffrey K. and Anson Shupe

1988   *Televangelism: Power and Politics on God's Frontier*. Henry
        Holt, New York

Hadden Jeffrey K., and C. W. Swann

1981   *Prime Time Preachers: The Rising Power of Televangelism*. Addi-
        son-Wesley, Reading, Massachusetts

Hague, George

1993   "Subtle Seduction: Why Some Christians are Turning to the New
        Age," *The Plain Truth* 58:8 (September):14–18.

Hall, John R.

1987   *Gone from the Promised Land: Jonestown in American Cultural
        History*. New Brunswick, New Jersey: Transaction.

Hall, Manly Palmer
1945   *An Encyclopedic Outline of Masonic, Hermetic, Qabbalistic and Rosicrucian Symbolic Philosophy*. Los Angeles: Philosophical Research Society.
Hancock, Graham
1995   *Fingerprints of the Gods*. New York: Crown.
Hansel, C. E. M.
1966   *ESP: A Scientific Evaluation*. New York: Scribner's.
Hao, Bai-Lin (ed.)
1984   *Chaos*. Singapore: World Scientific. [Some libraries catalogue this by author under Bai-Lin, Hao.]
Hardcastle, F.
1982   *The Chalice Well*. Glastonbury, England: Chalice Well Trust.
Hardyck, Jane Allyn, and Marcia Braden
1962   "Prophecy Fails Again: A Report of a Failure to Replication," *Journal of Abnormal and Social Psychology* 65:136–141.
Hargrove, Barbara
1983   "Social Sources and Consequences of the Brainwashing Controversy." Pp. 299-308 in *The Brainwashing/Deprogramming Controversy: Sociological, Psychological, Legal and Historical Perspectives*, edited by David G. Bromley and James T. Richardson. New York: Edwin Mellen.
Harris, George
1873   *Civilization Considered as a Science*. New York:Appleton.
Hartshorne, Hugh, and Mark A. May
1928   *Studies in Deceit*. New York:Macmillan.
Hayes, Brian
1994   "The World Wide Web," *American Scientist* 82:416–420.
Heider, Fritz
1958   *The Psychology of Interpersonal Relations*. New York: Wiley.
Heinlein, Robert A.
1942   *Beyond This Horizon. Astounding Science-Fiction* 29 (April):9–50; (May):55–97.
Herberg, Will
1955   *Protestant, Catholic, Jew*. Garden City, New York: Doubleday.
Herrigel, Eugen
1953   *Zen in the Art of Archery*. New York: Pantheon.
Higgins, Paul C., and Gary L. Albrecht.
1977   "Hellfire and Delinquency Revisited," *Social Forces* 952–58.
Hines, Terence M.
1981   Biorhythm Theory: A Critical Review. Pp. 208–218 in *Paranormal Borderlands of Science*, edited by Kendrick Frazer. Buffalo, New York: Prometheus.

Hirschi, Travis
   1969   *Causes of Delinquency.* Berkeley: University of California Press.
Hirschi, Travis, and Rodney Stark
   1969   "Hellfire and Delinquency," *Social Problems* 17:202–213.
Hoffman, Charles
   1970   *The Depression of the Nineties: An Economic History.* Westport, Connecticut: Greenwood.
Hoge, Dean R.
   1994   "Introduction: The Problem of Understanding Church Giving." *Review of Religious Research* 36:101–110.
Holmes, Thomas Rice Edward
   1888   *A History of the Indian Mutiny* London: W. H. Allen.
Homans, George C.
   1967   *The Nature of Social Science.* New York: Harcourt, Brace and World.
   1974   *Social Behavior: Its Elementary Forms.* New York: Harcourt Brace Jovanovich.
Horner, Jack, and Jan Ridolphi
   1972   *A Descriptive Dictionary of Eductivism.* Westwood Village, California: Personal Creative Freedoms Foundation.
Hostetler, John A.
   1968   *Amish Society.* Baltimore: Johns Hopkins Press.
   1974   *Hutterite Society.* Baltimore: Johns Hopkins Press.
Houghton, Walter R.
   1893   *Neely's History of the Parliament of Religions and Religious Congresses at the World's Columbian Exposition.* Chicago: Neely.
Howard-Gordon, Frances
   1982   *Glastonbury—Maker of Myths.* Glastonbury, England: Gothic Image.
Hoyt, Edwin P.
   1969   *The Goulds: A Social History.* New York: Weybright and Talley.
Hubbard, L. Ron
   1975   *Dianetics and Scientology Technical Dictionary.* Los Angeles: Church of Scientology of California, Publications Organization.
Iannaccone, Laurence R.
   1994   "Why Strict Churches are Strong," *American Journal of Sociology* 99:1180 1211.
Introvigne, Massimo
   1994   "Ordeal by Fire: The Tragedy of the Solar Temple." Torino, Italy: Center for Studies on New Religions.
Isaac, Larry W. and Larry J. Griffin
   1989   "Ahistoricism in Time-series Analyses of Historical Process: Critique, Redirection, and Illustrations from U.S. Labor History," *American Sociological Review* 54: 873–890.

James, William
    1986   *Essays in Psychical Research*. Cambridge: Harvard University Press.

Janis, Irving L.
    1982   *Groupthink: Psychological Studies of Policy Decisions and Fiascoes*. Boston: Houghton Mifflin.

Jevons, David, and Ann Jevons
    1978   *The Revelation of Ramala*. St. Helier, Jersey: Spearman.

Johnson, Benton
    1957   "A Critical Appraisal of the Church-Sect Typology," *American Sociological Review* 22:88–92.
    1963   "On Church and Sect," *American Sociological Review* 28:539–549.
    1971   "Church and Sect Revisited," *Journal for the Scientific Study of Religion* 10:124–137.

Johnson, Douglas W., Paul R. Picard, and Bernard Quinn
    1974   *Churches and Church Membership in the United States—1971*. Washington, D.C.: Glenmary Research Center.

Judah, J. Stillson
    1974   *Hare Krishna and the Counterculture*. New York: John Wiley and Sons.

Judd, Wayne R.
    1987   "William Miller: Disappointed Prophet" In *The Disappointed: Millerism and Millenarianism in the Nineteenth Century*, edited by Ronald L. Numbers and Jonathan M. Butler. Bloomington: Indiana University Press. 17–35.

Kalat, James
    1986   *Introduction to Psychology*. Belmont, California: Wadsworth.

Kanter, Rosabeth Moss
    1972   *Commitment and Community*. Cambridge:Harvard University Press.

Kapitza, Sergei
    1991   "Antiscience Trends in the U.S.S.R." *Scientific American* 265(2):32–38

Kay, Jane Holtz
    1982   "Last of the Shakers." *Historic Preservation* 34 (March/April): 14–21.

Keim, Albert N. (ed.)
    1975   *Compulsory Education and the Amish*. Boston: Beacon.

Kelley, Dean M.
    1983   "Deprogramming and Religious Liberty." In *The Brainwashing/Deprogramming Controversy: Sociological, Psychological, Legal and Historical Perspectives*, edited by David G. Bromley and James T. Richardson. New York: Edwin Mellen. 309–318.

441

Kelley, Jonathan
  1978   "Sexual Permissiveness: Evidence for a Theory," *Journal of Marriage and the Family* 40:455–468.
Keniston, Kenneth
  1968   *Young Radicals*. New York: Harcourt, Brace and World.
Kennedy, John G.
  1967   "Nubian Zar Ceremonies as Psychotherapy," *Human Organization* 26:185–194.
Kennedy, Joseph C. G. (ed.)
  1864   *Population of the United States in 1860*. Washington: Government Printing Office.
King, Francis
  1975   Magic—The Western Tradition. New York: Avon.
King, Martin Luther, Jr.
  1986   *A Testament of Hope: The Essential Writings of Martin Luther King, Jr.* Edited by James Melvin Washington. New York: Harper and Row.
Kipp, Jacob W.
  1994   "The Ukraine's Socio-Economic Crisis," *Military Review* 74(3): 32–37.
Kliever, Lonnie D.
  1987   "Religion and the Democratization of Culture." In *Spirit Matters: The Worldwide Impact of Religion on Contemporary Politics*, edited by Richard L. Rubenstein. New York: Paragon House. 35–53.
  1991   "Radical Democratization and Radical Monotheism: Mannheim and Niebuhr on Global Order." In *Religion and Global Order*, edited by Roland Robertson and William R. Garrett. New York: Paragon House. 245–261.
Kluckhohn, Clyde
  1951   "Values and Value-Orientations in the Theory of Action." In *Toward a General Theory of Action*, edited by Talcott Parsons and Edward Shils. Cambridge, Massachusetts: Harvard University Press.
Knudsen, Dean D., John R. Earle, and Donald W. Shriver, Jr.
  1978   "The Conception of Sectarian Religion: An Effort at Clarification," *Review of Religious Research* 20:44–60.
Konolige, Kit, and Frederica Konolige
  1978   *The Power of Their Glory: America's Ruling Class: The Episcopalians*. New York: Wyden/Simon and Schuster.
Korzybski, Alfred
  1948   *Science and Sanity*. Lakeville, Connecticut: International Non-Aristotelian Library.
  1950   *Manhood of Humanity* Lakeville, Connecticut: International Non-Aristotelian Library.

Kowalewski, David
   1991   "Cultism, Insurgency, and Vigilantism in the Philippines," *Sociological Analysis* 52:241–253.
Kvaraceus, William C.
   1954   *The Community and the Delinquent.* Yonkers-on-Hudson, New York: World Book Company.
Kwak, Chung Hwan
   1980   *Outline of the Principle: Level 4.* New York: Holy Spirit Association for the Unification of World Christianity.
La Barre, Weston
   1969   *They Shall Take Up Serpents.* New York: Schocken.
   1972   *The Ghost Dance.* New York: Dell.
La More, George E.
   1975   "The Secular Selling of a Religion," *Christian Century*, December 10: 1133 1137.
La Vey, Anton
   1969   *The Satanic Bible.* New York: Avon.
Lanchester, Frederick William
   1956   "Mathematics in Warfare." In *The World of Mathematics*, edited by James R. Newman. New York: Simon and Schuster. 2138–2157.
Land, Kenneth C., Glenn Deane, and Judith R. Blau
   1991   "Religious Pluralism and Church Membership: A Spatial Diffusion Model," *American Sociological Review* 56:237–249.
Langone, Michael D. (ed.)
   1993   *Recovery from Cults: Help for Victims of Psychological and Spiritual Abuse.* New York: W. W. Norton.
LaPiere Richard T.
   1934   "Attitudes versus Actions," *Social Forces* 13:230–237.
Lauer, Jeanette C., and Robert H. Lauer
   1983   "Sex Roles in Nineteenth-Century American Communal Societies," *Communal Societies* 3:16–28.
Leary, Timothy
   1983   *Flashbacks: An Autobiography.* Los Angeles: J. P. Tarcher.
Lewis, Gordon R.
   1966   *Confronting the Cults.* Grand Rapids, Michigan: Baker.
Lewis, Ioan M.
   1971.   *Ecstatic Religion.* Baltimore: Penguin.
Lewis, James R. and J. Gordon Melton (eds.)
   1994   *Sex, Slander, and Salvation: Investigating The Family/Children of God.* Stanford, California: Center for Academic Publication.
Lewis, Lionel Smithett
   1922   *St. Joseph of Arimathea at Glastonbury.* Cambridge, England: Clarke.

Lightman, Alan P., Jon D. Miller, and Bonnie J. Leadbeater
  1987 "Contemporary Cosmological Beliefs." Cambridge, Massachusetts: Center for Astrophysics, Harvard College Observatory, preprint #2479.
Lilliston, Lawrence, and Gary Shepherd
  1994 "Psychological Assessment of Children in The Family." In *Sex, Slander, and Salvation: Investigating The Family/Children of God*. Stanford, California: Center for Academic Publication. 47–56.
Lipset, Seymour Martin
  1971 *Rebellion in the University*. Boston: Little, Brown.
  1994 "The Social Requisites of Democracy Revisited," *American Sociological Review* 59:1–22.
Liska, Allen E.
  1974 "Emergent Issues in the Attitude-Behavior Consistency Controversy," *American Sociological Review* 39: 261–272.
Lofland, John
  1966 *Doomsday Cult*. Englewood Cliffs, New Jersey: Prentice-Hall.
  1977 *Doomsday Cult, Enlarged Edition*. New York: John Wiley.
Lofland, John, and Rodney Stark
  1965 "Becoming a World-Saver: A Theory of Conversion to a Deviant Perspective," *American Sociological Review* 30:862–875.
Long, Theodore E., and Jeffrey K. Hadden
  1983 "Religious Conversion and the Concept of Socialization: Integrating the Brainwashing and Drift Models," *Journal for the Scientific Study of Religion* 22:1–14.
Lucas George
  1977 *Star Wars—Episode IV: A New Hope*. Lucasfilm Ltd./Twentieth Century Fox Film Corporation.
  1980 *Star Wars—Episode V: The Empire Strikes Back*. Lucasfilm Ltd./Twentieth Century Fox Film Corporation.
  1983 *Star Wars—Episode VI: Return of the Jedi*. Lucasfilm Ltd./Twentieth Century Fox Film Corporation.
Lunan, Duncan
  1974 *Interstellar Contact*. Chicago: Henry Regnery.
Lyons, Arthur
  1970 *The Second Coming: Satanism in America*. New York: Dodd, Mead.
Macy, Michael
  1990 "Learning Theory and the Logic of Critical Mass," *American Sociological Review* 55:809–826.
  1991a "Chains of Cooperation: Threshold Effects in Collective Action," *American Sociological Review* 56:730–747.
  1991b "Learning to Cooperate: Stochastic and Tacit Collusion in Social Exchange," *American Journal of Sociology* 97:808–843.

Magruder, Jeb Stuart
  1978   *From Power to Peace.* Waco, Texas: Word Books.
Malony, H. Newton, and Samuel Southard
  1992   *Handbook of Religious Conversion.* Birmingham, Alabama: Religious Education Press.
Maltwood, Katherine E.
  1964   *Glastonbury's Temple of the Stars.* Cambridge, England: Clarke.
Mandelbrot, Benoit B.
  1983   *The Fractal Geometry of Nature.* San Francisco: W. H. Freeman.
Mannheim, Karl
  1936   *Ideology and Utopia.* New York: Harcourt, Brace and World.
Markovsky, Barry
  1992   "Network Exchange Outcomes: Limits of Predictability," *Social Networks* 14:267–286.
Marshall, Mary (Mary M. Dyer)
  1847   *The Rise and Progress of the Serpent from the Garden Eden.* Concord, New Hampshire, Mary Marshall.
Masaryk, Thomas G.
  1881   *Suicide and the Meaning of Civilization.* Chicago: University of Chicago Press [1970].
Maxwell, William Quentin
  1956   *Lincoln's Fifth Wheel: The Political History of the United States Sanitary Commission.* New York: Longmans, Green.
Mayer, Ann Elizabeth
  1991   *Islam and Human Rights.* Boulder, Colorado: Westview.
McCarthy, John D.
  1987   "Pro-Life and Pro-Choice Mobilization: Infrastructure Deficits and New Technologies." In *Social Movements in an Organizational Society*, edited by Mayer N. Zald and John D. McCarthy. New Brunswick, New Jersey: Transaction. 49–66.
McCarthy, John D. and Meyer N. Zald
  1973   *The Trend of Social Movements in America: Professionalization and Resource Mobilization.* Morristown, New Jersey: General Learning Press.
McClelland, Doug
  1989   *Down the Yellow Brick Road: The Making of the Wizard of Oz.* New York: Bonanza.
McClenon, James
  1994   *Wondrous Events: Foundations of Religious Belief.* Philadelphia: University of Pennsylvania Press.
McCloskey, Michael
  1983   "Intuitive Physics," *Scientific American* 248(4): 122–130.
McCready, William C. and Andrew M. Greeley
  1976   *The Ultimate Values of the American Population.* Sage, Beverly Hills, California

445

Bibliography

McGuire, Meredith B.
  1992   *Religion: The Social Context.* Belmont, California: Wadsworth.
McIntosh, Christopher
  1969   *The Astrologers and their Creed: An Historical Outline.* London: Hutchinson.
  1980   *The Rosy Cross Unveiled.* Wellingsborough, Northhamptonshire, England: Aquarian Press.
  1992   *The Rose Cross and the Age of Reason.* New York: E. J. Brill.
McKinney, Alexander H.
  1932   *Triumphant Christianity: The Life and Work of Lucy Seaman Bainbridge.* New York: Fleming H. Revell.
McPherson, J. Miller, Pamela A. Popielarz, and Sonja Drobnic
  1992   "Social Networks and Organizational Dynamics," *American Sociological Review* 57:153–170.
McQuaid, Donald A.
  1979   *The International Psychic Register.* Erie, Pennsylvania:Ornion Press.
Melcher, Marguerite Fellows
  1941   *The Shaker Adventure.* Princeton:Princeton University Press.
Melton, J. Gordon
  1985   "The Revival of Astrology in the United States." In Rodney Stark ed. *Religious Movements: Genesis, Exodus, and Numbers.* New York: Rose of Sharon. 279–299.
  1986   *Biographical Dictionary of American Cult and Sect Leaders.* New York: Garland.
  1987   "How New is New? The Flowering of the 'New' Religious Consciousness since 1965." In *The Future of New Religious Movements*, edited by David G. Bromley and Phillip E. Hammond. Macon, Georgia: Mercer University Press. 46–56.
  1989   "The Attitude of Americans toward Hinduism from 1883 to 1983 with Special Reference to the International Society for Krishna Consciousness." In *Krishna Consciousness in the West*, edited by David G. Bromley and Larry D. Shinn. 79–101.
  1993   *Encyclopedia of American Religions.* Detroit: Gale Research.
Mernissi, Fatima
  1992   *Islam and Democracy: Fear of the Modern World.* Reading, Massachusetts: Addison-Wesley.
Merton, Robert K.
  1968   *Social Theory and Social Structure.* Free Press, New York
Messing, Simon D.
  1958   "Group Therapy and Social Status in the Zar Cult of Ethopia," *American Anthropologist* 60:1120–1126.
Miller, Amy Bess, and Persis Fuller
  1970   *The Best of Shaker Cooking.* New York: Macmillan.

446

Miller, Kenneth D. and Ethel Prince Miller
  1962   *The People are the City: 150 Years of Social and Religious Concern in New York City*. New York: Macmillan.
Millikan, David
  1994   "The Children of God, Family of Love, The Family." In *Sex, Slander, and Salvation: Investigating the Family/Children of God*, edited by James R. Lewis and J. Gordon Melton. Stanford, California: Center for Academic Publication. 181–252.
Miyakawa, T. Scott
  1964   *Protestants and Pioneers: Individualism and Conformity on the American Frontier*. Chicago: University of Chicago Press.
Morselli, Henry
  1879   *Suicide: An Essay on Comparative Moral Statistics*. New York: Appleton (1882).
Morris, B. F.
  1864   *Christian Life and Character of the Civil Institutions of the United States, Developed in the Official and Historical Annals of the Republic*. Philadelphia: George W. Childs.
Morris, Robert L.
  1978   "A Survey of Methods and Issues in ESP Research." In *Extrasensory Perception*, edited by Stanley Krippner. New York: Plenum. 7–58.
Morrison, Theodore
  1974   *Chautauqua* Chicago: University of Chicago Press.
Muncy, Raymond Lee
  1973   *Sex and Marriage in Utopian Communities*. Bloomington:Indiana University Press.
Murray, John E.
  1993   "A Demographic Analysis of Shaker Mortality Trends," *Communal Societies* 13:22–44.
  1995   "Determinants of Membership Levels and Duration in a Shaker Commune, 1780–1880," *Journal for the Scientific Study of Religion* 34:35–48.
Nash, Jay Robert
  1976   *Darkest Hours* Chicago: Nelson-Hall.
Nasir, Jamal J.
  1990   *The Status of Women Under Islamic Law and Under Modern Islamic Legislation*. London: Graham and Trotman.
Nees, L. Guy
  1991   *Winds of Change, 1980–85: The Church in Transition*. Kansas City, Missouri: Nazarene Publishing House.
Neuhaus, Richard John
  1984   *The Naked Public Square: Religion and Democracy in America*. Grand Rapids, Michigan: William B. Eerdmans.

Neumeyer, Martin H.
  1955 *Juvenile Delinquency in Modern Society.* Princeton, New Jersey:
         D. van Nostrand.
Nevius, Helen S. Coan
  1869 *Our Life in China.* New York: Robert Carter.
  1895 *The Life of John Livingston Nevius.* New York: Fleming H. Revell.
Nevius, John L.
  1869 *China and the Chinese.* New York: Harper.
  1896 *Demon Possession and Allied Themes, Being an Inductive Study
         of Phenomena of Our Own Times.* New York: Fleming H. Revell.
Newman, Cathy and Sam Abell
  1989 "The Shakers' Brief Eternity," *National Geographic* 176(3):
         302–325.
Nichol, Francis D.
  1944 *The Midnight Cry.* Washington, D. C.: Review and Herald.
Niebuhr, H. Richard
  1929 *The Social Sources of Denominationalism.* New York: Holt.
Nietzsche, Friedrich
  1872 *The Birth of Tragedy.* New York: Random House [1967].
Nordhoff, Charles
  1875 *The Communistic Societies of the United States.* London: John
         Murray.
Noyes, John Humphrey
  1870 *History of American Socialisms.* Philadelphia: Lippincott.
  1872 *Male Continence.* New York: Gordon Press [1975].
  1875 *Essay on Scientific Propagation.* Oneida, New York: Oneida
         Community.
Noyes, Pierrepont
  1937 *My Father's House: An Oneida Boyhood.* New York: Farrar and
         Reinhart.
Numbers, Ronald L.
  1992 *Prophetess of Health: Ellen G. White and the Origins of Seventh-
         day Adventist Health Reform.* Knoxville: University of Tennessee
         Press.
Numbers, Ronald L., and Janet S. Numbers
  1987 "Millerism and Madness: A Study of 'Religious Insanity' in Nine-
         teenth-Century America." In *The Disappointed: Millerism and Mil-
         lenarianism in the Nineteenth Century*, edited by Ronald L. Numbers
         and Jonathan M. Butler. Bloomington: Indiana University Press.
         92–117.
  1992 "Ellen White on the Mind and the Mind of Ellen White." In
         *Prophetess of Health: Ellen G. White and the Origins of Seventh-day
         Adventist Health Reform* by Ronald L. Numbers. Knoxville: Univer-
         sity of Tennessee Press. 202–227.

Numbers, Ronald L., and Jonathan M. Butler (eds.)
  1987   *The Disappointed: Millerism and Millenarianism in the Nine-teenth Century*. Bloomington: Indiana University Press.
Obershall, Anthony
  1973   *Social Conflict and Social Movements*. Englewood Cliffs, New Jersey: Prentice-Hall.
O'Connor, Richard
  1973   *The Spirit Soliders: A Historical Narrative of the Boxer Rebellion*. New York: G. P. Putnam's Sons.
O'Dea, Thomas F.
  1966 *The Sociology of Religion*. Englewood Cliffs, New Jersey: Prentice-Hall.
Ogburn, William Fielding
  1922   *Social Change*. New York: Huebsch.
Okugawa, Otohiko
  1983   "Intercommunal Relationships among Nineteenth-century Communal Societies in America," *Communal Societies* 3:68–82.
Oliver, Edmund Henry
  1930   *The Winning of the Frontier*. Toronto, Canada: United Church Publishing House.
Olsen, M. Ellsworth
  1925   *A History of the Origin and Progress of Seventh-Day Adventists*. Washington, D.C.: Review and Herald Publishing Company.
Omohundro, John T.
  1976   "Von Däniken's Chariots: A Primer in the Art of Cooked Science," *The Zetetic* 1 (Fall/Winter):58–68.
O'Neil, Barbara, and Richard Phillips
  1975   *Biorhythms—How to Live With Your Life Cycles*. Pasadena, California: Ard Ritchie Press.
O'Neill, John J.
  1944   *Prodigal Genius: The Life of Nikola Tesla*. New York: David McKay.
Onions, C. T. (ed.)
  1966   *The Oxford Dictionary of English Etymology*. London: Oxford University Press.
Pagano, Robert R., Richard M. Rose, Robert M. Stivers, and Stephen Warrenburg
  1976   "Sleep during Transcendental Meditation," *Science* 191:308–310.
Paik, L. George
  1970   *The History of Protestant Missions in Korea, 1832–1910*. Seoul, Korea: Yonsei University Press.
Palmer, John
  1978   "Extrasensory Perception: Research Findings." In *Extrasensory Perception*, edited by Stanley Krippner. New York: Plenum. 59–243.

Palmer, Phoebe
  1845 *The Way of Holiness*. New York: G. Lane and C. B. Tippett.
  1988 *Selected Writings*, edited by Thomas C. Oden. New York: Paulist Press.
Palmer, Susan J.
  1994 " 'Heaven's Children:' The Children of God's Second Generation." In *Sex, Slander, and Salvation: Investigating The Family/Children of God*. Stanford, California: Center for Academic Publication. 1–25.
Parsons, Talcott
  1964 "Evolutionary Universals in Society," *American Sociological Review* 29:339–357.
Patrick, Ted and Tom Dulack
  1976 *Let Our Children Go!* New York: E. P. Dutton.
Pearson, Elmer R. and Julia Neal
  1974 *The Shaker Image*. Boston: New York Graphic Society.
Pearson, Michael
  1990 *Millennial Dreams and Moral Dilemmas*. Cambridge, England: Cambridge University Press.
Pemble, John
  1977 *The Raj, the Indian Mutiny and the Kingdom of Oudh, 1801–1859* Rutherford, New Jersey: Fairleigh Dickenson University Press.
Pitts, William L.
  1994 "The Davidian Tradition." In *From the Ashes: Making Sense of Waco*, edited by James R. Lewis. Lanham, Maryland: Roman and Littlefield. 33–39.
  1995 "Davidians and Branch Davidians." In *Armageddon in Waco*, edited by Stuart A. Wright. Chicago: University of Chicago Press. 20–42.
Pole, Wellesley Tudor
  1983a *The Enigma of Good Versus Evil*. Glastonbury, England: Chalice Well Trust.
  1983b *God is Love*. Glastonbury, England: Chalice Well Trust.
  1983c *Message for the Coming Time*. Glastonbury, England: Chalice Well Trust.
  1983d *Notes on Healing*. Glastonbury, England: Chalice Well Trust.
Pollock, Dale
  1983 *Skywalking: The Life and Films of George Lucas, the Creator of Star Wars*. New York: Ballantine.
Pope, Liston
  1942 *Millhands and Preachers*. New Haven, Connecticut: Yale University Press.

Pope, Whitney
 1976   *Durkheim's Suicide: A Classic Analyzed*. Chicago: University of
 Chicago Press.
Premananda
 1960   *Prayers of Self-Revelation*. Washington, D.C.: Self-Revelation
 Church.
Preston, Douglas J.
 1986   *Dinosaurs in the Attic: An Excursion into the American Museum
 of Natural History*. New York: St. Martin's Press.
Quinn, Bernard, Herman Anderson, Martin Bradley, Paul Goetting, and
 Peggy Schriver
 1982   *Churches and Church Membership in the United States, 1980*.
 Atlanta, Georgia: Glenmary Research Center.
Rachman, Stanley
 1971   *Effects of Psychotherapy*. Oxford: Pergamon.
Rack, Henry D.
 1993   *Reasonable Enthuisiast*. Nashville, Tennessee: Abingdon.
Radford, C. A. Raleigh
 1973   *Glastonbury Abbey*. London: Pitkin.
Ranney, David James
 1910   *Dave Ranney, or Thirty Years on the Bowery*. New York: Ameri-
 can Tract Society.
Rao, K. Ramakrishna
 1978   "Theories of Psi." In *Extrasensory Perception*, edited by Stanley
 Krippner. New York: Plenum. 245–295.
Raser, Harold E.
 1987   *Phoebe Palmer: Her Life and Thought*. Lewiston, New York: Ed-
 win Mellen.
Ray, Isaac
 1863   *Mental Hygiene*. Boston: Ticknor and Fields.
 1871   *Treatise on the Medical Jurisprudence of Insanity*. Boston: Little,
 Brown.
Redford, M. E.
 1958   *The Rise of the Church of the Nazarene*. Kansas City, Missouri:
 Nazarene Publishing House.
Reif, Rita
 1981   "Auction and Exhibition Point Up Shaker Popularity," *New York
 Times* November 5: C6.
Reiterman, Tim and John Jacobs
 1982   *Raven: The Untold Story of the Rev. Jim Jones and His People*.
 New York: E. P. Dutton.
Reps, Paul, and Nyogen Senzaki
 1957   *Zen Flesh, Zen Bones*. Rutland, Vermont: Charles E. Tuttle.

Rhine, Joseph B.
    1934   *Extra-Sensory Perception*. Boston: Bruce Humphries [1964].
    1937   *New Frontiers of the Mind*. New York: Farrar and Rinehart.
Richardson, James T.
    1994   "Lessons from Waco: When Will We Ever Learn?" In *From the Ashes: Making Sense of Waco*, edited by James R. Lewis. Lanham, Maryland: Roman and Littlefield. 181–184.
Richardson, James T., Joel Best, and David G. Bromley (ed.)
    1991   *The Satanism Scare*. New York: Aldine de Gruyter.
Richardson, James T., and Brock Kilbourne
    1983   "Classical and Contemporary Applications of Brainwashing Models: A Comparison and Critique." In *The Brainwashing/Deprogramming Controversy: Sociological, Psychological, Legal and Historical Perspectives*, edited by David G. Bromley and James T. Richardson. New York: Edwin Mellen. 29–45.
Richardson, James T., and Rex Davis
    1983   "Experiential Fundamentalism: Revisions of Orthodoxy in the Jesus Movement," *Journal of the American Academy of Religion* 51:397–525.
Richardson, James T., Mary White Stewart, and Robert B. Simmonds
    1979   *Organized Miracles*. New Brunswick, New Jersey: Transaction.
Richardson, John G., and Georgie A. Weatherby
    1983   "Belief in an Afterlife as Symbolic Sanction," *Review of Religious Research* 25:162–169.
Richey, Russell E.
    1991   *Early American Methodism*. Bloomington: Indiana University Press.
Robbins, Thomas, Dick Anthony, and James McCarthy
    1983   "Legitimating Repression." In *The Brainwashing/Deprogramming Controversy: Sociological, Psychological, Legal and Historical Perspectives*, edited by David G. Bromley and James T. Richardson. New York: Edwin Mellen. 319–328.
Roberts, Anthony
    1978 (ed.)   *Glastonbury*. London: Rider.
    1984   *Sacred Glastonbury*. Westhay, England: Zodiac House.
Robinson, Charles Edison
    1893   *A Concise History of the United Society of Believers*. East Canterbury, New Hampshire: United Society of Believers.
Robison, Sophia M.
    1960   *Juvenile Delinquency: Its Nature and Control*. New York: Holt, Rinehart and Winston.
Rochford, E. Burke, Jr.
    1982   "Recruitment Strategies, Ideology, and Organization in the Hare Khrishna Movement," *Social Problems* 29:399–410.

1987 "Dialectical Processes in the Development of Hare Krishna: Tension, Public Definition, and Strategy. In *The Future of New Religious Movements*, edited by David G. Bromley and Phillip E. Hammond. Macon, Georgia: Mercer University Press. 109–122.

1995 "Family Structure, Commitment, and Involvement in the Hare Krishna Movement," *Sociology of Religion* 56:153–175.

Rogers, Everett M.
1983 *Diffusion of Innovations*. New York: Free Press.

Rogerson, Alan
1969 *Millions Now Living Will Never Die: A Study of Jehovah's Witnesses*. London: Constable.

Roheim, Geza
1955 *Magic and Schizophrenia*. Bloomington: Indiana University Press.

Rowe, David L.
1987 "Millerites: A Shadow Portrait." In *The Disappointed: Millerism and Millenarianism in the Nineteenth Century*, edited by Ronald L. Numbers and Jonathan M. Butler. Bloomington: Indiana University Press. 1–16.

Runciman, Steven
1947 *The Medieval Manichee: A Study of the Christian Dualist Heresy*. Cambridge, England: Cambridge University Press.

Rupert, James
1995a "Burial Feud Signals Trouble for Kiev," *Washington Post*, August 24: A30.

1995b "Ukraine Patriarch's Unruly Burial Brings Church-State Ties to a Low," *Washington Post*, July 23: A16.

Salter, Andrew
1972 *The Case Against Psychoanalysis*. New York: Harper and Row.

Sanders, Ed
1971 *The Family: The Story of Charles Manson's Dune Buggy Attack Battalion*. New York: E. P. Dutton. (First edition only)

Sawyer, J. F. A.
1994 "Religion." In *The Encyclopedia of Language and Linguistics*. Oxford: Pergamon. 3531–3534.

Schachter, Stanley, and Jerome E. Singer
1962 "Cognitive, Social and Physiological Determinants of Emotional State," *Psychological Review* 69:379–399.

Schafer, Stephen, and Richard D. Knudten
1970 *Juvenile Delinquency: An Introduction*. New York: Random House.

Schauffler, Adolph Frederick
1919 *Memories of a Happy Boyhood*. New York: Fleming H. Revell.

Schauffler, Robert McE.
1951 *Schauffler Chronicle*. Published by the author, no place given.

Schein, Edgar F., Inge Schneier, and Curtis H. Becker.
  1961   *Coercive Persuasion*. New York: W. W. Norton.
Schervish, Paul G.
  1990   "Wealth and the Spiritual Secret of Money." In *Faith and Philanthropy in America*, edited by Robert Wuthnow and Virginia A. Hodgkinson. 63–90. San Francisco: Jossey-Bass.
Schiffer. Herbert F.
  1979   *Shaker Architecture*. Exton, Pennsylvania: Schiffer.
Schudson, Michael
  1992   *Watergate in American Memory*. New York: Basic Books.
Schulz, Barbara, George W. Bohrnstedt, Edgar F. Borgatta, and Robert R. Evans
  1977   "Explaining Premarital Sexual Intercourse among College Students," *Social Forces* 56:148–165.
Schuman, Howard, and Michael P. Johnson
  1976   "Attitudes and Behavior," *Annual Review of Sociology* 2: 161–207.
Schuman, Howard, and Stanley Presser
  1980   "Public Opinion and Public Ignorance: The Fine Line between Attitudes and Nonattitudes," *American Journal of Sociology* 85: 1214–1225
Scott, John Finley
  1971   *Internalization of Norms*. Englewood Cliffs, New York: Prentice-Hall.
Scruggs, Richard, Steven Zipperstein, Robert Lyon, Victor Gonzalez, Herbert Cousins, and Roderick Beverly
  1993   Report to the Deputy Attorney General on the Events at Waco, Texas, February 28 to April 19, 1993, Redacted Version. Washington, D. C.: Department of Justice.
Seager, Richard Hughes
  1995   *The World's Parliament of Religions*. Bloomington: Indiana University Press.
Seoane, Consuelo Andrew
  1960   *Beyond the Ranges* New York: Robert Spellar.
Seta (Seta U.S.A., Inc.)
  1993   *The Wizard of Oz for Super Nintendo*. Reno, Nevada: Seta.
Shapiro, David
  1965   *Neurotic Styles*. New York: Basic Books.
Shea, John D.
  1992   "Religion and Sexual Adjustment." In *Religion and Mental Health*, edited by John F. Schumaker. New York: Oxford University Press. 70–84.

Shea, John Gerald
1971   *The American Shakers and their Furniture*. New York: Van Nostrand.
Shepherd, Gary, and Lawrence Lilliston
1994   "Field Observations of Young People's Experience and Role in The Family." In *Sex, Slander, and Salvation: Investigating The Family/Children of God*. Stanford, California: Center for Academic Publication. 1–25.
Sherwood, Carlton
1991   *Inquisition: The Persecution and Prosecution of the Reverend Sun Myung Moon*. Washington, D.C.: Regnery Gateway.
Shinn, Larry D.
1983   "The Many Faces of Krishna." In *Alternatives to American Mainline Churches*, edited by Joseph H. Fichter. 113–135.
1985   "Conflicting Networks: Guru and Friend in ISKCON." In *Religious Movements: Genesis, Exodus, and Numbers*, edited by Rodney Stark. New York: Rose of Sharon. 95–114.
1987   "The Future of an Old Man's Vision: ISKCON in the Twenty-First Century." In *The Future of New Religious Movements*, edited by David G. Bromley and Phillip E. Hammond. Macon, Georgia: Mercer University Press. 123–140.
1994   "Why Did Waco Happen." In *From the Ashes: Making Sense of Waco*, edited by James R. Lewis. Lanham, Maryland: Roman and Littlefield. 185–188.
Shriver, Donald W., Jr.
1976   "Preface." In *Spindles and Spires: A Re-Study of Religion and Social Change in Gastonia* by John R. Earle, Dean D. Knudsen and Donald W. Shriver, Jr. Atlanta, Georgia: John Knox Press. 13–29.
Shupe, Anson D.
1976   " 'Disembodied Access' and Technological Constraints on Organizational Development: A Study of Mail-Order Religions," *Journal for the Scientific Study of Religion* 15:177–185.
Shupe, Anson D., and David G. Bromley
1980   *The New Vigilantes: Deprogrammers, Anti-Cultists, and the New Religions*. Beverly Hills, California: Sage.
Simpson, John H.
1990   "The Stark-Bainbridge Theory of Religion," *Journal for the Scientific Study of Religion* 29:367–371.
Singh, Parmatma (Howard Weiss)
1974   *Spiritual Community Guide, 1975–76*. San Rafael, California: Spiritual Community Publications.
1978   *Spiritual Community Guide, 1979*. San Rafael, California: Spiritual Community Publications.

1981 *A Pilgrim's Guide to Planet Earth*. San Rafael, California: Spiritual Community Publications.

Skvoretz, John, and Thomas J. Fararo
1995 "The Evolution of Systems of Social Interaction," *Current Perspectives in Social Theory*, 15:275–299.

Slesin, Suzanne
1981 "Bringing Shaker-Style Furniture Back to Life," *New York Times* November 5: C1, C6.

Smelser, Neil J.
1962 *Theory of Collective Behavior*. New York: Free Press.

Smith, Robert E.
1976 *The Complete Book of Biorhythm Life Cycles*. New York: Aardvark.

Snow, David A., Louis A. Zurcher, and Sheldon Ekland-Olson
1980 "Social Network and Social Movements: A Microstructural Approach to Differential Recruitment," *American Sociological Review* 45:787–801.

Snow, David A., and Richard Machalek
1983 "The Convert as a Social Type." In *Sociological Theory—1983*, edited by Randall Collins. San Francisco: Jossey-Bass. 259–288.
1984 "The Sociology of Conversion," *Annual Review of Sociology* 10:167–190.

Sorokin, Pitirim A.
1937 *Social and Cultural Dynamics*. 4 vols. New York: American Book Company.

Soskice, J. Martin
1994 "Religious Language." In *The Encyclopedia of Language and Linguistics*. Oxford: Pergamon. 3534–3536.

Spence, Lewis
1960 *An Encyclopedia of Occultism*. New Hyde Park, New York: University Books.

Spielberg, Steven
1978 *Close Encounters of the Third Kind*. ("fotonovel") New York: Dell.

Spiro, Melford E.
1979 *Gender and Culture: Kibbutz Women Revisited*. Durham, North Carolina: Duke University Press.

Stack, Steven
1983 "The Effect of the Decline in Institutionalized Religion on Suicide, 1954-1978, *Journal for the Scientific Study of Religion* 22:239-252.

Stark, Rodney
1965a "Social Contexts and Religious Experience," *Review of Religious Research* 7:17–28.

1965b "A Taxonomy of Religious Experience," *Journal for the Scientific Study of Religion* 5:97–116.

1975 *Social Problems*. New York: Random House.

1987 "How New Religions Succeed: A Theoretical Model." In *The Future of New Religious Movements*, edited by David G. Bromley and Phillip E. Hammond. Macon, Georgia: Mercer University Press. 11–29.

1994 "Rational Choice Theories of Religion," *The Agora* 2(1):1–5.

Stark, Rodney, Bruce D. Foster, Charles Y. Glock, and Harold E. Quinley

1971 *Wayward Shepherds*. New York: Harper and Row.

Stark, Rodney, and Charles Y. Glock

1968 *American Piety: The Nature of Religious Commitment*. Berkeley: University of California Press.

Stark, Rodney, Daniel P. Doyle, and Lori Kent

1980 "Rediscovering Moral Communities: Church Membership and Crime." In *Understanding Crime: Current Theory and Research*, edited by Travis Hirschi and Michael Gottfredson. Beverly Hills, California: Sage. 43–52.

Stark, Rodney, Daniel P. Doyle, and Jesse Lynn Rushing

1983 "Beyond Durkheim:Religion and Suicide," *Journal for the Scientific Study of Religion* 22:120–131.

Stark, Rodney, Lori Kent, and Daniel P. Doyle

1982 "Religion and Delinquency: The Ecology of a 'Lost' Relationship." *Journal of Research in Crime and Delinquency* 18 (2):4–24.

Stark, Rodney, and Lynne Roberts

1982 "The Arithmetic of Social Movements: Theoretical Implications," *Sociological Analysis* 43:53–68.

Stark, Rodney, and Roger Finke

1988 "American Religion in 1776: A Statistical Portrait," *Sociological Analysis* 49:39–51.

Stark, Rodney, and William Sims Bainbridge

1979 "Of Churches, Sects, and Cults," *Journal for the Scientific Study of Religion* 18:117–133.

1980 "Networks of Faith," *American Journal of Sociology* 86:1376–1395.

1981 "American-Born Sects: Initial Findings," *Journal for the Scientific Study of Religion* 20:130–149.

1985 *The Future of Religion*. Berkeley: University of California Press.

1987 *A Theory of Religion*. New York: Toronto/Lang.

1996 Religion, Deviance and Social Control. New York: Routledge.

Stein, Stephen J.

1992 *The Shaker Experience in America*. New Haven, Connecticut: Yale University Press.

Steinberg, Stephen
    1965   "Reform Judaism: The Origin and Evolution of a Church Move-
            ment," *Journal for the Scientific Study of Religion* 5:117–129.
Stephan, Karen H. and G. Edward Stephan
    1973   "Religion and the survival of Utopian communities." *Journal for
            the Scientific Study of Religion* 12: 89–100.
Story, Ronald
    1977   "Von Däniken's Chariots of the Gods," *The Zetetic* 2 (Fall/Win-
            ter):22–35.
Stowasser, Barbara Freyer
    1994   *Women in the Qur'an, Traditions and Interpretations.* New York:
            Oxford University Press.
Sullivan, Lawrence E.
    1993   "Recommendations Concerning Incidents such as the Branch Da-
            vidian Standoff in Waco." Letter reprinted in *Recommendations of
            Experts for Improvement in Federal Law Enforcement After Waco.*
            Washington, D.C.: Department of Justice and Department of the Trea-
            sury.
Sutherland, Edwin H., and Donald R. Cressey
    1974   *Principles of Criminology.* New York: Lippincott.
Suzuki, Daisetz Teitaro
    1956   Zen Buddhism. Garden City, New York: Doubleday.
Suzuki, Daisetz Teitaro, Erich Fromm, and Richard De Martino
    1960   *Zen Buddhism and Psychoanalysis.* New York: Harper & Row,
Symonds, John
    1958   *The Magic of Aleister Crowley.* London: Muller.
Szasz, Thomas
    1961   *The Myth of Mental Illness.* New York: Delta.
    1970   *The Manufacture of Madness.* New York: Harper and Row.
Tabor, James D.
    1994   "The Waco Tragedy: An Autobiographical Account of One At-
            tempt to Avert Disaster." In *From the Ashes: Making Sense of Waco*,
            edited by James R. Lewis. Lanham, Maryland: Roman and Littlefield.
            13–21.
    1995   "Religious Discourse and Failed Negotiations. In *Armageddon in
            Waco*, edited by Stuart A. Wright. Chicago: University of Chicago
            Press. 263–281.
Tappan, Paul W.
    1949   *Juvenile Delinquency.* New York: McGraw-Hill.
Tarde, Gabriel
    1903   *The Laws of Imitation.* New York: Henry Holt.
Taylor, David
    1983   "Thought Reform and the Unification Church." In *The Brain-
            washing/Deprogramming Controversy: Sociological, Psychological,*

Legal and Historical Perspectives, edited by David G. Bromley and James T. Richardson. New York: Edwin Mellen. 73–90.

Tealdo, Lydia L.
1928   "Reflections of Forty Years of Service with the Woman's Branch," *New York City Mission Monthly* 51(4): 15–17.

Tennov, Dorothy
1975   *Psychotherapy: The Hazardous Cure.* New York: Abelard-Schuman.

Thommen, George S.
1973   *Is This Your Day?* New York: Avon.

Tilly, Charles
1978   *From Mobilization to Revolution.* Reading, Massachusetts: Addison-Wesley.

Time magazine
1974   "The Psychic Scandal," August 26, p. 74.

Titelman, Carol (ed.)
1977   *The Art of Star Wars.* New York: Ballantine.

Toch, Hans
1965   *The Social Psychology of Social Movements.* Indianapolis: Bobbs-Merrill.

Trager, Helen G.
1966   *Burma Through Alien Eyes.* New York: Frederick A. Praeger.

Tribe, Laurence
1990   *Abortion: The Clash of Absolutes.* New York: W. W. Norton.

Trice, Harrison M. and Paul Michael Roman
1970   "Delabeling, Relabeling, and Alcoholics Anonymous," *Social Problems* 17:538–546.

Tipton, Steven M.
1982   *Getting Saved from the Sixties.* Berkeley: University of California Press.

Troeltsch, Ernst
1911   *The Social Teaching of the Christian Churches.* Translated by Olive Wyon. New York: Harper [1960].

Turner, Jonathan H.
1986   *The Structure of Sociological Theory.* Chicago: Dorsey Press.

Turner, Jonathan H., Leonard Beeghley, and Charles H. Powers
1989   *The Emergence of Sociological Theory.* Chicago: Dorsey Press.

Tworkov, Helen
1994   *Zen in America.* New York: Kodansha International.

Ulansey, David
1989   "The Mythraic Mysteries," *Scientific American* 261 (December): 130–135.

Van Vogt, A. E.
  1940   *Slan. Astounding Science-Fiction* 26 (September):9–40; (October):9–42; (November):119–160; (December):119–162.
  1948   *The World of Null-A*. New York: Ace.
Van Zandt, David E.
  1991   *Living in the Children of God*. Princeton, New Jersey: Princeton University Press.
Villiers, Oliver G.
  1977   *Wellesley Tudor Pole*. Canterbury, England: Bells.
Vincent, John H.
  1885   *The Chautauqua Movement*. Freeport, New York: Books for Libraries Press [1971].
Vivekananda
  1893   "Hinduism." In *The World's Parliament of Religions*, edited by John Henry Barrows. Chicago: Parliament Publishing Company. 968–978.
  1953   *The Yogas and Other Works*. New York: Ramakrishna-Vivekananda Center.
Wagner, Adolf Heinrich Gotthilf
  1864   *Die Gesetzmaessigkeit in den Scheinbar Willkuerlichen Menschlichen Handlungen vom Standpunkte der Statistik*. Hamburg: Boyes und Geisler.
Wallace, Anthony F. C.
  1966   *Religion: An Anthropological View*. New York: Random House.
Wallace, Robert Keith
  1970   "Physiological Effects of Transcendental Meditation," *Science* 167:1251–1754.
Wallace, Robert Keith, and Herbert Benson
  1972   "The Physiology of Meditation," *Scientific American* 226(2): 84–90.
Wallis, Roy
  1979a   "Millennialism and Community: Observations on the Children of God. In *Salvation and Protest: Studies of Social and Religious Movements*. New York: St. Martin's Press. 51–73.
  1979b   "Sex, Marriage and the Children of God." In *Salvation and Protest: Studies of Social and Religious Movements*. New York: St. Martin's Press. 74–90.
  1981   "Yesterday's Children: Cultural and Structural Change in a New Religious Movement." In *The Social Impact of New Religious Movements*, edited by Bryan Wilson. New York: Rose of Sharon. 97–133.
  1985   "The Dynamics of Change in the Human Potential Movement.." In Rodney Stark ed. *Religious Movements: Genesis, Exodus, and Numbers*. New York: Rose of Sharon. 129–156.

1986   "Figuring Out Cult Receptivity," *Journal for the Scientific Study of Religion* 25:494–503.

1987   "Hostages to Fortune: Thoughts on the Future of Scientology and the Children of God." In *The Future of New Religious Movements*, edited by David G. Bromley and Phillip E. Hammond. Macon, Georgia: Mercer University Press. 80–90.

Warner, R. Stephen

1993   "Work in Progress toward a New Paradigm for the Sociological Study of Religion in the United States," *American Journal of Sociology* 98:1044–1093.

Watch Tower Bible and Tract Society

1952   *Let God Be True.* New York: Watch Tower Bible and Tract Society, International Bible Students Association.

1959   *Jehovah's Witnesses in the Divine Purpose.* New York: Watch Tower Bible and Tract Society, International Bible Students Association.

Watts, Alan W.

1957   *The Way of Zen.* New York: Pantheon.

Weber, Max

1958   *The Protestant Ethic and the Spirit of Capitalism.* Translated by Talcott Parsons. New York: Scribner's.

1968   *Max Weber on Charisma and Institution Building.* Chicago: University of Chicago Press.

Welch, Michael R.

1977   "Analyzing Religious Sects: An Empirical Examination of Wilson's Sect Typology," *Journal for the Scientific Study of Religion* 16:125–139.

Weisbrot, Robert

1983   *Father Divine and the Struggle for Racial Equality.* Urbana: University of Illinois Press.

Westhues, Kenneth

1976   "Religious Organization in Canada and the United States," *International Journal of Comparative Sociology* 17:206–225.

1978   "Stars and Stripes, the Maple Leaf, and the Papal Coat of Arms," *Canadian Journal of Sociology* 3:245–261.

Wheatley, Richard

1881   *The Life and Letters of Mrs. Phoebe Palmer.* New York: W. C. Palmer.

White, Anna and Leila S. Taylor

1904   *Shakerism, Its Meaning and Message.* Columbus, Ohio: Heer.

White, Charles Edward

1986   *The Beauty of Holiness: Phoebe Palmer As Theologian, Revivalist, Feminist, and Humanitarian.* Grand Rapids, Michigan: Francis Asbury Press.

White, Elizabeth H.
  1978   "Legal Reform as an Indicator of Women's Status in Muslim Nations." In *Women in the Muslim World*, edited by Lois Beck and Nikki Keddie. Cambridge: Harvard University Press. 52–68.
White, Ellen G.
  1888   *The Great Controversy Between Christ and Satan*. Mountain View, California: Pacific Press Publishing Association [1950].
White, John
  1976a   "A Critical Look at TM," *New Age Journal*, January:30–35.
  1976b   "Second Thoughts: What's Behind TM?" *Human Behavior*, October:70–71.
White, Robert W.
  1964   *The Abnormal Personality*. New York: Ronald Press.
White, Theodore H.
  1975   *Breach of Faith: The Fall of Richard Nixon*. New York: Laurel/Dell [1986].
Whitworth, John McKelvie
  1975   *God's Blueprints*. London: Routledge and Kegan Paul.
Whyte, Martin King
  1992   "Prospects for Democratization in China," *Problems of Communism* 42:58–70.
Wilson, Bryan
  1961   *Sects and Society*. Berkeley: University of California Press.
  1970   *Religious Sects*. New York: McGraw-Hill.
  1979   "The Return of the Sacred," *Journal for the Scientific Study of Religion* 18:268–280.
  1993   "Historical Lessons in the Study of Sects and Cults." I *The Handbook on Cults and Sects in America*, edited by David G. Bromley and Jeffrey K. Hadden. Greenwich, Connecticut: JAI Press. 53–73.
Wilson, Clifford
  1970   *Crash Go the Chariots*. New York: Lancer.
  1975   *The Chariots Still Crash*. New York: Signet.
Wilson, E. O.
  1971   *The Insect Societies*. Cambridge: Harvard University Press.
  1975   *Sociobiology—The New Synthesis*. Cambridge: Harvard University Press.
Wilson, John and Thomas Janoski
  1995   "The Contribution of Religion to Volunteer Work," *Sociology of Religion* 56:137–152.
Wilson, Stephen
  1978   *Informal Groups*. Englewood Cliffs, New Jersey: Prentice-Hall.
Wright, Stuart
  1983   "Defection from New Religious Movements: A Test of Some The-

oretical Propositions," In *The Brainwashing/Deprogramming Contro-versy: Sociological, Psychological, Legal and Historical Perspectives*, edited by David G. Bromley and James T. Richardson. New York: Edwin Mellen. 106–121.

1995 "Construction and Escalation of a Cult Threat." In *Armageddon in Waco*, edited by Stuart A. Wright. Chicago: University of Chicago Press. 75–94.

Wuthnow, Robert
1976 *The Consciousness Reformation.* Berkeley: University of California Press.
1978 *Experimentation in American Religion.* Berkeley:University of California Press.
1988 *The Restructuring of American Religion.* Princeton, New Jersey: Princeton University Press.
1991 *Acts of Compassion: Caring for Others and Helping Ourselves.* Princeton, New Jersey: Princeton University Press.

Yatsubuchi, Banriu
1893 "Buddhism." Pp. 716–723 in *The World's Parliament of Religions*, edited by John Henry Barrows. Chicago: Parliament Publishing Company.

Yellen, Samuel
1936 *American Labor Struggles.* New York: Arno [1969].

Zablocki, Benjamin
1980 *Alienation and Charisma: A Study of Contemporary American Communes.* New York: Free Press.

Zald, Mayer N., and John D. McCarthy
1987 "Religious Groups as Crucibles of Social Movements." In *Social Movements in an Organizational Society*, edited by Mayer N. Zald and John D. McCarthy. New Brunswick, New Jersey: Transaction. 67–95.

Zweig, Stefan
1932 *Mental Healers.* New York: Viking.

Index

Index

Index

Index